# The Enlightenment

## A sourcebook and reader

At the beginning of the eighteenth century a distinctly modern vision of life was emerging; by its close, revolutions in America and France had revealed the power of new beliefs about human nature, rights and duties, nature and culture, the natural and material worlds, and a new faith in science, technology and the idea of progress. As people began to change the way they thought about themselves and the world around them, a whole new way of thinking developed, which still has an overwhelming impact two centuries on.

*The Enlightenment: A sourcebook and reader* brings together the work of major thinkers, such as Locke, Rousseau, Diderot and Kant, to illustrate the full importance and achievements of this period in history. Extracts from a wide range of sources are gathered thematically into sections on such aspects of the Enlightenment as political theory, religion and belief, art and nature, gender and society. All texts are introduced and a final section on 'Critical Reflections' provides a selection of modern critical opinions on the period by writers including Foucault, Habermas and Lyotard.

Containing illustrations from the work of artists such as Hogarth and Gainsborough, a chronology of the Enlightenment, and a detailed bibliography, *The Enlightenment: A sourcebook and reader* is a rich source of information and inspiration for all those studying this great period of change.

**Paul Hyland** is Head of the School of Historical and Cultural Studies at Bath Spa University College. He is a specialist in eighteenth-century studies and has taught and published widely in literary, historical and cultural studies. He recently became the first historian in Britain to be awarded a National Teaching Fellowship.

**Olga Gomez** is a Teaching Fellow in European Languages and Cultures at the University of Lancaster.

**Francesca Greensides** is a Lecturer in Early Modern History at Bath Spa University College.

# The

# Enlightenment

## A sourcebook and reader

*Edited by*
**Paul Hyland**

with Olga Gomez and Francesca Greensides

Routledge
Taylor & Francis Group

LONDON AND NEW YORK

First published 2003
by Routledge
2 Park Square, Milton Park, Abingdon, Oxon, OX14 4RN

Simultaneously published in the USA and Canada
by Routledge
270 Madison Ave, New York NY 10016

*Routledge is an imprint of the Taylor & Francis Group*

Transferred to Digital Printing 2007

Typeset in Bell Gothic and Perpetua by Taylor & Francis Ltd

*British Library Cataloguing in Publication Data*
A catalogue record for this book is available from the British Library

*Library of Congress Cataloging in Publication Data*
The Enlightenment: a sourcebook and reader / edited by Paul Hyland,
with the assistance of Olga Gomez and Francesca Greensides.
Includes bibliographical references and index.
1. Enlightenment. 2. Europe–Intellectual life–18th century. I Hyland,
Paul, 1965– II. Gomez, Olga. III. Greensides, Francesca.
B802 .E543 2003
940.2'5–dc21

2002032464

ISBN 0–415–20448–8 (hbk)
ISBN 0–415–20449–6 (pbk)

# Contents

# Illustrations

# Preface

The tradition of trying to define the Enlightenment stretches back to the eighteenth century itself, and has given rise to many different theories, approaches and assessments. Some important examples of these are introduced and included here in a selection of Modern Critical Reflections. Most of this book, however, is devoted to providing a selection of sources from the historical period of the Enlightenment – sources which, for the most part, stimulated or depicted great contemporary debates and which have subsequently inspired extensive modern critical discussions. Any selection from the thousands of fascinating texts and topics that can now be studied in relation to the Enlightenment is, however, fraught with difficulties, for there is no scholarly consensus about who or what of the Enlightenment – not to mention when and where – should be given preference. Nor then is there agreement about what might constitute a 'balanced' or 'representative' collection. At one level, a glance at the Chronology and Furhter Reading here reveals a rich array of texts and subjects whose inclusion would have been greatly welcomed, were space permitting. At another level, every choice of passage from a selected text, its introduction and its juxtaposition to other texts raises questions about what ideas, interpretations and approaches are being foregrounded. Within these limitations, the aim here has not been to foreclose debate about how the Enlightenment may be explored and understood, but rather to provide a structure that helps to facilitate and open up discussion from a number of directions. If this book helps and encourages readers to look further into the Enlightenment it will have served its purpose.

# Acknowledgements

This book could not have been produced without the help of many people, especially the many students whose enjoyment and criticism of Enlightenment texts and ideas has silently contributed to its design. No less humbling, and far too numerous to record, are the debts owed to modern scholars upon whose work a collection such as this must ultimately depend. Throughout this project, many students and scholars have also been directly consulted, and I am very grateful to each for all the generous advice that has been given. In particular, I should like to thank Alan Marshall, Elaine Chalus, Nick Drew, Terry Rodgers and Mpalive Msiska for help and support, as well as Vicky Peters and her colleagues at Routledge. I am also very grateful to Olga Gomez at Lancaster University and Francesca Greensides at Bath Spa University College for assisting with the selection of some texts and providing advice about how they should be introduced. Responsibility for all introductory and supporting material and editorial work is nevertheless my own. Above all, I should like to thank Nicky Wilson for unflagging enthusiasm, assistance and support in seeing this book through every stage of its development, and for her work on several translations included here. Many personal thanks are also due to Pauleen and to family and friends — not least for all the immeasurable things.

I am very grateful to the following authors, publishers and institutions for kindly granting permission to reproduce material from copyrighted works:

Jean d'Alembert, *Preliminary Discourse to the Encyclopedia of Diderot*, translated by Richard N. Schwab (Chicago: University of Chicago Press, 1995), © The University of Chicago Press, 1995.

Theodor Adorno and Max Horkheimer, *The Dialectic of Enlightenment*, translated by John Cumming (London: Verso, 1995, and New York: The Continuum Publishing Company, 1995), © Verso and Continuum International Publishing Group, 1995.

Ernst Cassirer, *The Philosophy of the Enlightenment* (Princeton: Princeton University Press, 1951), © Princeton University Press, 1951.

Catherine the Great, 'Instructions', from *Documents of Catherine the Great*, edited by W.F. Reddaway (Cambridge: Cambridge University Press, 1971), © Cambridge University Press, 1971.

Robert Darnton, *The Business of the Enlightenment: A Publishing History of the Encyclopédie, 1755–1800* (Cambridge, Mass.: Harvard University Press, 1979), © the President and Fellows of Harvard College, 1979.

Denis Diderot, 'A Supplement to the Voyage of Bougainville', from *Diderot: Political Writings*, translated and edited by J. Hope Mason and R. Wokler (Cambridge: Cambridge University Press, 1992), © Cambridge University Press, 1992.

Denis Diderot, *Salons*, edited by. J. Seznec and J. Adhémer, 4 vols (Oxford: Clarendon Press, 1957–67), © Oxford University Press, 1957–67. For permission to translate selected passages.

Denis Diderot, *Thoughts on the Interpretation of Nature; and other philosophical works*, introduced and annotated by David Adams (Manchester: Clinamen, 1999), © Clinamen Press Ltd, 1999.

Michel Foucault, 'What is Enlightenment?', from *The Foucault Reader*, edited by Paul Rabinow (Harmondsworth: Penguin, 1984), © as an unpublished work Michel Foucault and Paul Rabinow, 1984.

Frederick the Great, 'Essay on the Forms of Government', from *Enlightened Absolutism (1760–1790): A Documentary Sourcebook*, edited by A. Lentin (Newcastle-upon-Tyne: Avero Publications Ltd, 1985), © Avero Publications Ltd, 1985.

Peter Gay, *The Enlightenment: An Interpretation*, vol. I, *The Rise of Modern Paganism*; vol. II, *The Science of Freedom* (London: Weidenfeld & Nicolson, 1967–69), © Peter Gay, 1967–69.

Jürgen Habermas, *The Structural Transformation of the Public Sphere: An Inquiry into a Category of Bourgeois Society*, translated by T. Burger (Cambridge: Polity Press, 1989), © Polity Press, 1989.

Louis Jaucourt, 'Invention', from Diderot and d'Alembert, *Encyclopedia Selections*, translated and introduced by N.S. Hoyt and T. Cassirer (Indianapolis: Library of Liberal Arts, Bobbs-Merrill Co. Inc, 1965), © Bobbs-Merrill Co. Inc., 1965.

Kant, 'What is Enlightenment?' from Immanuel Kant, *On History*, translated by Lewis White Beck (Indianapolis: Liberal Arts Press, 1963), © Liberal Arts Press, 1963.

Gottfried Wilhelm Leibniz, *Theodicy*, from G. W. Leibniz, *Essays on the Goodness of God and the Freedom of Man and the Origin of Evil*, translated by E.M. Huggard (London: Routledge & Kegan Paul, 1951), © Routledge & Kegan Paul, 1951.

Jean-François Lyotard, *The Postmodern Condition: A Report on Knowledge*, translated by Geoff Bennington and Brian Massumi (Manchester: Manchester University Press, 1984 and Minneapolis: University of Minnesota Press, 1984), © Manchester University Press and University of Minnesota Press, 1984.

Jean Meslier, *Common Sense*, translated by Anna Knoop (New York: Arno Press and The New York Times, 1972), © Arno Press and the New York Times, 1972; translation © Anna Knoop.

Jean-Jacques Rousseau, *Discourse on the Arts and Sciences*, translated by G.D.H. Cole (London: J.M. Dent & Sons Ltd, 1913).

Marquis de Sade, *Philosophy in the Bedroom,* from *The Complete Justine Philosophy in the*

*Bedroom and Other Writings*, translated by Richard Seaver and Austryn Wainhouse (New York: Grove Press, Inc.,1966), © Richard Seaver and Austryn Wainhouse, 1965.

Sylvana Tomaselli, 'The Enlightenment Debate on Women', from *History Workshop Journal*, 20 (Autumn 1985), © *History Workshop Journal,* 1985.

Giambattista Vico, *New Science*, translated by David Marsh (Harmondsworth: Penguin, 1999). © Penguin, 1999.

Voltaire, *Poem on the Lisbon Disaster, or an Examination of the Axiom 'All is Well'*, translated by Joseph McCabe (London: Watts & Co., 1911).

Voltaire, 'Theist', from *Philosophical Dictionary*, with special introduction by William F. Fleming (E.R. Dumont, 1901), © E.R. Dumont, 1901.

Joan Wallach Scott, 'French Feminists and the Rights of "Man": Olympe de Gouges's Declarations', from *History Workshop Journal*, 28 (Autumn 1989), © *History Workshop Journal*, 1989.

## Illustrations

Copplestone Warre Bampfylde, *Bridge, Lake and South Bank at Stourhead*, c.1770 (photo: National Trust Photographic Library / John Bethell), © National Trust.

Jean-Baptiste Siméon Chardin, *La Raie* (1725–26) and *Le Bénédicité* (1740), (photos: Musée du Louvre), © Réunion des Musées Nationaux Agence photographique, Paris.

Thomas Gainsborough, *Mr and Mrs Robert Andrews*, 1748–50 (photo: National Gallery, London), © National Gallery, London.

Thomas Gainsborough, *Girl with Pigs*, 1782 (photo: black and white photographic print by permission of the Castle Howard Collection), © Castle Howard Estate Ltd.

Giambattista Vico, *Di Una Scienza* [*New Science*], 1744 (photo: by permission of the British Library; 8468.C.8), © The British Library.

Joseph Wright, *An Experiment on a Bird in an Air Pump*, 1768 (photo: Tate Gallery Picture Library), © Tate Gallery, London.

Every effort has been made to obtain permission for the use of copyright items. Editor and publisher would be glad to hear from any copyright holders not so acknowledged.

Paul Hyland,
Bath,
2002

# A note on the texts

Many of the Enlightenment works selected here have a long and complex history of production, publication, dissemination, suppression, revision and translation. Questions about what constitutes the 'best' or most 'authentic' edition of a text are therefore often difficult to answer. These questions are not made easier by what today may appear to be the very liberal practices of many eighteenth-century publishers and printers with regard to such matters as spelling, punctuation and typography. In terms of readership and impact, it is also worth noting that cheap, abridged, popularised and pirated versions of works sometimes enjoyed much wider circulation than expensively-produced subscription or authorially-sanctioned editions. Good modern English-language editions of most of the works selected here are now available, and these are listed under the author's name in the Further Reading section. In a few cases where no modern English-language edition has been produced, the Further Reading section provides information on the most recent English edition.

The texts presented here come from a variety of sources. Most extracts are taken from British eighteenth-century editions and translations into English. No attempt has been made to standardise these extracts according to modern English usage and conventions. However, silent editorial changes have been made to reduce what may now appear to be awkward and erratic forms of capitalisation, spelling and punctuation. Some extracts have been taken from modern editions and translations of the following works: d'Alembert's 'Preliminary Discourse' to the *Encyclopédie*, Catherine II's *Instruction*, Diderot's *Supplement to the Voyage of Bougainville*, Frederick II's *Essay on the Forms of Government*, Jaucourt's 'Invention' from the *Encyclopédie*, Kant's 'What is Enlightenment?', Leibniz's *Theodicy*, Rousseau's *Discourse on the Arts and Sciences*, de Sade's *Philosophy in the Boudoir*, and Vico's *New Science*. Bibliographical information about these modern editions is provided in the Acknowledgements. Four extracts have also been translated for this collection by Nicky Wilson and Paul Hyland. These passages are taken from Diderot's *Salons* (vols I–IV, ed. Jean Seznec and Jean Adhémer, Oxford,

Clarendon Press, 1957–67), de Gouges' *Les Droits de la Femme et de la Citoyenne* (1791), Laugier's *Essai sur l'Architecture* (1753) and Rousseau's *Rêveries du Promeneur Solitaire* (1782).

In addition to short biographical headnotes for each source, to assist the student reader some brief editorial notes have occasionally been inserted within the selected texts. These editorial interpolations are marked by the use of square brackets [thus], and usually refer to proper names, dates, published works, or obscure and archaic words. Similarly, ellipses, the editorial omission of sentences or passages within the texts selected here, are indicated by three dots within square brackets: [...]. Unless stated otherwise, in all title headings, editorial commentary and the Chronology, works are dated according to the year of their first publication or performance.

PART ONE

# Sources

# Chapter 1

# Human nature

**A** CENTRAL FEATURE OF THE ENLIGHTENMENT was the emphasis that all kind of scholars began to place upon the study of human nature. Important, and often new and exciting, ideas about human nature were therefore suffused within almost every kind of Enlightened work. Human nature was regarded as a subject of special significance largely because it was believed to provide the foundation for all knowledge. Hence the Scottish historian and philosopher David Hume wrote, 'Tis evident, that all the sciences have a relation, greater or less, to human nature; and that however wide any of them may seem to run from it, they still return back by one passage or another.' He continued: 'In pretending [claiming] therefore to explain the principles of human nature, we in effect propose a complete system of the sciences built upon a foundation almost entirely new, and the only one upon which they can stand with any security' (*A Treatise of Human Nature*, 1739).

To understand human nature, scholars tried to observe and analyse human conduct and the processes of the mind. This new emphasis on the study of man and the nature of woman led to the emergence of philosophical questions about the self, and to the rise of social sciences such as psychology, sociology and anthropology. Of course, there were a variety of views about the best ways of investigating the subject; whether it be through the medical sciences, by examining past societies or 'primitive' cultures (such as those of the newly-discovered Pacific islanders), or by uncovering the 'natural' laws that were believed to govern social, political and economic relations. For Hume, it was most important that all enquiries should be based upon 'a cautious observation of human life ... in the common course of the world', rather than religious beliefs or grand philosophical principles established without the support of experience and observation. However, some scholars, such as the Italian philosopher Giambattista Vico, questioned the very idea of a uniform human nature. In his view, humans could only be understood by recognising their profound differences according to the kind of societies in which they lived. Thus the idea that there was a human nature that could be isolated and examined independently of the plethora of human conditions and of the impact of environment and culture was not shared by all. Most, however, would probably have leaned more towards Hume's view:

> It is universally acknowledged that there is a great uniformity among the actions of men, in all nations and ages, and that human nature remains still the same, in its principles and operations ... Mankind are so much the same, in all times and places that history informs us of nothing new or strange in this particular. Its chief use is only to discover the constant and universal principles of human nature.
>
> (*An Enquiry Concerning Human Understanding*, 1748)

Whatever the preferred method of investigation, the poet Alexander Pope spoke for the Enlightenment generally in proposing that, rather than trying to fathom the mysteries of God, 'The proper study of mankind is man', and that the past neglect of this most essential subject had been responsible for what appeared to be centuries of no or slow progress in most other fields of knowledge.

Since the ancient Greeks, the idea of a human-centred (anthropocentric) cosmos had dominated European thought. Later, Christian theology had portrayed humans as flawed by the original sin of the Fall, and argued that it was through the redemption of Christ that man could hope to attain salvation. Many Enlightenment figures attempted to construct a natural 'secular' history of man to replace this traditional 'sacred' history based upon the Old Testament, and many thinkers rejected the Christian doctrine of innate sinfulness as 'unscientific'. This new approach, based upon the rise of confidence in knowledge gained from observation and experiment (empiricism), was inspired and aided by advances in astronomy and cosmology during the seventeenth century, when the work of scientists such as Bacon, Galileo, Kepler and Newton had brought into question long-accepted theological notions of an anthropocentric cosmos. Hence the earth, and more importantly, man's place on it, rather than being at the centre of a divine creation, could appear to be quite insignificant – if Christian teachings were ignored.

In the seventeenth century, the atheistic Thomas Hobbes had argued in his *Leviathan* (1651) that men are naturally and fundamentally self-seeking, individually existing units, who have to learn to co-operate within a society. Men, conceived by Hobbes as individuals, had formed and entered into civil society (agreeing to live under human-made rules and laws) simply because it furthered their own selfish interests to do so. Society, he claimed, could help ward off the dangers of the original 'state of nature' (when no civil laws and government existed) and could be constructed for everyone's benefit, even though no one was principally interested in the welfare of others. By the mid-eighteenth century, this view of man as a wholly selfishly-motivated and selfishly-reasoning creature came under sustained attack. Adam Ferguson and the Marquis de Condorcet, for example, had faith in the secular perfectibility of humans, believing that they had already risen from savagery to civilisation. Passions such as sex, ambition, pride, and even aggression, came to be viewed as not necessarily sinful and harmful. The Scottish philosopher and economist Adam Smith even claimed that some natural selfish passions did not have to be viewed as sinful or unhelpful. Some selfish desires, if appropriately directed, would inevitably lead to greater social harmony and prosperity.

As new worlds were being discovered, revealing extraordinary scenes of exotic, pagan and 'savage' life, there was a growing sense of confidence among some scholars that a real understanding of human nature would unfold. New confidence emerged in the human capacity for learning, the ability to direct change and make material improvements in the world. Many Enlightenment thinkers followed the English philosopher John Locke's claim that the human mind begins from birth as a clean slate, drawing from sensory experience and reflection to form ideas. The implications of this notion that humans have no innate ideas (e.g. of mother, colour or self) and that knowledge is fundamentally derived from individuals' sensory experience had a tremendous impact upon eighteenth-century thinking. First, it led some scholars to insist that, though distinctive individuals, humans begin life as fundamentally alike and equal. So, for example, belief in a common humanity inspired intellectuals such as Baron de Montesquieu to condemn slavery, and d'Alembert to believe in the improvement of all humankind through education. Secondly, it focused attention upon the nature of human understanding, for Locke had emphasised that the great majority of our ideas and the words used in communication are not directly related to things that have a material existence in the world, but are of our own invention. Thirdly, Locke's views seemed to imply that humans are not just the product of their environment, but that they can, in turn, transform their surroundings, thereby becoming to some extent their own maker. In this sense, human nature was not as uniform and constant as it might at first have seemed.

Crediting humans with more control over their own destiny led some radical thinkers such as Baron d'Holbach and La Mettrie to expound various kinds of materialist philosophies, claiming that the universe was simply matter, or matter in motion; that humans (not having souls) were nothing more than highly intricate pieces of machinery. Determinists such as French scholar Denis Diderot suggested that events (including human actions) were the result of causes that were beyond human control or choice. Even Diderot, however, felt the need to publish a refutation of some kinds of materialism and determinism such as that expressed by the Swiss-born philosopher Claude-Adrien Helvétius in his *De l'Esprit* (*Of the Mind*, 1758). Having seen his work condemned by most authorities, burned by the *parlement* of Paris, and having made several public recantations, Helvétius was prepared to postpone the publication of a sequel. Yet, when *De l'Homme* appeared posthumously in 1773, the views that it expressed continued to outrage not only Christian conceptions of humankind but most Enlightenment reasonings. Assaulting Jean-Jacques Rousseau's view of the natural goodness of mankind, and most Christian teachings, Helvétius insisted:

> Natural man is his own butcher, his own cook. His hands are always dripping with blood. Accustomed to killing, he must be deaf to the cry of pity ... The

most pleasant melody to the ears of the Inquisitor are the shrieks of pain. He laughs next to the stake on which the heretic is expiring. The Inquisitor, an assassin authorized by law, keeps within the civilized community the ferocity of natural man: he is a man of blood. The closer we draw to the natural state, the more we grow accustomed to murder, the easier it is.

For Helvétius, such truths were revealed both by 'the spectacle of nature' and by reflection. He reminded readers that 'born without ideas, without a character, indifferent to moral good and evil, we have only physical sensitivity as a gift from nature; that man in the cradle is nothing, that his vices, his virtues, his artificial passions, his talents, finally, his prejudices, even as far as self-love – everything is acquired by him' (*De l'Homme*). Helvétius liked to portray humans as vicious animals. When, towards the end of the eighteenth century, the Marquis de Sade asked the question 'What is man, and what difference is there between him and the other animals of the earth?' he concluded 'Decidedly none' (*Philosophy in the Boudoir*, 1795).

Despite the great attention that human nature received in the period, many scholars were concerned with the problems of such an investigation. Rousseau, Hume and Ferguson, for example, all expressed concern at attempts to distinguish 'natural' from 'social' man. And whereas some thinkers regarded humans as fundamentally the same, regardless of time, place and culture, Diderot viewed the study of mankind as worthy but inconclusive, because there could be no strictly defined model of human nature, given that there was no single human type. Discourses on race, and representations of racial difference, were also commonplace throughout the century, and clearly occupied the attention of many major thinkers. Yet, discussion of race has seldom figured in modern formulations of the Enlightenment. Even so, it may be thought that many of the fundamental questions about human nature and society that dogged and divided the scholars required answers to equally fundamental questions about the origins, diversity, history, rights and relationships of the various peoples of the world.

In the Christian tradition, all humans owed their origin to one pair, Adam and Eve, whose descendants had been dispersed and punished by an inevitable degeneration over a few thousand years since the Creation. An original unity and equality, in God's eyes, was thus assured; and this would provide an inspiration for many reformers, as in the anti-slavery movements. But as travellers and researchers throughout the century learned more about non-European peoples, examined ancient societies and 'discovered' many new and hitherto unimagined ones, the need for greater and more secular explanation became overwhelming. Were all humans descended from one source (monogenesis) or many (polygenesis), and how were they related? Was there an immutable and universal 'human nature'? Was life in 'natural' settings as 'nasty, brutish and short' as Hobbes had contested, or happier and more virtuous than in so-called 'civilised' societies as Rousseau protested?

Few scholars before the German philosopher and critic Johann Gottfried Herder would question the presumption of 'white' cultural and racial superiority at the head of a universal progress of humankind, perhaps in three or four stages from 'primitivism' to 'civilisation', as defined and measured by the reasonableness of 'white' Europeans. In *Ideas for a Philosophy of the History of Mankind* (1784–91) he wrote:

> For each genus Nature has done her share and to each she has given its prop-er progeny. She has divided the ape into as many species and varieties as pos-sible, and extended these as far as she could. But thou, o man, honour thyself: neither the pongo nor the gibbon is thy brother, but the [native] American and the Negro *are*. These, therefore, thou shouldst not oppress, or murder, or rob; for they are men like thee; with the ape thou canst not enter into fraternity.

Yet, while the work of writers such as Herder and Rousseau raised many questions about the often presumed inferiority of 'savage' peoples and non-Europeans, in many respects this was largely because their ideas challenged the mainstream of scholarly opinion. In his *System of Nature* (1735), the Swedish botanist Linnaeus classified human races according to what he believed to be a God-given hierarchy of nature (see p. 102). David Hume reflected in a footnote: 'I am apt to suspect the negroes and in general all the other species of men (for there are four or five different kinds) to be naturally inferior to the whites. There never was a civilised nation of any other complexion than white' ('Of National Characters', 1748). The great German philosopher Immanuel Kant wrote extensively on race, citing Hume's authority for his own observation that 'The Negroes of Africa have by nature no feeling that rises above the trifling' (*Observations on the Feeling of the Beautiful and Sublime*, 1764). In another highly influential work, *On the Natural Varieties of Mankind* (1776), the German anthropologist Blumenbach identified 'five principal varieties of mankind', of which four were of 'degenerated' stock. It was not surprising, then, that the first American edition (1798) of the *Encyclopaedia Britannica* stated in the entry for 'Negro': 'They are strangers to every sentiment of compassion, and are an awful example of the corruption of man when left to himself'.

While almost every Enlightenment thinker had something to say about the nature of 'civilised' societies, and their difference from those of 'savage', 'barbar-ian', 'primitive' other peoples, in discussions of race, the 'negro' (a term general-ly used to signify all black Africans) attracted particular attention. Throughout the century, slave empires and new nations would be built upon the transportation of some six to ten million 'Africans' (maybe many more) to the New World, and the vast profits generated by the Atlantic trades would fuel the industrial and eco-nomic development of Europe. Yet, if all humans were born free, with natural rights, as Locke, Montesquieu, Rousseau and others stated, the slave trade and all that depended upon it could not be tolerated. Many Enlightenment figures, from John Locke to Thomas Jefferson, had little difficulty in condemning slavery, at least in theory, though some were directly involved in its perpetuation, and most still thought of 'non-whites' as being profoundly inferior. Directly related to these views were long discussions about racial distinctions based upon skin colour, and in particular the origins of negritude. The natural historian Buffon offered an environmental explanation, but one that reflected his conviction in the superiority of white Europeans: 'The most temperate climate lies between the 40$^{th}$ and 50$^{th}$ degree of latitude, and it produces the most handsome and beautiful men. It is from this climate that the ideas of the genuine colour of mankind, and of the various degrees of beauty, ought to be derived. The two extremes [of climate] are equally remote from truth and from beauty' (*Natural History*, 1749–67). Diderot, a forceful critic of colonialism and the widely-presumed superiority of modern Europeans, tried to explain how negritude might be discussed by the Enlightened, and how the prevalence of slavery exposed the rhetoric of claims that all men were brethren.

## THOMAS HOBBES

Thomas Hobbes (1588–1679) was born in Malmesbury, Wiltshire, in the year of the Spanish Armada during Elizabeth I's reign. His father, a minister of the Church of England, was forced to flee following a brawl at church, never to see his family again. Hobbes attended Oxford University for five years, graduating in 1608. His lifelong connection with the Devonshire family began when he was appointed tutor-companion to the son of William Cavendish, Earl of Devonshire. This connection enabled him to travel and to meet influential people. He associated with Galileo, served as secretary to Francis Bacon, and had an acquaintance with Descartes, albeit one of mutual dislike. The outbreak of Civil War, leading to the execution of Charles I in 1649, drove Hobbes into self-imposed exile at Paris in 1640, but he returned to England in 1657, a few years before the Restoration of Charles II in 1660. Hobbes wrote on many subjects, including geometry and physics, but it was in political philosophy that he gained his reputation, publishing *De Cive* (1642), *Elements of Law, Natural and Politic* (1640) and *Leviathan* (1651). He died in 1679 at the age of ninety-one.

   The extract which follows is taken from Hobbes' most famous work, *Leviathan, or the Matter, Form, and Power of a Commonwealth, Ecclesiastical and Civil* (1651). Here, he considers what humans are 'by nature' and, more particularly, how they would behave if all social and legal restraints were removed. As an avowed atheist, he was greatly impressed with the scientific advances of his time and it was his aim to provide a secular explanation of human beings. He insisted that without the rules and punishments of civil society, there would be 'a war of every man, against every man', claiming that man is his material body, programmed for self-preservation. Humans are portrayed as innately and wholly self-seeking. Any seemingly altruistic or benevolent conduct is, in truth, an act which is rationally calculated to serve an individual's best personal desires and interests. Such uncompromising atheistic and materialist views in *Leviathan* made Hobbes many enemies, but established his reputation as an important philosopher, and though his work pre-dates the main period of the Enlightenment, his ideas influenced many of its major thinkers. Some later philosophers, such as Shaftesbury,

Rousseau and Hume, rejected his view of human nature, but others such as the materialist Helvétius (1715–71) in his scandalous *De l'Esprit* (*Of the Mind*, 1758) presented views of mankind that were no less deflating than those of Hobbes, arguing that the human mind was akin to that of an animal, and that it was governed by physical sensations and activated by self-interest.

## *Leviathan* (1651)

### 'Of the Natural Condition of Mankind, as concerning their Felicity and Misery'

From this equality of ability [among men], ariseth equality of hope in the attaining of our ends. And therefore if any two men desire the same thing, which nevertheless they cannot both enjoy, they become enemies; and in the way to their end (which is principally their own conservation, and sometimes their delectation only) endeavour to destroy, or subdue one another. And from hence it comes to pass, that where an invader hath no more to fear, than another man's single power; if one plant, sow, build, or possess a convenient seat, others may probably be expected to come prepared with forces united, to dispossess, and deprive him, not only of the fruit of his labour, but also of his life, or liberty. And the invader again is in the like danger of another.

And from this diffidence of one another, there is no way for any man to secure himself, so reasonable, as anticipation; that is, by force, or wiles, to master the persons of all men he can, so long, till he see no other power great enough to endanger him. And this is no more than his own conservation requireth, and is generally allowed. Also because there be some, that taking pleasure in contemplating their own power in the acts of conquest, which they pursue farther than their security requires; if others, that otherwise would be glad to be at ease within modest bounds, should not by invasion increase their power, they would not be able, long time, by standing only on their defence, to subsist. And by consequence, such augmentation of dominion over men, being necessary to a man's conservation, it ought to be allowed him.

Again, men have no pleasure (but on the contrary a great deal of grief) in keeping company, where there is no power able to overawe them all. For every man looketh that his companion should value him, at the same rate he sets upon himself: and upon all signs of contempt, or undervaluing, naturally endeavours, as far as he dares (which amongst them that have no common power to keep them in quiet, is far enough to make them destroy each other) to extort a greater value from this contemners, by dommage; and from others, by the example.

So that in the nature of man, we find three principal causes of quarrel. First, Competition; secondly, Diffidence; thirdly, Glory.

The first, maketh men invade for Gain; the second, for Safety; and the third, for Reputation. The first use violence, to make themselves masters of other men's persons, wives, children, and cattle; the second, to defend them; the third, for trifles, as a word, a smile, a different opinion, and any other sign of undervalue, either direct in their persons, or by reflection in their kindred, their friends, their nation, their profession, or their name.

Hereby it is manifest, that during the time men live without a common Power to keep them all in awe, they are in that condition which is called war; and such a war, as is of every man against every man. For war, consisteth not in battle only, or the act of fighting; but in a tract of time, wherein the will to contend by battle is sufficiently known: and therefore the notion of time is to be considered in the nature of war; as it is in the nature of weather. For as the nature of foul weather lyeth not in a shower or two of rain; but in an inclination thereto of many days together, so the nature of war, consisteth not in actual fighting, but in the known disposition thereto, during all the time there is no assurance to the contrary. All other time is peace.

Whatsoever therefore is consequent to a time of war, where every man is enemy to every man; the same is consequent to the time, wherein men live without other security, than what their own strength, and their own invention shall furnish them withal. In such condition, there is no place for industry; because the fruit thereof is uncertain: and consequently no culture of the earth; no navigation, nor use of the commodities that may be imported by sea; no commodious building; no instruments of moving and removing such things as require much force; no knowledge of the face of the earth; no account of time; no arts; no letters; no society; and which is worst of all, continual fear, and danger of violent death; and the life of man, solitary, poor, nasty, brutish, and short.

It may seem strange to some man, that has not well weighed these things, that Nature should thus dissociate, and render men apt to invade, and destroy one another: and he may therefore, not trusting to this inference, made from the passions, desire perhaps to have the same confirmed by experience. Let him therefore consider with himself, when taking a journey, he arms himself, and seeks to go well accompanied; when going to sleep, he locks his doors; when even in his house he locks his chests; and this when he knows there be laws, and public officers, armed, to revenge all injuries shall be done him; what opinion he has of his fellow subjects, when he rides armed; of his fellow citizens, when he locks his doors; and of his children, and servants, when he locks his chests. Does he not there as much accuse mankind by his actions, as I do by my words? But neither of us accuse man's nature in it. The desires, and other passions of man, are in themselves no sin. No more are the actions, that proceed from those passions, till they know a law that forbids them: which till laws be made they cannot know: nor can any law be made, till they have agreed upon the person that shall make it.

It may peradventure be thought, there was never such a time, nor condition of war as this; and I believe it was never generally so, over all the world: but there are many places, where they live so now. For the savage people in many places of America, except the government of small families, the concord whereof dependeth on natural lust, have no government at all; and live at this day in that brutish manner, as I said before. Howsoever, it may be perceived what manner of life there would be, where there were no common power to fear; by the manner of life, which men that have formerly lived under a peaceful government, use to degenerate into, in a civil war.

But though there had never been any time, wherein particular men were in a condition of war one against another; yet in all times, kings, and persons of sovereign authority, because of their independency, are in continual jealousies, and in the state and posture of gladiators; having their weapons pointing, and their eyes fixed on one another; that is, their forts, garrisons, and guns, upon the frontiers of their kingdoms;

and continual spies upon their neighbours; which is a posture of war. But because they uphold thereby, the industry of their subjects; there does not follow from it, that misery, which accompanies the liberty of particular men.

To this war of every man against every man, this also is consequent; that nothing can be unjust. The notions of right and wrong, justice and injustice have there no place. Where there is no common power, there is no law: where no law, no injustice. Force, and fraud, are in war the two cardinal virtues. Justice and injustice are none of the faculties neither of the body, nor mind. If they were, they might be in a man that were alone in the world, as well as his senses, and passions. They are qualities that relate to men in society, not in solitude. It is consequent also to the same condition, that there be no propriety, no dominion, no Mine and Thine distinct; but onely that to be every man's, that can get; and for so long, as he can keep it. And thus much for the ill condition, which man by mere Nature is actually placed in; though with a possibility to come out of it, consisting partly in the passions, partly in his reason.

The passions that encline men to peace, are fear of death; desire of such things are as necessary to commodious living; and a hope by their industry to obtain them. And Reason suggesteth convenient Articles of Peace, upon which men may be drawn to agreement. These Articles, are they, which otherwise are called the Laws of Nature.

(*Leviathan*, ch. XIII)

## ALEXANDER POPE

Alexander Pope (1688–1744) was England's leading poet in the early Enlightenment. Son of a linen draper, he was born in London but, due to a childhood illness, his growth was stunted, distorting his spine, so that for the rest of his life he was a hunchbacked cripple, encumbered, as he famously put it, by 'this long Disease, my Life'. He received a Roman Catholic education, and his continued commitment to Catholicism barred him from politics, the professions, and the universities, which meant that, latterly, he was self-taught. However, he did not learn and work in isolation. From his home in Twickenham (as a Catholic, he was not permitted to own a house within ten miles of London) he cultivated a close circle of intellectual and literary friends, such as Jonathan Swift, John Gay, and his neighbour Lord Burlington at Chiswick. He came to be regarded throughout Europe in the eighteenth century as a major moralist and poet. He was also one of the first poets to have made a good independent living from the commercial sale of his literary works (rather than from dependence upon private or institutional patrons), most notably from his translations of Homer's *Iliad* and *Odyssey*. Other important works include: *An Essay on Criticism* (1711), *The Rape of the Lock* (1714), *The Dunciad* (1728), and *Epistle to Burlington* (1731).

In his long philosophical poem *An Essay on Man* (1733–34) Pope tries to explain the seemingly contradictory nature of humankind (torn between reason and passion), and the role and place of humans in the perfectly designed world of God's creation. A key theme of the *Essay* is the attempt to reconcile man's self-loving nature and limited reasoning and knowledge with the infinite wisdom of a

God of love and reason. Pope portrays the world as a harmonious structure, a 'Great Chain of Being' with angels at the top of a long hierarchy that very gradually descends to the lowliest form of plant life. Humankind is regarded as the middle link in this chain, between angel and beast. The divine plan of nature cannot be fully known, seen or experienced by mankind, but, because it is God's creation, it must be perfect:

> All Nature is but Art, unknown to thee;
> All Chance, Direction, which thou canst not see;
> All Discord, Harmony, not understood;
> All partial Evil, universal Good:
> And, spite of Pride, in erring Reason's spite,
> One truth is clear, 'Whatever is, is right'.
>
> (*Essay on Man*, Epistle I, ll. 289–94)

Although the *Essay on Man* was later to come under attack from scholars such as the Swiss philosopher Jean-Pierre de Crousaz, and later from Voltaire (see p. 76), it was widely read and acclaimed, being translated into at least fifteen European languages during the eighteenth century. The *Essay* consists of four 'Epistles', and the extract here is taken from the beginning of Epistle II, 'Man, with respect to Himself, as an Individual'.

## An Essay on Man (1733–34)

> Know then thyself, presume not God to scan;
> The proper study of Mankind is Man.
> Plac'd on this isthmus of a middle state,
> A being darkly wise, and rudely great;
> With too much knowledge for the Sceptic side,      5
> With too much weakness for the Stoic's pride,
> He hangs between; in doubt to act, or rest,
> In doubt to deem himself a God, or Beast;
> In doubt his Mind or Body to prefer,
> Born but to die, and reas'ning but to err;      10
> Alike in ignorance, his reason such,
> Whether he thinks too little, or too much:
> Chaos of Thought and Passion, all confus'd;
> Still by himself abus'd, or disabus'd;
> Created half to rise, and half to fall;      15
> Great lord of all things, yet a prey to all;
> Sole judge of Truth, in endless Error hurl'd:
> The glory, jest, and riddle of the world!
>     Go, wond'rous creature! mount where Science guides,
> Go, measure earth, weigh air, and state the tides      20
> Instruct the planets in what orbs to run,

Correct old Time, and regulate the Sun.
Go, soar with Plato to th' empyreal sphere,
To the first good, first perfect, and first fair;
Or tread the mazy round his follow'rs trod,                    25
And quitting sense call imitating God,
As Eastern priests in giddy circles run,
And turn their heads to imitate the Sun.
Go, teach Eternal Wisdom how to rule;
Then drop into thyself, and be a fool!                         30
        Superior beings, when of late they saw
A mortal Man unfold all Nature's law,
Admir'd such wisdom in an earthly shape,
And show'd a Newton as we show an Ape.
        Could he, whose rules the rapid Comet bind,            35
Describe, or fix one movement of his Mind?
Who saw its fires here rise, and there descend,
Explain his own beginning, or his end?
Alas what wonder! Man's superior part
Uncheck'd may rise, and climb from art to art;                40
But when his own great work is but begun,
What Reason weaves, by Passion is undone.
        Trace Science then, with Modesty thy guide;
First strip off all her equipage of Pride,
Deduct what is but Vanity, or Dress,                           45
Or Learning's Luxury, or Idleness;
Or tricks to shew the stretch of human brain,
Mere curious pleasure, or ingenious pain:
Expunge the whole, or lop th' excrescent parts
Of all, our Vices have created Arts:                          50
Then see how little the remaining sum,
Which serv'd the past, and must the times to come!

        II. Two Principles in human nature reign;
*Self-love*, to urge, and *Reason*, to restrain;
Nor this a good, nor that a bad we call,                       55
Each works its end, to move or govern all:
And to their proper operation still,
Ascribe all Good; to their improper, Ill.
*Self-love*, the spring of motion, acts the soul;
*Reason*'s comparing balance rules the whole.                 60
Man, but for that, no action could attend,
And, but for this, were active to no end.
Fix'd like a plant on his peculiar spot,
To draw nutrition, propagate and rot;
Or, meteor-like, flame lawless thro' the void,                65

Destroying others, by himself destroy'd.
    Most Strength the moving Principle requires,
Active its Task, it prompts, impels, inspires:
Sedate and quiet the comparing lies,
Form'd but to check, delib'rate, and advise.       70
Self-Love still stronger, as its Objects nigh;
Reason's at distance and in prospect lie;
That sees immediate Good, by present Sense,
Reason, the future, and the consequence;
Thicker than Arguments, Temptations throng,      75
At best more watchful this, but that more strong.
The Action of the stronger to suspend,
Reason still use, to Reason still attend:
Attention, Habit and Experience gains,
Each strengthens Reason, and Self-Love restrains.    80
          (*Essay on Man*, Epistle II, 'Man, with respect to Himself,
as an Individual', ll. 1–80)

## JULIEN OFFRAY DE LA METTRIE

The French physician and philosopher La Mettrie (1709–51) was born and raised at St Malo in Brittany, the son of a prosperous textile merchant. Contrary to his parents' wishes that he should become a member of the clergy, he studied medicine at Paris and Reims, and also under the great Dutch physician and philosopher Hermann Boerhaave at Leiden University. Though he returned to St Malo and practised there as a physician, La Mettrie's medical education had led him to become one of the first and most radical of the French materialists. Knowledge of recent medical discoveries had persuaded him that muscular motion is a property inherent in matter. Moreover, he had become convinced that, to a large extent, ideas were also determined by physical states: that 'the brain has its muscles for thinking, as the legs have muscles for walking'. Such claims soon earned him notoriety and, as a result, he spent several years in exile in Holland. After *L'Homme Machine* (*Man a Machine*) was published anonymously at Leiden in 1747, he even had to leave there, taking refuge in Prussia under the protection of Fredrick the Great. In addition to translating Boerhaave's major works for publication in France, La Mettrie's principal works include *Natural History of the Soul* (1745), *Man a Machine* (1747) and *Discourse on Happiness* (1750).

    La Mettrie's most influential work *Man a Machine*, with its frankly atheist and materialist arguments, provoked outrage and angry protests. However, he seemed to take delight in shocking people whom he considered to have a pious outlook. Unable to suppress him, his enemies portrayed La Mettrie as a hedonistic monster, deprived of all morality. When he died unexpectedly, at Potsdam in 1751, shortly after eating game pie, it gave rise to the rumour that his death had been caused by over-indulgence, leading some contemporaries to console themselves with the belief that this was proof of the Providential punishment that atheists deserve.

In *Man a Machine* La Mettrie set out to repudiate the relationship between the body and the spiritual soul (metaphysical dualism) expounded by Descartes, Leibniz and Pope. He argued that all human faculties, including the soul, could be explained by the organisation of matter. Indeed, it was his view that the soul, mechanical in nature, was materially dependent on the body. In 1742, having contracted a fever, and observing the symptoms, he became convinced that thought is simply a physical mechanism. Hence, he claimed man was a 'thinking machine', whilst recognising the sensitive and mental life of the individual. Despite La Mettrie's notoriety, and the many attempts to suppress or discredit his ideas, his materialist philosophy influenced the works of Denis Diderot and Baron d'Holbach. By the end of the nineteenth century, he was regarded as one of the key forerunners of modern materialism, and his theory clearly has similarities to the principles underlying the science of cybernetics.

The extract here, based upon an English translation published in London in 1750, is taken from the early part of *Man a Machine*. La Mettrie has set the scene by claiming that the Optimists (followers of Leibniz and Pope) and the Cartesians (followers of Descartes' metaphysical dualism) have mistakenly 'spiritualized matter, rather than materialized the soul'. What is necessary in seeking the truth about human nature, he argues, is to be guided only by empirical findings based on experience and observation. The work concludes by advocating the arbitrariness and subjectivity of moral standards, maintaining that, as individuals, humans are totally governed by physical impulses.

## Man a Machine (1747)

Man is a machine so compound, that it is impossible to form at first a clear idea thereof, and consequently to define it. This is the reason that all the enquiries the philosophers have made *a priori*, that is, by endeavouring to raise themselves on the wings of the understanding, have proved ineffectual. Thus it is only *a posteriori*, or as it were disentangling the soul from the organs of the body, that we can discover with evidence the nature of man, and obtain the greatest degree of probability the subject will admit of.

Let us then follow the direction of experience, and not trouble our heads with the vain history of the opinions of philosophers. To be blind, and to think that one can do without this guide, is the very height of infatuation. Very justly has it has been observed by a modern writer [David Hume], that nothing but vanity can hinder us from drawing from second causes, what we pretend to infer from the first. We may, and even ought to admire all these subtle geniuses in their most useless labours; I mean Descartes [1596–1650], Malebranche [1638–1715], Leibniz [1646–1716]. But what benefit has mankind reaped from their profound meditations, and from all their works? Let us then see, not what others have thought, but what we ought to think ourselves for the tranquillity of our own lives.

As there are many different constitutions amongst men, so there are many different minds, characters, and manners. Even Galen [born *c*.130 AD] knew this truth which Descartes carried so far as to say, that physic alone could change the minds and manners, together with the body. [...]

The body and the soul seem to fall asleep together. In proportion as the motion of the blood grows calm, a soft soothing sense of peace and tranquillity spreads itself over the whole machine; the soul finds itself sweetly weighed down with slumber and sinks with the fibres of the brain: it becomes thus paralytic, as it were, by degrees, together with the muscles of the body. The latter are no longer able to support the head; the head itself can no longer bear the weight of thought; the soul is, during sleep, as if it had no existence.

If the circulation goes on with too great rapidity, the soul cannot sleep. If the soul be thrown into too great an agitation, the blood loses its calm, and rushes through the veins with a noise that sometimes may be distinctly heard. Such are the two reciprocal causes of insomnia. A frightful dream makes the heart beat double, and tears us from the sweet necessity of rest, as effectively as a lively pain, or pressing want. In a word, just as the cessation of the functions of the soul produces sleep, man is subject, even during some waking moments (when in reality the soul is no more than half awake) to certain sorts of reverie or slumbers of the soul, which are very frequent, and which sufficiently prove that the soul does not wait for the body to fall sleep. For if the soul does not entirely sleep, how much of it does it want! It is impossible for her to recollect one object, to which she gave attention amidst the innumerable crowd of confused ideas, as so many vanishing clouds had filled up, if I may say so, the atmosphere of the brain. [...]

The human body is a machine that winds up its own springs: it is the living image of perpetual motion. Food nourishes what a fever heats and excites. Without proper food the soul languishes, raves, and dies with faintness. It is like a taper, which revives in the moment it is going to be extinguished. Give but good nourishment to the body, pour into its tubes vigorous juices and strong liquors, then the soul, generous as these, arms itself with courage – as a soldier, whom water would have made run away, becoming undaunted, meets death with alacrity amidst the rattle of drums. Thus it is that a hot drink agitates the blood, which cold water would have calmed. [...]

We need only have eyes to see the necessary influence which age has over reason. The soul follows the progress of the body, as well as of education. In the fair sex, the soul adapts itself to the delicacy of constitution: thence flows that tenderness, that affection, those lively sentiments founded rather upon passion than reason; and those prejudices and superstitions whose impression is so hard to be effaced. Man, on the contrary, whose brain and nerves participate of the firmness of all solids, has a mind, as well as the features of his face, that is more vigorous. Education, which women are deprived of by custom, adds still new degrees of strength to the man's soul. [...]

What I have now mentioned, shows that the best company for an ingenious man is his own, if he cannot find his equals. Wit contracts decay amongst those who have none: for want of exercise at tennis, the ball is undextrously returned to him who knows not how to strike it. I would rather choose for a companion a sensible man, though unimproved by education, than a person who had had the misfortune of a bad one, provided the former had but sufficient youth on his side. An ill-tutored wit is like a strolling actor, whom the country has spoiled.

The different states of the soul are therefore always co-relative to the states of the body. But the better to show all this dependency and its causes, let us make use of comparative anatomy, and open the entrails of men and brutes. What method can we have of knowing the human structure, but by being enlightened by a just comparison of the animal economy of both?

In general, the form and composition of the brains of quadrupeds are very near the same with those of man. There is the same figure, the same composition throughout: with this essential difference, that man of all animals has the most brains, and fullest of windings and folds in proportion to the bulk of his body; next to him are the ape, the beaver, the elephant, the dog, the fox, the cat etc. [...]

These are the animals that resemble man the most; for we observe likewise amongst them the same gradual analogy, in relation to the callous body, in which Lancisi [1654–1720] had placed the seat of the soul. [...]

I shall only conclude what evidently follows from these incontestible observations. First, that the more savage animals are, the less brains they have. Secondly, that this organ seems to be greater in some measure, in proportion to their docility. Thirdly, that there is a constant and very surprising law of nature, that the more is gained on the side of understanding and wit, the more is lost of the side of instinct.

(*Man a Machine*)

## JEAN-JACQUES ROUSSEAU

Following the death of his mother at his birth, the Swiss philosopher Rousseau (1712–78) was brought up by his father, a watchmaker, until he was orphaned at the age of ten. He received little formal education, so he was virtually a self-taught writer and philosopher. Apprenticed to an engraver, who allegedly beat him, Rousseau ran away in 1728. He left the small Calvinist republic of Geneva where he had been born, and converted to Catholicism at Turin. This apparent change of faith was perhaps largely a consequence of a new influence in his life, Madame de Warens, a maternal figure who, in 1733, would also become Rousseau's lover. At the age of thirty, Rousseau set off for Paris in search of fortune and fame. Although he would later write on a great range of subjects – including music, politics, philosophy, nature, education, botany, himself – it was as a commentator on human nature in his prizewinning *Discours sur les Sciences et les Arts* (*Discourse on the Arts and Sciences*, 1750) that he first won great attention (see p. 261). This powerful critique of the alleged progress of modern society provided the first celebrated attack of what would later be called the Romantic movement against what it saw as the rise of rationalism in the Enlightenment. Rousseau's hostility to claims about man's progress and moral improvement led Voltaire and others to satirize him, and he began to feel persecuted by many of the *philosophes*. Nevertheless, he stood by his views. His famous treatise on education *Emile* (1762) begins with the statement: 'Everything is good as it leaves the hands of the Author of things; everything degenerates in the hands of man'.

Like Hobbes, Rousseau in his *Discours sur l'Origine de l'Inégalité Parmi les Hommes* (*Discourse upon the Origin and Foundation of the Inequality among Mankind*, 1755) examines the character and condition of man in the hypothetical 'state of nature' (pre-dating the formation of civil society in which people live under laws and government), but he attacks Hobbes, arguing that man's natural state is neither one of war nor misery. He presents an almost idyllic view of primitive man. For Rousseau, humans are naturally equal; possessing differences, but not inequalities. He attributes a special innate sympathy to humankind, and claims that in a 'natural state' we have limited wants, so our interests are few and easily met, without resorting to competition. He takes a radical position in stating that hierarchies, aggression, private possessions and moral degradation occur only as a consequence of the development and trappings of civil society. To explain his theory of human nature, he provides an 'historical' account of how human nature has been corrupted. The following extract is taken from the English translation (1761) of the *Discourse on Inequality*, which Rousseau dedicated to the Republic of Geneva.

## *Discourse on Inequality* (1755)

All animals must be allowed to have ideas, since all animals have senses. They even combine their ideas to a certain degree, and, in this respect, it is only the difference of such degree, that constitutes the difference between man and beast: some philosophers have even advanced, that there is more difference between some men than between some men and some beasts. Therefore it is not so much the understanding which is man's specific distinction among animals as it is the quality of being a free agent. Nature speaks to all animals, and the animal obeys. Man feels the same impulsion, but he perceives that he is free to acquiesce or to resist; and it is in the consciousness of this liberty, that the spirituality of his soul is evident. For physics explains, in some measure, the mechanism of the senses and the formation of ideas; but in the power of willing, or rather of choosing, and in the consciousness of this power, nothing can be discovered but acts, that are purely spiritual, and cannot be explained by the laws of mechanics.

But though the difficulties, involved in all these questions, should leave some room to dispute this difference between man and beast, there is another, very specific quality which distinguishes them, and a quality which will admit of no dispute; this is the faculty of improvement. This faculty which, with the help of circumstances, successively unfolds all other faculties, and resides among us not only in the species, but in the individual; whereas a beast is, after several months, all that he will be during his whole life; and his species, after a thousand years, precisely what it was in the first year of that long period. Why is man alone subject to the loss of his mental faculties? Is it not because he returns to his primitive condition? And, because the beast, who has acquired nothing and has nothing to lose, always retains his instinct. Man, losing in consequence of age or other accidents all that his perfectibility had enabled him to acquire, falls even lower than the beast. It would be sad for us to be forced to admit that this distinctive and almost unlimited faculty is the source of all of man's misfortunes; that it is this faculty that draws him out of that original condition, in which he would otherwise pass days in peace and innocence; that, causing his knowledge and his errors, his vices and his virtues to bloom with the passing of centuries, it renders him, in the end, both his own and nature's tyrant. It would be shocking to be obliged to commend as a benevolent being the man who first suggested to the Orinoco Indians the use of those boards which they bind on their children's temples in order to conserve at least a part of their original imbecility and happiness. [...]

Whatever these origins [of man] may have been, we can at least infer, from the little care which nature has taken to bring men together by mutual wants or to make the use of speech easy to them, how little she prepared them to be sociable, and how little she has contributed to anything they themselves have done to become so. In fact, it is impossible to imagine why, in that primitive state, a man would need another man any more than a monkey or a wolf needs his fellows; or supposing that he had, what motive might induce the other man to satisfy it; nor even, in the latter case, how they could agree among themselves on the conditions. I know that we are constantly told that in this state man would have been a most miserable creature; and if it is true, as I believe I have proved, that he could have had the desire and the opportunity to leave it only after many centuries, it would be a grievance against nature and not against the man she made thus. But, if I understand the term *miserable*, it is a meaningless word, or one which signifies only a painful privation and the suffering of the body or the soul. Now I should like someone to explain to me what kind of misery could be felt by a free being, whose heart enjoys perfect peace, and whose body is in perfect health. I ask whether civil life or natural life is more likely to become unbearable to those who enjoy it. I ask whether anyone has ever heard of a free savage even thinking of complaining about life and of putting an end to it. Let us judge, then, with less pride, where the true misery lies. [...]

It appears, first of all, that there was no kind of moral relations between men in this state, nor any known duties, they could not have been either good or bad, and had neither vices nor virtues; unless, we take these words in a physical sense, and call vices, in the individual, the qualities which may prove detrimental to his own preservation, and virtues, those which may contribute to it; in which case, we should be obliged to call him most virtuous, who least resists the simple impulses of nature. But without deviating from the usual meaning, it is proper for us to suspend our judgement about such a situation, and to be aware of our prejudice, until we have examined, on balance, whether there are more virtues than vices among civilized men; or whether their virtues are more beneficial to them than their vices are fatal; or whether the progress of their knowledge is a sufficient indemnity for the hurts they constantly do to each other even as they learn about the good they ought to do to each other; or whether they would not be, all in all, in a happier situation where they had nothing to fear nor good to hope from anyone, rather than having submitted to universal subserviency, and obliged themselves to depend for everything from those who feel no obligation to give them anything in return.

But above all, let us not conclude with Hobbes, that man, having no idea of goodness, must be naturally bad; or that he is vicious, because he does not know virtue, or that he always refuses his fellows services; or that he believes that none is due to them; nor that because of the right which he justly attributes to himself over the things he needs, he foolishly looks upon himself as the sole proprietor of the whole universe. Hobbes very plainly saw the flaw in all modern definitions of natural right; but the consequences which he draws from his own definition, show that he takes it in a sense which is no less false. In his reasoning about the principles which he establishes, that writer should have said that the state of nature being the state in which our self-preservation involves least harm to that of others, it is, consequently, the most conducive to peace and the most suited to the human kind. He says exactly the opposite because he improperly injected into the savage's self-preservation the need to satisfy numberless passions which are the work of society and which have rendered its laws necessary. The bad man, he says, is a robust child, and even if this were granted, what could this philosopher conclude from it? That, being robust, if he were as dependent on others as when he was weak, there is no excess that he would be guilty of. He would make nothing of beating his mother when she was too slow in giving her breast; that he would strangle one of his younger brothers without remorse when he was annoyed by him; that he would bite another's leg, when he would be bumped or annoyed by him. However, there are two contradictory suppositions in the state of nature; to be robust and independent. Man is weak when he is dependent, and before he becomes robust, he is emancipated. Hobbes did not consider that the same cause which prevents savages from using their reason, as our jurisconsults claim they do, also hinders them from making abusive use of their faculties, as he claims, so that we may say that savages are not bad precisely because they do not know what it is to be good; for it is neither the development of knowledge, nor the brake of law, but the absence of passions and ignorance of vice that prevents them from doing evil. There is, besides, another principle which Hobbes did not grasp, which, having been given to man to soften in certain circumstances the ferocity of his self-love, before its birth, or the desire of self-preservation, allays the ardour for his wellbeing, with an innate abhorrence to see his fellow man suffer. I shall not surely be contradicted, in granting to man the only natural virtue which the most extreme detractor of human virtues was forced to recognize. I mean that of pity, a characteristic suitable to beings as weak and liable to as many ills as we are; a virtue which is all the more universal and useful to man in that it is prior in him to all reflection; and so natural, that even the beasts themselves give evident signs of it.

(*Discourse on Inequality*, Part I)

## DENIS DIDEROT

Denis Diderot (1713–84) was born at Langres, the son of a prosperous master cutler. Initially interested in becoming a priest, he was sent to college in Paris from where he graduated in 1732. For the next ten years he scratched a living working as a hack writer and a tutor. In 1741 he met Antoinette Champion, daughter of a linen draper, and secretly married her in 1743, against his father's wishes. It was not a happy marriage, though it produced one surviving daughter, Angélique, to whom Diderot was devoted. In 1745 he published a translation of Lord Shaftesbury's *Inquiry Concerning Virtue* (1699) and in the following year *Pensées Philosophiques* (*Thoughts on Philosophy*) which was condemned by the *parlement* of Paris for 'putting all religions on virtually the same level' and rejecting all of them. Another clandestine publication *Lettre sur les Aveugles* (*Letter on the Blind*) appeared in 1749, exploring the Lockean idea that our knowledge would be different if we were deprived of any of our five senses. This work led to Diderot's arrest and imprisonment for three months at Vincennes. Although he was well treated (in part, due to Voltaire's expression of interest), and visited by Rousseau, the experience left an indelible impression, making him ever-fearful of publishing and acknowledging his most original writings. Many of his greatest works would therefore remain unpublished during his lifetime. However, he became internationally renowned and respected as the editor of the *Encyclopédie* (1751–72).

In 1747 Diderot was appointed editor of what many scholars would come to regard as the single most important textual achievement of the Enlightenment – the monumental *Encyclopédie, ou Dictionnaire Raisonné des Sciences, des Arts, et des Métiers* (*Encyclopedia, or Rational Dictionary of the Sciences, Arts and Trades*). Though the project owed its origins to the Parisian publisher, Le Breton, who in 1745 had planned a French translation of Ephraim Chambers' *Cyclopaedia* (1727), under Diderot's direction and D'Alembert's co-editorship (see p. 49), Le Breton's proposal was transformed into a far more original and ambitious work. The bold aim, as Diderot explained in his article 'Encyclopaedia', was 'to collect all the knowledge scattered over the face of the earth, to explain its general system to the men with whom we live, and to transmit this to the men who will come after us, so that the labour of past centuries may not be useless for the centuries to come, that our descendants, by becoming more educated may consequently be more virtuous and happier, and that we may not die without having deserved well of the human race' (vol. V, 1755). To accomplish such a goal, 'All things must be examined, debated and investigated, without exception and without regard to any-one's feelings', and this required authors who were prepared to write as though they were 'of no country, of no sect, of no rank'. Thus Diderot and d'Alembert (until 1758) drew upon the knowledge and views of scores of experts, to form 'a society of men of letters' that included *philosophes* such as Rousseau, Montesquieu, Voltaire, Jaucourt, Raynal and Condillac, during the twenty years that the twenty-eight volumes of *Encyclopédie* were in production.

Following the appearance of the first volume in 1751, the *Encyclopédie* soon became embroiled in a controversy with Jesuit censors over the alleged heresy of one of its contributors, Abbé de Prades. Though this led to a royal edict banning further publication and the attempted confiscation of manuscripts in 1752, with the help of Louis XV's director of publications (the censor) Malesherbes, produc-tion was cautiously resumed. Another major crisis occurred on the publication of volume VII in 1757, when d'Alembert's entry on 'Geneva' offended its Protestant clergy with the claim that they were akin to Enlightened deists. The attempted assassination of Louis XV by Damiens in 1757 (blamed on liberal thinking), and the publication of Helvétius' scandalously materialist work *De l'Esprit* (*Of the Mind*, 1758) inflamed conservative opinion, leading to a further ban on the *Encyclopédie*'s publication and its condemnation by the Pope. Though d'Alembert now resigned as co-editor, and even Voltaire advised closure, Diderot continued to oversee the production of ten more volumes of articles and eleven volumes of engravings which were finally completed in 1772 (see p. 138).

In the name of humanity, the *Encyclopédie* often challenged Christianity and traditional ways of thinking, but it did not advocate social or political revolution.

Nor were Diderot's many articles on philosophy, politics, religion, trade, manufacture and other topics among his most radical writings. Even so, he was enraged
to find out in 1764 that Le Breton had been silently censoring his articles to
remove material that might be deemed objectionable. Despite these and many
other difficulties in its tortuous history, the *Encyclopédie* was not only an outstanding intellectual achievement but a great commercial success. Though officially banned from sale in Paris, it was purchased (often surreptitiously) in its
original form or in several follow-up editions by many thousands of people from a
wide range of occupations, and was talked about and circulated throughout the
'Enlightened' world.

In the mid-1750s Diderot met his mistress and lifelong friend Sophie Volland
(1716–84) with whom he conducted a long and exceptionally vivid correspondence. He also wrote plays and theatre criticism, and the highly acclaimed study
of nature and scientific method *Pensées sur l'Interprétation de la Nature*
(*Thoughts on the Interpretation of Nature*), published anonymously in 1753 (see
p. 112). In the 1760s he turned at first to prose fiction, writing *La Religieuse*
(*The Nun*, 1796), his masterpiece *Le Neveu de Rameau* (*Rameau's Nephew*,
translated by Goethe in 1805) and *Jacques le Fataliste* (1796), and then developed his materialist philosophies and imaginative use of dialogue to produce *Le
Rêve de d'Alembert* (*D'Alembert's Dream*, 1830). He had also begun to write
reviews of the biennial art exhibitions at the Louvre, giving rise to a new kind of
literary art criticism (see p. 271), and in 1772 he produced what would later
become the famous *Supplement to the Voyage of Bougainville* (see p. 319).
None of these major works were published during Diderot's lifetime, but they
would later testify to his remarkable creativity, humanity, and breadth and flex-
ibility of thought. In 1773 he travelled to St Petersburg to thank Catherine the
Great for her patronage, and was very warmly received. After returning to
France in 1774, notwithstanding his own materialist and determinist views, he
wrote a refutation of what he regarded as the simplistic materialism of
Helvétius' *De l'Homme* (1773), and made substantial contributions to the
revised edition of Raynal's extraordinary study of Europeans and the wider
world (see p. 304). A few months after the death of Sophie Volland in 1784,
Diderot died at his home in Paris.

The following extracts are taken from an English translation (1783) of Abbé
Raynal's *A Philosophical and Political History of the Settlements* (first published
in 1772, but enlarged by 1780 to include many anonymous contributions from
Diderot). Although *History of the Settlements* was generally quite loosely organised, Book XI was wholly focused upon slavery and the slave trade. The first passage here is from Diderot's chapter 10: 'Colour of the Inhabitants of the Western
Coast of Africa, known by the name of Guinea. Enquiry into the cause of this phenomenon'. The second extract is from chapter 22: 'Wretched Condition of the
Slaves in America'. Two further extracts from *History of the Settlements* are provided in Chapter 11, 'Europeans and the Wider World'.

## 'Colour of the Inhabitants'

from Raynal's *History of the Settlements* ([1772], 1780)

Men! you are all brethren. How long will you defer to acknowledge each other? How long will it be before you perceive that Nature, your common mother, offers nourishment equally to all her children? Why must you destroy each other; and why must the hand that feeds you be continually stained with your blood? The acts that would excite your abhorrence in animals, you have been committing almost ever since you exist. Are you apprehensive of becoming too numerous? And do you not think that you will be exterminated fast enough by pestilential diseases, by the inclemency of the elements, by your labours, by your passions, by your vices, by your prejudices, by the weakness of your organs, and by the natural shortness of your life? The wisdom of the Being to whom you owe your existence, hath prescribed limits to your population, and to that of all living creatures, which will never be broken through. Have you not, in your wants, which are incessantly renewed, a sufficient number of enemies conspiring against you, without entering into a league with them? Man boasts of his superior excellence to all natural beings; and yet, with a spirit of ferociousness, which is not observed even in the race of tigers, man is the most terrible scourge of man. If his wishes were to be accomplished, there would soon remain no more than one single being of the same species upon the whole face of the globe.

This being, so cruel and so compassionate, so odious and so interesting, unhappy in the northern part of Africa, experiences a destiny infinitely more dreadful in the western part of this vast region.

Upon this coast, which extends from the Straight of Gibraltar to the Cape of Good Hope, the inhabitants have all, beyond the Niger, an oblong head; the nose large, flattened and spread out; thick lips; and curled hair, like the wool of our sheep. They are born white; and the only brown colour they at first exhibit, is round the nails and the eyes, with a small spot formed at the extremity of the genitals. Towards the eighth day after their birth the children begin to change colour, their skin darkens, and at length grows black, but of a dirty, sallow, and almost livid black; which, in process of time, becomes glossy and shining.

The flesh, however, the bones, the viscera, and all the internal parts, are of the same colour in Negroes as in white people. The lymph is equally white and limpid; and the milk of the nurses is everywhere the same.

The most palpable difference between them is, that the Negroes have the skin much hotter, and, as it were, oily, the blood of a blackish hue, the bile very deep coloured, the pulse quicker, a sweat which yields a strong and disagreeable smell, and a perspiration which often blackens the substance it comes in contact with. One of the inconveniences of this black colour, the image of night, which confounds all objects, is, that it hath, in some measure, obliged these people to scar their face and breast, and to stain their skin with various colours, in order that they may know each other at a distance. There are some tribes in which this practice is universal; among others, it appears to be a distinction reserved to superior rank. But as we see this custom established among the people of Tartary, of Canada, and of other savage nations, it may be doubted, whether it be not rather the effect of their wandering way of life, than of their complexion.

This colour proceeds from a mucous substance, which forms a kind of network between the epidermis and the skin. This substance, which is white in Europeans, brown in people of an olive complexion, and sprinkled over with reddish spots among light-haired or carroty people, is blackish among the Negroes.

The desire of discovering the causes of this colour, hath given rise to a variety of systems.

Theology, which hath taken possession of the human mind by opinion; which hath availed itself of the first fears of infancy, to inspire reason with eternal apprehensions; which hath altered everything, geography, astronomy, philosophy, and history; which hath introduced the marvellous and the mysterious in everything, in order to arrogate to itself the right of explaining everything: theology, after having made a race of men guilty and unfortunate from the fault of Adam, hath made a race of black men, in order to punish the fratricide of his son. The Negroes are the descendants of Cain. If their father was an assassin, it must be allowed that his posterity have made a severe atonement for his crime; and that the descendants of the pacific Abel have thoroughly avenged the innocent blood of their father.

Reason hath attempted to explain the colour of the Negroes, from consequences deduced from the phenomenon of chemistry. According to some naturalist, it is a vitriolic fluid contained in the lymph of the Negroes, and being too gross to pass through the pores of the skin, it ferments and unites with the mucous body, which it colours. It is then urged, why is the hair curled, and why are the eyes and teeth of negroes so white? For, the authors of this system do not consider that a vitriolic salt of such power and activity, would at length destroy all organisation. This, however, is as perfect in Negroes, as in the whitest of the human race.

Anatomy hath thought to have discovered the origin of the blackness of Negroes in the principles of generation. Nothing more, it should seem, would be necessary to prove, that Negroes are a particular species of men. For if anything discriminates the species, or the classes in each species, it is certainly the difference of the semen. But upon considering the matter more attentively, this hath been found to be a mistake, so that this explanation of the colour of Negroes, hath been given up. Neither have the consequences, pretended to be deduced from the difference between their figure and that of other people, appeared more convincing. Some of these forms are owing to the climate, most of them to ancient customs. It hath been conceived, that these barbarians might possibly have formed some extravagant ideas of beauty, according to which they had endeavoured to form their children; that this habit, in process of time, had been turned into nature, so that it was very seldom necessary to have recourse to art, in order to obtain these singular forms.

There are other causes of the colour of Negroes, more satisfactory than these: the seat of it, as we have observed, is in the *rete mucosum* [under-portion of the epidermis], under the epidermis, or cuticle. The substance of this network, which is mucous in the first instance, is afterwards changed into a web of vessels, the diameter of which is considerable enough to admit either a portion of the colouring part of the blood or of the bile, which is said to have a peculiar tendency towards the skin. From hence proceeds among white people, in whom this *rete mucosum* is more lax, the more vivid complexion of the cheeks. From hence also, that yellow or copper-colour which distinguishes whole nations, while under another climate, it is confined to one person, and produced by disease. The existence of one or of the other of these fluids is sufficient to colour the Negroes, especially if we add that the epidermis and the *rete mucosum* is thicker in them; that the blood is blackish, and the bile deeper coloured, and that their sweat, which is more plentiful, and less fluid, must necessarily thicken under the epidermis, and increase the darkness of the colour.

This system is also supported by natural philosophy, which observes that the parts of the body exposed to the sun are most deeply coloured, and that travellers, and people who dwell in the country, and who lead a wandering life (all those, in a word, who live continually in the open air, and under a more burning sky), have darker complexions. Philosophy thinks, from these observations, that the primitive cause of the colour of the Negroes may be attributed to the climate, and to the ardour of the sun. There are no Negroes, it is said, except in hot climates; their colour becomes darker in proportion as they approach the equator. It grows lighter at the extremities of the torrid zone. All the human species, in general, whitens in the snow, and is tanned in the sun. We perceive the different shades from white to black, and those from black to white, marked, as it were, by the parallel degrees which cut the earth in the direction from the equator to the poles. If the zones, contrived by the inventors of the sphere, were represented by real bands, we should see the black ebony colour insensibly changing to the right and left as far as the tropics, and from thence the brown colour would be seen to grow paler and lighter as far as the polar circles, by shades of white continually increasing in clearness.

As the shades of black are, however, deeper upon the western coasts of Africa, than in other regions perhaps as much heated, the ardour of the sun must certainly be combined with other causes, which have an equal influence upon organisation. Such of the Europeans as have made the longest residence in those countries, attribute this greater degree of blackness to the nitrous, sulphureous, or metallic particles, that are continually exhaling from the surface or from the bowels of the earth, to the custom of going naked, to the proximity of burning sands, and to other particulars which do not occur elsewhere in the same degree.

The circumstance that seems to confirm the opinion, that the colour of the Negroes is the effect of the climate, of the air, of the water, and of the food of Guinea, is, that this colour changes when the inhabitants are removed into other countries. The children they procreate in America are not so black as their parents were. After each generation the difference becomes more palpable. It is possible that after a numerous succession of generations, the men come from Africa, would not be distinguished from those of the country into which they may have been transplanted.

Although the opinion, which ascribes to the climate the first cause of the colour of the inhabitants of Guinea, be almost generally adopted, all the objections that may be urged against this system, have not yet been answered. This is one proof, added to a multitude of others, of the uncertainty of our knowledge.

And, indeed, how is it possible that our knowledge should not be uncertain and circumscribed? Our organs are so feeble, and our means so insufficient, our studies so much interrupted, our life so much agitated, and the object of our inquiries is of so immense an extent! Let naturalists, philosophers, chemists, and accurate observers of nature in all her works, persevere in their labours incessantly; and after ages of united and continual efforts, the secrets of nature which they will have discovered, when compared to her immense treasures, will be no more than as a drop of water to the vast ocean. [...]

(*History of the Settlements*, Book XI, ch. 10)

## 'Wretched Condition of the Slaves in America'

from Raynal's *History of the Settlements* (1780)

All Europe hath for this century past, been filled with the most sublime, and the soundest sentiments of morality. Writings, which will be immortal, have established in the most affecting manner, that all men are brethren. We are filled with indignation at the cruelties, whether civil or religious, of our ferocious ancestors, and we turn away our eyes from those ages of horror and blood. Those among our neighbours, whom the inhabitants of Barbary have loaden with irons, obtain our pity and assistance. Even imaginary distresses draw tears from our eyes, both in the silent retirement of the closet, and especially at the theatre. It is only the fatal destiny of the Negroes which doth not concern us. They are tyrannized, mutilated, burnt, and put to death, and yet we listen to these accounts coolly and without emotion. The torments of a people, to whom we owe our luxuries, can never reach our hearts.

The condition of these slaves, though everywhere deplorable, is something different in the colonies. In those where there are very extensive territories, a portion of land is generally given them, to supply them with the necessaries of life. They are allowed to employ a part of the Sunday in cultivating it, and the few moments that on other days they spare from the time allotted for their meals. In the more confined islands, the colonist himself furnishes their food, the greatest part of which hath been imported by sea from other countries. Ignorance, avarice, or poverty, have introduced into some colonies a method of providing for the subsistence of Negroes, equally destructive both to the men and the plantation. They are allowed on Saturday, or some other day, to work in the neighbouring plantations, or to plunder them, in order to procure a maintenance for the rest of the week.

Beside these differences arising from the particular situation of the settlements in the American islands, each European nation hath a manner of treating slaves peculiar to itself. The Spaniards make them the companions of their indolence; the Portuguese, the instruments of their debauchery; the Dutch, the victims of their avarice. By the English, they are considered merely as natural productions, which ought neither to be used, nor destroyed without necessity; but they never treat them with familiarity; they never smile upon them, nor speak to them. One would think they were afraid of letting them suspect that nature could have given any one mark of resemblance betwixt them and their slaves. This makes them hate the English. The French, less haughty, less disdainful, consider the Africans as a species of moral beings; and these unhappy men, sensible of the honour of seeing themselves almost treated like rational creatures, seem to forget that their master is impatient of making his fortune, that he always exacts labours from them above their strength, and frequently lets them want subsistence.

The opinions of the Europeans have also some influence on the condition of the Negroes of America. The Protestants, who are not actuated by a desire of making proselytes, suffer them to live in Mohammedism, or in that idolatry in which they were born, under a pretence, that it would be injurious to keep their *brethren in Christ* in a state of slavery. The Catholics think themselves obliged to give them some instruction, and to baptize them; but their charity extends no further than the bare ceremonies of a baptism, which is wholly useless and unnecessary to men who dread not the pains of hell, to which, they say, they are accustomed in this life.

We will not here so far debase ourselves as to enlarge the ignominious list of those writers who devote their abilities, to justify by policy what is reprobated by morality. In an age where so many errors are boldly exposed, it would be unpardonable to conceal any truth that is interesting to humanity. If whatever we have hitherto advanced hath seemingly tended only to alleviate the burthen of slavery, the reason is that it was first necessary to give some comfort to those unhappy beings whom we cannot set free; and convince their oppressors that they are cruel to the prejudice of their real interests. But, in the mean time, until some considerable revolution shall make the evidence of this great truth felt, it may not be improper to pursue this subject further. We shall then first prove, that there is no reason of state that can authorise slavery. We shall not be afraid to cite to the tribunal of reason and justice those governments which tolerate this cruelty, or which even are not ashamed to make it the basis of their power.

(*History of the Settlements*, Book XI, ch. 22)

## MARQUIS DE CONDORCET

The French mathematician, historian, political theorist and social reformer, Marie-Jean-Antoine-Nicolas de Caritat (1743–1794) is better known as the Marquis de Condorcet. Born in Picardy, the son of a nobleman who was killed in battle a few weeks after Nicolas was born, he was brought up by his mother and educated by Jesuits at the College of Navarre. In recognition of his work in mathematics, he was elected to the Académie des Sciences at the age of twenty-six, and soon became friends with many *philosophes*, including d'Alembert, Helvétius, Voltaire and Turgot. In 1785 he published a major work on the theory of probability and in the following year he married Sophie de Grouchy (1764–1822), whose *salon* at their house in Paris soon became one of the most influential of the period. He was the only prominent *philosophe* to participate actively in the French Revolution, campaigning for economic freedom, religious tolerance, legal and educational reform and the abolition of slavery. A firm republican, Condorcet was elected to represent Paris in the Legislative Assembly in 1791, and became its secretary. However, his opposition to the death penalty compelled him to vote against the execution of Louis XVI. The Jacobin rise to power in June 1793 forced him into hiding, and it was during this time, particularly from July to October 1793, that he wrote what would become his most famous work, *Esquisse d'un Tableau*

*Historique des Progrès de l'Esprit Humain* (*Sketch of a Historical Picture of the Human Mind*), published posthumously in 1795. After being captured on 27 March 1794, Condorcet died during his first night of imprisonment, possibly from poison.

Though the author of many works on mathematics, science, politics and philosophy, Condorcet's name and influence has been chiefly associated with the *Sketch*, and it is from a modern translation of this text that the following passages have been selected. In this work Condorcet propounded his idea of unlimited human progress and great confidence in the future, explaining his belief that human emancipation lay in the destruction of all the obstacles which have hindered it – most notably, reliance on revelation and authority. By understanding human nature and the value of science and popular education, advances in sciences and technology could be made, and the ignorance which had led to the inequalities, tyrannies and prejudices of former times would eventually be overcome. The *Sketch* tells a story of human progress as though it were a universal and inevitable history of humankind from barbarism to European Enlightenment. Thus in the 'first stage' Condorcet tells us 'Men are united in tribes', and in the second stage they become 'Pastoral peoples' who define their property rights. The eighth stage or epoch begins with the invention of printing, and the ninth stage runs 'From Descartes to the foundation of the French Republic', in which Newton, Locke, Condillac, d'Alembert, Rousseau and others lead the process of liberation: 'The philosophers of different nations who considered the interests of the whole of humanity without distinction of country, race or creed, formed a solid phalanx bonded together against all forms of error, against all manifestations of tyranny, despite their differences in matters of theory.' In the last and most original chapter of the *Sketch*, 'The Tenth Stage', Condorcet reflects upon 'The Future Progress of the Human Mind'. The following passages are three extracts from this final chapter.

## Sketch of a Historical Picture of the Human Mind (1795)

### 'The future progress of the human mind'

If man can, with almost complete assurance, predict phenomena when he knows their laws, and if, even when he does not, he can still, with great expectation of success, forecast the future on the basis of his experience of the past, why, then, should it be regarded as a fantastic undertaking to sketch, with some pretence to truth, the future destiny of man on the basis of his history? The sole foundation for belief in the natural sciences is this idea, that the general laws directing the phenomena of the universe, known or unknown, are necessary and constant. Why should this principle be any less true for the development of the intellectual and moral faculties of man than for the other operations of nature? Since beliefs founded on past experience of like conditions provide the only rule of conduct for the wisest of men, why should the philosopher be forbidden to base his conjectures on these same foundations, so long as he does not attribute to them a certainty superior to that warranted by the number, the constancy, and the accuracy of his observations?

Our hopes for the future condition of the human race can be subsumed under three important heads: the abolition of inequality between nations, the progress of equality within each nation, and the true perfection of mankind. Will all nations one day attain that state of civilization which the most enlightened, the freest and the least burdened by prejudices, such as the French and the Anglo-Americans have attained already? Will the vast gulf that separates these peoples from the slavery of nations under the rule of monarchs, from the barbarism of African tribes, from the ignorance of savages, little by little disappear?

Is there on the face of the earth a nation whose inhabitants have been debarred by nature herself from the enjoyment of freedom and the exercise of reason?

Are those differences which have hitherto been seen in every civilized country in respect of the enlightenment, the resources, and the wealth enjoyed by the different classes into which it is divided, is that inequality between men which was aggravated or perhaps produced by the earliest progress of society, are these part of civilization itself, or are they due to the present imperfections of the social art? Will they necessarily decrease and ultimately make way for a real equality, the final end of the social art, in which even the effects of the natural differences between men will be mitigated and the only kind of inequality to persist will be that which is in the interests of all and which favours the progress of civilization, of education, and of industry, without entailing either poverty, humiliation, or dependence? In other words, will men approach a condition in which everyone will have the knowledge necessary to conduct himself in the ordinary affairs of life, according to the light of his own reason, to preserve his mind free from prejudice, to understand his rights and to exercise them in accordance with his conscience and his creed; in which everyone will become able, through the development of his faculties, to find the means of providing for his needs; and in which at last misery and folly will be the exception, and no longer the habitual lot of a section of society?

Is the human race to better itself, either by discoveries in the sciences and the arts, and so in the means to individual welfare and general prosperity; or by progress in the principles of conduct or practical morality; or by a true perfection of the intellectual, moral, or physical faculties of man, an improvement which may result from a perfection either of the instruments used to heighten the intensity of these faculties and to direct their use or of the natural constitution of man?

In answering these three questions we shall find in the experience of the past, in the observation of the progress that the sciences and civilization have already made, in the analysis of the progress of the human mind and of the development of its faculties, the strongest reasons for believing that nature has set no limit to the realization of our hopes.

If we glance at the state of the world today we see first of all that in Europe the principles of the French constitution are already those of all enlightened men. We see them too widely propagated, too seriously professed, for priests and despots to prevent their gradual penetration even into the hovels of their slaves; there they will soon awaken in these slaves the remnants of their common sense and inspire them with that smouldering indignation which not even constant humiliation and fear can smother in the soul of the oppressed.

As we move from nation to nation, we can see in each what special obstacles impede this revolution and what attitudes of mind favour it. We can distinguish the nations where we may expect it to be introduced gently by the perhaps belated wisdom of their governments, and those nations where its violence intensified by their resistance must involve all alike in a swift and terrible convulsion.

Can we doubt that either common sense or the senseless discords of European nations will add to the effects of the slow but inexorable progress of their colonies, and will soon bring about the independence of the New World? And then will not the European population in these colonies, spreading rapidly over that enormous land, either civilize or peacefully remove the savage nations who still inhabit vast tracts of its land?

Survey the history of our settlements and commercial undertakings in Africa or in Asia, and you will see how our trade monopolies, our treachery, our murderous contempt for men of another colour or creed, the insolence of our usurpations, the intrigues or the exaggerated proselytic zeal of our priests, have destroyed the respect and goodwill that the superiority of our knowledge and the benefits of our commerce at first won for us in the eyes of the inhabitants. But doubtless the moment approaches when, no longer presenting ourselves as always either tyrants or corrupters, we shall become for them the beneficent instruments of their freedom.

The sugar industry, establishing itself throughout the immense continent of Africa, will destroy the shameful exploitation which has corrupted and depopulated that continent for the last two centuries. [...]

The degree of equality in education that we can reasonably hope to attain, but that should be adequate, is that which excludes all dependence, either forced or voluntary. We shall show how this condition can be easily attained in the present state of human knowledge even by those who can study only for a small number of years in childhood, and then during the rest of their life in their few hours of leisure. We shall prove that, by a suitable choice of syllabus and of methods of education, we can teach the citizen everything that he needs to know in order to be able to manage his household, administer his affairs and employ his labour and his faculties in freedom; to know his rights and to be able to exercise them; to be acquainted with his duties and fulfil them satisfactorily; to judge his own and other men's actions according to his own lights and to be a stranger to none of the high and delicate feelings which honour human nature; not to be in a state of blind dependence upon those to whom he must entrust his affairs or the exercise of his rights; to be in a proper condition to choose and supervise them; to be no longer the dupe of those popular errors which torment man with superstitious fears and chimerical hopes; to defend himself against prejudice by the strength of his reason alone; and, finally, to escape the deceits of charlatans who would lay snares for his fortune, his health, his freedom of thought and his conscience under the pretext of granting him health, wealth and salvation.

From such time onwards the inhabitants of a single country will no longer be distinguished by their use of a crude or refined language; they will be able to govern themselves according to their own knowledge; they will no longer be limited to a mechanical knowledge of the procedures of the arts or of professional routine; they will no longer depend for every trivial piece of business, every insignificant matter of instruction on clever men who rule over them in virtue of their necessary superiority; and so they will attain a real equality, since differences in enlightenment or talent can no longer raise a barrier between men who understand each other's feelings, ideas and language, some of whom may wish to be taught by others but, to do so, will have no need to be controlled by them, or who may wish to confide the care of government to the ablest of their number but will not be compelled to yield them absolute power in a spirit of blind confidence.

This kind of supervision has advantages even for those who do not exercise it, since it is employed for them and not against them. Natural differences of ability between men whose understanding has not been cultivated give rise, even in savage tribes, to charlatans and dupes, to clever men and men readily deceived. These same differences are truly universal, but now they are differences only between men of learning and upright men who know the value of learning without being dazzled by it; or between talent or genius and the common sense which can appreciate and benefit from them; so that even if these natural differences were greater, and more extensive than they are, they would be only the more influential in improving the relations between men and promoting what is advantageous for their independence and happiness.

These various causes of equality do not act in isolation; they unite, combine and support each other and so their cumulative effects are stronger, surer and more constant. With greater equality of education there will be greater equality in industry and so in wealth; equality in wealth necessarily leads to equality in education; and equality between the nations and equality within a single nation are mutually dependent.

So we might say that a well directed system of education rectifies natural inequality in ability instead of strengthening it, just as good laws remedy natural inequality in the means of subsistence, and just as in societies where laws have brought about this same equality, liberty, though subject to a regular constitution, will be more widespread, more complete than in the total independence of savage life. Then the social art will have fulfilled its aim, that of assuring and extending to all men enjoyment of the common rights to which they are called by nature.

The real advantages that should result from this progress, of which we can entertain a hope that is almost a certainty, can have no other term than that of the absolute perfection of the human race; since, as the various kinds of equality come to work in its favour by producing ampler sources of supply, more extensive education, more complete liberty, so equality will be more real and will embrace everything which is really of importance for the happiness of human beings. [...]

Among the causes of the progress of the human mind that are of the utmost importance to the general happiness, we must number the complete annihilation of the prejudices that have brought about an inequality of rights between the sexes, an inequality fatal even to the party in whose favour it works. It is vain for us to look for a justification of this principle in any differences of physical organization, intellect or moral sensibility between men and women. This inequality has its origin solely in an abuse of strength, and all the later sophisticated attempts that have been made to excuse it are vain.

We shall show how the abolition of customs authorized, laws dictated by this prejudice, would add to the happiness of family life, would encourage the practice of the domestic virtues on which all other virtues are based, how it would favour the progress of education, and how, above all, it would bring about its wider diffusion; for not only would education be extended to women as well as to men, but it can only really be taken proper advantage of when it has the support and encouragement of the mothers of the family. Would not this belated tribute to equity and good sense, put an end to a principle only too fecund of injustice, cruelty and crime, by removing the dangerous conflict between the strongest and most irrepressible of all natural inclinations and man's duty or the interests of society? Would it not produce what has until now been no more than a dream, national manners of a mildness and purity, formed not by proud asceticism, not by hypocrisy, not by the fear or shame or religious terrors but by freely contracted habits that are inspired by nature and acknowledged by reason?

Once people are enlightened they will know that they have the right to dispose of their own life and wealth as they choose; they will gradually learn to regard war as the most dreadful of scourges, the most terrible of crimes. The first wars to disappear will be those into which usurpers have forced their subjects in defence of their pretended hereditary rights.

Nations will learn that they cannot conquer other nations without losing their own liberty; that permanent confederations are their only means of preserving their independence; and that they should seek not power but security. Gradually mercantile prejudices will fade away, and a false sense of commercial interest will lose the fearful power it once had of drenching the earth in blood and of ruining nations under pretext of enriching them. When at last the nations come to agree on the principles of politics and morality, when in their own better interests they invite foreigners to share equally in all the benefits men enjoy either through the bounty of nature or by their own industry, then all the causes that produce and perpetuate national animosities and poison national relations will disappear one by one; and nothing will remain to encourage or even to arouse the fury of war.

Organizations more intelligently conceived than those projects of eternal peace which have filled the leisure and consoled the hearts of certain philosophers, will hasten the progress of the brotherhood of nations, and wars between countries will rank with assassinations as freakish atrocities, humiliating and vile in the eyes of nature and staining with indelible opprobrium the country or the age whose annals record them.

(*Sketch of a Historical Picture*, 'The Tenth Stage')

# Chapter 2

# The search for knowledge

**P**HILOSOPHERS HAVE ALWAYS ASKED QUESTIONS about knowledge: What is to count as knowledge? How is knowledge acquired and can anything be known for certain? Such questions belong to the branch of philosophy known as epistemology or the theory of knowledge. In the Christian tradition, the epistemological answer was that Revelation is the source of knowledge. We know for certain only that which God has revealed to us through the life of Christ and the scriptures. In their teachings, emphasising faith and obedience, Christian churches were keen to perpetuate this tradition and often suppressed ideas and experimental methods of enquiry that seemed to confront or jeopardise it.

In the seventeenth century a potent influence in the development of epistemology came from the work of the French philosopher René Descartes (1596–1650). Descartes demanded to know whether any claim to knowledge could be upheld against the possibility of doubt. In *Meditations* (1641), he devised a systematic method of doubt: anything that can be called into question must be discarded. He dismissed any previous beliefs acquired via the senses on the grounds that the senses have sometimes proved unreliable (they may deceive us, or we may be dreaming). But, Descartes concluded, there is one innate truth that cannot be doubted: that I exist, simply because I am able to doubt my existence. It is, then, only that which we know innately that can be guaranteed. On this basis, Descartes claimed that reason must be the only reliable source of knowledge (rationalism).

The rationalist theory of innate ideas has a very long history, going back to Plato, but towards the end of the seventeenth century the English philosopher John Locke launched a fundamental assault upon rationalism. He argued that it is the five senses which are the primary sources of knowledge. Without these senses, one could not know anything (even that one existed), and without particular senses (e.g. of sight) one could not have access to particular experiences and therefore to particular kinds of knowledge (e.g. of yellowness). Thus, for Locke:

The senses at first let in particular ideas, and furnish the yet empty cabinet, and the mind by degrees growing familiar with some of them, they are lodged in the memory, and names got to them. Afterwards, the mind, proceeding further, abstracts them, and by degrees learns the use of general names. In this manner the mind comes to be furnished with ideas and language, the materials about which to exercise its discursive faculty, and the use of reason becomes daily more visible, as these materials, that give it employment, increase.

(*Essay Concerning Human Understanding*, 1690, Book I, ch. II)

This theory is generally known as empiricism (from the Greek word for experience). Locke asserted that sensory perceptions, plus the mind's reflections on those perceptions, provide us with all the knowledge that we have, or can ever have. Rationalists, on the contrary, claimed that knowledge of the world was based on reason – that we can learn things solely by thinking, independently of sense experience.

As an empiricist, the Scottish philosopher and historian David Hume looked to Locke for inspiration, but tried to improve upon his predecessor's achievement. He redefined and analysed Locke's use of the word 'idea', preferring the term 'perceptions of the mind', which he subdivided into 'impressions' (primary) and 'ideas' (derivative). He also agreed with Locke's criticism of rationalism, on the basis that it underestimates the role of the senses in forming our understanding. However, Hume's criticism went further, for he regarded all religious belief as quite unreasonable, rejected Locke's idea of justice and property as being 'natural', and argued that reason is always 'subservient' to the emotions, for it can only ever be 'a slave to the passions'.

Hume's view of the role of reasoning in human affairs warns us that although the Enlightenment has often been referred to as 'The Age of Reason', this can be very misleading – not least because it suggests that what constitutes reasoning, and what is reasonable, can be determined independently of real people, living in real time and place, and that the eighteenth century saw the emergence of the *correct* form of reasoning, in place of various erroneous forms that had persisted in earlier times. Furthermore, reason was regarded as the most reliable source of knowledge by rationalists long before the eighteenth century, and the *philosophes* were by no means agreed in their views about the use of reasoning, let alone advocates of a strict rationalism that saw all learning as based solely or primarily upon thinking without regard to observation and experience. It was Locke and Newton who inspired many of the *philosophes* in their general preference for empiricism; a conviction that all knowledge is based in and derived from sensory experience. Empiricists such as Hume therefore favoured *a posteriori* (inductive) reasoning; a method of arriving at general truths following the evidence of lots of particular observations or experiments. This was considered opposed to the *a priori* (deductive) method of reasoning that was undertaken *before* experience, an approach upheld by rationalists such as the German philosopher G.W. Leibniz (see p. 68) and his pupil and populariser Christian Wolff (1679–1754).

Wolff, believing that mathematics provided the correct model for reasoning, developed a deductive method in an attempt to establish a strictly rationalist system of philosophy. This led him into disputes with Newtonians such as the French scientist Pierre Maupertius, and with devout reformist Lutherans (pietists) which resulted in him leaving the University of Halle for a post at Marburg in Saxony. However, following the accession of 'the philosopher-king' Frederick the Great in 1740, Wolff returned to Prussia where he consolidated his influence upon the course of the Enlightenment in Germany. The belief that knowledge and truths could be established with certitude, like mathematical calculations, appealed to rationalists such as Leibniz and Wolff. *A priori* reasonings could lead to logical and firm conclusions that were not contingent upon the vagaries of sensory experience. By contrast, *a posteriori* reasoning could only achieve provisional truths, as these were dependent upon propositions that were liable to change in the light of further (sensory) observation, experiment and experience. Tolerance of such uncertainty required confidence that reasoning from experiment and observation was preferable to reasoning solely from hypotheses, and for most *philosophes* (a term used here to refer generally to all kind of Enlightenment thinkers) it was Newton's methods and achievements that eventually provided the most persuasive evidence. This is how he put the case for 'experimental philosophy' in his *Optics* (1704):

> As in mathematics, so in natural philosophy, the investigation of difficult things by the method of analysis ought ever to precede the method of compositions. This analysis consists in making experiments and observations, and in drawing general conclusions from them by induction, and admitting of no objections against the conclusions but such as are taken from experiment, or other certain truths. For hypotheses are not to be regarded in experimental philosophy. And although the arguing from experiments and observations by induction be no demonstration of general conclusions, yet it is the best way of arguing which the nature of things admits of, and may be looked upon as so much the stronger by how much the induction is more general. And if no exception occur from phenomena, the conclusion may be pronounced generally.

Like Newton, Locke and Hume, the French philosopher Jean d'Alembert was strongly opposed to systems of philosophy built upon deductive reasoning from metaphysical hypotheses or propositions, as evidenced in the work of scholars such as Descartes and Leibniz. In his 'Preliminary Discourse' (1751) to the *Encyclopédie* d'Alembert recognised that Descartes, an 'inventive genius', had shown 'great courage in battling the most generally accepted prejudices', made a major contribution to mathematics, and prepared the ground for Newtonian physics and philosophy. In short, although Descartes had 'concluded by believing that he could explain everything, he at least began by doubting everything'. Similarly, Leibniz was commended for setting out the problems of understanding 'the union of body and soul, Providence, and the nature of matter'. But, like Descartes, his metaphysics could not solve them. Indeed, 'his system of Optimism is perhaps dangerous because of the alleged advantage that it has of explaining everything'. In this famous essay on the rise of Enlightenment, it was Bacon, Locke and Newton who became d'Alembert's heroes; and they would remain first in the hall of fame of many Enlightenment figures, such as Thomas Jefferson. These were the men who, after many centuries of ignorance and 'theological despotism', had 'prepared from afar the light which gradually, by imperceptible degrees would illuminate the world'.

D'Alembert, even more than Voltaire, saw Francis Bacon (1561–1621) as 'the greatest, the most universal and the most eloquent' of the modern philosophers. Though 'born in the depths of the most profound night', Bacon is celebrated for dividing science into different branches, being 'hostile to systems', trying to use philosophy 'to make us better or happier', studying nature, and conducting experiments. Newton is celebrated for 'inventing calculus', creating 'an entirely new optics' and 'discovering gravitation'. Most important, though, he 'gave philosophy a form which apparently it is to keep'. Finally, Locke is presented as having 'successfully carried through what Newton had not dared to do ... he reduced metaphysics to what it really ought to be: the experimental physics of the soul'.

D'Alembert believed passionately that the history of science and philosophy that he constructed for the 'Preliminary Discourse' reflected the fact that a revolution had recently taken place in human knowledge, and that the foundations were now laid for much further progress in the future. Like most Enlightenment texts, his essay was in part an act of rhetoric as it boldly proclaimed, for example, that 'the taste for [philosophical] systems ... is today almost entirely banished from works of merit'. However, a belief that the advancement of knowledge through new ways of reasoning would lead to great progress and improvement in human welfare and happiness became a hallmark of most Enlightenment thinking. It was an idea that d'Alembert, in particular, never tired of reciting. Thus, a few years later, he declared:

> Our century is called the century of philosophy *par excellence* ... If one considers without bias the present state of our knowledge, one cannot deny that philosophy among us has shown progress ... The discovery and application of a new method of philosophizing, the kind of enthusiasm which accompanies discoveries, a certain exultation of ideas which the spectacle of the universe produces in us – all these causes have brought about a lively fermentation of minds. Spreading through nature in all directions like a river which has burst its dams, this fermentation has swept with a sort of violence everything along with it which stood in its way ... Thus from the principles of the secular sciences to the foundations of religious revelation, from metaphysics to matters of taste, from music to morals, from the scholastic disputes of theologians to matters of trade, from the laws of princes to those of peoples, from natural law to the arbitrary laws of nations ... everything has been discussed and analysed, or at least mentioned. The fruit or sequel of this general effervescence of minds has been to cast new light on some matters and new shadows on others, just as the effect of the ebb and flow of the tides is to leave some things on the shores and to wash others away.
>
> (*Elements of Philosophy*, 1759)

Towards the end of the century the German philosopher Immanuel Kant recast problems of epistemology by proposing that there was some knowledge which was not derived from experience but that was a necessary apparatus for understanding the external world. This entailed both a powerful critique of rationalism and empiricism, as propounded by philosophers such as Leibniz and Locke and their respective followers. However, like d'Alembert and his metaphor of a river that had burst its dams, in reflecting on the century, Kant too saw Enlightenment (Aufklärung) as a dynamic and liberating process. Self-emancipation was by no means complete, but the process had begun: 'If we are asked "Do we now live in an *enlightened age*?" the answer is "No, but we do live in an *age of enlightenment*" ' ('What is Enlightenment?', 1785).

## ISAAC NEWTON

Sir Isaac Newton (1642–1727) was a natural philosopher who revolutionised the study of the physical world and laid many of the foundations of modern science. He was born in Lincolnshire and studied at Trinity College, Cambridge, graduating in 1665, apparently without distinction. However, his genius was soon recognised. When only twenty-three years old he worked out the fundamentals of calculus (which would later lead to a major controversy with Leibniz over who deserved the credit for first discovering it), and in 1669 he was appointed Lucasian Professor of Mathematics at Cambridge.

Newton's greatest work, the *Philosophiae Naturalis Principia Mathematica* (*Mathematical Principles of Natural Philosophy*), was first published in Latin in 1687, revised in 1713, followed by a third edition in 1726, and translated into English in 1729. It provided mathematical proof of the universal force of gravitation. The *Principia* is written in the form of three books: the first concerns itself with laws of motion; the second repudiates Descartes' (Cartesian) cosmology; and the third uses empirical method to explain the universalisation of the laws of gravity. Being outwardly a conventional Christian (though he secretly rejected the Trinity), Newton did not intend his work to undermine faith in God. Indeed, he undertook considerable theological researches, and his followers and supporters often used his theories as evidence of God's rational design of Nature. However, his findings were also cited by materialists who claimed that, if matter were active (for, according to the law of gravity, every particle of matter is attracted to all other matter in the universe), the natural world did not need to be directed (or even originally put in motion) by a Divine Being. Newton's methods of enquiry represented only part of his contribution to epistemology. Many of the *philosophes* were so impressed by his methods and theories, which were widely popularised by Voltaire, the Marquise du Châtelet and others, that his authority came to be regarded as a test of scientific truth. Clearly, his outstanding accomplishments in science now overshadow his deep and sustained interests in theology, ancient chronology and alchemy. Leaving Cambridge in 1696, he later became Master of the Royal Mint, President of the Royal Society in 1703, and was knighted in 1705.

In 1704 he published *Optics*, a major treatise on the composition of light and the use of the experimental method of enquiry.

The term 'Newtonian' represents a view of nature as a universal system explicable in terms of mathematical reasoning, divinely created and ordered. Many *philosophes* were inspired by Newton's methods and achievements, not only in their studies of the material world but also in their examinations of society and culture. Yet, while Newton's work gave rise to a tremendous confidence that the mysteries of Nature could be revealed and utilised for the benefit of humans, it seems that Newton was more circumspect: 'I do not know what I may appear to the world, but to myself I seem to have been only like a boy playing on the sea-shore, and diverting myself in now and then finding a smoother pebble or a prettier shell than ordinary, whilst the great ocean of truth lay all undiscovered before me.'

The following extract, based upon the English translation of 1729, is taken from the 'The System of the World', the third book of the *Principia*, in which Newton examines cause and effect, and draws particular attention to the importance of the senses in the work of philosophy, claiming that (in contrast to Descartes' method), his own method is empirical *and* deductive. In a short section at the beginning of Book Three, Newton sets out four rules for the study of natural philosophy. The first two rules appeared as hypotheses in the first edition (1687) of *Principia*; rule III, that attributes the property of gravity to heavenly bodies, upon which we cannot experiment, appeared in the 1713 revision; and rule IV, which states that the results of induction should not be preferred to mere hypotheses, was included in the third edition, in 1726.

## Mathematical Principles of Natural Philosophy (1687)

### 'Rules of Reasoning in Philosophy'

Rule I. *We are to admit no more causes of natural things than such as are both true and sufficient to explain their appearances.*

To this purpose the philosophers say that Nature does nothing in vain, and more is in vain when less will serve; for Nature is pleased with simplicity, and affects not the pomp of superfluous causes.

Rule II. *Therefore to the same natural effects we must, as far as possible, assign the same causes.*

As to respiration in a man and in a beast; the descent of stones in Europe and in America; the light of our culinary fire and of the sun; the reflection of light on the earth, and in the planets.

Rule III. *The qualities of bodies, which admit neither intension nor remission of degrees* [i.e. that cannot be increased or reduced], *and which are found to belong to all bodies within the reach of our experiments, are to be esteemed the universal qualities of all bodies whatsoever.*

For since the qualities of bodies are only known to us by experiments, we are to hold for universal all such as universally agree with experiments, and such as are not liable to diminution can never be quite taken away. We are certainly not to relinquish the evidence of experiments for the sake of dreams and vain fictions of our own devising; nor are we to recede from the analogy of Nature, which uses to be simple, and always consonant to itself. We no other way know the extension of bodies than by our senses, nor do these reach it in all bodies; but because we perceive extension in all that are sensible, therefore we ascribe it universally to all others also. That abundance of bodies are hard, we learn by experience; and because the hardness of the whole arises from the hardness of the parts, we therefore justly infer the hardness of the undivided particles not only of the bodies we feel but of all others. That all bodies are impenetrable, we gather not from reason, but from sensation. The bodies which we handle we find impenetrable, and thence conclude impenetrability to be an universal property of all bodies whatsoever. That all bodies are moveable, and endowed with certain powers (which we call the *vires inertiae* [forces of inertia]) of persevering in their motion, or in their rest, we only infer the like properties observed in the bodies which we have seen. The extension, hardness, impenetrability, mobility, and *vis inertiae* [force of inertia] of the whole, result from the extension, hardness, impenetrability, mobility, and *vires inertiae* of the parts; and thence we conclude the least particles of all bodies to be also all extended, and hard, and impenetrable, and moveable, and endowed with their proper *vires inertiae*. And this is the foundation of all philosophy. Moreover, that the divided but contiguous particles of bodies may be separated from one another, is matter of observation; and, in the particles that remain undivided, our minds are able to distinguish yet lesser parts, as is mathematically demonstrated. But whether the parts so distinguished, and not yet divided, may, by the powers of Nature, be actually divided and separated from one another, we cannot certainly determine. Yet, had we the proof of but one experiment that any undivided particle, in breaking a hard and solid body, suffered a division, we might by virtue of this rule conclude that the undivided as well as the divided particles may be divided and actually separated to infinity.

Lastly, if it universally appears by experiments and astronomical observations, that all bodies about the earth gravitate towards the earth, and that in proportion to the quantity of matter which they severally contain; that the moon likewise, according to the quantity of its matter, gravitates towards the earth; that, on the other hand, our sea gravitates towards the moon; and all the planets mutually one towards another; and the comets in like manner towards the sun; we must, in consequence of this rule, universally allow that all bodies whatsoever are endowed with a principle of mutual gravitation. For the argument from the appearances concludes with more force for the universal gravitation of all bodies than for their impenetrability; of which, among those in the celestial regions, we have no experiments, nor any manner of observation. Not that I affirm gravity to be essential to bodies; by their *vis insita* [inherent force] I mean nothing but their *vis inertiae*. This is immutable. Their gravity is diminished as they recede from the earth.

Rule IV. *In experimental philosophy we are to look upon propositions collected by general induction from phenomena as accurately or very nearly true, notwithstanding any contrary hypotheses that may be imagined, till such time as other phenomena occur, by which they may either be made more accurate, or liable to exceptions.*

This rule must follow, [so] that the argument of induction may not be evaded by hypotheses.

(*Mathematical Principles*, Book Three,
'The System of the World')

# JOHN LOCKE

The English philosopher, John Locke (1632–1704) was born in Somerset, ten years before the outbreak of the Civil War. The son of a lawyer and small landowner who served in the Parliamentary army, Locke was sent to Westminster School and, in 1652, to Christ Church College, Oxford, where he took up various teaching posts. Though trained in the philosophical orthodoxies of the day, he was inspired by experimental science and medicine. In 1667 he moved to London and became secretary and physician to the Earl of Shaftesbury, then Chancellor of the Exchequer. At this time he wrote an essay on toleration, which would form the basis for his *Letter Concerning Toleration*, published in 1689. In 1683, following Shaftesbury's fall from power in 1673 and the series of unsuccessful plots and efforts to exclude James, Duke of York, Charles II's Catholic brother, from the succession, Locke fled to Holland. During his exile, he redrafted *Two Treatises of Government* and *An Essay Concerning Human Understanding*, both of which were published in 1690. This was shortly after his return to England in 1689, when the Catholic James II (1685–9) was forced into exile by the invasion and succession of his Protestant son-in-law William of Orange. Shortly after his return to England, Locke met and befriended Newton, with whom he shared an interest in biblical criticism. Locke became a financial advisor to the government and wrote economic and other influential works, including *Some Thoughts concerning Education* (1693) and *The Reasonableness of Christianity* (1695). From 1696 to 1700 he served as a Commissioner for the Board of Trade. Locke's works soon exercised a profound influence upon the Enlightenment, providing the epistemological foundations for modern empiricism.

The *Essay Concerning Human Understanding* is divided into four 'books': (I) 'Of Innate Notions', (II) 'Of Ideas', (III) 'Of Words', and (IV) 'Of Knowledge and Opinion'. The following extracts are taken from books II and IV of the *Essay*. Locke expresses his opposition to Descartes' argument in support of the existence of innate ideas, and hence opens the way for much subsequent thinking by Hume, Kant and others in their understanding of what constitutes true knowledge. The aim and the method of the *Essay* are clearly stated in the introductory chapter, where Locke says that he will 'inquire into the origin, certainty and extent of human knowledge, together with the grounds and degrees of belief, opinion and assent'. Though convinced of the value of empiricism, Locke recognised that sometimes we seem to conceive of things outside our experience. But, he claimed, when we have ideas which do not appear to link directly to our experience, they are in fact made up by some sort of extrapolation from ideas that *are* based in our sensory experience. Locke asserts that the senses alone provide knowledge, without need for verification or interpretation by reason.

## An Essay Concerning Human Understanding (1690)

### 'Of Ideas in General, and their Original'

*Idea is the Object of Thinking.* Every man being conscious to himself that he thinks, and that which his mind is applied about whilst thinking being the *ideas* that are there, it is past doubt that men have in their minds several ideas, such as are those expressed by the words 'whiteness', 'hardness', 'sweetness', 'thinking', 'motion', 'man', 'elephant', 'army', 'drunkenness', and others. It is in the first place then to be inquired, How he come by them?

I know it is a received doctrine that men have native [innate] ideas, and original characters stamped upon their minds in their very first being. This opinion I have at large examined already; and, I suppose what I have said in the foregoing book [One] will be much more easily admitted, when I have shown whence the understanding may get all the ideas it has, and by what ways and degrees they may come into the mind; for which I shall appeal to everyone's own observation and experience.

*All ideas come from Sensation or Reflection.* Let us then suppose the mind to be, as we say, white paper, void of all characters, without any ideas; how comes it to be furnished? Whence comes it by that vast store which the busy and boundless fancy of man has painted on it with an almost endless variety? Whence has it all the materials of reason and knowledge? To this I answer, in one word, from *experience*. In that all our knowledge is founded, and from that it ultimately derives itself. Our observation employed either about external sensible objects, or about the internal operations of our minds perceived and reflected on by ourselves, is that which supplies our understandings with all the materials of thinking. These two are the fountains of knowledge, from whence all the ideas we have, or can naturally have, do spring.

(*Essay*, Book Two, ch. I, sections 1–2)

### 'Of Simple Ideas'

*Uncompounded Appearances.* The better to understand the nature, manner, and extent of our knowledge, one thing is carefully to be observed concerning the ideas we have; and that is, that some of them are *simple* and some *complex*.

Though the qualities that affect our senses are, in the things themselves, so united and blended that there is no separation, no distance between them, yet it is plain, the ideas they produce in the mind enter by the senses simple and unmixed. For, though the sight and touch often take in from the same object, at the same time, different ideas, as a man sees at once motion and colour, the hand feels softness and warmth in the same piece of wax; yet the simple ideas thus united in the same subject are as perfectly distinct as those that come in by different senses. The coldness and hardness which a man feels in a piece of ice being as distinct ideas in the mind as the smell and whiteness of a lily, or as the taste of sugar, and smell of a rose. And there is nothing can be plainer to a man than the clear and distinct perception he has of those simple ideas; which, being each in itself uncompounded, contains in it nothing but *one uniform appearance, or conception in the mind*, and is not distinguishable [divisible] into different ideas.

*The mind can neither make nor destroy them*. These simple ideas, the materials of all our knowledge, are suggested and furnished to the mind only by those two ways above mentioned, viz. sensation and reflection. When the understanding is once stored with these simple ideas, it has the power to repeat, compare, and unite them, even to an almost infinite variety, and so can make at pleasure new complex ideas. But it is not in the power of the most exalted wit, or enlarged understanding, by any quickness or variety of thought, to *invent* or *frame* one new simple idea in the mind, not taken in by the ways before mentioned: nor can any force of the understanding *destroy* those that are there. I would have anyone try to fancy any taste which had never affected his palate, or frame the idea of a scent he had never smelt: and when he can do this, I will also conclude that a blind man hath ideas of colours, and a deaf man true distinct notions of sounds.

This is the reason why I think it is not possible for anyone to imagine any other qualities in bodies, howsoever constituted, whereby they can be taken notice of, besides sounds, tastes, smells, visible and tangible qualities. And had mankind been made with but four senses, the qualities then which are the objects of the fifth sense had been as far from our notice, imagination, and conception, as now any belonging to a sixth, seventh, or eighth sense can possibly be; which, whether yet some other creatures, in some other parts of this vast and stupendous universe, may not have, will be a great presumption to deny. He that will not set himself proudly at the top of all things, but will consider the immensity of this fabric, and the great variety that is to be found in this little and inconsiderable part of it which he has to do with, may be apt to think that in other mansions of it there may be other and different intelligent beings, of whose faculties he has as little knowledge or apprehension as a worm shut up in one drawer of a cabinet hath of the senses or understanding of a man, such variety and excellency being suitable to the wisdom and power of the Maker. I have here followed the common opinion of man's having but five senses, though, perhaps, there may be justly counted more; but either supposition serves equally to my present purpose.

(*Essay*, Book Two, ch. II, sections 1–3)

### 'Some Further Considerations Concerning our Simple Ideas'

Whatsoever the mind perceives in itself, or is the immediate object of perception, thought, or understanding, that I call *idea*; and the power to produce any idea in our mind I call *quality* of the subject wherein that power is. Thus a snowball having the power to produce in us the ideas of white, cold, and round, the powers to produce those ideas in us, as they are in the snowball, I call qualities; and as they are sensations or perceptions in our understandings, I call them ideas; which ideas, if I speak of sometimes as in the things themselves, I would be understood to mean those qualities in the objects which produce them in us.

*Primary Qualities*. Qualities thus considered in bodies are, first, such as are utterly inseparable from the body, in what estate soever it be; and such as in all the alterations and changes it suffers, all the force can be used upon it, it constantly keeps; and such as sense constantly finds in every particle of matter which has bulk enough to be perceived; and the mind finds inseparable from every particle of matter, though less than to make itself singly be perceived by our senses. For example, take a grain of wheat, divide it into two parts: each part has still solidity, extension, figure, and mobility; divide it again, and it retains still the same qualities; and so divide it on, till the parts become insensible; they must retain still each of them all those qualities. For division (which is all that a mill, or pestle, or any other body, does upon another, in reducing it to insensible parts) can never take away either solidity, extension, figure, or mobility from any body, but only makes two or more distinct separate masses of matter, of that which was but one before; all which distinct masses, reckoned as so many distinct bodies, after division, make a certain number. These I call *original* or *primary qualities* of body, which I think we may observe to produce simple ideas in us, viz. solidity, extension, figure, motion or rest, and number.

Secondly, such qualities which in truth are nothing in the objects themselves but powers to produce various sensations in us by their primary qualities, i.e. by the bulk, figure, texture, and motion of their insensible parts, as colours, sounds, tastes, &c. These I call *secondary qualities*. To these might be added a third sort, which are allowed to be barely powers, though they are as much real qualities in the subject as those which I, to comply with the common way of speaking, call qualities, but for distinction, secondary qualities. For the power in fire to produce a new colour, or consistency, in wax or clay, by its primary qualities, is as much a quality in fire, as the power it has to produce in me a new idea or sensation of warmth or burning, which I felt not before, by the same primary qualities, viz. the bulk, texture, and motion of its insensible parts.

*How Primary Qualities produce Ideas*. The next thing to be considered is, how bodies produce ideas in us; and that is manifestly by impulse, the only way which we can conceive bodies operate in.

If then external objects be not united to our minds when they produce ideas therein, and yet we perceive these *original qualities* in such of them as singly fall under our senses, it is evident, that some motion must be thence continued by our nerves or animal spirits, by some parts of our bodies, to the brain, or the seat of sensation, there to produce in our minds the particular ideas we have of them. And since the extension, figure, number, and motion of bodies of an observable bigness, may be perceived at a distance by the sight, it is evident some singly imperceptible bodies must come from them to the eyes, and thereby convey to the brain some motion; which produces these ideas which we have of them in us.

*How secondary*. After the same manner that the ideas of these original qualities are produced in us, we may conceive that the ideas of *secondary qualities* are also produced, viz. by the operation of insensible particles on our senses. For, it being manifest, that there are bodies, and good store of bodies, each whereof are so small, that we cannot, by any of our senses, discover either their bulk, figure, or motion; as is evident in the particles of the air and water, and other extremely smaller than those, perhaps as much smaller than the particles of air or water, as the particles of air or water are smaller than peas or hail-stones. Let us suppose at present, that the different motions and figures, bulk and number, of such particles, affecting the several organs of our senses, produce in us those different sensations which we have from the colours and smells of bodies; for example, that a violet, by the impulse of such insensible particles of matter, of peculiar figures and bulks, and in different degrees and modifications of their motions, causes the ideas of the blue colour and sweet scent of that flower to be produced in our minds; it being no more impossible to conceive that God should annex such ideas to such motions, with which they have no similitude, than that he should annex the idea of pain to the motion of a piece of steel dividing our flesh, with which that idea hath no resemblance.

(*Essay*, Book Two, ch. VIII, sections 8–13)

### 'Of Our Knowledge of the Existence of Other Things'

*It is to be had only by Sensation.* The knowledge of our own being we have by intuition [ch. IX]. The existence of a God reason clearly makes known to us, as has been shown [ch. X].

The knowledge of the existence of any other thing we can have only by *sensation*; for, there being no necessary connexion of real existence with any *idea* a man hath in his memory, nor of any other existence but that of God with the existence of any particular man, no particular man can know the existence of any other being, but only when, by actual operating upon him, it makes itself perceived by him. For, the having the idea of anything in our mind no more proves the existence of that thing, than the picture of a man evidences his being in the world, or the visions of a dream make thereby a true history.

*Instance: Whiteness of this Paper.* It is therefore the actual receiving of ideas from without, that gives us notice of the existence of other things, and makes us know that something doth exist at that time without us, which causes that idea in us, though perhaps we neither know nor consider how it does it. For it takes not from the certainty of our senses, and the ideas we receive by them, that we know not the manner wherein they are produced. For example, whilst I write this, I have, by the paper affecting my eyes, that idea produced in my mind, which, whatever object causes, I call *white*; by which I know that that quality or accident (i.e. whose appearance before my eyes always causes that idea) doth really exist, and hath a being without me. And of this the greatest assurance I can possibly have, and to which my faculties can attain, is the testimony of my eyes, which are the proper and sole judges of this thing; whose testimony I have reason to rely on as so certain, that I can no more doubt, whilst I write this, that I can see white and black, and that something really exists that causes that sensation in me, than that I write or move my hand: which is a certainty as great as human nature is capable of, concerning the existence of anything but a man's self alone, and of God.

*This though not so certain as Demonstration, yet may be called Knowledge, and proves the Existence of Things without us.* The notice we have by our senses, of the existing of things without us, though it be not altogether so certain as our intuitive knowledge, or the deductions of our reason employed about the clear abstract ideas of our own minds; yet it is an assurance that deserves the name of *knowledge*. If we persuade ourselves that our faculties act and inform us right concerning the existence of those objects that affect them, it cannot pass for an ill-grounded confidence: for I think nobody can, in earnest, be so sceptical, as to be uncertain of the existence of those things which he sees and feels. At least, he that can doubt so far (whatever he may have with his own thoughts), will never have any controversy with me; since he can never be sure I say anything contrary to his opinion. As to myself, I think God has given me assurance enough of the existence of things without me; since, by their different application, I can produce in myself both pleasure and pain, which is one great concernment of my present state. This is certain: the confidence that our faculties do not herein deceive us is the greatest assurance we are capable of concerning the existence of material beings. For we cannot act anything but by our faculties; nor talk of knowledge itself, but by the help of those faculties which are fitted to apprehend even what knowledge is. But besides the assurance we have from our senses themselves, that they do not err in the information they give us of the existence of things without us, when they are affected by them, we are further confirmed in this assurance by other concurrent reasons.

(*Essay*, Book Four, ch. XI, sections 1–3)

## DAVID HUME

David Hume was born in Edinburgh in 1711. His father's death two years later left him to be raised by his devoted mother at their small estate in Berwickshire. Just before Hume's twelfth birthday, he was admitted to Edinburgh University, and although he left without taking a degree, his early writings revealed his academic prowess. This prompted his family to encourage him to enter the legal profession. However, he found 'an insurmountable aversion to everything but the pursuits of philosophy'. In 1745 he accepted the job of tutor to the Marquess of Annandale, who turned out to be certifiably insane. In 1752 Hume became librarian to the Faculty of Advocates in Edinburgh, and was hence able to work on his literary career which led to the publication of a celebrated six-volume *History of England* (1754–62). By 1761 his European reputation was sufficient for all his works to be entered in the Catholic Church's *Index* of forbidden books. Between 1763 and 1766 he lived in France, making friends with many *philosophes* and enjoying the intellectual life of Parisian salons. During the last year of his life, although desperately ill, he remained cheerful and continued to devote time to his works and to welcome friends. He died in 1776, surviving just long enough to hear the welcome news of the American Revolution. In that year, he wrote a brief autobiography, concluding:

> I was, I say, a man of mild dispositions, of command of temper, of an open, social, and cheerful humour, capable of attachment, but little susceptible of enmity, and of great moderation in all my passions. Even my love of literary fame, my ruling passion, never soured my temper, notwithstanding many frequent disappointments.
>
> (*My Own Life*, 1777)

The debate between rationalists and empiricists over the origins of knowledge was a central concern of Hume. He came down firmly on the side of empiricism and the principle that 'nothing is in the mind that was not first in the senses'. His first and eventually most famous work, the three-volume *Treatise of Human Nature* (1739–40), was a great disappointment to him. In his own words, it 'fell dead-born from the press, without reaching such distinction as even to excite a murmur among the zealots'. The aim of the *Treatise* was to explore the pitfalls of previous philosophies, which, in Hume's view, 'depend more upon invention than experience', and to establish empirical science as the foundation of knowledge. Although he clearly embraces the empiricist principles of Locke, he goes on to assert that consistent application of these principles will inevitably lead to scepticism. His own scepticism led him to challenge all religious beliefs (see p. 71) and traditional explanations of the origins and nature of moral distinctions (see p. 213). The following extract is from the opening section of Book I, 'Of the Understanding', of Hume's *Treatise*.

## A Treatise of Human Nature (1739)

### 'Of the Origin of our Ideas'

All the perceptions of the human mind resolve themselves into two distinct kinds, which I shall call impressions and ideas. The difference betwixt these consists in the degrees of force and liveliness with which they strike upon the mind, and make their way into our thought or consciousness. Those perceptions, which enter with most force and violence, we may name *impressions*; and under this name I comprehend all our sensations, passions and emotions, as they make their first appearance in the soul. By *ideas* I mean the faint images of these in thinking and reasoning; such as, for instance, are all the perceptions excited by the present discourse, excepting only, those which arise from the sight and touch, and excepting the immediate pleasure or uneasiness it may occasion. I believe it will not be very necessary to employ many words in explaining this distinction. Everyone of himself will readily perceive the difference betwixt feeling and thinking. The common degrees of these are easily distinguished; though it is not impossible but in particular instances they may very nearly approach to each other. Thus in sleep, in a fever, in madness, or in any very violent emotions of soul, our ideas may approach to our impressions. As on the other hand it sometimes happens, that our impressions are so faint and low, that we cannot distinguish them from our ideas. But notwithstanding this near resemblance in a few instances, they are in general so very different, that no one can make a scruple to rank them under distinct heads, and assign to each a peculiar name to mark the difference.

There is another division of our perceptions, which it will be convenient to observe, and which extends itself both to our impressions and ideas. This division is into simple and complex. Simple perceptions or impressions and ideas are such as admit of no distinction nor separation. The complex are the contrary to these, and may be distinguished into parts. Though a particular colour, taste, and smell are qualities all united together in this apple, 'tis easy to perceive they are not the same, but are at least distinguishable from each other.

Having by these divisions given an order and arrangement to our objects, we may now apply ourselves to consider with the more accuracy their qualities and relations. The first circumstance, that strikes my eye, is the great resemblance betwixt our impressions and ideas in every other particular, except their degree of force and vivacity. The one seem to be in a manner the reflexion of the other; so that all the perceptions of the mind are double, and appear both as impressions and ideas. When I shut my eyes and think of my chamber, the ideas I form are exact representations of the impressions I felt; nor is there any circumstance of the one, which is not to be found in the other. In running over my other perceptions, I find still the same resemblance and representation. Ideas and impressions appear always to correspond to each other. This circumstance seems to me remarkable, and engages my attention for a moment.

Upon a more accurate survey I find I have been carried away too far by the first appearance, and that I must make use of the distinction of perceptions into *simple* and *complex*, to limit this general decision, *that all our ideas and impressions are resembling*. I observe that many of our complex ideas never had impressions that corresponded to them, and that many of our complex impressions never are exactly copied in ideas. I can imagine to myself such a city as the New Jerusalem, whose pavement is gold and walls are rubies, though I never saw any such. I have seen Paris; but shall I affirm I can form such an idea of that city, as will perfectly represent all its streets and houses in their real and just proportions?

I perceive, therefore, that though there is, in general, a great resemblance betwixt our *complex* impressions and ideas, yet the rule is not universally true, that they are exact copies of each other. We may next consider how the case stands with our *simple* perceptions. After the most accurate examination of which I am capable, I venture to affirm, that the rule here holds without any exception, and that every simple idea has a simple impression, which resembles it; and every simple impression a correspondent idea. That idea of red, which we form in the dark, and that impression which strikes our eyes in sunshine, differ only in degree, not in nature. That the case is the same with all our simple impressions and ideas, 'tis impossible to prove by a particular enumeration of them. Everyone may satisfy himself in this point by running over as many as he pleases. But if anyone should deny this universal resemblance, I know no way of convincing him, but by desiring him to show a simple impression that has not a correspondent idea, or a simple idea, that has not a correspondent impression. If he does not answer this challenge, as it is certain he cannot, we may, from his silence and our own observation establish our conclusion.

Thus we find, that all simple ideas and impressions resemble each other; and as the complex are formed from them, we may affirm in general, that these two species of perception are exactly correspondent. Having discovered this relation, which requires no farther examination, I am curious to find some other of their qualities. Let us consider, how they stand with regard to their existence, and which of the impressions and ideas are causes, and which effects.

The full examination of this question is the subject of the present Treatise; and, therefore, we shall here content ourselves with establishing one general proposition, *That all our simple ideas in their first appearance are derived from simple impressions, which are correspondent to them, and which they exactly represent.* [...]

There is however one contradictory phenomenon, which may prove, that 'tis not absolutely impossible for ideas to go before their correspondent impressions. I believe it will readily be allowed, that the several distinct ideas of colours, which enter by the eyes, or those of sounds, which are conveyed by the hearing, are really different from each other, though at the same time resembling. Now if this be true of different colours, it must be no less of the different shades of the same colour, that each of them produces a distinct idea, independent of the rest. For if this should be denied, 'tis possible, by the continual gradation of shades, to run a colour insensibly into what is most remote from it; and, if you will not allow any of the means [intermediates] to be different, you cannot without absurdity, deny the extremes to be the same. Suppose therefore a person to have enjoyed his sight for thirty years, and to have become perfectly well acquainted with colours of all kinds, excepting one particular shade of blue, for instance, which it never has been his fortune to meet with. Let all the different shades of that colour, except that single one, be placed before him, descending gradually from the deepest to the lightest; 'tis plain, that he will perceive a blank, where that shade is wanting, and will be sensible, that there is a greater distance in that place betwixt the contiguous colours, than in any other. Now I ask, whether 'tis possible for him, from his own imagination, to supply this deficiency, and raise up to himself the idea of that particular shade, though it had never been conveyed to him by his senses? I believe there are few but will be of opinion that he can; and this may serve as a proof, that the simple ideas are not always derived from the correspondent impressions; though the instance is so particular and singular, that 'tis scarce worth our observing, and does not merit that for it alone we should alter our general maxim.

But besides this exception, it may not be amiss to remark on this head, that the principle of the priority of impressions to ideas must be understood with another limitation, viz. that as our ideas are images of our impressions, so we can form secondary ideas, which are images of the primary; as appears from this very reasoning concerning them. This is not, properly speaking, an exception to the rule so much as an explanation of it. Ideas produce the images of themselves in new ideas; but as the first ideas are supposed to be derived from impressions, it still remains true, that all our simple ideas proceed either mediately or immediately from their correspondent impressions.

This then is the first principle I establish in the science of human nature; nor ought we to despise it because of the simplicity of its appearance. For 'tis remarkable, that the present question concerning the precedency of our impressions or ideas, is the same with what has made so much noise in other terms, when it has been disputed whether there be any *innate ideas*, or whether all ideas be derived from sensation and reflexion. We may observe, that in order to prove the ideas of extension and colour not to be innate, philosophers do nothing but show, that they are conveyed by our senses. To prove the ideas of passion and desire not to be innate, they observe that we have a preceding experience of these emotions in ourselves. Now if we carefully examine these arguments, we shall find that they prove nothing but that ideas are preceded by other more lively perceptions, from which they are derived, and which they represent. I hope this clear stating of the question will remove all disputes concerning it, and will render this principle of more use in our reasonings, than it seems hitherto to have been.

(*Treatise*, Book I 'Of the Understanding', Part I, sect. 1)

## JEAN D'ALEMBERT

Jean Le Rond d'Alembert (1717–83), an illegitimate child, was abandoned by his mother, the literary hostess Madame de Tencin, on the steps of the baptistry of Saint Jean-Le-Rond in Paris, from where he received his name. Brought up by a glazier's wife, he was educated at a Jansenist college, studied law and medicine, but exhibited an exceptional talent and fascination for mathematics. His brilliance in this field led to him becoming a member of the Académie des Sciences in 1741, and to the publication of the acclaimed *Traité de Dynamique* (*Treatise on Dynamics*) in 1743. Both Frederick the Great and Catherine the Great wanted d'Alembert to lead their scientific academies, but (apart from visiting Frederick in 1763) he stayed in France with his lover, the *salon* hostess Julie de Lespinasse, and in 1772 became Secretary to the Académie des Sciences. From 1747, d'Alembert was co-editor with Diderot of the *Encyclopédie* (see p. 21), for which he wrote about 1,400 articles, including the important 'Discours Préliminaire' ('Preliminary Discourse') to the first volume (1751), outlining the whole project and providing an influential account of the history of science and knowledge, which championed Bacon, Locke and Newton. He became one of the leading *philosophes*, a friend of Voltaire, and a firm believer in the role of reason as the instrument of the Enlightenment and the improvement of society. Many *philosophes* would have agreed with Frederick that 'the little good sense of which our species is capable can only reside in a tiny minority of the nation, beyond the reach of the remainder, and that consequently superstitious beliefs will always prevail among the majority.' But, reflecting on this letter in 1770, d'Alembert replied: 'Doubtless the common people is a stupid animal which lets itself be led into the shadows when nothing better is offered to it. But offer it the truth; if this truth is simple, and especially if it goes straight to the heart [...] it seems to me that it will definitely seize on it and will want none other'. In 1758 he fell out with Diderot over his friend's materialism and atheism, and resigned from editing the *Encyclopédie*.

In the following extract from a modern translation of the 'Preliminary Discourse', d'Alembert begins by affirming his faith in the reliability of evidence derived from the senses. He traces the development of knowledge, from the sense impressions to complex forms of expression, such as conceptual ideas. He was convinced that as all knowledge can be reduced to its origin in sensory experience, it appeared that all humans have the capacity to be taught any art or science. This was the basis for his belief in the power of education gradually to spread the ideas and values of the Enlightenment.

## 'Preliminary Discourse' to the *Encyclopédie* (1751)

We can divide all our knowledge into direct and reflective knowledge. We receive direct knowledge immediately, without any operation of our will; it is the knowledge which finds all the doors of our souls open, so to speak, and enters without resistance and without effort. The mind acquires reflective knowledge by making use of direct knowledge, unifying and combining it.

All our direct knowledge can be reduced to what we receive through our senses; whence it follows that we owe all our ideas to our sensations. This principle of the first philosophers was for a long time regarded as an axiom by the scholastic philosophers. They respected it merely because it was ancient, and they would have defended 'substantial forms' and 'occult qualities' with equal vigor. Consequently, during the renaissance of philosophy this true principle received the same treatment as the absurd opinions from which it should have been distinguished: it was proscribed along with them, because nothing is more detrimental to truth, and nothing exposes it more to misinterpretation, than the intermingling or proximity of error. The system of innate ideas, which is attractive in several respects, and the more striking perhaps because it was less familiar, replaced the axiom of the scholastic philosophers [that we owe all our ideas to our sensations]; and after having reigned for a long time, the system of innate ideas still retains some partisans – so great are the difficulties hindering the return of truth, once prejudice or sophism has routed it from its proper place. Of late, however, it has been almost generally agreed that the ancients were right, nor is this the only matter on which we are beginning to draw closer to them.

Nothing is more indisputable than the existence of our sensations. Thus, in order to prove that they are the principle of all our knowledge, it suffices to show that they can be; for in a well-constructed philosophy, any deduction which is based on facts or recognized truths is preferable to one which is supported only by hypotheses, however ingenious. Why suppose that we have purely intellectual notions at the outset [innate ideas], if all we need do in order to form them is to reflect upon our sensations? The discussion which follows will demonstrate that these notions, in fact, have no other origin.

The fact of our existence is the first thing taught us by our sensations and, indeed, is inseparable from them. From this it follows that our first reflective ideas must be concerned with ourselves, that is to say, must concern that thinking principle which constitutes our nature and which is in no way distinct from ourselves. The second thing taught us by our sensations is the existence of external objects, among which we must include our own bodies, since they are, so to speak, external to us even before we have defined the nature of the thinking principle within us. These innumerable external objects produce a powerful and continued effect upon us which binds us to them so forcefully that, after an instant when our reflective ideas turn our consciousness inward, we are forced outside again by the sensations that besiege us on all sides. They tear us from the solitude that would otherwise be our lot. The multiplicity of these sensations, the consistency that we note in their evidence, the degrees of difference we observe in them, and the involuntary reactions that they cause us to experience – as compared with that voluntary determination we have over our reflective ideas, which is operative only upon our sensations themselves – all of these things produce an irresistible impulse in us to affirm that the objects we relate to these sensations, and which appear to us to be their cause, actually exist. This impulse has been considered by many philosophers to be the work of a Superior Being and the most convincing argument for the existence of these objects. And indeed, since there is no connection between each sensation and the object that occasions it, or at least the object to which we relate it, it does not seem that any possible passage from one to the other can be found through reasoning. Only a kind of instinct, surer than reason itself, can compel us to leap so great a gap. This instinct is so strong in us that even if one were to suppose for a moment that it subsisted while all external objects were destroyed, the reconstitution of those objects could not add to its strength. Therefore, let us believe without wavering that in fact our sensations have the cause outside ourselves which we suppose them to have; because the effect which can result from the real existence of that cause could not differ in any way from the effect we experience. Let us not imitate those philosophers of whom Montaigne [1533–92] speaks, who, when asked about the principle of men's actions, were still trying to find out whether there are men. Far from wishing to cast shadows on a truth recognized even by the skeptics when they are not debating, let us leave the trouble of working out its principle to the enlightened metaphysicians. It is for them to determine if that be possible, what gradation our soul observes when it takes that first step outside itself, impelled, so to speak, and held back at the same time by a crowd of perceptions, which, on the one hand, draw it toward external objects, and on the other hand (since these perceptions belong properly only the soul itself) seem to circumscribe it in a narrow space from which they do not permit it to withdraw.

Of all the objects that affect us by their presence, the existence of our body strikes us most vividly because it belongs to us most intimately. But hardly do we become aware of the existence of our body before we become aware of the attention it demands of us in warding off the dangers that surround it. Subject to endless needs, extremely sensitive to the action of external bodies, it would soon be destroyed were it not for the care we take in preserving it. Not that all external bodies give us disagreeable sensations; some seem to compensate by the pleasure which their action brings to us. But such is the misfortune of the human condition that pain is our most lively sentiment; pleasure affects us less than pain and hardly ever suffices to make up to us for it. In vain did some philosophers assert, while suppressing their groans in the midst of sufferings, that pain was not an evil at all. In vain did others place supreme happiness in sensuality – of which they nevertheless deprived themselves through fear of its consequences. All of them would have known our nature better if they had been content to limit their definition of the sovereign good of the present life to the exemption from pain, and to agree that, without hoping to arrive at this sovereign good, we are allowed only to approach it more or less, in proportion to our vigilance and the precautions we take. Reflections as natural as these will inevitably strike any man who is left alone and free of the prejudices of education or study. They will be the consequence of the first impression he receives from external objects, and they can be placed among the number of those first exertions of the soul which are deemed most valuable and worthy of observation by those who are truly wise, but which are neglected or rejected by ordinary philosophy, whose first principles are almost always contradicted by them.

The necessity of protecting our own bodies from pain and destruction causes us to examine which among the external objects can be useful or harmful to us, in order to seek out some and shun others. But hardly have we begun to survey these objects when we discover among them a large number of beings who seem entirely similar to ourselves, that is, whose forms are entirely like ours and who seem to have the same perceptions as we do, so far as we can judge at first glance. All this causes us to think that they also have the same needs that we experience and consequently the same interest in satisfying them. Whence we conclude that we should find it advantageous to join them

*Figure 2.1*   Frontispiece of the *Encyclopédie, or Reasoned Dictionary of the Sciences, Arts and Trades*

*Source*: Engraved by B.L. Prevost, from a 1764 drawing by Charles-Nicolas Cochin.

*Note*: For the essay entitled 'Encyclopédie', Diderot wrote: 'our *Encyclopédie* could only have been the endeavour of a philosophical century; that age has dawned'. The frontispiece depicts Reason and Philosophy pulling the veil away from Truth, radiating light from the centre and dispersing the clouds. Imagination (left) offers Truth a garland on behalf of all the Arts and Sciences.

in finding out what can be beneficial to us and what can be detrimental to us in Nature. The communication of ideas is the principle and support of this union, and necessarily requires the invention of signs — such is the source of the formation of societies, with which must have come the birth of languages.

('Preliminary Discourse' to the *Encyclopédie*)

## IMMANUEL KANT

Immanuel Kant (1724–1804), one of the greatest and most influential philosophers of the Enlightenment, was born into a relatively poor family in Königsberg (now Kaliningrad) in East Prussia, the son of a saddler. His parents were devout reformist (pietist) Lutherans, with a strong sense of conscience and duty, and his schooling was strictly religious. In person, Kant was short and remarkably thin; however, he placed great emphasis on his health and appearance and had a reputation for dressing elegantly. A student from the age of sixteen, and later tutor and Professor of Logic and Metaphysics (1770) at the University of Königsberg, he evidently never travelled more than about forty miles from his birthplace throughout his life. Even so, his interest in the politics of the age is apparent in his sympathy with both the American and French revolutionaries, and in works such as *Zum Ewigen Frieden* (*On Perpetual Peace*, 1795) in which he tried to show how independent nations, like moral persons, could and should form an international community committed to live in harmony and peace: 'The peoples of the earth have thus entered in varying degrees into a universal community, and it has developed to the point where a violation of rights in *one* part of the world is felt *everywhere*'. He was influenced by Newton, d'Alembert, Rousseau (who, in 1764, he called 'the Newton of the moral world') and, in particular, Hume. It was Hume's account of causality, that, according to Kant, 'first interrupted my dogmatic slumber and gave me a completely different direction to my enquiries in the field of speculative philosophy'. This led to a trilogy of major works, *Kritik der Reinen Vernunft* (*Critique of Pure Reason*, 1781), *Kritik der Praktischen Vernunft* (*Critique of Practical Reason*, 1788), and *Kritik der Urteilskraft* (*Critique of Judgement*, 1790), which established his international reputation.

The first *Critique*, though described by Kant himself as 'dry, obscure and contrary to all ordinary ideas', is generally regarded as a landmark in modern philosophy. In this work, Kant asks what can be known by pure (i.e. *a priori*) reasoning. While he agreed with empiricists such as Locke and Hume that there were no innate ideas, he did not accept that all knowledge could be derived solely from experience. In order to understand our experiences we have to have some concepts or tools ('categories' such as quantity and causation) that are not learnt from experience, but that enable us to make sense of the natural world through our experiences. The order and coherence of the natural world, the laws of nature, are not then inherent in nature but constructs imposed upon it by our minds: 'the order and regularity in objects, which we entitle *nature*, we ourselves introduce. The understanding is itself the lawgiver of nature.'

Having tackled our understanding of nature and scientific knowledge in the first *Critique*, in the second and in the *Grundlegung zur Metaphysik der Sitten* (*Fundamental Principles of the Metaphysic of Morals*, 1785) Kant examined action and ethics (see p. 220). He did not believe that Hume was right in attributing moral action to feelings. Rather, he argued, every person has a free will that enables them to decide what action to take. However, an action is only moral if it is undertaken for the sake of duty. The third *Critique* contained an important essay on aesthetics, discussing judgements of taste and beauty.

In 1784 Kant entered a competition held by the Enlightenment journal *Berlinische Monatsschrift* (*Berlin Monthly*) to answer the question 'Was ist Aufklärung?' ('What is Enlightenment?') In reflecting on the previous century, he argued that Enlightenment was a complex and on-going process, and summed up his view of the central aspiration of the *philosophes* in what would become the most commonly recited formulation (derived from the Roman poet Horace) of the Enlightenment: 'Dare to know! Have courage to use your own reason!'

## 'What is Enlightenment?' (1784)

Enlightenment is man's release from his self-incurred tutelage. Tutelage is man's inability to make use of his understanding without direction from another. Self-incurred is this tutelage when its cause lies not in lack of reason but in lack of resolution and courage to use it without direction from another. *Sapere aude*! [Dare to know!] 'Have courage to use your own reason!' – that is the motto of enlightenment.

Laziness and cowardice are the reasons why so great a portion of mankind, after nature has long since discharged them from external direction (*naturaliter maiorennes* [those who have come of age by course of nature]), nevertheless remains under lifelong tutelage, and why it is so easy for others to set themselves up as their guardians. It is so easy not to be of age. If I have a book which understands for me, a pastor who has a conscience for me, a physician who decides my diet, and so forth, I need not trouble myself. I need not think, if I can only pay – others will readily undertake the irksome work for me.

That the step to competence is held to be very dangerous by the far greater portion of mankind (and by the entire fair sex) – quite apart from its being arduous – is seen to by those guardians who have so kindly assumed superintendence over them. After the guardians have first made their domestic cattle dumb and have made sure that these placid creatures will not dare take a single step without the harness of the cart to which they are confined, the guardians then show them the danger which threatens if they try to go alone. Actually, however, this danger is not so great, for by falling a few times they would finally learn to walk alone. But an example of this failure makes them timid and ordinarily frightens them away from all further trials.

For any single individual to work himself out of the life under tutelage which has become almost his nature is very difficult. He has come to be fond of this state, and he is for the present really incapable of making use of his reason, for no one has ever let him try it out. Statutes and formulas, those mechanical tools of the rational employment or rather misemployment of his natural gifts, are the fetters of an everlasting tutelage. Whoever throws them off makes only an uncertain leap over the narrowest ditch because he is not accustomed to that kind of free motion. Therefore, there are only few who have succeeded by their own exercise of mind both in freeing themselves from incompetence and in achieving a steady pace.

But that the public should enlighten itself is more possible; indeed if only freedom is granted, enlightenment is almost sure to follow. For there will always be some independent thinkers, even among the established guardians of the great masses, who, after throwing off the yoke of tutelage from their own shoulders, will disseminate the spirit of the rational appreciation of both their own worth and every man's vocation for thinking for himself. But be it noted that the public, which has first been brought under this yoke by their guardians, forces the guardians themselves to remain bound when it is incited to do so by some of the guardians who are themselves capable of some enlightenment — so harmful is it to implant prejudices, for they later take vengeance on their cultivators or on their descendants. Thus the public can only slowly attain enlightenment. Perhaps a fall of personal despotism or of avaricious or tyrannical oppression may be accomplished by revolution, but never a true reform in ways of thinking. Rather, new prejudices will serve as well as old ones to harness the great unthinking masses.

For this enlightenment, however, nothing is required but freedom, and indeed the most harmless among all the things to which this term can properly be applied. It is the freedom to make public use of one's reason at every point. But I hear on all sides, 'Do not argue!' The officer says: 'Do not argue but drill!' The tax collector: 'Do not argue but pay!' The cleric: 'Do not argue but believe!' Only one prince [Frederick the Great] in the world says, 'Argue as much as you will, and about what you will, but obey!' Everywhere there is restriction on freedom.

Which restriction is an obstacle to enlightenment, and which is not an obstacle but a promoter of it? I answer: The public use of one's reason must always be free, and it alone can bring about enlightenment among men. The private use of reason, on the other hand, may often be very narrowly restricted without particularly hindering the progress of enlightenment. By the public use of one's reason I understand the use which a person makes of it as a scholar before the reading public. Private use I call that which one may make of it in a particular civil post or office which is intrusted to him. Many affairs which are conducted in the interest of the community require a certain mechanism through which some members of the community must passively conduct themselves with an artificial unanimity, so that the government may direct them to public ends, or at least prevent them from destroying those ends. Here argument is certainly not allowed — one must obey. But so far as a part of the mechanism regards himself at the same time as a member of the whole community or of a society of world citizens, and thus in the role of a scholar who addresses the public (in the proper sense of the word) through his writings, he certainly can argue without hurting the affairs for which he is in part responsible as a passive member. Thus it would be ruinous for an officer in service to debate about the suitability or utility of a command given to him by his superior; he must obey. But the right to make remarks on errors in the military service and to lay them before the public for judgment cannot equitably be refused him as a scholar. The citizen cannot refuse to pay the taxes imposed on him; indeed, an impudent complaint at those levied on him can be punished as a scandal (as it could occasion general refractoriness). But the same person nevertheless does not act contrary to his duty as a citizen when, as a scholar, he publicly expresses his thoughts on the inappropriateness or even the injustice of these levies. Similarly a clergyman is obligated to make his sermon to his pupils in catechism and his congregation conform to the symbol of the church which he serves, for he has been accepted on this condition. But as a scholar he has complete freedom, even the calling, to communicate to the public all his carefully tested and well-meaning thoughts on that which is erroneous in the symbol and to make suggestions for the better organization of the religious body and church. In doing this, there is nothing that could be laid as a burden on his conscience. For what he teaches as a consequence of his office as a representative of the church, this he considers something about which he has no freedom to teach according to his own lights; it is something which he is appointed to propound at the dictation of and in the name of another. He will say, 'Our church teaches this or that; those are the proofs which it adduces.' He thus extracts all practical uses for his congregation from statutes to which he himself would not subscribe with full conviction but to the enunciation of which he can very well pledge himself because it is not impossible that truth lies hidden in them, and, in any case, there is at least nothing in them contradictory to inner religion. For if he believed he had found such in them, he could not conscientiously discharge the duties of his office; he would have to give it up. The use, therefore, which an appointed teacher makes of his reason before his congregation is merely private, because this congregation is only a domestic one (even if it be a large gathering); with respect to it, as a priest, he is not free, nor can he be free, because he carries out the orders of another. But as a scholar, whose writings speak to his public, the world, the clergyman in the public use of his reason enjoys an unlimited freedom to use his own reason and to speak in his own person. That the guardians of the people (in spiritual things) should themselves be incompetent is an absurdity which amounts to the eternalization of absurdities.

But would not a society of clergymen, perhaps a church conference or a venerable classis (as they call themselves among the Dutch), be justified in obligating itself by oath to a certain unchangeable symbol in order to enjoy an unceasing guardianship over each of its members and thereby over the people as a whole, and even to make it eternal? I answer that this is altogether impossible. Such a contract, made to shut off all further enlightenment from the human race, is absolutely null and void even if confirmed by the supreme power, by parliaments, and by the most ceremonious of peace treaties. An age cannot bind itself and ordain to put the succeeding one into such a condition that it cannot extend its (at best very occasional) knowledge, purify itself of errors, and progress in general enlightenment. That would be a crime against human nature, the proper destination of which lies precisely in this progress; and the descendants would be fully justified in rejecting those decrees as having been made in an unwarranted and malicious manner.

The touchstone of everything that can be concluded as a law for a people lies in the question whether the people could have imposed such a law on itself. Now such a religious compact might be possible for a short and definitely limited time, as it were, in expectation of a better. One might let every citizen, and especially the clergyman, in the role of scholar, make his comments freely and publicly, i.e., through writing, on the erroneous aspects of the present institution. The newly introduced order might last until insight into the nature of these things had become so general and widely approved that through uniting their voices (even if not unanimously) they could bring a proposal to the throne to take those congregations under protection which had united into a changed religious organization according to their better ideas, without, however, hindering others who wish to remain in the order. But to unite in a permanent religious institution which is not to be subject to doubt before the public even in the lifetime of one man, and thereby to make a period of time fruitless in the progress of mankind toward improvement, thus working to the disadvantage of posterity – that is absolutely forbidden. For himself (and only for a short time) a man can postpone enlightenment in what he ought to know, but to renounce it for himself, and even more to renounce it for posterity, is to injure and trample on the rights of mankind.

And what a people may not decree for itself can even less be decreed for them by a monarch, for his lawgiving authority rests on his uniting the general public will in his own. If he only sees to it that all true or alleged improvement stands together with civil order, he can leave it to his subjects to do what they find necessary for their spiritual welfare. This is not his concern, though it is incumbent on him to prevent one of them from violently hindering another in determining and promoting this welfare to the best of his ability. To meddle in these matters lowers his own majesty, since by the writings in which his subjects seek to present their views he may evaluate his own governance. He can do this when, with deepest understanding, he lays upon himself the reproach: *Caesar non est supra grammaticos* [Caesar is not above the grammarians (i.e. the rules of grammar)]. Far more does he injure his own majesty when he degrades his supreme power by supporting the ecclesiastical despotism of some tyrants in his state over his other subjects.

If we are asked, 'Do we now live in an *enlightened age?*' the answer is, 'No,' but we do live in an *age of enlightenment*. As things now stand, much is lacking which prevents men from being, or easily becoming, capable of correctly using their own reason in religious matters with assurance and free from outside direction. But, on the other hand, we have clear indications that the field has now been opened wherein men may freely deal with these things and that the obstacles to general enlightenment or the release from self-imposed tutelage are gradually being reduced. In this respect, this is the age of enlightenment, or the century of Frederick [the Great].

A prince who does not find it unworthy of himself to say that he holds it to be his duty to prescribe nothing to men in religious matters but to give them complete freedom while renouncing the haughty name of *tolerance,* is himself enlightened and deserves to be esteemed by the grateful world and posterity as the first, at least from the side of government, who divested the human race of its tutelage and left each man free to make use of his reason in matters of conscience. Under him venerable ecclesiastics are allowed, in the role of scholars, and without infringing on their official duties, freely to submit for public testing their judgments and views which here and there diverge from the established symbol. And an even greater freedom is enjoyed by those who are restricted by no official duties. This spirit of freedom spreads beyond this land, even to those in which it must struggle with external obstacles erected by a government which misunderstands its own interest. For an example gives evidence to such a government that in freedom there is not the least cause for concern about public peace and the stability of the community. Men work themselves gradually out of barbarity if only intentional artifices are not made to hold them in it.

I have placed the main point of enlightenment – the escape of men from their self-incurred tutelage – chiefly in matters of religion because our rulers have no interest in playing the guardian with respect to the arts and sciences and also because religious incompetence is not only the most harmful but also the most degrading of all. But the manner of thinking of the head of a state who favours religious enlightenment goes further, and he sees that there is no danger to his lawgiving in allowing his subjects to make public use of their reason and to publish their thoughts on a better formulation of his legislation and even their open-minded criticisms of the laws already made. Of this we have a shining example wherein no monarch is superior to him whom we honour.

But only one who is himself enlightened, is not afraid of shadows and has a numerous and well-disciplined army to assure public peace can say: 'Argue as much as you will, and about what you will, only obey!' A republic could not dare say such a thing. Here is shown a strange and unexpected trend in human affairs in which almost everything, looked at in the large, is paradoxical. A greater degree of civil freedom appears advantageous to the freedom of mind of the people, and yet it places inescapable limitations upon it; a lower degree of civil freedom, on the contrary, provides the mind with room for each man to extend himself to his full capacity. As nature has uncovered from under this hard shell the seed for which she most tenderly cares – the propensity and vocation to free thinking – this gradually works back upon the character of the people, who thereby gradually become capable of managing freedom; finally, it affects the principles of government, which finds it to its advantage to treat men, who are now more than machines, in accordance with their dignity.

('What is Enlightenment?')

# Chapter 3

# Religion and belief

**T**HE ENLIGHTENMENT IS OFTEN CHARACTERISED as having a highly critical attitude toward religion – or, more specifically, the Christian faith and the authority of its churches – and there is no lack of evidence in the writings of many of the *philosophes* to support this point of view. Many argued that progress towards greater human happiness depended upon the rejection of Revelation (the disclosure of knowledge to humans by divine or supernatural agency) and of faith in the veracity of the scriptures and the teachings of the clergy. Many also commonly depicted the church and clergy as self-serving and corrupt. Some *philosophes* such as Baron d'Holbach became notorious for claiming that 'all religion is a castle in the air' and that the terror and ignorance fostered by religions accounted for most of the needless cruelties and sufferings of humankind. Nor were such views confined to radicals in Catholic France. In the Dutch republic, a few obscure authors, inspired by the 'atheistic' philosophies of Hobbes and Spinoza, published *Traité des Trois Imposteurs* (*Treatise of the Three Imposters*, 1719), explaining to their covert readers that the teachings of Moses, Jesus and Muhammad were 'the greatest impostures which anyone has been able to hatch, and which you should flee if you love the truth'. This was largely because 'The founders of Religions, sensing clearly that the basis of their impostures was the ignorance of the Peoples, resolved to keep them in it.' In England, another staunchly Protestant country, Edward Gibbon created a storm of protest by his account of the early Christians as a bunch of poor, irrational, intolerant, philistine, anti-social, hypocritical and miserable fanatics, whose unnatural beliefs and practices were both 'painful to the individual and useless to mankind'. Worse still, in his view, Christianity had contributed to the downfall of Roman civilisation, as a seemingly 'pure and humble religion gently insinuated itself into the minds of men, grew up in silence and obscurity, derived new vigour from opposition, and finally erected the triumphant banner of the Cross on the ruins of the Capitol' (*Decline and Fall of the Roman Empire*, ch. XV, 1776).

Such hostility to Christianity and, indeed, all 'revealed' religions, undoubtedly reflected an important vein of Enlightenment thinking, but it was by no means the only, nor the most common, line of thought. At the beginning of the century, the Anglo-Irish bishop and philosopher George Berkeley (1685–1753) attacked scepticism, materialism and irreligion in his famous *Treatise Concerning the Principles of Human Knowledge* (1710). From quite a different angle, the German rationalist philosopher and mathematician Leibniz provided an account of how Christianity was in strict keeping with scientific reasoning. This philosophy of 'Optimism' was popularised by Leibniz's pupil Christian Wolff (1679–1754) and by the Catholic poet Alexander Pope, whose *Essay on Man* (1733–34) became one of the most frequently reprinted and widely translated works of the Enlightenment. From an empiricist's point of view, for Locke, too, the use of reason (a divine gift) seemed not only to demonstrate God's existence but to validate the essential truths of Christianity as revealed through the Bible. Thus, in *The Reasonableness of Christianity, as Delivered in the Scriptures* (1695) he wrote anonymously of his 'hope of doing service to decaying piety, and mistaken and slandered Christianity', developing his earlier claim that 'Reason is natural revelation, whereby the eternal Father of Light, and foundation of all knowledge, communicates to mankind that portion of truth which he has lain within the reach of their natural faculties' (*Essay Concerning Human Understanding*, 1690). Newton's Christianity was no less devout, and his discovery of universal gravitation seemed at first to boost belief in a Supreme Being who had made and still regulated the laws of nature, rather than to feed the doubts sown by atheists such as Hobbes. Similarly, many figures such as the English scientist Stephen Hales and the French philosopher Condillac held quite orthodox religious views. Others, such as Thomas Jefferson and Joseph Priestley, though often critical of orthodox Christianity, still proclaimed a powerful commitment to a Christian faith. Reflecting upon 'that anti-Christian system imputed to me by those who know nothing of my opinions', in a private letter in 1803 Jefferson explained: 'To the corruptions of Christianity I am, indeed, opposed; but not to the genuine precepts of Jesus himself. I am a Christian, in the only sense he wished any one to be; sincerely attached to his doctrines, in preference to all others.'

Not all Enlightenment figures, however, thought that reason and revelation went largely hand in hand, and many used Locke's and Newton's findings to repudiate traditional Christian teachings. Figures such as the Catholic-born Irish heretic John Toland (1670–1722) and the English academic Matthew Tindal (1657–1733) became notorious for their determination to make religion more rational. In *Christianity not Mysterious* (1696), Toland claimed that 'there is nothing in the Gospel contrary to reason or above it', and called for religion to be stripped of anything that smacked of mystery. In *Christianity as Old as the Creation. Or the Gospel a Republication of the Religion of Nature* (1730), Tindall insisted that God's will was 'clearly and fully manifested in the Book of Nature', and reduced the Bible to a curious old story corrupted by the clergy. Such views were usually described as 'deism' – a belief in what appeared to be a simpler, more rational, natural and original religion, based upon a Supreme Being who was the creator of the world. Having designed the universe, most deists believed that the 'divine architect' had then withdrawn, leaving humans to their own devices but with the ability to use their reasonings to discover the laws of nature that accounted for the great order, variety and harmony of the world. Thus Voltaire granted that 'the whole philosophy of Newton leads of necessity to the knowledge of a Supreme Being, who created everything, arranged all things of his own free will' (*Elements of the Philosophy of Newton*, 1738). But he also became the great scourge of Christian teachings and clerical authority in France. Furthermore, following the Lisbon earthquake of 1755, he mocked popular Optimism and Leibniz's attempt to explain the existence of evil to Christians by use of the principle of 'sufficient reason' that 'Nothing happens without a reason why it should be so, rather than otherwise'. In his *Poem on the Lisbon Disaster, or an Examination of the Axiom 'All is Well'* (1756) and in the satirical tale *Candide* (1759), Voltaire sought to expose the ridiculousness of Optimism, 'a doctrine of despair under a consoling name', since it accepted that evil was just a necessary part of what was nevertheless 'the best of all possible worlds'.

While deists such as Toland and Voltaire undermined faith in the authority of the clergy, the Scottish sceptic David Hume launched a powerful assault not only upon Christianity and the claim that its truths could be verified by the miracles recounted in Scripture, but also upon all forms of deism and natural religion. This was part of a wider examination of the concept of causation, in which he argued that knowledge about the relationship between cause and effect is derived entirely from observation and experience, and that 'When we infer any particular cause from an effect, we must proportion the one to the other, and can never be allowed to ascribe to the cause any qualities, but what are exactly sufficient to produce that effect.' Thus, for example, on seeing a weight raised upon a scale, we can say that a sufficient force (cause) or forces must have been exerted to produce that effect. But (without prior knowledge from experience, or further observations and experiments) we could not know whether the force(s) could ever act again or lift a heavier weight, let alone attribute to it any reasonings or intentions. Since, unlike humankind, 'the Deity is known to us only by his productions', we cannot infer anything about 'the authors of the existence or order of the universe' other than what appears in the works of nature. Hume did not deny that there could be a god or gods, and that 'the divinity may *possibly* be endowed with attributes, which we have never seen exerted', but this was merely speculation. Deism was really no more reasonable than the Christian religion:

> You find certain phenomena in nature. You seek a cause or author. You imagine that you have found him. You afterwards become so enamoured of this offspring of your brain, that you imagine it impossible, but he must produce something greater and more perfect than the present scene of things, which is so full of ill and disorder. You forget, that this superlative intelligence and benevolence are entirely imaginary, or, at least, without any foundation in reason;

and that you have no ground to ascribe to him any qualities, but what you see he has actually exerted and displayed in his productions.

(*An Enquiry Concerning Human Understanding*, Section XI, 1748)

Hume's reasonings were shocking, not least in Presbyterian Scotland, but the materialism and atheism of scholars such as the French physician La Mettrie and the German-born aristocrat Baron d'Holbach proved an embarrassment even to most *philosophes*, many of whom also feared the social consequences of propagating irreligion. For, as Voltaire reflected: 'The institution of religion exists only to keep mankind in order, and to make men merit the goodness of God by their virtue' (*Philosophical Dictionary*, 1764). Most Enlightenment thinkers were generally agreed, however, on the need to increase freedom of expression, particularly in relation to religious opinions, and, in this respect at least, by mid-century Voltaire was their outstanding spokesman. In addition to his famous campaigns on behalf of victims of persecution and injustice such as Jean Calas and the Sirven family, he argued that 'Of all religions, the Christian ought doubtless to inspire the most toleration, although hitherto the Christians have been the most intolerant of all men.' Having asked 'What is toleration?' he answered: 'It is the natural attribute of humanity. We are all full of weakness and error: let us mutually pardon each other's follies. It is the first law of nature' (*Philosophical Dictionary*). Such views echoed Locke's proposition that 'The toleration of those that differ from others in matters of religion is so agreeable to the Gospel of Jesus Christ, and to the genuine reason of mankind, that it seems monstrous for men to be so blind, as not to perceive the necessity and advantage of it in so clear a light' (*A Letter Concerning Toleration*, 1689). Locke was keen to demonstrate that civil governments should not try to dictate or meddle with men's faith: 'The care of the salvation of men's souls cannot belong to the magistrate' as that would not contribute at all 'to the salvation of their souls'. A limited 'toleration', such as that offered under the Toleration Act of 1689 to some Protestant subjects who dissented from the Church of England, could therefore be envisioned. But even Locke did not recommend the inclusion of Roman Catholics (whose loyalty to the civil authority could not be trusted as they 'deliver themselves up to the service and protection of another prince') or 'those who deny the being of a God' (as 'Promises, covenants, and oaths, which are the bonds of human society, can have no hold upon an atheist') in his otherwise extraordinary but modest plans.

Written, while exiled to the relatively tolerant society of Holland, in 1685 – the year of the Catholic James II's succession in Britain, and of the outbreak of renewed persecution and emigration of French Protestants following Louis XIV's Revocation of the Edict of Nantes – Locke's *Letter Concerning Toleration* was not a statement in favour of a general freedom of expression. Nor was it the most liberal call for religious toleration: in the 1680s the French Huguenot refugee Pierre Bayle argued clearly that all religions should show and enjoy a spirit of tolerance within a peaceful society. Nevertheless, in highlighting the political implications of granting some degree of toleration to religious minorities within a state, Locke was addressing what would become a characteristic topic of Enlightenment discussion. Monarchs had traditionally regarded it as part of their sacred duty to promote religious uniformity throughout their lands, and there was no lack of legal and brutal effort to that effect in most of Europe in the eighteenth century. Yet while Maria Theresa of Austria deported thousands of Protestants in the name of Catholicism, her Catholic son Joseph II adopted what were regarded as more Enlightened policies. In addition to granting some toleration to Jews and some Protestant minorities, on the grounds that 'toleration helps to populate lands and make them prosperous', he also suppressed hundreds of monasteries, turning many into workhouses and hospitals. Similarly, Catherine the Great welcomed Jesuits (expelled from France and Spain in the 1760s) and introduced greater toleration of Jews and Muslims. However, among the Enlightened monarchs, it was Frederick the Great, Head of the Lutheran Church and an admirer of Bayle's writings, who best exemplified a new way of thinking about the relationship of politics and religion. He granted toleration to the Catholic subjects of invaded lands (such as Silesia, seized from Maria Theresa in 1740), welcomed Jesuits as teachers, increased the rights of Jews, and even founded a Catholic cathedral in Berlin. Of course, there were good political and economic reasons for these actions. Yet they were indicative of a new conviction that 'a society could not exist without laws, but it could certainly exist without religion' (Frederick to Voltaire, 1766). In his *Essay on the Forms of Government* (1777), Frederick recognised that 'persecution has given rise to the bloodiest longest and most destructive civil wars', and rejected it in the light of both practical and ethical considerations: 'One can force some poor wretch to pronounce a certain formula, from which he withholds his inner consent; so that the persecutor has gained nothing. But if we go back to the origin of society, it is perfectly clear that the monarch has no right to dictate the citizens' beliefs.'

Although the eighteenth century witnessed the growth of deism, scepticism and atheism, particularly among some intellectuals, and some places saw the codification of greater toleration of religions – as through Thomas Jefferson's Virginia Bill for Establishing Religious Freedom (1786), and the Declaration of the Rights of Man and the Citizen (1789) – the Enlightenment did not de-Christianise or secularise European society and philosophy. In addition to the many Enlightenment figures who held quite orthodox beliefs, some, such as the scientist Joseph Priestley, were positively enthusiastic about their faith. Indeed, the century saw the rise not only of various religious revival movements such as Pietism in Germany, the 'Great Awakening' in North America, and Methodism in Britain, but also of new Christian missions within and beyond European states. For Giambattista Vico, the belief that religion was central to the understanding of humanity and history led him to close his *New Science* (1725) with the comment: 'In sum, all the observations contained in this work lead to one conclusion. My *New Science* is indissolubly linked to the study of piety, and unless one is pious, one cannot be truly wise.' Furthermore, through the work of some central figures, such as Rousseau, the religious experiences of humankind were placed at the heart of Enlightenment debates:

God is good: this is certain. But man finds his happiness in the love of his fellows and God's happiness consists in the love of order; for it is through order that he maintains what is, and unites each part in the whole. God is just; of this I am sure, it is a consequence of his goodness; man's injustice is not God's work, but his own; that moral disorder which seems to the philosophers a presumption against Providence is to me a proof of its existence.

(*Emile*, Book IV, 1762)

## JOHN TOLAND

Born into a Gaelic-speaking Irish Catholic family in County Donegal, John Toland (1670–1722) would become one of the most controversial, influential and enigmatic writers of the early Enlightenment. According to his own accounts he was named 'Janus Junius' (he also once signed himself *Cosmopoli*: 'one who belongs to the world'), but it seems more likely that he was christened 'Seán Eoghain'. After working as a shepherd-boy, attending school in Derry, and renouncing his Catholicism in 1686, he travelled to Scotland where he studied theology, first at Glasgow and then at Edinburgh University where he was awarded an MA in 1690. After further studies at Leyden and Utrecht (1692–94), he left Holland, moving to Oxford and then to London where he published a short book *Christianity not Mysterious* in 1696. On a brief return to Ireland in 1697, he saw his work denounced by the clergy and burned by the common hangman. Threatened with arrest, he went into exile for the rest of his life.

Toland spoke many languages and travelled widely in Britain and the continent, including visits to Hanover (1702), where he debated religion and politics with Leibniz, and won the support of the Electress, Sophia; and Prague (1708), where he persuaded the Irish Franciscans to authenticate his claim to noble Gaelic ancestry. Even though he was an alleged atheist and a reprinter of seventeenth-century republican tracts, he acquired the patronage of several leading politicians including Robert Harley, whom he served as a pamphleteer and spy. Above all, however, it was for his many radical and extraordinary writings on religion, politics and philosophy that he became both famous and notorious. These included: *A Letter to a Member of Parliament, shewing that a Restraint on the Press is inconsistent with the Protestant Religion, and dangerous to the Liberties of the Nation* (1698); *The Life of John Milton* (1698); the materialist work, *Letters to Serena* (1704); *Reasons for Naturalizing the Jews in Great Britain and Ireland, on the same foot with all other Nations* (1714); *Nazarenus: or Jewish, Gentile, and Mahometan Christianity* (1718); *Pantheisticon: or the Form of Celebrating the Socratic Society* (in Latin, 1720; English translation, 1751), allegedly lampooning the liturgy of the Church of England; and a *History of the Druids* (1726) 'containing an account of the ancient Celtic religion and literature'. Ruined by the South Sea Bubble (1720), he died in poverty in London.

The following passages are taken from Toland's most famous work: *Christianity not Mysterious: or a Treatise showing that there is nothing in the Gospel contrary to Reason, nor above it* (1696). Though Locke rejected Toland's arguments, *Christianity not Mysterious* was clearly inspired by Locke's theory of knowledge in

*An Essay Concerning Human Understanding* (1690). Accepting that there are limits to knowledge and that it is impossible to understand fully the nature of anything, Toland claims that the mysteries and miracles of the Christian religion are an imposition and quite unreasonable. This assault upon revelation and traditional teachings sparked several controversies, but though Toland was vigorously opposed by some philosophers, such as George Berkeley, Bishop of Cloyne, his ideas became influential not only in Britain but on the continent, particularly in the works of Voltaire, d'Holbach, Montesquieu, Diderot and Herder. Variously described as a deist, a pantheist (a word Toland coined to describe himself), an atheist, or indeed a highly unorthodox Christian, Toland was always anticlerical. He was also thoroughly polemical, defending his work with several further publications. In considering objections to his arguments, in *Christianity not Mysterious* he noted:

> It may be objected, that the poor and illiterate cannot have such *Faith* as I maintain. Truly, if this can be made out, it may pass for a greater *Mystery* than any system of *Divinity* in *Christendom* can afford: for what can seem more strange and wonderful, than that the common people will sooner believe what is unintelligible, incomprehensible, and above their Reasons, than what is easy, plain, and suited to their capacities? But the vulgar are more obliged to *Christ*, who had a better opinion of them than these men; for he preached his *Gospel* to them in a special manner; and they, on the other hand, *heard him gladly* [1. Pet. 1. 9–12]; because, no doubt, they understood his instructions better than the *mysterious* lectures of their *Priests* and *Scribes*. The uncorrupted doctrines of *Christianity* are not above their reach or comprehension, but the gibberish of your *Divinity Schools* they understand not.
>
> (section 3, ch. 4)

The following extracts from *Christianity not Mysterious* are from the opening chapter 'The State of the Question', and from Section 3 'That there is nothing Mysterious, or above Reason in the Gospel'.

## *Christianity not Mysterious* (1696)

### '*The State of the Question*'

There is nothing that men make a greater noise about, in our time especially, than what they generally profess least of all to understand. It may be easily concluded, I mean *the mysteries of the Christian religion*. The *divines*, whose peculiar province it is to explain them to others, almost unanimously own their ignorance concerning them. They gravely tell us *we must adore what we cannot comprehend*: and yet some of 'em press their dubious comments upon the rest of mankind with more assurance and heat, than could be tolerably justified, though we should grant them to be absolutely infallible. The worst on't is, they are not all of a mind. If you be *orthodox* to those, you are a *heretic* to these. He that sides with a party is adjudged to hell by the rest; and if he declares for none, he receives no milder sentence from all.

Some of 'em say the *mysteries of the Gospel* are to be understood only in the sense of the *Ancient Fathers*. But that is so multifarious, and inconsistent with itself, as to make it impossible for anybody to believe so many contradictions at once. They themselves did caution their readers from leaning upon their authority, without the evidence of *reason*: and thought as little of becoming a rule of faith to their posterity, as we do to ours. Moreover, as all the *Fathers* were not authors, so we cannot properly be said to have their genuine sense. The works of those that have written are wonderfully corrupted and adulterated, or not entirely extant: and if they were, their meaning is much more obscure, and subject to controversy, than that of the *Scripture*.

Others tell us we must be of the mind of some *particular* Doctors [of the Church], pronounced orthodox by the authority of the *Church*. But as we are not a whit satisfied with any authority of that nature, so we see these same *particular Doctors* could not more agree than the whole herd of the *Fathers*; but tragically declaimed against one another's practices and errors: that they were as injudicious, violent, and factious as other men; that they were for the greatest part very credulous and superstitious in religion, as well as pitifully ignorant and superficial in the minutest punctilios of literature. In a word, that they were of the same nature and make with ourselves; and that we know of no privilege above us bestowed upon them by Heaven, except priority of birth, if that be one, as it's likely few will allow.

Some give a decisive voice in the unravelling of *mysteries*, and the interpretation of *Scripture*, to a *General Council*; and others to one man whom they hold to be the Head of the *Church* universal upon earth, and the infallible judge of all controversies. But we do not think such *Councils* possible, nor (if they were) to be of more weight than the *Fathers*; for they consist of such, and others as obnoxious altogether to mistakes and passions. And besides, we cannot have recourse, as to a standing rule, for the solution of our difficulties, to a wonder by God's mercy now more rarely seen than the secular games of old. As for the *one Judge of all Controversies*, we suppose none but such as are strongly prepossessed by interest or education can in good earnest digest those chimerical supreme Headships and monsters of infallibility. We read nowhere in the *Bible* of such delegate judges appointed by *Christ* to supply his *office*: and reason manifestly proclaims them frontless usurpers. Nor is their power finally distinguished from that of *Councils* to this hour, by the miserable admirers of both.

They come nearest the thing who affirm, that we are to keep to what the *Scriptures* determine about these matters: and there is nothing more true, if rightly understood. But ordinarily 'tis an equivocal way of speaking, and nothing less than the proper meaning of it is intended by many of those that use it. For they make the *Scriptures* speak either according to some spurious *philosophy*, or they conform them right or wrong to the bulky systems and formularies of their several communions.

Some will have us always believe *what the literal sense imports*, with little or no consideration for *reason*, which they reject as not fit to be employed about the revealed part of religion. Others assert, that we may use *reason* as the instrument, but not the rule of our belief. The first contend, some *mysteries* may be, or at least seem to be *contrary to reason*, and yet be received by faith. The second, that no *mystery* is contrary to *reason*, but that all are *above* it. Both of 'em from different principles agree, that several doctrines of the *New Testament* belong no farther to the enquiries of *reason*, than to prove 'em divinely revealed, and that they are properly *mysteries* still.

On the contrary, we hold that *reason* is the only foundation of all certitude: and that nothing revealed, whether as to its *manner* or *existence*, is more exempted from its disquisitions, than the ordinary phenomena of nature. Wherefore, we likewise maintain, according to the title of this discourse, that *there is nothing in the Gospel contrary to reason, nor above it; and that no Christian doctrine can be properly called a mystery*.

(*Christianity not Mysterious*, 'The State of the Question')

### 'That nothing ought to be called a mystery, because we have not an adequate idea of all its properties, nor any at all of its essence'

I shall discuss this point with all the perspicuity I am able. And, at first, I affirm, *that nothing can be said to be a mystery, because we have not an adequate idea of it, or a distinct view of all its properties at once; for then everything would be a mystery*. The knowledge of finite creatures is gradually progressive, as objects are presented to the understanding. *Adam* did not know so much in the twentieth as in the hundredth year of his age; and *Jesus Christ* is expressly recorded to have *increased in wisdom as well as in stature* [Luke 2.52]. We are said to know a thousand things, nor can we doubt of it; yet we never have a full conception of whatever belongs to them. I understand nothing better than this *table* upon which I am now writing: I conceive it divisible into parts beyond all imagination; but shall I say it is *above my reason* because I cannot count these parts, nor distinctly perceive their quantity and figures? I am convinced that *plants* have a regular contexture, and a multitude of vessels, many of them equivalent or analogous to those of *animals*, whereby they receive a juice from the earth, and prepare it, changing some into their own substance, and evacuating the excrementitious parts. But I do not clearly comprehend how all these operations are performed, though I know very well what is meant by a *tree*.

The reason is, because *knowing nothing of bodies but their properties, God has wisely provided we should understand no more of these than are useful and necessary for us*; which is all our present condition needs. Thus our eyes are not given us to see all quantities, nor perhaps anything as it is in itself, but as it bears some relation to us. What is too minute, as it escapes our sight, so it can neither harm nor benefit us: and we have a better view of bodies the nearer we approach them, because then they become more convenient or inconvenient; but as we remove farther off we lose their sight with their influence. I'm persuaded there's no motion which does not excite some sound in ears disposed to be affected with proportionable degrees of force from the air; and, it may be, the small animals concerned can hear the steps of the *spider*, as we do those of men and cattle. From these and millions of other instances it is manifest, that we have little certainty of anything but as it is noxious or beneficial to us.

Rightly speaking then, we are accounted to *comprehend* anything when its chief properties and their several uses are known to us: for to *comprehend* in all correct authors is nothing else but *to know*; and as of what is not knowable we can have no idea, so it is nothing to us. It is improper therefore to say a thing is above our reason, because we know no more of it than concerns us, and ridiculous to supercede our disquisitions about it upon that score. What should we think of a man that would stiffly maintain *water* to be above his reason, and that he would never enquire into its nature, nor employ it in his house or grounds, because he knows not how many particles go to a drop; whether the air passes through it, is incorporated with it, or neither? This is for all the world as if I could not go because I cannot fly. Now, seeing *the denominations of things are borrowed from their known properties, and that no properties are knowable but what concern us, or serve to discover such as we do*, we cannot be accountable for comprehending no other, nor justly required more by reasonable men, much less by the all-wise Deity.

The most compendious method therefore to acquire sure and useful knowledge, is *neither to trouble ourselves with what is useless, were it known; or what is impossible to be known at all*. Since I easily perceive the good or bad effects of rain upon the earth, what should I be the better did I comprehend its generation in the clouds? For, after all, I could make no rain at my pleasure, nor prevent its falling at any time. A probable hypothesis will not give satisfaction in such cases: the hands, for example, of two dials may have the same motion, though the disposition of the latent springs which produce it should be very different. And to affirm this or that to be the way, will not do, unless you can demonstrate that no other possible way remains. Nay, should you hit upon the real manner, you can never be sure of it, because the evidence of matters of fact solely depends upon testimony: and it follows not that such a thing is so, because it may be so.

The application of this discourse to my subject admits of no difficulty; and it is, first, *That no Christian doctrine, no more than any ordinary piece of nature, can be reputed a mystery, because we have not an adequate or complete idea of whatever belongs to it*. Secondly, *that what is revealed in religion, as it is most useful and necessary, so it must and may be as easily comprehended, and found as consistent with our common notions, as what we know of wood or stone, of air, of water, or the like*. And, thirdly, *That when we do as familiarly explain such doctrines, as what is known of natural things* (which I pretend we can), *we may then be as properly said to comprehend the one as the other*.

(*Christianity not Mysterious*, section 3, ch. 2)

## GOTTFRIED WILHELM LEIBNIZ

The German metaphysical philosopher and mathematician, Leibniz (1646–1716) was born in Leipzig towards the end of the Thirty Years War which had ravaged Europe. He was the son of the Professor of Moral Philosophy at Leipzig, and at the age of fifteen he entered the university, studying law and jurisprudence, graduating in 1663. In the early 1670s he served diplomatic missions to France and England, where he met distinguished scientists and philosophers, before becoming librarian to the Duke of Brunswick and, later, official historian to the House of Hanover. In 1700, he became the first president of the new Berlin Academy of Sciences. As a scientist, he shares with Newton the honour of having independently discovered the differential calculus, and of contributing to the concept of kinetic energy. However, he is best known for his work in metaphysics and as a foremost advocate of Optimism.

Leibniz wrote and published essays on a great variety of subjects, but his *Essais de Théodicée* (*Essays on Theodicy*, 1710) was the only book-length work that he published during his lifetime. It was based upon discussions that Leibniz had had with his philosophical sparring-partner, Pierre Bayle (1647–1706), a French Calvinist thinker and author of the influential *Historical and Critical Dictionary* (1697). *Theodicy* became famous for its espousal of the doctrine of Optimism, which states that this is 'the best of all possible worlds'. Optimism attempts to deal with the problem of the existence of evil, whilst maintaining a belief in an omnipotent and benevolent God. Leibniz claimed that evil forms a requisite part in the most complex fulfilment of God's providential plan in choosing to create this world, which was the most perfect of all possible worlds. Leibniz's pupil Christian Wolff and Pope's *Essay on Man* (1733) helped to popularise Optimism, but the philosophy was later rejected by most *philosophes* and brilliantly ridiculed by Voltaire in his comic novel *Candide, or Optimism* (1759).

After a lengthy Preface and a 'Preliminary Dissertation on the Conformity of Faith with Reason', *Theodicy* consists of 'Essays on the Justice of God and the Freedom of Man in the Origin of Evil, in Three Parts', followed by several Appendices. The extract here, from a modern translation, is taken from Part One of 'Essays on the Justice of God'.

## Essays on Theodicy (1710)

Our end is to banish from men the false ideas that represent God to them as an absolute prince employing a despotic power, unfitted to be loved and unworthy of being loved. These notions are the more evil in relation to God inasmuch as the essence of piety is not only to fear him but also to love him above all things: and that cannot come about unless there be knowledge of his perfections capable of arousing the love which he deserves, and which makes the felicity of those that love him. Feeling ourselves animated by a zeal such as cannot fail to please him, we have cause to hope that he will enlighten us, and that he will himself aid us in the execution of a project undertaken for his glory and for the good of men. A cause so good gives confidence: if there are plausible appearances against us, there are proofs on our side, and I would dare to say to an adversary:

*Aspice, num mage sit nostrum penetrabile telum*

[Look whether my weapon is not far more wounding (Virgil, *Aeneid*, 10.481)]

*God is the first reason of things*: for such things as are bounded as all that which we see and experience, are contingent and have nothing in them to render their existence necessary, it being plain that time, space and matter, united and uniform in themselves and indifferent to everything, might have received entirely other motions and shapes, and in another order. Therefore one must seek the reason for the existence of the world, which is the whole assemblage of *contingent* things, and seek it in the substance which carries with it the reason for its existence, and which in consequence is *necessary* and eternal. Moreover, this cause must be intelligent: for this existing world being contingent and an infinity of other worlds being equally possible, and holding, so to say, equal claim to existence with it, the cause of the world must needs have had regard or reference to all these possible worlds in order to fix upon one of them. This regard or relation of an existent substance to simple possibilities can be nothing other than the *understanding* which has the ideas of them, while to fix upon one of them can be nothing other than the act of the *will* which chooses. It is the *power* of this substance that renders its will efficacious. Power relates to *being*, wisdom or understanding to *truth*, and will to *good*. And this intelligent cause ought to be infinite in all ways, and absolutely perfect in *power*, in *wisdom* and in *goodness*, since it relates to all that which is possible. Furthermore, since all is connected together, there is no ground for admitting more than *one*. Its understanding is the source of *essences*, and its will is the origin of *existences*. There in few words is the proof of one only God with his perfections, and through him of the origin of things.

Now this supreme wisdom, united to a goodness that is no less infinite, cannot but have chosen the best. For as a lesser evil is a kind of good, even so a lesser good is a kind of evil if it stands in the way of a greater good; and there would be something to correct in the actions of God if it were possible to do better. As in mathematics, when there is no maximum nor minimum, in short nothing distinguished, everything is done equally, or when that is not possible nothing at all is done: so it may be said likewise in respect of perfect wisdom, which is no less orderly than mathematics, that if there were not the best (*optimum*) among all possible worlds, God would not have produced any. I call 'World' the whole succession and the whole agglomeration of all existent things, lest it be said that several worlds could have existed in different times and different places. For they must needs be reckoned all together as one world or, if you will, as one Universe. And even though one should fill all times and all places, it still remains true that one might have filled them in innumerable ways, and that there is an infinitude of possible worlds among which God must needs have chosen the best, since he does nothing without acting in accordance with supreme reason.

Some adversary not being able to answer this argument will perchance answer the conclusion by a counter-argument, saying that the world could have been without sin and without sufferings; but I deny that then it would have been *better*. For it must be known that all things are *connected* in each one of the possible worlds: the universe, whatever it may be, is all of one piece, like an ocean: the least movement extends its effect there to any distance whatsoever, even though this effect become less perceptible in proportion to the distance. Therein God has ordered all things beforehand once for all, having foreseen prayers, good and bad actions, and all the rest; and each thing *as an idea* has contributed, before its existence, to the resolution that has been made upon the existence of all things; so that nothing can be changed in the universe (any more than in a number) save its essence or, if you will, save its *numerical individuality*. Thus, if the smallest evil that comes to pass in the world were missing in it, it would no longer be this world; which, with nothing omitted and all allowance made, was found the best by the Creator who chose it.

It is true that one may imagine possible worlds without sin and without unhappiness, and one could make some like Utopian or Sevarambian romances: but these same worlds again would be very inferior to ours in goodness. I cannot show you this in detail. For can I know and can I present infinities to you and compare them together? But you must judge with me *ab effectu* [from the effects], since God has chosen this world as it is. We know, moreover, that often an evil brings forth a good whereto one would not have attained without that evil. Often indeed two evils have made one great good.

*(Theodicy*, 'Essays on the Justice of God', Part I)

## DAVID HUME

David Hume (see p. 45) was a sceptic with regard to religion. He recognised the vulnerability of Christianity to empirical analysis, given that much of the identity and significance of Christ was traditionally based on the 'miraculous evidences' of the New Testament. In the extract here, from the highly controversial essay 'Of Miracles' in his *Enquiry Concerning Human Understanding* (1748), Hume is concerned primarily with the nature of evidence and proof regarding claims about the world. He states: 'A wise man ... proportions his belief to the evidence', and that experience is 'our only guide in reasoning concerning matters of fact'. He aims to show how unreasonable it is to believe claims about a past event (such as the Resurrection) when that event is so clearly contrary to 'the laws of nature' established by all other human testimony, based upon one's own and all other impartial people's experiences.

'Of Miracles' is divided into two parts, reflecting two phases of the argument: the first part is largely philosophical, the second historical. In the first extract, from the opening of Part I, Hume begins by mischievously citing the argument of the former Archbishop of Canterbury, John Tillotson (1630–94): that belief in Christ's real presence in the bread and wine of a Catholic mass is unreasonable, as it confounds 'the clear evidence of a man's senses'. That empirical argument is then used by Hume to help discredit all Christian miracles. He notes how a reasonable person 'proportions his belief', and how knowledge about the causes of events (the relationship of cause and effect) can only be acquired from experience. Thus, to cite one of Hume's examples, no amount of *a priori* reasoning about what may happen to water in cold climates would ever lead an Indian prince to knowledge of the fact that water freezes at low temperatures. The prince requires experience (or the reliable testimony of others). If he has no experience of the phenomenon, he has no evidence for or against the law of nature that water freezes in cold climates. In the second extract, also from Part I, Hume claims that a miracle is, by definition, 'a violation of the laws of nature'. In the final extract, taken from the end of Part II, he proposes: 'we may establish it as a maxim that no human testimony can have such force as to prove a miracle ... so as to be the foundation of a system of religion'.

## *An Enquiry Concerning Human Understanding* (1748)

### *'Of Miracles'*

There is, in Dr Tillotson's writing, an argument against the *real presence*, which is as concise, and elegant, and strong as any argument can possibly be supposed against a doctrine [transubstantiation], so little worthy of a serious refutation. It is acknowledged on all hands, says that learned prelate, that the authority, either of the scripture or of tradition, is founded merely in the testimony of the apostles, who were eye-witnesses to those miracles of our Saviour, by which he proved his divine mission. Our evidence, then, for the truth of the Christian religion is less than the evidence for the truth of our senses; because, even in the first authors of our religion, it was no greater; and it was evident it must diminish in passing from them to their disciples; nor can any one rest such confidence in their testimony, as in the immediate object of his senses. But a weaker evidence can never destroy a stronger; and therefore, were the doctrine of the real presence ever so clearly revealed in scripture, it were directly contrary to the rules of just reasoning to give our assent to it. It contradicts sense, though both the scripture and tradition, on which it is supposed to be built, carry not such evidence with them as sense; when they are considered merely as external evidences, and are not brought home to every one's breast, by the immediate operation of the Holy Spirit.

Nothing is so convenient as a decisive argument of this kind, which must at least *silence* the most arrogant bigotry and superstition, and free us from their impertinent solicitations. I flatter myself, that I have discovered an argument of a like nature, which, if just, will, with the wise and learned, be an everlasting check to all kinds of superstitious delusion, and consequently, will be useful as long as the world endures. For so long, I presume, will the accounts of miracles and prodigies be found in all history, sacred and profane.

Though experience be our only guide in reasoning concerning matters of fact; it must be acknowledged, that this guide is not altogether infallible, but in some cases is apt to lead us into errors. One, who in our climate, should expect better weather in any week of June than in one of December, would reason justly, and conformably to experience; but it is certain, that he may happen, in the event, to find himself mistaken. However, we may observe that, in such a case, he would have no cause to complain of experience; because it commonly informs us beforehand of the uncertainty, by that contrariety of events, which we may learn from a diligent observation. All effects follow not with like certainty from their supposed causes. Some events are found, in all countries and all ages, to have been constantly conjoined together. Others are found to have been more variable, and sometimes to disappoint our expectations; so that, in our reasonings concerning matter of fact, there are all imaginable degrees of assurance, from the highest certainty to the lowest species of moral evidence.

A wise man, therefore, proportions his belief to the evidence. In such conclusions as are founded on an infallible experience, he expects the event with the last degree of assurance, and regards his past experience as a full *proof* of the future existence of that event. In other cases, he proceeds with more caution. He weighs the opposite experiments: he considers which side is supported by the greater number of experiments: to that side he inclines, with doubt and hesitation; and when at last he fixes his judgement, the evidence exceeds not what we properly call *probability*. All probability, then, supposes an opposition of experiments and observations, where the one side is found to overbalance the other, and to produce a degree of evidence, proportioned to the superiority. A hundred instances or experiments on one side, and fifty on another, afford a doubtful expectation of any event; though a hundred uniform experiments, with only one that is contradictory, reasonably beget a pretty strong degree of assurance. In all cases, we must balance the opposite experiments, where they are opposite, and deduct the smaller number from the greater, in order to know the exact force of the superior evidence.

To apply these principles to a particular instance; we may observe, that there is no species of reasoning more common, more useful, and even necessary to human life, than that which is derived from the testimony of men, and the reports of eye-witnesses and spectators. This species of reasoning, perhaps, one may deny to be founded on the relation of cause and effect. I shall not dispute about a word. It will be sufficient to observe that our assurance in any argument of this kind is derived from no other principle than our observation of the veracity of human testimony, and of the usual conformity of facts to the reports of witnesses. It being a general maxim, that no objects have any discoverable connexion together, and that all the inferences, which we can draw from one to another, are founded merely on our experience of their constant and regular conjunction; it is evident, that we ought not to make an exception to this maxim in favour of human testimony, whose connexion with any event seems, in itself, as little necessary as any other. Were not the memory tenacious to a certain degree; had not men commonly an inclination to truth and a principle of probity; were they not sensible to shame, when detected in a falsehood: were not these, I say, discovered by *experience* to be qualities, inherent in human nature, we should never repose the least confidence in human testimony. A man delirious, or noted for falsehood and villany, has no manner of authority with us.

And as the evidence, derived from witnesses and human testimony, is founded on past experience, so it varies with the experience, and is regarded either as a *proof* or a *probability*, according as the conjunction between any particular kind of report and any kind of object has been found to be constant and variable. There are a number of circumstances to be taken into consideration in all judgements of this kind; and the ultimate standard, by which we determine all disputes, that may arise concerning them, is always derived from experience and observation. Where this experience is not entirely uniform on any side, it is attended with an unavoidable contrariety in our judgements, and with the same opposition and mutual destruction of argument as in every other kind of evidence. We frequently hesitate concerning the reports of others. We balance the opposite circumstances, which cause any doubt or uncertainty; and when we discover a superiority on any side, we incline to it; but still with a diminution of assurance, in proportion to the force of its antagonist.

This contrariety of evidence, in the present case, may be derived from several different causes; from the opposition of contrary testimony; from the character or number of the witnesses; from the manner of their delivering their testimony; or from the union of all these circumstances. We entertain a suspicion concerning any matter of fact, when the witnesses contradict each other; when they are but few, or of a doubtful character; when they have an interest in what they affirm; when they deliver their testimony with hesitation, or on the contrary, with too violent asseverations. There are many other particulars of the same kind, which may diminish or destroy the force of any argument, derived from human testimony.

(*An Enquiry Concerning Human Understanding*,
Section X, 'Of Miracles', Part I, sections 86–89)

A miracle is a violation of the laws of nature; and as a firm and unalterable experience has established these laws, the proof against a miracle, from the very nature of the fact, is as entire as any argument from experience can possibly be imagined. Why is it more than probable, that all men must die; that lead cannot, of itself, remain suspended in the air; that fire consumes wood, and is extinguished by water; unless it be, that these events are found agreeable to the laws of nature, and there is required a violation of these laws, or in other words, a miracle to prevent them? Nothing is esteemed a miracle, if it ever happen in the common course of nature. It is no miracle that a man, seemingly in good health, should die on a sudden: because such a kind of death, though more unusual than any other, has yet been frequently observed to happen. But it is a miracle, that a dead man should come to life; because that has never been observed in any age or country. There must, therefore, be a uniform experience against every miraculous event, otherwise the event would not merit that appellation. And as a uniform experience amounts to a proof, there is here a direct and full *proof*, from the nature of the fact, against the existence of any miracle; nor can such a proof be destroyed, or the miracle rendered credible, but by an opposite proof, which is superior.

The plain consequence is (and it is a general maxim worthy of our attention), 'That no testimony is sufficient to establish a miracle, unless the testimony be of such a kind, that its falsehood would be more miraculous, than the fact, which it endeavours to establish; and even in that case there is a mutual destruction of arguments, and the superior only gives us an assurance suitable to that degree of force, which remains, after deducting the inferior.' When anyone tells me, that he saw a dead man restored to life, I immediately consider with myself, whether it be more probably, that this person should either deceive or be deceived, or that the fact, which he relates, should really have happened. I weigh the one miracle against the other; and according to the superiority, which I discover, I pronounce my decision, and always reject the greater miracle. If the falsehood of his testimony would be more miraculous, than the event which he relates; then, and not till then, can he pretend to command my belief or opinion.

(*An Enquiry Concerning Human Understanding*,
Section X, 'Of Miracles', Part I, sections 90–91)

I am the better pleased with the method of reasoning here delivered, as I think it may serve to confound those dangerous friends or disguised enemies to the *Christian Religion*, who have undertaken to defend it by the principles of human reason. Our most holy religion is founded on *Faith*, not on reason; and it is a sure method of exposing it to put it to such a trial as it is, by no means, fitted to endure. To make this more evident, let us examine those miracles, related in scripture; and not to lose ourselves in too wide a field, let us confine ourselves to such as we find in the *Pentateuch* [the first five books of the Old Testament, traditionally attributed to Moses], which we shall examine, according to the principles of these pretended Christians, not as the word or testimony of God himself, but as the production of a mere human writer and historian. Here then we are first to consider a book, presented to us by a barbarous and ignorant people, written in an age when they were still more barbarous, and in all probability long after the facts which it relates, corroborated by no concurring testimony, and resembling those fabulous accounts, which every nation gives of its origin. Upon reading this book, we find it full of prodigies and miracles. It gives an account of a state of the world and of human nature entirely different from the present: of our fall from that state; of the age of man, extended to near a thousand years; of the destruction of the world by a deluge; of the arbitrary choice of one people, as the favourites of heaven, and that people the countrymen of the author; of their deliverance from bondage by prodigies the most astonishing imaginable. I desire any one to lay his hand upon his heart, and after a serious consideration declare, whether he thinks that the falsehood of such a book, supported by such a testimony, would be more extraordinary and miraculous than all the miracles it relates; which is, however, necessary to make it be received, according to the measures of probability above established.

What we have said of miracles may be applied, without any variation, to prophecies; and indeed, all prophecies are real miracles, and as such only, can be admitted as proofs of any revelation. If it did not exceed the capacity of human nature to foretell future events, it would be absurd to employ any prophecy as an argument for a divine mission or authority from heaven. So that, upon the whole, we may conclude, that the *Christian Religion* not only was at first attended with miracles, but even at this day cannot be believed by any reasonable person without one. Mere reason is insufficient to convince us of its veracity. And whoever is moved by *Faith* to assent to it, is conscious of a continued miracle in his own person, which subverts all the principles of his understanding, and gives him a determination to believe what is most contrary to custom and experience.

> (*An Enquiry Concerning Human Understanding*,
> Section X, 'Of Miracles', Part II, sections 100–101)

## VOLTAIRE

Born in Paris, the son of a successful lawyer, Voltaire, the pen name of François-Marie Arouet (1694–1778), received a classical education at a Jesuit College. He came to be regarded as the best playwright in France, and later as a leading figure of the Enlightenment, especially famous for his campaigns for justice and religious tolerance. His philosophical views were inspired by the works of Pierre Bayle (1647–1706) and Fontenelle (1657–1757) and developed during his visit to England (1726–29), where he learned English and published his anticlerical poem on Henry IV of France, *La Henriade* in 1728. During the two-and-a-half years that he spent in England he was impressed by the apparent freedom and prosperity of the country, and by English science and philosophy – particularly the works of Bacon, Newton and Locke. Returning to France, a country dominated by Bourbon absolutism and Catholicism, he daringly fought against religious intolerance and persecution: 'I am tired of hearing that twelve men were able to establish Christianity; I should like to prove that one is capable of destroying it.' Though highly critical of organised religion and the superstition, ignorance and cruelties that he believed that it perpetrated, he retained a form of religious belief that was akin to deism.

Voltaire's many satirical works cost him several banishments from Paris, a period of exile in Holland, and eleven months' imprisonment in the Bastille from 1717.

On his release in 1718, his first play *Oedipe* (*Oedipus*) was performed at the Théâtre Français. When his *Lettres Philosophiques* (*Philosophical Letters*) appeared in France in 1734, praising English and satirising French society and institutions, he fled to live at the home of his lover, the scientist Madame du Châtelet at Cirey in Champagne. During the years there, he wrote plays and, with Mme du Châtelet, a treatise on Newtonian science. Following the distress caused by her sudden death in 1749, he accepted Frederick II's invitation to stay at the king's palace in Potsdam (1750–53). However, after several quarrels with Frederick and other *philosophes* at the royal court, Voltaire soon became disillusioned with the 'philosopher-king'. He also conducted long correspondences with Catherine the Great and many other *philosophes*. On his return to France in 1754 he found himself effectively barred from living in or near Paris. After moving in 1755 to Les Délices on the outskirts of Geneva, he wrote a *Poème sur le Désastre de Lisbonne* (*Poem on the Lisbon Disaster*, 1756) and the celebrated satirical tale *Candide* (1759). However, he fell out with the authorities in Geneva, and in 1759 he moved to a large estate a few miles away at Ferney (just over the Swiss border, in France), where he lived and worked for the next twenty years. Living very comfortably and maintaining an open house for visitors from all over Europe, he launched a series of famous campaigns against *l'infâme* (injustice). Thus, in the Calas affair in 1762, he challenged the Toulouse *parlement*'s decision to have the Protestant Jean Calas broken on the wheel, after the alleged murder of his Catholic son. Similarly, in 1766 he campaigned in the case of the young Chevalier de la Barre, who was tried, tortured and executed for blasphemous conduct. It was ordered that a copy of Voltaire's *Dictionnaire Philosophique* (*Philosophical Dictionary*, 1764) should be burned with La Barre's corpse. A prolific writer on a great range of subjects, Voltaire exercised a powerful influence upon the character of the Enlightenment throughout Europe. After a twenty-eight year absence, in 1778 he returned to Paris where he was fêted, but he died a few months later. In 1791 his remains (excluding his heart which had been sent to Ferney) were transferred to the Panthéon in Paris.

The first extract selected here, is from a modern (1911) translation of *Poem on the Lisbon Disaster, or an Examination of the Axiom 'All is Well'* (1756) – Voltaire's emotional response to the death and suffering of innocent people in Lisbon's earthquake on All Saints Day in 1755. This natural disaster, followed by fire and floods, took the lives of many thousands, scores of whom were crushed while at worship in their churches. Voltaire aims to undermine what he regards as the callous and foolish philosophy of Leibniz's Optimism, popularised by Pope's *Essay on Man* (1733–34), on the grounds that such a tragedy is inconsistent with belief in a benevolent and omnipotent Christian God. Rousseau promptly responded with a *Lettre de J.J. Rousseau à Monsieur de Voltaire, Le 18 Août 1756*, in which he explained how 'Mr Pope's poem alleviates my evils, and induces me to patience; yours [Voltaire] embitters my sorrows, excites my complaints, and, depriving me of everything but a doubtful hope, reduces me to despair'. He also argued that God was not responsible for the fact that the city was badly built: 'nature never assembled there twenty thousand houses of six or seven stories high; and that, if the inhabitants of that great city had been more equally dispersed, and more lightly lodged, the damage would have been much less, and perhaps none at all'. In the second extract, the entry entitled 'Theist' from his *Philosophical Dictionary*, Voltaire portrays the theist (akin to the deist) as someone who accepts the existence of a Supreme Being who is the author of the natural world and a model for goodness and justice.

## Poem on the Lisbon Disaster (1756)

Unhappy mortals! Dark and mourning earth!
Affrighted gathering of human kind!
Eternal lingering of useless pain!
Come, ye philosophers, who cry, 'All's well,'
And contemplate this ruin of a world.                              5
Behold these shreds and cinders of your race,
This child and mother heaped in common wreck,
These scattered limbs beneath the marble shafts—
A hundred thousand whom the earth devours,
Who, torn and bloody, palpitating yet,                            10
Entombed beneath their hospitable roofs,
In racking torment end their stricken lives,
To those expiring murmurs of distress,
To that appalling spectacle of woe,
Will ye reply: 'You do but illustrate                             15
The iron laws that chain the will of God'?
Say ye, o'er that yet quivering mass of flesh:
'God is avenged: the wage of sin is death'?
What crime, what sin, had those young hearts conceived
That lie, bleeding and torn, on mother's breast?                  20
Did fallen Lisbon deeper drink of vice
Than London, Paris or sunlit Madrid?
In these men dance; at Lisbon yawns the abyss.
Tranquil spectators of your brothers' wreck,
Unmoved by this repellent dance of death,                         25
Who calmly seek the reason of such storms,
Let them but lash your own security;
Your tears will mingle freely with the flood.
When earth its horrid jaws half open shows,
My plaint is innocent, my cries are just.                         30
Surrounded by such cruelties of fate,
By rage of evil and by snares of death,
Fronting the fierceness of the elements,
Sharing our ills, indulge me my lament.
'This pride,' ye say—'the pride of rebel heart,                   35
To think we might fare better than we do.'
Go, tell it to the Tagus' stricken banks;

Search in the ruins of that bloody shock;
Ask of the dying in that house of grief,
Whether 'tis pride that calls on heaven for help          40
And pity for the sufferings of men.
'All's well,' ye say, 'and all is necessary.'
Think ye this universe had been the worse
Without this hellish gulf in Portugal?
Are ye so sure the great eternal cause,                   45
That knows all things, and for itself creates,
Could not have placed us in this dreary clime
Without volcanoes seething 'neath our feet?
Set you this limit to the power supreme?
Would you forbid it use its clemency?                     50
Are not the means of the great artisan
Unlimited for shaping his designs?
The master I would not offend, yet wish
This gulf of fire and sulphur had outpoured
Its baleful flood amid the desert wastes.                 55
God I respect, yet love the universe.
Not pride, alas, it is, but love of man,
To mourn so terrible a stroke as this.


Would it console the sad inhabitants
Of these aflame and desolated shores                      60
To say to them: 'Lay down your lives in peace;
For the world's good your homes are sacrificed;
Your ruined palaces shall others build,
For other peoples shall your walls arise;
The North grows rich on your unhappy loss;               65
Your ills are but a link in general law;
To God you are as those low creeping worms
That wait for you in your predestined tombs'?
What speech to hold to victims of such ruth!
Add not such cruel outrage to their pain.                 70


Nay, press not on my agitated heart
These iron and irrevocable laws,
This rigid chain of bodies, minds, and worlds.
Dreams of the bloodless thinker are such thoughts.
God holds the chain: is not himself enchained;           75
By his indulgent choice is all arranged;
Implacable he's not, but free and just.
Why suffer we, then, under one so just?
There is the knot your thinkers should undo.

Think ye to cure our ills denying them?                       80
All peoples, trembling at the hand of God,
Have sought the source of evil in the world.
When the eternal law that all things moves
Doth hurl the rock by impact of the winds,
With lightning rends and fires the sturdy oak,               85
They have no feeling of the crashing blows;
But I, I live and feel, my wounded heart
Appeals for aid to him who fashioned it.


Children of that Almighty Power, we stretch
Our hands in grief towards our common sire.                  90
The vessel, truly, is not heard to say:
'Why should I be so vile, so coarse, so frail?'
Nor speech nor thought is given unto it.
The urn that, from the potter's forming hand,
Slips and is shattered has no living heart                   95
That yearns for bliss and shrinks from misery.
'This misery,' ye say, 'is other's good.'
Yes; from my mouldering body shall be born
A thousand worms, when death has closed my pain.
Fine consolation this in my distress!                        100
Grim speculators on the woes of men,
Ye double, not assuage, my misery.
In you I mark the nerveless boast of pride
That hides its ill with pretext of content.


I am a puny part of the great whole.                         105
Yes; but all animals condemned to live,
All sentient things, born by the same stern law,
Suffer like me, and like me also die.


The vulture fastens on his timid prey,
And stabs with bloody beak the quivering limbs:             110
All's well, it seems, for it. But in a while
An eagle tears the vulture into shreds;
The eagle is transfixed by shaft of man;
The man, prone in the dust of battlefield,
Mingling his blood with dying fellow men,                   115
Becomes in turn the food of ravenous birds.
Thus the whole world in every member groans:
All born for torment and for mutual death.
And o'er this ghastly chaos you would say
The ills of each make up the good of all!                   120

What blessedness! And as, with quaking voice,
Mortal and pitiful, ye cry, 'All's well,'
The universe belies you, and your heart
Refutes a hundred times your mind's conceit.


All dead and living things are locked in strife.          125
Confess it freely — evil stalks the land
Its secret principle unknown to us.
Can it be from the author of all good?
Are we condemned to weep by tyrant law
Of black Typhon or barbarous Ahriman?                     130
These odious monsters, whom a trembling world
Made gods, my spirit utterly rejects.


But how conceive a God supremely good,
Who heaps his favours on the sons he loves,               135
Yet scatters evil with as large a hand?
What eye can pierce the depth of his designs?
From that all-perfect Being came not ill:
And came it from no other, for he's lord:
Yet it exists. O stern and numbing truth!
O wondrous mingling of diversities!                       140
A God came down to lift our stricken race:
He visited the earth, and changed it not!
One sophist says he had not power to change;
'He had,' another cries, 'but willed it not:
In time he will, no doubt.' And, while they prate,        145
The hidden thunders, belched from underground,
Fling wide the ruins of a hundred towns
Across the smiling face of Portugal.
God either smites the inborn guilt of man,
Or, arbitrary lord of space and time,                     150
Devoid alike of pity and of wrath,
Pursues the cold designs he has conceived.
Or else this formless stuff, recalcitrant,
Bears in itself inalienable faults;
Or else God tries us, and this mortal life                155
Is but the passage to eternal spheres.
'Tis transitory pain we suffer here,
And death its merciful deliverance.
Yet, when this dreadful passage has been made,
Who will contend he has deserved the crown?               160
Whatever side we take we needs must groan;
We nothing know, and everything must fear.

Nature is dumb, in vain appeal to it,
The human race demands a word of God.
'Tis his alone to illustrate his work,                                    165
Console the weary, and illume the wise.
Without him man, to doubt and error doomed,
Finds not a reed that he may lean upon.


From Leibnitz learn we not by what unseen
Bonds, in this best of all imagined worlds,                               170
Endless disorder, chaos of distress,
Must mix our little pleasures thus with pain;
Nor why the guiltless suffer all this woe
In common with the most abhorrent guilt.
'Tis mockery to tell me all is well.                                      175
Like learned doctors, nothing do I know.


Plato has said that men did once have wings
And bodies proof against all mortal ill;
That pain and death were strangers to their world.
How have we fallen from that high estate!                                 180
Man crawls and dies: all is but born to die:
The world's the empire of destructiveness.
This frail construction of quick nerves and bones
Cannot sustain the shock of elements;
This temporary blend of blood and dust                                    185
Was put together only to dissolve;
This prompt and vivid sentiment of nerve
Was made for pain, the minister of death:
Thus in my years does nature's message run.
Plato and Epicurus I reject,                                              190
And turn more hopefully to learned Bayle.
With even poised scale Bayle bids me doubt.
He, wise enough and great to need no creed,
Has slain all systems — combats even himself:
Like that blind conqueror of Philistines,                                 195
He sinks beneath the ruin he has wrought.
What is the verdict of the vastest mind?
Silence: the book of fate is closed to us.
Man is a stranger to his own research;
He knows not whence he comes, nor whither goes                            200
Tormented atoms in a bed of mud,
Devoured by death, a mockery of fate.
But thinking atoms, whose far-seeing eyes,
Guided by thought, have measured the faint stars,

Our being mingles with the infinite;                              205
Ourselves we never see, or come to know.
This word, this theatre of pride and wrong,
Swarms with sick fools who talk of happiness.
With plaints and groans they follow up the quest,
To die reluctant, or be born again.                              210
At fitful moments in our pain-racked life
The hand of pleasure wipes away our tears;
But pleasure passes like a fleeting shade,
And leaves a legacy of pain and loss.
The past for us is but a fond regret,                            215
The present grim, unless the future's clear.
If thought must end in darkness of the tomb,
All will be well one day — so runs our hope.
All now is well, is but an ideal dream.
The wise deceive me: God alone is right.                         220
With lowly sighing, subject in my pain,
Once did I sing, in less lugubrious tone,
The sunny ways of pleasure's genial rule;
The times have changed, and, taught by growing age,
And sharing of the frailty of mankind,                           225
Seeking a light amid the deepening gloom,
I can but suffer, and will not repine.


A caliph once, when his last hour had come,
This prayer addressed to him he reverenced:
'To thee, sole and all-powerful king, I bear                     230
What thou dost lack in thy immensity —
Evil and ignorance, distress and sin.'
He might have added one thing further — hope.

(Poem on the Lisbon Disaster)

## 'Theist'

from *Philosophical Dictionary* (1764)

The theist is a man firmly persuaded of the existence of a Supreme Being equally good and powerful, who has formed all extended, vegetating, sentient, and reflecting existences, who perpetuates their species, who punishes crimes without cruelty, and rewards virtuous actions with kindness.

The theist does not know how God punishes, how He rewards, how He pardons; for he is not presumptuous enough to flatter himself that he understands how God acts, but he knows that God does act, and that He is just. The difficulties opposed to a providence do not stagger him in his faith, because they are only great difficulties, not proofs. He submits himself to that providence, although he perceives some of its effects and some appearances; and judging of the things he does not see from those he does see, he thinks that this providence pervades all places and all ages.

United in this principle with the rest of the universe, he does not embrace any of the sects, who all contradict themselves; his religion is the most ancient and the most extended; for the simple adoration of God has preceded all the systems in the world. He speaks a language that all nations understand, while they are unable to understand each other's. He has his brethren from Peking to Cayenne, and he reckons all the wise his brothers. He believes that religion consists neither in the opinions of incomprehensible metaphysics, nor in vain decorations, but in adoration and justice. To do good — that is his worship; to submit oneself to God – that is his doctrine. The Mahometan cries out to him: 'Take care of yourself, if you do not make the pilgrimage to Mecca.' 'Woe be to thee,' says a Franciscan, 'if thou dost make a journey to our Lady of Loretto.' He laughs at Loretto and Mecca; but he succours the indigent and defends the oppressed.

(*Philosophical Dictionary*, 'Theist')

## JEAN-JACQUES ROUSSEAU

Rousseau (see p. 17) struck a note of defiance which set him at odds with several of the *philosophes* on account of his profound faith in God and his delight in what he saw as the divine spectacle of nature. He often criticised the materialism of some of the *philosophes*, and even the deism of Voltaire. In *Emile* (1762), the book that he referred to as 'his greatest and best work', he mapped out a programme of 'natural' education and religion, based upon the belief that 'all the first impulses of nature are good and right'. This education aimed to free children from the tyranny of adult prejudice and expectation, so that they could develop in their own good time and retain their inherent goodness. He does not make an exception of religious instruction, but explains the importance of reserving religious education until a child is eighteen, claiming that this will deter the adult from seeing God in childlike terms. The child should also not be taught any specific religion, so he or she can be left to choose by the use of reason. Though evidently initially conceived as a work of 'a few pages', *Emile* grew into a substantial text consisting of five books: Books I–III explore infancy and childhood into adolescence; Book IV explores adulthood and includes the 'Profession of Faith'; and Book V deals with love and the responsibilities of adulthood, including a controversial section on female education. Book I begins with the famous observation: 'Everything is good coming from the hands of the Author of things, everything degenerates in the hands of man'. Offensive to Catholic and Protestant churches alike, *Emile* was condemned in Paris, Geneva, Amsterdam and Rome, and within weeks of its publication, a warrant was issued for the arrest of its author.

The extracts here, based upon the 1763 English translation of *Emile*, are taken from 'The Profession of a Savoyard Priest' in Book IV, in which Rousseau breaks off from the story of Emile to provide an autobiographical reflection upon natural religion. The kindly Catholic priest offers Rousseau spiritual guidance, but the 'profession' is Rousseau's own. In the discussion, he denounces the materialist doctrines of *philosophes* such as d'Holbach and Helvétius, as well as religious dogmas that are dependent on Revelation. He concludes that the 'inner light' is all that is required to give humans direction in religion, and stresses that religion should be a spiritual rather than ritualistic experience: 'I serve God in the simplicity of my heart.'

## 'The Profession of Faith of a Savoyard Priest'

from *Emile* (1762)

Though I have often experienced very great hardships, yet I never led a life so disagreeable as that which I passed during those times of perturbation and anxiety, when incessantly wandering from doubt to doubt, and brought back from my long meditations only uncertainty, obscurity, and contradictions in regard to the cause of my existence, and the rule of my human duty.

I cannot comprehend how it is possible to be a sceptic by system, and bona fide [in good faith]. Either there are no such philosophers, or they are the most wretched of all mankind. Doubt about the things it is important for us to know, is too violent a state for the human mind, which does not hold out in this state for long. It decides in spite of itself one way or the other and prefers to be deceived rather than not to believe at all.

What added to my perplexity was that I was educated in a church which decides everything and permits no doubt; the rejection of a single point made me reject all the rest, and the impossibility of assenting to so many absurd decisions, unhinged my belief from those which were not absurd. By being ordered to believe everything, I was prevented from giving my assent to anything, and I knew not where to stop.

I consulted the philosophers. I searched through their books, examined their different opinions, but found them all conceited and dogmatic, and even in their pretended scepticism, extremely ignorant, proving nothing, and laughing at one another; and in this they all agreed, and it seemed to be the only point in which they had reason on their side. Victorious whenever they attack, [they are] but weak and spiritless in defending themselves. If you weigh their reasons, they turn out to be good only at destructive criticism. If you reckon voices, each stands by himself; and they agree only to dispute: to listen to them was not the way to get rid of my uncertainty. [...]

The love of the truth now all my philosophy, and my whole method being reduced to a plain rule that exempts me from the vain subtlety of arguments, I resumed my inquiry into those parts of knowledge that interest me. I determined to admit as evident all knowledge to which in the sincerity of my heart I cannot refuse my consent; and as true all that, which appears to me to have a connection with the former; but to leave the rest as uncertain, without either rejecting or admitting it, and without troubling my head at their explanation, when attended with no utility to clarify it if it leads to nothing useful for practice.

But who am I? What right have I to judge of things, and who is it that determines my judgment? If it be involuntary, and a consequence of the impressions I receive, in vain do I puzzle my head at these idle researches; either they will be of no effect, or they will succeed of themselves, without my pretending to direct them. I must therefore turn my thoughts upon myself, [as] I propose to make use of [myself], and [know] how far I may depend on it.

I exist, and I have sense by which I am affected. This is the first truth that strikes me and to which I am obliged to acquiesce. Have I a proper idea of my existence, or do I perceive it only through my sensations? This is my first doubt, which it is impossible for me at present to solve. Continually affected by sensations, whether immediately or by memory, how is it possible for me to know whether the idea I have of self is something extraneous to those sensations, and may be independent of them?

My sensations are formed within me, since they make me perceive my existence; but their cause is external, since they affect me without my having anything to do with it, and I have nothing to do with producing or annihilating them. I therefore clearly perceive, that my sensation, which is something within me, and its cause or object, which is something external, are not the same thing.

Hence, not only do I exist, but there exist other beings, the objects of my sensations; and even if these objects were no more than ideas, still it is true, that those ideas are not myself.

Now, all that I sense extraneous to myself, acting upon my senses, I call *matter*; and every portion of matter, which I conceive to be united in individuals, I distinguish by the name of *body*. Thus all the disputes of idealists and materialists signify nothing to me. Their distinctions in regard to the appearance and reality of bodies are mere chimeras.

I am fully convinced of the existence of the universe, as of my own. I reflect on the objects of my sensations; and finding I have the faculty of comparing them, I sense myself endued with an active force, of which I knew nothing before. [...]

Remember always that I am not inculcating, but stating my principles. Whether matter be eternal or not, whether there is (or is not) a passive principle, still it is very certain that there is a unity throughout the whole, which proclaims a single intelligence; for I see nothing which is not ordered according to the same system and does not contribute to the same end, namely, towards preserving of the established order of the universe. This Being, who has will and power, this Being who is self-active, this Being in short whoever he be that directs the motion of the universe, and has ordained all things, I distinguish by the name of *God*. To this name I join the ideas of intelligence, power, and will which my reason hath discovered, and that of goodness, which flows from them as a necessary consequence. Yet He is imperceptible alike both to my senses and to my understanding; the more I think about it, the more I am confounded. I know most certainly that He exists, and that He is self-existent. I know that my existence is subordinate to His, and that everything around me is absolutely in the same case. I perceive God in all His works; I feel Him with myself; I see Him all around me, but as soon as I want to contemplate His nature, as soon as I want to find out where He is, what He is, His substance, He escapes me, my imagination is overwhelmed and my perception is lost. [...]

If man is a free agent, he acts of himself; whatever he does freely, neither interferes with, nor can be imputed to the ordered system of providence. Providence wills not the evil a man commits in abusing the liberty received from above; but it does not hinder him from doing it, whether because this evil, coming from a being so insignificant, is nothing in the Deity's eyes, or need not hinder it, without restraining his liberty, and doing a greater evil, by degrading his nature. He has made his creature free, not that he might do evil but good by choice. It has put him in a proper situation for this choice, by making good use of the faculties with which he was endowed, but he has limited his force that the abuse of the freedom cannot disturb the general order. The evil that man does falls back on him without changing anything in the system of the world, without hindering the human species from preserving itself even against its will. To complain that God does not hinder the commission of evil, is the same as complaining about His having given him an excellent nature, about His having put in men's actions the morality which ennobles them, and dignified them with virtue. Supreme enjoyment is inward content of mind; to merit this content we are placed upon earth and, endued with liberty, tempted by passions, and restrained by reason and conscience. What could the divine goodness do more in our favour? Could He make our nature contradictory and give the reward for having done well to him who did not have the power to act amiss? What! To prevent man from being vicious, must the Deity confine him to instinct and make him a brute? No, my divine maker, I shall never find fault that thou has created me after thy own image, to the end that I might be free, good, and happy like thyself!        —

It is the abuse of our faculties which renders us vicious and unhappy. Our vexations, our cares, and our sufferings come to us from ourselves. Moral evil is certainly our own work, and physical evil would be nothing without our vices, which render us sensible of it. Was it not for our preservation that nature gave us a sensibility to our wants? Is not bodily pain of the body a sign that the machine is out of order and a warning to remedy it? Death ... Do not the wicked embitter our lives and their own? Who would choose to live forever? Death is the remedy against the evils you create to yourself; nature did not want you to suffer forever. How few ills there are to which the man living in primitive simplicity is subject! He is free from distempers, as well as passions, and neither foresees nor fears death. When he feels it approaching, his miseries render it desirable to him; from then on it is no longer an evil. Were we satisfied to be what we are, we would not have to lament our fate, but pursuing an imaginary good, we expose ourselves to countless real evils. Whoever does not know how to endure a bit of hardship must expect a great deal. When someone has ruined his constitution by a disorderly life, he wants to restore it with remedies. To the evil he senses, he adds the evil he fears. Foresight of death makes it horrible and accelerates it. The more he wants to flee it, the more he senses it, and he dies of terror throughout his whole life, while blaming nature for evils which he has made for himself by offending it. [...]

If the soul be immaterial, it is capable of surviving the body; and if so, providence is justified. Had I no other proof of the immateriality of the soul, than the triumph of the wicked, and the oppression of the just upon earth, this alone would hinder me from doubting it. So grating a discord in the universal harmony, would set me on my inquiry how to account for it. I should say to myself, 'everything does not end with life; everything reverts into order at our death'. There would in truth be the quandary of wondering where man is when everything which can be sensed about him is dissolved. [...]

I was told that a revelation was necessary for pointing out the manner in which God thought fit to be served: and in support of this, I was informed of the extravagant modes of worship instituted by man, and those who told me so, did not advert that this very diversity of religions is owing to pretended revelations. As soon as people took it into their heads to have a revelation from the Deity, every man had a communication after his own way, and made the Deity say what he pleased. If one had paid attention only to what God says to the heart of man, there would never have been more than one religion on earth.

(*Emile*, Book IV, 'Profession of a Savoyard Priest')

## BARON D'HOLBACH

Born at Edesheim, of German aristocracy, Paul Heinrich Dietrich, Baron d'Holbach (1723–89) studied law at the University of Leiden (1744–48), before settling in Paris. Little is known about his parents, and it was from his maternal uncle that he inherited great wealth and a title. In Paris, Holbach worked as a financier and became a major contributor to the *Encyclopédie*. Initially his contribution to the Enlightenment was that of an expert on natural sciences and as a translator of German texts. Fluent in several languages, he translated German scientific works and English anti-Christian pamphlets into French, as well as authoring many philosophical essays. Like the greater part of his works, his most famous text, the notoriously materialist *Le Système de la Nature* (*The System of Nature*, 1770), dubbed 'the atheist's Bible', was written under a pseudonym 'Mirabaud', and published with great care so as to protect his anonymity. To many observers, Holbach's role in the Enlightenment was thus confined to that of co-host, with his wife, at the sumptuous Thursday and Sunday dinner parties at their Paris home and their country estate of Grandval, a few miles from Paris. These parties served as a social centre and intellectual forum for the Enlightenment, where *philosophes* such as d'Alembert, Diderot, Raynal and Buffon met regularly, and occasionally with visitors such as David Hume and Horace Walpole. This salon was described as the *café de l'Europe*. Few *philosophes* held opinions as radical as Holbach's: he espoused the view that atheism and morality were compatible, whereas religion and virtue were not.

The extract here is from the Preface to *Common Sense, or Natural Ideas Opposed to Supernatural* (1772). In this work, as in *The System of Nature*, Holbach attacked religious beliefs and argued for the sole reality of the material world. He claimed that notions of God (and all other religious ideas) are unnecessary and contrary to common sense. The world consisted entirely of matter in motion: 'matter always existed; that it moves by virtue of its essence; that all the phenomena of Nature are ascribable to the diversified motion of the variety of matter she contains; and which, like the phoenix, is continually regenerating out of its own ashes' (*System of Nature*). Apart from challenging the ideas of deists such as Rousseau, Holbach's works were regarded as so materialist and anti-religious that they even shocked other radicals. Voltaire summed up 'moderate' opinion by agreeing with Frederick the Great that *The System of Nature* 'is a pernicious work, alike for princes and people'.

## *Common Sense* (1772)

When we wish to examine in a cool, calm way the opinions of men, we are very much surprised to find that in those which we consider the most essential, nothing is more rare than to find them using common sense; that is to say, the portion of judgement sufficient to know the most simple truths, to reject the most striking absurdities, and to be shocked by palpable contradictions. We have an example of this in Theology, a science revered in all times, in all countries, by the greatest number of mortals; an object considered the most important, the most useful, and the most indispensable to the happiness of society. If they would but take the trouble to sound the principles upon which this pretended science rests itself, they would be compelled to admit that the principles which were considered incontestable, are but hazardous suppositions, conceived in ignorance, propagated by enthusism or bad intention, adopted by timid credulity, preserved by habit, which never reasons, and revered solely because it is not comprehended. Some, says Montaigne [1533–92], make the world believe that which they do not themselves believe a greater number of others make themselves believe, not comprehending what it is to believe. In a word, whoever will consult common sense upon religious opinions, and will carry into this examination the attention given to objects of ordinary interest, will easily perceive that these opinions have no solid foundation; that all religion is but a castle in the air; that Theology is but ignorance of natural causes reduced to a system; that it is but a long tissue of chimeras and contradictions; that it presents to all the different nations of the earth only romances devoid of probability, of which the hero himself is made up of qualities impossible to reconcile, his name having the power to excite in all hearts respect and fear, is found to be but a vague word, which men continually utter, being able to attach to it only such ideas or qualities as are belied by the facts, or which evidently contradict each other.

The notion of this imaginary being, or rather the word by which we designate him, would be of no consequence did it not cause ravages without number upon the earth. Born into the opinion that this phantom is for them a very interesting reality, men, instead of wisely concluding from its incomprehensibility that they are exempt from thinking of it, on the contrary, conclude that they cannot occupy themselves enough about it, that they must meditate upon it without ceasing, reason without end, and never lose sight of it. The invincible ignorance in which they are kept in this respect, far from discouraging them, does but excite their curiosity; instead of putting them on guard against their imagination, this ignorance makes them positive, dogmatic, imperious, and causes them to quarrel with all those who oppose doubts to the reveries which their brains have brought forth. What perplexity, when we attempt to solve an unsolvable problem! Anxious meditations upon an object impossible to grasp, and which, however, is supposed to be very important to him, can but put a man into bad humour, and produce in his brain dangerous transports. When interest, vanity, and ambition are joined to such a morose disposition, society necessarily becomes troubled. This is why so many nations have often become the theatres of extravagances caused by nonsensical visionists, who, publishing their shallow speculations for the eternal truth, have kindled the enthusism of princes and of people, and have prepared them for opinions which they represented as essential to the glory of divinity and to the happiness of empires.

We have seen, a thousand times, in all parts of our globe, infuriated fanatics slaughtering each other, lighting the funeral piles, committing without scruple, as a matter of duty, the greatest crimes. Why? To maintain or to propagate the impertinent conjectures of enthusiasts, or to sanction the knaveries of impostors on account of a being who exists only in their imagination, and who is known only by the ravages, the disputes, and the follies which he has caused upon the earth.

Originally, savage nations, ferocious, perpetually at war, adored (under various names) some God conformed to their ideas; that is to say, cruel, carnivorous, selfish, greedy of blood. We find in all the religions of the earth a God of armies, a jealous God, an avenging God, an exterminating God, a God who enjoys carnage and whose worshippers make it a duty to serve him to his taste. Lambs, bulls, children, men, heretics, infidels, kings, whole nations, are sacrificed to him. The zealous servants of this barbarous God go so far as to believe that they are obliged to offer themselves as a sacrifice to him. Everywhere we see zealots who, after having sadly meditated upon their terrible God, imagine that, in order to please him, they must do themselves all the harm possible, and inflict upon themselves, in his honour, all imaginable torments. In a word, everywhere, the baneful ideas of Divinity, far from consoling men for misfortunes incident to their existence, have filled the heart with trouble, and given birth to follies destructive to them. How could the human mind, filled with frightful phantoms and guided by men interested in perpetuating its ignorance and its fear, make progress? Man was compelled to vegetate in his primitive stupidity; he was preserved only by invisible powers, upon whom his fate was supposed to depend. Solely occupied with his alarms and his unintelligible reveries, he was always at the mercy of his priests, who reserved for themselves the right of thinking for him and of regulating his conduct.

Thus man was, and always remained, a child without experience, a slave without courage, a loggerhead who feared to reason, and who could never escape from the labyrinth into which his ancestors had misled him; he felt compelled to groan under the yoke of his Gods, of whom he knew nothing except the fabulous accounts of their ministers. These, after having fettered him by the ties of opinion, have remained his masters or delivered him up defenceless to the absolute power of tyrants, no less terrible than the Gods, of whom they were the representatives upon the earth. Oppressed by the double yoke of spiritual and temporal power, it was impossible for the people to instruct themselves and to work for their own welfare. Thus, religion, politics, and morals became sanctuaries, into which the profane were not permitted to enter. Men had no other morality than that which their legislators and their priests claimed as descended from unknown empyrean [heavenly] regions. The human mind, perplexed by these theological opinions, misunderstood itself, doubted its own powers, mistrusted experience, feared truth, disdained its reason, and left it to blindly follow authority. Man was a pure machine in the hands of his tyrants and his priests, who alone had the right to regulate his movements. Always treated as a slave, he had at all times and in all places the vices and dispositions of a slave.

These are the true sources of the corruption of habits, to which religion never opposes anything but ideal and ineffectual obstacles; ignorance and servitude have a tendency to make men wicked and unhappy. Science, reason, liberty, alone can reform them and render them more happy; but everything conspires to blind them and to confirm them in their blindness. The priests deceive them, tyrants corrupt them in order to subjugate them more easily. Tyranny has been, and always will be, the chief source of the depraved morals and habitual calamities of the people. These, almost always fascinated by their religious notions or by metaphysical fictions, instead of looking upon the natural and visible causes of their miseries, attribute their vices to the imperfections of their nature, and their misfortunes to the anger of their Gods; they offer to Heaven vows, sacrifices, and presents, in order to put an end to their misfortunes, which are really due only to the negligence, the ignorance, and to the perversity of their guides, to the folly of their institutions, to their foolish customs, to their false opinions, to their unreasonable laws, and especially to their want of enlightenment. Let the mind be filled early with true ideas; let man's reason be cultivated; let justice govern him; and there will be no need of opposing to his passions the powerless barrier of the fear of Gods. Men will be good when they are well taught, well governed, chastised or censured for the evil, and justly rewarded for the good which they have done to their fellow-citizens. It is idle to pretend to cure mortals of their vices if we do not begin by curing them of their prejudices. It is only by showing them the truth that they can know their best interests and the real motives which will lead them to happiness. Long enough have the instructors of the people fixed their eyes on heaven; let them at last bring them back to the earth. Tired of an incomprehensible theology, of ridiculous fables, of impenetrable mysteries, of puerile ceremonies, let the human mind occupy itself with natural things, intelligible objects, sensible truths, and useful knowledge.

(*Common Sense*, Preface)

# Chapter 4

# The natural world

**T**HE TERMS 'NATURE' AND 'NATURAL' were used in a great variety of ways and in every kind of writing and enquiry during the Enlightenment. Indeed, throughout the arts and sciences, and from politics to aesthetics, ideas about 'nature' and 'the natural' not only permeated most discussions, but became a scholarly obsession. While this aggravated some thinkers, such as the Scottish philosopher Adam Ferguson who declared that 'Of all the terms that we employ in treating of human affairs, those of *natural* and *unnatural* are the least determinate in their meaning' (*Essay on the History of Civil Society*, 1767), almost everyone found that use of the words was unavoidable. Nature could be used to mean the whole world and its workings as a unified system. It could be used to equate God with nature, as in the pantheism of the great Dutch philosopher Baruch Spinoza (1632–77); to refer to God as the creator of the world and its universal laws, as in John Locke's claim that 'the works of Nature everywhere sufficiently evidence a Deity'; or simply to contrast with ideas of the supernatural. It could be used to stand for whatever appeared to be the essential qualities of a particular thing, or whatever humans had not created and constructed through their learning, technologies and societies. It could be presented as stable or dynamic, intelligible or mysterious; as a complex material resource, to be improved, managed or exploited for human benefit; as a wild and hostile environment that needed to be tamed and mastered. It was often represented as the source of beauty and morality, to inspire the human spirit and imagination and to guide society, and it was frequently gendered (usually as feminine), and depicted in relation to other general concepts such as art, reason, culture and society. All of these and many other senses and uses of the word can be found within this book. Furthermore, while some figures tended to use the term in a broadly consistent manner – as in Rousseau's urge to portray nature as authentic, spiritual and beneficial – others, such as Denis

Diderot, used the word quite enigmatically to convey many different kind of thoughts and feelings.

Even though there were many ways in which writers and artists conceived of nature, at the beginning of the eighteenth century it was 'the mechanical philosophy' that dominated most scholarly discussions. This view of the world as particles of matter that had been created and set in motion (like the mechanisms of a perfect clock) by a God who thereafter made no interventions, owed much to René Descartes' writings in the seventeenth century. What constituted matter, and how it was kept in motion to produce all the observable phenomena, all the changes that took place throughout this seemingly self-regulating and self-sustaining system, were matters of contention. Even so, the idea of nature as a mechanical system that could be explained by the use of numbers, weights and measures led to a general confidence that its laws and secrets would be revealed by mathematical and physical analyses. Newton's discovery of the laws of motion and his use of mathematics in the *Principia* (1687) gave a tremendous boost to such convictions. But as his *Optics* (1704), a more discursive and experimental work, revealed, the acquisition of knowledge about nature required not only careful reasoning and quantification but also observation and experiment. Even in the 1670s Newton had written: 'The best and safest method of philosophising seems to be, first, to inquire diligently into the properties of things and to establish those properties by experiments, and to proceed later to hypotheses for the explanation of things themselves. For hypotheses ought to be applied only in the explanation of the properties of things.'

Newton's insistence upon the importance of investigating nature by observation and experiment inspired a great wave of physical, chemical, botanical and biological experiments. Thus Hermann Boerhaave (1668–1738), Europe's leading teacher of medicine at the University of Leiden, declared:

> Chemistry is no science formed *a priori*; 'tis no production of the human mind, framed by reasoning and deduction. It took its rise from a number of experiments casually made, without any expectation of what followed, and was only reduced into an art or system by collecting and comparing the effects of such unpremeditated experiments, and observing the uniform tendency thereof. So far, then, as a number of experiments agree to establish any undoubted truth; so far they may be considered as constituting the theory of chemistry.
>
> (*A New Method of Chemistry*, 1727)

Similarly, in introducing his celebrated experiments on plants and animals, the English cleric Stephen Hales explained:

> The wonderful and secret operations of Nature are so involved and intricate, so far out of reach of our senses, as they present themselves to us in their natural order, that it is impossible for the most sagacious and penetrating genius to pry into them, unless he will be at pains of analysing Nature, by a numerous and regular series of experiments; which are the only solid foundation

whence we may reasonably expect to make any advance, in the real knowledge of the nature of things.

(*Vegetable Statics,* 1727)

Like Hales' hero, Newton, throughout the century many scientists continued to stress their commitment to understanding nature by observation and experiment. The great chemist Antoine Lavoisier (1743–94), for example, declared that his research was based upon 'the rigorous law from which I have never deviated, of forming no conclusions which are not fully warranted by experiment' (*Elements of Chemistry,* 1789). Such claims seemed wholly consistent with Locke's view, a century earlier, that all knowledge sprang originally from the senses, and with the empiricist outcry against the metaphysical systems of philosophers such as Descartes and Leibniz that claimed that truths and knowledge about the world could be established quite independently of sense-experience. By mid-century, the Scottish philosopher David Hume was even proclaiming that 'Men are now cured of their passion for hypotheses and systems in natural philosophy, and will hearken to no arguments but those which are derived from experience' (*Enquiry Concerning the Principles of Morals,* 1751). However, this was more rhetorical than strictly truthful. For, as well as inspiring all kind of experiments, Newton's achievement in demonstrating that the motion of all bodies on and beyond the earth could be explained by the laws of motion and gravitation (by which there was a mutual attraction between any two bodies within the universe) seemed to support the idea that nature itself was a kind of rational system. Indeed, part of the *Principia* had even been entitled 'The System of the World'. Contrary to Newton's belief in a Supreme Being, for some materialists such as Baron d'Holbach this meant that there was no need for 'supernatural powers to account for the formation of things', or for their movement and development, since 'the idea of Nature necessarily includes that of motion'. Even life itself, generated by the combination of inanimate substances, was not a mystery – and human life was no exception. In his *System of Nature* (1770), d'Holbach reasoned:

> If flour be wetted with water, and the mixture closed up, it will be found, after some lapse of time (by the aid of a microscope) to have produced organised beings that enjoy life, of which the water and the flour were believed incapable. It is thus that inanimate matter can pass into life, or animate matter, which in itself is only an assemblage of motion. [...] The production of a man [...] would not be more astonishing than that of an insect with flour and water.

For some modern scholars, this kind of thinking led to the 'disenchantment' of the natural world during the Enlightenment. Yet love and respect for what often appeared to be the wondrous beauty, mystery and variety of nature were everpresent aspects of Enlightenment arts and crafts. The idea, for example, of nature as a garden was central to much eighteenth-century writing, from poetry to philosophy, and to the decorative and visual arts, from Meissen porcelain to landscape painting. In their constructions of the natural world, Enlightened scholars and artists often imagined it as a more beneficent and malleable resource than had their predecessors. Writers and artists recorded how nature was being exploited and land and stock enthusiastically 'improved' to produce unprecedented agricultural and industrial development – particularly in Britain. Expeditions were mounted to many relatively unknown places such as Siberia, Africa and the Pacific in the name of science, trade and commerce. Specimens of newly discovered plants and animals (and races) were gathered to be proudly exhibited and studied in botanical and zoological gardens. Visual records of specimens and expeditions, such as William Hodges' drawings of Tahiti during Captain Cook's voyages (see p. 311), helped the public to conceptualise the extraordinary world that was being presented and defined for European audiences. No less important, Enlightenment figures also saw nature increasingly as a source of pleasure as well as knowledge – a place for feeling as well as reasoning. Designers such as 'Capability' Brown and William Kent celebrated the beauty and sympathetic mastery of nature by landscaping the environs of their patrons' houses to show that 'all nature was a garden'. Painters such as George Stubbs (1724–1806), in his studies of horses, showed how scientific knowledge and investigation could be married with precise artistic expression. It was not just 'scientists', therefore, who carefully examined nature in order to reveal its elements and understand its workings. Nature – however imagined, represented, analysed or debated – was also generally believed to hold the keys to the advancement of all the arts and social sciences, and to human happiness, morality and self-fulfilment.

The extracts which follow here exemplify some of the ways that influential figures responded to and constructed nature in the period. The scientist Stephen Hales anatomised it and designed several series of experiments on plants and animals to explore some of its operations. The Swedish botanist Linnaeus devised a hierarchical system of classification of all living things, to aid identification and memorisation. This system, which largely depended upon the assumed stability of species since the Creation, was based upon the classification of plants and animals according to a few characteristics, such as the flowering parts of plants. Although it was widely used by collectors, scholars and explorers, the Linnaean system was strongly criticised for being abstract and artificial by some naturalists, such as the Comte de Buffon at the Paris Academy of Sciences. Buffon believed that while species were fixed, the 'genera, orders and classes' of the Linnaean system were simply human inventions, rather than 'natural' distinctions: 'If we descend by degrees from the great to the small, from the strong to the weak, we shall find that Nature has uniformly maintained a balance; that attentive only to the preservation of each species, she creates a profusion of individuals' (*Natural History*). He preferred to take a view of nature as 'historical' (rather than fixed and 'artificial'), considering it as changing over millions of years, quite contrary to Christian teachings about the history of the earth from the Creation some six thousand years ago. For Buffon, the living world was populated only by individuals that had gradually emerged through their natural (reproductive) history and that were linked in a Great Chain of Being (*scala naturae*) that descended by almost imperceptible degrees from 'the most perfect creature', 'man'. The idea that a Supreme Being had '*specified* in his Creation every degree of life', reflected the thoughts of Locke. It was a view that was echoed by Pope in his *Essay on Man* (1733) and by Joseph Addison (1672–1719), co-editor with Richard Steele of the tremendously popular and influential journal, the *Spectator*: 'The whole chasm in Nature, from a plant to a man, is filled up with diverse kinds of creatures, rising one over another, by such a gentle and easy ascent, that the little transitions and deviations from one species to another, are almost insensible' (*Spectator*, no. 519, 1712). However, Buffon's idea of nature as having and being a historical record that changed over millions of years was shocking. Not only did it challenge biblical teachings, but it raised the prospect that no life-forms were immutable or, indeed, original.

The final extracts here are taken from the writings of Diderot and Rousseau. Like Buffon, Diderot also rejected the Linnaean and all other 'systems' of nature, and the mechanical materialism of philosophers such as his friend d'Holbach. Writing in the 1770s, Diderot protested: 'The animal is a hydraulic machine. What idiotic things can be said following this one supposition.' Awed by the sheer multiplicity of natural phenomena, he wondered if 'man and all the animals be kinds of monsters', for 'sometimes the universe seems to me only an assemblage of monstrous beings' (*Elements of Physiology*). Exploring life as a dynamic force of nature, in his earlier *Thoughts on the Interpretation of Nature* (1753), he speculated that whole species might be transformed, for 'if nature is still at work ... All our natural science becomes as transitory as our words'.

In the final years of his life, Rousseau, estranged from friends and *philosophes*, found solace in his nature rambles and reflected on the joys of learning botany with the aid of Linnaeus' *Systema Naturae*. Yet Rousseau's thirst for knowledge about nature went far beyond an interest in its categorisation and operations. In his *Reveries of the Solitary Walker* (1782) he searched for truths about himself through his personal communion with the natural world.

## STEPHEN HALES

Born in Kent, Stephen Hales (1677–1761) went to study at Cambridge University in 1696, where he lived until he took holy orders in 1709 and became lifelong minister of the parish of Teddington in Middlesex. It was during his time at Cambridge that he began to conduct experiments on animals; at first on dogs, and later at Teddington on horses and other creatures. Building upon the work of scientists such as William Harvey (1578–1657) and Giovanni Borelli (1608–79), these experiments were designed 'to find out the real force of blood in the arteries'. By comparing the blood pressure of various animals, and measuring heart size and pulse rate, Hales was able to calculate cardiac output, and to relate this to an animal's weight and size. In the light of this work, in 1718 he was elected a Fellow of the Royal Society, and began his extensive researches into plant physiology. Through dozens of carefully constructed and innovative experiments, he examined the quantities of sap and moisture consumed by various plants, and the role of roots and leaves. He observed that plants without leaves only take in a little moisture, and suggested that leaves 'seem also designed for many other noble and important services'. This gradually led him to compare the leaves of plants to the lungs of animals, believing that both drew upon air for nourishment. Having presented his findings on plants to a meeting of the Royal Society in 1725, he delayed the publication of his work in order to conduct a series of additional experiments (many involving animals) into the nature of air. These and the discoveries on plants were finally published in *Vegetable Statics* in 1727.

Although Hales' experiments on animals evidently worried his Catholic friend and neighbour Alexander Pope, he believed that such studies would not only 'entertain the mind' but reveal 'the wonderful hand of the divine Architect'. Thus, like Newton, he maintained: 'The searching into the works of Nature, while it delights and enlarges the mind, and strikes us with the strongest assurance of the wisdom and power of the divine Architect, in framing for us so beautiful and well regulated a world, it does at the same time convince us of his constant benevolence and goodness towards us' (*Vegetable Statics*). He also believed that just as studies of plant physiology would lead to improvements in the 'delightful and beneficial' arts of gardening and agriculture, so vivisection would lead to better medical knowledge and practices. Indeed, like many other scientists whose ideas were based upon the mechanical philosophy, it seems that Hales saw little distinction between animals and vegetables – other than in the degree of their complexity. In this way of thinking, it appeared that (aside from humans) all living and non-living things were merely collections of matter, and animals were just machines or automata – matter in motion. Understanding the universal laws and workings of nature required such scientists to examine things in largely physical and 'statical' (pertaining to the science of weighing) terms, but also – in the light of Newton's methods and achievements – to experiment.

After the publication of *Vegetable Statics* and an important study of blood pressure, *Haemastatics* (1733), Hales became a notable public figure: supporting the activities of the Society for the Propagation of Christian Knowledge, pamphleteering against alcohol abuse, acting as a Trustee of the Colony of Georgia, and inventing a ventilator to provide fresh air in prisons, hospitals and ships. *Vegetable Statics* was translated into several European languages, and in 1753 Hales was elected a foreign member of the French Académie des Sciences. The discoveries reported in *Vegetable Statics* would provide a platform for the advancement of chemistry through the work of Henry Cavendish and Antoine Lavoisier later in the century, and Hales' inventions (such as the pedestal apparatus illustrated in Plate 16, Fig. 35 of *Vegetable Statics* – see Figure 4.1 below) were widely used and developed by scientists such as Joseph Priestley. Three extracts from *Vegetable Statics* are selected here. The first is Hales' 'Introduction' to his book. The second and third extracts are taken from chapter six, which provided a long account of his various experiments on 'air' – still regarded as a single element. In these passages Hales records some of his experiments on animals and on himself.

## Vegetable Statics (1727)

### 'Introduction'

The farther researches we make into this admirable scene of things, the more beauty and harmony we see in them: and the stronger and clearer convictions they give us, of the being, power and wisdom of the divine Architect, who has made all things to concur with a wonderful conformity, in carrying on, by various and innumerable combinations of matter, such a circulation of causes, and effects, as was necessary to the great ends of nature.

And since we are assured that the all-wise Creator has observed the most exact proportions, *of number, weight and measure*, in the make of all things; the most likely way therefore, to get any insight into the nature of those parts of the creation which come within our observation, must in all reason be to number, weigh and measure. And we have much encouragement to pursue this method of searching into the nature of things, from the great success that has attended any attempts of this kind.

Thus, in relation to those planets which revolve about our sun, the great philosopher [Isaac Newton] of our age has, by numbering and measuring, discovered the exact proportions that are observed in their periodical revolutions and distances from their common centres of motion and gravity: and that God has not only *comprehended the dust of the earth in a measure, and weighed the mountains in scales, and the hills in a balance*, Isaiah xl. 12, but that he also holds the vast revolving globes of this our solar system, most exactly poised on their common centre of gravity.

And if we reflect upon our discoveries that have been made in the animal economy [organisation], we shall find that the most considerable and rational accounts of it have been chiefly owing to the statical examination of their fluids, and solids dissolved into fluids, the animal daily takes in for its support and nourishment: and with what force and different rapidities those fluids are carried about in their proper channels, according to the different secretions that are to be made from them: and in what proportion the recrementitious fluid [e.g. saliva] is conveyed away, to make room for fresh supplies; and what proportion of this recrement [waste] nature allots to be carried off, by the several kinds of emunctories [waste-disposal parts] and excretory ducts.

And since in vegetables, their growth and the preservation of their vegetable life is promoted and maintained, as in animals, by the very plentiful and regular motion of their fluids, which are the vehicles ordained by nature, to carry proper nutriment to every part; it is therefore reasonable to hope, that in them also, by the same method of inquiry, considerable discoveries may in time be made, there being, in many respects a great analogy between plants and animals.

### 'Experiment CVII'

May 18, which was a very hot day, I repeated Dr. [John] Mayow's [1641–79] experiment, to find how much air is absorbed by the breath of animals inclosed in glasses,

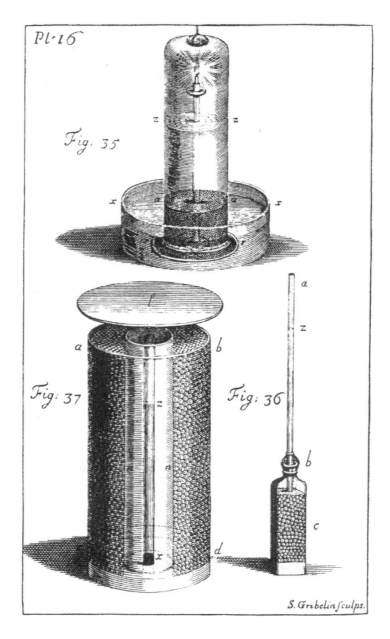

*Figure 4.1*  'Plate 16' from S. Hales, *Vegetable Statics* (1727)

*Note*: To aid understanding of many of his 124 experiments and the apparatus that he had designed and developed to conduct them, Hales provided 20 illustrative plates, each often consisting of several figures. Here, Fig. 35 (designed to estimate the quantity of air absorbed by burning material or the breath of an animal) shows a tall glass inverted in a vessel full of water; Fig. 36 (designed to measure the absorption of water by matter) shows a sealed bottle filled with mercury, peas and water; and Fig. 37 (designed to experiment with air pressure and absorption) shows a small iron pot containing a mercury gauge, set inside an iron cylinder filled with peas and water and covered by a lead lid.

which he found with a mouse to be 1/14 part of the whole air in the glass vessel (*de sp[iritus] nitro-aereo*, p. 104).

I placed on the pedestal, under the inverted glass *z z a a* (Fig: 35) a full grown rat. At first the water subsided a little, which was occasioned by the rarefaction of the air, caused by the heat of the animal's body. But after a few minutes the water began to rise, and continued rising as long as the rat lived, which was about 14 hours. The bulk of the air in which the rat lived so many hours was 2024 cubic inches; the quantity of elastic air [i.e. in a gaseous state] which was absorbed was 73 cubic inches, above 1/27 part of the whole, nearly what was absorbed by a candle in the same vessel, in Experiment 106.

I placed at the same time in the same manner another almost half grown rat under a vessel, whose capacity above the surface of the water *z z* (Fig: 35) was but 594 cubic inches, in which it lived 10 hours; the quantity of elastic air which was absorbed, was equal to 45 cubic inches, *viz.* 1/13 part of the whole air, which the rat breathed in. A cat of 3 months old lived an hour in the same receiver, and absorbed 16 cubic inches of air, *viz.* 1/30 part of the whole; an allowance being made in this estimate for the bulk of the cat's body. A candle in the same vessel continued burning but one minute, and absorbed 54 cubic inches, 1/11 part of the whole air.

And as in the case of burning *brimstone* [sulphur] and *candles*, more air was found to be absorbed in large vessels, than in small ones, and *vice versa*, more air in proportion to the capacity of the vessel was absorbed in small, than in large vessels, so the same holds true here too in the case of animals.

### 'Experiment CVIII'

The following Experiment will shew, that the elasticity of the air is greatly destroyed by the *respiration of human lungs*, viz.

I made a bladder very supple by wetting of it, and then cut off so much of the neck as would make a hole wide enough for the biggest end of a large fosset [faucet: vent-peg] to enter, to which the bladder was bound fast. The bladder and fosset contained 74 cubic inches. Having blown up the bladder, I put the small end of the fosset in my mouth; and at the same time pinched my nostrils close that no air might pass that way, so that I could only breath to and fro the air contained in the bladder. In less than half a minute I found a considerable difficulty in breathing, and was forced after that to fetch my breath very fast; and at the end of the minute, the suffocating uneasiness was so great that I was forced to take away the bladder from my mouth. Towards the end of the minute the bladder was become so flaccid, that I could not blow it above half full with the greatest expiration that I could make: and at the same time I could plainly perceive that my lungs were much fallen, just in the same manner as when we breathe out of them all the air we can at once. Whence it is plain that a considerable quantity of the elasticity of the air contained in my lungs, and in the bladder was destroyed: which supposing it to be 20 cubic inches, it will be 1/13 part of the whole air, which I breathed to and fro; for the bladder contained 74 cubic inches, and the lungs, by the following Experiment, about 166 cubic inches, in all 240.

These effects of respiration on the elasticity of the air, put me upon making an attempt to measure the inward surface of the lungs, which by a wonderful artifice are admirably contrived by the divine artificer, so as to make their inward surface to be commensurate to an expanse of air many times greater than the animal's body; as will appear from the following estimate.

(*Vegetable Statics*, ch. VI, 'Analysis of the Air')

### 'Experiment CXIII'

I tied down a live *dog* on his back, near the edge of a table, and then made a small hole through the intercostal muscles into his *thorax*, near the *diaphragm*. I cemented fast into this hole the incurvated end of a glass tube, whose orifice was covered with a little cap full of holes, that the dilatation of the lungs might not at once stop the orifice of the tube. A small vial [vessel] full of spirit of wine was tied to the bottom of the perpendicular tube, by which means the tube and vial could easily yield to the motion of the dog's body, without danger of breaking the tube, which was 36 inches long. The event was, that in ordinary inspirations, the spirit rose about six inches in the tube; but in great and laborious inspirations, it would rise 24 and 30 inches, *viz.* when I stopped the dog's nostrils and mouth, so that he could not breathe. This Experiment shews the force with which the lungs are raised by the dilatation of the *thorax*, either in ordinary or extraordinary and laborious inspirations. When I blew air with some force into the *thorax*, the dog was just ready to expire.

By means of another short tube, which had a communication with that which was fixed to the *thorax* near its insertion into the *thorax*, I could draw the air out of the *thorax*, the height of the *mercury*, instead of spirit in the tube, shewing to what degree the *thorax* was exhausted of air. The *mercury* was hereby raised nine inches, which would gradually subside as the air got into the *thorax* through the lungs.

I then laid bare the windpipe, and having cut it off a little below the *larynx*, I affixed to it a bladder full of air, and then continued sucking air out of the *thorax*, with a force sufficient to keep the lungs pretty much dilated. As the *mercury* subsided in the gauge, I repeated the suction for a quarter of an hour, till a good part of the air in the bladder was either drawn through the substance of the lungs into the *thorax*, or had lost its elasticity. When I pressed the bladder, the *mercury* subsided the faster; the dog was all the while alive, and would probably have lived much longer, if the Experiment had been continued; as is likely from the following Experiment, *viz.*

### 'Experiment CXIV'

I tied a middle-sized dog down alive on a table, and having laid bare his windpipe, I cut it asunder just below the *larynx*, and fixed fast to it the small end of a common fosset; the other end of the fosset had a large bladder tied to it, which contained 162 cubic inches; and to the other end of the bladder was tied the great end of another fosset, whose orifice was covered with a valve, which opened inward, so as to admit any air that was blown into the bladder, but none could return that way; yet for further security, that passage was also stopped with spiggot [peg].

As soon as the first fosset was tied fast to the wind-pipe, the bladder was blown full of air through the other fosset; when the dog had breathed the air in the bladder to and fro for a minute or two, he then breathed very fast, and shewed great uneasiness, as being almost suffocated.

Then with my hand I pressed the bladder hard, so as to drive the air into his lungs with some force; and thereby make his *abdomen* rise by the pressure of the *diaphragm*, as in natural breathings. Then taking alternately my hand off the bladder, the lungs with the *abdomen* subsided. I continued in this manner to make the dog breathe for an hour; during which time I was obliged to blow fresh air into the bladder every five minutes, three parts in four of that air being either absorbed by the vapours of the lungs, or escaping through the ligatures, upon my pressing hard on the bladder.

During this hour the dog was frequently near expiring, whenever I pressed the air but weakly into his lungs; as I found by his pulse, which was very plain to be felt in the great crural artery near the groin, which place an assistant held his finger on most part of the time; but the languid pulse was quickly accelerated, so as to beat fast; soon after I dilated the lungs much, by pressing hard upon the bladder, especially when the motion of the lungs was promoted by pressing alternately the *abdomen* and the bladder, whereby both the contraction and dilatation of the lungs was increased.

And I could by this means rouse the languid pulse whenever I pleased, not only at the end of every 5 minutes, when more air was blown into the bladder from a man's lungs, but also towards the end of the 5 minutes, when the air was fullest of fumes.

At the end of the hour, I intended to try whether I could by the same means have kept the dog alive some time longer, when the bladder was filled with the fumes of burning *brimstone*. But being obliged to cease for a little time from pressing the air into his lungs, while matters were preparing for this additional Experiment, in the meantime the dog died, which might otherwise have lived longer, if I had continued to force air into his lungs.

Now though this Experiment was so frequently disturbed, by being obliged to blow more air into the bladder twelve times during the hour; yet since he was almost suffocated in less than two minutes, by breathing of himself to and fro the first air in the bladder, he would by Experiment 106 on candles, have died in less than two minutes, when one fourth of the old air remained in the bladder, immediately to taint the new admitted air from a man's lungs; so that his continuing to live through the whole hour, must be owing to the forcible dilatation of the lungs, by compressing the bladder, and not to the *vivifying spirit of air*. For without that forcible dilatation, he had, after the first 5 or 10 minutes, been certainly dead in less than a minute, when his pulse was so very low and weak, which I did not find to be revived barely by blowing 3 parts in 4 of new air from the lungs of a man into the bladder. But it was constantly roused and quickened, whenever I increased the dilatations of the lungs, by compressing the bladder more vigorously; and that whether it was at the beginning or end of each 5 minutes, yet it was more easily quickened, when the bladder was at any time newly filled, than when it was near empty.

From these violent and fatal effects of very noxious vapours on the respiration and life of animals, we may see how the respiration is proportionably incommoded, when the air is loaded with lesser degrees of vapours, which vapours do in some measure clog and lower the air's elasticity; which it best regains by having these vapours dispelled by the ventilating motion of the free open air, which is rendered wholesome by the agitation of winds. Thus what we call a close warm air, such as has been long confined in a room, without having the vapours in it carried off by communicating with the open air, is apt to give us more or less uneasiness, in proportion to the quantity of vapours which are floating in it. For which reason the *German* stoves, which heat the air in a room without a free admittance of fresh air to carry off the vapours that are raised, as also the modern invention to convey heated air into rooms through hot flues, seem not so well contrived, to favour a free respiration, as our common method of fires in open chimneys, which fires are continually carrying a large stream of heated air out of the rooms up the chimney, which stream must necessarily be supplied with equal quantities of fresh air, through the doors and windows, or the crannies of them.

And thus many of those who have weak lungs, but can breathe well enough in the fresh country air, are greatly incommoded in their breathing, when they come into large cities where the air is full of fuliginous [thick] vapours, arising from innumerable coal fires, and stenches from filthy lay-stalls and sewers: And even the most robust and healthy in changing from a city to a country air, find an exhilarating pleasure, arising from a more free and kindly inspiration, whereby the lungs being less loaded with con-densing air and vapours, and thereby the vesicles [bladder-like vessels] more dilated, with a clearer and more elastic air, a freer course is thereby given to the blood, and probably a purer air mixed with it; and this is one reason why in the country a serene dry constitution of the air is more exhilarating than a moist thick air.

(*Vegetable Statics*, ch. VI, 'Analysis of the Air')

## CAROLUS LINNAEUS

Linnaeus (Carl von Linné, 1707–78) was born in Sweden, the son of a curate. He developed an interest in botany during his childhood and while studying medicine at the universities of Lund and Uppsala. After a journey to Lapland, further stud-ies in the Netherlands where he met the Dutch physician Hermann Boerhaave (1668–1738), and travels to England where he met the naturalist Sir Hans Sloane, he returned to Sweden and became a practising physician. In 1739 he married, and in 1741 was appointed to the chair of medicine at Uppsala University, where he remained for the rest of his life. He became the first presi-dent of the Royal Swedish Academy of Sciences (1739), physician to the royal family, and was ennobled, Carl von Linné in 1761. As his fame spread, his student-disciples were sent on expeditions, such as those of Captain Cook, to the remotest regions of the world in order to collect specimens of flora and fauna, thereby seek-ing to advance scientific knowledge and Swedish trade and commerce.

Most of Linnaeus' many important works on botany, such as *Philosophia Botanica* (1751) and *Species Plantarum* (1753), were published in Latin, as was his most famous work *Systema Naturae* in 1735. This text, first published at Leiden, would later be revised and extended into a multi-volume work which pio-neered the modern classification of all living things. Moving away from a system of classification in which the genus was followed by an elaborate description of the species, Linnaeus adopted a two-word (binomial) system, giving one name for the genus and one for the species. This nomenclature was used throughout the tenth edition of the *System of Nature* in 1758.

Following Classical traditions, Linnaeus divided the natural world into animal, vegetable and mineral kingdoms. The animal kingdom, in which he boldly included man as *homo sapiens*, was subdivided into six classes, of which *mammalia* (mammals) are the first. This class has seven orders: *primates* are the first, *belluae* (brute beasts) are the sixth, and *cete* (whales) are the seventh. The first genus in the order of *belluae* is *equus* (horse) which is comprised of six species (e.g. horse, ass, zebra), some of which have a number of varieties. In his general classification of plants Linnaeus based his taxonomy (principles of classification) on the number and arrangement of their reproductive parts. The twenty-four 'classes' of plants are grouped according to the number, proportion or situation of the stamens, the 'male' parts of the plants. The plant's pistils, its 'female' parts, determine the 'orders'. Some classes are termed 'hermaphrodite', as both stamen and pistil exist in the same flower or plant, or in different plants. Plants with no observable sexual parts (such as algae and ferns) are classified as 'cryptogamia' (hidden marriage). By basing his taxonomy upon an essential but nevertheless single observable characteristic of plants (their sexual parts), Linnaeus recognised that he was creating a somewhat 'artificial' system, as opposed to a more 'natural' one, based upon all of the characteristics that determine the form of plants. The Linnaean system of classification became widely used, even by Rousseau, but it was severely criticised by Buffon who preferred to classify species 'naturally', according to whether or not two animals or plants could produce fertile offspring.

The following extracts are from the beginning of the English edition of *Systema Naturae*, published as *A General System of Nature* in 1802. In the first extract, from the 'Introduction', Linnaeus explains why it is the duty of man 'to affix to every object its proper name'. In the second extract he explains the 'natural division of animals into six classes' and the subdivision of the first class 'Mammalia' into seven orders. Humans are then divided into two species: *Homo sapiens* and *Homo monstrosus*.

## System of Nature (1735)

### 'Introduction'

Man, when he enters the world, is naturally led to enquire who he is; whence he comes; whither he is going; for what purpose he is created; and by whose benevolence he is preserved. He finds himself descended from the remotest creation; journeying to a life of perfection and happiness; and led by his endowments to a contemplation of the works of nature.

Like other animals who enjoy life, sensation, and perception; who seek for food, amusements, and rest, and who prepare habitations convenient for their kind, he is curious and inquisitive: but, above all other animals, he is noble in his nature, in as much as, by the powers of his mind, he is able to reason justly upon whatever discovers itself to

his senses; and to look, with reverence and wonder, upon the works of Him who created all things.

That existence is surely contemptible, which regards only the gratification of instinctive wants, and the preservation of a body made to perish. It is therefore the business of
a thinking being, to look forward to the purposes of all things; and to remember that
the end of creation is, that God may be glorified in all his works.

Hence it is of importance that we should study the works of nature, than which, what
can be more useful, what more interesting? For, however large a portion of them lies
open to our present view; a still greater part is yet unknown and undiscovered.

All things are not within the immediate reach of human capacity. Many have been made
known to us, of which those who went before us were ignorant; many we have heard of,
but know not what they are; and many must remain for the diligence of future ages.

It is the exclusive property of man, to contemplate and to reason on the great book
of nature. She gradually unfolds herself to him, who with patience and perseverance,
will search into her mysteries; and when the memory of the present and of past generations shall be entirely obliterated, he shall enjoy the high privilege of living in the minds
of his successors, as he has been advanced in the dignity of his nature, by the labours of
those who went before him. [...]

The study of natural history, simple, beautiful, and instructive, consists in the collection, arrangement, and exhibition of the various productions of the earth. These are
divided into the three grand kingdoms of nature, whose boundaries meet together in
the Zoophytes [plant-like animals].

Minerals inhabit the interior parts of the earth in rude and shapeless masses; are
generated by salts, mixed together promiscuously, and shaped fortuitously. They are
bodies concrete, without life or sensation.

Vegetables clothe the surface with verdure, imbibe nourishment through bibulous
roots, breathe by quivering leaves, celebrate their nuptials in a genial metamorphosis,
and continue their kind by the dispersion of seed within prescribed limits. They are bodies organized, and have life and not sensation.

Animals adorn the exterior parts of the earth, respire, and generate eggs; are
impelled to action by hunger, congeneric affections, and pain; and by preying on other
animals and vegetables, restrain within proper proportion the numbers of both. They
are bodies organized, and have life, sensation and the power of locomotion.

Man, the last and best of created works; formed after the image of his Maker,
endowed with a portion of intellectual divinity, the governor and subjugator of all other
beings, is, by his wisdom alone, able to form just conclusions from such things as present themselves to his senses, which can only consist of bodies merely natural. Hence the
first step of wisdom is to know these bodies; and to be able, by those marks imprinted
on them by nature, to distinguish them from each other, and to affix to every object its
proper name.

These are the elements of all science; this is the great alphabet of nature: for if the
name be lost, the knowledge of the object is lost also; and without these, the student
will seek in vain for the means to investigate the hidden treasures of nature.

Method, the soul of science, indicates that every natural body may, by inspection, be
known by its own peculiar name; and this name points out whatever the industry of man

has been able to discover concerning it: so that amidst the greatest apparent confusion, the greatest order is visible.

System is conveniently divided into five branches, each subordinate to the other; *class, order, genus, species*, and *variety*, with their names and characters. For he must first know the name who is willing to investigate the object.

The science of nature supposes an exact knowledge of the nomenclature, and a systematic arrangement of all natural bodies. In this arrangement, the *classes* and *orders* are arbitrary; the *genera* and *species* are natural. All true knowledge refers to the species, all solid knowledge to the genus.

Of these three grand divisions the animal kingdom ranks highest in comparative estimation, next the vegetable, and the last and lowest is the mineral kingdom.

(*System of Nature*, Introduction)

### 'Animals'

Animals enjoy *sensation* by means of a living organization, animated by a medullary [bone marrow] substance; *perception* by nerves; and *motion* by the exertion of the will. They have *members* for the different purposes of life; *organs* for their different senses; and *faculties* or powers for the application of their different perceptions. They all originate from an egg. Their external and internal structure; their comparative anatomy, habits, instincts, and various relations to each other, are detailed in authors who professedly treat on these subjects.

The natural division of animals is into six classes, formed from their internal structure.

Heart with 2 auricles, 2 ventricles; blood warm, red:

    viviparous ... Mammalia (1);
    oviparous ... Birds (2).

Heart with 1 auricle, 1 ventricle, blood cold, red:

    lungs voluntary ... Amphibia (3);
    external gills ... Fishes (4).

Heart with 1 auricle, ventricle 0, sanies [blood] 0, cold, white:

    have antennae ... Insects (5);
    tentacula ... Worms (6).

1. Mammalia. *Lungs* respire alternately; *jaws* incumbent [resting], covered; *teeth* usually within; *teats* lactiferous; *organs of sense*, tongue, nostrils, eyes, ears, and papillæ of the skin; *covering*, hair, which is scanty in warm climates, and hardly any on aquatics; *supporters*, 4 feet, except in aquatics; and in most a *tail*; *walk* on the earth, and *speak*.

2. Birds. *Lungs* respire alternately; *jaws* incumbent, naked, extended, without teeth; *eggs* covered with a calcareous shell; *organs of sense*, tongue, nostrils, eyes and ears without auricles; *covering*, incumbent, imbricate [overlapping] feathers; *supporters*, feet 2, wings 2; and a heart-shaped rump; *fly* in the air, and *sing*.

3. Amphibia. *Jaws* incumbent; *penis* (frequently) double; *eggs* (usually) membranaceous; *organs of sense*, tongue, nostrils, eyes, ears; *covering*, a naked skin; *supporters* various, in some 0; *creep* in warm places, and *hiss*.

4. Fishes. *Jaws* incumbent; *penis* (usually) 0; *eggs* without white; *organs of sense*, tongue, nostrils, eyes, ears; *covering*, imbricate scales; *supporters*, fins; *swim* in the water, and *smack*.

5. Insects. *Spiracles* [air-holes], lateral pores; *jaws*, lateral; *organs of sense*, tongue, eyes, antennæ on the head, brain 0, ears 0, nostrils 0; *covering*, a bony coat of mail; *supporters*, feet, and in some, wings; *skip* on dry ground, and *buzz*.

6. Worms. *Spiracles*, obscure; *jaws*, various; frequently *hermaphrodites*; *organs of sense* tentacula, (generally) eyes, brain 0, ears 0, nostrils 0; *covering*, calcareous or 0, except spines; *supporters*, feet 0, fins 0; *crawl* in moist places, and are *mute*.

## Class *I.* Mammalia *[Mammals]*

These suckle their young by means of lactiferous teats. In external and internal structure they resemble man: most of them are quadrupeds; and with man, their natural enemy, inhabit the surface of the earth. The largest, though fewest in number, inhabit the ocean. They are distributed into seven *orders*, the characters of which are taken from the number, situation, and structure of the teeth.

1. Primates. *Fore-teeth* cutting, upper 4 parallel (except in some species of bats which have 2 or 0); *tusks*, solitary, that is, one on each side, in each jaw; *teats* 2, pectoral; *feet*, 2 arc-hands; *nails* (usually) flattened, oval; *food*, fruits, except a few who use animal food.

2. Bruta [Brutes]. *Fore-teeth* 0 in either jaw; *feet* with strong hoof-like nails; *motion*, slow; *food* (mostly) masticated vegetables.

3. Feræ [Wild Beasts]. *Fore-teeth* conic, usually 6 in each jaw; *tusks* longer; *grinders* with conic projections; *feet* with claws; *claws* subulate; *food*, carcases and preying on other animals.

4. Glires [Mice]. *Fore-teeth* cutting, 2 in each jaw; *tusks* 0; *feet* with claws formed for running and bounding; *food*, bark, roots, vegetables, &c which they gnaw.

5. Pecora [Cattle]. *Fore-teeth*, upper 0, lower cutting, many; *feet*, hoofed, cloven; *food*, herbs which they pluck, *chew* the cud; *stomachs* 4, the *paunch* to macerate and ruminate the food, the *bonnet*, reticulate to receive it, the *omasus*, or maniples of numerous folds to digest it, and the *abomasus*, or caille, fasciate to give it acescency and prevent putrefaction.

6. Belluæ [Brute beasts]. *Fore-teeth* obtuse; *feet* hoofed; *motion* heavy; *food* gathering vegetables.

7. Cete [Whales]. *Fins* pectoral instead of feet; *tail* horizontal, flattened; *claws* 0; *hair* 0; *teeth*, in some cartilaginous, in some bony; *nostrils* 0, instead of which is a fistulous opening in the anterior and upper part of the head; *food* molluscæ and fish; *habitation*, the ocean.

## Order *I.* Primates

Fore-teeth cutting: upper 4; parallel teats 2, pectoral
HOMO

Sapiens. Diurnal; varying by education and situation.

1. Four-footed, mute, hairy. *Wild man.*

2. Copper-coloured, choleric, erect. *American. Hair* black, straight, thick; *nostrils* wide; *face* harsh; *beard* scanty; obstinate, content, free. *Paints* himself with fine red lines. *Regulated* by customs.

3. Fair, sanguine, brawny. *European. Hair* yellow, brown, flowing; *eyes* blue; gentle, acute, inventive. *Covered* with close vestments. *Governed* by laws.

4. Sooty, melancholy, rigid. *Hair* black; *eyes* dark; *severe*, haughty, covetous. *Covered* with loose garments. *Governed* by opinions.

5. Black, phlegmatic, relaxed. *Hair* black, frizzled; *skin* silky; *nose* flat; *lips* tumid; crafty, indolent, negligent. *Anoints* himself with grease. *Governed* by caprice.

Monstrosus [Monstrous]. Varying by climate or art

1. Small, active, timid. *Mountaineer*
2. Large, indolent. *Patagonian*
3. Less fertile. *Hottentot*
4. Beardless. *American*
5. Head conic. *Chinese*
6. Head flattened. *Canadian*

The anatomical, physiological, natural, moral, civil, and social histories of man, are best described by their respective writers.

(*System of Nature*, 'Animals')

## COMTE DE BUFFON

Georges-Louis Leclerc, Comte de Buffon (1707–88), the son of an upper-middle-class magistrate, was born at Montbard. His early education was by the Jesuits of Dijon, and he later studied law and medicine. He allegedly took the life of an opponent in a duel, and then fled through France and Italy, returning to Montbard in 1731, after his mother's death. He inherited her wealth, and from this time assumed the name 'de Buffon'. In 1733, having presented a paper on mathematical probability, he was elected to the Academy of Sciences. His reputation as a natural scientist was promoted by his translation of Hales's *Vegetable Statics* in 1735 and of Newton's *Fluxions* in 1740. Having undertaken considerable research on forestry, in 1739 he was appointed to the prestigious post of supervisor of the Royal Botanic Gardens in Paris. He now began work on his hugely ambitious *Histoire Naturelle, générale et particulière* (Paris, 1749–1804), of which thirty-six volumes would be published in his lifetime, and a further eight volumes after his death. The *Natural History* considered a great range of subjects, including animals, birds, fish, fossils and minerals, but it led to an outcry in response to the challenges that it posed to traditional explanations of the origin of the world as depicted in the Book of Genesis. Even so, it was soon abridged and translated into many European languages, and hailed as a great scientific achievement.

As befits a work designed to promote the study of nature, Buffon began his *Histoire Naturelle* with a discourse on 'How to Study Natural History'. In this essay he stressed the importance of careful observation and description of particular objects, and the need to make generalisations. However, he warned against 'reducing nature to the status of petty systems' of classification. Rather, nature was 'a world of infinite combinations', and it was 'impossible to describe her accurately by such divisions, as she passes from one species to another, and often from one genus to another, by imperceptible nuances'. Having exposed what he regarded as the folly of the Linnaean classification of plants, he poured scorn on the Swedish naturalist's division of quadrupeds into orders. Thus he noted that the order of 'Ferae' (savage beasts) included such 'ferocious animals' as moles and hedgehogs, as well as lions and tigers. Similarly, the order of 'Glires' (mice) had to include porcupines, hares and beavers. It was, he concluded, both simpler and more natural to 'call an ass an ass, and a cat a cat'. Echoing Lockean views, Buffon claimed that 'Only individuals exist in nature ... genera, orders and classes exist only in our imagination.'

Twelve of the first fifteen volumes (1749–67) of the *Natural History* were devoted to the discussion of quadrupeds. This *Histoire Naturelle des Quadrupèdes* (translated as *History of Man and the Quadrupeds*) contained further criticism of the Linnaean system of classification on the grounds that the 'families' that Linnaeus claimed to have identified had no actual existence in the natural world. Thus Buffon maintained:

> If these families really existed, they could only be produced by the mixture and successive variation and degeneration of the primary species; and if it be once admitted, that there are families among plants and animals, that the ass belongs to the family of the horse, and differs from him only by degeneration; with equal propriety may it be concluded that the monkey belongs to the family of man; that the monkey is a man degenerated; that the man and the monkey have sprung from common stock.
>
> ('History of Man and the Quadrupeds', from *Natural History*, vol. IV, 1753)

The extracts here, from the 1781 Edinburgh edition of *History of Man and the Quadrupeds*, part of *Histoire Naturelle*, are from Buffon's introductory essays to his studies of domestic and wild animals.

## History of Man and the Quadrupeds (1753)

### 'Of Domestic Animals'

Man changes the natural condition of animals, by forcing them to obey and to serve him. A domestic animal is a slave destined to the amusement, or to aid the operations of men. The abuses to which he is too frequently subjected, joined to the unnatural mode of his living, induce great alterations both in his manners and dispositions. But a savage animal, obedient to Nature alone, knows no laws but those of appetite and independence. Thus the history of savage animals is limited to a small number of facts, the results of pure Nature. But the history of domestic animals is complicated, and warped with everything relative to the arts employed in taming and subduing the native wildness of their tempers: and, as we are ignorant what influence habit, restraint, and example, may have in changing the manners, determinations, movements, and inclinations of animals, it is the duty of the naturalist to examine them with care, and to distinguish those facts which depend solely on instinct from those that originate from education; to ascertain what is proper to them from what is borrowed; to separate artifice from Nature; and never to confound the animal with the slave, the beast of burden with the creature of God.

Man holds a legitimate dominion over the brute animals, which no revolution can destroy. It is the dominion of mind over matter; a right of Nature founded upon unalterable laws, a gift of the Almighty, by which man is enabled at all times to perceive the dignity of his being: for his power is not derived from his being the most perfect, the strongest, or the most dexterous of all animals. If he hold only the first rank in the order of animals, the inferior tribes would unite, and dispute his title to sovereignty. But man reigns and commands from the superiority of his nature: he thinks; and therefore he is master of all beings who are not endowed with this inestimable talent. Material bodies are likewise subject to his power: to his will they can oppose only a gross resistance, or an obstinate inflexibility, which his hand is always able to overcome, by making them act against each other. He is master of the vegetable tribes, which, by his industry he can, at pleasure, augment or diminish, multiply or destroy. He reigns over the animal creation; because, like them, he is not only endowed with sentiment and the power of motion, but because he thinks, distinguishes ends and means, directs his actions, concerts his operations, overcomes force by ingenuity, and swiftness by perseverance.

Among animals, however, some are more soft and gentle, others more savage and ferocious. When we compare the docility and submissive temper of the dog with the fierceness and rapacity of the tiger, the one appears to be the friend, and the other the enemy of man. Thus his empire over the animals is not absolute. Many species elude his power, by the rapidity of their flight, by the swiftness of their course, by the obscurity of their retreats, by the element which they inhabit: others escape him by the minuteness of their bodies; and others, instead of acknowledging their sovereign, attack him with open hostility. He is likewise insulted with the stings of insects, and the poisonous bites of serpents; and he is often incommoded with impure and useless creatures, which seem to exist for no other purpose but to form the shade between good and evil, and to make man feel how little, since his Fall, he is respected.

But the empire of God must be distinguished from the limited dominion of man. God, the creator of all being, is the sole governor of Nature. Man has no influence on the universe, the motions of the heavenly bodies, or the revolutions of the globe which he inhabits. He has no general dominion over animals, vegetables, or minerals. His power extends not to species, but is limited to individuals; for species and the great body of matter belong to, or rather constitute Nature. Everything moves on, perishes, or is renewed, by an irresistible power. Man himself, hurried along by the torrent of time, cannot prolong his existence. Connected, by means of his body, to matter, he is forced to submit to the universal law, and, like all other organized beings, he is born, grows, and perishes.

But the ray of divinity with which man is inspired, ennobles and animates him above every material's existence. This spiritual substance, so far from being subject to matter, is entitled to govern it; and though the mind cannot command the whole of Nature, she rules over individual beings. God, the source of all light and of all intelligence, governs the universe, and every species, with infinite power: man, who possesses only a ray of this intelligence, enjoys, accordingly, a power limited to individuals, and to small portions of matter.

It is, therefore, apparent that man has been enabled to subdue the animal creation, not by force, or the other qualities of matter, but by the powers of his mind. In the first ages of the world, all animals were equally independent. Man, after he became criminal and savage, was not in a condition to tame them. Before he could distinguish, choose, and reduce animals to a domestic state, before he could instruct and command them, he required to be civilized himself; and the empire over the animals, like all other empires, could not be established previous to the institution of society.

Man derives all his power from society, which matures his reason, exercises his genius, and unites his force. Before the formation of society, man was perhaps the most savage and the least formidable of all animals. Naked, without shelter, and destitute of arms, the earth was to him only a vast desert peopled with monsters, of which he often became the prey: and, even long after this period, history informs us, that the first heroes were only destroyers of wild beasts.

But, when the human species multiplied and spread over the earth, and when, by means of society and the arts, man was enabled to conquer the universe, he made the wild beasts gradually retire; he purged the earth of those gigantic animals, whose enormous bones are still to be found; he destroyed, or reduced to a small number, the voracious and hurtful species; he opposed one animal to another; subdued some by address, and others by force; and, attacking all by reason and art, he acquired to himself perfect security, and established an empire, which knows no other limits than inaccessible solitudes, burning sands, frozen mountains, or dark caverns, which serve as retreats to a few species of ferocious animals.

(*Natural History*, 'Of Domestic Animals')

### *'Of Wild Animals'*

Wild and free animals, without excepting man, are, of all animated beings, least subject to changes or variations of any kind. As they are at absolute liberty in the choice of their food and their climate, their nature is more permanent than that of domestic animals, which are enslaved, transported, maltreated, and fed, without consulting their inclination or taste. Wild animals live perpetually in the same manner. They never wander from climate to climate. The wood where they are brought forth is a country to which they are faithfully attached, and they never depart from it, unless they perceive that they can no longer live there in safety. They fly not so much from their natural enemies, as from the presence of man. Nature has furnished them with resources against the other animals, and put them on a level; they know their strength, their address, their designs, their haunts, and, if unable to avoid them, oppose force to force: in a word, they are species of the same genius. But how can they defend themselves against a being who is able to seize without seeing, and kill without approaching them?

It is man, therefore, who disturbs and disperses wild animals, and renders them a thousand times more savage than they would naturally be; for most of them require tranquillity only, and a moderate use of the air and earth. Nature even teaches them to live together, to unite into families, and to form societies. In countries not totally engrossed by man, some vestiges of these societies still remain. We there perceive common works carried on, designs that, though not founded on reason, appear to be projected upon rational conventions, the execution of which supposes union at least, and a joint co-operation of labour. It is not by force of physical necessity, like the ants, the bees, &c., that the beavers labour and build houses; for they are neither constrained by space, nor time, nor number, but unite from choice. Those which agree, remove; and some of them have been remarked, which, being constantly repulsed by others, were obliged to betake themselves to a solitary life. It is only in distant and desert countries, where they dread not the approach of man, that they incline to render their dwellings more fixed and commodious, by constructing houses, or a kind of villages, which have no small resemblance to the feeble and primitive efforts of a nascent republic. In countries, on the contrary, spread over by men, they carry terror along with them. The society of animals is then at an end. All industry ceases, and every art is stifled. They think no more of building, and neglect every conveniency. Perpetually pressed by fear and necessity, their only desire is the bare preservation of life, and their only occupation is flight and concealment. If the human species, as is reasonable to suppose, shall, in the progress of time, people equally the whole surface of the earth, the history of the beaver, in a few ages, will be regarded as a ridiculous fable.

We may, therefore, conclude, that the talents and faculties of animals, instead of augmenting, are perpetually diminishing. Time fights against them. The more the human species multiplies and improves, the more will the wild animals feel the effects of a terrible and absolute tyrant, who, hardly allowing them an individual existence, deprives them of liberty, of every associating principle, and destroys the very rudiments of their intelligence. What advances they have made, or may still make, convey little information of what they have been, or might acquire. If the human species were annihilated, to which of the animals would the sceptre of the earth belong?

(*Natural History*, 'Of Wild Animals')


## DENIS DIDEROT

In 1753, two years after the appearance of the first volume of the *Encyclopédie*, Diderot (see p. 20) published – tentatively and anonymously – the first version of what would become his extraordinary *Pensées sur l'Interprétation de la Nature* (*Thoughts on the Interpretation of Nature*), which was revised and enlarged in 1754. In this speculative work (inspired by Francis Bacon's writings), consisting of fifty-eight loosely structured sections, Diderot rejected the rationalist method of scholars such as Descartes and, more particularly, Linnaeus, whose static 'system' was based upon the classification of nature according to a few fixed ideas. He reflected that nature, portrayed as a thinking and feeling whole, was the source of knowledge, though its scale and complexity made it difficult to understand. It was therefore necessary to adopt an open-minded approach to the acquisition of knowledge about the natural world, as he explained at the beginning of the first section: 'Nature is to be my theme. I shall let my thoughts flow from my pen in the order in which things occur to me, to give a better picture of the workings of my mind.'

The following extracts from a modern translation of the 1754 edition of *Thoughts on the Interpretation of Nature* are selected here to illustrate some of the character of Diderot's conjectures. Following a short preface to young readers, in Sections VI to XII Diderot reflects on the difficulties of understanding the phenomena of nature, for which, he later suggests, 'we have three principal means: the observation of nature, thought and experiment. Observation collects the facts, thought combines them, and experiment verifies the result of the combination' (*Thoughts*, XV). In Section XXIII he explains his preference for empirical philosophy. In Section XXXII he speculates on sexuality and reproduction. In Section XLIX he ridicules the reasoning of Linnaeus, 'a systematist who has put man at the head of the quadrupeds in his system' with the result that 'he no longer sees him in nature except as an animal with four feet' (*Thoughts*, XLVIII). Finally, in Section LVIII, under the guise of asking 'Questions', he expresses his ideas about evolution, suggesting that nature is still at work and 'what we take for natural history is merely the far-from-complete history of a single instant' (*Thoughts*, LVIII).

## Thoughts on the Interpretation of Nature (1753)

### 'To young persons preparing to study Natural Philosophy'

Young man, open this book and read on. If you can manage to reach the end, better books than this will not be beyond you. Since my purpose is not so much to instruct you as to exercise your mind, it matters little to me whether you adopt or reject my ideas, so long as you give them your full attention. Someone more able than myself will teach you how to become acquainted with the power of nature; I shall be content if I have helped you to try out your own powers. And so farewell.

PS. One more word before I take my leave. Always bear in mind that *nature* is not *God*, that a *man* is not a *machine* and that a *hypothesis* is not a *fact*; you may be sure that if you think you have found something here which conflicts with these principles, you will have failed to understand me.

(*Thoughts*, prefatory address)

VI. When we compare the infinite number of phenomena in nature with the limitations of our own intelligence and the frailty of our organs, how could we ever expect to discover — in view of the slowness of our work, the long and frequent interruptions which it suffers, and the scarcity of creative spirits — anything but a few broken, isolated parts of the great chain which links everything together. Even if experimental science continued to work for century after century, the materials which it accumulated would eventually have become too great to fit into any system, and the inventory of them would still be far from complete. How many volumes would be needed to encompass just the terms intended to designate different sets of phenomena, once these phenomena had been ascertained? How long will it take for the language of philosophy to be complete? And, even if it were complete, what man could possibly master it? [...] It is also true that the idea of 'usefulness' sets boundaries on everything. The criterion of usefulness is about to place limits on geometry, and in a few centuries from now, it will do the same for experimental science. I estimate that this field of study will last for some centuries yet, because it has an infinitely broader spectrum of use than any abstract science, and because it is indisputably the basis of everything which we know for certain.

VII. So long as something exists only in the mind, it remains there as an opinion, or a notion which may be either true or false, and which can be accepted or contradicted. It becomes meaningful only when linked to things which are external to it. This linkage is achieved either by an uninterrupted series of experiments, or by an uninterrupted line of reasoning, one end of which is rooted in observation and the other in experimentation; or else by a series of experiments scattered at intervals in a reasoned argument, as weights may be attached along a thread held by its two ends. Without these weights, the thread would be at the mercy of the slightest breath of air.

VIII. Concepts which have no foundation in nature may be compared to those Northern forests where the trees have no roots. It needs nothing more than a gust of wind, or some trivial event, to bring down a whole forest of trees — and of ideas.

IX. Men have scarcely begun to realise how rigorous are the laws governing enquiry into the truth, and how few are the means at our disposal. The whole enterprise comes down to proceeding from the senses to reflection, and from reflection back to the senses: an endless process of withdrawing into oneself, and re-emerging. This is how bees work. We will have foraged in vain if we do not return to the hive loaded with beeswax. All this wax will have been accumulated in vain, unless we know how to make honeycombs.

X. Unfortunately, however, it is quicker and easier to commune with oneself than to consult nature. That is why reason tends to remain cloistered, whereas instinct wants to reach outside itself. Instinct never ceases to watch, to sample, to touch and to listen; there may be more experimental science to be learnt from studying animals than by following the courses given by a professor. There is no artifice in what they do. They set about achieving their purposes, careless of what is around them; if they do take us by surprise, that is not their intention. Astonishment is the first reaction to any great phenomenon; it is the task of philosophy to dispel it. The purpose of a course in experimental philosophy is to send the listener away better informed, not stunned. To pride oneself on natural phenomena, as though one had invented them oneself, would be to imitate the [self-important] stupidity of an editor [Pierre Coste, 1668–1747] of the *Essais*, who could never hear the name of Montaigne [1533–92] without blushing. There is a fundamental lesson which there is often occasion to teach: the recognition of one's own inadequacy. Would it not be better to win the confidence of others by frankly admitting 'I simply do not know', than to keep babbling on and cover oneself with embarrassment by endeavouring to find explanations for everything? Anyone who openly admits his ignorance of something he knows nothing about makes me more inclined to believe what he does try to explain to me.

XI. Astonishment often arises from imagining several extraordinary events when only one has taken place, and from imagining as many discrete occurrences in nature as there are phenomena, whereas perhaps there has never been more than a single act of nature. It further appears that if nature had been obliged to produce more than one such act, the differing results of these acts would have remained separate; moreover, there would be sets of phenomena unrelated to one another, and the common connecting chain, which philosophy takes to be continuous, would be broken at several points. The total separateness of an individual fact is incompatible with the concept of a whole, and without that philosophy would cease to exist.

XII. It would appear that nature has chosen to use the same mechanism in an infinite number of different ways [Diderot cites Buffon's *Histoire Naturelle*, and other works]. She never abandons one type of creation before replicating that genus in all its possible variations. If we consider the animal kingdom, and observe that, among the quadrupeds, every single one possesses functions and bodily parts – especially internal organs – fully resembling those of any other quadruped, is it not easy to believe that in the beginning there was only a single animal which served as prototype for all the others, and that all nature has done is to lengthen, shorten, alter, multiply or eliminate certain organs. Imagine the fingers of the hand joined together, with the substance of the nails so extended and thickened that it engulfs and covers the whole body; then, instead of a human hand, you would have a horse's hoof. When we observe the successive outward metamorphoses which take place in this prototype, whatever it may be, pushing one realm of life closer to another by imperceptible stages, and populating the regions where these two realms border on each other (if they can be referred to as 'borders' in the absence of any true divisions); and, populating, as I said, the border regions of the two realms with vague, unidentifiable beings, largely devoid of the forms, qualities and functions of one region and assuming the forms, qualities and functions of the other; who, then, would not be persuaded that there had never been more than one single prototype for every being? But whether one accepts this philosophical conjecture as true, like Doctor Baumann [the pseudonym used by Maupertius for his *Dissertatio[...] de Universali Systemata Naturae*, 1751], or rejects it as false, in common with Monsieur de Buffon, no-one will deny that it should be adopted as an essential hypothesis for the advancement of experimental physics, of rationalist philosophy and for the discovery and explanation of phenomena which depend on being organised. Obviously, nature could never have preserved such a degree of similarity amongst its constituent parts, and introduced such variety in the forms it adopts, without frequently bringing out something in one organism which has been suppressed in another. In this, nature resembles a woman who likes to dress up, and whose different disguises, exposing first one part of herself and then another, give some hope to her ardent admirers that they may one day get to know the whole person.

(*Thoughts*, VI–XII)

XXIII. We have identified two types of philosophy – one is empirical and the other rationalist. One of the two goes blindfolded, always groping its way, grasping everything which comes to hand and finally encountering precious things. The other assembles these precious materials and attempts to fashion them into a flaming torch; but this would-be torch has, until now, served less well than the gropings of the rival camp – and this is as it should be. Experimentation moves endlessly, and is forever active; it devotes as much time to seeking out phenomena as reason spends on seeking analogies. Experimental science does not know what its work will produce and what it will not, but it nonetheless labours without respite. Rationalist philosophy, in contrast, weighs up the alternatives, pronounces on them and stops there. It boldly states that '*light cannot be split*'; meanwhile the experimental philosopher merely listens without rejoinder throughout the centuries and then, suddenly, he brings out the prism, with the words '*light can be split*'.

(*Thoughts*, XXIII)

XXXII.  1. There is a certain body known as a mola [an ectopic pregnancy]. Some maintain that this singular body is engendered in the female without the assistance of the male. However the mystery of generation may be accomplished, both sexes are certainly involved. Could the mola not be an assembly, either of every element emanating from the female in the production of a male, or of all the elements emanating from the male in his different approaches to the female? Could these elements which are quiescent in the male, but widespread and sustained in certain females with a hot temperament and a vivid imagination, not be fired and stirred into activity? And could those elements which are quiescent in the female not be activated either by an arid and sterile presence, and by seemingly barren and purely carnal movements of the male, or else by the violence and the repression of desires induced by the female; could they not then leave their storage site for the womb where they remain, and combine of their own accord? Could the mola not be the combination of elements emanating from the female alone, or those originating just from the male? If the mola results from a combination such as I envisage, however, the laws governing this combination will be just as invariable as the laws of generation itself ... The organisation of the mola will therefore remain invariable. If we were to take up a scalpel and perform dissections on these molæ, we might even discover some which bore traces associated with the difference between the sexes. This might be described as the art of proceeding from the relatively unknown to the completely unknown. It is an irrational form of behaviour found to a surprising degree in those who have acquired, or who possess naturally, a gift for the experimental sciences; dreams of this sort have led to a number of discoveries. It is this sort of guesswork which should be taught to learners – if, indeed, it can be taught at all.

2. However, if it is discovered in the course of time that the mola is never engendered in the female without the involvement of the male, then a number of new and far more convincing conjectures can be formulated on the subject of this singular body. The web of blood-vessels which we call the placenta is known to be a mushroom-shaped segment of a sphere, adhering by its convex area to the womb throughout the pregnancy, with the umbilical cord serving as a stalk; it comes away from the womb during the contractions of childbirth; its surface is smooth in a healthy woman who has had a successful delivery. In its generation, its bodily conformation and its behaviour, a living being is never anything but what the constraints of its existence, the laws of motion, and the universal order of things determine that it shall be; should this segment of a sphere – which

appears to adhere to the womb only through being placed in contact with it — happen gradually to come away at the edges from the start of the pregnancy, and continue to do so at a rate directly proportional to its increase in volume, it occurred to me that these edges, once free of any attachment, would draw closer and closer together, and assume a spherical shape. The umbilical cord, tugged by two opposing forces – one caused by the convex and detached edges of the segment, which would tend to shorten it, and the other by the weight of the foetus, which would tend to lengthen it – would then be much shorter than under normal conditions. A time would come when these edges would meet and knit together, forming a type of ovum, in the centre of which a foetus, as abnormal in its organisation as in its production, would be found, obstructed, constricted and suffocated. This ovum would feed until the small surface area still connecting it came away entirely under its weight, and it fell into the womb unattached, whence it would be ejected by being laid, rather as a hen lays an egg (an object to which the ovum, at least by its shape, has some similarity). If these conjectures could be tested in a mola, and if it were nonetheless demonstrated that this mola is engendered in the female without any assistance from the male, it would then clearly follow that the foetus is formed in the female and that the male only becomes involved at the development stage.

(*Thoughts*, XXXII)

XLIX. Man, says Linnaeus in the preface to his *Fauna Suecica* [1746], is neither a stone nor a plant; he must therefore be an animal. He does not have only one foot, so he cannot be a worm. He is not an insect because he has no antennae, nor a fish, because he has no fins, nor a bird, because he has no feathers. So what is man? He has a mouth like a quadruped. He has four feet; he uses the two fore-feet to touch with, and the two hind-feet to walk with. So he must be a quadruped. The Linnaean goes on to say: 'It is true that, as a consequence of my theories about natural history, I have never been able to distinguish between man and ape, because there are certain apes which have less hair than certain men: these apes walk on two legs and use their hands and feet like men. Nor do I consider speech to be a distinguishing feature; my method only allows for those features which are dependent on number, contour, proportion and situation.' 'So your logic must be wrong', the logician will say; and the naturalist will conclude that man is a four-footed animal.

### LVIII. Questions

1. If there is no link from one phenomenon to another, there can be no philosophy. Even if all phenomena were interlinked, the state of each of them might still not be permanent. But if each living being is in a perpetual state of change, even as a result of the workings of nature, then despite the chain which links phenomena together, there is still no philosophy. All our natural sciences become as transitory as the words we utter. What we take for natural history is merely the far-from-complete history of a single instant. I ask, therefore, whether metals always have been, and always will be, as they now are; whether plants always have been, and always will be, as they now are; whether animals always have been, and always will be, as they now are; and so on. A word to sceptics: having meditated profoundly on certain phenomena, you may understandably

question not so much the fact that the world was created, but whether it now is as it used to be, and as it will be in the future.

2. Just as in the animal and vegetable kingdoms, an individual comes into being, so to speak, grows, remains in being, declines and passes on, will it not be the same for the entire species? If our faith did not teach us that animals left the Creator's hands just as they now appear and, if it were permitted to entertain the slightest doubt as to their beginning and their end, may not a philospher, left to his own conjectures, suspect that, from time immemorial, animal life had its own constituent elements, scattered and intermingled with the general body of matter, and that it happened that these constituent elements came together because it was possible for them to do so; that the embryo formed from these elements went through innumerable arrangements and developments, successively acquiring movement, feeling, ideas, thought, reflection, consciousness, feelings, emotions, signs, gestures, sounds, articulate sounds, language, laws, arts and sciences; that millions of years passed between each of these developments, and there may be other developments or kinds of growth still to come of which we know nothing; that a stationary point either has been or will be reached; that the embryo either is, or will be, moving away from this point through a process of everlasting decay, during which its faculties will leave it in the same way as they arrived; that it will disappear for ever from nature – or rather, that it will continue to exist there, but in a form and with faculties very different from those it displays at this present point in time? Religion saves us from many deviations, and a good deal of work. Had religion not enlightened us on the origin of the world and the universal system of being, what a multitude of different hypotheses we would have been tempted to take as nature's secret! Since these hypotheses are all equally wrong, they would all have seemed almost equally plausible. The question of why anything exists is the most awkward that philosophy can raise – and Revelation alone provides an answer.

(*Thoughts*, LVIII)

## JEAN-JACQUES ROUSSEAU

Having been driven out of many places due to the notoriety of his works and his own irascibility, in 1770 Rousseau (see p. 17) returned to Paris. He felt isolated and estranged from society now, and needed to 'clamber up rocks and mountains … to rid myself as much as possible of the memory of men'. As he explained at the beginning of his last major work, the *Rêveries du Promeneur Solitaire* (*Reveries of the Solitary Walker*), published posthumously in 1782: 'Here I am now, alone in the world; having no brother, neighbour, friend or company but myself. The most sociable and loving of men has with unanimous agreement been rejected by all the rest.' In these final years, 'living between myself and nature', he dedicated his time and energy to recording his thoughts about himself and his life and the many pleasures that he found in botany during his ramblings through nature.

Written during the last two years of his life, 1777 and 1778, but never completed, the *Reveries* extols the 'natural' and the spontaneous, Rousseau's emotions and his appreciation of the natural environment as he tries to record 'all the strange ideas which pass through my head when I am walking'. Personal, lyrical and ostensibly written only for himself – rather than to argue a point or to persuade a reader – the ten loosely structured 'walks' or essays of the *Reveries* clearly express Rousseau's romanticism. In the extract translated here from the Fifth Walk, Rousseau, mixing imagination and reflection, writes about his communion with nature through his experience of the plants and landscapes of the little island of Saint-Pierre on Lake Bienne in Switzerland, where he had stayed for several weeks in the autumn of 1765. As he recalled in his *Confessions* (see p. 357), he had fled to St Peter's Island after the pastor of Môtiers had denounced his *Letters from the Mountain* (1764) and his house had been stoned by villagers in the middle of the night. However, the island was under the jurisdiction of Berne, and he was soon ordered to leave.

## Reveries of the Solitary Walker (1782)

Of all the homes I have lived in (and I have had some charming ones) none has made me so truly happy and left me with such tender regrets as the island of Saint-Pierre in the middle of the Lake of Bienne. That little island which at Neuchâtel goes by the name of the island of La Motte is very little known, even in Switzerland. No traveller, to my knowledge, mentions it. It is, however, very pleasant and uniquely situated to provide happiness to the man who enjoys being self-contained; for, although I may perhaps be the only person in the world whose destiny has imposed this on him, I cannot believe that I am the only one who has so natural a taste, though, so far, I have never found it in anyone else.

The banks of the Lake of Bienne are wilder and more romantic than those of Lake Geneva, because the rocks and woods are closer to the water, but I find them no less agreeable. There is less cultivation of fields and vines, fewer towns and houses, but there is more natural grassland, there are more meadows, more retreats shaded by trees, more frequent contrasts and closer undulations. As these happy banks do not have large tracks that would aid transport, the country is visited little by travellers, but it is attractive to those solitary dreamers who love, at their leisure, to become intoxicated by the charms of nature and to collect their thoughts in a silence disturbed by no other sound than the cry of eagles, interspersed by the warbling of birds and the rolling streams falling from the mountain. This beautiful, almost round lake nestles at its centre two small islands, one inhabited and cultivated, about half a league round, and another which is smaller, deserted and fallow, which will be destroyed in time by the removal of earth in order to repair the damage that waves and storms do to the larger island. Thus it is that the substance of the weak is always used to benefit the powerful. [...]

It was on this small island [on 12 September 1765] that I found refuge after being stoned at Môtiers [on 6 September 1765]. I found the place so charming, I lived a life there that so agreed with my temperament that I resolved to end my days there. [...]

I was barely allowed to spend two months on this island, but I would have spent two years, two centuries, and all eternity there without a moment's boredom, although I and my companion [Thérèse Levasseur] did not have any other company [living on the island] but the tax officer, his wife and their servants, who were, in truth, very good people and nothing more, but this was precisely what I needed. I consider those two months the happiest of my life, so very happy that they would have sufficed for the rest of my existence without giving birth to any desire in my soul for any other state.

What was it then, this happiness, and in what did this pleasure consist? When I describe the life I led there, I will leave the men of this century guessing. A precious *far niente* [doing nothing] was the first and principal pleasure that I wished to taste in all its sweetness, and all that I did during my stay was, in effect, be a man devoted to the delicious and necessary task of idleness. [...]

One of my great delights was, above all, to leave my books in their boxes and to have no writing desk. When I was forced to pick up my pen and reply to unfortunate letters, I borrowed the writing desk of the tax officer, muttering under my breath, and hastening to return it, in the vain hope of never again having to borrow it. Instead of all those wretched papers and poring over old books, I filled the room with flowers and hay; for I had just become enamoured with botany in those days, for which Dr [Jean-Antoine] d'Ivernois [1703–65] had inspired me and which soon became a passion. I did not want any more work, and I needed a diversion that I enjoyed that would require the kind of effort that a lazy man would like to make. I undertook to produce the *flora petrinsularis* [*flora of the island of Saint-Pierre*] and to describe all of the plants on the island with no omissions, in sufficient detail to keep me busy for the rest of my days. It is said that a German has written a book about lemon peel. I would have written one on each grain of the fields, each moss in the woods, each lichen which carpets the rocks, in fact, I did not want to leave one blade of grass, or one atom of plant-life not fully described. In pursuance of this beautiful project, every morning after breakfast, which we all took together, I went out with a magnifying glass in my hand and my *Systema Naturae* [by Linnaeus] under my arm, and visited a section of the island which I had, for this purpose, divided up into small squares, with the intention of exploring them one after another in each season. Nothing is more remarkable than the raptures and the ecstasies that I experienced with each study that I made of the structure and organisation of plants, and of the role the sexual parts play in fructification, as this system was entirely new to me. The distinguishing of generic characteristics, of which, previously, I had not had the slightest idea, enchanted me as I checked them against common species, in the hope that it would turn up a rare species. The forking of the two long stamens of the prunella [self-heal], the resilience of those of the nettle and wallflower, the bursting of fruit of the garden-balsam and of the pod of the boxwood, a thousand small tricks of fructification, which I observed for the first time, filled me with joy, and I went around asking people if they had seen the horns of the prunella, as [Jean de] La Fontaine [1621–95] asked people if they had read [the Book of the prophet] Habakkuk. After two or three hours I would return carrying an ample harvest, a supply of enjoyment for the afternoon at the house, should it rain. I would spend the rest of the morning with the tax collector, his wife and Thérèse, visiting their workers and their crops, more often than not turning my hand to work with them, and often the people of Bern who came to see me, would find me perched in big trees, girded with a sack which I would fill with fruit and then lower to the ground by rope. The morning exercise and the good mood which is inseparable from it, made the break for lunch very pleasant for me. But when it went on for too long and the fine weather tempted me, I could no longer wait, and, while the others were still at the table, would slip away and would jump alone into a boat, which I would row to the middle of the lake when the water was calm, and there, stretching myself at full length in the boat, my eyes looking up at the sky, I would let myself go and drift at the mercy of the water, sometimes spending several hours, immersed in a thousand confused, but delicious reveries, which, while having no determined focus or constancy, were to me one hundred times better than all that I had found the most sweet in what one calls the pleasures of life. [...]

When the lake was too rough for me to go on it, I spent the afternoon walking across the island, botanising to the right and to the left, sitting myself down, sometimes in the most attractive and remote retreats to dream at my leisure, sometimes on a terrace or hillock, so that I could run my eyes over the superb and entrancing view of the lake and its banks, crowned on one side by the nearby mountains and on the other enlarged by rich, fertile plains, over which the view extended to the distant, bluish mountains beyond.

When the evening approached, I came down from the peaks of the island and happily sat in some hidden place on the bank at the edge of the lake; there the noise of the waves and the movement of the water engaged my senses, and chased all other restlessness from my soul, and plunged it into a delicious reverie, the night often surprising me without my having noticed it. The ebb and the flow of this water, its continuous sound, now and then increasing, struck my ears and my eyes constantly, compensating for the internal movements which the reverie had extinguished within me, and was sufficient to make me feel my existence with pleasure, without taking the trouble to think. From time to time the surface of the water showed me the image of a weak and short reflection on the instability of earthly things: but soon these light impressions were washed away by the uniformity of the continual movement which rocked me to the point that, without any active assistance from my soul, I found it difficult, when called at the appointed hour with the agreed signal, to detach myself from that place without effort.

After dinner when the evening was fine, we would again all go together to take a stroll on the terrace to breathe in the fresh breezes of the lake. We would rest on the pavilion, we would laugh and chat, and sing an old song, which was every bit as good as any modern intrigues, and at last we would go to bed, happy with our day, and wishing only the same for tomorrow. Leaving aside unforeseen and unwelcome visits, this is the manner in which I spent my time on the island during my stay there. Let someone tell me now what there is which is sufficiently alluring to stir in my heart regrets so vivid, tender and lasting, that, even after fifteen years, it is impossible for me to think of this cherished place without each time feeling myself carried away again by outbursts of desire.

I have noticed in the vicissitudes of a long life that the periods of sweetest pleasure and most keen enjoyment are not, however, those whose memory attracts and touches me the most. These short moments of delirium and of passion, however vivid they may be, are nevertheless, by their very vivacity, just well-scattered points in the line of a life. They are too rare and too quick to constitute a state of being, and the happiness that my heart misses is not made of passing moments, but of a pure and permanent state, which has nothing vivid in it, but its duration increases its charm to the point that one finds in it the highest form of happiness.

Everything on earth is in a continual state of flux: nothing keeps a constant and fixed form, and our affections which become attached to external things, inevitably pass and change like them. Always in front of us or behind us, they remember the past which is no longer, or foresee the future, which is often not to be: there is nothing solid there to which the heart can attach itself. There is scarcely a pleasure here on earth which does not pass; I doubt there is such a thing known to man as lasting happiness. In our most vivid enjoyment there is hardly one moment when the heart can truly say to us: I would like this moment to last for ever; and how can one call happiness that transitory state which still leaves the heart anxious and empty, which makes us regret something beforehand, or still desire something afterwards?

But if there is a state where the soul finds a position secure enough in which to rest completely, and to gather there all its being, without having to recall the past or to encroach on the future; where time is nothing for it, where the present lasts for ever, yet without marking its duration and without any trace of succession, with no other feeling of deprivation or enjoyment, of pleasure or pain, of desire or fear, except that alone of our existence, and that this feeling alone can fill it completely; so far as this state lasts, he who finds it can call himself happy, not with an imperfect, poor and relative happiness, such as that which one finds in the pleasures of life, but with a sufficient, perfect and full happiness, which does not leave such emptiness in the soul, that it feels the need to fill. Such is the state in which I found myself often on the island of Saint-Pierre in my solitary reveries, either lying in my boat, letting it drift at the mercy of the water, or sitting on the shore of the rough lake, or elsewhere on the bank of a beautiful river or a stream murmuring over the gravel.

In such a situation, what does a man enjoy? Nothing outside himself, nothing if not himself and his own existence; while such a state lasts he is self-sufficient, like God. The feeling of an existence stripped of all other affection is by itself a precious feeling of contentment and of peace, which alone is enough to make this existence dear and sweet to anyone who is able to separate himself from all sensual and earthly impressions which come unceasingly to distract us from it and to upset our sweetness here on earth. But the majority of men, perturbed by continual passions, have little knowledge of such a state, and, having only tasted it imperfectly during a few instants, conserve nothing of it but a vague and confused idea that does not make its charms felt to them. It would not even be good, in the present state of things, that, hungry for those sweet ecstasies, they were to be put off the activity-filled life, that their ever-emerging needs stipulate to them as their duty. But an unfortunate man, who has been excluded from human society, and can no longer do anything useful or good either for others or himself down here, can find in this state, compensation for all the human happiness that fortune and men have taken from him.

(*Reveries*, 'Fifth Walk')

# Chapter 5

# Science and invention

**I**N THE EARLY EIGHTEENTH CENTURY, not only was the use of science as a means of describing and understanding the natural world still in its infancy, but its subject matter and utility were still generally uncertain. The fact that the words 'science' and 'scientist' were not widely used in their modern senses until the nineteenth century gives some indication of the transformation in the status of science which has since taken place. During the Enlightenment, 'scientific' views of the world were discussed largely within a framework of studies known as 'natural philosophy', which included the study of 'physics' ('natural things') and philosophical discussions about human understanding of natural phenomena. Science, then, was not a field of research or cultural investment that was generally regarded as clearly separate from other bodies of knowledge, or from literary, moral and theological studies, let alone divided into discrete and distinctive 'disciplines' such as biology, geology, zoology and botany (parts of 'natural history'), though these branches were beginning to emerge.

What would later be depicted by Jean d'Alembert, Voltaire and other *philosophes* as a 'scientific revolution' had begun in the seventeenth century with the work of scholars such as Francis Bacon (1561–1621), Galileo Galilei (1564–1642), Johannes Kepler (1571–1630), René Descartes (1596–1650), and Isaac Newton (1642–1727). According to d'Alembert (see p. 35) the methods of study and findings of these thinkers laid the foundations for eighteenth-century scientific enquiries and many of the Enlightenment's debates about the natural world. Since Ancient Greek times, the world had been looked upon largely as a living and mysterious entity, an orderly and integrated whole. However, in the seventeenth century a less organic but more mechanical and mathematical view of nature had emerged. Thus the German astronomer Kepler wrote: 'My goal is to show that the heavenly machine is not a kind of divine living being but is similar to a clockwork.' In the main, early eighteenth-century scientists struggled with variations of the mechanical philosophy (seeking to explain changes in nature in terms of matter) that they inherited from discussions about Descartes. However, by mid-century there was a growing number of exceptions as scholars such as the Comte de Buffon and Denis Diderot criticised the use of mechanical systems and mathematics as means of explaining the living world. By the close of the century, men such as Erasmus Darwin had come to see nature itself as dynamic, gradually changing over millions of years. Moreover, far from seeing humans as machines, and as having a fixed place in a static 'Great Chain of Being', Darwin and others raised the prospect of unlimited progress for man and nature. As he optimistically noted in his *Zoonomia* (1794–96), 'All nature exists in a state of perpetual improvement.'

At the beginning of the eighteenth century, the work of two English scholars (commonly paired together during the Enlightenment) gradually made a particularly powerful impact upon the course of scientific thinking. John Locke broke away from Cartesian (from Descartes) philosophies by emphasising the key role of sensory experience as the foundation of knowledge (empiricism), and Isaac Newton produced mathematical descriptions and explanations of the cosmic order and of universal gravitation, and put forward the idea of space as infinite. His celebrated *Optics* (1704), for example, was intended 'to explain the properties of light … by reason and experiment', and his work on gravity in the *Principia* (1687) demonstrated that the motion of planets was due to the same laws as governed the movement of all matter upon earth. The success of Newton's work – not least in the importance that was now given to mathematics in the light of his and Leibniz's work – seemed clearly to justify his experimental method of research, and it inspired scores of curious scholars to conduct extraordinary investigations and experiments in many fields. Some of these enquiries were conducted at universities by members of faculty such as Hermann Boerhaave (1668–1738), the head of medicine at Leiden, and Joseph Black (1728–99), professor of Chemistry at Glasgow and later Edinburgh. However, in universities where clerical authority was often strong, as in France, it was generally harder to develop a secular curriculum. Experimental research was therefore often conducted by members of scientific associations such as the Royal Society at London (founded in 1662), the smaller and more exclusive, state-directed Paris Académie des Sciences (1666–1793), the Russian Academy of Sciences at St Petersburg (1724), and the Berlin Academy of Sciences (1700), which was reorganised by Frederick the Great who appointed the French scientist and mathematician Pierre Maupertius (1698–1756) as its president in 1746. Dozens of smaller national academies and regional associations, such as the Lunar Society of Birmingham and the Academy of Dijon (which awarded Rousseau the prize for his famous essay in 1750), also sprang up throughout Europe and played a vital part in fostering the spirit of intellectual inquiry that so characterised the century.

According to Voltaire and d'Alembert it was Bacon and Newton who, above all, had sparked the tremendous growth of enthusiasm for experiment in the investigations of nature by amateur and professional natural philosophers alike. So, for example, following Newton's revolutionary findings on attraction, electricity became an important and popular subject of research. In England, the amateur experimenter Stephen Gray (1666–1736) demonstrated the attractive power of electricity by using silk cords to suspend a boy from a ceiling and charging him with static electricity so that his body would draw up objects from below. This was among the experiments that Benjamin Franklin witnessed (see p. 367) at the demonstration given by Dr Archibald Spencer at Boston in 1743, and it would become part of the standard repertoire of displays of scientific wonders performed at private and public entertainments. Thus, having amused the French royal court by electrifying dozens of gendarmes, Franklin's rival, the physicist Abbé Nollet (1700–70) would later send an electric charge along a line of two hundred Carthusian monks. Less spectacular, but perhaps no less dramatic for an audience at close quarters, were the parlour demonstrations of popular science, such as the experiment on a bird in an air-pump, portrayed in a painting by Joseph Wright (see p. 295). In Philadelphia, Franklin and his friends performed their own extraordinary experiments, famously attracting lightning strikes by connecting a wire to a kite. Such experiments, whether conducted in the open air or in laboratories, were sometimes lethal and often dangerous, as experimenters found in 1746, when they accidentally discovered the Leyden jar, a device that could store large quantities of static electricity. The curiosity and credulity of many of these scientists and their projects may now appear ridiculous, and their great rash of speculative thinking and experimentation was sometimes savagely satirised by contemporaries. Thus, in *Gulliver's Travels* (1727) Jonathan Swift, the dean of St Patrick's Cathedral, Dublin, ridiculed the Royal Society and its famous journal *Philosophical Transactions* by portraying the mad scientists of the Academy of Lagado inflating a dog with a pair of bellows and trying to extract sunbeams out of cucumbers. Yet, however strange such investigations must often have appeared, some would yield important and useful findings, as did the experiments on plant and animal physiology conducted by the English cleric Stephen Hales and Franklin's invention of lightning rods.

Newton (who became President of the Royal Society in 1703) became an icon of the Enlightenment, and hence much eighteenth-century science and research was influenced by what were believed to be his methods. Many scholars aimed to complete what they regarded as his project – the identification of the 'natural laws' which evidently governed the physical world, and that could be used to predict future events – by extending his methods of research to all branches of human enquiry. In England, Newton's achievements were celebrated and popularised by followers such as J.T. Desaguliers, who not only conducted numerous public lectures and demonstrations but published texts such as *The Newtonian System of the World: the Best Model of Government* (1728), a poem which purportedly revealed the political principles and policies that corresponded with Newton's physics. In France, Voltaire simplified and popularised Newton's ideas, as did his colleague, the physicist and philosopher Gabrielle Émilie, Marquise du Châtelet, who published a French translation of the *Principia* in the 1750s. Similarly, in Italy the writer and fleeting lover of Lady Mary Wortley Montagu, Francesco Algarotti, produced the very popular *Il Neutonianismo per le Dame* (*Newtonianism for Ladies*) in 1733.

This widespread dissemination and discussion of Newton's work reflected not only its scientific importance but its extraordinary impact upon philosophy in general and the rise of what would later become the disciplines of the social sciences. Thus in mid-century, the Scottish historian and philosopher David Hume aimed to become the 'Newton of the moral sciences', and a group of reformers in France, known as the physiocrats, led by François Quesnay (1694–1774), were advising that economic policy should be radically revised in the light of scientific principles – derived, of course, from the immutable laws of nature. Although *physiocratie* ('rule of nature') in economic affairs was criticised by many figures, including Voltaire and Rousseau, and had a limited impact on state policy, in their search for economic theories and policies that were founded upon 'scientific' reasonings the physiocrats were not alone, as Adam Smith would show in *The Wealth of Nations* (1776). Thus, throughout the Enlightenment, to most *philosophes* it seemed that the keys to progress and improvement consisted, above all, in revising thought and practice so that they were in keeping with what were reckoned to be the laws of nature, as revealed and codified by scientific study. Even towards the close of the century, one of the greatest exponents of human advancement, the Marquis de Condorcet, was still convinced that 'All the errors in politics and in morals are founded upon philosophical mistakes, which, themselves, are connected with physical errors. There does not exist any religious system, or supernatural extravagance which is not founded on an ignorance of the laws of nature' (*Sketch of a Historical Picture of the Human Mind*, 1795).

At the beginning of the century, scientists such as Newton and Hales had envisaged scientific research as partly serving religious ends – demonstrating the design and purpose of the Creation. Thus, in an *Epitaph. Intended for Isaac Newton* (1730), Pope could proclaim that Newton's achievements had helped to reveal God's benevolence and omniscience:

Nature, and Nature's Laws lay hid in Night.
God said, *Let Newton be!* and All was Light.

Later in the century, the dissenting preacher, philosopher and scientist Joseph Priestley (1733–1804) could still maintain that 'A philosopher ought to be something greater and better than another man. The contemplation of the works of God should give a sublimity to his virtue, should expand his benevolence, extinguish everything mean, base and selfish in his nature, give a dignity to all his sentiments, and teach him to aspire to the moral perfections of the great author of all things' (*History of Electricity*, 1775). Yet, during the course of the century, for many scholars it became less necessary to think of nature and justify scientific enquiries in religious terms. Thus, in mid-century, Buffon offered a 'natural' history of the earth that he believed was based upon observation (notably of fossil evidence) rather than hypothetical systems and long-established religious doctrines. Ever gaining in momentum was the idea that useful knowledge was secular and concerned with the sensory world. As scientific knowledge grew, so scientific enquiry and experiment increasingly came to be regarded as the most useful means of acquiring knowledge of humans, society and the material world. In this respect, even the radical theology and politics of Priestley seemed to spring from Newton's method. In his *Disquisitions Relating to Matter and Spirit* (1777), Priestley professed 'an uniform and rigorous adherence ... to the universally received rules of philosophizing, such as are laid down by Sir Isaac Newton at the beginning of his Third Book of *Principia'*. This rise of a more secular approach to scientific studies did not, however, lead to a lack of serious and passionate disputes. On the contrary, throughout the century there were always many competing theories and philosophies of science (such as the mechanical, materialist and vitalist views of matter), many scientific controversies (such as those concerning the classification of nature), and many scientific practices (such as alchemy and mesmerism) that today would generally be regarded as quite 'unscientific'.

A celebration of the advancement of science and technology was one of the distinctive goals of the *Encyclopédie* (1751–72), edited by Diderot and d'Alembert (see p. 21). This hugely ambitious work, comprising twenty-eight folio volumes (seventeen of text and eleven of illustrations), provided an unrivalled collection of current knowledge in arts and crafts, science and technology, industry and agriculture. It was also the first encyclopaedia to recruit dozens of experts, each contributing articles in their chosen fields, thereby offering a forum for an astonishing range of new methods, findings and ideas. In particular, the *Encyclopédie* championed technological inventions which sought to lighten workloads and increase the volume and efficiency of production. In his essay on 'Invention', a major contributor Louis Jaucourt even proposed that 'If we scan history we will see that inventors were the first to be deified; the world adored them as visible gods.' Throughout the century, scientists such as Hales, Franklin and Darwin were always looking for ways to innovate as a means of promoting public welfare and improvement. Similarly, engineers such as James Watt (1736–1819), whose steam-engine design would help to put Britain at the forefront of what would become known as the Industrial Revolution, were at the heart of innovations in industrial technology. In his 'Preliminary Discourse' to the *Encyclopédie*, d'Alembert proudly proclaimed that nothing – except bigotry and superstition – now stood in the way of progress. Once the proper scientific methods were adopted and applied to all problems and enquiries, knowledge would flourish and a steady improvement of society would result. The work of Watt's friend and colleague, the materialist physician, inventor, scientist and poet Erasmus Darwin well illustrates this general confidence, and new-found belief in the power and right of science and invention to transform almost everything.

## VOLTAIRE

Voltaire (see p. 75) was greatly impressed by the achievements of English philosophy and science, especially the spirit of empiricism that he found in the works of Bacon, Newton and Locke. Although he was not a scientist, many of Voltaire's works were devoted to disseminating scientific knowledge to French readers, and in this respect he played a vital role in the popularisation of Newtonian science and its discoveries. His *Letters Concerning the English Nation* was first published in

London in 1733, but when it was revised to appear in France, clandestinely published at Rouen as *Lettres Philosophiques* in the following year, a warrant was issued for the author's arrest and the book was burned for being 'dangerous to religion and civil order'. The general tone of this work was critical of the *ancien régime*, for Voltaire partly used his review of Britain's arts and liberties to highlight what he regarded as the many shortcomings of French society. So, for example, in discussing the rise of empiricism, Voltaire turned this into an English tradition to contrast very favourably with what he presented as a French rationalist tradition as exemplified by Descartes. This was a view that would be echoed by d'Alembert in his 'Preliminary Discourse' (1751) to the *Encyclopédie* and that would become ingrained in many Enlightenment accounts of the history of science and philosophy.

The extracts here from *Letters Concerning the English Nation* are taken from Letters XII and XVI. Letter XII, 'On the Lord Bacon', champions Francis Bacon (1561–1621), to whom Voltaire attributed the rise of experimental science. It was Bacon's view, as reported by Voltaire and d'Alembert, that human progress would develop once the illusions of traditional theories and methods were shaken off. In Letter XVI, 'On Sir Isaac Newton's *Optics*', Voltaire reflects upon Newton's seminal *Optics* (1704), in which he rejected Descartes' theory and set out this own account of the properties of light, inspiring scientific investigations into light, heat and electricity throughout the century.

## Letters Concerning the English Nation (1733)

### 'On the Lord Bacon'

Not long since, the trite and frivolous question following was debated in a very polite and learned company, *viz.* who was the greatest man, Caesar, Alexander, Tamerlane, Cromwell, &c.

Somebody answered, that Sir Isaac Newton excelled them all. The gentleman's assertion was very just; for if true greatness consists in having received from Heaven a mighty genius, and in having employed it to enlighten our own minds and that of others; a man like Sir Isaac Newton, whose equal is hardly found in a thousand years, is the truly great man. And those politicians and conquerors (and all ages produce some) were generally so many illustrious wicked men. That man claims our respect, who commands over the minds of the rest of the world by the force of truth, not those who enslave their fellow creatures; he who is acquainted with the universe, not they who deface it.

Since therefore you desire me to give you an account of the famous personages which England has given birth to, I shall begin with Lord Bacon, Mr Locke, Sir Isaac Newton, &c. Afterwards the warriors and ministers of state shall come in their order.

I must begin with the celebrated Viscount Verulam, known in Europe by the name of Bacon, which was that of his family. [...]

He is the father of experimental philosophy. It must indeed be confessed, that very surprising secrets had been found out before his time. The sea-compass, printing, engraving on copper plates, oil-painting, looking-glasses; the art of restoring, in some measure, old men to their sight by spectacles; gun-powder, &c had been discovered. A new world had been sought for, found, and conquered. Would not one suppose that these sublime discoveries had been made by the greatest philosophers, and in ages much more enlightened than the present? But 'twas far otherwise; all these great changes happened in the most stupid and barbarous times. Chance only gave birth to most of those inventions; and 'tis very probable that what is called chance, contributed very much to the discovery of America; at least it has been always thought, that Christopher Columbus undertook his voyage, merely on the relation of a captain of a ship, which a storm had drove as far westward as the Caribee [Caribbean] islands. Be this as it will, men had sailed round the world, and could destroy cities by an artificial thunder more dreadful than the real one. But, then they were not acquainted with the circulation of the blood, the weight of the air, the laws of motion, light, the number of our planets, &c. And a man who maintained a thesis on Aristotle's *Categories*; on the universals *a parte rei* ['from the part of the matter', a term used in scholastic philosophy] or suchlike nonsense, was looked upon as a prodigy.

The most astonishing, the most useful inventions, are not those which reflect the greatest honour on the human mind. 'Tis to a mechanical instinct, which is found in many men, and not to true philosophy, that most arts owe their origin.

The discovery of fire, the art of making bread, of melting and preparing metals, of building houses, and the invention of the shuttle, are infinitely more beneficial to mankind than printing or the sea-compass. And yet these arts were invented by uncultivated, savage men.

What a prodigious use the Greeks and Romans made afterwards of mechanics! Nevertheless, they believed that there were crystal heavens; that the stars were small lamps which sometimes fell into the sea; and one of their greatest philosophers [Anaxagoras], after long researches found that the stars were so many flints which had been detached from the earth.

In a word, no one, before the Lord Bacon, was acquainted with experimental philosophy, nor with the several physical experiments which have been made since his time. Scarce one of them but is hinted at in his work, and he himself had made several. He made a kind of pneumatic engine, by which he guessed the elasticity of the air. He approached, on all sides as it were, to the discovery of its weight, and had very near attained it, but some time after [Evangelista] Torricelli [1608–47] seized upon this truth. In a little time experimental philosophy began to be cultivated on a sudden in most parts of Europe. 'Twas a hidden treasure which the Lord Bacon had some notion of, and which all the philosophers, encouraged by his promises, endeavoured to dig up.

But that which surprized me most was to read in his work, in express terms, the new attractions, the invention of which is ascribed to Sir Isaac Newton.

We must search, says Lord Bacon, whether there may not be a kind of magnetic power, which operates between the earth and heavy bodies, between the moon and the ocean, between the planets, &c. In another place he says, either heavy bodies must be carried toward the centre of the earth, or must be reciprocally attracted by it; and in the latter case 'tis evident, that the nearer bodies, in their falling, draw towards the earth, the stronger they will attract one another. We must, says he, make an experiment to see whether the same clock will go faster on the top of a mountain or at the bottom of a mine. Whether the strength of the weights decreases on the mountain, and increases in the mine. 'Tis probable that the earth has a true attractive power.

This forerunner in philosophy was also an elegant writer, an historian and a wit.

(*Letters Concerning the English Nation*, Letter XII)

## 'On Sir Isaac Newton's *Optics*'

The philosophers of the last age found out a new universe; and a circumstance which made its discovery more difficult, was, that no one had so much as suspected its existence. The most sage and judicious were of opinion, that 'twas a frantic rashness to dare so much as to imagine that it was possible to guess the laws by which the celestial bodies move, and the manner how light acts. Galileo [1564–1642] by his astronomical discoveries, Kepler by his calculation [*Tabulae Rudolphinae*, 1627], Descartes (at least in his *Dioptrics*) [1637] and Sir Isaac Newton in all his works, severally saw the mechanism of the springs of the world. The geometricians have subjected infinity to the laws of calculation. The circulation of the blood in animals, and of the sap in vegetables, have changed the face of nature with regard to us. A new kind of existence has been given to bodies in the air-pump. By the assistance of telescopes, bodies have been brought nearer to one another. Finally, the several discoveries which Sir Isaac Newton has made on light, are equal to the boldest things which the curiosity of man could expect, after so many philosophical novelties.

Till [Marco] Antonio de Dominis [1560–1626], the rainbow was considered as an inexplicable miracle. This philosopher guessed that it was a necessary effect of the sun and rain. Descartes gained immortal fame, by his mathematical explication of this so natural a phenomenon. He calculated the reflexions and refractions of light in drops of rain; and his sagacity on this occasion was at that time looked upon as next to divine.

But what would he have said had it been proved to him that he was mistaken in the nature of light; that he had not the least reason to maintain that 'tis a globular body: that 'tis false to assert, that this matter spreading itself through the whole, waits only to be projected forward by the sun, in order to be put in action, in like manner as a long staff acts at one end when pushed forward by the other? That light is certainly darted by the sun; in fine [finally], that light is transmitted from the sun to the earth in about seven minutes, though a cannon ball, which were not to lose any of its velocity, could not go that distance in less than twenty-five years? How great would have been his astonishment, had he been told, that light does not reflect directly by impinging against the solid parts of bodies; that bodies are not transparent when they have large pores; and that a man should arise, who would demonstrate all these paradoxes, and anatomize a single ray of light with more dexterity than the ablest artist dissects a human body. This man is come. Sir Isaac Newton has demonstrated to the eye, by the bare assistance of the prism, that light is a composition of coloured rays, which, being united, form the white colour. A single ray is by him divided into seven, which all fall upon a piece of linen, or a sheet of white paper, in their order one above the other, and at unequal distances. The first is red, the second orange, the third yellow, the fourth green, the fifth blue, the sixth indigo, the seventh a violet purple. Each of these rays transmitted afterwards by an hundred other prisms, will never change the colour it bears; in like manner as gold, when completely purged from its dross, will never change afterwards in the crucible. As a superabundant proof that each of these elementary rays has inherently in itself that which forms its colour to the eye, take a small piece of yellow wood for instance, and set it in the ray of a red colour, this wood will instantly be tinged red; but set it in the ray of a green colour, it assumes a green colour, and so of all the rest.

From what cause therefore do colours arise in nature? 'Tis nothing but the disposition of bodies to reflect the rays of a certain order, and to absorb all the rest.

What then is the secret disposition? Sir Isaac Newton demonstrates, that 'tis nothing more than the density of the small constituent particles of which a body is composed. And how is this reflexion performed? 'Twas supposed to arise from the rebounding of the rays, in the same manner as a ball on the surface of a solid body; but this is a mistake, for Sir Isaac taught the astonished philosophers, that bodies are opaque for no other reason, but because their pores are very large; that light reflects on our eyes from the very bosom of those pores; that the smaller the pores of a body are, the more such a body is transparent. Thus paper which reflects the light when dry, transmits it when oiled, because the oil, by filling its pores, makes them much smaller.

'Tis there that examining the vast porosity of bodies, every particle having its pores, and every particle of those particles having its own; he shows we are not certain that there is a cubic inch of solid matter in the universe, so far are we from conceiving what matter is. Having thus divided, as it were, light into its elements, and carried the sagacity of his discoveries so far, as to prove the method of distinguishing compound colours from such as are primitive; he shows, that these elementary rays separated by the prism, are ranged in their order for no other reason but because they are refracted in that very order; and 'tis this property (unknown till he discovered it) of breaking or splitting in this proportion; 'tis this unequal refraction of rays, this power of refracting the red less than the orange colour, &c. which he calls the different refrangibility. The most reflexible rays are the most refrangible, and from hence he evinces that the same power is the cause both of the reflection and refraction of light.

But all these wonders are merely but the opening of his discoveries. He found out the secret to see the vibrations or fits of light, which come and go incessantly, and which either transmit light or reflect it according to the density of the parts they meet with. He has presumed to calculate the density of the particles of air necessary between two glasses, the one flat, the other convex on one side, set one upon the other; in order to operate such a transmission or reflexion, or to form such and such a colour.

From all these combinations he discovers the proportion in which light acts on bodies, and bodies act on light.

He saw light so perfectly, that he has determined to what degree of perfection the art of increasing it, and of assisting our eyes by telescopes can be carried.

Descartes, from a noble confidence, that was very excusable considering how strongly he was fired at the first discoveries he made in an art which he almost first found out; Descartes, I say, hoped to discover in the stars, by the assistance of telescopes, objects as small as those we discern upon the earth.

But Sir Isaac has shown, that dioptric telescopes cannot be brought to a greater perfection; because of that refraction, and of that very refrangibility, which at the same time that they bring objects nearer to us, scatter too much the elementary rays. He has calculated in these glasses the proportion of the scattering of the red and of the blue rays; and proceeding so far as to demonstrate things which were not supposed even to exist, he examines the inequalities which arise from the shape or figure of the glass, and that which arises from the refrangibility. He finds, that the object glass of the telescope being convex on one side and flat on the other, in case the flat side be turned towards the object, the error which arises from the construction and position of the glass, is above five thousand times less than the error which arises from the refrangibility. And therefore, that the shape or figure of the glasses is not the cause why telescopes cannot be carried to a greater perfection, but arises wholly from the nature of light.

For this reason he invented a telescope, which discovers objects by reflection and not by refraction. Telescopes of this new kind are very hard to make, and their use is not easy. But according to the English, a reflective telescope of but five feet has the same effect as another of an hundred feet in length.

(*Letters Concerning the English Nation*, Letter XVI)

## COMTE DE BUFFON

When Buffon (see p. 107) published the first volume of his *Histoire Naturelle* in 1749, after an initial discourse on 'How to Study Natural History' he turned to a major essay on 'The History and Theory of the Earth'. This was a subject that, throughout the century, scientists and theologians would explore with great enthusiasm. Scholars such as René Descartes (1596–1650), Thomas Burnet (*c.*1635–1715), William Whiston (1667–1752) and John Woodward (1665–1728), all believed that scientific investigation of the earth would provide the evidence to substantiate Christian claims, and they had formed 'systems' and 'hypotheses' to prove their propositions. For Buffon, however, knowledge of the earth was fundamentally about understanding the life and natural history of the animals and plants that lived on its surface and in its seas. Unlike the *a priori* methods employed by theologians in their attempts to support accounts of the earth derived from the Bible, Buffon wanted to provide a 'natural' (rather than a 'sacred') history of the earth that could exclude the Flood. However, he believed it to be 'an incontrovertible fact' that 'the dry land which we now inhabit, and even the summits of the highest mountains, were formerly covered with the waters of the seas'. No less important was Buffon's claim that fossil evidence indicated that the world and life itself were far older than the Church had recognised. He calculated that the earth was about eighty thousand years old, rather than the traditional (Christian) estimate of six thousand years; though his unpublished manuscripts show that he actually estimated the earth to be as much as three million years old. Even so, his claims led to his work being condemned by the Faculty of Theology at the Sorbonne. He went on to claim in his *Époques de la Nature* (*Epochs of Nature*, 1778) that planetary temperature is the all-important condition of life, and that it took thousands of years for the earth to cool sufficiently for water to condense on its surface and life to begin. He deduced that the negro, more able than the white man to withstand the heat, must have inhabited the earth first.

Buffon's work contains many ideas that would later influence the work of scientists such as Charles Darwin and the development of the theory of the evolution of species. In the following extract, based upon the 1781 English translation of the *History and Theory of the Earth*, from *Histoire Naturelle*, Buffon begins with criticism of some of the 'fanciful systems' of three recent scholars.

## History and Theory of the Earth (1749)

In subjects of an extensive kind, the relations of which it is difficult to trace, where some facts are but partially known, and others obscure, it is more easy to form a fanciful system, than to establish a rational theory. Thus the theory of the earth has never hitherto been treated but in a vague and hypothetical manner. I shall, therefore, exhibit a cursory view only of the notions of some authors who have written upon this subject.

The first hypothesis [by William Whiston] I shall mention is more conspicuous for its ingenuity than solidity. It is the production of an English astronomer, who was an enthusiastic admirer of Sir Isaac Newton's system of philosophy. Convinced that every possible event depends upon the motions and direction of the stars, he endeavours to prove, by means of mathematical calculations, that all the changes this earth has undergone have been produced by the tail of a comet.

For another hypothesis we are indebted to a heterodox divine [Thomas Burnet], whose brain was so fully impregnated with poetical illusions, that he imagined he had seen the universe created. After telling us the state of the earth when it first sprung from nothing, what changes have been introduced by the deluge [the Flood], what the earth has been, and what it now is, he assumes the prophetic style, and predicts what will be its condition after the destruction of the human kind.

A third writer [John Woodward], a man of more extensive observation than the two former, but equally crude and confused in his ideas, explains the principal appearances of the globe by the aid of an immense abyss in the bowels of the earth, which, in his estimation, is nothing but a thin crust enclosing this vast ocean of fluid matter.

These hypotheses are all constructed on tottering foundations. The ideas they contain are indistinct, the facts are confounded, and the whole is a motley jumble of physics and fable. They, accordingly, have never been adopted but by men who embrace opinions without examination, and who, incapable of distinguishing the degrees of probability, are more deeply impressed with marvellous chimeras than with the genuine force of truth.

My ideas on this subject will be less extraordinary, and may even appear unimportant, when compared with the grand systems of such hypothetical writers. But it should not be forgotten, that it is the business of an historian to describe, not to invent; that no gratuitous suppositions are to be admitted in subjects which depend upon fact and observation; and that, in historical compositions, the imagination cannot be employed, except for the purpose of combining observations, of rendering facts more general, and of forming a connected whole, which presents to the mind clear ideas and probable conjectures: I say, probable; for it is impossible to give demonstrative evidence on this subject. Demonstration is confined to the mathematical sciences. Our knowledge in physics and natural history depends entirely on experience, and is limited to the method of reasoning by induction.

With regard to the history of the earth, therefore, we shall begin with such facts as have been universally acknowledged in all ages, not omitting those additional truths which have fallen within our own observation.

The surface of this immense globe exhibits to our observation heights, depths, plains, seas, marshes, rivers, caverns, gulfs, volcanoes; and, on a cursory view, we can discover, in the disposition of these objects, neither order nor regularity. If we penetrate into the bowels of the earth, we find metals, minerals, stones, bitumens, sands, earths, waters, and matter of every kind, seemingly placed by mere accident, and without any apparent design. Upon a nearer and more attentive inspection, we discover sunk mountains, caverns filled up, shattered rocks, whole countries swallowed up, new islands emerged from the ocean, heavy substances placed above light ones, hard bodies inclosed within soft bodies; in a word, we find matter in every form, dry and humid, warm and cold, solid and brittle, blended in a chaos of confusion, which can be compared to nothing but a heap of rubbish, or the ruins of a world.

These ruins, however, we inhabit with perfect security. The different generations of men, of animals, and of plants, succeed one another without interruption: the productions of the earth are sufficient for their sustenance; the motions of the sea, and the currents of the air, are regulated by fixed laws; the returns of the seasons are uniform, and the rigours of winter invariably give place to the verdure of the spring. With regard to us, everything has the appearance of order: the earth, formerly a chaos, is now a tranquil, an harmonious, a delightful habitation, where all is animated and governed by such amazing displays of power and intelligence, as fill us with admiration, and elevate our minds to the contemplation of the great Creator. But let us not decide precipitantly concerning the irregularities on the surface of the earth, and the apparent disorder in its bowels: we shall soon perceive the utility, and even the necessity of this arrangement. With a little attention, we shall perhaps discover an order of which we had no conception, and general relations that cannot be apprehended by a slight examination. Our knowledge, indeed, with regard to this subject, must always be limited. We are entirely unacquainted with many parts of the surface of this globe, and have partial ideas only concerning the bottom of the ocean, which, in many places, has never been sounded. We can only penetrate the rind of the earth. The greatest caverns, the deepest mines, descend not above the eight thousandth part of its diameter. Our judgement is therefore confined to the upper stratum, or mere superficial part. We know, indeed, that, bulk for bulk, the earth is four times heavier than the sun: we likewise know the proportion its weight bears to that of the other planets. But still this estimation is only relative. We have no standard. Of the real weight of the materials we are so ignorant, that the internal part of the globe may be either a void space, or it may be composed of matter a thousand times heavier than gold. Neither is there any method of making farther discoveries on this subject. It is even with difficulty that rational conjectures can be formed.

We must therefore confine ourselves to an accurate examination and description of the surface of the earth, and of such inconsiderable depths as we have been able to penetrate. The first object which attracts attention, is that immense collection of waters with which the greatest part of the globe is covered. These waters occupy the lowest grounds; their surface is always level; and, notwithstanding their uniform tendency to equilibrium and rest, they are kept in perpetual agitation by a powerful agent, which counteracts their natural tranquillity, which communicates to them a regular periodic motion, alternately elevating and depressing their waves, and which produces a concussion or vibration in the whole mass, even to the most profound depths. This motion of the waters is coeval with time, and will endure as long as the sun and moon, by which it is produced.

In examining the bottom of the sea, we perceive it to be equally irregular as the surface of the dry land. We discover hills and valleys, plains and hollows, rocks and earths of every kind. We discover, likewise, that islands are nothing but the summits of vast mountains, whose foundations are buried in the ocean; we find other mountains whose tops are nearly on a level with the surface of the water; and rapid currents which run contrary to the general movement. These currents sometimes run in the same direction; at other times their motion is retrograde; but they never exceed their natural limits, which seem to be as immutable as those which bound the efforts of land-rivers. On one hand, we meet with tempestuous regions, where the winds blow with irresistible fury, where the heavens and the ocean, equally convulsed, are mixed and confounded in the general shock; violent intestine motions, tumultuous swellings, water spouts, and strange agitation produced by volcanoes, whose mouths, though many fathoms below the surface, vomit forth torrents of fire, and push, even to the clouds, a thick vapour, composed of water, sulphur, and bitumen; and dreadful gulfs or whirlpools which seem to attract vessels for no other purpose than to swallow them up. On the other hand, we discover vast regions of an opposite nature, always smooth and calm, but equally dangerous to the mariner. Here the winds never exert their force; the nautical art is of no utility; the becalmed voyagers must remain immoveably fixed, till death relieve them from misery. To conclude, directing our eyes toward the southern or northern extremities of the globe, we discover huge masses of ice, which, detaching themselves from the polar regions, advance, like floating mountains, to the more temperate climates, where they dissolve and vanish from our view.

Beside these grand objects, the ocean presents us with myriads of animated beings, almost infinite in variety: some, clothed in light scales, swim with amazing swiftness; others, loaded with thick shells, trail heavily along, leaving their traces in the sand: to others, Nature has given fins resembling wings, with which they support themselves in the air, and fly before their enemies to considerable distances. Lastly, the sea gives birth to other animals, which, totally deprived of motion, live and die immovably fixed to the same rocks: all, however, find abundance of food in this fluid element. The bottom of the ocean, and the shelving sides of rocks, produce plentiful crops of plants of many different species; its soil is composed of sand, gravel, rocks, and shells; in some places, it is a fine clay, in others, a compact earth; and, in general, the bottom of the sea has an exact resemblance to the dry land which we inhabit.

(*Natural History*, vol. I, 'History and Theory of the Earth')

## LOUIS JAUCOURT

Chevalier de Jaucourt (1704–80) was born in Paris into an old aristocratic but Protestant family. He was sent to Geneva for his education, and after studying at the University of Geneva he went on to study under the Dutch physician Boerhaave at the University of Leiden (matriculating in 1728), though he never practised. In 1736 he left Holland to return to France, having produced an edition of Leibniz's *Essays on Theodicy*, published at Amsterdam in 1734. It was as one of the leading contributors to the *Encyclopédie*, however, that he rose to modest fame, and it has been estimated that he composed twenty-eight per cent of all articles in the seventeen text volumes of that work (see p. 21). These essays were on a wide range of subjects, including philosophy, politics and war. When Jean d'Alembert withdrew from co-editing the *Encyclopédie* in 1758, Jaucourt became the general manager of the work under Denis Diderot's guidance. Despite his great contribution to this work, Jaucourt is seldom mentioned in most standard histories of the Enlightenment.

The following extract from the *Encyclopédie* is an entry entitled 'Invention', and it discusses a subject which the *philosophes* believed could play a crucial role in contributing to the progress and happiness of humankind. The full impact of many eighteenth-century inventions such as John Harrison's marine chronometer for determining longitude, Thomas Newcomen's steam engine (which was greatly improved by James Watt and put to commercial use in England in the 1770s), and Richard Arkwright's water-frame for spinning cotton (used throughout the spinning-mills of northern Britain, and central to the rise of the factory system) could not have been envisaged by Jaucourt in mid-century. However, the value of earlier discoveries, such as the invention of printing – upon which the Enlightenment depended both for scholarly and mass communication – filled him with enthusiasm.

## 'Invention'

from the *Encyclopédie* (1765)

A general term which can be applied to everything that is found, invented, or discovered, and which is of use or interest in the arts, sciences, and crafts. To some extent this term is synonymous with 'discovery,' though less striking; I should like to be permitted here to use them interchangeably, without repeating the interesting things the reader should already have read under the word 'Discovery.'

We owe inventions to time, pure chance, to lucky and unforeseen speculations, mechanical instincts, as well as to the patience and resourcefulness of those who work. The useful inventions of the thirteenth and fourteenth centuries did not at all result from the researches of those who are known as wits in polite society, nor did they come from speculative philosophers. They were the fruit of that mechanical instinct with which nature has endowed some men, independently from philosophy. The invention of spectacles, known as *besicles,* to assist the weakened sight of old men dates from the end of the thirteenth century. It is said that we owe it to Alexandro [della] Spina [died 1313]. In that same century the Venetians already possessed the secret of making crystal mirrors; Faience earthenware which was used in Europe instead of porcelain, was discovered in Faenza; windmills date from approximately the same period. The making of paper from pounded and boiled cloth was invented in the early fourteenth century.

Cortusius speaks of a certain Pax who established the first paper-making factory in Padua a century before the invention of printing. This is how early discoveries happily produce their first fruit, and often thanks to men who remain unknown.

I say the first fruit, for it has to be observed that the most interesting and useful things that we possess today in the arts were not found in the state in which we see them now. Everything was discovered in rough form or in parts and has been gradually brought to greater perfection. At least this seems to be the case for those inventions of which we have spoken, and it can be proven for the invention of glass, the compass, printing, clocks, mills, telescopes, and many others.

I shall not mention the discoveries in the sciences that could have been prepared by the labours of preceding centuries; this would be a subject for too extensive a research. Nor shall I speak of discoveries that are supposedly modern, yet are merely old theories, put forward once again, and more clearly. In any case, such discussions would prove very little. In order to remain within the framework of the arts, I shall be satisfied to observe that a shorter or longer time lapse was needed to perfect the inventions which originally, in uncivilized centuries, were the products of chance or mechanical genius.

Guttenburg only invented movable characters, carved in relief on wood and on metal. It was [Peter] Schoffer [1425–1502] who improved this invention and found the secret of casting these characters. How much this art has been perfected since Schoffer is well known.

The invention of the compass in the twelfth century is of the same order as the invention of printing, whether its use was first discovered by the mariner Goya, a native of Malfi, or by the English, or the French, or the Portuguese. In the beginning men knew only how to place the magnetized needle on a piece of cork floating on water; later this needle was suspended on a pivot inside a box that in its turn was suspended. Finally it was fixed onto a mariner's card or a piece of talc upon which had been traced a circle divided into thirty-two equal parts to mark the thirty-two wind directions, together with another concentric circle divided into 360 degrees, which measured the angles and separations of the compass.

The invention of windmills (perhaps originating in Asia) only became successful when geometry perfected the machine, which is based entirely upon the theory of compound movement.

How many centuries have elapsed between the moment when Cresieius made the first watch run by a movement, probably around 613 in Rome, and the most recent pendulum clock made in England by [George] Graham [1673–1751] or in France by Julien Le Roy [1686–1759]. Did not [Christiaan] Huygens [1629–95] or Leibniz [1646–1716] and many others contribute to their perfection?

I could say almost as much about the development of the small telescope, from [Jacobius] Metius [1580–1628] to the Benedictine Dom Noel. Can there be any doubt about the difference between the rough cut of the [Sancy] diamond discovered by chance three centuries ago by Louis de Berquen, and the beautiful brilliant or rose cut our gem cutters are able to execute today? Usage and practice have taught them all kinds of ways of cutting stones, and their eyes and their hands are the guides. It is the forty-seventh proposition of the first book [of *Elements of Geometry*] of Euclid [lived *c.*300 BC] which has made possible the achievement of such beautiful proportions when cutting these precious stones into lozenges, triangles, facets, and bevels, which give them their brilliance and glittering effect. Thus those men who were fortunate enough to be born at the right time, had a perfect knowledge of mechanics and have taken advantage of the sketchy simplicity of early inventions; and slowly, thanks to their shrewdness, they brought them to the degree of perfection where we see them today.

Inventions are the children of time, but, if I may say so, industriousness can speed the delivery. How many centuries did men walk on silk without knowing how to make use of it, how to adorn themselves with it. No doubt nature has in her storehouse treasures which are as precious and which she keeps for the moment when we least expect them; let us always be prepared to take advantage of them.

Often an invention illuminates a preceding one and throws a few flickers of light on one that is to follow. I am not saying that any invention is always productive in itself. Great rivers do not always rise in the waters of other great rivers. But inventions which seem to be without any general relationship still cross-fertilize each other; they re-appear in a thousand ways that shorten and assist men's labours, and there is nothing more gratifying than the invention or perfection of arts that aim at the happiness of mankind. Such inventions have the advantage over political enterprises in that they bring about the public good without harming anyone. The most spectacular conquests are bathed only in sweat, tears, and blood. He who discovers some secret useful to life, such as, for example, the dissolution of stones in the bladder, would not have to fear the remorse that is inseparable from glory where crime and unhappiness are mingled. The invention of the compass and the printing press opened wider horizons and beautified and enlightened the world. If we scan history we will see that inventors were the first to be deified; the world adored them as visible gods.

After this we need not be astonished that inventors are sensitive to the honour of being discoverers. It is the last thing of which a man would want to divest himself. After Thales [of Miletus, c.575–532 BC] discovered the relationship between the sun's diameter and the circle this star describes around the earth, he communicated this discovery to someone who offered him anything he would desire for it. Thales asked only to be allowed to keep the honour of the discovery. This wise man of Greece, poor and old, was left untouched by the thought of money or profit or any kind of advantage, but he feared the injustice that might deprive him of his deserved glory.

Moreover, all those who, thanks to their astuteness, their labours, their talents, and their diligence, will be able to combine research and observation, profound theory and experimentation, will continually enrich existing inventions and discoveries and will have the glory of paving the way for new ones.

If I may repeat here the words which the editors of this work wrote in the Introduction to volume III:

> The *Encyclopédie* will write the history of our century's wealth in this subject; it will do so for our own century, which is ignorant of this history, and for the centuries to come, which thus will be able to go further. Discoveries in the arts will no longer run the danger of being forgotten; facts will become known to the philosophers, and reflection will be able to simplify and enlighten blind practice.

For the success of this enterprise, however, it is necessary that an enlightened government be willing to grant it a powerful and constant protection against injustice, persecution, and the calumny of enemies.

('Invention', *Encyclopédie*, vol. VIII, 1765)

## Engravings of Technology, from the *Encyclopédie*

In addition to its comprehensive examination of the arts and sciences, the *Encyclopédie* (see p. 21) included detailed entries and illustrations on the work and skills of tradespeople and master craftsmen. Contrary to the traditional downgrading of the 'mechanical' arts, the *Encyclopédie* attempted to raise their status by emphasising their usefulness in maintaining human welfare and supporting economic progress. The editor, Denis Diderot, himself the son of a master cutler, interviewed master craftsmen regarding their trades, tools and methods of production. Meticulous drawings were made for the *Encyclopédie*'s 2,500 engravings, contained in eleven volumes of plates, including illustrations of what were considered to be contemporary best practices. Diderot exclaimed, 'How strangely we judge! We demand that people should be usefully engaged, and we disdain useful men!'

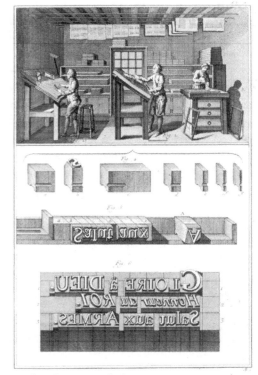

*Imprimerie en Lettres, L'Opération de la Casse*

*Figure 5.1* 'Printing Press'

*Source*: *Encyclopédie* vol. VII, plate I.

*Note*: Printing presses were essential tools for the communication and dissemination of ideas and knowledge in the eighteenth century, so it is no surprise that the editors of the *Encyclopédie* took a special interest in surveying all aspects of printing and book production. The Enlightenment both depended upon and promoted the growth of a print culture, disseminating ideas largely through the media of newspapers, pamphlets, journals, novels, scholarly books and engravings. Moreover, the long and complex history of the production of the *Encyclopédie* itself was testimony to the difficulty and importance of maintaining scholarly publication. It was prohibited in 1752, and again in 1759 when it was also placed upon the Catholic Index of forbidden books. Despite its importance, however, the technological development of printing was slow in the eighteenth century. The traditional, usually family-run, handpress remained dominant, though many printing-houses became larger in the course of the century.

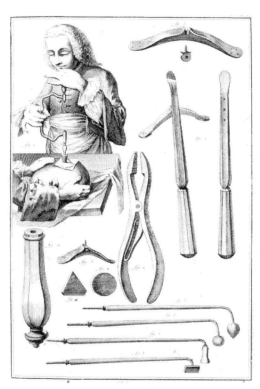

*Figure 5.2* 'Drilling Head'

*Source*: *Encyclopédie* vol. XII, plate XVII.

*Note*: Apart from a vast array of 'quacks', in the eighteenth century the medical 'profession' consisted of three groups: physicians (university-educated practitioners who diagnosed and prescribed for patients); surgeons (usually trained through apprenticeships, who performed most surgery, from extracting teeth to amputating limbs); and apothecaries (trained by apprenticeship, who kept shops and dispensed the physicians' prescriptions). Surgeons and apothecaries were regarded as craftsmen and tradesmen, and were therefore not generally held in high esteem. In presenting the methods and instruments employed in surgery, the *Encyclopédie* helped to raise the prestige of the practice, and prompted further scientific investigation into surgical methods.

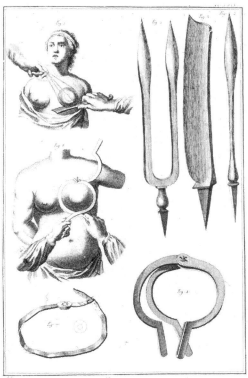

*Figure 5.3* 'Mastectomy'

*Source*: *Encyclopédie* vol. XII, plate XXIX.

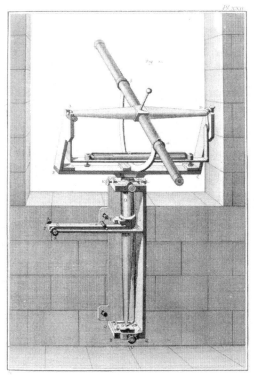

*Figure 5.4* 'Instruments of Astronomy'

*Source*: *Encyclopédie* vol. V, plate XXII.

*Note*: Most Enlightenment scholars regarded Newton's explanation of the motion of the planets as an outstanding achievement, and astronomy came to symbolise the great value of his scientific method. With the benefit of more refined equipment, eighteenth-century astronomers observed the positions, motions and the distances of the stars with greater accuracy. The popularity of astronomy was reflected in the discovery of Uranus in 1781 by the German-born musician and amateur astronomer William Herschel.

*Astronomie, Instrumens* *Instrument des Paisages en Perspective*

## ERASMUS DARWIN

Erasmus Darwin (1731–1802) was born near Nottingham, the son of a lawyer. After studying at Cambridge and Edinburgh universities, in 1756 he set up a medical practice at Lichfield, where he lived for the next twenty-five years. He fathered fourteen children in the course of his two marriages and, in addition to his renown as a fine and kind physician, he became an acclaimed poet, major scientist and prolific inventor, as well as a founder-member of one of the Enlightenment's most productive associations, the Lunar Society of Birmingham. He was also a founder of the Lichfield Botanical Society, which published his translation of Linnaeus' *Genera Plantarum* (*The Families of Plants*) in 1787. He was made a fellow of the Royal Society in 1761, and met Rousseau in England in 1766. A tireless and very sociable figure, Darwin's friendships with men such as Matthew Boulton, Josiah Wedgwood, James Watt and Joseph Priestley led to many collaborative enterprises. After his second marriage, in 1781, he moved to Derby where he founded a philosophical society (1783) and wrote his most important works. Joseph Wright painted naturalistic portraits of him in 1770 and 1793.

As a polymath, deist and materialist who believed in human progress; a supporter of liberal causes such as female education, the abolition of the slave trade, and the French Revolution; and a lifelong opponent of cruelty, war and despotism, Darwin has often been portrayed as the embodiment of late eighteenth-century

Enlightenment values. Though upset by Darwin's anti-Christian views, Samuel Coleridge visited him in 1796, and wrote: 'Derby is full of curiosities, the cotton, the silk mills, Wright, the painter, and Dr. Darwin, the everything, except the Christian! Dr. Darwin possesses, perhaps, a greater range of knowledge than any other man in Europe, and is the most inventive of philosophical men.'

Darwin's most important writings are the long poem *The Botanic Garden* (1789–91), a vast compendium of the age's scientific knowledge; *Zoonomia; or The Laws of Organic Life* (1794–96); *Phytologia* (1800), on plant life; and the epic poem *The Temple of Nature* (1803), tracing the origins and evolution of life from microscopic specks 'beneath the waves', 'perhaps millions of ages before the commencement of the history of mankind'. Darwin's ideas about evolution (foreshadowing the work of his grandson, Charles Darwin) were raised in his great treatise on the theory and practice of medicine, *Zoonomia*, volume II of which provided a catalogue of diseases and their possible cures. In the following extract from volume I (1794), Darwin draws upon his scientific knowledge, medical experience and artistic interests in an extraordinarily wide-ranging discussion of instinct. The analysis is based upon meticulous research, reasoning and reflection. Darwin numbers each part of his text and, as in modern scholarly practice, he cites the sources of his knowledge, abbreviated in parentheses, as he proceeds.

## *Zoonomia* (1794–96)

### *'Instinct'*

I. All those internal motions of animal bodies, which contribute to digest their aliment, produce their secretions, repair their injuries, or increase their growth, are performed without our attention or consciousness. They exist as well in our sleep, as in our waking hours, as well as in the foetus during the time of gestation, as in the infant after nativity, and proceed with equal regularity in the vegetable as in the animal system. These motions have been shown in a former part of this work to depend on the irritations of peculiar fluids, and as they have never been classed amongst the instinctive actions of animals, are precluded from our present disquisition.

But all those actions of men or animals, that are attended with consciousness, and seem neither to have been directed by their appetites, taught by their experience, nor deduced from observation or tradition, have been referred to the power of instinct. And this power has been explained to be a *divine something*, a kind of inspiration; whilst the poor animal, that possesses it, has been thought little better than *a machine*.

The *irksomeness* that attends a continued attitude of the body, or the *pains* that we receive from heat, cold, hunger or other injurious circumstances, excite us to *general locomotion*: and our senses are so formed and constituted by the hand of nature, that certain objects present us with pleasure, others with pain, and we are induced to approach and embrace these, to avoid and abhor those, as such sensations direct us.

Thus the palates of some animals are gratefully affected by the mastication of fruits, others of grains, and others of flesh; and they are thence instigated to attain, and to consume those materials; and are furnished with powers of muscular motion, and of digestion proper for such purposes.

These *sensations* and *desires* constitute a part of our system, as our *muscles* and *bones* constitute another part: and hence they may alike be termed *natural* or *connate*; but neither of them can properly be termed *instinctive*: as the word instinct in its usual acceptation refers only to the *actions* of animals, as above explained. The origin of these *actions* is the subject of our present enquiry.

The reader is intreated carefully to attend to this definition of *instinctive actions*, lest by using the word instinct without adjoining any accurate idea to it, he may not only include the natural desires of love and hunger, and the natural sensations of pain or pleasure, but the figure and contexture of the body, and the faculty of reason itself under this general term.

II. We experience some sensations, and perform some actions before our nativity; the sensations of cold and warmth, agitation and rest, fullness and inanition, are instances of the former; and the repeated struggles of the limbs of the foetus, which begin about the middle of gestation, and those motions by which it frequently wraps the umbilical chord around its neck or body, and even sometimes ties it in a knot; are instances of the latter (Smellie's *Midwifery*, vol. 1, p. 182).

By a due attention to these circumstances many of the actions of young animals, which at first sight seemed only referable to an inexplicable instinct, will appear to have been acquired like all other animal actions that are attended with consciousness, *by the repeated efforts of our muscles under the conduct of our sensations or desires*.

The chick in the shell begins to move its feet and legs on the sixth day of incubation (Mattreican, p. 138); or on the seventh day (Langley); afterwards they are seen to move themselves gently in the liquid that surrounds them, and to open and shut their mouths (Harvei, *de Generat*. p. 62, and 197; *Form de Poulet*. ii, p. 129). Puppies before the membranes are broken, that involve them, are seen to move themselves, to put out their tongues, and to open and shut their mouths (Harvey, Gipson, Riolan, Haller). And calves lick themselves and swallow many of their hairs before their nativity: which however puppies do not (Swammerden, p. 319; Flemyng, *Phil. Trans.* Ann. 1755. 42). And towards the end of gestation, the foetus of all animals are proved to drink part of the liquid in which they swim (Haller, *Physiol*. T. 8, 204). The white of egg is found in the mouth and gizzard of the chick, and is nearly or quite consumed before it is hatched (Harvei, *de Generat*. 58). And the liquor amnii is found in the mouth and stomach of the human foetus, and of calves; and how else should that excrement be produced in the intestines of all animals, which is voided in great quantity soon after their birth (Gipson, *Med. Essays*, Edinb. V.i. 13. Haller, *Physiolog*. T. 3, p. 318, and T. 8). In the stomach of a calf the quantity of this liquid amounted to about three pints, and the hairs amongst it were of the same colour with those on its skin (Blasii, *Anat. Animal*, p. m. 122). These facts are attested by many other writers of credit, besides those above mentioned.

III. It has been deemed a surprising instance of instinct, that calves and chickens should be able to walk by a few efforts almost immediately after their nativity: whilst the human infant in those countries where he is not incumbered with clothes, as in India, is five or six months, and in our climate almost a twelvemonth, before he can safely stand upon his feet.

The struggles of all animals in the womb must resemble their mode of swimming, as by this kind of motion they can best change their attitude in water. But the swimming of the calf and the chicken resembles their manner of walking, which they have thus in part acquired before their nativity, and hence accomplish it afterwards with very few efforts, whilst the swimming of the human creature resembles that of a frog, and totally differs from his mode of walking.

There is another circumstance to be attended to in this affair, that not only the growth of those peculiar parts of animals, which are first wanted to secure their subsistence, are in general furthest advanced before their nativity: but some animals come into the world more completely formed throughout their whole system than others, and are thence much forwarder in all their habits of motion. Thus the colt, and the lamb, are much more perfect animals than the blind puppy, and the naked rabbit; and the chick of the pheasant, and the partridge, has more perfect plumage, and more perfect eyes, as well as greater aptitude to locomotion, than the callow nestlings of the dove, and of the wren. The parents of the former only find it necessary to show them their food, and to teach them to take it up; whilst those of the latter are obliged for many days to obtrude it into their gaping mouths.

IV. From the facts mentioned in No. 2 of this Section, it is evinced that the foetus learns to swallow before its nativity; for it is seen to open its mouth, and its stomach is found filled with the liquid that surrounds it. It opens its mouth, either instigated by hunger, or by the irksomeness of a continued attitude of the muscles of its face; the liquor amnii, in which it swims, is agreeable to its palate, as it consists of a nourishing material (Haller, *Phys.* T. 8, p. 204). It is tempted to experience its taste further in the mouth, and by a few efforts learns to swallow, in the same manner as we learn all other animal actions which are attended with consciousness, *by the repeated efforts of our muscles under the conduct of our sensations or volitions*.

The inspiration of air into the lungs is so totally different from that of swallowing a fluid in which we are immersed, that it cannot be acquired before our nativity. But at this time, when the circulation of the blood is no longer continued through the placenta, that suffocating sensation, which we feel about the precordia, when we are in want of fresh air, disagreeably affects the infant: and all the muscles of the body are excited into action to relieve this oppression; those of the breast, ribs, and diaphragm are found to answer this purpose, and thus respiration is discovered, and is continued throughout our lives, as often as the oppression begins to recur. Many infants, both of the human creature, and of quadrupeds, struggle for a minute after they are born before they begin to breathe (Haller, *Phys.* T. 8, p. 400, *ib.* pt. 2 p.1). Mr. Buffon thinks the action of the dry air upon the nerves of smell of new-born animals, by producing an endeavour to sneeze, may contribute to induce this first inspiration, and that the rarefaction of the air by the warmth of the lungs contributes to induce expiration (*Hist. Nat.* Tom. 4, p. 174). Which latter it may effect by producing a disagreeable sensation by its delay, and a consequent effort to relieve it. Many children sneeze before they respire, but not all, as far as I have observed, or can learn from others.

At length, by the direction of its sense of smell, or by the officious care of its mother, the young animal approaches the odoriferous rill of its future nourishment, already experienced to swallow. But in the act of swallowing, it is necessary nearly to close the mouth, whether the creature be immersed in the fluid it is about to drink, or not. Hence, when the child first attempts to suck, it does not slightly compress the nipple between its lips, and suck as an adult person would do, by absorbing the milk; but it takes the whole nipple into its mouth for this purpose, compresses it between its gums, and thus repeatedly chewing (as it were) the nipple, presses out the milk; exactly in the same manner as it is drawn from the teats of cows by the hands of the milkmaid. The celebrated [William] Harvey [1578–1657] observes, that the fœtus in the womb must have sucked in a part of its nourishment, because it knows how to suck the minute it is born, as any one may experience by putting a finger between its lips, and because in a few days it forgets this art of sucking, and cannot without some difficulty again acquire it (*Exercit. de Gener. Anim.* 48). The same observation is made by Hippocrates [died *c.* 375 BC].

A little further experience teaches the young animal to suck by absorption, as well as by compression; that is, to open the chest as in the beginning of respiration, and thus to rarefy the air in the mouth, that the pressure of the denser external atmosphere may contribute to force out the milk.

The chick yet in the shell has learnt to drink by swallowing a part of the white of the egg for its food; but not having experienced how to take up and swallow solid seeds, or grains, is either taught by the solicitous industry of its mother; or by many repeated attempts is enabled at length to distinguish and to swallow this kind of nutriment.

And puppies, though they know how to suck like other animals from their previous experience in swallowing, and in respiration; yet are they long in acquiring the art of lapping with their tongues, which from the flaccidity of their cheeks, and length of their mouths, is afterwards a more convenient way for them to take in water.

V. The senses of smell and taste in many other animals greatly excel those of mankind, for in civilized society, as our victuals are generally prepared by others, and are adulterated with salt, spice, oil, and empyreuma [the taste and smell left by fire], we do not hesitate about eating whatever is set before us, and neglect to cultivate these senses; whereas other animals try every morsel by the smell, before they take it into their mouths, and by the taste before they swallow it: and are led not only each to his proper nourishment by this organ of sense, but it also at a maturer age directs them in the gratification of their appetite of love. Which may be further understood by considering the sympathies of these parts described in Class IV. 2. 1. 7. While the human animal is directed to the object of his love by his sense of beauty, as mentioned in No. VI. of this Section. Thus Virgil, *Georg.* III, 250. [...]

The following curious experiment is related by Galen [*c.* 129–199 AD]. 'On dissecting a goat great with young I found a brisk embryon, and having detached it from the matrix, and snatching it away before it saw its dam, I brought it into a certain room, where there were many vessels, some filled with wine, others with oil, some with honey, others with milk, or some other liquor; and in others were grains and fruits; we first observed the young animal get upon its feet, and walk, then it shook itself, and afterwards scratched its side with one of its feet. Then we saw it smelling to every one of these things, that were set in the room; and when it had smelt to them all, it drank up the milk' (L. 6, *de locis.* cap. 6).

Parturient quadrupeds, as cats, and bitches, and sows, are led by their sense of smell to eat the placenta as other common food; why then do they not devour their whole progeny, as is represented in an ancient emblem of time? This is said sometimes to happen in the unnatural state in which we confine sows; and indeed nature would seem to have endangered her offspring in this nice circumstance! But at this time the stimulus of the milk in the tumid teats of the mother excites her to look out for, and to desire some unknown circumstance to relieve her. At the same time the smell of the milk attracts the exertions of the young animals towards its source, and thus the delighted mother discovers a new appetite, as mentioned in Sect. XIV, 8, and her little progeny are led to receive and to communicate pleasure by this most beautiful contrivance.

VI. But though the human species in some of their sensations are much inferior to other animals, yet the accuracy of the sense of touch, which they possess in so eminent a degree, gives them a great superiority of understanding; as is well observed by the ingenious Mr. Buffon. The extremities of other animals terminate in horns, and hoofs, and claws, very unfit for the sensation of touch; whilst the human hand is finely adapted to encompass its object with this organ of sense.

The elephant is indeed endued with a fine sense of feeling at the extremity of his proboscis, and hence has acquired much more accurate ideas of touch and of sight than most other creatures. The two following instances of the sagacity of these animals may entertain the reader, as they were told me by some gentlemen of distinct observation, and undoubted veracity, who had been much conversant with our eastern settlements. First, the elephants that are used to carry the baggage of our armies, are put each under the care of one of the natives of Indostan, and whilst himself and his wife go into the woods to collect leaves and branches of trees for his food, they fix him to the ground by a length of chain, and frequently leave a child yet unable to walk, under his protection: and the intelligent animal not only defends it, but as it creeps about, when it arrives near the extremity of his chain, he wraps his trunk gently round its body, and brings it again into the centre of his circle. Secondly, the traitor elephants are taught to walk on a narrow path between two pit-falls, which are covered with turf, and then to go into the woods, and to seduce the wild elephants to come that way, who fall into these wells, whilst he passes safe between them: and it is universally observed, that those wild elephants that escape the snare, pursue the traitor with the utmost vehemence, and if they can overtake him, which sometimes happens, they always beat him to death.

The monkey has a hand well enough adapted for the sense of touch, which contributes to his great facility of imitation; but in taking objects with his hands, as a stick or an apple, he puts his thumb on the same side of them with his fingers, instead of counteracting the pressure of his fingers with it: from this neglect he is much slower in acquiring the figures of objects, as he is less able to determine the distances or diameters of their parts, or to distinguish their vis inertiæ from their hardness. Helvétius [1715–71] adds, that the shortness of his life, his being fugitive before mankind, and his not inhabiting all climates, combine to prevent his improvement (*De l'Esprit*, T. 1. p.). There is however at this time an old monkey shown in Exeter Change, London, who having lost his teeth, when nuts are given him, takes a stone in his hand, and cracks them with it one by one; thus using tools to effect his purpose like mankind.

The beaver is another animal that makes much use of his hands, and if we may credit the reports of travellers, is possessed of amazing ingenuity. This however, Mr. Buffon affirms, is only where they exist in large numbers, and in countries thinly populated with men; while in France in their solitary state they show no uncommon ingenuity.

Indeed all the quadrupeds that have collar-bones (claviculae) use their fore-limbs in some measure as we use our hands, as the cat, squirrel, tiger, bear and lion; and as they exercise the sense of touch more universally than other animals, so are they more sagacious in watching and surprising their prey. All those birds, that use their claws for hands, as the hawk, parrot and cuckoo, appear to be more docile and intelligent; though the gregarious tribes of birds have more acquired knowledge.

Now as the images that are painted on the retina of the eye are no other than signs, which recall to our imaginations the objects we had before examined by the organ of touch, as is fully demonstrated by Dr. [George] Berkeley [1685–1753] in his treatise on vision; it follows that the human creature has greatly more accurate and distinct sense of vision than that of any other animal. Whence as he advances to maturity he gradually acquires a sense of female beauty, which at this time directs him to the object of his new passion.

Sentimental love, as distinguished from the animal passion of that name, with which it is frequently accompanied, consists in the desire or sensation of beholding, embracing, and saluting a beautiful object.

The characteristic of beauty therefore is that it is the object of love; and though many other objects are in common language called beautiful, yet they are only called so metaphorically, and ought to be termed agreeable. A Grecian temple may give us the pleasurable idea of sublimity, a Gothic temple may give us the pleasurable idea of variety, and a modern house the pleasurable idea of utility; music and poetry may inspire our love by association of ideas; but none of these, except metaphorically, can be termed beautiful, as we have no wish to embrace or salute them.

Our perception of beauty consists in our recognition by the sense of vision of those objects, first, which have before inspired our love by the pleasure which they have afforded to many of our senses; as to our sense of warmth, of touch, of smell, of taste, hunger and thirst; and, secondly, which bear any analogy of form to such objects.

When the babe, soon after it is born into this cold world, is applied to its mother's bosom; its sense of perceiving warmth is first agreeably affected; next its sense of smell is delighted with the odour of her milk; then its taste is gratified by the flavour of it; afterwards the appetites of hunger and of thirst afford pleasure by the possession of their objects, and by the subsequent digestion of the aliment; and, lastly, the sense of touch is delighted by the softness and smoothness of the milky fountain, the source of such variety of happiness.

All these various kinds of pleasure at length become associated with the form of the mother's breast; which the infant embraces with its hands, presses with its lips, and watches with its eyes; and thus acquires more accurate ideas of the form of its mother's bosom, than of the odour and flavour or warmth, which it perceives by its other senses. And hence in our maturer years, when any object of vision is presented to us, which by its waving or spiral lines bears any similitude to the form of the female bosom, whether it be found in a landscape with soft gradations of rising and descending surface, or in the forms of some antique vases, or in other works of the pencil or the chissel, we feel a general glow of delight, which seems to influence all our senses; and, if the object be not too large, we experience an attraction to embrace it with our arms, and to salute it with our lips, as we did in our early infancy the bosom of our mother. And thus we find, according to the ingenious idea of Hogarth [1697–1764], that the waving lines of beauty were originally taken from the temple of Venus.

This animal attraction is love; which is a sensation, when the object is present; and a desire, when it is absent. Which constitutes the purest source of human felicity, the cordial drop in the otherwise vapid cup of life, and which overpays mankind for the care and labour, which are attached to the pre-eminence of his situation above other animals.

(*Zoonomia*, vol. I, sect. XVI, 'Of Instinct', nos 1–6)

# Chapter 6

# Political rights and responsibilities

**M**ANY OF THE MOST FAMOUS SAYINGS from the Enlightenment – such as 'Man was born free, and everywhere he is in chains' (Rousseau), 'No man has received from nature the right to command others' (Diderot), 'Enlightenment is man's release from his self-incurred tutelage' (Kant) – have sometimes been put together to create an impression of the Enlightenment as an international movement possessing a united political purpose and conviction. From such a picture it is possible to see (as, indeed, some of the French *philosophes* proposed) the Enlightenment as a heroic struggle against the injustices and oppressions that had arisen from the excessive traditional authority exercised by most eighteenth-century states and the infamous (cruel and irrational) practices of their privileged and powerful churches. In this struggle, key figures, such as Voltaire with his cry of 'Ecrasez l'infâme' (a call to resist injustices), waged campaigns to liberate humankind, often enduring personal sacrifices, such as imprisonment and exile, in the process. How far humankind, mostly illiterate and deeply divided (not least in Europe) by religion, nation, class, gender and race, knew of or subscribed to Enlightenment thinking could not be determined – though in recent years the social composition and penetration of the Enlightenment has been carefully examined. Even so, the key political values believed to be embedded in Enlightened thought, and the historical trajectory suggested by the metaphor of light, implied a linear 'progress of humanity' to which all free and reasonable humans could or should be expected to aspire.

As a moving picture, this grand narrative of the Enlightenment could be seen as beginning with a questioning of religious teachings. It would gather momentum through the development and public dissemination of new (liberal) ideas, sometimes aided by the follies and failures of contemporary governments. And it would lead to 'popular' and/or 'democratic' movements and rebellions against the status quo, most notably in North America and France. There, revolutions spoke both of an earlier, far better and more 'natural' state of human affairs that could be restored, and of the creation of a radically *new* order that would signal a fundamental break with the past. Thus, from its supposed intellectual roots the Enlightenment was often believed to have yielded radical and revolutionary political fruits, largely inspired in America by the liberal ideals of the Englishman John Locke, and in France by the republican and democratic ideals of the self-styled 'citizen of Geneva', Jean-Jacques Rousseau.

It was not difficult to link the first phase of the French Revolution, beginning with the overthrow of the old order and the formulation of the Declaration of the Rights of Man and the Citizen in 1789, to the political ideals of some Enlightenment thinkers. For, although Montesquieu, Voltaire, Rousseau and most of the French *philosophes* never advocated revolution, all had been opposed to many of the political practices of the *ancien régime* and all had wanted to see laws in place that would protect individuals from what were regarded as the state's wilful misuse and abuse of power. A few scholars, such as Denis Diderot and the Marchese di Beccaria, warned of the dangers that would befall society should the authorities fail to seize the opportunity afforded by Enlightened thinking to introduce reforms. But most wanted to see reforms springing from within the existing social order, rather than as a result of its general overthrow. The ideas of *philosophes* such as Rousseau and Voltaire could and would, of course, be bent to serve all kinds of revolutionary purposes. But their 'original' political intent, it could be claimed, had been largely to avert a crisis, to save society from the injustices and oppressions that were the hallmarks of despotic rule. Following the founding of the Republic in 1792, the leaders of the Revolution corrupted or abandoned the *philosophes'* ideals, and unleashed a new kind of terror on the nation. Thus, though closely related to the Revolution, the political ideals of the *philosophes* were not responsible for it. Indeed, the French Revolution could be variously attributed to a range of groups (aristocracy, bourgeoisie, peasantry) and factors (national bankruptcy, ministerial mismanagement, poor harvests) in which the *philosophes* played little or no part.

Though equally keen to represent the Enlightenment as a united political movement, conservative commentators, such as Edmund Burke in his *Reflections on the Revolution in France* (1790), and some modern critics, painted a rather different picture. Even the first phase of the Revolution could be seen as the dreadful consequence of permitting a conspiracy of misguided idealists to undermine religion and the status quo. Certainly, this was not the dawn of a more just and rational society based upon a true understanding of liberty and equality, as the followers of the *philosophes* had hoped. Moreover, as the Revolution became more radical, violent and international, introducing 'a new era in the world's history' (Goethe) in 1792, and with leaders who apparently looked back to Voltaire and Rousseau for inspiration, so the continuity of the Enlightenment as a story primarily about the subversion of authority (paradoxically culminating in the revolutionary tyranny of the Terror, 1793–94) seemed clear. In America, leaders of political revolt, such as Thomas Jefferson, had evidently championed Locke, in saying: 'We hold these truths to be sacred and undeniable; that all men are created equal and independent, that from that equal creation they derive rights inherent and inalienable, among which are the preservation of life, and liberty, and the pursuit of happiness' (draft of the American Declaration of Independence). And even holders of traditional power, such as Catherine the Great, a good friend to many *philosophes*, had eventually repudiated the Enlightenment; writing in 1794 that 'the sole aim of the whole movement, as experience is proving, is to destroy ... authority'. So, for some commentators, the responsibility of *philosophes* for the revolutions that would mark the birth of modern Western political history seemed clear enough.

To sustain such grand accounts requires a determination to emphasise the continuity of the Enlightenment as a fundamentally homogeneous and autonomous political movement, based upon a set of similar ideas that was not subject to various interpretations, and whose development and articulation were largely unaffected by particular historical contexts and the vicissitudes of time and place. Yet, a great range of forces and traditions, such as cameralism (the systematic analysis of state policy and administration to promote economic growth) in central Europe and Puritanism in America, helped to shape the changing 'national contexts' of colonies, republics, monarchies, empires, city-states and principalities within which many kinds of political debate and change in the eighteenth century actually took place. Furthermore, in their political writings the French *philosophes* were never agreed about who should govern, and throughout the century their views ranged from apologies for benevolent absolutism and social conservatism to appeals for republicanism, democracy, and anarchism. Outside France too, there were theorists such as Giambattista Vico who were firm advocates of absolutist monarchy. Indeed, it can be argued that the development of Enlightenment political thought depended as much upon major disagreements between leading thinkers over key issues such as the origins of justice (Locke and Hume), rights to private property (Voltaire and Rousseau), the proper role of the state (Frederick the Great and Adam Smith) and the French Revolution (Burke and Paine), for example, as upon some broad agreements about the proper terms of these debates.

In the course of these long discussions many important figures revised and sometimes radically altered their positions. Thus Catherine the Great changed her opinion of the Enlightenment, and Frederick the Great tempered many of his beliefs once he had taken on the responsibilities of government. Furthermore, the views of the French *philosophes* were no less subject to change in the light of their experiences and reflections. Having initially been impressed by Frederick's rule, following a visit to Prussia in the 1750s, Voltaire changed his mind about the philosopher-king and his regime. Similarly, after a visit to Catherine's court in the 1770s, Diderot revised his thoughts on Enlightened absolutism in Russia. Earlier in the century, visits to England by Voltaire (1726–28) and Montesquieu (1721–33) had inspired key texts of the Enlightenment, championing what seemed like Britain's relatively open, egalitarian, peaceful, tolerant, prosperous and progressive society, safeguarded by political representation and the rule of law – in marked contrast with the *ancien régime*. But, by the end of the century, in the light of the American and French Revolutions and the British conservative reaction and suppression of political radicalism (such as that of the United Irishmen) in the

1790s, it seemed to many that Britain with its monarchy, church and aristocracy was more akin to the 'old order' than to a new model society and constitution. Thus, throughout the century, individuals, new generations and whole nations would change their political perceptions of others and themselves, sometimes to an extraordinary extent. In this respect, even the idea of the Enlightenment as a united political movement (for good or ill) can be seen as partly a creation of the furore set in motion by the French Revolution, as well as an underlying cause of the crises of the final decades of the century.

As many of the *philosophes* who lived in France were sometimes at odds with the authorities there (usually over the publication of their works) and several consequently spent some time in exile, it is not difficult to represent them as political outcasts and subversives. Indeed, many radical political thinkers fled to places such as the Dutch Republic where they could live and publish their thoughts in far greater freedom than in France. Yet 'moderate' *philosophes* such as Buffon, Montesquieu, Turgot (Minister of Finance, 1774–76) and even Voltaire (as Royal Historiographer, 1745–47) were appointed to official posts, and many enjoyed the patronage and protection of Europe's Enlightened monarchs. Outside France, Newton, Locke, Leibniz, Linnaeus, Beccaria, Adam Smith and other writers also served their governments – as would Franklin and Jefferson, of course – in various capacities. Rather than being outsiders, key figures in the Enlightenment were thus very much 'insiders', part of the recognised political elite. Some, such as Rousseau, Diderot and d'Alembert came from relatively humble social origins. But in addition to those of royal birth, several leading figures also came from noble families and, with one very notable exception, Rousseau, many evidently felt quite comfortable in aristocratic circles. Many spoke boldly of the natural rights and equality of all men, and believed that they wrote and acted in the service of humanity. But, for most *philosophes* this did not mean that they were prepared to put their faith in the opinions and judgements of the common people. A few adopted radical positions. Diderot wrote that 'Individual wills are suspect; they may be good or they may be bad. But the general will is always good. It has never been wrong, and will never mislead' ('Natural Law', *Encyclopédie*, vol. V, 1755). Rousseau too, in the *Social Contract* (1762), spoke of the supreme authority of the 'general will' of the people, to be exercised in the interests of the common good, once civil society had been formed:

> The general will is always rightful and always tends to the public good; but it does not follow that the decisions of the people are always equally right. We always want what is advantageous but we do not always discern it. The people is never corrupted, but it is often misled; and only then does it seem to will what is bad.
>
> (*Social Contract*, Book 2, ch. 3)

Even so, these were radical opinions. What, across Europe, millions of poor illiterate peasants steeped in centuries of religious superstition, ignorance, and ancient custom could contribute to the progress of Enlightenment was not always immediately apparent from the comforts of the study or the salon. Nor did most of the *philosophes* embrace the prospect of educating 'the beasts of burden of human society' with much enthusiasm. While Diderot and d'Alembert were quite enthusiastic (the former proclaiming that 'security consists in ruling over educated men'), Voltaire and Frederick were more circumspect (the latter insisting that 'the little good sense of which our species is capable can only reside in a tiny minority of the nation'). Even so, Enlightened monarchs such as Frederick, Catherine and Joseph II were all keen not only to found new academies to enlighten the privileged classes, but also to provide some public elementary education for the masses. For Frederick, at least, the logic of this was simple: 'The true benefit of the State, its advantage and glory demand that the people in it should be as well educated and enlightened as possible, in order to furnish it, in every field, with a number of trained subjects capable of acquitting themselves expertly in the different tasks entrusted to them' ('Speech to the Berlin Academy of Sciences', 1772).

Although there was no agreed political theory that emerged from the Enlightenment, its major figures did share a number of key ideas, interests and concerns. Many of these were expressed in the highly influential works of Locke and Montesquieu, and in the writings and policies of Frederick the Great and Catherine the Great as they sought to govern their states as Enlightened monarchs. Influenced by the work of natural law theorists such as the Dutch jurist Hugo Grotius (1583–1645), and Thomas Hobbes (1588–1679), Locke in his *Two Treatises of Government* (1690), sought to explain the origins of government by social contract, and the rights and responsibilities of individuals as citizens of their own societies rather than as mere subjects to a sovereign. In particular, he was keen to counter the claims expressed in works such as Robert Filmer's *Patriarcha* (1680) that it could be shown from Scripture that – like Adam and all fathers over their children – monarchs derived an absolute authority from (and were only accountable to) God. Equally keen to counter despotism, and its ruling ethos 'fear', in *The Spirit of the Laws* (1748) Montesquieu sought to show how the prosperity and happiness of a society depended upon its laws and type of government, and how these themselves were influenced by history, geography and climate. His theories exercised a powerful influence upon Catherine II in her attempt to reform the laws of Russia through her famous *Nakaz* (*Instruction*) presented to a Legislative Commission in 1767. Similarly, inspired by Locke's writings and the example of the Roman Emperor Marcus Aurelius (ruled 161–180 AD), Frederick set out to govern Prussia by what he took to be Enlightened thinking, and to distinguish his own kind of regime from that of countries such as France.

The term 'Enlightened absolutism' was not used widely in the eighteenth century, and has given rise to considerable controversy among historians in modern times. However, there can be little doubt that in their political rhetoric, if not always in their policies, monarchs such as Catherine and Frederick were greatly influenced by the *philosophes* and sought to mould various aspects of their regimes in accordance with what they believed were the hallmarks of Enlightened thinking. Thus Catherine took a secular view of her responsibilities: 'Since Natural Law commands us to strive as much as we can for the welfare of all men, we are bound to relieve the position of those under our sway, as far as common sense permits' (*Nakaz*, no. 252). And Frederick eschewed any religious justification for his authority based upon the divine right of kings, arguing instead that 'The monarch is the first servant of the State'. In a private memorandum in 1752 he gave a typically secular explanation of this thinking:

> A well-run government must have a system as coherent as a system of philosophy; all the measures taken must be well reasoned; finances, foreign policy and military affairs must work to the same end, namely the consolidation of the State and the increase of its power. Now a system can only emanate from one mind; and this must be the monarch's. Idleness, luxury or stupidity prevent rulers from pursuing the noble task of bringing about their people's happiness. Such monarchs make themselves so contemptible ... Their negligence towards their peoples even becomes criminal.

Such views encouraged many *philosophes* to believe that Enlightened monarchs held the keys to progress in much of Europe; though many who, like Voltaire and Diderot, travelled to Prussia or Russia would return home rather disillusioned. Thus on his return from Russia in 1774, Diderot penned his *Observations sur le Nakaz* (*Observations on the Nakaz*) which would later be posted to his patron, Catherine. In this extensive critique of Catherine's proposal, Diderot began with the contention 'There is no true sovereign except the nation; there can be no true legislator except the people', and concluded with the observation

> I see in Her Imperial Majesty's Instruction a plan for an excellent Code, but not a word on the means of ensuring its stability. I see in it the name of the despot abdicated, but the thing itself preserved, and despotism called monarchy.
>
>     I see no provision in it for the emancipation of the body of the nation; but without emancipation, or without liberty, there is no property; without property, no agriculture; without agriculture, no strength, greatness, prosperity, wealth.
>
>     But the Empress has a great soul, insight, enlightenment, a very extensive genius; justice, goodness, patience and resolution.

## JOHN LOCKE

In 1690, shortly after the overthrow of James II (1685–89) by his Protestant son-in-law William of Orange, John Locke (see p. 40) published, anonymously, what would become one of the most influential political works of the Enlightenment and a founding text in liberal philosophy: *Two Treatises of Civil Government*. The book, largely written in the early 1680s when there were several attempts to exclude the Catholic James from succeeding to his brother Charles II's throne, consisted of two tracts. In the first, Locke set out to refute the widely accepted claims of the Royalist writer Sir Robert Filmer (1588–1653) in his *Patriarcha* (1680), written before the Civil War, that kings possessed an absolute authority over their subjects, inheriting this patriarchal power by primogeniture from Adam, to whom God had originally entrusted it. It was thus the sacred duty of all people, born into subjection to their king, to obey their sovereign who was only ever accountable to God. In the second tract, 'an Essay concerning the True Original, Extent, and End of Civil Government', Locke set out his own radical and highly controversial account of the origins and nature of political rights and power. Drawing upon the work of natural law theorists such as Hugo Grotius and Samuel Pufendorf, and James Tyrrell's *Patriarcha non Monarchia* (1681), Locke argued that political authority arose from individuals who, living originally free and equal in a state of nature, then agreed to form and live under the rules of civil society in order to protect and promote their God-given individual rights. The whole purpose of this social contract was to protect the natural (God-given) property rights of individuals; rights which existed prior to the formation of political society: 'The great and chief end, therefore, of men's uniting into commonwealths, and putting themselves under government, is the preservation of their property.' When, in extreme circumstances, governments failed to uphold life and property, the people have the right to resist the tyranny, and to reform society to preserve their fundamental rights.

Locke's ideas about natural rights, social contract, popular sovereignty, government and the right of resistance exercised a powerful influence on the course of political thinking during the Enlightenment, and his work has given rise to intense scholarly debates in modern times. The extracts here are taken from the second of the *Two Treatises*, beginning with his account of 'the state of nature', in which 'being all equal and independent, no one ought to harm another in his life, health, liberty, or possessions'.

## Two Treatises of Government (1690)

### 'Of the State of Nature'

To understand political power right, and derive it from its original, we must consider what state all men are naturally in, and that is a state of perfect freedom to order their actions and dispose of their possessions and persons as they think fit, within the bounds of the law of nature, without asking leave, or depending upon the will of any other man. [...]

But though this be a state of liberty, yet it is not a state of licence, though man in that state have an uncontrollable liberty to dispose of his person or possessions, yet he has not liberty to destroy himself, or so much as any creature in his possession, but where some nobler use than its bare preservation calls for it. The state of nature has a law of nature to govern it, which obliges everyone. And reason, which is that law, teaches all mankind who will but consult it that, being all equal and independent, no one ought to harm another in his life, health, liberty, or possessions. For men being all the workmanship of one omnipotent and infinitely wise maker, all the servants of one sovereign master, sent into the world by his order and about his business, they are his property whose workmanship they are, made to last during his, not one another's, pleasure. And being furnished with like faculties, sharing all in one community of nature, there cannot be supposed any such subordination among us that may authorize us to destroy one another, as if we were made for one another's uses, as the inferior ranks of creatures are for ours. Everyone, as he is bound to preserve himself, and not to quit his station wilfully, so by the like reason when his own preservation comes not in competition, ought he, as much as he can, to preserve the rest of mankind, and may not, unless it be to do justice on an offender, take away or impair the life, or what tends to the preservation of the life, liberty, health, limb, or goods of another.

(Two Treatises, II, ch. II, paras 4 and 6)

### 'Of the State of War'

The state of war is a state of enmity and destruction. And, therefore, declaring by word or action, not a passionate and hasty, but a sedate, settled design upon another man's life, puts him in a state of war with him against whom he has declared such an intention, and so has exposed his life to the other's power, to be taken away by him, or anyone that joins with him in his defence and espouses his quarrel: it being reasonable and just I should have a right to destroy that which threatens me with destruction. For by the fundamental law of nature, man being to be preserved, as much as possible, when all cannot be preserved the safety of the innocent is to be preferred. And one may destroy a man who makes war upon him, or has discovered an enmity to his being, for the same reason that he may kill a wolf or lion: because such men are not under the ties of the common law of reason, have no other rule but that of force and violence, and so may be treated as beasts of prey, those dangerous and noxious creatures, that will be sure to destroy him whenever he falls into their power. [...]

To avoid this state of war (wherein there is no appeal but to Heaven, and wherein every the least difference is apt to end, where there is no authority to decide between the contenders) is one great reason of men's putting themselves into society, and quitting the state of nature. For where there is an authority, a power on earth from which relief can be had by appeal, there the continuance of the state of war is excluded, and the controversy is decided by that power.

(Two Treatises, II, ch. III, paras 16 and 21)

### 'Of Slavery'

The natural liberty of man is to be free from any superior power on earth, and not to be under the will or legislative authority of man, but to have only the law of nature for his rule. The liberty of man, in society, is to be under no other legislative power but that established, by consent, in the commonwealth, nor under the dominion of any will, or restraint of any law, but what the legislative shall enact, according to the trust put in it. Freedom, then, is not what Sir R[obert] F[ilmer] tells us, O[bservations on] A[ristotle], [p.]55: 'A liberty for everyone to do what he lists, to live as he pleases, and not to be tied by any laws.' But freedom of men under government is to have a standing rule to live by, common to everyone of that society, and made by the legislative power erected in it; a liberty to follow my own will in all things where the rule prescribes not; and not to be subject to the inconstant, uncertain, unknown, arbitrary will of another man. As freedom of nature is to be under no other restraint but the law of nature.

(*Two Treatises*, II, ch. IV, para. 22)

### 'Of Property'

Though the earth and all inferior creatures be common to all men, yet every man has a property in his own person. This nobody has any right to but himself. The labour of his body, and the work of his hands, we may say, are properly his. Whatsoever then he removes out of the state that nature hath provided and left it in, he hath mixed his labour with, and joined to it something that is his own, and thereby makes it his property. It being by him removed from the common state nature placed it in, it hath by this labour something annexed to it that excludes the common right of other men. For this labour being the unquestionable property of the labourer, no man but he can have a right to what that is once joined to, at least where there is enough and as good left in common for others.

He that is nourished by the acorns he picked up under an oak, or the apples he gathered from the trees in the wood, has certainly appropriated them to himself. Nobody can deny but the nourishment is his. I ask then, When did they begin to be his? When he digested? Or when he ate? Or when he boiled? Or when he brought them home? Or when he picked them up? And 'tis plain if the first gathering made them not his, nothing else could. That labour put a distinction between them and common. That added something to them more than nature, the common mother of all, had done; and so they became his private right. And will anyone say he had no right to those acorns and apples he thus appropriated, because he had not the consent of all mankind to make them his? Was it a robbery thus to assume to himself what belonged to all in common? If such a consent as that was necessary, man had starved, notwithstanding the plenty God had given him. We see in commons, which remain so by compact, that 'tis the taking any part of what is common, and removing it out of the state nature leaves it in, which begins the property; without which the common is of no use. And the taking of this or that part does not depend on the express consent of all the commoners. Thus the grass my horse has bit, the turfs my servant has cut, and the ore I have digged in any place where I have a right to them in common with others, become my property, without the assignation or consent of anybody. The labour that was mine, removing them out of that common state they were in, hath fixed my property in them. [...]

But the chief matter of property being now not the fruits of the earth, and the beasts that subsist on it, but the earth itself, as that which takes in and carries with it all the rest, I think it is plain that property in that too is acquired as the former. As much land as a man tills, plants, improves, cultivates, and can use the product of, so much is his property. He by his labour does, as it were, enclose it from the common. Nor will it invalidate his right to say 'Everybody else has an equal title to it, and therefore he cannot appropriate, he cannot enclose, without the consent of all his fellow-commoners, all mankind.' God, when he gave the world in common to all mankind, commanded man also to labour, and the penury of his condition required it of him. God and his reason commanded him to subdue the earth, i.e. improve it for the benefit of life, and therein lay out something upon it that was his own, his labour. He that in obedience to this command of God, subdued, tilled and sowed any part of it, thereby annexed to it something that was his property, which another had not title to, nor could without injury take from him.

(*Two Treatises*, II, ch. V, paras 27, 28 and 32)

### 'Of the Beginning of Political Societies'

Men being, as has been said, by nature all free, equal and independent, no one can be put out of this estate and subjected to the political power of another without his own consent. The only way whereby anyone divests himself of his natural liberty and puts on the bonds of civil society is by agreeing with other men to join and unite into a community for their comfortable, safe, and peaceable living one amongst another in a secure enjoyment of their properties, and a greater security against any that are not of it. This any number of men may do, because it injures not the freedom of the rest; they are left as they were, in the liberty of the state of nature. When any number of men have so consented to make one community or government, they are thereby presently incorporated, and make one body politic, wherein the majority have a right to act and conclude the rest.

For when any number of men have, by the consent of every individual, made a community, they have thereby made that community one body, with a power to act as one body, which is only by the will and determination of the majority. For that which acts any community being only the consent of the individuals of it, and it being necessary to that which is one body to move one way, it is necessary the body should move that way whither the greater force carries it, which is the consent of the majority; or else it is impossible it should act or continue one body, one community, which the consent of every individual that united into it agreed that it should; and so everyone is bound by that consent to be concluded by the majority. And therefore we see that in assemblies empowered to act by positive laws where no number is set by that positive law which empowers them, the act of the majority passes for the act of the whole, and of course determines, as having by the law of nature and reason the power of the whole.

And thus every man, by consenting with others to make one body politic under one government, puts himself under an obligation to everyone of that society to submit to the determination of the majority, and to be concluded by it; or else this original compact, whereby he with others incorporates into one society, would signify nothing, and be no compact, if he be left free, and under no other ties than he was in before, in the state of nature. For what appearance would there be of any compact? What new engagement if he were no further tied by any decrees of the society than he himself thought fit and did actually consent to? This would still be as great a liberty as he himself had before his compact, or anyone else in the state of nature hath, who may submit himself and consent to any acts of it if he thinks fit.

(*Two Treatises*, II, ch. VIII, paras 95–97)

### 'Of the Ends of Political Society and Government'

If man in the state of nature be so free as has been said; if he be absolute lord of his own person and possessions, equal to the greatest, and subject to nobody, why will he part with his freedom? Why will he give up this empire, and subject himself to the dominion and control of any other power? To which 'tis obvious to answer that, though in the state of nature he hath such a right, yet the enjoyment of it is very uncertain, and constantly exposed to the invasion of others. For all being kings as much as he, every man his equal, and the greater part no strict observers of equity and justice, the enjoyment of the property he has in this state is very unsafe, very unsecure. This makes him willing to quit this condition which, however free, is full of fears and continual dangers. And 'tis not without reason that he seeks out, and is willing to join in society with others who are already united, or have a mind to unite for the mutual preservation of their lives, liberties, and estates, which I call by the general name *property*.

The great and chief end, therefore, of men's uniting into commonwealths, and putting themselves under government, is the preservation of their property, to which in the state of nature there are many things wanting.

First, there wants an established, settled, known law, received and allowed by common consent to be the standard of right and wrong, and the common measure to decide all controversies between them. For though the law of nature be plain and intelligible to all rational creatures; yet men being biased by their interest, as well as ignorant for want of study of it, are not apt to allow of it as a law binding to them in the application of it to their particular cases.

Secondly, in the state of nature there wants a known and indifferent judge, with authority to determine all differences according to the established law. For everyone in that state being both judge and executioner of the law of nature, men being partial to themselves, passion and revenge is very apt to carry them too far, and with too much heat, in their own cases; as well as negligence and unconcernedness to make them too remiss in other men's.

Thirdly, in the state of nature there often wants power to back and support the sentence when right, and to give it due execution. They who by any injustice offended, will seldom fail, where they are able, by force to make good their injustice. Such resistance many times makes the punishment dangerous, and frequently destructive, to those who attempt it. [...]

But though men when they enter into society give up the equality, liberty, and executive power they had in the state of nature into the hands of the society, to be so far disposed of by the legislative as the good of the society shall require; yet it being only with an intention in everyone the better to preserve himself his liberty and property (for no rational creature can be supposed to change his condition with an intention to be worse), the power of the society, or legislative constituted by them, can never be supposed to extend further than the common good; but is obliged to secure everyone's property by providing against those three defects abovementioned that made the state of nature so unsafe and uneasy. And so whoever has the legislative or supreme power of any commonwealth is bound to govern by established standing laws, promulgated and known to the people, and not by extemporary decrees; by indifferent and upright judges, who are to decide controversies by those laws; and to employ the force of the community at home only in the execution of such laws, or abroad to prevent or redress foreign injuries, and secure the community from inroads and invasion. And all this to be directed to no other end, but the peace, safety, and public good of the people.

(*Two Treatises*, II, ch. IX, paras 123–126 and 131)

### 'Of the Forms of a Commonwealth'

The majority having, as has been showed, upon men's first uniting into society, the whole power of the community naturally in them, may employ all that power in making laws for the community from time to time, and executing those laws by officers of their own appointing; and then the form of the government is a perfect democracy. Or else may put the power of making laws into the hands of a few select men and their heirs or successors, and then it is an oligarchy. Or else into the hands of one man, and then it is a monarchy; if to him and his heirs, it is an hereditary monarchy; if to him only for life, but upon his death the power only of nominating a successor to return to them, an elective monarchy. And so accordingly of these the community may make compounded and mixed forms of government, as they think good. And if the legislative power be at first given by the majority to one or more persons only for their lives, or any limited time, and then the supreme power to revert to them again, when it is so reverted the community may dispose of it again anew into what hands they please, and so constitute a new form of government. For the form of government depending upon the placing the supreme power, which is the legislative, it being impossible to conceive that an inferior power should prescribe to a superior, or any but the supreme make laws, according as the power of making laws is placed, such is the form of the commonwealth.

(*Two Treatises*, II, ch. X, para. 132)

### 'Of the Extent of the Legislative Power'

The great end of men's entering into society being the enjoyment of their properties in peace and safety, and the great instrument and means of that being the laws established in that society, the first and fundamental positive law of all commonwealths is the establishing of the legislative power; as the first and fundamental natural law, which is to govern even the legislative itself, is the preservation of the society, and (as far as will consist with the public good) of every person in it. This legislative is not only the supreme power of the commonwealth, but sacred and unalterable in the hands where the community have once placed it; nor can any edict of anybody else, in what form soever conceived, or by what power soever backed, have the force and obligation of a law which has not its sanction from that legislative which the public has chosen and appointed. For without this the law could not have that which is absolutely necessary to its being a law, the consent of the society, over whom nobody can have a power to make laws, but by their own consent, and by authority received from them; and therefore all the obedience which by the most solemn ties anyone can be obliged to pay ultimately terminates in this supreme power, and is directed by those laws which it enacts; nor can any oaths to any foreign power whatsoever, or any domestic subordinate power, discharge any member of the society from his obedience to the legislative, acting pursuant to their trust, nor oblige him to any obedience contrary to the laws so enacted, or further than they do allow; it being ridiculous to imagine one can be tied ultimately to obey any power in the society which is not the supreme. [...]

These are the bounds which the trust that is put in them by the society, and the law of God and nature, have set to the legislative power of every commonwealth, in all forms of government.

First, they are to govern by promulgated, established laws, not to be varied in particular cases, but to have one rule for rich and poor, for the favourite at court and the country man at plough.

Secondly, these laws also ought to be designed for no other end ultimately but the good of the people.

Thirdly, they must not raise taxes on the property of the people without the consent of the people, given by themselves or their deputies. And this properly concerns only such governments where the legislative is always in being, or at least where the people have not reserved any part of the legislative to deputies, to be from time to time chosen by themselves.

Fourthly, the legislative neither must nor can transfer the power of making laws to anybody else, or place it anywhere but where the people have.

(*Two Treatises*, II, ch. XI, paras 134 and 142)

### 'Of the Subordination of the Powers of the Commonwealth'

Though in a constituted commonwealth, standing upon its own basis, and acting according to its own nature, that is, acting for the preservation of the community, there can be but one supreme power, which is the legislative, to which all the rest are and must be subordinate, yet the legislative being only a fiduciary power to act for certain ends, there remains still in the people a supreme power to remove or alter the legislative when they find the legislative act contrary to the trust reposed in them. For all power given with trust for the attaining an end, being limited by that end, whenever that end is manifestly neglected or opposed the trust must necessarily be forfeited, and the power devolve into the hands of those that gave it, who may place it anew where they shall think best for their safety and security. And thus the community perpetually retains a supreme power of saving themselves from the attempts and designs of anybody, even of their legislators, whenever they shall be so foolish or so wicked as to lay and carry on designs against the liberties and properties of the subject. For no man, or society of men, having a power to deliver up their preservation, or consequently the means of it, to the absolute will and arbitrary dominion of another, whenever anyone shall go about to bring them into such a slavish condition, they will always have a right to preserve what they have not a power to part with; and to rid themselves of those who invade this fundamental, sacred, and unalterable law of self-preservation for which they entered into society. And thus the community may be said in this respect to be always the supreme power, but not as considered under any form of government, because this power of the people can never take place till the government be dissolved.

(*Two Treatises*, II, ch. XIII, para. 149)

### 'Of Conquest'

Though governments can originally have no other rise than that before mentioned, nor polities be founded on anything but the consent of the people; yet such has been the disorders ambition has filled the world with, that in the noise of war, which makes so great a part of the history of mankind, this consent is little taken notice of; and therefore many have mistaken the force of arms for the consent of the people, and reckon conquest as one of the originals of government. But conquest is as far from setting up any government as demolishing an house is from building a new one in the place. Indeed it often makes way for a new frame of a commonwealth by destroying the former; but, without the consent of the people, can never erect a new one.

That the aggressor, who puts himself into the state of war with another, and unjustly invades another man's right, can, by such an unjust war, never come to have a right over the conquered, will be easily agreed by all men, who will not think that robbers and pirates have a right of empire over whomsoever they have force enough to master; or that men are bound by promises which unlawful force extorts from them. Should a robber break into my house and, with a dagger at my throat, make me seal deeds to convey my estate to him, would this give him any title? Just such a title by his sword has an unjust conqueror who forces me into submission. The injury and the crime is equal, whether committed by the wearer of a crown or some petty villain. The title of the offender, and the number of his followers, make no difference in the offence, unless it be to aggravate it. [...]

The short of the case in conquest is this: the conqueror, if he have a just cause, has a despotical right over the persons of all that actually aided and concurred in the war against him, and a right to make up his damage and cost out of their labour and estates, so he injure not the right of any other. Over the rest of the people, if there were any that consented not to the war, and over the children of the captives themselves, or the possessions of either, he has no power; and so can have, by virtue of conquest, no lawful title himself to dominion over them, or derive it to his posterity; but is an aggressor if he attempts upon their properties, and thereby puts himself in a state of war against them.

(*Two Treatises*, II, ch. XVI, paras 175–176 and 196)

### 'Of Tyranny'

As usurpation is the exercise of power which another hath a right to, so tyranny is the exercise of power beyond right, which nobody can have a right to. And this is making use of the power anyone has in his hands, not for the good of those who are under it, but for his own private separate advantage. When the governor, however entitled, makes not the law but his will the rule, and his commands and actions are not directed to the preservation of the properties of his people, but the satisfaction of his own ambition, revenge, covetousness, or any other irregular passion. [...]

Wherever law ends tyranny begins, if the law be transgressed to another's harm. And whosoever in authority exceeds the power given him by the law, and makes use of the force he has under his command to compass that upon the subject which the law allows not, ceases in that to be a magistrate, and acting without authority, may be opposed, as any other man who by force invades the right of another. [...]

May the commands then of a prince be opposed? May he be resisted as often as anyone shall find himself aggrieved, and but imagine he has not right done him? This will unhinge and overturn all polities, and instead of government and order leave nothing but anarchy and confusion.

To this I answer: That force is to be opposed to nothing but to unjust and unlawful force. Whoever makes any opposition in any other case draws on himself a just condemnation both from God and man, and so no danger or confusion will follow, as is often suggested.

(Two Treatises, II, ch. XVIII, paras 199, 202–204)

### 'Of the Dissolution of Government'

To conclude, the power that every individual gave the society, when he entered into it, can never revert to the individuals again, as long as the society lasts, but will always remain in the community; because without this there can be no community, no commonwealth, which is contrary to the original agreement. So also when the society hath placed the legislative in any assembly of men, to continue in them and their successors, with direction and authority for providing such successors, the legislative can never revert to the people whilst that government lasts: because having provided a legislative with power to continue for ever, they have given up their political power to the legislative, and cannot resume it. But if they have set limits to the duration of their legislative, and made this supreme power in any person or assembly only temporary, or else when, by the miscarriages of those in authority, it is forfeited, upon the forfeiture of their rulers, or at the determination of the time set, it reverts to the society, and the people have a right to act as supreme, and continue the legislative in themselves, or erect a new form, or under the old form place it in new hands, as they think good.

(Two Treatises, II, ch. XIX, para. 243)

## BARON DE MONTESQUIEU

Charles Louis de Secondat (1689–1755) was born at La Brède, near Bordeaux, the eldest son of a Catholic noble family from which he inherited his title in 1716. After studying law at the University of Bordeaux and at Paris, he became a magistrate and president of the criminal division of the *parlement* of Bordeaux. In 1721 he produced an epistolary novel *Les Lettres Persanes* (*The Persian Letters*, published anonymously at Amsterdam), satirising French politics, society and manners through the fictional letters of Persian travellers. Following the success of this book, in the late 1720s he was elected to the Académie Française and undertook a tour of European states, including England (1729–31) where he lived for two years, studying Locke and the British constitution. His *Considérations sur les Causes de la Grandeur des Romains et leur Décadence* (*Considerations on the Causes of the Greatness of the Romans and their Decline*) was published in 1734.

Despite increasing blindness, on his return to France he worked on *De l'Esprit des Lois* (*The Spirit of the Laws*), published at Geneva in 1748. Although he claimed in the Preface, to 'give thanks to the Supreme that I was born a subject of that government under which I live', and that 'I have not drawn my principles from my prejudices, but from the nature of things', the book was banned by the Catholic church. Even so, it was a great success; provoking such criticism and controversy as to lead Montesquieu to publish a defence of it in 1751. His ideas exercised a powerful influence upon political theorists and reformers, from Catherine the Great to the framers of the Constitution of the United States, and upon various constitutions adopted during the French Revolution.

In *The Spirit of the Laws*, Montesquieu analysed the differences between three forms of government (republican, monarchic, despotic) and what he saw as the dominant ethos (virtue, honour, fear) of each form. In this account, mixing historical commentary, philosophy and political theory, he particularly praised the British constitution for its separation of powers (e.g. the independence of the judiciary), and warned of the dangers of despotism. In the second part of the book, he developed his theory of how the environment (including geography, custom, resources and climate) helped to shape the culture and laws of each society. The extracts here, based upon a popular eighteenth-century translation of the *Spirit of the Laws*, are taken from both parts of the book. In the last three extracts he explains how slavery and polygamy are related to climate.

## The Spirit of the Laws (1748)

### 'Of Positive Laws'

As soon as mankind enter into a state of society, they lose the sense of their weakness; the equality ceases, and then commences the state of war.

Each particular society begins to feel its strength, whence arises a state of war betwixt different nations. The individuals likewise of each society become sensible of their strength; hence the principal advantages of this society they endeavour to convert to their own emolument, which constitutes between them a state of war.

These two different kinds of hostile states give rise to human laws. Considered as inhabitants of so great a planet, which necessarily implies a variety of nations, they have laws relative to their mutual intercourse, which is what we call the law of nations. Considered as members of a society that must be properly supported, they have laws relative to the governors and the governed; and this we call political law. They have also another sort of laws relating to the mutual communication of citizens: by which is understood the civil law.

The law of nations is naturally founded on this principle, that different nations ought in time of peace to do one another all the good they can, and in time of war as little harm as possible, without prejudicing their real interests.

The object of war is victory; victory aims at conquest; conquest at preservation. From this and the preceding principle, all those rules are derived which constitute the law of nations.

All countries have a law of nations, not excepting the Iroquois themselves, though they devour their prisoners; for they send and receive ambassadors, and understand the rights of war and peace. The mischief is, that their law of nations is not founded on true principles.

Besides the law of nations relating to all societies, there is a politic law for each particularly considered. No society can subsist without a form of government. 'The conjunction of the particular forces of individuals', as [Giovanni Vincenzo] Gravina [1664–1718] well observes, 'constitutes what we call a political state'.

The general force may be in the hands of a single person, or of many. Some think that nature having established paternal authority, the government of a single person was most conformable to nature. But the example of paternal authority proves nothing. For if the power of a father is relative to a single government, that of brothers after the death of a father, or that of cousins-german after the decease of brothers, are relative to a government of many. The political power necessarily comprehends the union of several families.

Better is it to say that the government most conformable to nature, is that whose particular disposition best agrees with the humour and disposition of the people in whose favour it is established.

The particular force of individuals cannot be united without a conjunction of all their wills. 'The conjunction of those wills', as Gravina again very justly observes, 'is what we call the civil state.'

Law in general is human reason, inasmuch as it governs all the inhabitants of the earth; the political and civil laws of each nation ought to be only the particular cases in which this human reason is applied.

They should be adapted in such a manner to the people for whom they are made, as to render it very unlikely for those of one nation to be proper for another.

They should be relative to the nature and principle of the actual, or intended government; whether they form it, as in the case of political laws, or whether they support it, as may be said of civil institutions.

They should be relative to the climate of each country, to the quality of the soil, to its situation and extent, to the manner of living of the natives, whether husbandmen, huntsmen, or shepherds; they should have a relation to the degree of liberty which the constitution will bear; to the religion of the inhabitants, to their inclinations, riches, number, commerce, manners, and customs. In fine, they have relations to each other, as also to their origin, to the intent of the legislator, and to the order of things on which they are established; in all which different lights they ought to be considered.

This is what I have undertaken to perform in the following work. These relations I shall examine, since all these together form what I call the spirit of laws.

(*Spirit of the Laws*, Book 1, ch. 3)

### 'Of the Nature of the three different Governments'

There are three species of government; the *republican*, *monarchical*, and *despotic*. In order to discover their nature, it is sufficient to recollect the common notion, which supposes three definitions, or rather three facts: that a *republican government is that in which the body, or only a part of the people, is possessed of the supreme power; a monarchical, that in which a single person governs by fixed and established laws; a despotic government that in which a single person, without law and without rule, directs everything by his own will and caprice.*

This is what I call the nature of each government; we must examine now which are those laws that follow this nature directly, and consequently are the first fundamental laws.

(*Spirit of the Laws,* Book 2, ch. 1)

### 'Of the Republican Government, and the Laws relative to Democracy'

When the body of the people in a republic are possessed of the supreme power, this is called a *democracy*. When the supreme power is lodged in the hands of a part of the people, it is then an *aristocracy*.

In a democracy the people are in some respects the sovereign, and in others the subject.

They can no way exercise sovereignty but by their suffrages, which are their own will; now, the sovereign's will is the sovereign himself. The laws therefore which establish the right of suffrage, are fundamental to this government. In fact, it is as important to regulate in a republic, in what manner, by whom, to whom, and concerning what suffrages are to be given, as it is in a monarchy to know who is the prince, and after what manner he ought to govern.

(*Spirit of the Laws,* Book 2, ch. 2)

### 'Of the Laws relative to the Nature of Aristocracy'

In an aristocracy, the supreme power is lodged in the hands of a certain number of persons. These are invested both with the legislative and executive authority; and the rest of the people are in respect to them the same as the subjects of a monarchy in regard to the monarch.

(*Spirit of the Laws*, Book 2, ch. 3)

### 'Of the Relation of Laws to the Nature of Monarchical Government'

The intermediate, subordinate, and dependent powers, constitute the nature of monarchical government, I mean of that in which a single person governs by fundamental laws. I said the *intermediate*, *subordinate*, and *dependent powers*. In fact, in monarchies the prince is the source of all power, political and civil. These fundamental laws necessarily suppose the intermediate channels through which the power flows; for if there be only the momentary and capricious will of a single person to govern the state, nothing can be fixed, and of course there can be no fundamental law.

The most natural, intermediate, and subordinate power is that of the nobility. This in some measure seems to be essential to a monarchy, whose fundamental maxim is, *no monarch, no nobility; no nobility, no monarch*; but there may be a despotic prince.

(*Spirit of the Laws*, Book 2, ch. 4)

### 'Of the Laws relative to the Nature of a Despotic Government'

From the nature of despotic power it follows, that the single person invested with this power, commits the execution of it also to a single person. A man whom his senses continually inform, that he himself is everything, and his subjects nothing, is naturally lazy, voluptuous, and ignorant.

In consequence of this he neglects the management of public affairs. But were he to commit the administration to many, there would be continually disputes among them; each would form intrigues to be his first slave, and he would be obliged to take the reins into this own hands.

*(Spirit of the Laws*, Book 2, ch. 5)

### 'Difference between the Nature and Principle of Government'

After having examined the laws relative to the nature of each government, we must investigate those that relate to its principle.

There is this difference between the nature and principle of government; its nature is that by which it is constituted, and its principle that by which it is made to act. One is its particular structure, and the other the human passions which set it in motion.

Now, laws ought to be no less relative to the principle than to the nature of each government. We must therefore inquire into this principle, which shall be the subject of this third book.

*(Spirit of the Laws*, Book 3, ch. 1)

### 'Of the Principle of Democracy'

There is no great share of probity necessary to support a monarchical or despotic government. The force of laws in one, and the prince's arm in the other, are sufficient to direct and maintain the whole. But in a popular state, one spring more is necessary, namely virtue.

What I have here advanced, is confirmed by the unanimous testimony of historians, and is extremely agreeable to the nature of things. For it is clear, that in a monarchy, where he who commands the execution of the laws generally thinks himself above them, there is less need of virtue than in a popular government, where the person intrusted with the execution of the laws, is sensible of being subject himself to their direction.

*(Spirit of the Laws*, Book 3, ch. 3)

### 'Of the Principle of Aristocracy'

As virtue is necessary in a popular government, so it is necessary also under an aristocracy. True it is that in the latter it is not so absolutely requisite.

The people, who in respect to the nobility are the same as the subjects with regard to the monarch, are restrained by their laws. They have therefore less occasion for virtue than the people in a democracy. But how are the nobility to be restrained? Those who are to execute the laws against their colleagues, will immediately perceive they are acting against themselves. Virtue is therefore necessary in this body by the very nature of the constitution.

(*Spirit of the Laws*, Book 3, ch. 4)

### 'That Virtue is not the Principle of Monarchical Government'

In monarchies, policy makes people do great things with as little virtue as she can. Thus in the finest machines, art has contrived as few movements, springs, and wheels, as possible.

The state subsists independently of the love of our country, of the thirst of true glory, of self-denial, of the sacrifice of our dearest interests, and of all those heroic virtues which we admire in the ancients, and which to us are known only by story.

(*Spirit of the Laws*, Book 3, ch. 5)

### 'In what Manner Virtue is supplied in a Monarchical Government'

But it is high time for me to have done with this subject, lest I should be suspected of writing a satire against monarchical government. Far be it from me; if monarchy wants one spring, it is provided with another. Honour, that is, the prejudice of every person and every rank, supplieth the place of virtue, and is everywhere here representative. Here it is capable of inspiring the most glorious actions, and joined with the force of laws may lead us to the end of government, as well as virtue itself.

Hence, in well-regulated monarchies, they are almost all good subjects, and very good men; for to be a good man, a good intention is necessary.

(*Spirit of the Laws*, Book 3, ch. 6)

### 'That Honour is not the Principle of Despotic Government'

Honour is far from being the principle of despotic government: men being here all upon a level, no one can prefer himself to another; men, being here all slaves, can give themselves no preference at all.

Besides, as honour has its laws and rules, as it knows not how to submit, as it depends in a great measure on a man's own caprice, and not on that of another person; it can be found only in countries in which the constitution is fixed, and where they are governed by settled laws.

(*Spirit of the Laws*, Book 3, ch. 7)

### 'Of the Principle of Despotic Government'

As virtue is necessary in a republic, and in a monarchy honour; so fear is necessary in despotic government. With regard to virtue, there is no occasion for it, and honour would be extremely dangerous.

Here the immense power of the prince is devolved entirely upon those to whom he is pleased to intrust it. Persons capable of setting a value upon themselves would be likely to create revolutions. Fear must therefore depress their spirits, and extinguish even the least sense of ambition.

(*Spirit of the Laws*, Book 3, ch. 9)

### 'Different Significations given to the Word Liberty'

There is no word that has admitted of more various significations, and has made more different impressions on human minds, than that of *liberty*. Some have taken it for a facility of deposing a person on whom they had conferred a tyrannical authority; others for the power of choosing a person whom they are obliged to obey; others for the right of bearing arms, and of being thereby enabled to use violence; others for the privilege of being governed by a native of their own country, or by their own laws. A certain nation for a long time thought that liberty consisted in the privilege of wearing a long beard. Some have annexed this name to one form of government, in exclusion of others. Those who had a republican taste, applied it to this government; those who liked a monarchical state, gave it to monarchies. Thus they all have applied the name of liberty to the government most conformable to their own customs and inclinations; and as in a republic people have no so constant and so present a view of the instruments of the evils they complain of, and likewise as the laws seem there to speak more, and the executors of the laws less, it is generally attributed to republics, and denied to monarchies. In fine [finally], as in democracies the people seem to do very near whatever they please, liberty has been placed in this sort of government, and the power of the people has been confounded with their liberty.

(*Spirit of the Laws*, Book 9, ch. 2)

### 'In what Liberty consists'

It is true, that in democracies the people seem to do what they please; but political liberty does not consist in an unrestrained freedom. In governments, that is, in societies directed by laws, liberty can consist only in the power of doing what we ought to will, and in not being constrained to do what we ought not to will.

We must have continually present to our minds the difference between independence and liberty. Liberty is a right of doing whatever the laws permit; and if a citizen could do what they forbid, he would no longer be possessed of liberty, because all his fellow citizens would have the same power.

(*Spirit of the Laws*, Book 9, ch. 3)

### 'The same Subject continued'

Democratic and aristocratic states are not necessarily free. Political liberty is to be met with only in moderate governments: yet even in these it is not always met with. It is there only when there is no abuse of power. But constant experience shows us, that every man invested with power is apt to abuse it; he pushes on till he comes to something that limits him. Is it not strange, though true, to say, that virtue itself has need of limits?

To prevent the abuse of power, it is necessary that, by the very disposition of things, power should be a check to power. A government may be so constituted, as no man shall be compelled to do things to which the law does not oblige him, nor forced to abstain from things which the law permits.

(Spirit of the Laws, Book 9, ch. 4)

### 'Of the end or View of different Governments'

Though all governments have the same general end, which is that of preservation, yet each has another particular view. Increase of dominion was the view of Rome; war, of Sparta; religion, of the Jewish laws; commerce, that of Marseilles; public tranquillity, that of the laws of China; navigation, that of the laws of Rhodes; natural liberty, that of the policy of the savages; in general, the pleasures of the prince that of despotic states; that of monarchies, the prince's and the kingdom's glory. The independence of individuals is the end aimed at by the laws of Poland, and from thence results the oppression of the whole.

One nation [England] there is also in the world, that has for the direct end of its constitution political liberty.

(Spirit of the Laws, Book 9, ch. 4)

### 'Of Civil Slavery'

Slavery, properly so called, is the establishment of a right which gives to one man such a power over another, as renders him absolute master of his life and fortune. The state of slavery is in its own nature bad. It is neither useful to the master nor the slave; not to the slave, because he can do nothing through a motive of virtue; not to the master, because, by having an unlimited authority over his slaves, he insensibly accustoms himself to the want of all moral virtues, and from thence grows fierce, hasty, severe, choleric, voluptuous, and cruel.

In despotic countries, where they are already in a state of political slavery, civil slavery is more tolerable than in other governments. Everyone ought to be satisfied in those countries with necessaries and life. Hence the condition of a slave is hardly more burdensome than that of a subject.

But in a monarchical government, where it is of the utmost importance that human nature should not be debased, or dispirited, there ought to be no slavery. In democracies where they are all upon an equality, and in aristocracies where the laws ought to use their utmost endeavours to procure as great an equality as the nature of the government will permit, slavery is contrary to the spirit of the constitution; it only contributes to give a power and luxury to the citizens which they ought not to have.

(Spirit of the Laws, Book 15, ch. 1)

### 'Of the Slavery of the Negroes'

Were I to vindicate our right to make slaves of the negroes, these should be my arguments.

The Europeans, having extirpated the Americans, were obliged to make slaves of the Africans, for clearing such vast tracts of land.

Sugar would be too dear, if the plants which produce it were cultivated by any other than slaves.

These creatures are all over black, and with such a flat nose, that they can scarcely be pitied.

It is hardly to be believed that God, who is a wise being, should place a soul, especially a good soul, in such a black ugly body.

It is so natural to look upon colour as the criterion of human nature, that the Asiatics, among whom eunuchs are employed, always deprive the *blacks* of their resemblance to us, by a more opprobrious distinction.

The colour of the skin may be determined by that of the hair, which, among the Egyptians, the best philosophers in the world, was of such importance, that they put to death all the red-haired men who fell into their hands.

The negroes prefer a glass necklace to that gold, which polite nations so highly value. Can there be a greater proof of their wanting common sense?

It is impossible for us to suppose these creatures to be men, because, allowing them to be men, a suspicion would follow, that we ourselves are not Christians.

Weak minds exaggerate too much the wrong done to the Africans. For were the case as they state it, would the European powers, who make so many needless conventions among themselves, have failed to make a general one, in behalf of humanity and compassion?

(*Spirit of the Laws*, Book 15, ch. 5)

### 'That in the Countries of the South there is a Natural Inequality between the two Sexes'

Women, in hot climates, are marriageable at eight, nine, or ten years of age; thus, in those countries, infancy and marriage almost always go together. They are old at twenty; their reason therefore never accompanies their beauty. When beauty demands the empire, the want of reason forbids the claim; when reason is obtained, beauty is no more. These women ought then to be in a state of dependence; for reason cannot procure in old age, that empire, which even youth and beauty could not give. It is therefore extremely natural, that in these places, a man, when no law opposes it, should leave one wife to take another, and that polygamy should be introduced.

In temperate climates, where the charms of women are best preserved, where they arrive later at maturity, and have children at a more advanced season of life, the old age of their husbands in some degree follows theirs; and as they have more reason and knowledge at the time of marriage, if it be only on account of their having continued longer in life, it must naturally introduce a kind of equality between the two sexes, and in consequence of this, the law of having only one wife.

In cold countries the almost necessary custom of drinking strong liquors, establishes intemperance amongst men. Women, who, in this respect, have a natural restraint, because they are always on the defensive, have therefore the advantage of reason over them.

Nature, which has distinguished men by their reason and bodily strength, has set no other bounds to their power than those of this strength and reason. It has given charms to women, and ordained that their ascendant over man shall end with these charms: but, in hot countries, these are found only at the beginning, and never in the progress of life.

Thus the law which permits only one wife, is physically conformable to the climate of Europe, and not to that of Asia. This is the reason why Mahometanism was established with such facility in Asia, and so difficultly extended in Europe; why Christianity is maintained in Europe, and has been destroyed in Asia; and, in fine, why the Mahometans have made such progress in China, and the Christians so little.

(*Spirit of the Laws*, Book 16, ch. 2)

## CATHERINE II

Catherine the Great (1729–96), daughter of a minor German prince, was born at Stettin and married to the future tsar Peter III in 1745. A few months after Peter's accession, in 1762, he was overthrown by Catherine who would now rule as Empress of Russia until her death. During her marriage, she read widely, including works such as Pierre Bayle's *Historical and Critical Dictionary* (1697) and Voltaire's historical writings. Later, in her voluminous correspondence with Voltaire, Diderot, Grimm, d'Alembert and others, she would declare the *Encyclopédie* 'an inexhaustible source of excellent things', delight in the *philosophes'* campaigns and achievements, and refer to Voltaire as her 'master'. Though possessing absolute authority, Catherine was committed to many of the values and reforms advocated by the *philosophes* (at least until the shock of the French Revolution made her more conservative) and, within what she considered the practical constraints of the empire, in many respects she tried to rule as an Enlightened monarch. She also amassed an outstanding collection of European works of art, including the purchase of Diderot's library. To many *philosophes*, her wars with Turkey, annexation of the Crimea and acquisition of lands through the Partitions of Poland seemed unenlightened; and, following his visit to her court in 1774, Diderot left disillusioned. After the French Revolution, Catherine changed her opinion of the *philosophes*, holding them responsible for the violence and destruction. In a letter to Melchior Grimm in 1794, she wrote: 'Do you remember that the late King of Prussia [Frederick II] claimed to have been told by Helvétius that the aim of the *philosophes* was to overturn all thrones, and that the *Encyclopédie* was written with no other end in view than to destroy all kings and all religions? Do you remember that you never wished to be included among the *philosophes*? Well, you were right [...] The sole aim of the whole movement, as experience is proving, is to destroy.' Even so, her life and reign were widely celebrated and became the stuff of legend. Like Peter the Great's Westernising policies at the beginning of the century, Catherine's desire to promote Russia's economic and political development was widely debated in Europe.

The text selected here is from a modern translation of Catherine's *Nakaz* (*Instruction*), the most important, frequently translated and disseminated statement of her political philosophy; presented in 1767 to a Legislative Commission that she had summoned in order to remodel the laws of Russia. As she acknowledged to Frederick II and other *philosophes*, the 526 items of the *Instruction* drew heavily on two main sources of inspiration: 'Most of it is taken from President Montesquieu's *The Spirit of the Laws* and the Marquis of Beccaria's *On Crimes and Punishments*.' The Legislative Assembly did not produce the radical reforms for which many *philosophes* had hoped. But, as a distillation of some *philosophes*' views and a clear expression of Catherine's own sympathies at that time, the *Instruction* played an important role in sowing ideas of the Enlightenment in Russian history.

## Instruction (1767)

### The Instructions to the Commissioners for Composing a New Code of Laws

1. The Christian Law teaches us to do mutual good to one another, as much as possibly we can.

2. Laying this down as a fundamental rule prescribed by that religion, which has taken, or ought to take root in the hearts of the whole people; we cannot but suppose, that every honest man in the community is, or will be, desirous of seeing his native country at the very summit of happiness, glory, safety, and tranquillity.

3. And that every individual citizen in particular must wish to see himself protected by laws, which should not distress him in his circumstances, but, on the contrary, should defend him from all attempts of others, that are repugnant to this fundamental rule.

4. In order therefore to proceed to a speedy execution of what *we* expect from such a general wish, *we*, fixing the foundation upon the above first-mentioned rule, ought to begin with an inquiry into the natural situation of this empire.

5. For those laws have the greatest conformity with nature, whose particular regulations are best adapted to the situation and circumstances of the people, for whom they are instituted.

6. Russia is a European state. [...]

9. The sovereign is absolute; for there is no other authority but that which centres in his single person, that can act with a vigour proportionate to the extent of such a vast dominion.

10. The extent of the dominion requires an absolute power to be vested in that person who rules over it. It is expedient so to be, that the quick dispatch of affairs, sent from distant parts, might make ample amends for the delay occasioned by the great distance of the places.

11. Every other form of government whatsoever would not only have been prejudicial to Russia, but would even have proved its entire ruin.

12. Another reason is; that it is better to be subject to the laws under one master, than to be subservient to many.

13. What is the true end of monarchy? Not to deprive people of their natural liberty; but to correct their actions, in order to attain the *supreme good*.

14. The form of government, therefore, which best attains this end, and at the same time sets less bounds than others to natural liberty, is that which coincides with the views and purposes of rational creatures, and answers the end, upon which we ought to fix a steadfast eye in the regulations of civil polity.

15. The intention and the end of monarchy, is the glory of the citizens, of the state and of the sovereign.

16. But, from this glory, a sense of liberty arises in a people governed by a monarch; which may produce in these states as much energy in transacting the most important affairs, and may contribute as much to the happiness of the subjects, as even liberty itself. [...]

32. It is the greatest happiness for a man to be so circumstanced, that, if his passions should prompt him to be mischievous, he should still think it more for his interest not to give way to them.

33. The laws ought to be so framed, as to secure the safety of every citizen as much as possible.

34. The equality of the citizens consists in this; that they should all be subject to the same laws.

35. This equality requires institutions so well adapted, as to prevent the rich from oppressing those who are not so wealthy as themselves, and converting all the charges and employments intrusted to them as magistrates only, to their own private emolument.

36. General or political liberty does not consist in that licentious notion, *that a man may do whatever he pleases*.

37. In a state or assemblage of people that live together in a community, where there are laws, liberty can only consist *in doing that which every one ought to do*, and *not to be constrained to do that which one ought not to do*.

38. A man ought to form in his own mind an exact and clear idea of what liberty is. *Liberty is the right of doing whatsoever the laws allow*: And if any one citizen could do what the laws forbid, there would be no more liberty; because others would have an equal power of doing the same.

39. The political liberty of a citizen is the peace of mind arising from the consciousness, that every individual enjoys his peculiar safety; and in order that the people might attain this liberty, the laws ought to be so framed, that no one citizen should stand in fear of another; but that all of them should stand in fear of the same laws.

(*Instruction*, nos 1–5, 9–16, 32–39)

# FREDERICK II

Frederick the Great (1712–86) inherited the throne of his domineering father, to become King of Prussia in 1740. Despite his father's strict Lutheranism and militarism, Frederick developed a love of foreign literature, philosophy, music and the arts, and began a lifelong correspondence with Voltaire who oversaw the publication of his first work *Anti-Machiavel*, a denunciation of unnecessary wars, published in Holland in 1740. On his accession, Frederick invaded Silesia; the first step in an expansionist foreign policy that would lead to the growth of a massive army and a series of bloody and destructive wars throughout his reign. In what he saw as the interests of the state, Frederick also reopened the Berlin Academy of Sciences, codified Prussian laws, abolished judicial torture, supported greater religious toleration and freedom of the press, encouraged large-scale immigration, protected and befriended many *philosophes*, and supervised state-directed economic growth. The continuity of many of Frederick's policies with those of his father – in particular his militarism and social and economic conservatism – frustrated many *philosophes* and has led some modern historians to reject the view that he was an Enlightened monarch. Rather, they see 'Enlightened absolutism' as a misnomer, and Frederick's philosophical postures as a sham. Even so, he played a key role in the eyes of most contemporaries – though they were also divided in their views of his regime.

As a 'philosopher-king', Frederick was keen to distinguish his enlightened absolutism from what he regarded as the wilful, decadent, self-serving, unjust and inefficient despotism of countries such as France. Though Frederick was no less powerful than a Bourbon king, he rejected religious (divine right) justifications of monarchy, and proclaimed that 'the monarch has no right to dictate the citizen's beliefs'. For Frederick, Christianity was 'an old metaphysical fiction, stuffed with fables, contradictions and absurdities'. He also emphasised the importance of the rule of law, revising the judicial system in his *Codex Fridericianus* of 1749, and worked tirelessly to promote what he regarded as the welfare and interests of the state and its citizens. In the extract here, from a modern translation of *Essai sur les Formes du Gouvernement* (*Essay on the Forms of Government*, 1777), one of his many public and private writings, Frederick sets out his view of Enlightened monarchy.

## Essay on the Forms of Government (1777)

The citizens only granted pre-eminence to one of their fellows in return for the services which they expected from him. These services consist in upholding the laws, ensuring that justice is scrupulously observed, opposing the corruption of manners as far as he can and defending the State against its enemies. The ruler must supervise agriculture, he must ensure abundant supplies for the community and promote industry and trade. He is like a sentry, permanently on guard against his neighbours and the activities of the enemies of the State [...] Just as all the springs of a watch operate to the same purpose, namely, to measure time, so too the springs of government should be set in such a way that all the different parts of the administration contribute equally to the greatest good of the State, that vital object that must never be lost sight of. [...]

The ruler is linked by indissoluble bonds to the body of the State; consequently he feels the repercussion of all the ills that afflict his subjects, and likewise, society suffers the misfortunes which affect its ruler. There is only one good, namely, that of the State in general. If the ruler loses some provinces, he is no longer in the same position as before to assist his subjects. If misfortune has driven him into debt, it is the poor citizens who must pay; on the other hand, if the population is very small, if the people languishes in poverty, the ruler lacks every resource. These are truths so incontrovertible that there is no need to stress them further. I repeat, then, the ruler represents the State; he and his peoples form a single body which can only be happy as long as they are both harmoniously united. The ruler is to the society he governs what the head is to the whole body: he must see, think and act for the whole community, in order to obtain for it all the benefits of which it is capable. If monarchical government is to be superior to republican, the monarch's decision is all-important; he must be active and upright, and must muster all his good qualities in order to fulfil his destined career.

This is my idea of his duties. He must acquire an accurate and detailed knowledge of his country's strengths and weaknesses, including monetary resources, population, finances, trade and the laws and character of the nation which he is to rule. [...]

Since any individual who fails to act according to principle is inconsistent in his conduct, it is all the more important that the ruler, who is responsible for the people's welfare, should act according to a fixed system of politics, war, finances, trade and law. [...]

These are the general duties that a ruler must carry out. In order not to fall short of them, he must constantly remind himself that he is a man, like the least of his subjects; if he is society's first judge, first general, first financier, first minister, it is not in order that he should merely symbolise their duties, but that he should carry them out. He is the first servant of the State, obliged to act with probity, wisdom, and complete disinterestedness, as if at any moment he were accountable to his citizens for his stewardship. So he is to blame, if he squanders the national revenue, which is the product of taxation, on luxury, ostentation and dissipation, when he should be promoting good moral conduct, which is the guardian of the laws, when he should be improving national education, and not undermining it by his bad example. [...] This is the true idea that should be held of the duties of a monarch and is the only way to make monarchical government good and beneficial. If many rulers behave differently, we must attribute this to their lack of reflection on the institution of monarchy and the duties attaching to it. They have assumed a responsibility whose onerousness and importance they have underestimated; they have erred through lack of knowledge; for in our day ignorance causes more errors than wickedness.

This portrait of a monarch will perhaps be seen in the eyes of critics to resemble the ideal of the sage depicted by the Stoics, an ideal which has never existed in fact, and to which Marcus Aurelius [Roman Emperor, 161–180 AD] alone came closest. We hope that this humble essay may be able to produce some Marcus Aureliuses: that would be the finest reward we could hope for, and it would benefit humanity at the same time.

(*Essay on the Forms of Government*)

# Chapter 7

# The development of civil society

**I**N SEEKING TO UNDERSTAND the characteristics and dynamics of the societies in which they lived, many *philosophes* became fascinated by the origins and histories of their own and other peoples. They did not want to rely upon scriptural accounts of the formation and diffusion of society, or upon theological approaches to history, such as Bishop Bossuet's *Discourse on Universal History* (1681), in which history was seen as the working out of God's will and purpose. Nor did a meticulous collection and discussion of the documentary evidence of the past prove particularly appealing, though many *philosophes* took an interest in the great range of new evidence about human history and societies that was being acquired from sources such as the excavation of ancient sites at Herculaneum and Pompeii; the translation of non-European texts and manuscripts; and the writings of travellers and settlers, such as those of Captain Cook and of the Jesuits in China. Rather, as Voltaire put it, to most *philosophes* it seemed that mere 'érudition' in historical research was akin to antiquarianism, and that close attention to details was 'a vermin which destroy great works'. Eager to demonstrate the progress and potential for improvement of the human race, there was a tendency of the Enlightened to look upon the past, and to represent it, with condescension or disdain. Despite his numerous historical writings, Voltaire therefore declaimed that 'history in general is a collection of crimes, follies and misfortunes, among which we have now and then met with few virtues, and some happy times; as we sometimes see a few scattered huts in a barren desert' (*Essay on the Customs and Spirit of Nations*, 1756).

In order to write the kind of history – 'philosophical history', as it came to be known – that the *philosophes* preferred, it was necessary to have a subject worthy of epic literary treatment and capable of sustaining a grand narrative of the progress of human society and selected nations. Voltaire's *Age of Louis XIV* (1751) and *Essay on the Customs* therefore focused on what appeared to be grand subjects – the unprecedented greatness of France during Louis' reign, and 'a sketch of universal history' drawn from a free-ranging comparison of the nations and cultures of the world. Similarly, although the century's most celebrated historian, Edward Gibbon, would later decry Voltaire's lack of respect for sources and occasional disregard for historical accuracy, he nevertheless agreed that Enlightenment history needed to be far more than a secular assemblage of facts and figures on specific topics. Echoing most other *philosophes*, Gibbon maintained that 'historians should be philosophers', and that: 'To the eyes of the philosopher, events are the least interesting part of history. It is the knowledge of man, morality and politics he finds there that elevates it in his mind'. Thus it was History on a grand scale that most appealed to the philosophical spirit of the Enlightened, and brought ambitious writers such as Gibbon to international acclaim. In addition to his magisterial study of Roman civilisation, and Voltaire's works, by mid-century the Enlightenment had produced a string of voluminous and popular texts, such as David Hume's *History of England* (1754–62), William Robertson's *History of the Reign of Emperor Charles V* (1769) and *History of America* (1776), and Abbé Raynal's *A Philosophical and Political History of the Settlements* (1772), through which its ideas and values were expressed.

A philosophical history was expected not only to be instructive about the past, but to have contemporary relevance, drawing out lessons that could be applied to modern settings. This was just as necessary when sources were scarce and unreliable as when they were fairly plentiful. Thus Robertson's *relatively* well-documented depiction of the American Indians as lazy, stupid and wretched savages, living without civilisation in a hostile environment, could be read as a cue for further colonisation. Similarly, Gibbon's *Decline and Fall of the Roman Empire* (1776–88) was infused with lessons about religious toleration, political liberty, poverty and prosperity, reason and desire (to name but a few) that both forged and reflected the opinions of Enlightened audiences. In the main, these history lessons depended upon a general confidence in the uniformity of human nature. As Hume explained: 'Mankind are so much the same, in all times and places, that history informs us of nothing new or strange in this particular. Its chief use is only to discover the constant and universal principles of human nature' (*Essays Moral and Political*, 1741–42). Even allowing for differences due to geographical and environmental factors, it was therefore possible to explain and judge human behaviour and societies by what appeared to be a timeless and universal standard. Thus, while Robertson could argue that 'the disposition and manners of men are formed by their situation' (*History of America*), and that 'the human mind, whenever it is placed in the same situation, will, in ages the most distant, assume the same form and be distinguished by the same manners' (*History of Charles V*), he nevertheless had little difficulty in judging American Indians by what he considered to be the standards of the Enlightened.

To account for the differences between, and changes that took place within, human societies, past and present, it was possible to employ a wide range of tools and methods – seemingly quite independent of the biblical evidence of monogenesis and Babel. Some were based upon the scientific classification and explanations of the living world proposed by writers such as Linnaeus and the Comte de Buffon. The Swedish botanist, Linnaeus, had divided humans into two species: *Homo Sapiens* and *Homo Monstrosus* (see p. 106). The French natural historian, Buffon, had argued that 'there was originally but one species', and that diversity was due largely to environmental factors. Others, such as the Scottish philosopher and historian, John Millar, in his *Origin of the Distinction of Ranks, or an Enquiry into the Circumstances which gave Rise to Influence and Authority in the Different Members of Society* (1771) placed greater emphasis upon the mode of subsistence – and, in particular, the treatment of women – as a means of explaining social differences and dynamics. Though equally controversial, almost all of these accounts began or ended with Europeans being placed at the top of a hierarchy of humans.

To base their explanations of the origins and development of societies on firm foundations, many *philosophes* drew upon the work of natural law theorists such as Hugo Grotius (1583–1645) and Samuel Pufendorf (1632–94). These writers had tried to establish universal systems of law and morality based upon reasoning about what appeared to be the fundamental drives and needs of humans living in an original 'state of nature' (generally regarded as God's creation), before rules and government had emerged. Isolation of what they took to be the key common features and circumstances of life in this hypothetical 'state of nature', pre-dating the formation of civil society, provided a powerful means by which Hobbes, Locke, Montesquieu, Rousseau, Adam Smith, Condorcet, Kant and many others drew up their largely conjectural and theoretical accounts of how and why civil society had emerged and – no less important – on what ethical and other foundations the modern nation or society should be based. Yet, while there was broad agreement among many over the importance of 'the law of nature' in reasoning about human rights and duties, there was much less agreement about the actual character of 'the state of nature', let alone about the kind of modern society and political state it seemed to legitimate. In particular, Rousseau's conjectures about human nature brought the whole idea of progress into question.

Rousseau rejected both the Hobbesian claim that life in a state of nature was 'nasty, brutish, and short', a 'war of everyone against everyone', and the Lockean view that property existed before the formation of society and was even essential to its creation. In the opening of the second part of his *Discourse on the Origins of Inequality* (1755) Rousseau famously declared:

> The first man who, having enclosed a piece of ground, took it into his head to say 'This is mine', and found people simple enough to believe him, was the real founder of civil society. From how many crimes, wars, and murders, from how many horrors and misfortunes might not any one have saved mankind, by pulling up the stakes, or filling up the ditch, and crying to his fellows: 'Beware of listening to this impostor; you are undone if you once forget that the fruits of the earth belong to us all, and the earth itself to nobody.'

Rather than seeing the natural state as a miserable condition from which humans would be grateful to escape, in his secular account of the fall of man it was 'the

origin of society and law, which bound new fetters on the poor, and gave new powers to the rich; which irretrievably destroyed natural liberty, externally fixed the
law of property and inequality, converted clever usurpation into inalienable right,
and, for the advantage of a few ambitious individuals, subjected all mankind to perpetual labour, slavery and wretchedness'. He concluded:

> If the reader thus discovers and retraces the lost and forgotten road, by which
> man must have passed from a state of nature to the state of society ... he can-
> not fail to be struck by the vast distance which separates the two states. It is in
> tracing this slow succession that he will find the solution to a number of prob-
> lems of politics and morals, which philosophers cannot settle ... In a word, he
> will explain how the soul and the passions of men alter unawares, changing their
> very nature; why our wants and pleasures in the end seek new objects; and why,
> the original man having vanished by degrees, society only offers to us an assem-
> bly of artificial men and factitious passions, which are the work of all these new
> relations, and without any real foundation in nature. We are taught nothing on
> this subject by reflection that is not entirely confirmed by observation. The sav-
> age and the civilised man differ so much in the bottom of their hearts and in
> their inclinations, that what constitutes the supreme happiness of one would
> reduce the other to despair. The former breathes only peace and liberty.

On reading the *Discourse*, Voltaire wrote wryly to Rousseau:

> I have received your new book against the human race ... Never has so much
> talent been used to want to make us into animals; you make one want to walk
> on all fours ... However, as it is more than sixty years since I lost the habit, I
> feel unfortunately that it will be impossible for me to regain it.

Criticism of Rousseau's ideas, particularly that savages lived free, healthy, honest and happy lives, was not confined to France. Frederick the Great, a protector
of Rousseau, noted in 1762 that 'my ideas are as far from his as the finite is from
the infinite. He will never persuade me to browse on the grass and walk on all
fours.' A decade later he told the Berlin Academy of Sciences:

> Compare a Canadian savage with any citizen of a civilised country of Europe,
> and all the advantage will be with the latter. How can one prefer crude nature
> to nature perfected, lack of means of subsistence to a life of ease, rudeness to
> politeness, the security of possessions enjoyed under the protection of the laws
> to the law of the jungle and to anarchy, which destroys the fortunes and con-
> ditions of families? Society, a community of men, could not do without either
> the arts or the sciences.

In Italy, Beccaria (see p. 216) reflected that 'All the feelings a man has, whatever
state he is in, are always natural to him', and that 'Man entered into the state of society from the state of savagery precisely because his natural feelings had changed'

and would continue to change along with sociability itself. It was therefore quite wrong to think that the feelings with which men entered society could later serve as a guide to the laws and morality of civilised nations. After reviewing the great debate on whether 'man' is happier in a savage or a social state, Beccaria concluded:

> Just as the natural philosopher sees the current order of things on the face of the globe, but can also read in its innards the traces of the past disorders that created it and whose effects are still discernible in nature, so the moralist, observing the advantages of our current state and the progress that has been made in the science of happiness, can perceive them as the outcome of ancient disorders; and he may dare to predict that current evils are just the inevitable tremors and upheavals arising from that process, after which the nations will march on towards a final, still very distant, state of equality and happiness.
>
> ('Reflections on Barbarousness and Civilisation', 1760s)

Such confidence in the progress of human society was expressed by many *philosophes* throughout the century. For the English scientist Joseph Priestley it sprang from a mixture of radical politics and religious convictions. Believing that 'The reign of reason will ever be the reign of peace', and that it had been 'foretold in many prophesies' that there would be a 'happy state of things' to come, he envisaged a future 'when nation shall no more rise up against nation, and when they shall learn war no more. This is a state of things which good sense, and the prevailing spirit of commerce, aided by Christianity and true philosophy cannot fail to effect in time' (*Letters to Edmund Burke occasioned by his Reflections on the Revolution in France*, 1791). For the French philosopher and mathematician Condorcet, greater education and equality would roll back the power of priests and despots in a universal process of advancement. It could be shown 'from reasoning and from facts' that 'the perfectibility of man is absolutely indefinite', and that 'the progress of this perfectibility, henceforth above the control of every power that would impede it, has no other limit than the duration of the globe upon which nature has placed us' (*Sketch of a Historical Picture of the Human Mind*, 1795). A little earlier, Gibbon had closed his 'General Observations on the Fall of the Roman Empire in the West' with 'the pleasing conclusion that every age of the world has increased and still increases the real wealth, the happiness, the knowledge, and perhaps the virtue, of the human race' (*Decline and Fall of the Roman Empire*, vol. II, 1781).

In often representing distant societies and cultures as 'primitive', 'ruder', 'underdeveloped', 'inferior' versions of contemporary European nations, many *philosophes* clearly expressed a belief in their own society's modernity and superiority, as well as their commitment to the idea and legitimacy of change. To some writers, the 'other' societies and cultures of the past and present were at least as strange and exotic as they were familiar, profoundly different in their ways of thinking, communicating and socialising. For Giambattista Vico, in Naples, memory and imagination were vital tools to unlock the history and diversity of nations. To the German philosopher and critic Herder, differences between nations were also central to the understanding of human society and history, and well worth maintaining against the growing prospect of a general and dismal uniformity, for 'every distinct community is a *nation*, having its own national culture as it has its own language' (*Ideas for a Philosophy of the History of Mankind*, 1784–91). However, in the work of many *philosophes* who were committed to the idea that human nature was fundamentally unchanging, there was a tendency to gloss over or dismiss the 'otherness' of distant peoples. As Vico put it: 'when people can form no idea of distant and unfamiliar things, they judge them by what is present and familiar'. Thus, in seeking to reveal the natural laws that governed the development of societies, Adam Smith portrayed all humans as being primarily motivated by what he took to be archetypal selfish and acquisitive desires, notwithstanding all the differences in beliefs and circumstances.

Together with writers such as Adam Ferguson and John Millar, Smith's ideas about social development formed part of what became known as the 'four-stage theory' that emerged most clearly in the works of the Scottish Enlightenment. Instead of using categories such as race, colour and religion to explain the diversity of societies, each was classified according to its dominant mode of subsistence; hunting and gathering, pastoral, agricultural, and commercial (capitalist). Each mode represented a key stage in the progress of civilisation, from the 'lowest and rudest' state of hunters, such as the native tribes of North America, who lived according to the laws of nature; to the pastoral stage as evidenced among the Tartars and Arabs; to the agricultural economies of feudal societies; to the most advanced stage, 'the age of commerce', which distinguished most European states. Though embedded in *The Wealth of Nations* (1776), a succinct expression of this theory was reported to have been given by Smith in his *Lectures on Jurisprudence* in the 1760s: 'There are four distinct states which mankind passes through: 1st, the age of hunters; 2nd, the age of shepherds; 3rd, the age of agriculture; 4th, the age of commerce.' Ferguson and others recognised that there were losses as well as gains in this grand progress of 'the species itself from rudeness to civilization', but there was little doubt about where the balance lay. In his *Essay on the History of Civil Society* (1767), he reported: 'We may, with good reason, congratulate our species on their having escaped from a state of barbarous disorder and violence, into a state of domestic peace and regular policy; when they have sheathed the dagger, and disarmed the animosities of civil contention; when the weapons with which they contend are the reasonings of the wise, and the tongue of the eloquent'. This history was also a moral progress: 'The wealth, the aggrandizement and power of nations, are commonly the effects of virtue; the loss of these advantages, is often a consequence of vice.'

Some of the ways in which the origins, history and development of civil society were portrayed during the Enlightenment can be examined here through extracts from the highly influential work of Ferguson, Smith and Gibbon. Further insights can be gained from the extracts in other chapters, particularly from the works of Locke (p. 154), Rousseau (p. 262) and Condorcet (p. 28). In this chapter, however, our selection of texts begins with an extract from Vico's extraordinary *New Science*, in which a very different approach to that of the Scottish Enlightenment was employed. Though no less convinced that there were key stages or periods in the history of all societies, for Vico these stages were the age of gods, the age of heroes, and finally the age of humanity.

## GIAMBATTISTA VICO

Giambattista Vico (1668–1744), son of a poor bookseller, was born, lived most of his life, and died in Naples. Educated by Jesuits, he worked as a private tutor before becoming a Professor of Rhetoric at Naples University in 1699. His wide-ranging interests in philosophy, history, literature, mythology and the law were reflected in his major works: *De Antiquissima Italorum Sapienta* (*On the Ancient Wisdom of the Italians*, 1710), the three-volume *Diritto Universale* (*On Universal Law*, 1720–22), and *Scienza Nuova* (*New Science*, 1725). None of these works earned Vico either the academic promotion or the international recognition for which he yearned. Frustrated by the financial strains of raising a large family, and a growing sense of intellectual isolation, he wrote his *Autobiography* (1729) and extensively revised the *New Science*, producing a second version in 1730 and a third version which was published in 1744, shortly after his death.

Although *New Science* was largely ignored by the *philosophes*, a century later the French historian Michelet drew attention to the book, and it is now considered a seminal – if challenging and controversial – text in the history of ideas. In the 1930s the historian Paul Hazard remarked that 'our intellectual history would have had a very different tale to tell' had Vico been listened to. In particular, 'our eighteenth-century ancestors would not have believed that everything that was clear was necessarily true. On the contrary they would have looked on clarity as a defect rather than a virtue in the matter of human reason. If an idea is clear, it means that it is finished, rounded off, over and done with. They would have given pride of place in the hierarchy of faculties, not to reason, but to the imagination' (*European Thought in the Eighteenth Century*). Emphasising the importance of memory and imagination, and drawing upon many scholarly traditions and debates, *New Science* argued that humans could only truly understand what they themselves had made (such as mathematics and human societies), rather than the natural world which was of God's creation. A new kind of philosophy should therefore be founded and directed towards understanding the history of nations. Due to failure to appreciate 'the poetic nature of the founders of nations', scholars had failed to see that human feelings, thoughts, language, customs and institutions were profoundly different in past societies. Consequently, a true understanding of ancient societies and the development of nations had not been attained. Revising and developing his insights and ideas throughout his life, Vico claimed that he could demonstrate, in a highly systematic manner, that there were three very different kinds of society – the age of the gods, the age of the heroes, and the age of men – each representing a distinctive stage in the development of each nation, and that there was a historical process that was inevitable and universal. From this account of human history (variously portrayed by modern commentators as conservative, anti-modern, radical, or unEnlightened), the study of the humanities and the idea of humanity itself would need to be fundamentally rethought.

The extracts published here, from a modern translation, are taken from the beginning of the third edition of *New Science*, in which Vico uses a frontispiece illustration to introduce his thoughts and provide readers with a general 'Idea of the Work'.

*Figure 7.1*   'Tableau of Civil Institutions'
*Source*: Frontispiece of the 1744 edition of *New Science*.

To help readers understand the extraordinary and challenging ideas of his *New Science*, in the third edition (1744) Vico provided a frontispiece engraving, opposite a portrait of himself. The engraving, depicting the world of nations, the world of nature, and the world of minds and of God, was followed by forty-two paragraphs in which Vico introduced the 'Idea of the Work'. In this, all elements of the picture, such as the items on the ground (e.g. purse, sword, plough, rudder, tablet inscribed with letters from two Latin alphabets), which denote 'the world of nations', are meticulously arranged and explained. Thus

> the tablet lies quite close to the plough and rather far from the rudder. This represents the origin of native languages, each of which was formed in its own land, where the founders of nations finally chanced to settle ... The tablet shows only the beginning of the alphabets, and lies facing the statue of Homer [*c*.1050–850 BC]. For Greek tradition tells us that the Greek letters were not all invented at one time.

The significance that Vico attached to some of the other elements of his 'tableau' is explored in the passages selected here.

## New Science ([1725], 1744)

### 'Idea of the Work'

Just as Cebes the Theban once made a *Tablet* of things moral [a first-century Greek dialogue in which an allegorical painting about human morality is described and analysed], so I present here a *Tableau of civil institutions*. Before reading my work, you may use this tableau to form an idea of my New Science. And after reading it, you will find that this tableau aids your imagination in retaining my work in your memory.

The woman with winged temples who stands on the celestial globe, meaning the world of nature, is Metaphysics: for her name in fact means 'above nature'. The radiant triangle with the seeing eye is God, shown in his manifestation as providence. In her state of ecstasy, Metaphysics contemplates God above the order of natural institutions, through which philosophers have previously contemplated him. In other words, Metaphysics in this work ascends higher and contemplates in God the world of human minds, which we call the metaphysical world. Metaphysics thus seeks to demonstrate God's providence in the world of the human spirit, which we call the civil world or the world of nations.

In the lower part of the picture are represented various hieroglyphs symbolizing the institutions which are the basic elements of the civil world. The globe, which represents the physical or natural world, rests on only one point of the altar. This means that previously the philosophers have contemplated and demonstrated divine providence only through the natural order, in which God is conceived as an eternal Mind who is the free and absolute sovereign of nature. To this God, humankind offers its worship, sacrifices, and other divine honours, because his eternal counsel naturally grants and preserves our existence. But no philosopher has yet contemplated God's providence under humankind's most characteristic property, which is its essentially social nature. Since original sin caused people to fall from a state of perfect justice, human intentions and actions generally follow different and even contrary paths. If people were left to pursue their private interests, they would live in solitude like wild beasts. But by His providential care, God ordered and arranged human institutions so that this same self-interest led people, even through these different and contrary ways, to live with justice like *human beings* and to remain in society. In my New Science, I shall show that this social nature is the true civil nature of humankind, and that law exists in nature. This role of divine providence is the first of the principal topics studied in my New Science. Viewed in this aspect, my work becomes a *rational civil theology of divine providence*. In the Zodiac belt circling the celestial globe, only the signs of Leo and Virgo, and no others, appear full-face or in what is called front view. The figure of Leo means that the principles of my New Science begin by contemplating Hercules, who is the archetype of the founder celebrated by every pagan nation of antiquity [...] As for Virgo, the astronomers adopted the poets' description of the goddess as crowned with ears of grain. This means that Greek history began in the Golden Age, which the poets clearly celebrate as the world's first age [...] During this Golden Age, the gods mingled with heroes on earth, as the ancient poets faithfully record. As we shall see, the earliest pagans, being simple and uncouth folk, were deceived by the fearful superstitions created by their vigorous imaginations, and so truly believed that they saw gods on earth [...]

You must not think it improper that the altar stands beneath the celestial globe and supports it. As we shall see, the world's first altars were raised by the pagans in the primitive, earthbound heaven sung by the ancient poets, whose myths faithfully record the tradition that Heaven once ruled on earth and bestowed great benefits on the human race [...]

The ray of divine providence, which illuminates the convex jewel adorning the breast of Metaphysics, signifies that metaphysics must have a clean and pure heart [...]

The ray of providence is reflected from the breast of Metaphysics to the statue of Homer [*c*.1050–850 BC], who is the earliest pagan author to come down to us. For metaphysics has its origins in the history of human ideas, beginning with humankind's very first civilised thoughts [...]

In addition, I note that my work employs a new form of criticism, which was previously lacking, in seeking to establish the truth about the founders of the pagan nations. For these founders in fact lived more than a thousand years before those writers with whom previous criticism has dealt. In my Science, philosophy undertakes to examine philology. (By philology, I mean the science of everything that depends on human volition: for example, all histories of the languages, customs, and deeds of various peoples in both war and peace.) Previously, philosophy has had almost a horror of discussing questions of philology, since they involve lamentably obscure cases and infinitely diverse effects. But here philosophy reduces philology to the form of a science, discovering in it the outlines of an *ideal eternal history*, along which the histories of all nations pass in time.

(*New Science*, 'Idea of the Work', paras 1–7)

Thus, by studying the common nature of nations in the light of divine providence, my *New Science*, or new metaphysics, discovers the origins of divine and human institutions in the pagan nations. And on the basis of these origins, my Science establishes a system of the natural law of the nations, which progresses with great regularity and consistency in all three ages through which the Egyptians said they had passed in the entire course of world history. These three ages are the following: (1) The age of the gods, when the pagan peoples believed that they were living under divine government, and that all their actions were commanded by auspices and oracles, which are the most ancient institutions in secular history. (2) The age of the heroes, when heroes ruled everywhere in aristocratic states by virtue of their presumed natural superiority to the plebeians. (3) And finally, the age of men, when all recognized their equality in human nature, so that they first established democracies and later monarchies, which are the two forms of human government.

Corresponding to these three types of nature and government, three kinds of language were spoken, which constitute the lexicon of my New Science: (1) The first dates from the age of families when pagan peoples had just embraced civilization. We find that it was a mute or wordless language which used gestures or physical objects bearing a natural relationship to the ideas they wanted to signify. (2) The second language used heroic emblems – such as similes, comparisons, images, metaphors, and descriptions of nature – as the principal lexicon of its heroic language, which was spoken in the age when heroes ruled. (3) The third language was the human or civilized language which used vocabulary agreed on by popular convention, and of which the people are the absolute lords. This language is proper to democracies and monarchies, for in those states it is the people who determine the meaning of the laws, which are binding for nobles and plebeians alike. Hence, once the laws of any nation are written in the common speech, knowledge of them is no longer in the hands of the nobility. Previously, the nobles of every nation, who were also priests, kept their laws in a secret language like a sacred object. This is the natural reason for the secrecy in which the Roman patricians kept their laws before popular liberty was established. These are precisely the three languages which the Egyptians said had been spoken earlier in their world, corresponding exactly in both number and order to the three ages through which their world had passed: (1) The first was the *hieroglyphic* language, a sacred and secret language using mute gestures, as befits religions, in which observance is more important than speech. (2) The second was the *symbolic* language using resemblances, like the heroic language I have just described. (3) Finally, the third was the *epistolary* or vernacular language, which was used for the common business of everyday life. These three kinds of language were found among the Chaldaeans, Scythians, Egyptians, Germanic peoples, and all the other nations of pagan antiquity. (Hieroglyphic writing persisted later among the Egyptians simply because they were closed to foreign nations longer, which also explains why the Chinese still use ideograms. But the use of hieroglyphics by other nations proves that the Egyptians' presumption of their own remote antiquity is groundless.)

My Science sheds light on the origins of both languages and letters, which were previously the despair of historians and philologists, whose bizarre and grotesque opinions I shall review. The unfortunate reason for their error is obvious: they simply assumed that nations developed languages first, and then letters. Yet languages and letters were born as twins and developed at the same pace through all three kinds. We find precise evidence for such origins in the stages of the Latin language which I discovered in the first edition of my *New Science*. (Earlier, I remarked that this work contains three sections which I do not regret writing; this is the second of them.) This evidence has offered me many discoveries about the history, government, and law of the ancient Romans, as the reader will find in countless passages of the present work. Following my example, scholars of Oriental languages, of Greek, and especially of German among the modern languages, which is a mother tongue, will be able to make discoveries about antiquities that surpass their expectations and mine.

In seeking the basic principle of the common origins of languages and letters, we find that the first peoples of pagan antiquity were, by a demonstrable necessity of their nature, *poets* who spoke by means of *poetic symbols*. This discovery provides the master key of my New Science, but making it has cost me nearly an entire scholarly career spent in tireless researches. For to our more civilized natures, the poetic nature of the first people is utterly impossible to imagine, and can be understood only with the greatest effort. Their symbols were certain *imaginative general categories*, or archetypes. These were largely images of animate beings, such as gods and heroes, which they formed in their imagination, and to which they assigned all the specifics and particulars comprised by each generic category. (In precisely this way, the myths of civilized ages, such as the plots of the New Comedy, are rational archetypes derived from moral philosophy; and from these myths, our comic poets create in their characters these imaginative archetypes, which are simply the most complete ideas of human types in each genre.) We find, then, that the divine and heroic symbols were true myths, or true mythical speech. And we discover that, in describing the early age of the Greek peoples, the meaning of their allegories is based on identity rather than analogy, and is thus historical rather than philosophical. These archetypes – which is what myths are in essence – were created by people endowed with vigorous imaginations but feeble powers of reasoning. So they prove to be true poetic statements, which are feelings clothed in powerful passions, and thus filled with sublimity and arousing wonder. We further find that poetic expression springs from two sources: the poverty of language, and the need to explain and be understood. This engendered the vividness of heroic speech, which was the direct successor of the mute language of the divine age, which had conveyed ideas through gestures and objects naturally related to them. Eventually, following the inevitable natural course of human institutions, the Assyrians, Syrians, Phoenicians, Egyptians, Greeks, and Romans developed languages, which began with heroic verse, then passed to iambics, and finally ended in prose. This progression is confirmed by the history of ancient poetry. And it explains why we find so many natural versifiers are born in German-speaking lands, particularly in the peasant region of Silesia; and why the first authors in Spanish, French, and Italian wrote in verse.

From these three languages, we may derive a conceptual dictionary, which properly defines words in all the different articulate languages. In this work, I shall refer, when necessary, to this dictionary, of which the reader will find a detailed sample in the first edition of my Science. In that passage, I studied the timeless attributes of the fathers who lived in the age when languages were formed, both in the state of families and in the first heroic cities. Then, in fifteen different languages, both living and dead, I derived proper definitions of the words for father, which varied according to their different attributes. (Of the three sections in that edition which satisfy me, this is the third.) This lexicon proves necessary if we are to learn the language of the ideal eternal history through which the histories of all nations in time pass. And it is necessary if we are to be scientific in citing authorities that confirm our observations about the natural law of nations, and about particular kinds of jurisprudence.

There were, then, *three* languages, proper to *three* ages in which *three* kinds of government ruled, conforming to *three* kinds of civil natures, which change as nations follow their course. And we find that these languages were accompanied by an appropriate kind of jurisprudence, which in each age followed the same order. [...]

In conclusion, let me summarise the idea of this work as briefly as possible. The entire picture represents three worlds in the order in which the human minds of pagan antiquity ascended from earth to heaven. (1) The symbols seen on the ground denote the world of nations, the very things to which people applied themselves. (2) The globe in the middle represents the world of nature, which was subsequently observed by natural scientists. (3) And the symbols above these signify the world of minds and of God, which were eventually contemplated by the metaphysicians.

(*New Science*, 'Idea of the Work', paras 31–36, 42)


## ADAM FERGUSON

Adam Ferguson (1723–1816), son of a Presbyterian minister, was born in Perthshire and educated at St Andrews University. After studying divinity at Edinburgh, in 1745 he became deputy chaplain to the Black Watch regiment, serving in Britain and abroad. In 1759 he was appointed professor of natural philosophy at Edinburgh University and five years later to the chair of moral philosophy there. After marrying, in 1767, he published his first major work, *An Essay on the History of Civil Society*. This was followed by two other major works: a three-volume *History of the Progress and Termination of the Roman Republic* (1783), and the two-volume *Principles of Moral and Political Science* (1792). In 1778 he travelled to Philadelphia as secretary to the British commissioners, and in 1793 to Italy and Germany where he was elected an honorary member of the Berlin Academy of Sciences. Thereafter he retired to St Andrews, where he died in 1816.

Though it did not impress his good friend David Hume, and was much-inspired by Montesquieu's work, *An Essay on the History of Civil Society* established Ferguson's reputation as an influential thinker and, later, as a founder of sociology. The *Essay* begins with an examination of 'the universal qualities of our nature', noting especially that 'society appears to be as old as the individual' and that careful observation suggests 'a principle of progression [improvement]', whereby 'the latest efforts of human invention are but a continuation of certain devices which were practised in the earliest ages of the world, and in the rudest state of mankind'. Thereafter, the *Essay* traces the evolution of society from primitive to commercial forms: each stage of development being due to a complex interaction of social, psychological and material factors; being only partly due to human reasoning and design, and entailing losses (such as the undermining of civic virtues, as the wealth of individuals increases) as well as gains from the collective inheritance of the wisdoms of previous generations. The two extracts from the *Essay* published here are from the first sections of Part I, 'Of the General Characteristics of Human Nature', and of Part II, 'Of the History of Rude Nations'.

## An Essay on the History of Civil Society (1767)

### 'Of the General Characteristics of Human Nature'

Mankind are to be taken in groups, as they have always subsisted. The history of the individual is but a detail of the sentiments and thoughts he has entertained in the view of his species: and every experiment relative to this subject should be made with entire societies, not with single men. We have every reason, however, to believe, that in the case of such an experiment made, we shall suppose, with a colony of children transplanted from the nursery, and left to form a society apart, untaught, and undisciplined, we should only have the same things repeated, which, in so many different parts of the earth, have been transacted already. The members of our little society would feed and sleep, would herd together and play, would have a language of their own, would quarrel and divide, would be to one another the most important objects of the scene, and, in the ardour of their friendships and competitions, would overlook their personal danger, and suspend the care of their self-preservation. Has not the human race been planted like the colony in question? Who has directed their course? Whose instruction have they heard? Or whose example have they followed?

Nature, therefore, we shall presume, having given to every animal its mode of existence, its dispositions and manner of life, has dealt equally with those of the human race; and the natural historian who would collect the properties of this species, may fill up every article now, as well as he could have done in any former age. Yet one property by which man is distinguished, has been sometimes overlooked in the account of his nature, or has only served to mislead our attention. In other classes of animals, the individual advances from infancy to age or maturity; and he attains, in the compass of a single life, to all the perfection his nature can reach: but, in the human kind, the species has a progress as well as the individual; they build in every subsequent age on foundations formerly laid; and, in a succession of years, tend to a perfection in the application of their faculties, to which the aid of long experience is required, and to which many generations must have combined their endeavours. We observe the progress they have made; we distinctly enumerate many of its steps; we can trace them back to a distant antiquity; of which no record remains, nor any monument is preserved, to inform us what were the openings of this wonderful scene. The consequence is, that instead of attending to the character of our species, where the particulars are vouched by the surest authority, we endeavour to trace it through ages and scenes unknown; and, instead of supposing that the beginning of our story was nearly of a piece with the sequel, we think ourselves warranted to reject every circumstance of our present condition and frame, as adventitious, and foreign to our nature. The progress of mankind from a supposed state of animal sensibility, to the attainment of reason, to the use of language, and to the habit of society, has been accordingly painted with a force of imagination, and its steps have been marked with a boldness of invention, that would tempt us to admit, among the materials of history, the suggestions of fancy, and to receive, perhaps, as the model of our nature in its original state, some of the animals whose shape has the greatest resemblance to ours.

It would be ridiculous to affirm, as a discovery, that the species of the horse was probably never the same with that of the lion; yet, in opposition to what has dropped from the pens of eminent writers, we are obliged to observe, that men have always appeared among animals a distinct and a superior race; that neither the possession of similar organs, nor the approximation of shape, nor the use of the hand, nor the continued intercourse with this sovereign artist, has enabled any other species to blend their nature or their inventions with his; that in his rudest state, he is found to be above them; and in his greatest degeneracy, never descends to their level. He is, in short, a man in every condition; and we can learn nothing of his nature from the analogy of other animals. If we would know him, we must attend to himself, to the course of his life, and the tenor of his conduct. With him the society appears to be as old as the individual, and the use of the tongue as universal as that of the hand or the foot. If there was a time in which he had his acquaintance with his own species to make, and his faculties to acquire, it is a time of which we have no record, and in relation to which our opinions can serve no purpose, and are supported by no evidence. [...]

We speak of art as distinguished from nature; but art itself is natural to man. He is in some measure the artificer of his own frame, as well as his fortune, and is destined, from the first age of his being, to invent and contrive. He applies the same talents to a variety of purposes, and acts nearly the same part in very different scenes. He would be always improving on his subject, and he carries this intention wherever he moves, through the streets of the populous city, or the wilds of the forest.

(*Essay*, Part I, Section 1, 'Of the question relating to the state of nature')

### 'Of the History of Rude Nations'

The history of mankind is confined within a limited period, and from every quarter brings an intimation that human affairs have had a beginning. Nations, distinguished by the possession of arts, and the felicity of their political establishments, have been derived from a feeble original, and still preserve in their story the indications of a slow and gradual progress, by which this distinction was gained. The antiquities of every people, however diversified, and however distinguished, contain the same information on this point.

In sacred history, we find the parents of the species, as yet a single pair, sent forth to inherit the earth, and to force a subsistence for themselves amidst the briers and thorns which were made to abound on its surface. Their race, which was again reduced to a few, had to struggle with the dangers that await a weak and infant species; and after many ages elapsed, the most respectable nations took their rise from one or a few families that had pastured their flocks in the desert.

The Grecians derive their own origin from unsettled tribes, whose frequent migrations are a proof of the rude and infant state of their communities; and whose warlike exploits, so much celebrated in story, only exhibit the struggles with which they disputed for the possession of a country they afterwards, by their talent for fable, by their arts, and their policy, rendered so famous in the history of mankind.

Italy must have been divided into many rude and feeble cantons, when a band of robbers, as we are taught to consider them, found a secure settlement on the banks of the Tiber, and when a people, yet composed only of one sex, sustained the character of a nation. Rome, for many ages, saw, from her walls, on every side, the territory of her enemies, and found as little to check or to stifle the weakness of her infant power, as she did afterwards to restrain the progress of her extended empire. Like a Tartar or a Scythian horde, which had pitched on a settlement, this nascent community was equal, if not superior, to every tribe in its neighbourhood; and the oak which has covered the field with its shade, was once a feeble plant in the nursery, and not to be distinguished from the weeds by which its early growth was restrained.

The Gauls and the Germans are come to our knowledge with the marks of a similar condition; and the inhabitants of Britain, at the time of the first Roman invasions, resembled, in many things, the present natives of North America: they were ignorant of agriculture; they painted their bodies; and used for cloathing, the skins of beasts.

Such therefore appears to have been the commencement of history with all nations, and in such circumstances are we to look for the original character of mankind. The inquiry refers to a distant period, and every conclusion should build on the facts which are preserved for our use. Our method, notwithstanding, too frequently, is to rest the whole on conjecture; to impute every advantage of our nature to those arts which we ourselves possess; and to imagine, that a mere negation of all our virtues is a sufficient description of man in his original state. We are ourselves the supposed standards of politeness and civilization; and where our own features do not appear, we apprehend, that there is nothing which deserves to be known. But it is probable that here, as in many other cases, we are ill qualified, from our supposed knowledge of causes, to prognosticate effects, or to determine what must have been the properties and operations, even of our own nature, in the absence of those circumstances in which we have seen it engaged. Who would, from mere conjecture, suppose, that the naked savage would be a coxcomb and a gamester?; that he would be proud and vain, without the distinctions of title and fortune; and that his principal care would be to adorn his person, and to find an amusement? Even if it could be supposed that he would thus share in our vices, and, in the midst of his forest, vie with the follies which are practised in the town; yet no one would be so bold as to affirm, that he would likewise, in any instance, excel us in talents and virtues; that he would have a penetration, a force of imagination and elocution, an ardour of mind, an affection and courage, which the arts, the discipline, and the policy of few nations would be able to improve. Yet these particulars are a part in the description which is delivered by those who have had opportunities of seeing mankind in their rudest condition: and beyond the reach of such testimony, we can neither safely take, nor pretend to give, information on the subject.

If conjectures and opinions formed at a distance, have not sufficient authority in the history of mankind, the domestic antiquities of every nation must, for this very reason, be received with caution. They are, for most part, the mere conjectures or the fictions of subsequent ages; and even where at first they contained some resemblance of truth, they still vary with the imagination of those by whom they are transmitted, and in every generation receive a different form. They are made to bear the stamp of the times through which they have passed in the form of tradition, not of the ages to which their pretended descriptions relate. The information they bring, is not like the light reflected from a mirror, which delineates the object from which it originally came; but, like rays that come broken and dispersed from an opaque or unpolished surface, only give the colours and features of the body from which they were last reflected.

When traditionary fables are rehearsed by the vulgar, they bear the marks of a national character; and though mixed with absurdities, often raise the imagination, and move the heart: when made the materials of poetry, and adorned by the skill and the eloquence of an ardent and superior mind, they instruct the understanding, as well as engage the passions. It is only in the management of mere antiquaries, or stript of the ornaments which the laws of history forbid them to wear, that they become even unfit to amuse the fancy, or to serve any purpose whatsoever.

It were absurd to quote the fable of the Iliad or the Odyssey, the legends of Hercules, Theseus, or Oedipus, as authorities in matter of fact relating to the history of mankind; but they may, with great justice, be cited to ascertain what were the conceptions and sentiments of the age in which they were composed, or to characterise the genius of that people, with whose imaginations they were blended, and by whom they were fondly rehearsed and admired.

In this manner fiction may be admitted to vouch for the genius of nations, while history has nothing to offer that is intitled to credit. The Greek fable accordingly conveying a character of its authors, throws light on an age of which no other record remains. The superiority of this people is indeed in no circumstance more evident than in the strain of their fictions, and in the story of those fabulous heroes, poets, and sages, whose tales, being invented or embellished by an imagination already filled with the subject for which the hero was celebrated, served to inflame that ardent enthusiasm with which this people afterwards proceeded in the pursuit of every national object.

It was no doubt of great advantage to those nations, that their system of fable was original, and being already received in popular traditions, served to diffuse those improvements of reason, imagination, and sentiment, which were afterwards, by men of the finest talents, made on the fable itself, or conveyed in its moral. The passions of the poet pervaded the minds of the people, and the conceptions of men of genius being communicated to the vulgar, became the incentives of a national spirit.

(*Essay*, Part II, Section 1, 'Of the informations
on this subject which are derived from Antiquity')

## ADAM SMITH

Adam Smith (1723–90), together with his friends David Hume and Adam Ferguson, was one of the leading figures of the Scottish Enlightenment. Born into the professional middle classes at Kirkcaldy in Fife, he studied at Glasgow and Oxford universities before becoming Professor of Logic (1751) and of Moral Philosophy (1752) at Glasgow. His first, highly successful book, *The Theory of Moral Sentiments* was published in 1759. As tutor to the young Duke of Buccleuch, he went to France in 1764, residing at Toulouse and Paris, meeting *philosophes* and visiting Voltaire at Geneva, before returning to London and Scotland in 1766. His celebrated *An Inquiry into the Nature and Causes of the Wealth of Nations* was first published in two volumes in 1776. Despite his fame, Smith lived a quiet life, working in Edinburgh as a customs commissioner for Scotland until his death.

In *The Wealth of Nations*, Smith identifies and explains what he sees as the fundamental 'natural' principles upon which economic growth, prosperity and social development are, and should be, based. Driven by an inherent desire to promote their own economic welfare, each person seeks to maximise the value and productivity of their labour, bargaining with others who are equally self-seeking in order to exchange goods and services. In this market place, provided that 'natural' conditions of 'perfect liberty' are upheld, each person is able to use their reasoning to strike deals and contracts to their own advantage, thereby producing benefits for both/all parties whenever an exchange or trade takes place. Through free trade, the pursuit of private gain is thus harmonised ('by an invisible hand') with social benefit, and this leads to the growing interdependence and prosperity of all. Paradoxically, when groups or governments, whatever their intentions, distort the 'natural' conditions which promote free trade (e.g. by granting monopolies, forming trade unions, or fixing 'artificial' prices), then public welfare and prosperity are undermined.

It is easy to caricature Smith's view of humans as instinctively competitive, selfish and acquisitive individuals, and his economic theory as a heartless legitimation of the inequalities of capitalism. But Smith's concern to alleviate the seemingly endemic poverty in all societies and nations by showing how they can (and need to) co-operate to raise productivity and maximise economic growth, and his hostility to many of the policies and competitive practices that eighteenth-century governments pursued, point to a more complex picture. Few works of the Enlightenment, or any other age, can have exercised such a powerful and pervasive influence upon the material conditions of people's lives in the modern world. The extracts here are taken from the beginning of *The Wealth of Nations*, where Smith sets out the general principles that underlie his work.

## The Wealth of Nations (1776)

### 'Introduction and Plan of the Work'

The annual labour of every nation is the fund which originally supplies it with all the necessaries and conveniences of life which it annually consumes, and which consist always, either in the immediate produce of that labour, or in what is purchased with that produce from other nations.

According therefore, as this produce, or what is purchased with it, bears a greater or smaller proportion to the number of those who are to consume it, the nation will be better or worse supplied with all the necessaries and conveniences for which it has occasion.

But this proportion must in every nation be regulated by two different circumstances; first, by the skill, dexterity, and judgment with which its labour is generally applied; and, secondly, by the proportion between the number of those who are employed in useful labour, and that of those who are not so employed. Whatever be the soil, climate, or extent of territory of any particular nation, the abundance or scantiness of its annual supply must, in that particular situation, depend upon those two circumstances.

The abundance or scantiness of this supply too seems to depend more upon the former of those two circumstances than upon the latter. Among the savage nations of hunters and fishers, every individual who is able to work, is more or less employed in useful labour, and endeavours to provide, as well as he can, the necessaries and conveniences of life, for himself, or such of his family or tribe as are either too old, or too young, or too infirm to go a hunting and fishing. Such nations, however, are so miserably poor, that, from mere want, they are frequently reduced, or, at least, think themselves reduced, to the necessity sometimes of directly destroying, and sometimes of abandoning their infants, their old people, and those afflicted with lingering diseases, to perish with hunger, or to he devoured by wild beasts. Among civilised and thriving nations, on the contrary, though a great number of people do not labour at all, many of whom consume the produce of ten times, frequently of a hundred times more labour than the greater part of those who work; yet the produce of the whole labour of the society is so great, that all are often abundantly supplied, and a workman, even of the lowest and poorest order, if he is frugal and industrious, may enjoy a greater share of the necessaries and conveniences of life than it is possible for any savage to acquire.

The causes of this improvement, in the productive powers of labour, and the order, according to which its produce is naturally distributed among the different ranks and conditions of men in the society, make the subject of the First Book of this Inquiry.

(*Wealth of Nations*, I, 'Introduction and Plan of the Work', paras. 1–5)

## 'Of the Division of Labour'

The greatest improvement in the productive powers of labour, and the greater part of the skill, dexterity, and judgment with which it is anywhere directed, or applied, seem to have been the effects of the division of labour.

The effects of the division of labour, in the general business of society, will be more easily understood, by considering in what manner it operates in some particular manufactures. It is commonly supposed to be carried furthest in some very trifling ones; not perhaps that it really is carried further in them than in others of more importance: but in those trifling manufactures which are destined to supply the small wants of but a small number of people, the whole number of workmen must necessarily be small; and those employed in every different branch of the work can often be collected into the same workhouse, and placed at once under the view of the spectator. In those great manufactures, on the contrary, which are destined to supply the great wants of the great body of the people, every different branch of the work employs so great a number of workmen, that it is impossible to collect them all into the same workhouse. We can seldom see more, at one time, than those employed in one single branch. Though in such manufactures, therefore, the work may really be divided into a much greater number of parts, than in those of a more trifling nature, the division is not near so obvious, and has accordingly been much less observed.

To take an example, therefore, from a very trifling manufacture; but one in which the division of labour has been very often taken notice of, the trade of the pin maker; a workman not educated to this business (which the division of labour has rendered a distinct trade), nor acquainted with the use of the machinery employed in it (to the invention of which the same division of labour has probably given occasion), could scarce, perhaps, with his utmost industry, make one pin in a day, and certainly could not make twenty. But in the way in which this business is now carried on, not only the whole work is a peculiar trade, but it is divided into a number of branches, of which the greater part are likewise peculiar trades. One man draws out the wire, another straightens it, a third cuts it, a fourth points it, a fifth grinds it at the top for receiving the head; to make the head requires two or three distinct operations; to put it on, is a peculiar business, to whiten the pins is another; it is even a trade by itself to put them into the paper; and the important business of making a pin is, in this manner, divided into about eighteen distinct operations, which, in some manufactories, are all performed by distinct hands, though in others the same man will sometimes perform two or three of them. I have seen a small manufactory of this kind where ten men only were employed, and where some of them consequently performed two or three distinct operations. But though they were very poor, and therefore but indifferently accommodated with the necessary machinery, they could, when they exerted themselves, make among them about twelve pounds of pins in a day. There are in a pound upwards of four thousand pins of a middling size. Those ten persons, therefore, could make among them upwards of forty-eight thousand pins in a day. Each person, therefore, making a tenth part of forty-eight thousand pins, might be considered as making four thousand eight hundred pins in a day. But if they had all wrought separately and independently, and without any of them having been educated to this peculiar business, they certainly could not each of them have made twenty, perhaps not one pin in a day; that is, certainly not the two hundred and fortieth, perhaps not the four thousand eight hundredth part of what they are at present capable of performing, in consequence of a proper division and combination of their different operations.

In every other art and manufacture, the effects of the division of labour are similar to what they are in this very trifling one; though, in many of them, the labour can neither be so much subdivided, nor reduced to so great a simplicity of operation. The division of labour, however, so far as it can be introduced, occasions, in every art, a proportionable increase of the productive powers of labour. The separation of different trades and employments from one another, seems to have taken place, in consequence of this advantage. This separation too is generally carried furthest in those countries which enjoy the highest degree of industry and improvement; what is the work of one man, in a rude state of society, being generally that of several in an improved one. In every improved society, the farmer is generally nothing but a farmer; the manufacturer, nothing but a manufacturer. The labour too which is necessary to produce any one complete manufacture, is almost always divided among a great number of hands. How many different trades are employed in each branch of the linen and woollen manufactures, from the growers of the flax and the wool, to the bleachers and smoothers of the linen, or to the dyers and dressers of the cloth! The nature of agriculture, indeed, does not admit of so many subdivisions of labour, nor of so complete a separation of one business from another, as manufactures. It is impossible to separate so entirely, the business of the grazier from that of the corn farmer, as the trade of the carpenter is commonly separated from that of the smith. The spinner is almost always a distinct person from the weaver; but the ploughman, the harrower, the sower of the seed, and the reaper of the corn, are often the same. The occasions for those different sorts of labour returning with the different seasons of the year, it is impossible that one man should be constantly employed in any one of them. This impossibility of making so complete and entire a separation of all the different branches of labour employed in agriculture, is perhaps the reason why the improvement of the productive powers of labour in this art, does not always keep pace with their improvement in manufactures. The most opulent nations, indeed, generally excel all their neighbours in agriculture as well as in manufactures; but they are commonly more distinguished by their superiority in the latter than in the former. [...]

This great increase of the quantity of work, which, in consequence of the division of labour, the same number of people are capable of performing, is owing to three different circumstances; first, to the increase of dexterity in every particular workman; secondly, to the saving of the time which is commonly lost in passing from one species of work to another; and lastly, to the invention of a great number of machines which facilitate and abridge labour, and enable one man to do the work of many.

First, the improvement of the dexterity of the workman necessarily increases the quantity of the work he can perform, and the division of labour, by reducing every man's business to some one simple operation, and by making this operation the sole employment of his life, necessarily increases very much the dexterity of the workman. [...]

Secondly, the advantage which is gained by saving the time commonly lost in passing from one sort of work to another, is much greater than we should at first view be apt to imagine it. It is impossible to pass very quickly from one kind of work to another, that is carried on in a different place, and with quite different tools. A country weaver, who cultivates a small farm, must lose a good deal of time in passing from his loom to the field, and from the field to his loom. When the two trades can be carried on in the same workhouse, the loss of time is no doubt much less. It is even in this case, however, very considerable. A man commonly saunters a little in turning his hand from one sort of employment to another. When he first begins the new work he is seldom very keen and hearty; his mind, as they say, does not go to it, and for some time he rather trifles than applies to good purpose. The habit of sauntering and of indolent careless application, which is naturally, or rather necessarily acquired by every country workman who is obliged to change his work and his tools every half hour, and to apply his hand in twenty different ways almost every day of his life; renders him almost always slothful and lazy, and incapable of any vigorous application even on the most pressing occasions. Independent, therefore, of his deficiency in point of dexterity, this cause alone must always reduce considerably the quantity of work which he is capable of performing.

Thirdly, and lastly, every body must be sensible how much labour is facilitated and abridged by the application of proper machinery. It is unnecessary to give any example. I shall only observe, therefore, that the invention of all those machines by which labour is so much facilitated and abridged, seems to have been originally owing to the division of labour. Men are much more likely to discover easier and readier methods of attaining any object, when the whole attention of their minds is directed towards that single object, than when it is dissipated among a great variety of things. But in consequence of the division of labour, the whole of every man's attention comes naturally to be directed towards some one very simple object. It is naturally to be expected, therefore, that some one or other of those who are employed in each particular branch of labour should soon find out easier and readier methods of performing their own particular work, wherever the nature of it admits of such improvement. A great part of the machines made use of in those manufactures in which labour is most subdivided, were originally the inventions of common workmen, who, being each of them employed in some very simple operation, naturally turned their thoughts towards finding out easier and readier methods of performing it. Whoever has been much accustomed to visit such manufactures, must frequently have been shown very pretty machines, which were the inventions of such workmen, in order to facilitate and quicken their own particular part of the work. In the first fire [steam] engines, a boy was constantly employed to open and shut alternately the communication between the boiler and the cylinder, according as the piston either ascended or descended. One of those boys, who loved to play with his companions, observed that, by tying a string from the handle of the valve, which opened this communication, to another part of the machine, the valve would open and shut without his assistance, and leave him at liberty to divert himself with his play-fellows. One of the greatest improvements that has been made upon this machine, since it was first invented, was in this manner the discovery of a boy who wanted to save his own labour.

All the improvements in machinery, however, have by no means been the inventions of those who had occasion to use the machines. Many improvements have been made by the ingenuity of the makers of the machines, when to make them became the business of a peculiar trade; and some by that of those who are called philosophers or men of speculation, whose trade it is, not to do anything, but to observe everything; and who, upon that account, are often capable of combining together the powers of the most distant and dissimilar objects. In the progress of society, philosophy or speculation becomes, like every other employment, the principal or sole trade and occupation of a particular class of citizens. Like every other employment too, it is subdivided into a great number of different branches, each of which affords occupation to a peculiar tribe or class of philosophers; and this subdivision of employment in philosophy, as well as in every other business, improves dexterity, and saves time. Each individual becomes more expert in his own peculiar branch, more work is done upon the whole, and the quantity of science is considerably increased by it.

It is the great multiplication of the productions of all the different arts, in consequence of the division of labour, which occasions, in a well-governed society, that universal opulence which extends itself to the lowest ranks of the people. Every workman has a great quantity of his own work to dispose of beyond what he himself has occasion for; and every other workman being exactly in the same situation, he is enabled to exchange a great quantity of his own goods for a great quantity, or, what comes to the same thing, for the price of a great quantity of theirs. He supplies them abundantly with what they have occasion for, and they accommodate him as amply with what he has occasion for, and a general plenty diffuses itself through all the different ranks of the society.

Observe the accommodation of the most common artificer or day-labourer in a civilised and thriving country, and you will perceive that the number of people of whose industry a part, though but a small part, has been employed in procuring him this accommodation, exceeds all computation. The woollen coat, for example, which covers the day-labourer, as coarse and rough as it may appear, is the produce of the joint labour of a great multitude of workmen. The shepherd, the sorter of the wool, the wool-comber or carder, the dyer, the scribbler, the spinner, the weaver, the fuller, the dresser, with many others, must all join their different arts in order to complete even this homely production. How many merchants and carriers, besides, must have been employed in transporting the materials from some of those workmen to others who often live in a very distant part of the country! How much commerce and navigation in particular, how many shipbuilders, sailors, sailmakers, ropemakers, must have been employed in order to bring together the different drugs made use of by the dyer, which often come from the remotest corners of the world! What a variety of labour too is necessary in order to produce the tools of the meanest of those workmen! To say nothing of such complicated machines as the ship of the sailor, the mill of the fuller, or even the loom of the weaver, let us consider only what a variety of labour is requisite in order to form that very simple machine, the shears with which the shepherd clips the wool. The miner, the builder of the furnace for smelting the ore, the feller of the timber, the burner of the charcoal to be made use of in the smelting house, the brickmaker, the bricklayer, the workmen who attend the furnace, the millwright, the forger, the smith, must all of them join their different arts in order to produce them.

(*Wealth of Nations*, I, ch.1, 'Of the Division of Labour', paras 1–11)

### 'Of the Principle which gives occasion to the Division of Labour'

This division of labour, from which so many advantages are derived, is not originally the effect of any human wisdom, which foresees and intends that general opulence to which it gives occasion. It is the necessary, though very slow and gradual consequence of a certain propensity in human nature which has in view no such extensive utility; the propensity to truck, barter, and exchange one thing for another.

Whether this propensity be one of those original principles in human nature, of which no further account can be given; or whether, as seems more probable, it be the necessary consequence of the faculties of reason and speech, it belongs not to our present subject to enquire. It is common to all men, and to be found in no other race of animals, which seem to know neither this nor any other species of contracts. Two greyhounds, in running down the same hare, have sometimes the appearance of acting in some sort of concert. Each turns her towards his companion, or endeavours to intercept her when his companion turns her towards himself. This, however, is not the effect of any contract, but of the accidental concurrence of their passions in the same object at that particular time. Nobody ever saw a dog make a fair and deliberate exchange of one bone for another with another dog. Nobody ever saw one animal by its gestures and natural cries signify to another, this is mine, that yours; I am willing to give this for that.

When an animal wants to obtain something either of a man or of another animal, it has no other means of persuasion but to gain the favour of those whose service it requires. A puppy fawns upon its dam, and a spaniel endeavours by a thousand attractions to engage the attention of its master who is at dinner, when it wants to be fed by him. Man sometimes uses the same arts with his brethren, and when he has no other means of engaging them to act according to his inclinations, endeavours by every servile and fawning attention to obtain their good will. He has not time, however, to do this upon every occasion. In civilised society he stands at all times in need of the cooperation and assistance of great multitudes, while his whole life is scarce sufficient to gain the friendship of a few persons. In almost every other race of animals each individual, when it is grown up to maturity, is entirely independent, and in its natural state has occasion for the assistance of no other living creature. But man has almost constant occasion for the help of his brethren, and it is in vain for him to expect it from their benevolence only. He will be more likely to prevail if he can interest their self-love in his favour, and shew them that it is for their own advantage to do for him what he requires of them. Whoever offers to another a bargain of any kind, proposes to do this. Give me that which I want, and you shall have this which you want, is the meaning of every such offer; and it is in this manner that we obtain from one another the far greater part of those good offices which we stand in need of. It is not from the benevolence of the butcher, the brewer, or the baker, that we expect our dinner, but from their regard to their own interest. We address ourselves, not to their humanity but to their self-love, and never talk to them of our own necessities but of their advantages. Nobody but a beggar chooses to depend chiefly upon the benevolence of his fellow-citizens. Even a beggar does not depend upon it entirely. The charity of well-disposed people, indeed, supplies him with the whole fund of his subsistence. But though this principle ultimately provides him with all the necessaries of life which he has occasion for, it neither does nor can provide him with them as he has occasion for them. The greater part of his occasional wants are supplied in the same manner as those of other people, by treaty, by barter, and by purchase. With the money which one man gives him he purchases food. The old clothes which another bestows upon him he exchanges for other old clothes which suit him better, or for lodging, or for food, or for money, with which he can buy either food, clothes, or lodging, as he has occasion.

As it is by treaty, by barter, and by purchase, that we obtain from one another the greater part of those mutual good offices which we stand in need of, so it is this same trucking disposition which originally gives occasion to the division of labour. In a tribe of hunters or shepherds a particular person makes bows and arrows, for example, with more readiness and dexterity than any other. He frequently exchanges them for cattle or for venison with his companions; and he finds at last that he can in this manner get more cattle and venison, than if he himself went to the field to catch them. From a regard to his own interest, therefore, the making of bows and arrows grows to be his chief business, and he becomes a sort of armourer. Another excels in making the frames and covers of their little huts or moveable houses. He is accustomed to be of use in this way to his neighbours, who reward him in the same manner with cattle and with venison, till at last he finds it his interest to dedicate himself entirely to this employment, and to become a sort of house-carpenter. In the same manner a third becomes a smith or a brazier, a fourth a tanner or dresser of hides or skins, the principal part of the cloth-ing of savages. And thus the certainty of being able to exchange all that surplus part of the produce of his own labour, which is over and above his own consumption, for such parts of the produce of other men's labour as he may have occasion for, encourages every man to apply himself to a particular occupation, and to cultivate and bring to per-fection whatever talent or genius he may possess for that particular species of business.

The difference of natural talents in different men is, in reality, much less than we are aware of; and the very different genius which appears to distinguish men of different professions, when grown up to maturity, is not upon many occasions so much the cause, as the effect of the division of labour. The difference between the most dissimilar char-acters, between a philosopher and a common street porter, for example, seems to arise not so much from nature, as from habit, custom, and education. When they came into the world, and for the first six or eight years of their existence, they were, perhaps, very much alike, and neither their parents nor play-fellows could perceive any remarkable difference. About that age, or soon after, they come to be employed in very different occupations. The difference of talents comes then to be taken notice of, and widens by degrees, till at last the vanity of the philosopher is willing to acknowledge scarce any resemblance. But without the disposition to truck, barter, and exchange, every man must have procured to himself every necessary and convenience of life which he want-ed. All must have had the same duties to perform, and the same work to do, and there could have been no such difference of employment as could alone give occasion to any great difference of talents.

As it is this disposition which forms that difference of talents, so remarkable among men of different professions, so it is this same disposition which renders that difference useful. Many tribes of animals acknowledged to be all of the same species, derive from nature a much more remarkable distinction of genius, than what, antecedent to custom and education, appears to take place among men. By nature a philosopher is not in genius and disposition half so different from a street porter, as a mastiff is from a grey-hound, or a greyhound from a spaniel, or this last from a shepherd's dog. Those differ-ent tribes of animals, however, though all of the same species, are of scarce any use to one another. The strength of the mastiff is not, in the least, supported either by the swiftness of the greyhound, or by the sagacity of the spaniel, or by the docility of the shepherd's dog. The effects of those different geniuses and talents, for want of the power or disposition to barter and exchange, cannot be brought into a common stock, and do not in the least contribute to the better accommodation and convenience of the species. Each animal is still obliged to support and defend itself, separately and independently, and derives no sort of advantage from that variety of talents with which nature has dis-tinguished its fellows. Among men, on the contrary, the most dissimilar geniuses are of use to one another; the different produces of their respective talents, by the general dis-position to truck, barter, and exchange, being brought, as it were, into a common stock, where every man may purchase whatever part of the produce of other men's talents he has occasion for.

(*Wealth of Nations*, I, ch.2, 'Of the Principle
which gives occasion to the Division of Labour', paras 1–5)

*'That the Division of Labour is limited by the Extent of the Market'*

As it is the power of exchanging that gives occasion to the division of labour, so the extent of this division must always be limited by the extent of that power, or, in other words, by the extent of the market. When the market is very small, no person can have any encouragement to dedicate himself entirely to one employment, for want of the power to exchange all that surplus part of the produce of his own labour, which is over and above his own consumption, for such parts of the produce of other men's labour as he has occasion for.

There are some sorts of industry, even of the lowest kind, which can be carried on nowhere but in a great town. A porter, for example, can find employment and subsistence in no other place. A village is by much too narrow a sphere for him; even an ordinary market town is scarce large enough to afford him constant occupation. In the lone houses and very small villages which are scattered about in so desert a country as the Highlands of Scotland, every farmer must be butcher, baker and brewer for his own family. In such situations we can scarce expect to find even a smith, a carpenter, or a mason, within less than twenty miles of another of the same trade. The scattered families that live at eight or ten miles distance from the nearest of them, must learn to perform themselves a great number of little pieces of work, for which, in more populous countries, they would call in the assistance of those workmen.

(*Wealth of Nations*, I, ch. 3, 'That the Division
of Labour is limited by the Extent of the Market', paras 1–2)

# EDWARD GIBBON

Edward Gibbon (1737–94), son of an Anglican squire, was born at Putney and educated at Westminster School. Sent to Oxford University in 1752, where he converted to Catholicism, his father dispatched him to the Calvinist city of Lausanne in 1753 where he reconverted and spent his time reading a vast array of literary and historical works. Returning from Switzerland to live at his family home in Hampshire in 1758, he published his first work *Essay on the Study of Literature*, in French, in 1761. After serving as a captain in the Hampshire militia, in 1763 he set off on the Grand Tour of Europe, meeting various *philosophes* at Paris, and 'musing amidst the ruins of the Capitol' at Rome where he was inspired by 'the idea of writing the decline and fall of the city'. Following his return to England in 1765, he began work on his masterpiece *The History of the Decline and Fall of the Roman Empire*, published in six large volumes, 1776–88. Having fulfilled his life-long ambition to become a famous historian, after his father's death in 1770, he moved to London and took a seat (though he never spoke) in parliament. In 1783 he migrated to Lausanne to complete *The Decline and Fall* and write his autobiography, published posthumously as his *Memoirs*. He died shortly after his return to London in 1793.

Even in an age of deep learning and interest in the Classics, *The Decline and Fall* represented an immense scholarly and literary achievement, for it is both one of the great history books of all time, and an outstanding narrative, infused with

complex ironies and rhetoric. Not only are the scale and scope of the work, span-
ning twelve centuries and several continents, truly epic, but its method, style and
themes signal a turning point in the writing of history. Adopting a sceptical view of
the veracity of historical sources, particularly of 'sacred' texts, Gibbon eschewed
the conventional practice of providing religious explanations of the past, preferring
a meticulous analysis and citation (in over 8,000 footnotes, omitted here) of the
evidence on which his claims were based. The implications of this secular approach
were most clearly marked in the notorious last two chapters (15 and 16) of volume one, in which Gibbon portrayed the early Christians as ignorant, irrational,
intolerant, anti-social and miserable fanatics. Yet, having 'insinuated itself into the
minds of men', this seemingly 'pure and humble religion' proceeded to undermine
many of the values upon which Roman civilisation was based.

The extracts published here from *The Decline and Fall* are from Volume One
(1776), in which Gibbon reflects on the greatness of the Empire in its 'Golden
Age', and the nature of the barbarian German tribes who would eventually overthrow the Empire; and from Volume Two (1781), in which he offers 'General
Observations' about the progress and security of eighteenth-century society. While
it may be tempting to see Gibbon's sympathies as lying wholly with the love of
learning, political liberty, religious tolerance, moderation and public spirit that he
sees as the original hallmarks of Roman civilisation, the subtle ironies of his magisterial rhetoric serve both to reassure the Enlightened reader and to raise fundamental questions about many Enlightenment ideas and distinctions.

## The Decline and Fall of the Roman Empire (1776–88)

### 'Introduction'

In the second century of the Christian Era, the empire of Rome comprehended the
fairest part of the earth, and the most civilized portion of mankind. The frontiers of that
extensive monarchy were guarded by ancient renown and disciplined valour. The gentle, but powerful, influence of laws and manners had gradually cemented the union of
the provinces. Their peaceful inhabitants enjoyed and abused the advantages of wealth
and luxury. The image of a free constitution was preserved with decent reverence: the
Roman senate appeared to possess the sovereign authority, and devolved on the emperors all the executive powers of government. During a happy period of more than
fourscore years [96–180 AD] the public administration was conducted by the virtue and
abilities of Nerva, Trajan, Hadrian, and the two Antonines.

(*Decline and Fall*, vol. 1, ch. I, 'Introduction', para. 1)

### 'Of the Union and Internal Prosperity of the Roman Empire in the Age of the Antonines'

It is not alone by the rapidity or extent of conquest that we should estimate the greatness of Rome. The sovereign of the Russian deserts commands a larger portion of the
globe. In the seventh summer after his passage of the Hellespont, Alexander [the

Great, 356–323 BC] erected the Macedonian trophies on the banks of the Hyphasis. Within less than a century, the irresistible Zingis, and the Mogul princes of his race, spread their cruel devastations and transient empire from the sea of China to the confines of Egypt and Germany. But the firm edifice of Roman power was raised and preserved by the wisdom of ages. The obedient provinces of Trajan and the Antonines were united by laws and adorned by arts. They might occasionally suffer from the partial abuse of delegated authority; but the general principle of government was wise, simple, and beneficent. They enjoyed the religion of their ancestors, whilst in civil honours and advantages they were exalted, by just degrees, to an equality with their conquerors.

I. The policy of the emperors and the senate, as far as it concerned religion, was happily seconded by the reflections of the enlightened, and by the habits of the superstitious, part of their subjects. The various modes of worship which prevailed in the Roman world were all considered by the people as equally true; by the philosopher as equally false; and by the magistrate as equally useful. And thus toleration produced not only mutual indulgence, but even religious concord. [...]

II. The narrow policy of preserving, without any foreign mixture, the pure blood of the ancient citizens, had checked the fortune and hastened the ruin of Athens and Sparta. The aspiring genius of Rome sacrificed vanity to ambition, and deemed it more prudent, as well as honourable, to adopt virtue and merit for her own wheresoever they were found, among slaves or strangers, enemies or barbarians. [...]

Whatever evils either reason or declamation have imputed to extensive empire, the power of Rome was attended with some beneficial consequences to mankind; and the same freedom of intercourse which extended the vices, diffused likewise the improvements, of social life. In the more remote ages of antiquity the world was unequally divided. The East was in the immemorial possession of arts and luxury: whilst the West was inhabited by rude and warlike barbarians, who either disdained agriculture, or to whom it was totally unknown. Under the protection of an established government, the productions of happier climates, and the industry of more civilised nations, were gradually introduced into the western countries of Europe; and the natives were encouraged, by an open and profitable commerce, to multiply the former, as well as to improve the latter. It would be almost impossible to enumerate all the articles, either of the animal or the vegetable reign, which were successively imported into Europe from Asia and Egypt; but it will not be unworthy of the dignity, and much less of the utility, of an historical work, slightly to touch on a few of the principal heads. (1) Almost all the flowers, the herbs, and the fruits, that grow in our European gardens, are of foreign extraction, which, in many cases, is betrayed even by their names: the apple was a native of Italy; and when the Romans had tasted the richer flavour of the apricot, the peach, the pomegranate, the citron, and the orange, they contented themselves with applying to all these new fruits the common denomination of apple, discriminating them from each other by the additional epithet of their country. (2) In the time of Homer [c. 1050–850 BC] the vine grew wild in the island of Sicily, and most probably in the adjacent continent; but it was not improved by the skill, nor did it afford a liquor grateful to the taste, of the savage inhabitants. A thousand years afterwards Italy could boast that, of the fourscore most generous and celebrated wines, more than two-thirds were produced from her soil. The blessing was soon communicated to the Narbonnese province of Gaul; but so intense was the cold to the north of the Cevennes, that, in the time of Strabo [c.64 BC–21 AD], it was thought impossible to ripen the grapes in those parts of Gaul. This difficulty, however, was gradually vanquished; and there is some reason to believe that the vineyards of Burgundy are as old as the age of the Antonines. (3) The olive, in the western world, followed the progress of peace, of which it was considered as the symbol. Two centuries after the foundation of Rome, both Italy and Africa were strangers to that useful plant; it was naturalised in those countries, and at length carried into the heart of Spain and Gaul. The timid errors of the ancients, that it required a certain degree of heat, and could only flourish in the neighbourhood of the sea, were insensibly exploded by industry and experience. (4) The cultivation of flax was transported from Egypt to Gaul, and enriched the whole country, however it might impoverish the particular lands on which it was sown. (5) The use of artificial grasses became familiar to the farmers both of Italy and the provinces, particularly the lucerne, which derived its name and origin from Media. The assured supply of wholesome and plentiful food for the cattle during winter multiplied the number of the flocks and herds, which in their turn contributed to the fertility of the soil. To all these improvements may be added an assiduous attention to mines and fisheries, which, by employing a multitude of laborious hands, serve to increase the pleasures of the rich and the subsistence of the poor. The elegant treatise [De re Rustica (c.65 AD)] of Columella describes the advanced state of the Spanish husbandry under the reign of Tiberius [ruled 14–37 AD]; and it may be observed that those famines which so frequently afflicted the infant republic were seldom or never experienced by the extensive empire of Rome. The accidental scarcity, in any single province, was immediately relieved by the plenty of its more fortunate neighbours.

Agriculture is the foundation of manufactures; since the productions of nature are the materials of art. Under the Roman empire, the labour of an industrious and ingenious people was variously, but incessantly, employed in the service of the rich. In their dress, their table, their houses, and their furniture, the favourites of fortune united every refinement of conveniency, of elegance, and of splendour, whatever could soothe their pride, or gratify their sensuality. Such refinements, under the odious name of luxury, have been severely arraigned by the moralist of every age; and it might perhaps be more conducive to the virtue, as well as happiness, of mankind, if all possessed the necessaries, and none the superfluities, of life. But in the present imperfect condition of society, luxury, though it may proceed from vice or folly, seems to be the only means that can correct the unequal distribution of property. [...]

It was scarcely possible that the eyes of contemporaries should discover in the public felicity the latent causes of decay and corruption. This long peace, and the uniform government of the Romans, introduced a slow and secret poison into the vitals of the empire. The minds of men were gradually reduced to the same level, the fire of genius was extinguished, and even the military spirit evaporated.

(*Decline and Fall*, vol. 1, ch. II, paras 1–2 and various passages)

### 'Of the Constitution of the Roman Empire in the Age of the Antonines'

If a man were called to fix the period in the history of the world during which the condition of the human race was most happy and prosperous, he would, without hesitation,
name that which elapsed from the death of Domitian to the accession of Commodus
[i.e. 96–180 AD]. The vast extent of the Roman empire was governed by absolute
power, under the guidance of virtue and wisdom. The armies were restrained by the
firm but gentle hand of four successive emperors whose characters and authority commanded involuntary respect. The forms of the civil administration were carefully preserved by Nerva, Trajan, Hadrian, and the Antonines, who delighted in the image of liberty, and were pleased with considering themselves as the accountable ministers of the
laws. Such princes deserved the honour of restoring the republic, had the Romans of
their days been capable of enjoying a rational freedom.

  The labours of these monarchs were overpaid by the immense reward that inseparably
waited on their success; by the honest pride of virtue, and by the exquisite delight of
beholding the general happiness of which they were the authors. A just but melancholy
reflection embittered, however, the noblest of human enjoyments. They must often have
recollected the instability of a happiness which depended on the character of a single man.
The fatal moment was perhaps approaching, when some licentious youth, or some jealous
tyrant, would abuse, to the destruction, that absolute power which they had exerted for
the benefit, of their people. The ideal restraints of the senate and the laws might serve to
display the virtues, but could never correct the vices, of the emperor. The military force
was a blind and irresistible instrument of oppression; and the corruption of Roman manners would always supply flatterers eager to applaud, and ministers prepared to serve, the
fear or the avarice, the lust or the cruelty, of their masters.

(Decline and Fall, vol. 1, two paragraphs from ch. III)

### 'The State of Germany till the Invasion of the Barbarians in the Time of the Emperor Decius'

The most civilised nations of modern Europe issued from the woods of Germany; and
in the rude institutions of those barbarians we may still distinguish the original principles of our present laws and manners. In their primitive state of simplicity and independence, the Germans were surveyed by the discerning eye, and delineated by the
masterly pencil, of Tacitus, the first of historians who applied the science of philosophy
to the study of facts. [...]

  The Germans, in the age of Tacitus [c.55–117 AD], were unacquainted with the use of
letters; and the use of letters is the principal circumstance that distinguishes a civilised
people from a herd of savages incapable of knowledge or reflection. Without that artificial help the human memory soon dissipates or corrupts the ideas intrusted to her
charge; and the nobler faculties of the mind, no longer supplied with models or with
materials, gradually forget their powers; the judgment becomes feeble and lethargic, the
imagination languid or irregular. Fully to apprehend this important truth, let us attempt,
in an improved society, to calculate the immense distance between the man of learning
and the *illiterate* peasant. The former, by reading and reflection, multiplies his own

experience, and lives in distant ages and remote countries; whilst the latter, rooted to a single spot, and confined to a few years of existence, surpasses but very little his fellow-labourer the ox in the exercise of his mental faculties. The same, and even a greater difference, will be found between nations than between individuals; and we may safely pronounce, that without some species of writing no people has ever preserved the faithful annals of their history, ever made any considerable progress in the abstract sciences, or ever possessed, in any tolerable degree of perfection, the useful and agreeable arts of life.

Of these arts the ancient Germans were wretchedly destitute. They passed their lives in a state of ignorance and poverty, which it has pleased some declaimers to dignify with the appellation of virtuous simplicity. [...]

If we contemplate a savage nation in any part of the globe, a supine indolence and a carelessness of futurity will be found to constitute their general character. In a civilised state every faculty of man is expanded and exercised; and the great chain of mutual dependence connects and embraces the several members of society. The most numerous portion of it is employed in constant and useful labour. The select few, placed by fortune above that necessity, can however fill up their time by the pursuits of interest or glory, by the improvement of their estate or of their understanding, by the duties, the pleasures, and even the follies of social life. The Germans were not possessed of these varied resources. The care of the house and family, the management of the land and cattle, were delegated to the old and the infirm, to women and slaves. The lazy warrior, destitute of every art that might employ his leisure hours, consumed his days and nights in the animal gratifications of sleep and food. And yet, by a wonderful diversity of nature (according to the remark of a writer who had pierced into its darkest recesses), the same barbarians are by turns the most indolent and the most restless of mankind. They delight in sloth, they detest tranquillity. The languid soul, oppressed with its own weight, anxiously required some new and powerful sensation; and war and danger were the only amusements adequate to its fierce temper. [...]

Although the progress of civilisation has undoubtedly contributed to assuage the fiercer passions of human nature, it seems to have been less favourable to the virtue of chastity, whose most dangerous enemy is the softness of the mind. The refinements of life corrupt while they polish the intercourse of the sexes. The gross appetite of love becomes most dangerous when it is elevated, or rather, indeed, disguised, by sentimental passion. The elegance of dress, of motion, and of manners, gives a lustre to beauty and inflames the senses through the imagination. Luxurious entertainments, midnight dances, and licentious spectacles, present at once temptation and opportunity to female frailty. From such dangers the unpolished wives of the barbarians were secured by poverty, solitude, and the painful cares of a domestic life. The German huts, open on every side to the eye of indiscretion or jealousy, were a better safeguard of conjugal fidelity than the walls, the bolts, and the eunuchs of a Persian haram. To this reason another may be added of a more honourable nature. The Germans treated their women with esteem and confidence, consulted them on every occasion of importance, and fondly believed that in their breasts resided a sanctity and wisdom more than human. Some of these interpreters of fate, such as Velleda, in the Batavian war, governed, in the name of the deity, the fiercest nations of Germany. The rest of the sex, without being adored as goddesses, were respected as the free and equal companions of soldiers;

associated even by the marriage ceremony to a life of toil, of danger, and of glory. In their great invasions the camps of the barbarians were filled with a multitude of women, who remained firm and undaunted amidst the sound of arms, the various forms of destruction, and the honourable wounds of their sons and husbands. Fainting armies of Germans have, more than once, been driven back upon the enemy by the generous despair of the women, who dreaded death much less than servitude. If the day was irrecoverably lost, they well knew how to deliver themselves and their children, with their own hands, from an insulting victor. Heroines of such a cast may claim our admiration; but they were most assuredly neither lovely nor very susceptible of love. Whilst they affected to emulate the stern virtues of *man*, they must have resigned that attractive softness in which principally consist the charm and weakness of *woman*. Conscious pride taught the German females to suppress every tender emotion that stood in competition with honour, and the first honour of the sex has ever been that of chastity. The sentiments and conduct of these high-spirited matrons may, at once, be considered as a cause, as an effect, and as a proof of the general character of the nation. Female courage, however it may be raised by fanaticism or confirmed by habit, can be only a faint and imperfect imitation of the manly valour that distinguishes the age or country in which it may be found.

The religious system of the Germans (if the wild opinions of savages can deserve that name) was dictated by their wants, their fears and their ignorance. They adored the great visible objects and agents of nature, the Sun and the Moon, the Fire and the Earth; together with those imaginary deities who were supposed to preside over the most important occupations of human life. They were persuaded that, by some ridiculous arts of divination, they could discover the will of the superior beings, and that human sacrifices were the most precious and acceptable offering to their altars. [...]

Such was the situation and such were the manners of the ancient Germans. Their climate, their want of learning, of arts, and of laws, their notions of honour, of gallantry, and of religion, their sense of freedom, impatience of peace, and thirst of enterprise, all contributed to form a people of military heroes.

(*Decline and Fall*, vol. 1, various passages from ch. IX)


### 'General Observations on the Fall of the Roman Empire in the West'

The savage nations of the globe are the common enemies of civilised society; and we may inquire, with anxious curiosity, whether Europe is still threatened with a repetition of those calamities which formerly oppressed the arms and institutions of Rome. Perhaps the same reflections will illustrate the fall of that mighty empire, and explain the probable causes of our actual security. [...]

Should these speculations be found doubtful or fallacious, there still remains a more humble source of comfort and hope. The discoveries of ancient and modern navigators, and the domestic history or tradition of the most enlightened nations, represent the *human savage* naked both in mind and body, and destitute of laws, or arts, of ideas, and almost of language. From this abject condition, perhaps the primitive and universal state of man, he has gradually arisen to command the animals, to fertilise the earth, to traverse the ocean, and to measure the heavens. His progress in the improvement and exercise of his mental and corporeal faculties has been irregular and various; infinitely slow in the beginning, and increasing by degrees with redoubled velocity: ages of laborious ascent have been followed by a moment of rapid downfall; and the several climates of the globe have felt the vicissitudes of light and darkness. Yet the experience of four thousand years should enlarge our hopes and diminish our apprehensions: we cannot determine to what height the human species may aspire in their advances towards perfection; but it may safely be presumed that no people, unless the face of nature is changed, will relapse into their original barbarism. The improvements of society may be viewed under a threefold aspect. (1) The poet or philosopher illustrates his age and country by the efforts of a *single* mind; but these superior powers of reason or fancy are rare and spontaneous productions; and the genius of Homer [*c.*1050–850 BC], or Cicero [106–43 BC], or Newton [1642–1727], would excite less admiration if they could be created by the will of a prince or the lessons of a preceptor. (2) The benefits of law and policy, of trade and manufactures, or arts and sciences, are more solid and permanent; and *many* individuals may be qualified, by education and discipline, to promote, in their respective stations, the interest of the community. But this general order is the effect of skill and labour; and the complex machinery may be decayed by time, or injured by violence. (3) Fortunately for mankind, the more useful, or, at least, more necessary arts, can be performed without superior talents or national subordination; without the powers of *one*, or the union of *many*. Each village, each family, each individual, must always possess both ability and inclination to perpetuate the use of fire and of metals; the propagation and service of domestic animals; the methods of hunting and fishing; the rudiments of navigation; the imperfect cultivation of corn or other nutritive grain; and the simple practice of the mechanic trades. Private genius and public industry may be extirpated; but these hardy plants survive the tempest, and strike an everlasting root into the most unfavourable soil. The splendid days of Augustus [27 BC–14 AD] and Trajan [98–177 AD] were eclipsed by a cloud of ignorance; and the barbarians subverted the laws and palaces of Rome. But the scythe, the invention or emblem of Saturn, still continued annually to mow the harvests of Italy; and the human feasts of the Læstrigons have never been renewed on the coast of Campania.

Since the first discovery of the arts, war, commerce, and religious zeal have diffused among the savages of the Old and New World these inestimable gifts: they have been successively propagated; they can never be lost. We may therefore acquiesce in the pleasing conclusion that every age of the world has increased and still increases the real wealth, the happiness, the knowledge, and perhaps the virtue, of the human race.

(*Decline and Fall*, vol. 2, various passages from ch. XXXVIII)

# Chapter 8

# Moral principles and punishments

**E**THICS OR MORAL PHILOSOPHY seeks to provide an understanding of the principles by which particular communities or societies live, and how they ought to live. In Christian theology and practice, moral distinctions and choices were seen as fundamental to human life and action, and to the understanding of God's will and purpose. Yet, in the eighteenth century, many notions of morality and punishment based upon God-given, universal and eternal precepts about good and evil, explained and enforced by religious customs, were challenged by some intellectuals. In many respects this process had begun in the seventeenth century as the alleged atheism and materialism of Thomas Hobbes and the Jewish heretic Baruch Spinoza (1632–77) challenged traditional teachings. Indeed, though Spinoza's works were read in secret by radicals, 'Spinozism' became a term of abuse, signifying a dangerous concoction of atheism and materialism, even among many *philosophes* and sceptics such as David Hume. In questioning the authority of the Church and the certainty of its doctrines, such as those concerning the immortality of the soul, original sin and divine justice, some thinkers felt obliged to make fresh enquiries into the origins, nature and validity of moral distinctions and the role of punishment. A great deal of attention was therefore devoted to these subjects, and new theories emerged which permeated many other Enlightenment discussions.

Many figures such as Newton, Locke, Rousseau, Kant, and key Jewish thinkers such as Moses Mendelssohn (1729–86) drew inspiration from their religious beliefs, and even sceptics like Hume attached importance to wrestling with religious ideas (if only to defeat them), so it would be misleading to suggest that the Enlightenment simply turned ethics into a secular debate. Furthermore, it would be quite disabling to think that on what today may be regarded as the most pressing 'moral' issues of the age, such as slavery and the slave-trade, and war and torture, the *philosophes* must have had an exclusive claim to the moral high-ground. In the eyes of traditionalists, the secular reasonings and lifestyles of many *philosophes* seemed rather to undermine morality. Yet, in the course of the Enlightenment, and often in the face of censorship, a more secular debate about morality did emerge in some important texts, and this opened up the possibility for some thinkers to claim that what constitutes morality may be subjective or culturally relative.

David Hume's moral philosophy was first published in his *Treatise of Human Nature* (1739) and later in his *Enquiry Concerning the Principles of Morals* (1751). The *Enquiry* is generally easier and clarifies many of the arguments made in the *Treatise*, though the *Treatise* would eventually become the more influential work. Hume attempted to show that particular moral distinctions and judgements were social constructions, and that they do not rest on rational truths that can be established *a priori* (prior to the evidence of experience), as René Descartes (1596–1650) had claimed. Rather, moral distinctions inevitably arise in all societies from humans' common possession of a natural benevolence which leads them to want to approve of things which promote the welfare and happiness of society. This is true at least when individuals have no personal or selfish interest in the particular case, and sometimes even when they do (as in a person's ability to praise a heroic act which is, nevertheless, against his or her immediate self-interest). Hume accepts that all people also have inherent selfish desires, but, as these are often different from one person to another, so they could never provide a basis for establishing shared criteria of moral judgement. Thus, the basis of morality lies in what Hume terms a 'common sympathy' (a shared passion) in human nature, which leads us to have an agreed yardstick (public welfare and utility) for the measurement of all human conduct. Our reasoning helps to inform us about whether or not an action enhances or damages public welfare. Thus the Greeks had reasoned that the killing of tyrants was a good thing, but modern Europeans now reckoned to the contrary as tyrannicide made it even more likely that despots would rule with greater cruelty. Even so, both ancient and modern societies used the same yardstick (public welfare) to reach their (different) moral judgements.

Hume was also the author of one of the great statements of religious scepticism in the period, *Dialogues Concerning Natural Religion* (1779), and it was largely his writings that inspired the German philosopher, Immanuel Kant. Contrary to Hume's thesis, it was reason, according to Kant, that was the paramount faculty, as some knowledge did not spring from experience. Thus, in the debate over the question of whether moral judgements could and should be made by reason, Kant disagreed with Hume's view that such judgements were based upon feelings. Not only did he emphasise the importance of reason, but he also stressed the importance of 'duty' in moral conduct. He believed that the individual should 'act as if his own maxim were to serve as a universal law' for all other rational beings. This provided a famous test of moral conduct, but it did not explain the source of moral principles.

Hume also highlighted another recurrent subject for ethical debate – pleasure. In the Christian tradition, the pursuit of pleasures for their own sake – such as all those of the flesh – was at best regarded with suspicion, and often taken as a sign of the depravity of humans. But as many *philosophes* questioned old models of human nature entailing original sin, and grew confident in the prospect of a continuous improvement in the material circumstances and conditions of people's lives, so the pursuit of pleasure became not only a more reasonable and legitimate goal of a free society based upon individual desires and interests, but also the chief goal or axiom (the *summum bonum*) of new moral systems. Thus, in his introduction to *On Crimes and Punishments* (1764), the Italian philosopher and penal reformer, the Marchese di Beccaria, could claim:

> We shall see, if we open histories, that laws, which are or ought to be contracts between free men, have generally been nothing but the instrument of the passions of a few men, or the result of some accidental and temporary necessity. They have not been dictated by a cool observer of human nature, able to concentrate the actions of a multitude of men to a single point of view, to determine whether or not they contribute to *the greatest happiness shared among the greater number.*

Finding ways to reform society in order to maximise each person's (and/or most people's) happiness became a major quest of many Enlightenment thinkers. This sprang from a new spirit of confidence in each person's birthright to pursue pleasure, and a desire to make the laws that governed civil society consistent with what were perceived to be the natural laws that governed the material world. Since the latter were widely regarded as evidence of God's reason and benevolence in the Creation, this could also be regarded as a religious or moral duty. In his celebrated *Essay on Man* (1733), Pope explained how the natural and personal pursuit of pleasure ('Oh Happiness! Our being's end and aim!') was ultimately harmonised with the wider public interest ('That true self-love and social are the same'), because God had ordered the world so that true happiness could only be attained by trying to do good for others ('Virtue alone is Happiness below' [on earth]). Yet, no less appealing to many *philosophes'* ways of thinking were the Classical precedents and arguments in favour of a hedonistic way of life.

The Greek philosopher Epicurus (341–270 BC) had held that human judgements are based on feelings of pain and pleasure, and the term 'hedonism' arose to describe a philosophy which makes happiness the goal of life. As an exponent of egoistic hedonism, Jeremy Bentham believed that people generally act so as to maximise their pleasure. However, he regarded himself as a philanthropist – but one who explained that he found pleasure in helping others. Questions about the relationship of self-interest and social welfare had concerned poets such as Pope and the Dutch-born radical Bernard Mandeville (1670–1733) in his celebrated *Fable of the Bees; or Private Vices, Public Benefits* (1714) since the beginning of the Enlightenment, and in works such as Madame du Châtelet's *Discourse on Happiness* (1779) they would continue to fascinate scholars throughout the century. A key question was whether selfishness was always immoral and damaging to society. There was no agreed answer, but the advantages of Enlightened self-interest were examined in many texts, such as Adam Smith's *The Wealth of Nations*, and the extent to which moral laws could be derived from the individual's pursuit of personal happiness (because the welfare of others is – ultimately – in each person's best interest) became a familiar subject of debate.

As many thinkers' belief in divine justice diminished, so questions about the morality and use of worldly punishment became the subject of intense debates. In *The Spirit of the Laws* (1751), Montesquieu had emphasised how important it was to the liberty of all individuals in society, that they were protected by a small number of strictly defined laws and an independent judiciary. For Montesquieu, laws were not needed to correct religious 'errors', for that was God's responsibility. Moreover, the scope of the criminal law should be clearly limited, and the penalties imposed for breaches of the law should not be excessively harsh or cruel. Even though, as a judge, Montequieu must have authorised the torture and execution of many people, he evidently believed that the innocent needed to be protected, that torture was cruel and useless, and that the death penalty was used far too freely. He was also a great admirer of English liberties, though these did not produce the kind of penal reforms that might have been expected. On the contrary, the number of crimes which carried the death penalty rose in England, so that by 1820 there were over two hundred capital offences – mostly to protect property rights. Similarly in France there were over a hundred capital offences at the outbreak of the Revolution. Montesquieu's ideas would inspire many subsequent reformers such as Beccaria, whose *On Crimes and Punishments* would be widely cited by the *philosophes*, but it was in Prussia that some of the most extraordinary penal reforms of the period were introduced.

Like Montesquieu and Beccaria, Frederick II (see p. 20) believed firmly in the rule of law – though with himself as absolute guarantor – rather than in the arbitrary power of princes. He also believed that all social classes should have equal access to justice and be equally subject to the laws of the land, and that it was better to spare an innocent person than to condemn a guilty one. Such views led to a systematic revision and codification of Prussian law in the *Codex Fridericianus* of 1749. But it was Frederick's views on crime and punishment that probably most shocked his contemporaries. Far from regarding torture as a just and necessary means of eliciting information from the accused, of obtaining a confession or of administering exemplary retribution, Frederick declared that it was 'as cruel as it is useless', and finally abolished it in 1754. He also reduced the number of capital offences and executions, and introduced reforms that would deter unmarried mothers from committing infanticide. He supported Voltaire's campaigns against religious persecution and intolerance in France, and awarded a fugitive accomplice of the notorious Chevalier de la Barre a commission in the Prussian army. In the celebrated case of the miller, Arnold, Frederick even imprisoned his High Court judges in the 1770s for what he (mistakenly) regarded as their failure to treat a poor man fairly. Of course, discipline and punishment in the army remained exceptionally brutal, and Frederick insisted upon his right to wage a 'just war' (in the essential interests of the state), notwithstanding the scathing criticisms of Voltaire and others. However, in discussing issues such as the legitimacy and inhumanity of war, the rule of law, freedom of expression and religious toleration, capital punishment and torture, in both his public pronouncements and his private correspondence with the *philosophes*, Frederick's concerns for the welfare of his subjects were invariably secular.

The new interest in investigating 'morality', rather than 'sin', and in secularising notions of crime and punishment was most famously expressed in the work of Beccaria. Horrified at the seeming arbitrariness of many sentences and the mistreatment of innocent people and criminals, Beccaria called for a fundamental review of the law and legal processes in order to preserve society and individuals' rights. He was opposed both to torture, which he regarded as 'a cruelty consecrated by custom', and to capital punishment, which (often combined with a selection of tortures) was still a public spectacle in most states. He also believed that punishments should be carefully adjusted in severity according to the seriousness of the crimes committed – an idea that Bentham would develop in the creation of a hedonic calculus.

Faced with the need to rethink the origins of morality and to establish secular moral systems that clearly demonstrated each person's rights and duties, many *philosophes* such as La Mettrie, Holbach and Helvétius adopted materialist positions, emphasising the 'artificial' nature of all moral judgements. Their works were widely challenged and condemned by traditional authorities, but it is probably in the writings of the Marquis de Sade that the shocking force of a new kind of thinking about morality can be most keenly felt today. The Marquis expressed, in highly graphic terms, the view that evil is part of the natural world, including the character of human beings. As a human construct, for Sade, morality could neither be objective nor absolute, but would always be relative and subjective.

## DAVID HUME

David Hume (see p. 45) attempted to provide a systematic account of morals, based upon the empirical study of human nature. In *An Enquiry Concerning the Principles of Morals* (1751), he tries to explain the origins of shared moral judgements in societies, and how these judgements change in the light of new experiences and further reasoning about experiences, though the criteria (human welfare and happiness) for determining what is and is not moral remain constant. Hume accepted that humans possessed selfish individual passions which often motivated their actions, but rejected the notion that humans possessed no other kind of feelings. He believed there was overwhelming empirical evidence that 'No man is absolutely indifferent to the happiness and misery of others', for 'there is some benevolence, however small, infused into our bosoms'. Thus he is keen to refute Hobbes' view of human nature. He states: 'There is a [Hobbesian] principle ... that all *benevolence* is mere hypocrisy, friendship a cheat, public spirit a farce, fidelity a snare to procure trust and confidence; and that while all of us, at bottom, pursue only our private interest, we wear these fair disguises, in order to put others off their guard, and expose them the more to our wiles and machinations.'

The following extracts are from *An Enquiry Concerning the Principles of Morals*, which Hume regarded 'of all my writings, historical, philosophical, or literary, incomparably the best' (*My Own Life*, 1777). The first extract focuses on natural sympathy, an inherent human capacity to be moved by evidence of the feelings (happiness and suffering) of others. According to Hume, sympathy is not in itself an object of moral approval, but rather the source from which we derive our shared criteria for reaching moral judgements. These benevolent sentiments are deeply embedded in our everyday language, which reflects our ability to understand one another, based upon our common feelings. By comparing moral approval with aesthetic preference, in the second extract Hume is suggesting that ethics may be a matter of taste; thus he promotes the possibility of subjective moral standards. Hume's thesis depends on sentiment (feelings, passions, desires) motivating our discussions and actions, which express and lead us to moral judgements. Reason (knowledge, thinking) cannot motivate us, for only passions can do this. (As he famously proclaimed: 'Tis not contrary to reason, to prefer the destruction of the whole world to the scratching of my finger.') However, reasoning plays a vital role in enabling us to reflect on and learn from our experiences and in informing us about how we might act to attain the objects of our desires.

## An Enquiry Concerning the Principles of Morals (1751)

### 'Why Utility Pleases'

The more we converse with mankind, and the greater social intercourse we maintain, the more we shall be familiarized to these general [moral] preferences and distinctions, without which our conversation and discourse could scarcely be rendered intelligible to each other. Every man's interest is peculiar to himself, and the aversions and desires, which result from it, cannot be supposed to affect others in a like degree. General language, therefore, being formed for general use, must be moulded on some more general views, and must affix the epithets of praise or blame, in conformity to sentiments, which arise from the general interests of the community. And if these sentiments, in most men, be not so strong as those, which have a reference to private good; yet still they must make some distinction, even in persons the most depraved and selfish; and must attach the notion of good to a beneficent conduct, and of evil to the contrary. Sympathy, we shall allow, is much fainter than our concern for ourselves, and sympathy with persons remote from us much fainter than that with persons near and contiguous; but for this very reason it is necessary for us, in our calm judgements and discourse concerning the characters of men, to neglect all these differences, and render our sentiments more public and social. Besides, that we ourselves often change our situation in this particular, we every day meet with persons who are in a situation different from us, and who could never converse with us were we to remain constantly in that position and point of view, which is peculiar to ourselves. The intercourse of sentiments, therefore, in society and conversation, makes us form some general unalterable standard, by which we may approve or disapprove of characters and manners. And though the heart takes not part entirely with those general notions, nor regulates all its love and hatred, by the universal abstract differences of vice and virtue, without regard to self, or the persons with whom we are more intimately connected; yet have these moral differences a considerable influence, and being sufficient, at least, for discourse, serve all our purposes in company, in the pulpit, on the theatre, and in the schools.

Thus, in whatever light we take this subject, the merit, ascribed to the social virtues, appears still uniform, and arises chiefly from that regard, which the natural sentiment of benevolence engages us to pay to the interests of mankind and society. If we consider the principles of the human make, such as they appear to daily experience and observation, we must, *a priori* [i.e. reasoning from principles independently of experience] conclude it impossible for such a creature as man to be totally indifferent to the well or ill-being of his fellow-creatures, and not readily, of himself, to pronounce, where nothing gives him any particular bias, that what promotes their happiness is good, what tends to their misery is evil, without any farther regard or consideration. Here then are the faint rudiments, at least, or outlines, of a *general* distinction between actions; and in proportion as the humanity of the person is supposed to increase, his connexion with those who are injured or benefited, and his lively conception of their misery or happiness; his consequent censure or approbation acquires proportionable vigour. There is no necessity, that a generous action, barely mentioned in an old history or remote gazette, should communicate any strong feelings of applause and admiration. Virtue, placed at such a distance, is like a fixed star, which, though to the eye of reason it may appear as luminous as the sun in his meridian, is so infinitely removed as to affect the senses, neither with light nor heat. Bring this virtue nearer, by our acquaintance or connexion with the persons, or even by an eloquent recital of the case; our hearts are immediately caught, our sympathy enlivened, and our cool approbation converted into the warmest sentiments of friendship and regard. These seem necessary and infallible consequences of the general principles of human nature, as discovered in common life and practice.

Again, reverse these views and reasonings: consider the matter *a posteriori* [i.e. reasoning from experience and observation]; and weighing the consequences, enquire if the merit of social virtue be not, in a great measure, derived from the feelings of humanity, with which it affects the spectators. It appears to be matter of fact, that the circumstance of *utility*, in all subjects, is a source of praise and approbation: That it is constantly appealed to in all moral decisions concerning the merit and demerit of actions: That it is the *sole* source of that high regard paid to justice, fidelity, honour, allegiance, and chastity: That it is inseparable from all the other social virtues, humanity, generosity, charity, affability, lenity, mercy, and moderation. And, in a word, that it is a foundation of the chief part of morals, which has a reference to mankind and our fellow creatures.

(Enquiry Concerning the Principles of Morals, Section V,<br>'Why Utility Pleases', Part II)

### *'Concerning Moral Sentiment'*

This doctrine [that reason 'is not alone sufficient to produce any moral blame or approbation'] will become still more evident, if we compare moral beauty with natural, to which in many particulars it bears so near a resemblance. It is on the proportion, relation, and position of parts, that all natural beauty depends; but it would be absurd thence to infer, that the perception of beauty, like that of truth in geometrical problems, consists wholly in the perception of relations, and was performed entirely by the understanding or intellectual faculties. In all the sciences our mind, from the known relations investigates the unknown. But in all decisions of taste or external beauty, all the relations are beforehand obvious to the eye; and we thence proceed to feel a sentiment of complacency or disgust, according to the nature of the object, and disposition of our organs.

Euclid [c. 300 BC] has fully explained all the qualities of the circle; but has not in any proposition said a word of its beauty. The reason is evident. The beauty is not a quality of the circle. It lies not in any part of the line, whose parts are equally distant from a common centre. It is only the effect which that figure produces upon the mind, whose peculiar fabric or structure renders it susceptible of such sentiments. In vain would you look for it in the circle, or seek it, either by your senses or by mathematical reasonings, in all the properties of that figure.

Attend to [Andrea] Palladio [1518–80] and [Claude] Perrault [1613–88], while they explain all the parts and proportions of a pillar. They talk of the cornice, and frieze, and base, and entablature, and shaft and architrave; and give the description and position of each of these members. But should you ask the description and position of its beauty, they would readily reply, that the beauty is not in any of the parts or members of a pillar, but results from the whole, when that complicated figure is presented to an intelligent mind, susceptible to those finer sensations. Till such a spectator appear, there is nothing but a figure of such particular dimensions and proportions: from his sentiments alone arise its elegance and beauty. [...]

Thus the distinct boundaries and offices of *reason* and of *taste* are easily ascertained. The former conveys the knowledge of truth and falsehood: the latter gives the sentiment of beauty and deformity, vice and virtue. The one discovers objects as they really stand in nature, without addition or diminution: the other has a productive faculty, and gilding or staining all natural objects with the colours, borrowed from internal sentiment, raises in a manner a new creation. Reason being cool and disengaged, is no motive to action, and directs only the impulse received from appetite or inclination, by showing us the means of attaining happiness or avoiding misery. Taste as it gives pleasure or pain, and thereby constitutes happiness or misery, becomes a motive to action, and is the first spring or impulse to desire and volition. From circumstances and relations, known or supposed, the former leads us to the discovery of the concealed and unknown after all circumstances and relations are laid before us, the latter makes us feel from the whole a new sentiment of blame or approbation. The standard of the one, being founded on the nature of things, is eternal and inflexible even by the will of the Supreme Being: the standard of the other, arising from the internal frame and constitution of animals, is ultimately derived from that Supreme Will, which bestowed on each being its peculiar nature and arranged the several classes and orders of existence.

(*Enquiry Concerning the Principles of Morals*,
Appendix I, 'Concerning Moral Sentiment')

## MARCHESE DI BECCARIA

The Italian criminologist, Cesare Bonesana, Marchese di Beccaria (1738–94), born in Milan of aristocratic parents, was educated at the Jesuit College in

Parma and at the University of Pavia, graduating in 1758. In the early 1760s he was greatly influenced by the small informal circle of Enlightened thinkers led by Pietro Verri, and contributed several essays to their journal *Il Caffe* (*The Coffee House*, 1764–66). Having been drawn to the work of the *philosophes* after reading Montesquieu's *Persian Letters* (1721) and Helvétius' *Essay on the Mind* (1758), he won their respect with his most important and influential work, *Dei Delitti e Delle Pene* (*On Crimes and Punishments*, 1764). Although it was first published anonymously out of fear of reprisals due to its attack on contemporary legal and judicial systems, it was soon translated into French (1766) and English (1767), and honoured with commentaries by Voltaire and Diderot. Indeed, so celebrated was the young Beccaria, he was invited to Paris to meet the *philosophes* there in 1766, but he became so homesick he soon returned to Milan.

The conditions that Beccaria had witnessed during his visit to a prison in Milan provided the information and moral stimulus for his writing. *On Crimes and Punishments* became a protest against the discretionary power of judges which produced inconsistency of sentencing, the use of torture to obtain confessions before persons had been proven guilty, and as a punishment, and the carrying out of capital punishment for minor, as well as serious, offences. Beccaria incorporated the concepts of social contract, utility and hedonism – ideas current in many Enlightenment works – into this carefully reasoned thesis. He argued that the law should be used as an instrument of social reform, and that it must be clearly defined to safeguard and promote individuals' happiness. Judges should not be allowed to interpret the law, but simply to establish whether or not it had been violated. He advocated that punishment should aim at deterrence, and that this is best achieved by a swift and certain punishment. In 1771, he became a senior public administrator for Lombardy, ruled by the Habsburgs since 1707, and was responsible for various legal and monetary reforms.

In helping to secularise the discussion of law, and ideas of crime and punishment, Beccaria's work had a profound impact on Enlightenment thinking about jurisprudence, and helped pave the way for major penal reforms over the next two centuries. His ideas were adopted by the National Assembly of France in 1789 as Article VIII of its 'Declaration of the Rights of Man and of the Citizen', and his influence can be seen in many legal reforms, such as Catherine the Great's *Instruction* (1767), and the Criminal Code of 1786 introduced by Grand Duke Leopold of Tuscany, which abolished capital punishment and torture. The two extracts selected here are from a nineteenth-century translation of *On Crimes and Punishments*. In the first extract, Beccaria argues that the primary objective of punishment is to ensure the existence of a stable society. Hence the seriousness of a crime should be judged in relation to the extent to which it harms society. Furthermore, punishment should be adjusted in severity to suit the seriousness of the crime. In the second extract, Beccaria argues that the death penalty is generally neither a just nor a useful form of punishment.

## On Crimes and Punishments (1764)

### 'The Proportion between Crimes and Punishments'

It is not only the common interest of mankind that crimes should not be committed, but that crimes of every kind should be less frequent, in proportion to the evil they produce to society. Therefore, the means made use of by the legislature to prevent crimes should be more powerful, in proportion as they are destructive of the public safety and happiness, and as the inducements to commit them are stronger. Therefore there ought to be a fixed proportion between crimes and punishments.

It is impossible to prevent entirely all the disorders which the passions of mankind cause in society. These disorders increase in proportion to the number of people, and the opposition of private interests. If we consult history, we shall find them increasing, in every state, with the extent of dominion. In political arithmetic, it is necessary to substitute a calculation of probabilities to mathematical exactness.

That force which continually impels us to our own private interest, like gravity, acts incessantly, unless it meets with an obstacle to oppose it. The effects of this force are the confused series of human actions. Punishments, which I would call political obstacles, prevent the fatal effects of private interest, without destroying the impelling cause, which is that sensibility inseparable from man. The legislator acts, in this case like a skilful architect, who endeavours to counteract the force of gravity by combining the circumstances which may contribute to the strength of his edifice.

The necessity of uniting in society being granted, together with the conventions, which the opposite interests of individuals must necessarily require, a scale of crimes may be formed, of which the first degree should consist of those which immediately tend to the dissolution of society, and the last, of the smallest possible injustice done to a private member of that society. Between these extremes will be comprehended all actions contrary to the public good, which are called criminal, and which descend by insensible degrees, decreasing from the highest to the lowest. If mathematical calculation could be applied to the obscure and infinite combinations of human actions, there might be a corresponding scale of punishments, descending from the greatest to the least; but it will be sufficient that the wise legislator mark the principal divisions, without disturbing the order, lest to crimes of the *first* degree, be assigned punishments of the *last*. If there were an exact and universal scale of crimes and punishments, we should then have a common measure of the degree of liberty and slavery, humanity and cruelty, of different nations.

Any action, which is not comprehended in the above mentioned scale, will not be called a crime, or punished as such, except by those who have an interest in the denomination. The uncertainty of the extreme points of this scale has produced a system of morality which contradicts the laws; a multitude of laws that contradict each other; and many which expose the best men to the severest punishments, rendering the ideas of *vice* and *virtue* vague and fluctuating, and even their existence doubtful. Hence that fatal lethargy of political bodies, which terminates in their destruction.

Whoever reads, with a philosophic eye, the history of nations, and their laws, will generally find that the ideas of virtue and vice, of a good or a bad citizen, change with the revolution of ages; not in proportion to the alteration of circumstances, and consequently conformable to the common good; but in proportion to the passions and errors by which the different lawgivers were successively influenced. He will frequently observe that the passions and vices of one age are the foundation of the morality of the following; that violent passion, the offspring of fanaticism and enthusiasm, being weakened by time, which reduces all the phenomena of the natural and moral world to an equality, become, by degrees, the prudence of the age, and a useful instrument in the hands of the powerful or artful politician. Hence the uncertainty of our notions of honour and virtue; an uncertainty which will ever remain, because they change with the revolutions of time, and names survive the things they originally signified; they change with the boundaries of states, which are often the same both in physical and moral geography.

Pleasure and pain are the only springs of action in beings endowed with sensibility. Even among the motives which incite men to acts of religion, the invisible Legislator has ordained rewards and punishments. From a partial distribution of these will arise that contradiction, so little observed, because so common; I mean, that of punishing by the laws the crimes which the laws have occasioned. If an equal punishment be ordained for two crimes that injure society in different degrees, there is nothing to deter men from committing the greater, as often as it is attended with greater advantage.

(*On Crimes and Punishments*, ch. VI)

### 'The Death Penalty'

The useless profusion of punishments, which has never made men better, induces me to inquire whether the punishment of death be really just or useful in a well governed state. What right, I ask, have men to cut the throats of their fellow-creatures? Certainly not that on which the sovereignty and laws are founded. The laws, as I have said before, are only the sum of the smallest portions of the private liberty of each individual, and represent the general will, which is the aggregate of that of each individual. Did anyone ever give to others the right of taking away his life? Is it possible, that in the smallest portions of the liberty of each, sacrificed to the good of the public, can be obtained the greatest of all good, life? If it were so, how shall it be reconciled to the maxim which tells us that a man has no right to kill himself? Which he certainly must have, if he could give it away to another.

But the punishment of death is not authorized by any right; for I have demonstrated that no such right exists. It is therefore a war of a whole nation against a citizen, whose destruction they consider as necessary or useful to the general good. But if I can further demonstrate that it is neither necessary nor useful, I shall have gained the cause of humanity.

The death of a citizen cannot be necessary but in one case. When, though deprived of his liberty, he has such power and connections as may endanger the security of the nation; when his existence may produce a dangerous revolution in the established form of government. But even in this case, it can only be necessary when a nation is on the verge of recovering or losing its liberty; or in times of absolute anarchy, when the disorders themselves hold the place of laws. But in a reign of tranquillity; in a form of government approved by the united wishes of the nation; in a state fortified from enemies without, and supported by strength within, and opinion, perhaps more efficacious; where all power is lodged in the hands of the true sovereign; where riches can purchase pleasures and not authority, there can be no necessity for taking away the life of a subject. [...]

A punishment, to be just, should have only that degree of severity which is sufficient to deter others. Now there is no man, who, upon the least reflection, would put in competition the total and perpetual loss of his liberty with the greatest advantages he could possibly obtain in consequence of a crime. Perpetual slavery, then, has in it all that is necessary to deter the most hardened and determined, as much as the punishment of death. I say, it has more. There are many who can look upon death with intrepidity and firmness; some through fanaticism, and others through vanity, which attends us even to the grave; others from a desperate resolution, either to get rid of their misery, or cease to live: but fanaticism and vanity forsake the criminal in slavery, in chains and fetters, in an iron cage; and despair seems rather the beginning than the end of their misery. The mind, by collecting itself and uniting all its force, can, for a moment, repel assailing grief; but its most vigorous efforts are insufficient to resist perpetual wretchedness. [...]

Let us, for a moment, attend to the reasoning of a robber or assassin, who is deterred from violating the laws by the gibbet or the wheel. I am sensible, that to develop the sentiments of one's own heart is an art which education only can teach; but although a villain may not be able to give a clear account of his principles, they nevertheless influence his conduct. He reasons thus: 'What are these laws that I am bound to respect, which make so great a difference between me and the rich man? He refuses me the farthing I ask of him, and excuses himself by bidding me have recourse to labour, with which he is unacquainted. Who made these laws? The rich and the great, who never deigned to visit the miserable hut of the poor; who have never seen him dividing a piece of mouldy bread, amidst the cries of his famished children, and the tears of his wife. Let us break those ties, fatal to the greatest part of mankind, and only useful to a few indolent tyrants. Let us attack injustice at its source. I will return to my natural state of independence. I shall live free and happy on the fruits of my courage and industry. A day of pain and repentance may come, but it will be short; and for an hour of grief, I shall enjoy years of pleasure and liberty. King of a small number, as determined as myself, I will correct the mistakes of fortune; and shall see those tyrants grow pale and tremble at the sight of him, whom, with insulting pride, they would not suffer to rank with dogs and horses.' [...]

The punishment of death is pernicious to society, from the example of barbarity it affords. If the passions, or necessity of war, have taught men to shed the blood of their fellow creatures, the laws which are intended to moderate the ferocity of mankind, should not increase it by examples of barbarity, the more horrible, as this punishment is usually attended with formal pageantry. Is it not absurd, that the laws, which detect and punish homicide, should, in order to prevent murder, publicly commit murder themselves?

(*On Crimes and Punishments*, ch. XXVIII)

# IMMANUEL KANT

The strongly pietist background of Kant (see p. 53) exercised a considerable influence on his moral philosophy, and provoked his assault upon the materialist ethics of writers such as Baron d'Holbach. Having been raised and educated as a Lutheran, Kant was very much concerned with duty and matters of conscience.

In the extracts here from a nineteenth-century translation of *Grundlegung zur Metaphysik der Sitten* (*Fundamental Principles of the Metaphysic of Morals*, 1785), Kant places the notion of duty at the centre of ethics (deontology), claiming that a moral act is an action undertaken from a sense of duty, regardless of its consequences of pain and pleasure. Hence, he asserts, an act must be motivated by duty in order to be morally worthy. He extended the concept of duty from specific to generalised duties. Incorporated into this deontological thesis is Kant's practical and objective guide for moral conduct, whereby we act only in such a way that we are prepared for everyone else to act in that same way, which he calls the 'categorical imperative': 'Act as if you wished the maxim by which you act to become a universal law'. He infers that application of the categorical imperative requires a negative test. So, actions which do *not* accord with the categorical imperative, are acts we ought *not* to perform, rather than that we *should* perform acts which *do* accord; it simply means these acts are morally permissible.

## Fundamental Principles of the Metaphysic of Morals (1785)

We have then to develop the notion of a will which serves to be highly esteemed for itself, and is good without a view to anything further, a notion which exists already in the sound natural understanding requiring rather to be cleared up than to be taught, and which in estimating the value of our actions always takes the first place, and constitutes the condition of all the rest. In order to do this we will take the notion of duty, which includes that of a good will, although implying certain subjective restrictions and hindrances. These, however, far from concealing it, or rendering it unrecognizable, rather bring it out by contrast, and make it shine forth so much the brighter.

I omit here all actions which are already recognized as inconsistent with duty, although they may be useful for this or that purpose, for with these the question whether they are done *from duty* cannot arise at all, since they even conflict with it. I also set aside those actions which really conform to duty, but to which men have no *direct inclination*, performing them because they are impelled thereto by some other inclination. For in this case we can readily distinguish whether the action which agrees with duty is done from *duty*, or from a selfish view. It is much harder to make this distinction when the action accords with duty, and the subject has besides a *direct* inclination to it. For example, it is always a matter of duty that a dealer should not overcharge an inexperienced purchaser, and wherever there is much commerce the prudent tradesman does not overcharge, but keeps a fixed price for everyone, so that a child buys of him as well as any other. Men are thus *honestly* served; but this is not enough to make us believe that the tradesman has so acted from duty and from principles of honesty: his own advantage required it; it is out of the question in this case to suppose that he might besides have a direct inclination in favour of the buyers, so that, as it were, from love he should give no advantage to one over another. Accordingly the action was done neither from duty nor from direct inclination, but merely with a selfish view.

On the other hand, it is a duty to maintain one's life; and, in addition, everyone has also a direct inclination to do so. But on this account the often anxious care which most men take for it has no intrinsic worth, and their maxim has no moral import. They preserve their life *as duty requires*, no doubt, but not *because duty requires*. On the other hand, if adversity and hopeless sorrow have completely taken away the relish for life; if the unfortunate one, strong in mind, indignant at his fate rather than desponding or dejected, wishes for death, and yet preserves his life without loving it – not from inclination or fear, but from duty – then his maxim has a moral worth.

To be beneficent when we can is a duty; and besides this, there are many minds so sympathetically constituted that, without any other motive of vanity or self-interest, they find a pleasure in spreading joy around them and can take delight in the satisfaction of others so far as it is their own work. But I maintain that in such a case an action of this kind, however proper, however amiable it may be, has nevertheless no true moral worth, but is on a level with other inclinations, e.g. the inclination to honour, which, if it is happily directed to that which is in fact of public utility and accordant with duty, and consequently honourable, deserves praise and encouragement, but not esteem. For the maxim lacks the moral import, namely, that such actions be *done from duty*, not from inclination. Put the case that the mind of that philanthropist were clouded by sorrow of his own, extinguishing all sympathy with the lot of others, and that while he still has the power to benefit others in distress, he is not touched by their trouble because he is absorbed with his own; and now suppose that he tears himself out of this dead insensibility, and performs the action without any inclination to it, but simply from duty, then first has his action its genuine moral worth. Further still; if nature has put little sympathy in the heart of this or that man; if he, supposed to be an upright man, is by temperament cold and indifferent to the sufferings of others, perhaps because in respect of his own he is provided with the special gift of patience and fortitude, and supposes, or even requires, that others should have the same and such a man would certainly not be the meanest product of nature – but if nature had not specially framed him for a philanthropist, would he not still find in himself a source from whence to give himself a far higher worth than that of a good-natured temperament could be? Unquestionably. It is just in this that the moral worth of the character is brought out which is incomparably the highest of all, namely, that he is beneficent, not from inclination, but from duty.

To secure one's own happiness is a duty, at least indirectly; for discontent with one's condition, under a pressure of many anxieties and amidst unsatisfied wants, might easily become a *great temptation to transgression of duty*. But here again, without looking to duty, all men have already the strongest and most intimate inclination to happiness, because it is just in this idea that all inclinations are combined in one total. But the precept of happiness is often of such a sort that it greatly interferes with some inclinations, and yet a man cannot form any definite and certain conception of the sum of satisfaction of all of them which is called happiness. It is not then to be wondered at that a single inclination, definite both as to what it promises and as to the time within which it can be gratified, is often able to overcome such a fluctuating idea, and that a gouty patient, for instance, can choose to enjoy what he likes, and to suffer what he may, since, according his calculation, on this occasion at least, he has [only] not sacrificed the enjoyment of the present moment to a possibly mistaken expectation of a happiness which is supposed to be found in health. But even in this case, if the general desire for happiness did not influence his will, and supposing that in his particular case health was not a necessary element in this calculation, there yet remains in this, as in all other cases, this law, namely, that he should promote his happiness not from inclination but from duty, and by this would his conduct first acquire true moral worth.

(Fundamental Principles, First Section, 'Transition from the common<br>rational Knowledge of Morality to the Philosophical')

There is therefore but one categorical imperative, namely this: *Act only on that maxim whereby thou canst at the same time will that it should become a universal law.*

Now if all imperatives of duty can be deduced from this one imperative as from their principle, then, although it should remain undecided whether what is called duty is not merely a vain notion, yet at least we shall be able to show what we understand by it and what this notion means.

Since the universality of the law according to which effects are produced constitutes what is properly called *nature* in the most general sense (as to form), that is the existence of things so far as it is determined by general laws, the imperative of duty may be expressed thus: *Act as if the maxim of thy action were to become by thy will a Universal Law of Nature*.

We will now enumerate a few duties, adopting the usual division of them into duties to ourselves and to others, and into perfect and imperfect duties.

A man reduced to despair by a series of misfortunes feels wearied of life, but is still so far in possession of his reason that he can ask himself whether it would not be contrary to his duty to himself to take his own life. Now he inquires whether the maxim of his action could become a universal law of nature. His maxim is: From self-love I adopt it as a principle to shorten my life when its longer duration is likely to bring more evil than satisfaction. It is asked then simply whether this principle founded on self-love can become a universal law of nature. Now we see at once that a system of nature of which it should be a law to destroy life by means of the very feeling whose special nature it is to impel to the improvement of life would contradict itself, and therefore could not exist as a system of nature; hence that maxim cannot possibly exist as a universal law of nature, and consequently would be wholly inconsistent with the supreme principle of all duty.

(Fundamental Principles, Second Section, 'Transition from popular<br>moral Philosophy to the Metaphysics of Morals')

## JEREMY BENTHAM

Born in London, Bentham (1748–1832) was expected to follow in the footsteps of his father and grandfather in becoming a lawyer. Thus, at the age of twelve he entered Queen's College, Oxford, and on graduating in 1763, he studied law at Lincoln's Inn, London. Although law remained central to Bentham's work throughout his life, he never practised it. He rebelled against the current legal procedure and devoted himself instead to jurisprudence, aiming to discover the fundamental principles of a just, rational, humane and simplified legal system. Disturbed by the social evils of his time, supported by a legal system he considered to be brutal, costly and incoherent, he developed the ideas of writers such as Beccaria, Helvétius and Hume to form a doctrine, Utilitarianism, which would serve as an effective philosophical basis for social reform. He took Hume's theory of social utility and transformed it into the 'greatest happiness' principle. At the beginning of his major work *An Introduction to the Principles of Morals and Legislation* (1789), Bentham states his principle: 'It is the greatest happiness for the greatest number, that is the measure of right and wrong'. He believed he had reworked a truth about human nature – that we are motivated by the pursuit of pleasure and the avoidance of pain – and that this truth was the correct foundation for a theory of morality. From his premises, punishment, in itself, must be wrong because it causes pain. Punishment can, therefore, only be justified when the pain it causes is outweighed by a greater pain that it averts by deterring others from causing misery. Since it was his view that the sole purpose of punishment is to minimise overall suffering, Bentham advocated a penal system based on deterrence and rehabilitation, as opposed to retribution. So committed was he to tackling the issue of punishment that, following a trip to Russia in 1785, he designed his famous prison, the Panopticon, with its central inspection tower. It was never built, but his ideas, particularly his insistence on the need for rehabilitation, acted as a spur to later penal reform.

In the first of the following extracts from *Principles of Morals and Legislation*, Bentham sets out the basis for his moral theory, explaining the 'Principle of Utility'. In the second extract he adds a psychological dimension to his theory, explaining how, being individuals, people's ideas of happiness will differ, and that the value of pleasure and pain varies with factors such as intensity, duration, certainty and remoteness. According to Bentham's principle, virtue can be measured by quantitative and qualitative levels of pleasure and pain. By developing an elaborate 'hedonic calculus', he claimed he could take these factors into account in the pleasure and pain an act promotes, hence precisely measuring an action's moral worth.

## *The Principles of Morals and Legislation* (1789)

### *'Of the Principle of Utility '*

Nature has placed mankind under the governance of two sovereign masters, *pain and pleasure*. It is for them alone to point out what we ought to do, as well as to determine what we shall do. On the one hand the standard of right and wrong, on the other the chain of causes and effects, are fastened to their throne. They govern us in all we do, in all we say, in all we think: every effort we can make to throw off our subjection, will serve but to demonstrate and confirm it. In words a man may pretend to abjure their empire: but in reality he will remain subject to it all the while. The *principle of utility* recognizes this subjection, and assumes it for the foundation of that system, the object of which is to rear the fabric of felicity by the hands of reason and of law. Systems which attempt to question it, deal in sounds instead of sense, in caprice instead of reason, in darkness instead of light.

But enough of metaphor and declamation: it is not by such means that moral science is to be improved.

The principle of utility is the foundation of the present work: it will be proper therefore at the outset to give an explicit and determinate account of what is meant by it. By the principle of utility is meant that principle which approves or disapproves of every action whatsoever, according to the tendency which it appears to have to augment or diminish the happiness of the party whose interest is in question: or, what is the same thing in other words, to promote or to oppose that happiness. I say of every action whatsoever; and therefore not only of every action of a private individual, but of every measure of government.

By utility is meant that property in any object, whereby it tends to produce benefit, advantage, pleasure, good, or happiness (all this in the present case comes to the same thing) or (what comes again to the same thing) to prevent the happening of mischief, pain, evil, or unhappiness to the party whose interest is considered: if that party be the community in general, then the happiness of the community: if a particular individual, then the happiness of that individual.

The interest of the community is one of the most general expressions that can occur in the phraseology of morals: no wonder that the meaning of it is often lost. When it has a meaning, it is this. The community is a fictitious *body*, composed of the individual persons who are considered as constituting as it were its *members*. The interest of the community then is, what? – the sum of the interests of the several members who compose it.

It is in vain to talk of the interest of the community, without understanding what is the interest of the individual. A thing is said to promote the interest, or to be *for* the interest, of an individual, when it tends to add to the sum total of his pleasures: or, what comes to the same thing, to diminish the sum total of his pains.

An action then may be said to be conformable to the principle of utility, or, for shortness sake, to utility (meaning with respect to the community at large) when the tendency it has to augment the happiness of the community is greater than any it has to diminish it.

A measure of government (which is but a particular kind of action, performed by a particular person or persons) may be said to be conformable to or dictated by the principle of utility, when in like manner the tendency which it has to augment the happiness of the community is greater than any which it has to diminish it.

When an action, or in particular a measure of government, is supposed by a man to be conformable to the principle of utility, it may be convenient, for the purposes of discourse, to imagine a kind of law or dictate, called a law or dictate of utility: and to speak of the action in question, as being conformable to such law or dictate.

A man may be said to be a partizan of the principle of utility, when the approbation or disapprobation he annexes to any action, or to any measure, is determined by, and proportioned to the tendency which he conceives it to have to augment or to diminish the happiness of the community: or in other words, to its conformity or unconformity to the laws or dictates of utility.

Of an action that is conformable to the principle of utility, one may always say either that it is one that ought to be done, or at least that it is not one that ought not be done. One may say also, that it is right it should be done; at least that it is not wrong it should be done: that it is a right action; at least that it is not a wrong action. When thus interpreted, the words *ought*, and *right* and *wrong*, and others of that stamp, have a meaning: when otherwise, they have none.

(Principles of Morals, ch. I, sections 1–10)

### 'Value of a lot of Pleasure or Pain, How to be Measured'

Pleasures then, and the avoidance of pains, are the *ends* which the legislator has in view: it behoves him therefore to understand their *value*. Pleasures and pains are the *instruments* he has to work with: it behoves him therefore to understand their force, which is again, in other words, their value.

To a person considered *by himself*, the value of a pleasure or pain considered *by itself*, will be greater or less, according to the four following circumstances:

1. Its *intensity*
2. Its *duration*
3. Its *certainty* or *uncertainty*
4. Its *propinquity* or *remoteness*

These are the circumstances which are to be considered in estimating a pleasure or a pain considered each of them by itself. But when the value of any pleasure or pain is considered for the purpose of estimating the tendency of any *act* by which it is produced, there are two other circumstances to be taken into the account; these are,

5. Its *fecundity*, or the chance it has of being followed by sensations of the *same* kind: that is, pleasures, if it be a pleasure: pains, if it be a pain.
6. Its *purity*, or the chance it has of *not* being followed by sensations of the *opposite* kind: that is, pains, if it be a pleasure: pleasures, if it be a pain.

These two last, however, are in strictness scarcely to be deemed properties of the pleasure or the pain itself; they are not, therefore, in strictness to be taken into the account of the value of that pleasure or that pain. They are in strictness to be deemed properties only of the act, or other event, by which such pleasure or pain has been produced; and accordingly are only to be taken into the account of the residency of such act or such event.

To a *number* of persons, with reference to each of whom the value of a pleasure or a pain is considered, it will be greater or less, according to seven circumstances: to wit, the six preceding ones; viz.

1. Its *intensity*
2. Its *duration*
3. Its *certainty* or *uncertainty*
4. Its *propinquity* or *remoteness*

5.  Its *fecundity*
6.  Its *purity*

And one other; to wit:

7.  Its *extent*; that is, the number of persons to whom it *extends*; or (in other words) who are affected by it.

To take an exact account then of the general tendency of any act, by which the interests of a community are affected, proceed as follows. Begin with any one person of those whose interests seem most immediately to be affected by it: and take an account,

1.  Of the value of each distinguishable *pleasure* which appears to be produced by it in the *first* instance.
2.  Of the value of each *pain* which appears to be produced by it in the *first* instance.
3.  Of the value of each pleasure which appears to be produced by it *after* the first. This constitutes the *fecundity* of the first *pleasure* and the *impurity* of the first *pain*.
4.  Of the value of each *pain* which appears to be produced by it after the first. This constitutes the *fecundity* of the first *pain*, and the *impurity* of the first pleasure.
5.  Sum up all the values of all the *pleasures* on the one side, and those of all the pains on the other. The balance, if it be on the side of pleasure, will give the *good* tendency of the act upon the whole, with respect to the interests of that *individual* person; if on the side of pain, the *bad* tendency of it upon the whole.
6.  Take an account of the *number* of persons whose interests appear to be concerned; and repeat the above process with respect to each. *Sum up* the numbers expressive of the degrees of *good* tendency, which the act has, with respect to each individual, in regard to whom the tendency of it is *good* upon the whole: do this again with respect to each individual, in regard to whom the tendency of it is *bad* upon the whole. Take the *balance;* which, if on the side of *pleasure*, will give the general *good tendency* of the act, with respect to the total number or community of individuals concerned; if on the side of pain, the general *evil tendency*, with respect to the same community.

It is not to be expected that this process should be strictly pursued previously to every moral judgement, or to every legislative or judicial operation. It may, however, be always kept in view: and as near as the process actually pursued on these occasions approaches to it, so near will such process approach to the character of an exact one.

The same process is alike applicable to pleasure and pain, in whatever shape they appear: and by whatever denomination they are distinguished: to pleasure, whether it be called *good* (which is properly the cause or instrument of pleasure), or *profit* (which is distant pleasure, or the cause or instrument of distant pleasure), or *convenience*, or *advantage, benefit, emolument, happiness*, and so forth: to pain, whether it be called *evil* (which corresponds to *good)*, or *mischief*, or *inconvenience*, or *disadvantage*, or *loss*, or *unhappiness*, and so forth.

Nor is this a novel and unwarranted, any more than it is a useless theory. In all this there is nothing but what the practice of mankind, wheresoever they have a clear view of their own interest, is perfectly conformable to. An article of property, an estate in land, for instance, is valuable, on what account? On account of the pleasures of all kinds which it enables a man to produce, and what comes to the same thing the pains of all kinds which it enables him to avert. But the value of such an article of property is universally understood to rise or fall according to the length or shortness of the time which a man has in it: the certainty or uncertainty of its coming into possession: and the nearness or remoteness of the time at which, if at all, it is to come into possession. As to the *intensity* of the pleasures which a man may derive from it, this is never thought of, because it depends upon the use which each particular person may come to make of it; which cannot be estimated till the particular pleasures he may come to derive from it, or the particular pains he may come to exclude by means of it, are brought to view. For the same reason, neither does he think of the *fecundity* or *purity* of those pleasures.

(Principles of Morals, ch. IV, sections 1–8)

## MARQUIS DE SADE

Donatien Alphonse François de Sade (1740–1814), born in Paris, the son of one of Louis XV's diplomats, became a French cavalry officer during the Seven Years War and later a notorious writer. He became famous for his sexual writings and perversions, including the inflicting of pain, and it is from his name that the term 'sadism' is derived. Sade's sexual acts cost him twenty-nine years spent in various prisons and asylums, beginning, just a few months after his marriage to Renée-Felagie de Montreuil in 1763, with punishment for 'excesses' committed in a brothel. In 1772 he was condemned to death for poisoning and sodomy. He escaped, travelled to Italy, but was later recaptured and imprisoned at Vincennes in 1777, and then transferred to the Bastille in 1784. In 1789 he was placed in a mental asylum from which he was released a year later, only to be re-arrested during the Revolutionary Terror. In the 1790s Sade was at last free to publish a few of his many writings, but their publication resulted in his return to prison and then to an asylum where he remained until his death. His works, largely unpublished during his lifetime, include *Justine, ou les Malheurs de la Vertu* (*Justine, or Good Conduct well Chastised*, 1791), and *La Philosophie dans le Boudoir* (*Philosophy in the Boudoir*, 1795).

Sade's works expound a philosophy that rejects both the existence of God, and Nature's inherent goodness. He uses highly graphic descriptions of sexual acts to affirm nature's apparent amoralism, on the basis that since humans are a part of nature, whatever they desire is 'natural', and hence he takes delight in the search for self-gratification. As Simone de Beauvoir observed: 'Sade made of his eroticism the meaning and expression of his whole existence.' Though challenging and disturbing, Sade's libertine writings do rest upon some philosophical propositions: notably, that cruelty is a fundamental characteristic of human nature, which is most evident during sexual activity. In 1783 he wrote to his wife: 'My manner of thinking stems straight from my considered reflections; it holds with my existence, with the way I am made. It is not in my power to alter it; and were it, I'd not do so. This manner of thinking you find fault with is my sole consolation in life; it alleviates all my sufferings in prison, it composes all my pleasures in the world outside, it is dearer to me than life itself.' In terms of ethics, he claimed that notions of right and wrong are merely human distinctions, devoid of any objective validity. In their *Dialectic of Enlightenment* (1947), Horkheimer and Adorno claimed that Sade's glorification of malevolence was the inevitable consequence of the pursuit of Enlightenment ideals.

The following extract is from a modern translation of *Philosophy in the Boudoir*, which was written as seven 'dialogues', and published anonymously in two volumes with four erotic engravings. In this work, the four protagonists discuss and enact their sexual fantasies, 'for no voice save that of passions can conduct you to happiness'. In the fifth dialogue, the young Eugénie says, 'I should like to know whether manners are truly necessary in a governed society'. A pamphlet 'Yet Another Effort, Frenchmen, If You Would Become Republicans', ostensibly just purchased outside the Palace of Equality, is then produced and read aloud by one of the debauchees. The text champions the freedoms that will be enjoyed after Christianity and conventional sexual moralities have been totally rejected. Having discussed sex crimes, the fifth dialogue then examines murder.

## Philosophy in the Boudoir (1795)

In the second category of man's crimes against his brethren, there is left to us only murder to examine, and then we will move on to man's duties toward himself. Of all the offenses man may commit against his fellows, murder is without question the cruelest, since it deprives man of the single asset he has received from Nature, and its loss is irreparable. Nevertheless, at this stage several questions arise, leaving aside the wrong murder does him who becomes its victim.

1.   As regards the laws of Nature only, is this act really criminal?
2.   Is it criminal with what regards the laws of politics?
3.   Is it harmful to society?
4.   What must be a republican government's attitude toward it?
5.   Finally, must murder be repressed by murder?

Each of these questions will be treated separately; the subject is important enough to warrant thorough consideration; our ideas touching murder may surprise for their boldness. But what does that matter? Have we not acquired the right to say anything? The time has come for the ventilation of great verities; men today will not be content with less. The time has come for error to disappear; that blindfold must fall beside the heads of kings. From Nature's point of view, is murder a crime? That is the first question posed.

It is probable that we are going to humiliate man's pride by lowering him again to the rank of all of Nature's other creatures, but the philosopher does not flatter small human vanities; ever in burning pursuit of truth, he discerns it behind stupid notions of pride, lays it bare, elaborates upon it, and intrepidly shows it to the astonished world.

What is man? And what difference is there between him and other plants, between him and all the other animals of the world? None, obviously. Fortuitously placed, like them, upon this globe, he is born like them; like them he reproduces, rises, and falls; like them he arrives at old age and sinks like them into nothingness at the close of his life span Nature assigns each species of animal, in accordance with its organic construction. Since the parallels are as exact that the inquiring eye of philosophy is absolutely unable to perceive any grounds for discrimination, there is then just as much evil in killing animals as men, or just as little, and whatever be the distinctions we make, they will be found to stem from our pride's prejudices, than which, unhappily, nothing is more absurd. Let us all the same press onto the question. You cannot deny it is one and the same, to destroy a man or a beast; but is not the destruction of all living animals decidedly an evil, as the Pythagoreans believed, and as they who dwell on the banks of the Ganges yet believe? Before answering that, we remind the reader that we are examining the question only in terms of Nature and in relation to her; later on, we will envisage it with reference to men.

Now then, what value can Nature set upon individuals whose making costs her neither the least trouble nor the slightest concern? The worker values his work according to the labour it entails and the time spent creating it. Does man cost Nature anything? And, under the supposition that he does, does he cost her more than as an ape or an elephant? I go further: what are the regenerative materials used by Nature? Of what are composed the beings which come into life? Do not the three elements of which they are formed result form the prior destruction of other bodies? If all individuals were possessed of eternal life, would it not become impossible for Nature to create any new ones? If Nature denies eternity to beings, it follows that their destruction is so useful to her that she absolutely cannot dispense with it, and that she cannot achieve her creation without drawing from the store of destruction which death prepares for her, from this moment onward the idea of annihilation which we attach to death ceases to be real; there is no more veritable annihilation; what we call the end of the living animal is no longer a true finis, but a simple transformation, a transmutation of matter, what every modern philosopher acknowledges as one of Nature's fundamental laws. According to these irrefutable principles, death is hence no more than a change of form, an imperceptible passage from one existence into another, and that is what Pythagoras called metempsychosis.

These truths once admitted, I ask whether it can ever be proposed that destruction is a crime? Will you dare tell me, with the design of preserving your absurd illusions, that transmutation is destruction? No, surely not; for, to prove that, it would be necessary to demonstrate matter inert for an instant, for a moment in repose. Well, you will never detect any such moment. Little animals are formed immediately a large animal expires, and these little animals' lives are simply one of the necessary effects determined by the large animal's temporary sleep. Given this, will you dare suggest that one pleases Nature more than another? To support that contention, you would have to prove what cannot be proven: that elongated or square are more useful, more agreeable to Nature than oval or triangular shapes; you would have to prove that, with what regards

Nature's sublime scheme, a sluggard who fattens in idleness is more useful than the horse, whose service is of such importance, or than a steer, whose body is so precious that there is no part of it which is not useful; you would have to say that the venomous serpent is more necessary than the faithful dog.

Now, as not one of these systems can be upheld, one must hence consent unreservedly to acknowledge our inability to annihilate Nature's works; in light of the certainty that the only thing we do when we give ourselves over to destroying is merely to effect an alteration in forms which does not extinguish life, it becomes beyond human powers to prove that there may exist anything criminal in the alleged destruction of a creature, of whatever age, sex, or species you may suppose it. Led still further in our series of inferences proceeding one from the other, we affirm that the act you commit in juggling the forms of Nature's different productions is of advantage to her, since thereby you supply her the primary material for her reconstructions, tasks which would be compromised were you to desist from destroying.

Well, let *her* do the destroying, they tell you; one ought to let her do it, of course, but they are Nature's impulses man follows when he indulges in homicide; it is Nature who advises him, and the man who destroys his fellow is to Nature what are the plague and famine, like them sent by her hand which employs every possible means more speedily to obtain of destruction this primary matter, itself absolutely essential to her works.

Let us deign for a moment to illumine our spirit by philosophy's sacred flame; what other than Nature's voice suggests to us personal hatreds, revenges, wars, in a word, all those causes of perpetual murder? Now, if she incites us to murderous acts, she has need of them; that once grasped, how may we suppose ourselves guilty in her regard when we do nothing more than obey her intentions?

But that is more than what is needed to convince any enlightened reader, that for murder ever to be an outrage to Nature is impossible.

Is it a political crime? We must avow, on the contrary, that it is, unhappily, merely one of policy's and politics' greatest instruments. Is it not by dint of murders that France is free today? Needless to say, here we are referring to the murders occasioned by war, not to the atrocities committed by plotters and rebels; the latter, destined to the public's execration, have only to be recollected to arouse forever general horror and indignation. What study, what science, has greater need of murder's support than that which tends only to deceive, whose sole end is the expansion of one nation at another's expense? Are wars, the unique fruit of this political barbarism, anything but the means whereby a nation is nourished, whereby it is strengthened, whereby it is buttressed? And what is war if not the science of destruction? A strange blindness in man, who publicly teaches the art of killing, who rewards the most accomplished killer, and who punishes him who for some particular reason does away with his enemy? Is it not high time errors so savage be repaired?

Is murder then a crime against society? But how could that reasonably be imagined? What difference does it make to this murderous society, whether it have one member more, or less? Will its laws, its manners, its customs be vitiated? Has an individual's death ever had any influence upon the general mass? And after the loss of the greatest battle, what am I saying? After the obliteration of half the world — or, if one wishes, of the entire world — would the little number of survivors, should there be any, notice even the faintest difference in things? No, alas. Nor would Nature notice any either, and the stupid pride of man, who believes everything created for him, would be dashed indeed, after the total extinction of the human species, were it to be seen that nothing in Nature had changed, and that the stars' flight had not for that been retarded.

(Philosophy in the Boudoir, 'Fifth Dialogue')

# Chapter 9

# Gender and society

**J**UST AS THERE WAS NO SINGLE VIEW of human nature, how it was formed and how (if at all) it might be 'improved', so too ideas about male and female bodies, about mental and moral differences between men and women, sexual identities and gendered roles, responsibilities and rights, did not stem from or lead to one common point of view during the Enlightenment. Nor, in the light of modern feminist research and studies of women's history and masculinities in the period, is there an agreed view about the extent and manner to which key ideas of the Enlightenment were gendered, and, in particular, their impact upon the lives of women. This does not mean, of course, that women and women's concerns were simply subsumed in male discourses about topics such as human nature (though they often were), or that they were just ignored. In texts as different as Steele's *Spectator* (1711–12) and Vico's *New Science* (1725), in the portrayal of Gibbon's barbarians or Cook's Polynesians, in the heroines of much eighteenth-century fiction, and in works of art from Chardin's domestic servants to Mozart's *The Marriage of Figaro* (Vienna, 1786) gender issues, such as those concerning women's role and nature, were clearly at the centre of attention. Women's fleeting appearance or near absence in other works could also be just as telling, when seen as evidence of the presumptions about gender that often underlay many *philosophes'* thinking. Above all, however, elite women were active participants in the development of Enlightened thinking, forging new images and ideals of their own identity, fashioning new social practices, and contributing to and critiquing Enlightenment debates, from Mary Astell's criticism of Locke's writings to Mme de Staël's assault upon Napoleon's regime.

In addition to the poverty and illiteracy that prevented most eighteenth-century men and women from engaging in Enlightenment discussions, the legal subordination of and practical discrimination against women in most public roles was unlikely to have stimulated their participation. Even so, throughout the century, women such as the Marquise du Châtelet (1706–49), Catharine Macaulay (1731–91), Mary Wollstonecraft (1759–97) and Mme de Staël (1766–1817) wrote important scientific, historical, philosophical and literary works of the Enlightenment. In Britain alone, writers such as Aphra Behn (1640–89), Eliza Haywood (1693–1756), Fanny Burney (1752–1840), Elizabeth Hamilton (1758–1816), Ann Radcliffe (1764–1823) and Maria Edgeworth (1768–1849) produced important drama, poetry and fiction. Painters such as the Swiss-born Angelica Kauffmann (1741–1807) and the Parisian Elisabeth Vigée-Lebrun (1755–1842) became renowned artists. Innumerable women were subscribers to and supporters of works such as the *Spectator* and the *Encyclopédie*, and many became members of new libraries, associations and debating societies. Moreover, in the person of Catherine the Great (and to some extent in Maria Theresa, too) the Enlightenment had a champion and female figure of the first importance.

At the end of the seventeenth century, influential writers such as the French theologian Fénelon in his *Treatise on the Education of Girls* (1687) and would-be reformers of female education such as Mary Astell in *A Serious Proposal to the Ladies* (1694) often drew upon biblical authority and social custom to circumscribe women's roles and aspirations. Thus in *The Lady's New Year Gift: or an Advice to a Daughter* (1688), the Marquis of Halifax could confidently proclaim: 'You must first lay it down for a foundation [of society] in general, that there is inequality in the sexes, and that for the better economy of this world, the men, who were to be the law-givers, had the larger share of reason bestowed upon them; by which means your [female] sex is the better prepared for the compliance that is necessary for the better performance of those [domestic] duties which seem to be most properly assigned to it.' Such views expressed the widespread convictions that women were, by nature, weaker than men in mind and body, less reasoning, best placed in the domestic sphere, and often inherently inclined to vanity, frivolity and wantonness (at least according to many contemporary satirists). A more rational position, that 'the mind has no sex', was well expressed in the essays of François Poulain de la Barre, as in *The Equality of Both Sexes* (1673). Furthermore, in 1719 Daniel Defoe would claim, 'I have often thought of it as one of the most barbarous customs in the world, considering us as a civilized and Christian country, that we deny the advantages of learning to women'. Yet it was most often conservative religious teachings and traditions that underlay the work of later reformers such as Hannah More (1745–1833).

Throughout the century, the socio-economic and cultural changes brought about by the growth of urbanisation, literacy and industrialisation in some parts of Europe had a significant impact on the lives of women. Many now entered the paid-labour market as domestic servants or as factory workers, though the growing middle classes not only generally supported the idea that families should be headed by male wage-earners, but idealised woman's role as carer for the home, for child-rearing and being the moral and religious fulcrum of family life. There was also a marked tendency in the work of writers such as Richard Steele (1672–1729) to idealise a matrimonial state and the happiness that could be derived from it, provided it were founded upon mutual love, companionship and fidelity. Clearly, this placed a new onus of responsibility for domestic harmony and sexual fulfilment upon most men and women, and these shifting patterns of thought and debates over gender roles and rights are well reflected in the arts and literature of the period. Thus, in popular novels, such as Samuel Richardson's *Pamela, or Virtue Rewarded* (1740) and Fanny Burney's *Evelina, or A Young Lady's Entrance into the World* (1778) there was a growing fascination with women's experience and subjectivity. There was also intense interest in the kind of education that would be deemed appropriate for men and women. This was expressed at the beginning of the period in works such as Locke's *Some Thoughts Concerning Education* (1693) and in the writings of reformers such as Mary Astell and Richard Steele, and it continued throughout the century. Thus in France, in 1777 the Academy of Besançon proposed a debate on women and education, to which the young Marie Phlipon (later Madame de Roland) contributed a discourse. Similarly, in 1783 the Academy of Châlons-sur-Marne proposed essays on the best ways to improve women's education. Such concerns were dramatised in Choderlos de Laclos' celebrated epistolary novel *Les Liaisons Dangereuses* (*Dangerous Acquaintances*, 1782) which drew extraordinary attention to the restricted social, sexual and mental worlds that privileged women were expected to inhabit, and against which some rebelled.

Increasingly, women came to be seen by some men and women as excluded from the Enlightenment culture of public reasoning and rights. While many Enlightenment thinkers identified what they claimed were 'universal' human attributes, much energy was also expended upon defining women's 'natural' difference, sometimes using new medical or scientific research as incontrovertible evidence. Thus many images and ideals of republican masculinity and domestic femininity were created, implicitly based upon gendered notions of culture/nature, public/private, reason/emotion. These often produced a range of ambiguous and contradictory assertions, such as the claim that femininity was 'natural' (i.e. not socially constructed), yet in order to preserve their feminine qualities women needed to be excluded or deterred from engaging in the artificial affairs of public life, to which most privileged men increasingly proclaimed their own natural right. One of the most striking and influential examples of the codification of sexual difference and sex-specific rights came from Rousseau's *Emile* (1762), a fictional account of the education of a boy, and an exposition of the moral philosophy that would ensure the development of a 'natural' man. Rousseau explained the education that he believed would protect goodness from being corrupted: from maternal breast-feeding, to Emile's learning of a trade, his aesthetic and moral development, his religious education, his courtship with Sophie, a period of travel through Europe, and the growth of an interest in politics. The text ends with Emile's marriage to Sophie and the news of his impending fatherhood. Rousseau was keen to show how the sexes complement each other, and in *Emile* he argued that 'if woman is made to please and to be in subjection to man, she ought to make herself pleasing in his eyes and not provoke him to anger; her strength is in her charms, by their means she should compel him to discover and use his strength. The surest way of arousing this strength is to make it necessary by resistance.' He also noted that 'Women do wrong to complain of the inequality of man-made laws; this inequality is not of man's making, or at any rate it is not the result of mere prejudice, but of reason.'

Notwithstanding Rousseau's highly patronising but very influential views, high-born ladies such as the Marquise du Châtelet and Lady Mary Wortley Montagu played a vital (if not always conspicuous) part in the progress of the Enlightenment. Most were also painfully aware of the difficulties that this entailed due to the poor education, limited public roles and low intellectual abilities that men had traditionally assigned to them. Thus the scientist and philosopher, Mme du Châtelet, Voltaire's friend, colleague and lover, probably spoke for many when she wrote: 'If I were king, I would redress an abuse which cuts back, as it were, one half of humankind. I would have women participate in all human rights, especially those of the mind.' In Britain, women could participate in public life through a wide range of artistic, social and philanthropic activities and interests – though, contrary to common thinking, and drawing on her own experiences as the wife of the British ambassador at Constantinople, Lady Mary still reckoned that even Turkish women enjoyed more freedoms (see p. 300). Such aristocratic ladies also exercised considerable influence through 'salons', in which artists, *philosophes* and their followers were regularly invited to private houses to debate and share their knowledge and opinions within contexts that were largely designed and managed by women. Thus ladies such as Elizabeth Montagu (1720–1800) 'Queen of the Bluestockings' in Britain, and Mademoiselle Lespinasse, the Marquise du Deffand, Madame de Geoffrin and Madame Condorcet in France, became powerful figures in the communicative practices of the Enlightenment, helping to develop an elite secular culture that was notably separate from that of the royal court. In this respect, though loathed by Rousseau, the Parisian salon has been regarded as the defining social institution of the discursive practices – polite conversation and letter writing – of the Enlightenment's 'Republic of Letters'. For *salonnières* can be seen as central to the formation of a new view of, and emphasis upon, sociability – a role that has sometimes tended to be obscured by the emphasis that is usually placed upon published philosophical works as the main expressions and instruments of the Enlightenment. In France too, despite opposition from the Catholic church, women also joined many of the masonic lodges that sprang up, debating and championing civic virtues, as Freemasonry spread rapidly across the continent from Britain.

In the latter part of the century, the politics of the American and French Revolutions encouraged a wave of fresh debates on the rights of women. In America, women in New Jersey and Pennsylvania acquired the franchise. In France, women became conspicuously involved in Parisian street politics and bread riots. Some political clubs during the French Revolution espoused 'feminist' causes such as the elimination of primogeniture, and divorce initiated by the wife. In 1793, Pauline Léon (a chocolate maker) and Claire Lacombe (an actress) even set up a 'women only' club, *Société de Citoyennes Révolutionnaires*. Later that year, however, political mobilisation was blocked by the National Assembly's dissolution of women's political organisations. Moreover, following disturbances, in 1795 it decreed that groups of women larger than five would be subject to arrest – an example of how women's exclusion from the 'public sphere' was sometimes reinforced rather than advanced by political upheaval and debate.

Although social change and the growth of commercial markets for literary and artistic works offered new opportunities for many female artists and authors, the situation of most women writers was more complex than that of the *salonnières*. Some, such as Lady Mary Wortley Montagu, were unwilling to publish under their own name. Others, such as Catharine Macaulay found themselves shunned or derided by other women for daring to take up a republican position or marrying a much younger man. Women artists, like those who strove for a political role, often cut across the gendered divisions of thought and society that permeated many Enlightened works, and it was in these tensions between, on the one hand, the formulation of universal rights and new forms of reasoning, and on the other hand, the active and sometimes hostile denial of these things to women, that much of the groundwork for modern feminism was laid.

The following extracts introduce a range of reforming and early 'feminist' voices from the eighteenth century. In the passage from *Letters on Education* (1790), Catharine Macaulay, while sharing some of Rousseau's criticisms of women's character and behaviour, argues firmly against his views of gender difference. Like many other writers, she argued that difference was not 'natural', but a product of the type of education that women had usually received. This view was often put in religious terms, as in the extract here from Astell's *Serious Proposal to the Ladies* (1694), and in the work of the educator and reformer Hannah More. Although the events of the French Revolution encouraged the formulation of women's rights in expressly political terms, in rejecting women's subjugation Mary Wollstonecraft did not call for votes for women. However, in her *Vindication of the Rights of Woman* (1792) she penned a thorough attack on conventional gendered thinking, arguing for greater roles and opportunities for women through education, and in married and family life. Like the *philosophe* Condorcet in his *On the Granting of Civil Rights to Women* (1790), Olympe de Gouges, in her *Declaration of the Rights of Woman* (1791), went further than Wollstonecraft and dared to imagine women exercising a direct political role and voice.

## MARY ASTELL

Mary Astell (1666–1731) was the daughter of a coal merchant from Newcastle. Orphaned at the age of twelve and educated by a clergyman uncle, she lived most of her life modestly in genteel poverty. In the 1680s she moved to London and gradually forged a literary career there. Like many women writers of the time, she chose to live a celibate life, often supported by female friends. In *The Christian Religion* (1705) she rejected Locke's contractual theory of government, and campaigned against granting Protestant dissenters from the Church of England greater religious and civil liberties. Even so, as a devout Anglican, much of her work attempted to give a religious foundation for the improvement of women's education. In addition to many religious tracts, her major works were *A Serious*

*Proposal to the Ladies, for the advancement of their true and greatest interest, by a lover of her sex*, in two parts (1694 and 1697), advocating female religious retreats as an alternative to marriage, and *Some Reflections on Marriage* (1700). In the latter work, reflecting on traditional interpretations of the subjection of women, based on male readings of the Scriptures, she noted: 'Sense is a portion that God Himself has been pleased to distribute to both sexes with an impartial hand, but learning is what men have engrossed to themselves, and one can't but admire their great improvements!' These bold works influenced contemporaries such as Lady Mary Chudleigh in her poem *The Ladies Defence* (1700) against the subjugation of wives, and Daniel Defoe, who took up the idea of an academy for women in his *Essay on Projects* (1697), arguing that 'the whole difference in mankind proceeds either from accidental difference in the make of their [women's] bodies, or from the foolish difference of education'. Many later writers, such as Mary Wortley Montagu (1689–1762) took up Astell's call for reform of female education, noting: 'We are educated in the grossest ignorance, and no art omitted to stifle our natural reason'. Astell died shortly after surgery at the age of sixty-five, following a mastectomy.

In the passages selected here, from the first part of *A Serious Proposal*, Astell explains the reasoning behind her proposal to establish an academy for women where they can live and study independently of men. Part II of *A Serious Proposal* is a more philosophical text, acknowledging the influence of Descartes and Malebranche, and criticising the ideas of Locke.

## A Serious Proposal to the Ladies (1694)

Since you [ladies] can't be so unkind to yourselves, as to refuse your *real* interest, I only entreat you to be so wise as to examine wherein it consists; for nothing is of worse consequence than to be deceived in a matter of so great concern. 'Tis as little beneath your grandeur as your prudence, to examine curiously what is in this case offered you; and to take care that cheating hucksters don't impose upon you with deceitful ware. This is a matter infinitely more worthy your debates, than what colours are most agreeable, or what's the dress becomes you best. Your *glass* [mirror] will not do you half so much service as a serious reflection on your own minds, which will discover irregularities more worthy your correction, and keep you from being either too much elated or depressed by the representations of the other. 'Twill not be near so advantageous to consult with your dancing-master as with your own thoughts, how you may with greatest exactness tread in the paths of virtue, which has certainly the most attractive *air*, and wisdom the most graceful and becoming *mien*. Let these attend you, and your carriage will be always well composed, and everything you do will carry its charm with it. No solicitude in the adornation of yourselves is discommended, provided you employ your care about that which is really your *self*, and do not neglect that particle of divinity within you, which must survive, and may (if you please) be happy and perfect when it's unsuitable and much inferior companion is mouldring into dust. Neither will any pleasure be denied you, who are only desired not to catch at the shadow and let the substance go. You may be as ambitious as you please, so you aspire to the best things; and contend with your neighbours as much as you can, that they may not out-do you in any commendable quality. Let it never be said, that they to whom pre-eminence is so very agreeable, can be tamely content that others should surpass them in *this*, and precede them in a *better* world! Remember, I pray you, the famous women of former ages, the *Orinda*s [a pseudonym used by a seventeenth-century woman writer] of late, and the more modern heroines and others, and blush to think how much is now, and will hereafter be said of them, when you yourselves (as great a figure as you make) must be buried in silence and forgetfulness! Shall your emulation fail *there only* where 'tis commendable? Why are you so preposterously humble, as not to contend for one of the highest mansions in the court of Heaven? Believe me, ladies, this is the only *place* worth contending for, you are neither better nor worse in yourselves for going before, or coming after *now*, but you are really so much the better, by how much the higher your station is in an orb of glory. How can you be content to be in the world like tulips in a garden, to make a fine *show* and be good for nothing; have all your glories set in the grave, or perhaps much sooner! [...]

Pardon me the seeming rudeness of this Proposal, which goes upon a supposition that there is something amiss in you, which it is intended to amend. My design is not to expose, but to rectify your failures. To be exempt from mistake, is a privilege few can pretend to, the greatest is to be past conviction, and too obstinate to reform. Even the *men*, as exact as they would seem, and as much as they divert themselves with our miscarriages, are very often guilty of greater faults, and such as considering the advantages they enjoy, are much more inexcusable. But I will not pretend to correct their errors, who either are, or at least *think* themselves too wise to receive instruction from a woman's pen. My earnest desire is, that you ladies, would be as perfect and happy as 'tis possible to be in this imperfect state; for I love you too well to endure a spot upon your beauties, if I can by any means remove and wipe it off. I would have you live up to the dignity of your nature, and express your thankfulness to GOD for the benefits you enjoy by a due improvement of them: As I know very many of you do, who countenance that piety which the men decry, and are the brightest patterns of religion that the age affords; 'tis my grief that all the rest of our sex do not imitate such illustrious examples, and therefore I would have them increased and rendered more conspicuous, that vice being put out of countenance, (because virtue is the only thing in fashion) may sneak out of the world, and its darkness be dispelled by the confluence of so many shining graces. The men perhaps will cry out that I teach you false doctrine, for because by their seductions some amongst us are become very mean and contemptible, they would fain persuade the rest to be as despicable and forlorn as they. We're indeed obliged to them for their management, in endeavouring to make us so, who use all the artifice they can to spoil, and deny us the means of improvement. So that instead of enquiring why all women are not wise and good, we have reason to wonder that there are any so. Were the men as much neglected, and as little care taken to cultivate and improve them, perhaps they would be so far from surpassing those whom they now despise, that they themselves would sink into the greatest stupidity and brutality. The preposterous returns that the most of them make, to all the care and pains that is bestowed on them, renders this no uncharitable, nor improbable conjecture. One would therefore almost think, that the wise disposer of all things, foreseeing how unjustly women are denied opportunities of improvement from *without*, has therefore by way of compensation endowed them with greater propensions to virtue and a natural goodness of temper *within*, which if duly managed, would raise them to the most eminent pitch of heroic virtue. Hither, ladies, I desire you would aspire, 'tis a noble and becoming ambition, and to remove such obstacles as lie in your way is the design of this Paper. We will therefore enquire what it is that stops your flight, that keeps you grovelling here below, catching flies when you should be busied in obtaining empires.

Although it has been said by men of more wit than wisdom, and perhaps of more malice than either, that women are naturally incapable of acting prudently, or that they are necessarily determined to folly, I must by no means grant it; that hypothesis would render my endeavours impertinent, for then it would be in vain to advise the one, or endeavour the reformation of the other. Besides, there are examples in all ages, which sufficiently confute the ignorance and malice of this assertion.

The incapacity, if there be any, is acquired not natural; and none of their follies are so necessary, but that they might avoid them if they pleased themselves. Some disadvantages indeed they labour under, and what these are we shall see by and by and endeavour to surmount; but women need not take up with mean things, since (if they are not wanting to themselves) they are capable of the best. Neither God nor Nature have excluded them from being ornaments to their families and useful in their generation; there is therefore no reason they should be content to be cyphers in the world, useless at the best, and in a little time a burden and nuisance to all about them. And 'tis very great pity that they who are so apt to over-rate themselves in smaller matters, should, where it most concerns them to know, and stand upon their value, be so insensible of their own worth.

The cause, therefore of the defects we labour under, is, if not wholly, yet at least in the first place, to be ascribed to the mistakes of our education; which like an error in the first concoction [understanding] spreads its influence through all our lives. [...]

Now as to the Proposal it is to erect a *monastery*, or if you will (to avoid giving offence to the scrupulous and injudicious, by names which though innocent in themselves, have been abused by superstitious practices) we will call it a *religious retirement*, and such as shall have a double aspect, being not only a retreat from the world for those who desire that advantage, but likewise, an institution and previous discipline, to fit us to do the greatest good in it; such an institution as this (if I do not mightily deceive myself) would be the most probable method to amend the present and improve the future age. For here, those who are convinced of the emptiness of earthly enjoyments, who are sick of the vanity of the world and its impertinencies, may find more substantial and satisfying entertainments, and need not be confined to what they justly loath. Those who are desirous to know and fortify their weak side, first do good to themselves, that hereafter they may be capable of doing more good to others; or for their greater security are willing to avoid *temptation*, may get out of that danger which a continual stay in view of the enemy and the familiarity and unwearied application of the temptation may expose them to; and gain an opportunity to look into themselves, to be acquainted at home and no longer the greatest strangers to their own hearts. Such as are willing in a more peculiar and undisturbed manner, to attend the great business they came into the world about, the service of GOD and improvement of their own minds, may find a convenient and blissful recess from the noise and hurry of the world. A world so cumbersome, so infectious, that although through the grace of GOD and their own strict watchful-ness, they are kept from sinking down into its corruptions, 'twill however damp their flight to heaven, [and] hinder them from attaining any eminent pitch of virtue.

You are therefore, ladies, invited into a place, where you shall suffer no other con-finement, but to be kept out of the road of sin: you shall not be deprived of your grandeur, but only exchange the vain pomps and pageantry of the world, empty titles and forms of state, for the true and solid greatness of being able to despise them. You will only quiet the chat of insignificant people for an ingenious conversation; the froth of flashy wit for real wisdom; idle tales for instructive discourses. The deceitful flatter-ies of those who under pretence of loving and admiring you, really served their own base ends, for the seasonable reproofs and wholesome counsels of your hearty well-wishers and affectionate friends, which will procure you those perfections your feigned lovers pretended you had, and kept you from obtaining. No uneasy task will be enjoined you, all your labour being only to prepare for the highest degrees of that glory, the very lowest of which is more than at present you are able to conceive, and the prospect of it sufficient to outweigh all the pains of religion, were there any in it, as really there is none. All that is required of you, is only to be as happy as possibly you can, and to make sure of a felicity that will fill all the capacities of your souls! A happiness, which when once you have tasted it, you'll be fully convinced you could never do too much to obtain it; nor be too solicitous to adorn your souls with such tempers and dispositions as will at present make you in some measure such holy and heavenly creatures as you one day hope to be in a more perfect manner; without which qualifications you can neither rea-sonably *expect*, nor are *capable* of enjoying the happiness of life to come. Happy retreat! which will be the introducing you into such a *Paradise* as your Mother *Eve* forfeited, where you shall feast on pleasures, that do not like those of the world, disappoint your expectations, pall your appetites, and by the disgust they give you, put you on the fruit-less search after new delights, which when obtained are as empty as the former; but such as will make you truly happy *now*, and prepare you to be *perfectly* so hereafter. Here are no serpents to deceive you, whilst you entertain yourselves in these delicious gar-dens. No provocations will be given in this amicable society, but to love and to good works, which will afford such an entertaining employment, that you'll have as little inclination as leisure to pursue those follies which in the time of your ignorance passed with you under the name of love; although there is not in nature two more different things, than *true love* and that *brutish passion* which pretends to ape it. Here will be no rivalling but for the love of God, no ambition but to procure his favour, to which noth-ing will more effectually recommend you, than a great and dear affection to each other.

(*A Serious Proposal*, Part One)

# RICHARD STEELE

Sir Richard Steele (1672–1729) was born in Dublin, the son of a poor Anglo-Irish attorney who died before Steele reached the age of five. Through the patronage of the Duke of Ormonde, Steele was educated at Charterhouse School, where he met Joseph Addison (1672–1719), and at Oxford University. In 1694 he entered the army, attaining the rank of captain (1700) before retiring from military duties in 1705. In 1701 he published his first highly-successful prose work, a moral essay *The Christian Hero: or, An Argument Proving that no Principles but those of Religion are Sufficient to make a Great Man.* This was followed by three comedies which were produced at Drury Lane, most notably *The Tender Husband* (1705). After marrying his second wife, and serving as editor of the government's official newsletter *The London Gazette* (1707–09), he founded a series of immensely popular journals: the tri-weekly *Tatler* (1709–11), the daily *Spectator* (1711–12) and the daily *Guardian* (1713). In 1713 he entered parliament as MP for Stockbridge, determined to use his great popularity and literary skills to promote the Hanoverian succession at the death of Queen Anne (1702–14). Though expelled from the House of Commons for seditious writings (including an issue of his political journal the *Englishman*), following the accession of George I (1714–27), Steele was rewarded by the Whigs with a knighthood, a safe seat in parliament and a patent to reform the Drury Lane Theatre. Even so, he fell out with leading ministers and, following the success of his play, *The Conscious Lovers* (1722), retired to his wife's estate in Wales, where he died in 1729.

As a political propagandist and populariser of Locke's views, Steele was often engaged in 'paper wars' with other journalists such as Daniel Defoe, Jonathan Swift and John Toland. However, as an essayist and editor of the *Tatler* and the *Spectator* he and his colleague Addison created a range of urbane, ironic and gently satiric characters and voices that exercised an important and pervasive influence upon the development of eighteenth-century literature and society. Through these journals (271 *Tatlers*, 555 *Spectators*, 175 *Guardians*), read in homes, coffee houses and taverns across the country, Steele not only brought a wide range of contemporary issues and ideas before the public, but did so in a manner that promoted public debate and ownership of discussion. As his famous editor-persona 'Mr Spectator' explained: 'I shall be ambitious to have it said of me, that I brought philosophy out of the closets and libraries, schools and colleges, to dwell in clubs and assemblies, at tea-tables and in coffee-houses' (*Spectator*, no. 10, 12 March 1711). Thus readers were invited to send letters to the editor (which were often published), and dozens of figures such as George Berkeley, Alexander Pope and Mary Wortley Montagu contributed essays. Though often focusing upon the seemingly small concerns and moments of contemporary life, the journals also addressed major social, religious, scientific and philosophical topics. Following their conclusion, the collected papers (particularly of the *Spectator*) reappeared in dozens of new editions, translations and imitations in Britain, across the continent and in North America. It seems that almost everyone, from Rousseau to Beccaria and Benjamin Franklin, enjoyed and studied them. Thus the *Spectator* became perhaps the most widely read, reproduced, and celebrated secular publication of the century.

Steele's journals were explicitly designed to appeal as much to women readers as to men, and they revelled in examining all kind of gender issues from a great variety of angles. In the extracts selected here, Steele reflects upon ill-natured husbands (*Tatler*, 149), answers a letter about the education of a country girl (*Spectator*, 66), and from the first series of his political journal the *Englishman*

(1713–14) examines the liberty of women (*Englishman*, 9). Though Addison was generally more conservative in his view of women's role and nature, during the political crisis of the Jacobite rebellion, in his journal the *Freeholder* (1715–16) he repeatedly called upon women to demonstrate their patriotism.

## *Tatler*, no. 149 (1710)

It has often been a solid grief to me, when I have reflected on this glorious nation, which is the scene of public happiness and liberty, that there are still crowds of private tyrants, against whom there neither is any law now in being, nor can there be invented any by the wit of man. These cruel men are ill-natured husbands. The commerce in the conjugal state is so delicate, that it is impossible to prescribe rules for the conduct of it, so as to fit ten thousand nameless pleasures and disquietudes which arise to people in that condition. But it is in this as in some other nice cases, where touching upon the malady tenderly, is half way to the cure; and there are some faults which need only to be observed to be amended. I am put into this way of thinking by a late conversation which I am going to give account of.

I made a visit the other day to a family for which I have a great honour, and found the father, the mother, and two or three of the younger children, drop off designedly to leave me alone with the eldest daughter, who was but a visitant there as well as myself, and is the wife of a gentleman of a very fair character in the world. As soon as we were alone, I saw her eyes full of tears, and methought she had much to say to me, for which she wanted encouragement. 'Madam', said I, 'You know I wish you all as well as any friend you have: speak freely what I see you are oppressed with, and you may be sure, if I cannot relieve your distress, you may at least reap so much present advantage, as safely to give yourself the ease of uttering it.' She immediately assumed the most becoming composure of countenance, and spoke as follows: 'It is an aggravation of affliction in a married life, that there is a sort of guilt in communicating it: for which reason it is, that a lady of your and my acquaintance, instead of speaking to you herself, desired me the next time I saw you, as you are a professed friend to our sex, to turn your thoughts upon the reciprocal complaisance [civility] which is the duty of a married state.

'My friend was neither in fortune, birth or education, below the gentleman whom she has married. Her person, her age, and her character, are also such as he can make no exception to. But so it is, that from the moment the marriage ceremony was over, the obsequiousness of a lover was turned into the haughtiness of a master. All the kind endeavours which she uses to please him, are at best but so many instances of her duty. This insolence takes away that secret satisfaction, which does not only excite to virtue, but also rewards it. It abates the fire of a free and generous love, and embitters all the pleasures of a social life.' The young lady spoke all this with such an air of resentment, as discovered how nearly she was concerned in the distress.

When I observed she had done speaking, 'Madam', said I, 'The affliction you mention is the greatest that can happen in human life, and I know but one consolation in it, if that be a consolation, that the calamity is a pretty general one. There is nothing so common as for men to enter into marriage, without so much as expecting to be happy in it. They seem to propose to themselves a few holidays in the beginning of it; after which, they are to return at best to the usual course of their life; and for ought they know, to constant misery and uneasiness. From this false sense of the state they are going into, proceeds the immediate coldness and indifference, or hatred and aversion, which attend ordinary marriages, or rather bargains to cohabit.' Our conversation was here interrupted by company which came in upon us.

The humour of affecting a superior carriage [behaviour], generally arises from a false notion of the weakness of a female understanding in general, or an overweening opinion that we have of our own: for when it proceeds from a natural ruggedness and brutality of temper, it is altogether incorrigible, and not to be amended by admonition. Sir Francis Bacon [1561–1621], as I remember, lays it down as a maxim, that no marriage can be happy in which the wife has no opinion of her husband's wisdom; but without offence to so great an authority, I may venture to say, that a sullen-wise man is as bad as a good-natured fool. Knowledge, softened with complacency [civility] and good breeding, will make a man equally beloved and respected; but when joined with a severe, distant and unsociable temper, it creates rather fear than love.

(*Tatler*, no. 149, 23 March 1710)

## *Spectator,* no. 66 (1711)

The general mistake among us in the educating our children is, that in our daughters we take care of their persons and neglect their minds; in our sons, we are so intent upon adorning their minds, that we wholly neglect their bodies. It is from this that you shall see a young lady celebrated and admired in all the assemblies about town; when her elder brother is afraid to come into a room. From this ill management it arises, that we frequently observe a man's life is half spent before he is taken notice of; and a woman in the prime of her years is out of fashion and neglected. The boy I shall consider upon some other occasion, and at present stick to the girl: and I am the more inclined to this, because I have several letters which complain to me that my female readers have not understood me for some days last past, and take themselves to be unconcerned in the present turn of my writings. When a girl is safely brought from her nurse, before she is capable of forming one simple notion of anything in life, she is delivered to the hands of her dancing-master; and with a [deportment] collar round her neck, the pretty wild [uncultivated] thing is taught a fantastical gravity of behaviour, and forced to a particular way of holding her head, heaving her breast, and moving with her whole body; and all this under pain of never having an husband, if she steps, looks or moves awry. This gives the young lady wonderful workings of imagination, what is to pass between her and this husband, that she is every moment told of, and for whom she seems to be educated. Thus her fancy is engaged to turn all her endeavours to the ornament of her person, as what must determine her good and ill in this life; and she naturally thinks, if she is tall enough, she is wise enough for anything for which her education makes her think she is designed. To make her an agreeable person is the main purpose of her parents; to that is all their cost, to that all their care directed; and from this general folly of parents we owe our present numerous race of coquets. These reflections puzzle me, when I think of giving my advice on the subject of managing the wild thing mentioned in the letter of my correspondent. But sure there is a middle way to be followed; the management of a young lady's person is not to be overlooked, but the erudition [cultivation] of her mind is much more to be regarded. According as this is managed, you will see the mind follow the appetites of the body, or the body express the virtues of the mind.

(*Spectator*, no. 66, 16 May 1711)

## *Englishman,* no. 9 (1713)

The Greek sentence [by Menander, 341–290 BC] on the front of this paper, is a piece of raillery on the fair sex, and the liberty they enjoyed in his country. He says in allusion to their manner of life, 'There is no one in this country knows his father; the son only suspects, or at best believes who is the man.'

For all this gentleman's pleasantry, the liberty of women is the source of all the gratifications which they give us. It is the freedom and regulation of the will which distinguishes human from bestial sensations; and he who is possessed of a woman of merit, whose heart is retained to him, not only by the laws of our religion and our country, but also by daily new obligations of civility, kindness and friendship, has an object on which to employ the best dispositions of the mind, and exercising in himself the highest generosity, in circumstances that seem, to the unconcerned, ordinary and indifferent.

The friendship which a generous husband has towards his wife, is as much above the friendship which man bears to man, as the conversation of a courtship is more pleasing than ordinary discourse. I have remarked, that in all nations their public affairs are conducted with more or less elegance, dexterity, and success, as they respectively restrain or give freedom to their women. In Turkey, where the whole race of mankind are begotten by slaves and masters of slaves, there is neither learning, commerce, religion nor liberty, but what are maintained by a rigid observance of such laws and restraints, as hinder the growth of any of those advantages to a perfection which would embellish human life. In Italy, where women are veiled from public view, and interdicted the pleasures of society and conversation, that behaviour has a suitable effect upon their lives: their love and their honour are of a piece; they taste the one only in brutal lust, and assert the other in base and barbarous murders. I will not here observe the greatness of Italian princes and potentates in comparison with other nations of more open converse.

Where the fair sex are treated with gallantry and superior civility, that treatment has its visible effect to the advantage of all public and private transactions. I will take upon me to say, the French principally owe their greatness to it. A certain liberality of heart and frankness in conversation, where both sexes are intermixed, is what insensibly insinuates their power among foreigners, and makes them appear, when they are raised above mere want, the happiest of all human race in themselves. If you examine Holland by the same rule, they also owe their prosperity to their treatment of women. As trade and commerce are essential to their very being, their women are their clerks and accomptants [accountants]; and the management of their cash is in the hands of those, who cannot squander, embezzle, or misapply it but to their own destruction. It is indeed a senseless imagination, to suppose the business of human life is to be carried on with an exclusion of half the species: and what makes the churlish behaviour in this kind more apparently absurd, is, that the nicest and greatest persons of all ages have had the greatest complaisance [civility] this way; and found their account from it in the success of their most important affairs.

It is the injustice of men to conceal all the good, and aggravate all the evil, which arises to them from the interposition of the other sex. There is no great incident recorded in Antiquity wherein a woman has had her part, if it be an ill one, but what is told with indignation that she was at all concerned. There is nothing laudable of women but what is related with an insinuation that it is matter of wonder that it came from her. But let morose men say what they please, and flatter themselves that it is because they are too wise they do not affect the conversation of the fair sex; they will find, upon an impartial examination, that their disinclination proceeds from want of taste, and that they are above other men from no other cause, but as they are less gentle.

From such considerations as these, the Englishman may very well triumph in his woman when he has obtained her: and I have hardly ever known an instance wherein he has failed of happiness, but from an unjust motive in his choice, or some ill-natured irregularity in his behaviour after he has chosen.

(*Englishman*, no. 9, 24 October 1713)

## CATHARINE MACAULAY

Catharine Macaulay, née Sawbridge (1731–91) was born into a wealthy merchant family at Wye in Kent. She lost her mother at the age of two, and was largely educated at home. In 1760, she married a Scottish physician, George Macaulay, who was in charge of a London hospital, and by whom she had a daughter. In 1766 George died, leaving Catharine a good inheritance. By then, she had already started her major work, *The History of England from the Accession of James I to that of the Brunswick Line*, which ran to eight volumes and was published from 1763 to 1783. Its republican stance won her both notoriety and respect as an intellectual and historian, and Horace Walpole, the poet Thomas Gray, William Pitt and George Washington were among her admirers. Madame de Roland, too, was impressed by Macaulay's erudition, as was Mary Wollstonecraft who wrote to her saying that she was 'the only female writer who I coincide in opinion with, respecting the rank our sex ought to endeavour to attain in this world'. In 1774, Macaulay moved to Bath, setting up a salon there. A few years later she married William Graham, twenty-six years younger than herself, and moved (amidst public ridicule) with him to live in Berkshire. During the political crises of the 1760s and 1770s, she was an active supporter of John Wilkes, and wrote pamphlets advocating universal male suffrage, opposing primogeniture and supporting the cause of American Independence. She also wrote two replies to Edmund Burke: *Observations on a Pamphlet entitled Thoughts on the Cause of the Present Discontent* (1770) and *Observations on the Reflections of the Right Hon. Edmund Burke, on the Revolution in France* (1790). She travelled to France (1775, 1777–78) and to the United States (1784) where her work was well received, and she corresponded with several Americans such as George Washington, John Adams, Ezra Stiles and Mercy Otis Warren.

Macaulay's *Letters on Education, with Observations on Religious and Metaphysical Subjects* was published in 1790. It provided critiques of women's education and of 'false ideas of female excellence', and influenced contemporaries such as Wollstonecraft in her writing of *A Vindication of the Rights of Woman* (1792). In the extract from *Letters on Education* selected here, Macaulay challenges notions of gender difference (Rousseau's in particular) and the attitudes that support such views. The passage, Letter XXII, 'No Characteristic Difference in Sex', is addressed to the fictional character Hortensia.

## *Letters on Education* (1790)

The great difference that is observable in the characters of the sexes, Hortensia, as they display themselves in the scenes of social life, has given rise to much false speculation on the natural qualities of the female mind. For though the doctrine of innate ideas, and innate affections, are in a great measure exploded by the learned, yet, few persons reason so closely and so accurately on abstract subjects as, through a long chain of deductions, to bring forth a conclusion which in no respect militates with their premises.

It is a long time before the crowd give up opinion they have been taught to look upon with respect; and I know many persons who will follow you willingly through the course of your argument, till they perceive it tends to the overthrow of some fond prejudice; and then they will either sound a retreat, or begin a contest in which the contender for truth, though he cannot be overcome, is effectually silenced, from the mere weariness of answering positive assertions, reiterated without end. It is from such causes that the notion of a sexual difference in the human character has, with a very few exceptions, universally prevailed from the earliest times, and the pride of one sex, and the ignorance and vanity of the other, have helped to support an opinion which a close observation of Nature, and a more accurate way of reasoning, would disprove.

It must be confessed, that the virtues of the males among the human species, though mixed and blended with a variety of vices and errors, have displayed a bolder and a more consistent picture of excellence than female nature has hitherto done. It is on these reasons that, when we compliment the appearance of a more than ordinary energy in the female mind, we call it masculine; and hence it is, that Pope has elegantly said *a perfect woman's but a softer man*. And if we take in the consideration, that there can be but one rule of moral excellence for beings made of the same materials, organized after the same manner, and subjected to similar laws of Nature, we must either agree with Mr [Alexander] Pope [1688–1744], or we must reverse the proposition, and say, that *a perfect man is a woman formed after a coarser mold*. The difference that actually does subsist between the sexes, is too flattering for men to be willingly imputed to accident; for what accident occasions, wisdom might correct; and it is better, says Pride, to give up the advantages we might derive from the perfection of our fellow associates, than to own that Nature has been just in the equal distribution of her favours. These are the sentiments of the men; but mark how readily they are yielded to by the women; not from humility I assure you, but merely to preserve with character those fond vanities on which they set their hearts. No; suffer them to idolize their persons, to throw away their life in the pursuit of trifles, and to indulge in the gratification of the meaner passions, and they will heartily join in the sentence of their degradation.

Among the most strenuous asserters of a sexual difference in character, Rousseau is the most conspicuous, both on account of that warmth of sentiment which distinguishes all his writings, and the eloquence of his compositions: but never did enthusiasm and the love of paradox, those enemies to philosophical disquisition, appear in more strong opposition to plain sense than in Rousseau's definition of this difference. He sets out with a supposition, that Nature intended the subjection of the one sex to the other; that consequently there must be an inferiority of intellect in the subjected party; but as man is a very imperfect being, and apt to play the capricious tyrant, Nature, to bring things nearer to an equality, bestowed on the woman such attractive graces, and such an insinuating address, as to turn the balance on the other scale. Thus Nature, in a giddy mood, recedes from her purposes, and subjects prerogative to an influence which must produce confusion and disorder in the system of human affairs. Rousseau saw this objection; and in order to obviate it, he has made up a moral person of the union of the two sexes, which, for contradiction and absurdity, outdoes every metaphysical riddle that was ever formed in the schools. In short, it is not reason, it is not wit; it is pride and sensuality that speak in Rousseau, and, in this instance, has lowered the man of genius to the licentious pedant.

But whatever might be the wise purpose intended by Providence in such a disposition of things, certain it is, that some degree of inferiority, in point of corporal strength, seems always to have existed between the two sexes; and this advantage, in the barbarous ages of mankind, was abused to such a degree, as to destroy all the natural rights of the female species, and reduce them to a state of abject slavery. What accidents have contributed in Europe to better their condition, would not be to my purpose to relate; for I do not intend to give you a history of women; I mean only to trace the sources of their peculiar foibles and vices; and these I firmly believe to originate in situation and education only: for so little did a wise and just Providence intend to make the condition of slavery an unalterable law of female nature, that in the same proportion as the male sex have consulted the interest of their own happiness, they have relaxed in their tyranny over women; and such is their use in the system of mundane creation, and such their natural influence over the male mind, that were these advantages properly exerted, they might carry every point of any importance to their honour and happiness. However, till that period arrives in which women will act wisely, we will amuse ourselves in talking of their follies.

The situation and education of women, Hortensia, is precisely that which must necessarily tend to corrupt and debilitate both the powers of mind and body. From a false notion of beauty and delicacy, their system of nerves is depraved before they come out of their nursery; and this kind of depravity has more influence over the mind, and consequently over morals, than is commonly apprehended. But it would be well if such causes only acted towards the debasement of the sex; their moral education is, if possible, more absurd than their physical. The principles and nature of virtue, which is never properly explained to boys, is kept quite a mystery to girls. They are told indeed, that they must abstain from those vices which are contrary to their personal happiness, or they will be regarded as criminals, both by God and man; but all the higher parts of rectitude, every thing that ennobles our being, and that renders us both innoxious and useful, is either not taught, or is taught in such a manner as to leave no proper impression on the mind. This is so obvious a truth, that the defects of female education have ever been a fruitful topic of declamation for the moralist; but no one of this class of writers have laid down any judicious rules for amendment. Whilst we still retain the absurd notion of a sexual excellence, it will militate against the perfecting a plan of education for either sex. The judicious [Joseph] Addison [1672–1719] animadverts on the absurdity of bringing a young lady up with no higher idea of the end of education than to make her agreeable to a husband, and confining the necessary excellence for this happy acquisition to the mere graces of person.

Every parent and tutor may not express himself in the same manner as is marked out by Addison; yet certain it is, that the admiration of the other sex is held out to women as the highest honour they can attain; and whilst this is considered as their *summum bonum* [supreme good], and the beauty of their persons the chief *desideratum* [object of desire] of men, Vanity, and its companion Envy, must taint, in their characters, every native and every acquired excellence. Nor can you, Hortensia, deny, that these qualities, when united to ignorance, are fully equal to the engendering and rivetting all those vices and foibles which are peculiar to the female sex; vices and foibles which have caused them to be considered, in ancient times, as beneath cultivation, and in modern days have subjected them to the censure and ridicule of writers of all descriptions, from the deep thinking philosopher to the man of ton [fashion] and gallantry, who, by the bye, sometimes distinguishes himself by qualities which are not greatly superior to those he despises in women. Nor can I better illustrate the truth of this observation than by the following picture, to be found in the polite and gallant Chesterfield [1694–1773]. 'Women,' says his Lordship [in *Letters to his Son* (1774)], 'are only children of larger growth. They have an entertaining tattle, sometimes wit; but for solid reasoning, and good sense, I never in my life knew one that had it, or who acted or reasoned in consequence of it for four and twenty hours together. A man of sense only trifles with them, plays with them, humours and flatters them, as he does an engaging child; but he neither consults them, nor trusts them in serious matters.'

(*Letters on Education*, Part 1, Letter XXII, 'No Characteristic Difference in Sex')

## OLYMPE DE GOUGES

Marie Olympe Aubry de Gouges (1748–93) was born Marie Gouze at Montauban in southern France. Her mother was evidently a former servant, and her father a butcher. She received very little formal education and at the age of sixteen married Louis Yves Aubry, a wealthy and much older man with whom she had a son. At the death of her husband, she resolved never to marry again, and rather than be known as the widow Aubry, she took her mother's middle name, changed her father's name and added the aristocratic 'de'. She later claimed that she was the illegitimate daughter of a local marquis. She moved to Paris where she became a prolific writer and pamphleteer, gradually gendering her image and campaigning on a great range of political, social and feminist issues, such as a women-only theatre, maternity hospitals, marriage and divorce, the rights of single mothers and orphans, and imprisonment for debt. In 1788 she published a melodrama *Zamore and Mirza*, which she later revised and presented as an anti-slavery text, *The Slavery of the Blacks* (1792).

At the height of the Revolution, in 1791, Gouges published a pamphlet, *Les Droits de la Femme et de la Citoyenne* (*The Rights of Woman and the Female Citizen*). It was dedicated to Marie Antoinette, for Gouges was a defender of constitutional monarchy, and perhaps hoped that the Queen would stand up for women's political rights. She also spoke at, and wrote letters to, the National Assembly and put up posters in Paris declaiming Marat and Robespierre which provoked controversy and ridicule. Her Declaration of the Rights of Woman both denies sexual difference (women should be given rights so that no difference is made between the sexes) and explores the particularities of women (women should be given rights because they show superior strength in childbirth). Gouges was guillotined during the Terror in the autumn of 1793 for composing writings that undermined the regime. It was officially reported that 'In her defence, the accused said that she had ruined herself in order to propagate the principles of the Revolution and that she was the founder of popular societies of her sex, etc.'

The following extract is from the beginning of *The Rights of Woman*, in which Gouges calls upon women to 'Wake up!' and 'Recognise your Rights'.

## *The Rights of Woman* (1791)

Man, are you capable of being just? It is a woman who is asking you this question; you will at least not take away this right from her. Tell me, what has given you the sovereign authority to oppress my sex? Your strength? Your talents? Observe the Creator in his wisdom; examine, in all its greatness, Nature, to which you appear to want to draw close, and give me, if you dare, an example of this tyrannical authority. Go back to the animals, consult the elements, study the plants, and finally cast an eye over all modifications of organic matter; surrender to the evidence when I offer you the means to do so. Search, probe, and distinguish, if you can, the sexes in the workings of nature. Everywhere you will find them mingled, everywhere they work together in a harmonious unity in this immortal masterpiece.

Man alone has made a principle from his exceptional circumstances. Bizarre, blind, swollen with science and, in this age of enlightenment and wisdom, having degenerated into the crassest ignorance, he wants to rule despotically over a sex which has all its intellectual faculties; he wants to benefit from the Revolution, and to claim his rights to equality, and then say nothing more.

DECLARATION OF THE RIGHTS OF WOMAN AND THE FEMALE CITIZEN

*To be enacted by the National Assembly in its closing sessions, or at a session of the next legislature.*

## Preamble

Mothers, daughters, sisters, representatives of the nation, demand to be made part of a National Assembly. Since ignorance, omission and contempt for the rights of woman are the only causes of public misfortune and of the corruption of governments, [they] have resolved to set out in a solemn declaration the natural, inalienable and sacred rights of woman, in order that this declaration constantly presented to all members of society, always reminds them of their rights and duties, in order that the exercise of power by women and the exercise of power by men may be compared with the objective of every political institution, thereby becoming more respected, so that the demands of women citizens, henceforth based on simple and incontestable principles, will always uphold the constitution, good morals and the happiness of all.

Consequently, the sex which is as superior in beauty as in courage during the sufferings of motherhood, recognises and declares, in the presence and under the auspices of the Supreme Being, the following Rights of Woman and Female Citizens.

## Article I

Woman is born free and lives equal to man in her rights. Social distinctions can be based only on common usefulness to the community.

## Article II

The purpose of all political associations is the preservation of the natural and inalienable rights of woman and man. These rights are liberty, property, security and above all, the right to resist oppression.

## Article III

The principle of all sovereignty lies essentially in the nation, which is nothing but the bringing together of woman and man. No body, no individual can exercise any authority that does not emanate expressly from it.

## Article IV

Liberty and justice lie in restoring everything that belongs to others. Thus the only restrictions to the exercise of the natural rights of woman come from man's perpetual tyranny; these restrictions must be reformed by the laws of nature and reason.

## Article V

The laws of nature and reason forbid any action which is harmful to society. Everything that is not prohibited by these wise and holy laws cannot be prevented, and nobody can be compelled to do what they [these laws] do not command.

## Article VI

The law must be the expression of the general will. All female and male citizens must contribute personally, or through their representatives, to its formation. It must be the same for everyone: all female and male citizens, being equal in its eyes, must be equally eligible for all high honours, public positions and employment, according to their abilities, and without other distinctions besides those of their virtues and talents.

## Article VII

No woman is an exception. She is accused, arrested, and detained as determined by the law. Women, like men, must obey this rigorous law.

## Article VIII

The law must prescribe only those punishments which are strictly and obviously necessary, and no one can be punished, except by virtue of a law decreed and promulgated prior to the offence, and legally applicable to women.

## Article IX

Any woman found guilty will be subject to the full rigour of the law.

## Article X

No body should be persecuted for their fundamental opinions. Woman has the right to mount the scaffold; she must equally have the right to mount the rostrum, provided that her demonstrations do not disturb public order established by the law.

## Article XI

The free communication of thoughts and opinions is one of the most precious rights of woman, since this freedom assures recognition of children by their fathers. Every female citizen can therefore say freely: 'I am the mother of a child who belongs to you', without being forced by a barbaric prejudice to conceal the truth, except when, in cases determined by the law, this freedom has been abused.

## Article XII

The guarantee of the rights of woman and of the female citizen implies a major benefit. This guarantee must be established for the advantage of all, and not just for those to whom it is particularly entrusted.

## Article XIII

Contributions by men and women towards the upkeep of the police force and for administration expenses are equal; woman has a share in all duties, in all laborious tasks;

she must therefore have the same share of the distribution of appointments, posts, offices, honours and jobs in industry.

### Article XIV

Female and male citizens have the right to establish for themselves, or through their representatives, what is necessary for taxation. This can only apply to women, if they are granted an equal share, not only in the riches, but also in the administration of public affairs, and the right to determine the level, the basis, the collection and the duration of taxation.

### Article XV

All women, united with men in matters of taxation, have the right to call any public servant to account for his administration.

### Article XVI

Any society in which the guarantee of rights is not assured, or the separation of powers is not determined has no constitution. The constitution is void if the majority of individuals who make up the nation have not participated in drafting it.

### Article XVII

Property belongs to both sexes whether united or separated. It is for each person an inviolable and sacred right. Nobody can be deprived of it, because it is the true legacy of Nature, unless public need, legally approved, requires it, and then only on condition of a fair and predetermined compensation.

### Postscript

Women, wake up! The tocsin of reason is being heard throughout the world. Discover your rights. The powerful rule of nature is no longer surrounded by prejudice, fanaticism, superstition and lies. The flame of truth has dispelled all the clouds of folly and usurpation. Enslaved man has gathered his strength, and needs yours to break his chains. Having become free, he has become unjust towards his companion. Oh women! Women! When will you cease to be blind?

(*The Rights of Woman*)

## MARY WOLLSTONECRAFT

Mary Wollstonecraft (1759–97) was born in London into a large middle-class family that had inherited wealth from her Irish paternal grandfather. From the age of twenty-one, she worked as a lady's companion, governess and teacher, setting up a school with her younger sister Eliza in 1783, before becoming a writer. She wrote on girls' education, notably *Thoughts on the Education of Daughters* (1787), and published a novel, *Mary, A Fiction* (1788) and children's fiction, *Original Stories from Real Life* (1788), before writing *A Vindication of the Rights of Man* (1790), a reply to Edmund Burke's criticisms of the French Revolution. She travelled to Paris, where she wrote *A Vindication of the Rights of Woman* (1792) and met an American explorer and author, Gilbert Imlay, there, by whom she had a daughter, Fanny. After travelling in Sweden, Denmark and Norway, she returned to London in 1795, separating from Imlay and trying to drown herself in the Thames. In 1796 she fell in love with the political radical William Godwin. They married in the following year, but five months later Wollstonecraft died after complications following the birth of another daughter, the future Mary Shelley. In 1798 William Godwin published Mary's *Posthumous Works*, in four volumes, including her love letters to Imlay.

*A Vindication of the Rights of Woman* is one of the first major explorations of women's subordination. Written in the midst of her personal experiences of the French Revolution, Wollstonecraft took many of the ideals of the Enlightenment and applied them to women, arguing that it was hypocritical not to do so. It is a passionately argued text, resolutely opposed to various forms of tyranny and control and thoroughly analysing the socialisation of women. Wollstonecraft states that the basis of good is Reason, Virtue and Knowledge, and it is access to education that is instrumental in allowing women to benefit from rational culture and in releasing them from the frivolous pleasures of the private sphere. The scandal surrounding Wollstonecraft's life limited the impact of *A Vindication* for many years. Nevertheless, it became and remains an influential feminist text. In the three extracts here from *A Vindication* Wollstonecraft discusses gender distinctions, women's reasoning, and the need for equality in education.

## *A Vindication of the Rights of Woman* (1792)

### 'The Prevailing Opinion of Sexual Character, Continued'

I wish to sum up what I have said in a few words, for I here throw down my gauntlet, and deny the existence of sexual virtues, not excepting modesty. For man and woman, truth, if I understand the meaning of the word, must be the same; yet the fanciful female character, so prettily drawn by poets and novelists, demanding the sacrifice of truth and sincerity, virtue becomes a relative idea, having no other foundation than utility, and of that utility men pretend arbitrarily to judge, shaping it to their own convenience.

Women, I allow, may have different duties to fulfil; but they are *human* duties, and the principles that should regulate the discharge of them, I sturdily maintain, must be the same.

To become respectable, the exercise of their understanding is necessary, there is no other foundation for independence of character; I mean explicitly to say that they must only bow to the authority of reason, instead of being the *modest* slaves of opinion.

In the superior ranks of life how seldom do we meet with a man of superior abilities, or even common acquirements? The reason appears to me clear; the state they are born in was an unnatural one. The human character has ever been formed by the employments the individual, or class, pursues; and if the faculties are not sharpened by necessity, they must remain obtuse. The argument may fairly be extended to women; for seldom occupied by serious business, the pursuit of pleasure gives that insignificance to their character that renders the society of the *great* so insipid. The same want of firmness, produced by a similar cause, forces them both to fly from themselves to noisy pleasures, and artificial passions, till vanity takes place of every social affection, and the characteristics of humanity can scarcely be discerned. Such are the blessings of civil governments, as they are at present organized, that wealth and female softness equally tend to debase mankind, and are produced by the same cause; but allowing women to be rational creatures, they should be incited to acquire virtues which they may call their own, for how can a rational being be ennobled by anything that is not obtained by its *own* exertions?

(*A Vindication*, ch. 3)

### 'Observations on the State of Degradation to which a Woman is Reduced by Various Causes'

The stamen of immortality, if I may be allowed the phrase, is the perfectibility of human reason; for, were man created perfect, or did a flood of knowledge break in upon him, when he arrived at maturity, that precluded error, I should doubt whether his existence would be continued after the dissolution of the body. But, in the present state of things, every difficulty in morals that escapes from human discussion, and equally baffles the investigation of profound thinking, and the lightning glance of genius, is an argument on which I build my belief of the immortality of the soul. Reason is, consequentially, the simple power of improvement; or, more properly speaking, of discerning truth. Every individual is in this respect a world in itself. More or less may be conspicuous in one being than another; but the nature of reason must be the same in all, if it be an emanation of divinity, the tie that connects the creature with the Creator; for, can that soul be stamped with the heavenly image, that is not perfected by the exercise of its own reason? Yet outwardly ornamented with elaborate care, and so adorned to delight man, 'that with honour he may love', the soul of woman is not allowed to have this distinction, and man, ever placed between her and reason, she is always represented as only created to see through a gross medium, and to take things on trust. But dismissing these fanciful theories, and considering woman as a whole, let it be what it will, instead of a part of man, the inquiry is whether she have reason or not. If she have, which, for a moment, I will take for granted, she was not created merely to be the solace of man, and the sexual should not destroy the human character.

Into this error men have, probably, been led by viewing education in a false light; not considering it as the first step to form a being advancing gradually towards perfection; but only as a preparation for life. On this sensual error, for I must call it so, has the false system of female manners been reared, which robs the whole sex of its dignity, and classes the brown and fair with the smiling flowers that only adorn the land. This has ever been the language of men, and the fear of departing from a supposed sexual character, has made even women of superior sense adopt the same sentiments. Thus understanding, strictly speaking, has been denied to woman; and instinct, sublimated into wit and cunning, for the purposes of life, has been substituted in its stead.

The power of generalising ideas, of drawing comprehensive conclusions from individual observations, is the only acquirement, for an immortal being, that really deserves the name of knowledge. Merely to observe, without endeavouring to account for anything, may (in a very incomplete manner) serve as the common sense of life; but where is the store laid up that is to clothe the soul when it leaves the body?

This power has not only been denied to women; but writers have insisted that it is inconsistent, with a few exceptions, with their sexual character. Let men prove this, and I shall grant that woman only exists for man. I must, however, previously remark that the power of generalising ideas, to any great extent, is not very common amongst men or women. But this exercise is the true cultivation of the understanding; and everything conspires to render the cultivation of the understanding more difficult in the female than the male world.

(*A Vindication*, ch. 4)


### 'On National Education'

True taste is ever the work of the understanding employed in observing natural effects; and till women have more understanding, it is vain to expect them to possess domestic taste. Their lively senses will ever be at work to harden their hearts, and the emotions struck out of them will continue to be vivid and transitory, unless a proper education store their mind with knowledge.

It is the want of domestic taste, and not the acquirement of knowledge, that takes women out of their families, and tears the smiling babe from the breast that ought to afford it nourishment. Women have been allowed to remain in ignorance and slavish independence many, very many, years, and still we hear of nothing but their fondness of pleasure and sway [power], their preference of rakes and soldiers, their childish attachment to toys, and the vanity that makes them value accomplishments more than virtues.

History brings forward a fearful catalogue of the crimes which their cunning has produced, when the weak slaves have had sufficient address to overreach their masters. In France, and in how many other countries, have men been the luxurious despots, and women the crafty ministers? Does this prove that ignorance and dependence domesticate them? Is not their folly the by-word of the libertines, who relax in their society; and do not men of sense continually lament that an immoderate fondness for dress and dissipation carries the mother of a family forever from home? Their hearts have not been debauched by knowledge, or their minds led away by scientific pursuits; yet they do not fulfil the peculiar duties which, as women, they are called upon by Nature to fulfil. On the contrary, the state of warfare which subsists between the sexes makes them employ those wiles that often frustrate the more open designs of force.

When therefore I call women slaves, I mean in a political and civil sense; for indirectly they obtain too much power, and are debased by their exertions to obtain illicit sway.

Let an enlightened nation [France] then try what effect reason would have to bring them back to nature, and their duty; and allowing them to share the advantages of education and government with man, see whether they will become better, as they grow wiser and become free. They cannot be injured by the experiment, for it is not in the power of man to render them more insignificant than they are at present.

To render this practicable, day-schools for particular ages should be established by the government, in which boys and girls might be educated together. The school for the younger children, from five to nine years of age, ought to be absolutely free and open to all classes. A sufficient number of masters should also be chosen by a select committee in each parish, to whom any complaints of negligence, &c. might be made, if signed by six of the children's parents.

Ushers would then be unnecessary; for I believe experience will ever prove that this kind of subordinate authority is particularly injurious to the morals of youth. What, indeed, can tend to deprave the character more than outward submission and inward contempt? Yet how can boys be expected to treat an usher with respect, when the master seems to consider him in the light of a servant, and almost to countenance the ridicule which becomes the chief amusement of the boys during the play hours?

But nothing of this kind could occur in an elementary day-school, where boys and girls, the rich and poor, should meet together. And to prevent any of the distinctions of vanity, they should be dressed alike, and all obliged to submit to the same discipline, or leave the school. The schoolroom ought to be surrounded by a large piece of ground, in which the children might be usefully exercised, for at this age they should not be confined to any sedentary employment for more than an hour at a time. But these relaxations might all be rendered a part of elementary education, for many things improve and amuse the senses, when introduced as a kind of show, to the principles of which, dryly laid down, children would turn a deaf ear. For instance, botany, mechanics, and astronomy. Reading, writing, arithmetic, natural history and some simple experiments in natural philosophy [science], might fill up the day; but these pursuits should never encroach on gymnastic plays in the open air. The elements of religion, history, the history of man, and politics, might also be taught by conversations in the Socratic form.

After the age of nine, girls and boys, intended for domestic employments, or mechanical trades, ought to be removed to other schools, and receive instruction, in some measure appropriated to the destination of each individual, the two sexes being still together in the morning; but in the afternoon the girls should attend a school, where plain work, mantua-making, millinery, etc., would be their employment.

The young people of superior abilities, or fortune, might now be taught, in another school, the dead and living languages, the elements of science, and continue the study of history and politics, on a more extensive scale, which would not exclude polite literature.

Girls and boys still together? I hear some readers ask: yes. And I should not fear any other consequence than that some early attachment might take place; which, whilst it had the best effect on the moral character of the young people, might not perfectly agree with the views of the parents, for it will be a long time, I fear, before the world will be so far enlightened that parents, only anxious to render their children virtuous, shall allow them to choose companions for life themselves.

Besides, this would be a sure way to promote early marriages, and from early marriages the most salutary physical and moral effects naturally flow. What a different character does a married citizen assume from the selfish coxcomb, who lives but for himself, and who is often afraid to marry lest he should not be able to live in a certain style. Great emergencies excepted, which would rarely occur in a society of which equality was the basis, a man can only be prepared to discharge the duties of public life, by the habitual practice of those inferior ones which form the man.

In this plan of education the constitution of boys would not be ruined by the early debaucheries, which now make men so selfish, or girls rendered weak and vain, by indolence, and frivolous pursuits. But, I presuppose, that such a degree of equality should be established between the sexes as would shut out gallantry and coquetry, yet allow friendship and love to temper the heart for the discharge of higher duties. These would be schools of morality — and the happiness of man, allowed to flow from the pure springs of duty and affection, what advances might not the human mind make? Society can only be happy and free in proportion as it is virtuous; but the present distinctions, established in society, corrode all private, and blast all public virtue.

(A Vindication, ch. 12)

# Chapter 10

# Art, architecture and nature

**I**N THE ENCYCLOPÉDIE'S 'tree of human knowledge' (a diagram designed in 1751 to illustrate the unity and structure of all learning in the arts, sciences and trades), the 'liberal arts' are listed as poetry, music, painting, sculpture and engraving. These arts are distinguished from the 'mechanical' ones (applied arts and crafts, such as 'practical architecture', 'practical sculpture' and 'glassmaking') on the grounds that the former are 'primarily created by the mind', and the others 'by the hands'. As the editors (d'Alembert in his 'Preliminary Discourse' and Diderot in his article on 'Art') explained, this distinction had led to great support and esteem being enjoyed by 'artists', but it had also led to a general disregard for the welfare and development of the more useful works of the 'artisan', much to the detriment of human happiness and progress.

The *Encyclopédie* was clearly designed to redress this disparity, by championing the value of practical and technical learning over that of mere scholasticism (the 'so-called science of the centuries of ignorance') and by drawing all the arts together by encouraging artists and scholars to engage, like artisans, more directly with the study of nature and its products, rather than with religious or mythological subjects. Thus Denis Diderot, the most influential art critic of the age, would repeatedly proclaim the primacy of nature, and in his reviews of the exhibitions at the Louvre, would lavish praise on the 'truthfulness' with which painters such as Chardin seemed to capture 'nature itself' (*Salons*). Rousseau, too, in his extraordinary *Discourse on the Arts and Sciences* (1750) would insist upon the goodness of what was 'natural', and castigate traditional arts and learning for helping to corrupt and enslave human beings.

Such commitment to the observation and celebration of the ordinary, particular and imperfect world of 'common nature' (echoing Locke's observation that 'All things that exist being [i.e. are] particulars') was typical of much Enlightened thinking. It could be seen in William Hogarth's choice of contemporary scenes and subjects, set in 'real' time and place, his enthusiasm for the mass production of his works, and in his 'intimate intuition into nature' as Horace Walpole noted in *Anecdotes on Painting* (1762). It could also be seen in Thomas Gainsborough's fascination with common folk and 'little dirty subjects', rather than with highly-polished historical or religious works in the grand style of the Italian masters. Even Sir Joshua Reynolds, first President of the Royal Academy and a firm believer in rules of art founded upon the study of Old Masters, praised Gainsborough's faithful portrayal of 'the living world' – though his genius, like that of Chardin and Hogarth, was still reckoned to lie firmly within 'the lower rank of art' (*Discourse XIV*, 1788). Towards the end of his career, Gainsborough would produce highly sentimentalised 'cottage' pictures such as *Girl with Pigs* (1782) in which 'common nature' was romantically idealised. While Reynolds still approved, this picturesque or 'Rousseauesque' portrayal of the natural world was a far cry from the grand style, derived from the study of Renaissance artists, in which a generalised and intellectually idealised view of Nature was normally preferred.

The discreet 'improvement' and sensory enjoyment of 'common nature' became a recurrent theme in the rise of landscape gardening (regarded by the poet Alexander Pope as one of the 'sister arts' with poetry and painting) in the period. Instead of formal gardens (such as Versailles) based upon strict geometry and symmetry, showing the submission of nature (as in topiary) to man's will and intellect, Pope and designers such as William Kent aimed to create gardens that appealed more to the senses. In their designs, serpentine shapes replaced straight lines, and a great variety of plants and vistas were carefully placed to suggest that 'all nature is a garden'. Such informal gardens, including classical monuments and statues, were added to new classically-inspired villas such as those at Stourhead and Chiswick. These Palladian mansions, following the classically-inspired work of the Italian Renaissance architect Andrea Palladio (1508–80), expressed the wealth, taste and self-confidence of their owners in a new age of imperial expansion. Moreover, by the 1750s the idea that the principles of good (classical) architecture were 'founded upon simple nature' was well embedded in architectural theory through Laugier's *Essay on Architecture* (1753) and William Chambers' *Treatise on Civil Architecture* (1759). In the second half of the century, buildings such as Thomas Jefferson's Monticello in Virginia, and Soufflot's Church of Ste Geneviève in Paris were testimony to the cultural impact of neoclassicism, as were paintings such as Jacques-Louis David's *Oath of the Horatii* (1784) and *Death of Marat* (1793) during the French Revolution.

In the course of the century, many important developments would take place in painting, architecture and gardening, as well as in the decorative and other arts, and new terms such as Baroque, Palladian, Rococo, Neoclassical, Gothic and Romantic would be used to describe these styles and movements. Many factors combined to produce these changes, including research, travel, trade and discovery; the growth of clubs, societies and salons; the birth of new academies, exhibitions and museums; the rise of middle-class wealth, literacy and consumerism; and, of course, shifting interests, tastes and fashions. Technological developments in the 'mechanical arts' were also often crucial, enabling an 'artist' such as Hogarth to make a living from the mass production of his prints, and an 'artisan' such as Josiah Wedgwood to make a fortune from the neoclassically-designed pottery produced by his ceramics factories in the Midlands. Paintings of factories, such as Richard Arkwright's cotton mills, together with scenes of blacksmiths' shops and iron forges would even become a small but distinctive part of the work of the artist Joseph Wright, to whom Wedgwood was a friend and patron. However, it is for a few great 'scientific' paintings, in particular *A Philosopher Giving a Lecture on the Orrery* (1766) and *An Experiment on a Bird in an Air Pump* (1768), two large exhibition pieces in the long tradition of candlelight painting, that Wright is best known today. In seeming to explore the complex relationships between art, ethics, nature, science and learning, these extraordinary paintings have been proclaimed as among the greatest visual expressions of the Enlightenment. For artists such as Wright and Hogarth not only portrayed and enriched a wide range of Enlightenment values and ideas, but also subverted and critiqued them.

## JEAN-JACQUES ROUSSEAU

In 1742, Rousseau (see p. 17), seeking work and fame at the age of thirty, left Chambéry and moved to Paris where he submitted his new method of annotating music to the Academy of Sciences and published a *Dissertation on Modern Music*. After a year working at the French Embassy in Venice, he returned to Paris, developing friendships with Condillac and Diderot; and writing a ballet, and articles on music for the projected *Encyclopédie*. He was now living with the chambermaid, Thérèse Levasseur, who would bear him children, all of whom he would take to an orphanage; a secret that Voltaire would later make public, much to Rousseau's anger and embarrassment. It was not until 1750, however, that Rousseau rose to fame. In considering this question, he was on his way to visit Diderot in prison at Vincennes, when he read of an essay competition set by the Academy of Dijon: 'Has the restoration of the arts and sciences helped to purify morals?' According to his own account, he was immediately shaken by the realisation that 'man is naturally good' but corrupted by false social systems. Though Diderot would hardly have agreed, he encouraged his friend to submit an essay, and in 1750 Rousseau's *Discours sur les Sciences et les Arts* (*Discourse on the Arts and Sciences*) won the prize.

The importance of the *Discourse* did not lie only in its exposition of ideas and arguments that would come to be seen as the hallmark of Rousseau's writings, or even in its assault upon the vices and follies that wealth, power and privilege had fostered. Critically, the *Discourse* challenged some of the most cherished notions of the early Enlightenment: including empiricism, neoclassicism, the role of traditional arts and learning, enthusiasm for science and technology, belief and confidence in social and cultural progress, and the moral superiority of 'civil' over 'savage' people – to name but a few. Thus the *Discourse* expressed a view of the world, and implicitly a preferred way of life, that would set Rousseau at odds with most other leading *philosophes*. He would now be both a major part of the

Enlightenment (vital to its development), and quite apart from it (subverting its achievements). In the two extracts from the *Discourse* selected here, Rousseau explains how the development of arts and sciences has contributed to the degeneration of human virtues and happiness.

## Discourse on the Arts and Sciences (1750)

It is a noble and beautiful spectacle to see man raising himself, so to speak, from nothing by his own exertions; dissipating, by the light of reason, all the thick clouds in which he was by nature enveloped; mounting above himself; soaring in thought even to the celestial regions; like the sun, encompassing with giant strides the vast extent of the universe; and, what is still grander and more wonderful, going back into himself, there to study man and get to know his own nature, his duties and his end. All these miracles we have seen renewed within the last few generations.

Europe had relapsed into the barbarism of the earliest ages; the inhabitants of this part of the world, which is at present so highly enlightened, were plunged, some centuries ago, in a state still worse than ignorance. A scientific jargon, more despicable than mere ignorance, had usurped the name of knowledge, and opposed an almost invincible obstacle to its restoration.

Things had come to such a pass, that it required a complete revolution to bring men back to common sense. This came at last from the quarter from which it was least expected. It was the stupid Mussulman [Muhammad, died 632 AD], the eternal scourge of letters, who was the immediate cause of their revival among us. The fall of the throne of Constantine [died 337 AD] brought to Italy the relics of Ancient Greece; and with these precious spoils France in turn was enriched. The sciences soon followed literature, and the art of thinking joined that of writing: an order which may seem strange, but is perhaps only too natural. The world now began to perceive the principal advantage of an intercourse with the Muses, that of rendering mankind more sociable by inspiring them with the desire to please one another with performances worthy of their mutual approbation.

The mind, as well as the body, has its needs: those of the body are the basis of society, those of the mind its ornaments.

So long as government and law provide for the security and well-being of men in their common life, the arts, literature and the sciences, less despotic though perhaps more powerful, fling garlands of flowers over the chains which weigh them down. They stifle in men's breasts that sense of original liberty, for which they seem to have been born; cause them to love their own slavery, and so make of them what is called a civilised people.

Necessity raised up thrones; the arts and sciences have made them strong. Powers of the earth, cherish all talents and protect those who cultivate them. Civilised peoples, cultivate such pursuits: to them, happy slaves, you owe that delicacy and exquisiteness of taste, which is so much your boast, that sweetness of disposition and urbanity of manners which make intercourse so easy and agreeable among you – in a word, the appearance of all the virtues, without being in possession of one of them.

It was for this sort of accomplishment, which is by so much the more captivating as it seems less affected, that Athens and Rome were so much distinguished in the boasted times of their splendour and magnificence: and it is doubtless in the same respect that our own age and nation will excel all periods and peoples. An air of philosophy without pedantry; an address at once natural and engaging, distant equally from Teutonic clumsiness and Italian pantomime; these are the effects of a taste acquired by liberal studies and improved by conversation with the world. What happiness would it be for those who live among us, if our external appearance were always a true mirror of our hearts; if decorum were but virtue; if the maxims we professed were the rules of our conduct; and if real philosophy were inseparable from the title of philosopher! But so many good qualities too seldom go together; virtue rarely appears in so much pomp and state.

Richness of apparel may proclaim the man of fortune, and elegance the man of taste; but true health and manliness are known by different signs. It is under the homespun of the labourer, and not beneath the gilt and tinsel of the courtier, that we should look for strength and vigour of body.

External ornaments are no less foreign to virtue, which is the strength and activity of the mind. The honest man is an athlete, who loves to wrestle stark naked; he scorns all those vile trappings, which prevent the exertion of his strength, and were, for the most part, invented only to conceal some deformity.

Before art had moulded our behaviour, and taught our passions to speak an artificial language, our morals were rude but natural; and the different ways in which we behaved proclaimed at the first glance the difference of our dispositions. Human nature was not at bottom better then than now; but men found their security in the ease with which they could see through one another, and this advantage, of which we no longer feel the value, prevented their having many vices.

In our day, now that more subtle study and a more refined taste have reduced the art of pleasing to a system, there prevails in modern manners a servile and deceptive conformity; so that one would think every mind had been cast in the same mould. Politeness requires this thing; decorum that; ceremony has its forms, and fashion its laws, and these we must always follow, never the promptings of our own nature.

(*Discourse*, Part 1)

We cannot reflect on the morality of mankind without contemplating with pleasure the picture of the simplicity which prevailed in the earliest times. This image may be justly compared to a beautiful coast, adorned only by the hands of nature; towards which our eyes are constantly turned, and which we see receding with regret. While men were innocent and virtuous and loved to have the gods for witnesses of their actions, they dwelt together in the same huts; but when they became vicious, they grew tired of such inconvenient onlookers, and banished them to magnificent temples. Finally, they expelled their deities even from these, in order to dwell there themselves; or at least the temples of the gods were no longer more magnificent than the palaces of the citizens. This was the height of the degeneracy; nor could vice ever be carried to greater lengths than when it was seen, supported, as it were, at the doors of the great, on columns of marble, and graven on Corinthian capitals.

As the conveniences of life increase, as the arts are brought to perfection, and luxury spreads, true courage flags, the virtues disappear; and all this is the effect of the sciences and of those arts which are exercised in the privacy of men's dwellings.[...]

Our gardens are adorned with statues and our galleries with pictures. What would you imagine these masterpieces of art, thus exhibited to public admiration, represent? The great men, who have defended their country, or the still greater men who have enriched it by their virtues? Far from it. They are the images of every perversion of heart and mind, carefully selected from ancient mythology, and presented to the early curiosity of our children, doubtless that they may have before their eyes the representations of vicious actions, even before they are able to read.

*(Discourse*, Part 2)

## MARC-ANTOINE LAUGIER

Marc-Antoine Laugier (1713–69), was born in Provence and became a lapsed Jesuit priest and the author of a famous treatise, *Essai sur L'Architecture*, translated into English and German shortly after its publication at Paris in 1753. In the *Essay* he sets out what he sees as the principles of good architectural design, based upon the hypothetical 'rustic cabin' of primitive man. For Laugier, the cabin was a natural and functional expression of man's need for shelter, and its three key elements (column, entablature and pediment) provided a perfect model 'founded upon simple nature', for later architecture. Laugier was not an architect, but his rationalist views were highly influential and can be seen in neoclassical buildings such as Soufflot's design of the church of Sainte-Geneviève in Paris, which in 1791 was adapted to become the secular Panthéon, where the bodies of Voltaire and Rousseau were disinterred and reburied during the Revolution. The extracts translated here are taken from the preface and first chapter of Laugier's book.

### *Essay on Architecture* (1753)

Architecture, of all the useful arts, demands the most eminent talents and the most extensive knowledge. As much genius, spirit and taste is perhaps required to make a great architect, as to make a first-rate painter or poet. It would be a great mistake to believe that only mechanics are involved; that it is all restricted to excavating foundations and building walls according to rules, the practice of which presupposes only eyes accustomed to judging lines, and hands made to use a trowel.

When speaking of the art of building, what presents itself to the imagination of the common people are jumbled heaps of inconvenient rubbish, immense piles of shapeless materials, a terrible noise of hammers, hazardous scaffolds, a terrifying set of machines, an army of dirty workmen, bespattered with mud. This is the external appearance, the least pleasant of an art, whose ingenious mysteries are perceived by few, but excite the admiration of those who discern them. There they discover inventions whose boldness implies a huge and productive genius; proportions, the use of which shows a severe and systematic precision; embellishments whose elegance discloses a delicate and exquisite sentiment. Whoever is capable of perceiving such real beauties, far from merging architecture with the lesser arts, will rather be tempted to place it in the ranks of the most profound sciences. The sight of a building built with all the perfection of the art, affords an irresistible pleasure and enchantment. This spectacle awakens in the soul noble and moving ideas. It causes us to experience that sweet emotion, that pleasing rapture aroused by such works, which bear the mark of a true superiority of genius. A beautiful building speaks eloquently for its architect. In his writings, M. [Claude] Perrault [1613–88] appears, at best, to be a learned man: the colonnade of the Louvre [designed by Perrault] determines that he is a great man.

Architecture owes all that is perfect in it to the Greeks, a nation privileged to be ignorant of nothing in the sciences, and to invent all in the arts. The Romans, worthy of admiration, capable of copying the excellent models provided for them by the Greeks, wanted to add their own to them, and show the whole world that, when perfection is achieved, it may only be copied, and not surpassed.

The barbarism of succeeding ages, having buried all the fine arts under the ruins of an empire, which alone retained its taste and principles, created a new system of architecture, where proportions were unknown, embellishments bizarrely shaped and ridiculously heaped together, producing only carved stones, shapeless, grotesque, excessive. This modern architecture has for too long been the delight of Europe. Most of our great churches are, unfortunately, destined to preserve traces of it for distant posterity. Let us speak the truth: with countless blemishes, this architecture has had some beauties. Although in its most magnificent productions there prevails a heaviness of spirit and a coarseness of sentiment which is quite shocking, we cannot but admire the boldness of the features, the delicacy of the chisel, the air of majesty and of disengagement which one notes in certain pieces, which, in all aspects, have something of the desperate and inimitable about them. But at length, more fortunate geniuses were able to glimpse in these ancient monuments proof of the universal misguidedness, and also the means of returning from it. Made to taste the wonders that, in vain, had been exposed to all eyes for centuries, they reflected on the reports of them, they imitated their skill. By means of research, examination and trial, they revived the study of good rules, and re-established architecture in all its former rights. They abandoned the ridiculous Gothic and Arabian rubbish, substituting it with manly and elegant Doric, Ionian and Corinthian ornaments. The French, slow to invent, but quick to follow favourable inventions, envied Italy the glory of reviving the magnificent creations of Greece.

(*Essay*, Introduction)

### 'General Principles of Architecture'

It is with Architecture as with all other arts; its principles are founded upon simple nature, and in the proceedings of this are clearly marked the rules of that. Let us consider original man without other help, without any other guide than the natural instinct of his needs. He wants a resting place. At the edge of a peaceful stream he notices some grass; its growing greenness is pleasing to his eye, the soft down looks inviting to him; he goes to it, and, softly extended on this flecked carpet, he dreams of nothing but to enjoy in peace the gifts of nature: he lacks nothing, he desires nothing. But soon the heat of the sun burns him and he seeks shade. He notices a forest which offers him the coolness of its shade; he runs to hide himself in its thickets and is happy there. In the meantime, a thousand vapours raised by chance meet and gather, thick clouds cover the air, a terrible, torrential rain falls on this delightful forest. The man, poorly covered by the shelter of the leaves, no longer knows how to protect himself from the uncomfortable humidity which penetrates from all sides. He sees a cave, he slides into it, and, finding himself dry, congratulates himself on his discovery. But new sources of annoyance make him dislike this shelter. He is in darkness, he is breathing unhealthy air; he leaves, resolved, by his own efforts, to make good the carelessness and negligence of nature. The man wants to make a shelter which will cover him without burying him. Several broken branches in the forest are the materials suitable for his project. He chooses four of the strongest which he raises perpendicularly and forms into a square. Above he puts four others crossways, and on these he raises some which slope and meet at a point from both sides. This type of roof is covered with leaves, woven together closely in a way that neither the sun, nor the rain can penetrate; and there the man lives. It is true that the cold and the heat make him uncomfortable in his house, which is open on all sides; but he will fill up the space between the pillars and find himself protected.

Such is the course of simple nature: art owes its origin to the imitation of her method of working. The small rustic cabin which I have just described is the model upon which all the splendours of architecture have been conceived. It is in keeping close to the simplicity of the first model in its execution that we avoid essential faults, that we reach real perfection. Pieces of wood raised perpendicularly gave us the idea of columns. The horizontal pieces that are laid upon them gave us the idea of entablatures. Finally, the sloping pieces which form the roof gave us the idea of the pediment. This is what all the masters of the art have recognised. But then we ought here to be very much on our guard. Never did a principle have more fruitful consequences. It is easy henceforth to distinguish the parts which are essential to the composition of an order of architecture, from those which have only been introduced by necessity, or added on a whim. All the beauty is contained in the essential parts; all the liberties are found in the parts introduced by necessity; all the defects are contained in the parts introduced on a whim.

(*Essay*, ch. 1)

## WILLIAM CHAMBERS

Sir William Chambers (1723–96) was born at Göteborg, Sweden, the son of a Scottish merchant. In his youth he travelled to India and China before studying architecture at the École des Arts in Paris, and then taking up residence in Rome. He moved to London in 1755, and in the following year was appointed tutor of architecture to the Prince of Wales (George III) who later appointed him to various posts with responsibility for official buildings. Among his many works, he was responsible for the design of Kew Gardens and of Somerset House in London.

Following the publication of his study of Chinese architecture, *Designs of Chinese Buildings* (1756), in 1759 Chambers published the first edition of his most important book, *Treatise on Civil Architecture*, which would become a standard text. Though clearly influenced by Laugier's work, Chambers objected to the 'French Jesuit's' general dislike of decorative features, 'as if, in the whole catalogue of arts, architecture should be the only one confined to its pristine simplicity, and secluded from any deviation or improvement'. The popularity of *Civil Architecture* led Chambers to issue a third, enlarged edition under the new title *A Treatise on the Decorative Part of Civil Architecture* in 1791, from which two extracts on the 'Orders of Architecture' are published here.

## *Treatise on Civil Architecture* ([1759], 1791)

As in many other arts, so in architecture, there are certain elementary forms, which, though simple in their nature, and few in number, are the principal constituent objects of every composition; however complicated or extensive it may be.

Of these there are in our art, two distinct sorts; the first consisting of such parts as represent those that were essentially necessary in the construction of the primitive huts, as the shaft of the column, with the plinth of its base, and the abacus of its capital; representing the upright tress, with the stones used to raise, and to cover them. Likewise the architrave and triglyph, representing the beams and joists; the mutules, modillions, and dentils either representing the rafters or some other pieces of timber employed to support the covering; and the corona, representing the beds of materials, which composed the covering itself. All these are properly distinguished by the appellation of essential parts, and form the first class. The subservient members, contrived for the use and ornament of these, and intended either to support, to shelter, or to unite them gracefully together, which are usually called mouldings, constitute the second class.

The essential parts were, most probably, the only ones employed, even in the first stone buildings; as may be collected from some ancient structures, yet remaining: for the architects of those early times, had certainly very imperfect ideas of beauty in the productions of art, and therefore contented themselves, with barely imitating the rude model before them; but coming in time to compare the works of their own hands, with animal and vegetable productions, each species of which is composed of a great diversity of forms, affording an inexhaustible fund of amusement to the mind, they could not but conceive a disgust at the frequent repetition of square figures in their buildings, and therefore thought of introducing certain intermediate parts which might seem to be of some use, and at the same time be so formed as to give a more varied, pleasing appearance to the whole composition: and this, in all probability, was the origin of mouldings.

(*Civil Architecture*, 'Of the Parts which Compose the Orders
of Architecture and of their Properties, Application, and Enrichments')

The orders of Architecture, as has been observed, are the basis upon which the whole decorative part of the art is chiefly built, and towards which the attention of the artist must ever be directed, even where no orders are introduced. In them, originate most of the forms used in decoration; they regulate most of the proportions; and to their combination multiplied, varied, and arranged in a thousand different ways, architecture is indebted for its most splendid productions.

These orders are different modes of building, said originally to have been imitated from the primitive huts; being composed of such parts as were essential in their construction, and afterwards also in the temples of antiquity; which, though at first

*Figure 10.1*   'The Primitive Buildings'

*Source*: W. Chambers, *A Treatise on Civil Architecture* (1759).

*Note*: This plate appears within the chapter 'Of the Origin and Progress of Building', where it serves to support Chambers' view: 'That the primitive hut was of a conic figure, it is reasonable to conjecture; from its being the simplest of solid forms, and most easily constructed ... but, as soon as the inhabitants discovered the inconvenience of the inclined sides, and the worst of upright space in the cone, they changed it for the cube ... they fixed in the ground several upright trunks of trees, to form the sides; filling the intervals between them with branches, closely interwoven, and spread over with clay ... By degrees, other improvements took place; and means were found to make the fabric lasting, neat and handsome, as well as convenient'.

simple and rude, were in the course of time, and by the ingenuity of succeeding architects, wrought up and improved, to such a pitch of perfection, that they were by way of
excellence distinguished by the name of orders.

Of these there are five: three said to be of Grecian origin, are called Grecian orders;
being distinguished by the names of Doric, Ionic, and Corinthian: they exhibit three distinct characters of composition; supposed to have been suggested, by the diversity of
character in the human frame. The remaining two being of Italian origin, are called Latin
orders; they are distinguished by the names of Tuscan and Roman, and were probably
invented with a view of extending the characteristic bounds, on one side, still farther
towards strength and simplicity; as on the other, towards elegance and profusion of
enrichments. [...]

The ingenuity of man has, hitherto, not been able to produce a sixth order, though
large premiums have been offered, and numerous attempts been made, by men of first
rate talents, to accomplish it. Such is the fettered human imagination, such the scanty
store of its ideas, that Doric, Ionic, and Corinthian, have ever floated uppermost; and
all that has ever been produced amounts to nothing more than different arrangements
and combinations of their parts, with some trifling deviations scarcely deserving
notice; the whole generally tending more to diminish than to increase the beauty of the
ancient orders.

The substitution of cocks, owls or lions' heads, &c. for roses; of trophies, cornu-
copias, lilies, sphinxes, or even men, women and children, for volutes; the introduction of feathers, lyres, flower de luces, or coronets, for leaves; are more alterations
than improvements; and the suspension of festoons of flowers, or collars of knighthood, over the other enrichments of a capital, like lace on embroidery, rather tends
to complicate and confuse the form, than to augment its grace or contribute to its
excellence.

The suppression of parts of the ancient orders, with a view to produce novelty,
has of late years been practised among us with full as little success. And though it is
not wished to restrain sallies of imagination, nor to discourage genius from attempting to invent, yet it is apprehended, that attempts to alter the primary forms invented by the ancients, and established by the concurring approbation of many ages, must
ever be attended with dangerous consequences, must always be difficult, and seldom, if ever, successful. It is like coining words, which, whatever may be their value,
are at first but ill received, and must have the sanction of time, to secure them a current reception.

An order is composed of two principal members, the column and the entablature,
each of which is divided into three principal parts. Those of the column are the base,
the shaft, and the capital; those of the entablature are the architrave, the frieze, and the
cornice. All these are again subdivided into many smaller parts, the disposition, number, forms, and dimensions of which characterise each order, and express the degree of
strength or delicacy, richness or simplicity, peculiar to it.

(*Civil Architecture*, 'Of the Orders of Architecture in General')

## JEAN-SIMÉON CHARDIN

Chardin (1699–1779), son of a cabinet maker, was born and lived most of his life in Paris. After serving an apprenticeship at the Académie de Saint-Luc, in 1728 he exhibited several paintings, two of which, *La Raie* (*The Rayfish*) and *Le Buffet* (*The Buffet*), were selected as 'reception pieces' which gained him admission to the prestigious Académie Royale, as a painter 'skilled in animals and fruit'. This entitled him to show his work at the Salon du Louvre and, following its reopening in 1737, he became a regular exhibitor of still life and genre paintings. Elected to the post of treasurer of the Académie in 1755, he became responsible for the hanging of paintings in the biennial exhibitions at the Salon, and was granted lodgings in the Louvre by Louis XV in 1757. Chardin's life was marked by the deaths of his first wife and two children, and of the daughter from his second marriage to a prosperous widow in 1744. By the end of his life he had produced fewer than three hundred paintings, of which about a third were variants on earlier works. He never travelled abroad, and died at his apartment in the Louvre.

As Chardin never attempted 'history painting', the most prestigious kind of painting encompassing great religious, mythological or historical subjects, and only tried his hand at the second category, portraiture, with limited critical success from 1746 to 1757, his

*Figure 10.2*　J-S. Chardin, *La Raie* (oil on canvas, 114.5 x 146 cm, 1725–26)

*Source*: Photo, Réunion des Musées Nationaux.

*Note*: The painting aroused great interest when it was exhibited and presented to the Académie Royale in 1728. It depicts ordinary human-made kitchen objects (jug, knife, pans) together with vegetable and animal life (onions, oysters, fish and cat). At the centre of attention is the 'disgusting' face and body of a gutted skate.

*Figure 10.3*   J-S. Chardin, *Le Bénédicité* (oil on canvas, 49.5 x 38.5 cm, 1740)

*Source*: Photo, Réunion des Musées Nationaux.

*Note*: Chardin began to paint human figures in the 1730s, and *Le Bénédicité* was exhibited and presented as a gift to Louis XV in 1740. Many of these genre scenes were depictions of domestic servants at work 'below stairs'. Others were portrayals of middle-class women and children at work or play within their homes. *Le Bénédicité* presents a 'family scene' (without a father-figure) in which a mother (or governess) and daughter pause while the son says a prayer before a simple meal. Chardin painted several versions of this scene, and it was engraved for popular prints.

work did not command the highest prices. However, within the lowly categories of 'genre scenes', and the lowest of all, still life and landscape, his domestic scenes were often highly prized for their 'naturalness' and 'truthfulness', and fetched good prices; and the 'genre scenes' sold well as popular prints. The paintings were purchased by artists, professionals, merchants, and art collectors – including Frederick II of Prussia and Catherine II of Russia. Selected here are two of Chardin's most famous works: a still life, *La Raie*, and a genre scene, *Le Bénédicité* (*Saying Grace*).

## DENIS DIDEROT

Diderot's pioneering work in art criticism began in 1759, when his friend the German-born diplomat and writer Melchior Grimm (1723–1807) invited him to review the Royal Academy of Painting and Sculpture's current exhibition at the Louvre. In 1753 Grimm, a contributor to the *Encyclopédie* and resident in Paris, had launched a manuscript newsletter on French cultural affairs, the *Correspondance Littéraire,* and it was for this highly exclusive journal, sent every two weeks to a small group of German princes and monarchs such as Catherine II, that Diderot's reviews of the biennial salons, from 1759 to 1781, were penned. Since the newsletters did not appear in print, they were not subject to official censorship or the laws of libel, and this encouraged Diderot to speak more freely about the works that he critiqued. Initially, in 1759, his commentary was fairly short, but by 1765 his review had grown to book-length proportions as he examined the patchwork of hundreds of paintings that were displayed from floor to ceiling along the salon's walls. Though written in a confidential manner for the most prestigious patrons and collectors of art in Europe, the exhibitions represented a new public space for the discussion and purchase of art, and Diderot showed great skill in conveying the sense of multiple approaches and responses to the exhibits through the subjective reflections of his conversational style.

The biennial exhibitions were open to the public for several weeks from 25 August, and they attracted a broad social range of French and foreign spectators. During the shows, Diderot would join the hundreds of visitors each day, working his way through the catalogue, taking notes, committing the paintings to his visual memory, and collecting 'the verdicts of old men and the thoughts of children, the judgements of men of letters, the opinions of the sophisticated, and the views of the people'. He would also chat with artists and collectors, and clearly held many discussions with Chardin, who, as the *tapissier*, was responsible for the hanging of exhibits. What always appealed to Diderot about Chardin's compositions was their evident purity of conception and their truthfulness to nature, both in terms of physical appearances and the moral or 'magical' qualities that he felt that the works embodied. In contrast, the famous François Boucher was often berated by Diderot for the decadence and folly of his voluptuous nudes and historical scenes.

Though Diderot generally respected the traditional hierarchy of paintings, he showed no great respect for artists' reputations. Nor did he propound a consistent theory of art. Nevertheless, his *Salon* writings mark a watershed in the development of art criticism and, though they were not published in France until the 1790s, he took great pride in them. Thus he told his mistress, Sophie Volland, that his review of the 1765 exhibition was 'undoubtedly the best thing I have done in all my literary career'. The following commentaries on Chardin's paintings, translated here, are taken from the six salons that Diderot reviewed from 1759 to 1769.

## 'Chardin'

from *Salons* (1759–69)

With Chardin we return to hunting; heads of game; a young pupil drawing, viewed from behind; a girl doing some tapestry; two small pictures of fruit. It is always nature and truth; you would take the bottles by the neck if you were thirsty; the peaches and grapes awaken the appetite and beckon. [...] This Chardin has a quick mind; he understands the theory of his art; he paints in a manner which is his own, and his paintings will one day be in great demand.

(*Salon of 1759*)

Chardin has painted a *Bénédicité* [*Saying Grace*], some *Animaux* [*Animals*], some *Vanneaux* [*Lapwings*], and a few other pieces. It is always a very faithful imitation of nature, using the technique which is this artist's own; an unpolished and abrupt technique; a base, common and domestic nature. It is a long time since this painter has finished anything; he no longer takes the trouble to paint the feet and the hands. He works like a man of the world who has the gift and talent, and who is content to sketch his thoughts with four strokes of the brush. He now tops the list of neglected painters, having produced many pieces which have earned him an eminent position among the first-rate painters. Chardin has a quick mind, and perhaps no one speaks better about painting than he. His reception piece at the Academy proves that he has understood the magic of colours. He has diffused this magic in several other compositions, and, together with the art of drawing, invention and extreme reality, so many qualities brought together have made these pieces very valuable now. Chardin has originality in his own genre. This originality runs from his paintings to his engravings. When you have seen one of his paintings, you can never mistake them; they are recognisable everywhere. Look at his *Gouvernante avec ses Enfants* [*Governess with her Children*] and you will have seen his *Bénédicité*.

*(Salon of 1761)*

There are several small paintings by Chardin in the Salon; they almost all show fruits with the accessories of a meal. It is nature itself; the objects stand out from the canvas with a reality which deceives the eye.

When climbing the stairs [of the Salon], there is one painting which is particularly worthy of attention. The artist has placed on a table an old Chinese porcelain vase, two biscuits, a jar filled with olives, a basket of fruit, two glasses half-filled with wine, a Seville orange and some pâté.

To look at paintings of other artists, it seems that I need to develop my sight; to look at those of Chardin, I have only to keep the eyes given to me by Nature and to make good use of them.

If I wanted my child to become a painter, this is the painting that I would buy. 'Copy this for me', I would say to him, 'copy this for me again'. But Nature herself is perhaps not more difficult to copy.

You see, this porcelain vase is made of porcelain; these olives are really separated from the eye by the water in which they are submerged; you only have to take these biscuits and eat them, to cut open this orange and squeeze it, to pick up this glass of wine and drink it, these fruits and peel them, and to cut this pâté with a knife.

He is the one who understands the harmony of colours and reflections. Oh, Chardin! It is not white, red or black that you mix on your palette; it is the very substance of the objects, it is the air and light that you take on the tip of your brush and apply to the canvas.

After my child had copied and recopied this painting, I would turn his attention to *La Raie Dépouillée* [*The Gutted Skate*] by the same master. The object is disgusting, but it is actually the flesh of the fish, its skin, its blood – the very appearance of the thing would not otherwise produce such an effect. Monsieur Pierre [Jean-Baptiste Pierre, 1713–89], look carefully at this painting when you next visit the Academy, and, if you can, learn the secret of using one's talent to stop certain natural beings from causing disgust.

*(Salon of 1763)*

If, as the philosophers say, it is true that there is nothing real but our sensations, that neither the emptiness of space, nor the very solidity of our bodies is perhaps anything in itself of what we experience, then let these philosophers tell me what is the difference, four feet away from your [Chardin's] paintings, between the Creator and you.

Chardin is so true, so true, so harmonious, that although one only sees inanimate nature on his canvases, vases, cups, bottles, bread, wine, water, grapes, fruits, pâtés, he holds his own against, and can perhaps take you away from, two of the most beautiful Vernets [Claude-Joseph Vernet, 1714–89], beside which he has not hesitated in placing his work. It is, my friend, as in the world, when the presence of a man, a horse, or an animal does not at all destroy the effect of rock, a tree, a stream. The stream, the tree and the rock are, without doubt, less interesting than the man, the woman, the horse, the animal; but they are equally real.

I must tell you, my friend, of an idea that has just come to me, and which will, perhaps, not come back to me at another time; it is that this type of painting that we call genre, is more suited to old men or those who are born old. It requires only study and patience. No animation; little genius, scarcely any poetry; much technique and truth; and that is all. Now, you know that the time when we start, what is commonly known as the search for truth, is exactly the time when our temples begin to grey and when we would find it unbecoming to write a love-letter. Regarding these grey hairs, my friend, I have this morning seen that my own head is completely silver, and I cried out like Sophocles when Socrates asked him how his love life was going: '*A domino agresti et furioso profugi*' [I am free of that savage and raging master].

I am happy now to chat with you, more especially as I will say only one thing about Chardin: and this is it. Choose a spot; arrange the objects on it just as I tell you, and you can be sure that you will have seen his paintings. [...]

*Une Corbeille de Raisins* [*A Basket of Grapes*]. This is all there is to the painting: just scatter a few individual grapes around the basket, a macaroon, a pear and two or three ladyapples; you will agree that some individual grapes, a macaroon and a few lady-apples are not promising in either shape or colour; nevertheless, just look at Chardin's painting. [...]

This man is the leading colourist in the Salon, and perhaps one of the finest colourists of painting. I cannot forgive that impertinent Webb [Daniel Webb, 1719–98] for having written a treatise [*An Enquiry into the Beauties of Painting*, 1760] on art without ever citing a single Frenchman. Nor can I forgive Hogarth for having said that the French School has not even a mediocre colourist. You have lied, Mr. Hogarth; either through ignorance or platitude. I know that your nation is in the habit of scorning an impartial author who dares to praise us: but must you so basely court your fellow citizens at the expense of the truth? Paint, paint better if you can. Learn to draw and do not write any more. The English and the French have two very different ways. Ours is to overrate the English compositions; theirs is to disparage ours. Hogarth was still alive two years ago. He visited France; and Chardin has been a great colourist for thirty years.

*(Salon of 1765)*

It is said that this painter has a technique which is his own, and that he uses his thumb as much as his brush. I do not know about this, but I am sure of one thing, that I have never known anyone who has watched him work. However that may be, his compositions appeal equally to the uninstructed and to the connoisseur. They have an incredible strength of colour, an overall harmony, a true and piquant effect, beautiful forms, a magic in their execution that makes you despair, and a mixture of diversity and arrangement. Move away, move closer, the illusion is the same, there is no confusion and no point of symmetry either, and no flittering effects; the eye is always pleased, because there is calm and tranquillity. One stops in front of a Chardin by instinct, just as a traveller, weary from his journey, goes to sit down, almost without noticing, in a spot that offers him a grassy seat, silence, the sound of water, some shade and coolness.

*(Salon of 1767)*

Chardin is such a strict imitator of nature, such a severe judge of himself, that I have seen one of his paintings of *Gibier* [*Game*] that he has never completed, because the small rabbits, on which he was working, had begun to decay; he despaired of achieving with others the harmony which was in his mind. All of those brought to him were either too dark or too light.

*(Salon of 1769)*

## WILLIAM HOGARTH

Hogarth (1697–1764) was born into a large family and spent most of his life in London and its environs. His father, an impoverished schoolmaster and Classicist, was sent to debtors' prison in 1707. In 1714, Hogarth was apprenticed to a silver plate engraver, and in 1720 he set up his own shop as an engraver, producing coats of arms, shop cards, book illustrations (notably for Samuel Butler's *Hudibras*) and satirical engravings on contemporary topics. Following his studies under the celebrated 'history painter' Sir James Thornhill, in the late 1720s Hogarth turned to oil painting, producing 'conversation pieces' (group portraits), and marrying Sir James's daughter. Eager to reach a wider public, raise his income, and gain independence from art connoisseurs and patrons, in 1731 he painted his first major narrative series *A Harlot's Progress*, which he then engraved and sold as popular prints, with great success. Though designed to expose the vices and follies of contemporary life – not least through the portrayal of class, race and gender struggles – in producing 'genre' series such as *A Harlot's Progress* (1732), *A Rake's Progress* (1735), *Marriage à la Mode* (1745), *Industry and Idleness* (1747), *The Four Stages of Cruelty* (1751), and *Four Prints of an Election* (1758), Hogarth hoped that his 'modern moral subjects' would be judged by the criteria applied to traditional 'history' paintings. Even so, he continued to produce portraits and 'history' paintings in the 1740s and '50s, though these works did not win the recognition he believed that they deserved.

Throughout his life, Hogarth (ever a patriot) railed both against the rules of taste and art laid down by largely foreign connoisseurs, and at the 'servile' artists who preferred to imitate Old Masters rather than to learn by 'studying from nature'. His belief that grace and beauty resided in nature itself, formed the basis of his treatise *The Analysis of Beauty* (1753) which challenged the conventions of art theory, and consequently was generally lampooned. Having purchased a house by the Thames at Chiswick, Hogarth was buried in the churchyard there, not far from what he regarded as a neoclassical monstrosity – Chiswick House.

In an advert for *Beer Street* and *Gin Lane*, Hogarth stated that, as they were 'calculated to reform some reigning vices peculiar to the lower classes of people, in hopes to render them of more extensive use, the author has published

*Figure 10.4*   W. Hogarth, *Beer Street* (engraving, 36 x 30.5 cm, 1751)

them in the cheapest manner possible'. Based upon his acute observation (but extraordinary representation) of the lives and activities of common people, Hogarth arranges two street scenes to contrast the 'idleness, poverty, misery and distress' produced by gin drinking, with the prosperity and pleasures of a beer-drinking society. Dozens of contrasting images and contemporary references are arranged to prompt the viewer to compare the figures and scenes depicted, and to draw the appropriate moral and social lessons.

In *Beer Street* 'all is joyous and thriving'. Under the sign of 'Health and the Barley Mow', a poor artist paints an advertisement for gin, from a gin bottle

*Figure 10.5*   W. Hogarth, *Gin Lane* (engraving, 36 x 30.5 cm, 1751)

hanging from the sign; two fishwives read a new ballad on 'Herring Fishery'; a porter rests a basket of books to be shredded, containing academic works such as 'Turnbul on Painting'; and a newspaper and king's speech to parliament lie on the table. In *Gin Lane* an emaciated ballad-singer has a copy of 'Downfall of Madm Gin'; and the gin vault advertises 'Drunk for a Penny. Dead drunk for two pence. Clean Straw for Nothing'.

## HORACE WALPOLE

Horace Walpole (1717–97) was the youngest son of the Prime Minister, Sir Robert Walpole, and became the 4th Earl of Orford in 1791. Educated at Eton and Cambridge University, in 1739 he undertook the Grand Tour of France and Italy, returning in 1741 to become an MP until 1768. From 1750 he was responsible for the revival of Gothic style at Strawberry Hill, his villa at Twickenham, which became a tourist attraction. He set up a private printing press there and published various literary works, including his tragedy *The Mysterious Mother* (1768). He is best known, however, as the author of the first Gothic novel *The Castle of Otranto* (1765). A tireless and highly influential art critic and collector, from 1762 to 1771 he published his four-volume *Anecdotes of Painting in England*, which included his famous essay 'On Modern Gardening'. His correspondence (some 3,000 letters) has recently been published in 48 volumes.

The following extracts are taken from the fourth volume (1771) of *Anecdotes of Painting in England*. In the first extract, Walpole reviews William Hogarth's work and achievements. He begins by comparing Hogarth's work with that of modern dramatists and authors. In the second extract Walpole celebrates the rise of landscape gardening and the innovative work of the painter, architect and designer William Kent (1684–1748), who had laid out the gardens for Chiswick House. This was the home of Kent's friend and the champion of Palladianism, Richard Boyle (1694–1753), Lord Burlington.

## *Anecdotes of Painting in England* (1762–71)

### 'William Hogarth'

Having dispatched the herd of our painters in oil, I reserved to a class by himself that great original genius, Hogarth; considering him rather as a writer of comedy with a pencil, than as a painter. If catching the manners and follies of an age *living as they rise*, if general satire on vices and ridicules, familiarized by strokes of nature, and heightened by wit, and the whole animated by proper and just expressions of the passions, be comedy, Hogarth composed comedies as much as Molière [1622–73]: in his *Marriage à la Mode* there is even an intrigue carried on throughout the piece. He is more true to character than Congreve [1670–1729]; each personage is distinct from the rest, acts in his sphere, and cannot be confounded with any other of the dramatis personæ. The alderman's footboy, in the last print of the set I have mentioned, is an ignorant rustic; and if wit is struck out from the characters in which it is not expected, it is from their acting conformably to their situation and from the mode of their passions, not from their having the wit of fine gentlemen. Thus there is wit in the figure of the alderman, who when his daughter is expiring in the agonies of poison, wears a face of solicitude, but it is to save her gold ring, which he is drawing gently from her finger. The thought is parallel to Molière's, where the miser puts out one of the candles as he is talking. Molière, inimitable as he has proved, brought a rude theatre to perfection. Hogarth had no model to follow and improve upon. He created his art; and used colours instead of language. His place is between the Italians, whom we may consider as epic poets and tragedians, and the Flemish painters, who are as writers of farce and editors of burlesque nature. They are the Tom Browns of the mob. Hogarth resembles Butler [1612–80], but his subjects are more universal, and amidst all his pleasantry, he observes the true end of comedy, reformation; there is always a moral to his pictures. Sometimes he rose to tragedy, not in the catastrophe of kings and heroes, but in marking how vice conducts insensibly and incidentally to misery and shame. He warns against encouraging cruelty and idleness in young minds, and discerns how the different vices of the great and vulgar lead by various paths to the same unhappiness. The fine lady in *Marriage à la Mode*, and Tom Nero in *The Four Stages of Cruelty*, terminate their story in blood – she occasions the murder of her husband, he assassinates his mistress. How delicate and superior too is his satire, when he intimates in the College of Physicians and Surgeons that preside at a dissection, how the legal habitude of viewing shocking scenes hardens the human mind, and renders it unfeeling. The president maintains the dignity of insensibility over an executed [Tom Nero] corpse, and considers it but as the object of a lecture. In the print of the Sleeping Judges [*The Bench*], this habitual indifference only excites our laughter.

It is to Hogarth's honour that in so many scenes of satire or ridicule, it is obvious that ill-nature did not guide his pencil. His end is always reformation, and his reproofs general. Except in the print of *The Times*, and the two portraits of Mr. Wilkes [John Wilkes] and Mr. Churchill [*The Bruiser*] that followed, no man amidst such a profusion of characteristic faces, ever pretended to discover or charge him with the caricatura of a real person; except of such notorious characters as Charteris and Mother Needham [in *A Harlot's Progress*], and a very few more, who are acting officially and suitably to their professions. As he must have observed carefully the operation of the passions on the countenance, it is even wonderful that he never, though without intention, delivered the very features of any identical person. It is at the same time a proof of his intimate intuition into nature: but had he been too severe, the humanity of endeavouring to root out cruelty to animals would atone for many satires. It is another proof that he drew all his stores from nature and the force of his own genius, and was indebted neither to models nor books for his style, thoughts or hints, that he never succeeded when he designed for the works of other men. I do not speak of his early performances at the time that he was engaged by booksellers, and rose not above those they generally employ; but in his maturer age, when he had invented his art, and gave a few designs for some great authors, as Cervantes, Gulliver [Swift], and even Hudibras [Butler], his compositions were tame, spiritless, void of humour, and never reach the merits of the books they were designed to illustrate. He could not bend his talents to think after anybody else. He could think like a great genius rather than after one. [...]

Another instance of this author's genius is his not condescending to explain his moral lessons by the trite poverty of allegory. If he had an emblematic thought, he expressed it with wit, rather than by a symbol. Such is that of the whore setting fire to the world in the *Rake's Progress*. Once indeed he descended to use an allegoric personage, and was not happy in it: in one of his *Election* prints Britannia's chariot breaks down, while the coachman and footman are playing at cards on the box. Sometimes too, to please his vulgar customers, he stooped to low images and national satire, as in the two prints of *France* and *England*, and that of *The Gates of Calais*. The last indeed has great merit, though the caricatura is carried to excess. In all these the painter's purpose was to make his countrymen observe the ease and affluence of a free government, opposed to the wants and woes of slaves. In *Beer Street* the English butcher tossing a Frenchman in the air with one hand [in an early version], is absolute hyperbole; and what is worse, was an afterthought, not being in the first edition. The Gin-alley [*Gin Lane*] is much superior, horridly fine, but disgusting.

His *Bartholomew-Fair* is full of humour; The *March to Finchley*, of nature: *The Enraged Musician* tends to farce. *The Four Parts of the Day*, except the last, are inferior to few of his works. *The Sleeping Congregation*, *The Lecture on the Vacuum*, *The Laughing Audience*, *The Consultation of Physicians* as a coat of arms, and *The Cockpit*, are perfect in their several kinds. The prints of *Industry and Idleness* have more merit in the intention than execution.

Towards his latter end he now and then repeated himself, but seldomer than most great authors who executed so much.

It may appear singular that of an author whom I call comic, and who is so celebrated for his humour, I should speak in general in so serious a style; but it would be suppressing the merits of his heart to consider him only as a promoter of laughter. I think I have shown that his views were more generous and extensive. Mirth coloured his pictures, but benevolence designed them. He smiled like Socrates, that men might not be offended at his lectures, and might learn to laugh at their own follies. When his topics were harmless, all his touches were marked with pleasantry, and fun. He never laughed like Rabelais [?1494–1553] at nonsense that he imposed for wit; but like Swift [1667–1745] combined incidents that divert one from their unexpected encounter, and illustrate the tale he means to tell. Such are the hens roosting on the upright-waves in the scene of the Strollers [*Strolling Actresses dressing in a Barn*], and the devils drinking porter on the altar. The manners or *costume* are more than observed in every one of his works. The very furniture of his rooms describe the characters of the persons to whom they belong; a lesson that might be of use to comic authors. It was reserved to Hogarth to write a scene of furniture. The rake's levee-room, the nobleman's dining-room, the apartments of the husband and wife in *Marriage à la Mode*, the alderman's parlour, the poet's bedchamber, and many others, are the history of the manners of the age.

(*Anecdotes*, vol. 4, ch. 4, 'Painters in the
Reign of George II: William Hogarth')

### 'On Modern Gardening'

Gardening was probably one of the first arts that succeeded to that of building houses, and naturally attended property and individual possession. Culinary, and afterwards medicinal herbs, were the objects of every head of a family: it became convenient to have them within reach, without seeking them at random in woods, in meadows, and on mountains, as often as they were wanted. When the earth ceased to furnish spontaneously all these primitive luxuries, and culture became requisite, separate inclosures for rearing herbs grew expedient. Fruits were in the same predicament, and those most in use or that demand attention, must have entered into and extended the domestic inclosure. The good man Noah, we are told, planted a vineyard, drank of the wine, and was drunken, and everybody knows the consequences. Thus we acquired kitchen-gardens, orchards, and vineyards. I am apprized that the prototype of all these sorts was the garden of Eden, but as that Paradise was a good deal larger than any we read of afterwards, being inclosed by the rivers Pison, Gihon, Hiddekel, and Euphrates, as every tree that was pleasant to the sight and good for food grew in it, and as two other trees were likewise found there, of which not a slip or sucker remains, it does not belong to the present discussion. After the Fall no man living was suffered to enter into the garden; and the poverty and necessities of our first ancestors hardly allowed them time *to make improvements on their estates* in imitation of it, supposing any plan had been preserved. A cottage and a slip of ground for a cabbage and a gooseberry-bush, such as we see by the side of a common, were in all probability the earliest seats and gardens: a well and bucket succeeded to the Pison and Euphrates. As settlements increased, the orchard and vineyard followed; and the earliest princes of tribes possessed just the necessaries of a modern farmer. [...]

From what I have said, it appears how naturally and insensibly the idea of a kitchen-garden slid into that which has for so many ages been peculiarly termed a garden, and by our ancestors in this country, distinguished by the name of a pleasure-garden. A square piece of ground was originally parted off in early ages for the use of the family – to exclude cattle and ascertain the property it was separated from the fields by a hedge. As pride and desire of privacy increased, the inclosure was dignified by walls, and in climes where fruits were not lavished by the ripening glow of nature and soil, fruit-trees were assisted and sheltered from surrounding winds by the like expedient; for the inundation of luxuries which have swelled into general necessities, have almost all taken their source from the simple fountain of reason.

When the custom of making square gardens inclosed with walls was thus established, to the exclusion of nature and prospect, pomp and solitude combined to call for something that might enrich and enliven the insipid and unanimated partition. Fountains, first invented for use, which grandeur loves to disguise and throw out of the question, received embellishments from costly marbles, and at last to contradict utility, tossed their waste of waters into air in spouting columns. Art, in the hands of rude man, had at first been made a succedaneum to nature; in the hands of ostentatious wealth, it became the means of opposing nature; and the more it traversed the march of the latter, the more nobility thought its power was demonstrated. Canals measured by the line were introduced in lieu of meandering streams, and terraces were hoisted aloft in opposition to the facile slopes that imperceptibly unite the valley to the hill. Balustrades defended these precipitate and dangerous elevations, and flights of steps rejoined them to the subjacent flat from which the terrace had been dug. Vases and sculpture were added to these unnecessary balconies, and statues finished the lifeless spot with mimic representations of the excluded sons of men. Thus difficulty and expence were the constituent parts of those sumptuous and selfish solitudes; and every improvement that was made was but a step farther from nature. The tricks of waterworks to wet the unwary, not to refresh the panting spectator, and parterres embroidered in patterns like a petticoat, were but the childish endeavours of fashion and novelty to reconcile greatness to what it had surfeited on. To crown these impotent displays of false taste, the shears were applied to the lovely wildness of form with which nature has distinguished each various species of tree and shrub. The venerable oak, the romantic beech, the useful elm, even the aspiring circuit of the lime, the regular round of the chestnut, and the almost moulded orange-tree, were corrected by such fantastic admirers of symmetry. The compass and square were of more use in plantations than the nurseryman. The measured walk, the quincunx, and the etoile imposed their unsatisfying sameness on every royal and noble garden. Trees were headed, and their sides pared away; many French groves seem green chests set upon poles. Seats of marble, arbours and summer-houses, terminated every visto [vista]; and symmetry, even where the space was too large to permit its being remarked at one view, was so essential, that, as Pope observed,

> —each alley has a brother,
> And half the garden just reflects the other.

Knots of flowers were more defensibly subjected to the same regularity. Leisure, as Milton expressed it,

> in trim gardens took his pleasure.

In the garden of Marshal de Biron at Paris, consisting of fourteen acres, every walk is buttoned on each side by lines of flowerpots, which succeed in their seasons. When I saw it, there were nine thousand pots of Asters, or la Reine Marguerite. [...]

I call a sunk fence [ha-ha] the leading step, for these reasons. No sooner was this simple enchantment made, than levelling, mowing and rolling, followed. The contiguous ground of the park without the sunk fence was to be harmonized with the lawn within; and the garden in its turn was to be set free from its prim regularity, that it might assort with the wilder country without. The sunk fence ascertained the specific garden, but that it might not draw too obvious a line of distinction between the neat and the rude, the contiguous out-lying parts came to be included in a kind of general design: and when nature was taken into the plan, under improvements, every step that was made, pointed out new beauties and inspired new ideas. At that moment appeared [William] Kent, painter enough to taste the charms of landscape, bold and opinionative enough to dare and to dictate, and born with a genius to strike out a great system from the twilight of imperfect essays. He leaped the fence, and saw that all nature was a garden. He felt the delicious contrast of hill and valley changing imperceptibly into each other, tasted the beauty of the gentle swell, or concave scoop, and remarked how loose groves crowned an easy eminence with happy ornament, and while they called in the distant view between their graceful stems, removed and extended the perspective by delusive comparison.

Thus the pencil of his imagination bestowed all the arts of landscape on the scenes he handled. The great principles on which he worked were perspective, and light and shade. Groups of trees broke too uniform or too extensive a lawn; evergreens and woods were opposed to the glare of the champaign [open plains], and where the view was less fortunate, or so much exposed as to be beheld at once, he blotted out some parts by thick shades, to divide it into variety, or to make the richest scene more enchanting by reserving it to a farther advance of the spectator's step. Thus selecting favourite objects, and veiling deformities by screens of plantation; sometimes allowing the rudest waste to add its soil to the richest theatre, he realized the compositions of the greatest masters in painting. Where objects were wanting to animate his horizon, his taste as an architect could bestow immediate termination. His buildings, his seats, his temples, were more the works of his pencil than of his compasses. We owe the restoration of Greece and the diffusion of architecture to his skill in landscape.

But of all the beauties he added to the face of this beautiful country, none surpassed his management of water. Adieu to canals, circular basins, and cascades tumbling down marble steps, that last absurd magnificence of Italian and French villas. The forced elevation of cataracts was no more. The gentle stream was taught to serpentize seemingly at its pleasure, and where discontinued by different levels, its course appeared to be concealed by thickets properly interspersed, and glittered again at a distance where it might be supposed naturally to arrive. Its borders were smoothed, but preserved their waving irregularity. A few trees scattered here and there on its edges sprinkled the tame bank that accompanied its meanders; and when it disappeared among the hills, shades descending from the heights leaned towards its progress, and framed the distant point of light under which it was lost, as it turned aside to either hand of the blue horizon.

Thus dealing in none but the colours of nature, and catching its most favourable features, men saw a new creation opening before their eyes. The living landscape was chastened or polished, not transformed. Freedom was given to the forms of trees; they extended their branches unrestricted, and where any eminent oak, or master beech had escaped maiming and survived the forest, bush and bramble was removed, and all its honours were restored to distinguish and shade the plain. Where the united plumage of an ancient wood extended wide its undulating canopy, and stood venerable in its darkness, Kent thinned the foremost ranks, and left but so many detached and scattered trees, as softened the approach of gloom, and blended a chequered light with the thus lengthened shadows of the remaining columns.

(*Anecdotes of Painting*, vol. 4, ch. 7, 'On Modern Gardening')

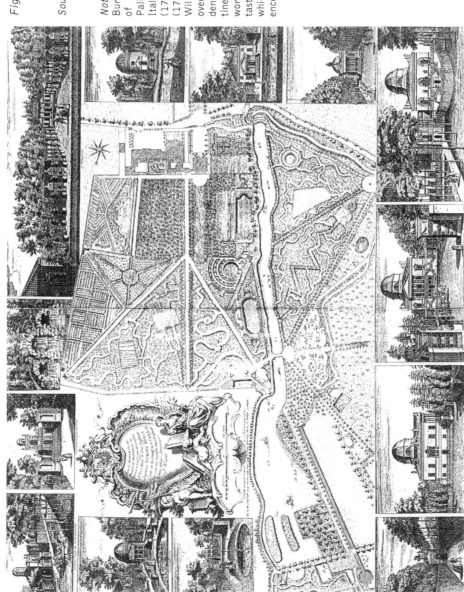

*Figure 10.6* J. Rocque, 'Plan of Chiswick Park', London (1736)

*Source:* From J. Badeslade and J. Rocque, *Vitruvius Britannicus*, vol. IV (1739).

*Note:* Chiswick Park was owned by Lord Burlington (1694–1753), a leading patron of the arts and the champion of Palladianism in Britain. Following visits to Italy, he laid out plans for the gardens (1715) and built a Palladian villa (1725–29). The interior was designed by William Kent (1684–1748) who also took over responsibility for the informal gardens in the 1730s and created the serpentine canal. Horace Walpole praised Kent's work and found the house 'a model of taste, though not without faults, some of which are occasioned by too strict adherence to rules and symmetry'.

Figure 10.7   Copplestone Warre
            Bampfylde, *Bridge,*
            *Lake and South Bank*
            *at Stourhead* (drawing,
            37.5 x 54.5 cm, c. 1770)

*Source:* Photo, National Trust
Photographic Library/John
Bethell.

*Note:* Following the building in the early
1720s of a Palladian mansion (designed by
Colen Campbell) at Stourhead, Wiltshire,
in the mid-1740s plans were laid out to
create a picturesque landscape garden.
This enormous project involved the
damming of the river Stour to form a lake,
the planting of the grounds, and the building and furnishing of classically-inspired
monuments, all to show how 'common
nature' could be 'improved' to provide a
variety of gentle, visually pleasing and
classically interesting walks and vistas.
Bampfylde's drawing shows the stone
bridge (1762) based upon Palladio's
bridge at Vicenza. Also shown are the
Pantheon (1754, right) and the Temple of
Apollo (1765, left), both designed by
Henry Flitcroft, a protégé of Lord
Burlington and a colleague of William
Kent.

## THOMAS GAINSBOROUGH

Gainsborough (1727–88) was baptised at Sudbury in Suffolk, the son of a local clothier. In 1740 he went to work for a French engraver in London where he probably also studied at the informal St Martin's Lane Academy, founded by Hogarth in 1735. After marrying, in 1748 he returned to Sudbury where he drew and painted the 'common nature' of the Suffolk countryside, before moving to Ipswich in search of more clients. Having gained a reputation for portraiture and landscapes, in 1759 he moved to the fashionable and increasingly neoclassical city of Bath, developing his 'peculiar style' to produce works such as his portrait of the actor David Garrick (1766) and *The Harvest Wagon* (1767). As a founder-member of the Royal Academy he often exhibited there, despite his rejection of the academic rules and conventions that Joshua Reynolds wanted to uphold. Returning to London in 1774, Gainsborough continued to experiment with his compositions, mixing his media and producing drawings and paintings of landscapes and his 'fancy pictures' of ordinary country people in what may appear to be romantically idealised rural settings.

### Note to figure 10.8

The most celebrated of Gainsborough's early (and commissioned) works, *Mr and Mrs Robert Andrews* mixes portraiture and landscape to depict the newly-married couple posed in front of an oak tree on their property near Sudbury. The squire, dressed for shooting, leans gently against a green bench while his pointer dutifully looks up at him. His wife, dressed in a pale-blue gown, is seated with one hand on what Gainsborough may originally have intended to be a pheasant, shot by her husband. The fertility and prosperity of their estate are indicated by the sheaves of corn, an enclosed flock of sheep and the plantation of oaks in the background.

### Note to figure 10.9

One of the first of Gainsborough's 'fancy pictures', Reynolds thought *Girl with Pigs* 'by far the best picture he ever painted, or perhaps ever will', and purchased it for a hundred guineas shortly before it was exhibited in 1782. Painted at Gainsborough's house in Pall Mall, London, where it was reported that several pigs had been seen 'gambolling about the painting room', the picture shows a young girl seated in a Classic pose of meditation while small pigs feed. Though a lowly subject for an oil painting, it invites questions not only about childhood, but also (like *Mr and Mrs Robert Andrews*) about nature, property and gender.

*Figure 10.8* T. Gainsborough, *Mr and Mrs Robert Andrews* (oil on canvas, 70 x 119.5 cm, 1748–50)

*Source:* Photo, National Gallery, London.

Figure 10.9   T. Gainsborough, *Girl with Pigs* (oil on canvas, 125.6 x 148.6 cm, 1782)

*Source:* Black and white photographic print, from the Castle Howard collection.

# JOSHUA REYNOLDS

Sir Joshua Reynolds (1723–92), born at Plympton in Devon, became the foremost portrait painter and art critic of his generation. After studying in Italy, in 1753 he set up his own studio in London where he won recognition for his Classically-posed portraits of rich and famous contemporaries. In 1769 he was elected first president of the newly founded Royal Academy (1768), and delivered the first of his fifteen lectures on the theory of art, the first seven published as *Discourses on Art* in 1778, and all included in the collection of his *Works* that appeared in 1797. In these lectures he stressed that painting was an intellectual activity involving the careful study of Old Masters, and the idealisation of Nature according to Classical traditions. Though keen to raise the status of British art, he argued in his first lecture that 'an implicit obedience to the Rules of Art, as established by the practice of the Great Masters, should be exacted from the young students'.

The extracts here are taken from *The Works of Sir Joshua Reynolds*, published in two volumes in 1797. The first extract is from one of his three short essays that appeared in Dr Johnson's *Idler* series in 1759. Here, Reynolds explains the relationship of Art to Nature, and why the 'grand style' is first in the hierarchy of painting. In the second extract, taken from his fourteenth Discourse, 'delivered to the students of the Royal Academy on the distribution of prizes' in 1788, and published in the following year, he praises Gainsborough's 'genius in a lower rank of art'.

## 'The Grand Style of Painting'

from Johnson's *Idler,* no. 79 (1759)

Sir, Your acceptance of a former letter on Painting, gives me encouragement to offer a few more sketches on the same subject.

Amongst the Painters and the writers on Painting, there is one maxim universally admitted, and continually inculcated. *Imitate Nature* is the invariable rule; but I know none who have explained in what manner this rule is to be understood; the consequence of which is, that everyone takes it in the most obvious sense — that objects are represented naturally, when they have such relief that they seem real. It may appear strange, perhaps, to hear this sense of the rule disputed; but it must be considered, that if the excellency of a Painter consisted only in this kind of imitation, Painting must lose its rank, and be no longer considered as a liberal art, and sister to Poetry; this imitation being merely mechanical, in which the slowest intellect is always sure to succeed best; for the Painter of genius cannot stoop to drudgery, in which the understanding has no part; and what pretence has the art to claim kindred with Poetry, but by its power over the imagination? To this power the Painter of genius directs his aim; in this sense he studies Nature, and often arrives at his end, even by being unnatural, in the confined sense of the word.

The grand style of Painting requires this minute attention to be carefully avoided, and must be kept as separate from it as the style of Poetry from that of History. Poetical ornaments destroy that air of truth and plainness which ought to characterize History; but the very being of Poetry consists in departing from this plain narration, and adopting every ornament that will warm the imagination. To desire to see the excellencies of each style united, to mingle the *Dutch* with the *Italian* School, is to join contrarieties which cannot subsist together, and which destroy the efficacy of each other. The *Italian* attends only to the invariable, the great, and general ideas which are fixed and inherent in universal Nature; the *Dutch*, on the contrary, to literal truth and a minute exactness in the detail, as I may say, of Nature modified by accident. The attention to these petty peculiarities is the very cause of this naturalness so much admired in the Dutch pictures, which, if we suppose it to be a beauty, is certainly of a lower order, that ought to give place to a beauty of a superior kind, since one cannot be obtained but by departing from the other.

(Idler, no. 79, 20 October 1759)

## Discourse XIV (1788)

### 'Gainsborough'

We have lately lost Mr. Gainsborough [1727–88], one of the greatest ornaments of our Academy. It is not our business here, to make panegyrics on the living, or even on the dead who were of our body. The praise of the former might bear appearance of adulation; and the latter, of untimely justice; perhaps of envy to those whom we have still the happiness to enjoy, by an oblique suggestion of invidious comparisons. In discoursing therefore on the talents of the late Mr. Gainsborough, my object is, not so much to praise or to blame him as to draw from his excellencies and defects, matter of instruction to the students in our academy. If ever this nation should produce genius sufficient to acquire to us the honourable distinction of an English School, the name of Gainsborough will be transmitted to posterity, in the history of the Art, among the very first of that rising name. That our reputation in the Arts is now only rising, must be acknowledged; and we must expect our advances to be attended with old prejudices, as adversaries, and not as supporters; standing in this respect in a very different situation from the late artists of the Roman School, to whose reputation ancient prejudices have certainly contributed: the way was prepared for them, and they may be said rather to have lived in the reputation of their country, than to have contributed to it; whilst whatever celebrity is obtained by English Artists, can arise only from the operation of a fair and true comparison. And when they communicate to their country a share of their reputation, it is a portion of fame not borrowed from others, but solely acquired by their own labour and talents. [...]

I am well aware how much I lay myself open to the censure and ridicule of the academical professors of other nations, preferring the humble attempts of Gainsborough to the works of those regular graduates in the great historical style. But we have the sanction of all mankind in preferring genius in a lower rank of art, to feebleness and insipidity in the highest. [...]

It may not be improper to make mention of some of the customs and habits of this extraordinary man; points which come more within the reach of an observer; I however mean such only as are connected with his art, and indeed were, as I apprehend, the causes of his arriving to that high degree of excellence, which we see and acknowledge in his works. Of these causes we must state, as the fundamental, the love which he had to his art; to which, indeed, his whole mind appears to have been devoted, and to which everything was referred; and this we may fairly conclude from various circumstances of his life, which were known to his intimate friends. Among others he had a habit of continually remarking to those who happened to be about him, whatever peculiarity of countenance, whatever accidental combination of figures, or happy effects of light and shadow, occurred in prospects, in the sky, in walking the streets, or in company. If, in his walks, he found a character that he liked, and whose attendance was to be obtained, he ordered him to his house: and from the fields he brought into his painting-room, stumps of trees, weeds, and animals of various kinds; and designed them, not from memory, but immediately from the objects. He even framed a kind of model of landskips, on his table; composed of broken stones, dried herbs, and pieces of looking glass, which he magnified and improved into rocks, trees, and water. How far this latter practice may be useful in giving hints, the professors of landskip can best determine. Like every other technical practice it seems to me wholly to depend on the general talent of him who uses it. Such methods may be nothing better than contemptible and mischievous trifling; or they may be aids. I think upon the whole, unless we constantly refer to real nature, that practice may be more likely to do harm than good. I mention it only, as it shews the solicitude and extreme activity which he had about everything that related to his art; that he wished to have his objects embodied as it were, and distinctly before him; that he neglected nothing which could keep his faculties in exercise, and derived hints from every sort of combination.

We must not forget whilst we are on this subject, to make some remarks on his custom of painting by night, which confirms what I have already mentioned, his great affection to his art; since he could not amuse himself in the evenings by any other means so agreeable to himself. I am indeed much inclined to believe that it is a practice very advantageous and improving to an artist for by this means he will acquire a new and a higher perception of what is great and beautiful in Nature. By candlelight, not only objects appear more beautiful, but from their being, in a greater breadth of light and shadow, as well as having a greater breadth and uniformity of colour, nature appears in a higher style; and even the flesh seems to take a higher and richer tone of colour. Judgment is to direct us in the use to be made of this method of study; but the method itself is, I am very sure, advantageous. I have often imagined that the two great colourists, Titian [c.1490–1576] and Correggio [c.1494–1534], though I do not know that they painted by night, formed their high ideas of colouring from the effects of objects by this artificial light: but I am more assured, that whoever attentively studies the first and best manner of Guercino [1591–1666], will be convinced that he either painted by this light, or formed his manner on this conception.

Another practice Gainsborough had, which is worth mentioning as it is certainly worthy of imitation; I mean his manner of forming all the parts of his picture together; the whole going on at the same time, in the same manner as nature creates her works. Though this method is not uncommon to those who have been regularly educated, yet probably it was suggested to him by his own natural sagacity. [...]

When such a man as Gainsborough arrives to great fame, without the assistance of an academical education, without travelling to Italy, or any of those preparatory studies which have been so often recommended, he is produced as an instance, how little such studies are necessary; since so great excellence may be acquired without them. This is an inference not warranted by the success of any individual; and I trust it will not be thought that I wish to make this use of it.

It must be remembered that the style and department of art which Gainsborough chose, and in which he so much excelled, did not require that he should go out of his own country for the objects of his study; they were everywhere about him; he found them in the streets, and in the fields; and from the models thus accidentally found, he selected with great judgment such as suited his purpose. As his studies were directed to the living world principally, he did not pay a general attention to the works of the various masters, though they are, in my opinion, always of great use, even when the character of our subject requires us to depart from some of their principles. It cannot be denied, that excellence in the department of the art which he professed may exist without them; that in such subjects, and in the manner that belongs to them, the want of them is supplied, and more than supplied, by natural sagacity, and a minute observation of particular nature. If Gainsborough did not look at nature with a poet's eye, it must be acknowledged that he saw her with the eye of a painter; and gave a faithful, if not a poetical, representation of what he had before him. [...]

Whether he most excelled in portraits, landskips, or fancy-pictures, it is difficult to determine: whether his portraits were most admirable for exact truth of resemblance, or his landskips for a portrait-like representation of nature, such as we see in the works of Rubens [1577–1640], Rysdale [Ruysdael, c.1602–70], and others of those Schools. In his fancy-pictures, when he had fixed on his object of imitation, whether it was the mean and vulgar form of a wood-cutter, or a child of an interesting character, as he did not attempt to raise the one, so neither did he lose any of the natural grace and elegance of the other; such a grace, and such an elegance, as are more frequently found in cottages than in courts. This excellence was his own, the result of his particular observation and taste; for this he was certainly not indebted to the Flemish School, nor indeed to any School; for his grace was not academical, or antique, but selected by himself from the great school of nature; and there are yet a thousand modes of grace, which are neither theirs, nor his, but lie open in the multiplied scenes and figures of life, to be brought out by skilful and faithful observers.

Upon the whole, we may justly say, that whatever he attempted he carried to a high degree of excellence. It is to the credit of his good sense and judgment that he never did attempt that style of historical painting, for which his previous studies had made no preparation.

And here it naturally occurs to oppose the sensible conduct of Gainsborough in this respect, to that of our late excellent Hogarth [1697–1764], who, with all his extraordinary talents, was not blessed with this knowledge of his own deficiency; or of the bounds which were set to the extent of his own powers. After this admirable artist had spent the greater part of his life in an active, busy, and we may add, successful attention to the ridicule of life; after he had invented a new species of dramatic painting, in which probably he will never be equalled, and had stored his mind with infinite materials to explain and illustrate the domestic and familiar scenes of common life, which were generally, and ought to have been always, the subject of his pencil; he very imprudently, or rather presumptuously, attempted the great historical style, for which his previous habits had by no means prepared him: he was indeed so entirely unacquainted with the principles of this style, that he was not even aware, that any artificial preparation was at all necessary. It is to be regretted, that any part of the life of such a genius should be fruitlessly employed. Let his failure teach us not to indulge ourselves in the vain imagination, that by a momentary resolution we can give either dexterity to the hand, or a new habit to the mind.

I have, however, little doubt, but that the same sagacity which enabled those two extraordinary men to discover their true object, and the peculiar excellence of that branch of art which they cultivated, would have been equally effectual in discovering the principles of the higher style; if they had investigated those principles with the same eager industry, which they exerted in their own department. As Gainsborough never attempted the heroic style, so neither did he destroy the character and uniformity of his own style, by the idle affectation of introducing mythological learning in any of his pictures. [...]

To return to Gainsborough; the peculiarity of his manner, or style, or we may call it the language in which he expressed his ideas, has been considered by many, as his greatest defect. But without altogether wishing to enter into the discussion, whether this peculiarity was a defect or not, intermixed, as it was, with great beauties, of some of which it was probably the cause, becomes a proper subject of criticism and enquiry to a painter.

A novelty and peculiarity of manner, as it is often a cause of our approbation, so likewise it is often a ground of censure; as being contrary to the practice of other painters, in whose manner we have been initiated, and in whose favour we have perhaps been prepossessed from our infancy; for, fond as we are of novelty, we are upon the whole creatures of habit. However, it is certain, that all those odd scratches and marks, which, on a close examination, are so observable in Gainsborough's pictures, and which even to experienced painters appear rather the effect of accident than design; this chaos, this uncouth and shapeless appearance, by a kind of magic, at a certain distance assumes form, and all the parts seem to drop into their proper places; so that we can hardly refuse acknowledging the full effect of diligence, under the appearance of chance and hasty negligence. That Gainsborough himself considered this peculiarity in his manner and the power it possesses of exciting surprise, as a beauty in his works, I think may be inferred from the eager desire which we know he always expressed, that his pictures, at the Exhibition, should be seen near, as well as at a distance.

The slightness which we see in his best works, cannot always be imputed to negligence. However they may appear to superficial observers, painters know very well that a steady attention to the general effect, takes up more time, and is much more laborious to the mind, than any mode of high finishing or smoothness, without such attention. His *handling, the manner of leaving the colours*, or in other words, the methods he used for producing the effect, had very much the appearance of the work of an artist who had never learned from others the usual and regular practice belonging to the art; but still, like a man of strong intuitive perception of what was required, he found out a way of his own to accomplish his purpose.

It is no disgrace to the genius of Gainsborough, to compare him to such men as we sometimes meet with, whose natural eloquence appears even in speaking a language, which they can scarce be said to understand; and who, without knowing the appropriate expression of almost any one idea, contrive to communicate the lively and forcible impressions of an energetic mind.

I think some apology may reasonably be made for his manner, without violating truth, or running any risk of poisoning the minds of the younger students, by propagating false criticism, for the sake of raising the character of a favourite artist. It must be allowed, that this hatching manner of Gainsborough did very much contribute to the lightness of effect which is so eminent a beauty in his pictures; as on the contrary, much smoothness, and uniting the colours, is apt to produce heaviness. Every artist must have remarked, how often that lightness of hand which was in his dead-colour, or first painting, escaped in the finishing, when he had determined the parts with more precision; and another loss he often experiences, which is of greater consequence; whilst he is employed in the detail, the effect of the whole together is either forgotten or neglected. The likeness of a portrait, as I have formerly observed, consists more in preserving the general effect of the countenance, than in the most minute finishing of the features, or any of the particular parts. Now Gainsborough's portraits were often little more, in regard to finishing, or determining the form of the features, than what generally attends a dead colour; but as he was always attentive to the general effect, or whole together, I have often imagined that this unfinished manner contributed even to that striking resemblance for which his portraits are so remarkable.

To conclude. However, we may apologize for the deficiencies of Gainsborough (I mean particularly his want of precision and finishing) who so ingeniously contrived to cover his defects by his beauties; and who cultivated that department of art, where such defects are more easily excused. You are to remember, that no apology can be made for this deficiency, in that style which this academy teaches, and which ought to be the object of your pursuit. It will be necessary for you, in the first place, never to lose sight of the great rules and principles of the art, as they are collected from the full body of the best general practice, and the most constant and uniform experience; this must be the ground-work of all your studies: afterwards you may profit, as in this case I wish you to profit, by the peculiar experience and personal talents of artists living and dead; you may derive lights, and catch hints from their practice; but the moment you turn them into models, you fall infinitely below them; you may be corrupted by excellencies, not so much belonging to the art as personal and appropriated to the artist; and become bad copies of good painters, instead of excellent imitators of the great universal truth of things.

(*Discourse XIV*, 10 December 1788)

## JOSEPH WRIGHT

Joseph Wright (1734–97) was born in Derby, the son of a lawyer. After an apprenticeship in London, he became a successful portrait painter in the Midlands. There he became good friends with many members of a new philosophical and scientific association, the Lunar Society, including scientists such as Erasmus Darwin and entrepreneurs such as Josiah Wedgwood. In 1773 he travelled to Italy to develop his understanding of Classical and Renaissance art, and in 1775 he moved to Bath for two years in the hope of gaining commissions following Gainsborough's recent departure for London. Living in Derby from 1783 until his death, his paintings included some portraits of industrialists such as Richard Arkwright and his cotton mills, as well as more classically and romantically inspired works.

*Figure 10.10* J. Wright, *An Experiment on a Bird in an Air Pump* (oil on canvas, 183 × 244 cm, 1768)

*Source*: Photo, National Gallery, London.

*Note*: Wright portrays a small group of people gathered together to observe the drama of a well-known scientific experiment. A natural philosopher prepares to lift the lid of a large glass bowl containing a bird (maybe a dove, representing the Holy Ghost) that has been temporarily deprived of air by a vacuum pump, in the expectation that the bird will be revived. In the high-art tradition of 'candlelight' painting, the contrast of light and shadow draws attention to the thoughts and feelings of those present. A boy draws a curtain at the window through which a full moon casts its light. This large, highly polished and uncommissioned work was painted for public exhibition at the Society of Artists in 1768, and sold for £200. In seeming to raise many questions about the relationship of art, nature, science, ethics and education, as well as the phenomenon of light, the painting has been widely used to represent modern ideas of the Enlightenment.

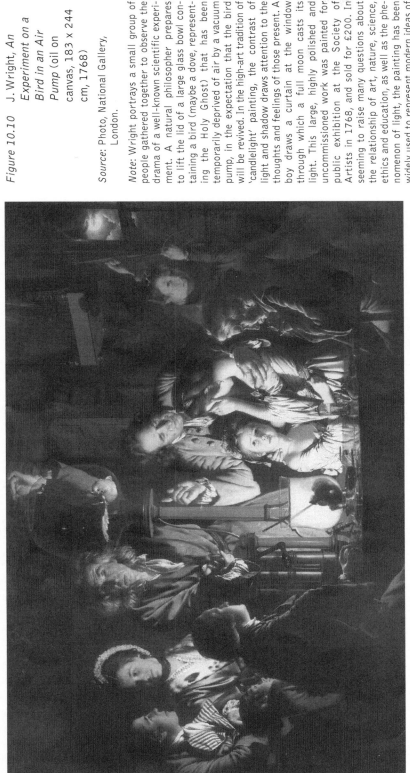

# Chapter 11

# Europeans and the wider world

**T**HE CULTURAL ENCOUNTERS between Europeans and non-Europeans in the eighteenth century were, in many respects, vital to the defining (and later to the undermining) of what it meant to be Enlightened. For it was often through these encounters, both real and imagined, that key questions about human nature, society and history; the classification and exploitation of nature; and many of the moral and practical problems of the modern world were shaped.

At the beginning of the century, the Spanish, French, British, Dutch and Portuguese had already established some trading posts, settlements and colonies across the continents. These served a great variety of purposes and, throughout the century, old colonies would grow (some to acquire independence, as in North America), new ones would be formed (as in Bengal under the East India Company), many more trading posts would be established (such as the slaving stations on the coast of West Africa), and new lands and peoples would be 'discovered' (particularly in the Pacific). Many of these overseas 'possessions' would also change hands in accordance with the shifting fortunes of the European powers. From a distance, a great range of eighteenth-century events and developments, such as the South Sea Bubble of 1720, the publication of an English translation of the Koran in 1734, the opening of the British Museum in 1759, the rise of Orientalism, the founding of a penal colony at Botany Bay in 1788, the massive increase in consumption of overseas products such as tea, cotton and tobacco, Napoleon's conquest of Egypt in 1798, and the Louisiana Purchase in 1803 can be seen as tiny fragments of what would later become an epic story of growing European engagement with, dependence upon, and exploitation of the peoples and resources of the wider world.

This new engagement can be traced in many ways, as in the growing appetite for contemporary accounts and histories of other peoples – a new kind of travel literature and history, often of highly variable accuracy, but written in more secular (though no less moral) terms for eighteenth-century readers. Thus, in addition to the fascinating observations and reflections of travellers such as Lady Mary Wortley Montagu, based upon her stay in Turkey, and the historical works of writers like Voltaire and Hume, the century witnessed the publication of hundreds of 'overseas' histories, such as those on Virginia (Beverly, 1705), the Saracens (Ockley, 1708–18), and Dahomey (Norris, 1789), to name a few. Among 'Enlightened' histories, one of the most important on the wider world was Raynal's *Philosophical and Political History of the Settlements*, first published in six volumes in 1772. Though ranging freely across the continents to reflect upon a large array of subjects, it was, of course, the Europeans who provided the common thread, and in many respects the ever-present anti-heroes of the text.

This tremendous thirst for knowledge and stories about foreign lands and people was fuelled by many factors, not least, commercial and strategic interests. But for those *philosophes* who were grounded in empiricism, learning about the geography, history, flora and fauna of the world, as well as other cultures, was both an intellectual necessity and a moral responsibility. Furthermore, as their confidence in an absolute, universal and eternal measure of what was true and reasonable (based upon Classical authority and Christian teachings) generally receded, it seemed that worldly knowledge often depended upon no more than human experience, itself contingent upon time and place – though the relativist implications of this were generally resisted. To see things from a non-European point of view was thus to gain a vital insight, to call upon an external 'other' witness for evidence and opinion. And, naturally, the *philosophes* could not always resist the temptation of rigging the testimony of the witnesses that they cited and invented, usually to serve Enlightened purposes by criticising the traditional beliefs and practices of most Europeans. Montesquieu's *Persian Letters* (1721) and Diderot's *Supplement to the Voyage of Bougainville* (1796) are famous examples of how fictitious 'foreigners' were brilliantly used to question European conventions. But 'foreign' figures and societies would regularly appear in almost every kind of Enlightened work, popping up whenever needed to voice or validate a *philosophe*'s opinions. What at first sight might seem strange and inexplicable, such as the customs of many non-Europeans, could, with a little Enlightened thinking, be rendered something altogether more revealing.

In order to understand the wider world, and to represent it to fellow Europeans, the travellers and scholars of the period needed to invent as much as they discovered. For everything (fossils, plants, animals and peoples) needed to be defined, described and catalogued in order to be put in its proper place within the new tree of knowledge that was to be constructed. Specimens had to be selected, collected and transported, including natives such as the Polynesians Auturu and Omai, whom Bougainville and Cook brought home to Paris and London. Later, many of the societies and nations of the world would find themselves redefined and 'mapped out' (culturally and geographically) by Europeans. But in the eighteenth century, even basic geographical knowledge of the continents, especially *Terra Australis* (southern land) was still very much 'under construction'. Thus aside from limited knowledge of ancient cultures such as those of China and Japan, until Cook's voyages in the 1770s, it was still believed that there was a great southern continent, rich in resources and opportunities, waiting to be discovered. Due to the work of explorers such as Bougainville and Cook, by the turn of the century the shape of the world's coastlines and many 'new' societies had been uncovered, but vast tracts of land, notably the interiors of Africa and Asia, had hardly been examined. So it seemed that when explorers such as William Dampier published highly popular accounts of their travels and adventures, as in his *New Voyage round the World* (1697), the extraordinary evidence presented (whether 'true' or 'false') would usually raise more questions than were answered.

Distinguishing between discovery and invention, material facts and verbal fictions about the wider world was never easy, for anybody. Even in the most 'authentic' chronicles of journeys and discoveries, such as those of Mary Wortley Montagu or James Cook and his colleagues, audiences had to be considered, as Cook found out when the account of his first circumnavigation of the word was 'improved' for publication. Moreover, the fact that large parts of the world remained unknown provided rich material for creative writing. Thus in one of the first great novels, *The Life and Strange Surprising Adventures of Robinson Crusoe* (1719), ostensibly 'Written by Himself' and set at the mouth of the Orinoco, Daniel Defoe freely adapted the 'true story' of the years that one Alexander Selkirk had spent on a desert island, to create a seemingly realistic account of Crusoe's heroic exploitation of nature, sale of a black slave Xury, and subjugation of the 'native' Man Friday. Shortly afterwards, Jonathan Swift published a famous satire on human nature, modern science and society, spoofing the pretence of descriptive realism in such writings. In his *Travels into Several Remote Nations of the World* (1726), the fictitious narrator Lemuel Gulliver prefers to relate 'plain matters of fact' about his experiences of giants, flying islands and horses governing humans, rather than entertain the reader with 'strange improbable tales'. At the end, in a stunning indictment of war and colonialism, Gulliver even answers the criticism that he had failed Britain by refusing to lay claim to the lands that he had visited. But, by then, the 'gentle reader' knows that this traveller who has lost his faith in humanity is now quite insane.

Throughout the century, all kind of literary works would be given foreign settings, but it was especially appropriate that *Gulliver's Travels*, which both stretched most readers' credulity and spawned dozens of science-fiction sequels, should have been partly 'set' in the South Seas. For it was here in the Pacific, most notably at Tahiti, that Europeans made perhaps their most important and fascinating discoveries about the wider world. According to Bougainville and others, Tahiti was an earthly paradise, populated by a friendly, cheerful, peaceful, free and sensual people. Yet, the mark of that society's very first encounter with the West would be the contraction of venereal disease. Though Cook tried hard to correct some of the more utopian impressions of the island that Bougainville had given, and found the Tongan islands rather more enchanting, a great torrent of romantic, exotic and erotic fantasies had been unleashed. Many questions would be asked about the Polynesians, and the dilemmas raised by the 'discovery' of them went to the heart of Enlightenment thinking. Cook and others were keen to protect the islanders from exploitation, but the material and political interests of Europeans went generally unchecked. Moreover, following the foundation of the London Missionary Society in 1795, missionaries were sent. Noting the 'complete change effected in the manners of the [Tahitian] people, from gross sensuality to the greatest decency and good behaviour', in 1821 two inspectors for the Society recorded their 'great satisfaction' at 'the progress which civilization has made in islands so lately in the depths of barbarism and the grossest superstition'.

## MARY WORTLEY MONTAGU

Lady Mary (1689–1762) was born in London, the eldest child of Lady Mary Fielding and Evelyn Pierrepont (later Duke of Kingston). Her mother died when she was four, so Mary was largely raised by a grandmother and educated by a governess, though she taught herself Latin. After a troubled courtship, in 1712 she eloped with Edward Wortley MP, and had a son by him in the following year. When her husband was appointed ambassador to Turkey in 1716, Lady Mary and her son accompanied him to Constantinople (Istanbul) where she wrote what would later become known as her *Embassy Letters*. After the birth of a daughter in 1718 she returned to London with her husband. In the aristocratic and literary circles in which she moved, Lady Mary became renowned for her wit and learning. She met Voltaire, became friends with John Gay and Alexander Pope (who was infatuated by her, until she probably rebuffed him), and was patron to the poet Edward Young and her cousin Henry Fielding. In 1736 she became passionate about the fashionable young bisexual Italian poet Francesco Algarotti, and planned to live with him on the continent. After leaving England in 1739, she spent most of the next twenty years in Italy, estranged from her husband, but writing home to her family and friends, while Algarotti travelled and later became Frederick the Great's lover. When her husband died in 1761, she returned to England where she died in 1762.

Although she wrote essays, poems, letters (including one on husbands, for Steele's *Spectator*) and criticism, due in part to her sense of her social position Montagu was reluctant to publish under her own name during her lifetime. She told her daughter (Lady Bute): 'I write only for myself'. Even so, she ensured that her *Embassy Letters* would be published in London shortly after her death. They appeared in 1763 as a three-volume collection of fifty-two *Letters of the Right Honourable Lady M—y W—y M—e: Written during her Travels in Europe, Asia and Africa, to Persons of Distinction, Men of Letters, &c., in different Parts of Europe. Which Contain, among other Curious Relations, Accounts of the Policy and Manners of the Turks; Drawn from Sources that have been inaccessible to other Travellers.* The letters were based upon two small albums (loaned to Mary Astell in 1724) of copies and adaptations of actual letters sent to various friends while Montagu was living in Istanbul, or travelling there and back. Instead of portraying the Turks according to Western European stereotypes and scholarship as a brutal and boorish people, living in terror under despotism and a false religion,

Montagu formed her own opinions and crafted them into a literary work that made a great impression upon most contemporaries, not least on Gibbon and Voltaire. On her return to England in 1718, she had contributed to the advancement of medicine by bringing back the Turkish practice of inoculating for smallpox (which she had contracted in 1715, leaving her face pitted with scars), and demonstrating its efficacy on her children. Now, after her death, she was hailed as one of the great letter writers of the century. In the following letter from her *Embassy Letters*, she reflects upon a range of Turkish and Armenian customs.

## Embassy Letters (1763)

### To the Countess of — [May 1718]

I am now preparing to leave Constantinople, and perhaps you will accuse me of hypocrisy, when I tell you, 'tis with regret; but as I am used to the air, and have learnt the language, I am easy here; and as much as I love travelling, I tremble at the inconveniences attending so great a journey, with a numerous family, and a little infant hanging at the breast. However, I endeavour, upon this occasion, to do as I have hitherto done in all the odd turns of my life; turn them, if I can to my diversion. In order to do this, I ramble every day, wrapped up in my ferige [ferace: overmantle] and asmack [yashmak], about Constantinople, and amuse myself with seeing all that is curious in it. I know you will expect that this declaration should be followed with some account of what I have seen. But I am in no humour to copy what has been writ so often over. To what purpose should I tell you, that Constantinople is the ancient Byzantium; that 'tis at present the conquest of a race of people, supposed Scythians; that there are five or six thousand mosques in it; that Sancta Sophia was founded by Justinian [Emperor of Constantinople, 527–65], I'll assure 'tis not for want of learning, that I forbear writing all these bright things. I could also, with very little trouble, turn over [Richard] Knolles [1550?–1610] and Sir Paul Rycaut [1628–1700], to give you a list of Turkish emperors; but I will not tell you what you may find in every author that has writ of this country. I am more inclined, out of a true female spirit of contradiction, to tell you the falsehood of a great part of what you find in authors; as for instance, in the admirable Mr [Aaron] Hill, who so gravely asserts [in *Present State of the Ottoman Empire* (1709)], that he saw in Sancta Sophia, a sweating pillar, very balsamic for disordered heads. There is not the least tradition of any such matter; and I suppose it was revealed to him in vision, during his wonderful stay in the Egyptian catacombs; for I am sure he never heard of any such miracle here. 'Tis also very pleasant to observe how tenderly he and all his brethren voyage-writers lament the miserable confinement of the Turkish ladies, who are perhaps more free than any ladies in the universe, and are the only women in the world that lead a life of uninterrupted pleasure, exempt from cares, their whole time being spent in visiting, bathing, or the agreeable amusement of spending money and inventing new fashions. A husband would be thought mad that exacted any degree of economy from his wife, whose expenses are no way limited but by her own fancy. 'Tis his business to get money, and her's to spend it; and this noble prerogative extends itself to the very meanest of the sex. Here is a fellow that carries embroidered handkerchiefs upon his back to sell. And as miserable a figure as you may suppose such a mean dealer; yet I'll assure you his wife scorns to wear anything less than cloth of gold; has her ermine furs and a very handsome set of jewels for her head. 'Tis true, they have no places but the bagnios, and these can only be seen by their own sex; however, that is a diversion they take great pleasure in.

I was, three days ago, at one of the finest in the town, and had the opportunity of seeing a Turkish bride received there, and all the ceremony used on that occasion, which made me recollect the Epithalamium [wedding-song] of Helen, by Theocritus [c.310–250 BC]; and it seems to me, that the same customs have continued ever since. All the she friends, relations and acquaintance of the two families, newly allied, meet at the bagnio; several others go, out of curiosity, and I believe there were that day two hundred women. Those that were, or had been married, placed themselves round the rooms on the marble sofas; but the virgins very hastily threw off their clothes, and appeared without other ornament or covering, than their own long hair braided with pearl or ribbon. Two of them met the bride at the door, conducted by her mother and another grave relation. She was a beautiful maid of about seventeen, very richly dressed, and shining with jewels, but was presently reduced to the state of nature. Two others filled silver gilt pots with perfume, and began the procession, the rest following in pairs, to the number of thirty. The leaders sung an epithalamium, answered by the others in chorus, and the two last led the fair bride, her eyes fixed on the ground, with a charming affectation of modesty. In this order they marched round the three large rooms of the bagnio. 'Tis not easy to represent to you the beauty of this sight, most of them being well proportioned and white skinned; all of them perfectly smooth, and polished by the frequent use of bathing. After having made their tour, the bride was again led to every matron round the rooms, who saluted her with a compliment and a present, some of jewels, others of pieces of stuff [cloth], handkerchiefs, or little gallantries of that nature, which she thanked them for, by kissing their hands. I was very well pleased with having seen this ceremony; and you may believe me, that the Turkish ladies have, at least, as much wit and civility, nay liberty, as among us. 'Tis true, the same customs that give them so many opportunities of gratifying their evil inclinations (if they have any) also put it very fully in the power of their husbands to revenge themselves, if they are discovered; and I do not doubt but they suffer sometimes for their indiscretions in a very severe manner. About two months ago, there was found at daybreak, not very far from my house, the bleeding body of a young woman, naked, only wrapped in a coarse sheet, with two wounds of a knife, one in her side, and another in her breast. She was not quite cold, and was so surprisingly beautiful, that there were very few men in Pera [now Beyoglu, part of Istanbul] that did not go to look upon her; but it was not possible for anybody to know her, no woman's face being known. She was supposed to have been brought, in the dead of night, from the Constantinople side, and laid there. Very little enquiry was made about the murderer, and the corpse was privately buried without noise. Murder is never pursued by the King's officers, as with us. 'Tis the business of the next relations to revenge the dead person; and if they like better to compound that matter for money (as they generally do) there is no more said of it. One would imagine this defect in their government should make such tragedies very frequent, yet they are extremely rare; which is enough to prove the people not naturally cruel. Neither do

I think in many other particulars, they deserve the barbarous character we give them. I am well acquainted with a Christian woman of quality, who made it her choice to live with a Turkish husband, and is a very agreeable sensible lady. Her story is so extraordinary, I cannot forbear relating it; but I promise you it shall be in as few words as I can possibly express it.

She is a Spaniard, and was at Naples with her family, when that kingdom was part of the Spanish dominion. Coming from thence in a felucca, accompanied by her brother, they were attacked by the Turkish admiral, boarded and taken — and now how shall I modestly tell you the rest of her adventure? The same accident [rape] happened to her, that happened to the fair Lucretia [daughter of the poet Lucretius, c.99–55 BC] so many years before her. But she was too good a Christian to kill herself, as that heathenish Roman did. The Admiral was so much charmed with the beauty, and long-suffering of the fair captive, that, as his first compliment, he gave immediately liberty to her brother and attendants, who made haste to Spain, and in a few months sent the sum of four thousand pounds sterling, as a ransom for his sister. The Turk took the money, which he presented to her, and told her she was at liberty. But the lady very discreetly weighed the different treatment she was likely to find in her native country. Her relations (as the kindest thing they could do for her in her present circumstances) would certainly confine her to a nunnery for the rest of her days. Her infidel lover was very handsome, very tender, very fond of her, and lavished at her feet all the Turkish magnificence. She answered him very resolutely, that her liberty was not so precious to her as her honour, that he could no way restore that but by marrying her, and she therefore desired him to accept the ransom as her portion, and give her the satisfaction of knowing that no man could boast of her favours without being her husband. The admiral was transported at this kind offer, and sent back the money to her relations, saying he was too happy in her possession. He married her, and never took any other wife, and (as she says herself) she never had reason to repent the choice she made. He left her some years after, one of the richest widows in Constantinople. But there is no remaining honourably a single woman, and that consideration has obliged her to marry the present Capitan Bassa (i.e. Admiral) his successor. I am afraid that you will think my friend fell in love with her ravisher; but I am willing to take her word for it, that she acted wholly on principles of honour, though I think she might be reasonably touched at his generosity, which is often found amongst the Turks of rank.

'Tis a degree of generosity to tell the truth, and 'tis very rare that any Turk will assert a solemn falsehood. I don't speak of the lowest sort; for as there is a great deal of ignorance, there is very little virtue amongst them; and false witnesses are much cheaper than in Christendom, those wretches not being punished (even when they are publicly detected) with the rigour they ought to be.

Now I am speaking of their law, I don't know whether I have ever mentioned to you one custom peculiar to their country, I mean adoption, very common amongst the Turks, and yet more amongst the Greeks and Armenians. Not having it in their power to give their estates to a friend or distant relation, to avoid its falling into the Grand Signior's treasury, when they are not likely to have any children of their own, they choose some pretty child of either sex, amongst the meanest people, and carry the child and its parents before the Cadi, and there declare they receive it for their heir. The parents, at the same time, renounce all future claim to it; a writing is drawn and witnessed, and a child thus adopted cannot be disinherited. Yet I have seen some common beggars, that have refused to part with their children in this manner, to some of the richest among the Greeks (so powerful is the instinctive affection that is natural to parents!), though the adopting fathers are generally very tender to these children of their souls, as they call them. I own this custom pleases me much better than our absurd one of following our name. Methinks, 'tis much more reasonable to make happy and rich, an infant whom I educate after my own manners brought up (in the Turkish phrase) upon my knees, and who has learnt to look upon me with a filial respect, than to give an estate to a creature without other merit or relation to me than that of a few letters. Yet this is an absurdity we see frequently practised.

Now I have mentioned the Armenians, perhaps it will be agreeable to tell you something of that nation, with which I am sure you are utterly unacquainted. I will not trouble you with the geographical account of the situation of their country, which you may see in the maps; or a relation of their ancient greatness, which you may read in the Roman history. They are now subject to the Turks; and, being very industrious in trade, and increasing and multiplying, are dispersed in great numbers through all the Turkish dominions. They were, as they say, converted to the Christian religion by St Gregory, and are perhaps the devoutest Christians in the whole world. The chief precepts of their priests enjoin the strict keeping of their Lents, which are, at least, seven months in every year, and are not to be dispensed with on the most emergent necessity; no occasion whatever can excuse them if they touch anything more than mere herbs or roots (without oil) and plain dry bread. That is their constant diet. Mr W[ortle]y has one of his interpreters of this nation, and the poor fellow was brought so low by the severity of his fasts, that his life was despaired of. Yet neither his master's commands, nor the doctor's entreaties (who declared nothing else could save his life) were powerful enough to prevail with him to take two or three spoonfuls of broth. Excepting this, which may rather be called a custom, than an article of faith, I see very little in their religion different from ours. 'Tis true, they seem to incline very much to Mr [William] Whiston's [1667–1752] doctrine [Arianism]; neither do I think the Greek church very distant from it, since 'tis certain, the Holy Spirit's proceeding only from the Father, is making a plain subordination in the Son. But the Armenians have no notion of transubstantiation, whatever account Sir Paul Rycaut gives of them (which account [*Present State of the Greek and Armenian Churches*] I am apt to believe was designed to compliment our court [Charles II's] in 1679) and they have a great horror for those amongst them that change to the Roman religion. What is most extraordinary in their customs, is their matrimony; a ceremony, I believe, unparalleled all over the world. They are always promised very young; but the espoused never see one another, till three days after their marriage. The bride is carried to church with a cap on her head, in the fashion of a large trencher, and over it a red silken veil, which covers her all over to her feet. The priest asks the bridegroom whether he is contented to marry that woman, be she deaf, be she blind? These are the literal words; to which having answered yes; she is led home to his house, accompanied with all the friends and relations on both sides, singing and dancing, and is placed on a cushion in the corner of the sofa; but her veil is not lifted up, not even by her husband. There is something so odd and monstrous in these ways, that I could not believe them till I had enquired of several Armenians myself, who all assured me of the truth of them, particularly one young fellow who wept when he spoke of it, being promised by his mother to a girl that he must marry in this manner, though he protested to me, he had rather die than submit to this slavery, having already figured his bride to himself, with all the deformities in nature. I fancy I see you bless yourself at this terrible relation. I cannot conclude my letter with a more surprising story, yet 'tis as seriously true, as that I am,

Dear sister, Yours, &c. &c,

*(Embassy Letters)*

## ABBÉ RAYNAL

Guillaume Thomas Raynal (1713–96) was born in southern France where he attended a Jesuit college at Rodez before becoming a teacher and a priest. In 1746 he moved to Paris, working as a journalist, attending salons and meeting *philosophes* such as Montesquieu and d'Holbach. With the assistance of other *philosophes*, in 1770 he published a six-volume *Histoire Philosophique et Politique des Établissements et du Commerce des Européens dans les Deux Indes* (*Philosophical and Political History of the Settlements and Trade of the Europeans in the Two* [East and West] *Indies*). The work was an immediate success and, though placed on the Index in 1774, it was reproduced in numerous French and English editions throughout Raynal's life. The reaction of 'Enlightened' monarchs was also telling. In 1773, Joseph II of Austria banned the text from bookshops and catalogues but permitted foreigners and natives to bring it 'quietly' through customs. In the same year, Catherine II wrote to Voltaire that not only was the book preventing her from reading Helvétius' posthumous and materialist *De l'Homme* (1773) – which had been dedicated to her – but that it was also giving her 'a great aversion to the conquerors of the New World'. By 1780 the text had been considerably enlarged and politically radicalised by anonymous contributions from Denis Diderot, and in the following year the *parlement* of Paris issued an order to ban the work and exile its famous author. Raynal fled to Prussia and Switzerland before returning to the South of France in 1784, and then to Paris after the outbreak of the Revolution.

The *History of the Settlements* provides both a great compendium of information about the nature, pattern and impact of European trade and colonialism, and extensive critical reflections upon the character, practices and beliefs of various peoples and nations throughout the world. Its purposes were multiple: not least to extend Europeans' knowledge of the wider world, to promote fair trade and commerce, and to call European nations to account for the destructive nature of many of their policies, most notably the slave trade. Inevitably, the text is Eurocentric, mixing a great range of historical, geographical, social and economic facts and fictions in its rhetorical descriptions of the lives of non-Europeans and the portraits of their nations. Yet in many respects the work well expresses Enlightenment values and opinions. Thus, in the last part (book XIX) of the 1780 edition, the author

(Diderot) insists that the work is, like his *Encyclopédie*, written 'in favour of all mankind, without distinction of sect or country'. He also expresses the hope that 'Under the auspices of philosophy, may there be one day extended, from one extremity of the world to the other, that chain of union and benevolence which ought to connect civilised people! May they never more carry among savage nations the example of vice and oppression!'

Two extracts from an English translation (1783) of the 1780 edition of the *History of the Settlements* are given here. The first, from book III, 'Settlements, Trade, and Conquests of the English in the East Indies', describes Arabia and 'the character of its inhabitants'. The second, from book VII, 'Conquest of Peru by the Spaniards. Changes that have happened in this Empire since that Revolution', describes the lives of women living in 'a state of nature' on the banks of the Orinoco river, Venezuela. (Two other extracts from *History of the Settlements*, by Diderot, are provided in the chapter on Human Nature.)

## A Philosophical and Political History of the Settlements ([1772], 1780)

### 'Description of Arabia'

All histories agree that this country [Arabia] was peopled at a most early period of antiquity. Its first inhabitants came probably from Syria and Chaldea. It is not known at what period they began to be civilized; whether their knowledge was derived from India, or whether they acquired it themselves. It appears that their religion was Sabeism, even before they were acquainted with the people of Upper Asia. They had conceived sublime ideas of the divinity at an early period; they worshipped the stars as bodies animated by celestial spirits: their religion was neither cruel nor absurd; and though they were liable to those sallies of enthusiasm so common among the southern nations, they do not seem to have been tainted with fanaticism till the time of Mohammed. The inhabitants of Arabia Deserta professed a less rational kind of worship. Many of them worshipped, and some offered human sacrifices to the sun. It is a truth that may be collected from the study of history, and the inspection of the globe, that the religious systems in barren countries, subject to inundations and volcanoes, have ever had a tincture of cruelty, and have always been of a milder cast in countries more favoured by nature. They take their character from the climate where they are formed.

When Mohammed had established a new religion in his country, it was no difficult task to infuse a spirit of zeal into his followers; and this zeal made them conquerors. They extended their dominion from the western seas to those of China, and from the Canaries to the Molucca islands. They also carried along with them the useful arts, which they improved. The Arabians did not equally succeed in the fine arts; they showed, indeed, some genius for them, but had not the least idea of that taste with which nature some time after inspired the people who became their disciples.

Perhaps genius, which is the offspring of a creative imagination, flourishes in hot countries, which abound with a variety of productions, grand scenes, and surprising events that excite enthusiasm; while taste, which selects and reaps the produce of the fields that genius has sown, seems rather to belong to people of a sedate, mild, and moderate disposition, who live under the influence of a temperate sky. Perhaps too, this same taste, which is the effect of reason refined and matured by time, requires a degree of stability in the government, united with a certain freedom of thinking, a gradual improvement of knowledge, which, affording a greater scope to genius, enables it to discern more exactly the relation one object has to another, and to combine with happier art those mixed sensations which give the highest entertainment to men of elegant minds. Accordingly, the Arabians, who were almost constantly forced into regions disturbed with war and fanaticism, never enjoyed that temperature of government and climate which gives birth to taste. But they introduced into the countries they conquered, sciences which they had pillaged, as it were, in the course of their ravages, and all the arts essential to the prosperity of nations.

No nation at that time understood commerce so well, or carried it to a greater extent. They attended to it even in the course of their conquests. Their merchants, manufactures, and staples, extended from Spain to Tonquin; and other people, at least those in the western part of the world, were indebted to them for arts and sciences, and all articles conducive to the convenience, the preservation, and the pleasures of life.

When the power of the Caliphs began to decline, the Arabians, after the example of several nations they had subdued, threw off the yoke of these princes, and the country re-assumed by degrees its ancient form of government, as well as its primitive manners. At this era, the nation being, as formerly, divided into tribes, under the conduct of different chiefs, returned to their original character, from which fanaticism and ambition had made them depart.

The stature of the Arabians is low, their bodies lean, and their voice slender; but they have robust constitutions, brown hair, a swarthy complexion, black sparkling eyes, a witty, but seldom an agreeable, countenance. This contrasted mixture of features and qualities, which seem incompatible, appear to have been united in this race of men, to constitute a singular nation, whose figure and character partake strongly of that of the Turks, Africans, and Persians, by whom they are surrounded. Grave and serious, they consider their long beards as marks of dignity; they speak little, use no gesture, make no pauses, nor interrupt one another in their conversation. They pique themselves on observing the strictest probity towards each other, which is the effect of that self-love, and that spirit of patriotism, which, united together, make any nation, clan, or society, esteem and prefer themselves to the rest of the world. The more carefully they preserve their phlegmatic character, so much the more formidable is their resentment when once it is raised. These people have abilities, and even a genius for the sciences; yet they cultivate them but little, either from want of assistance, or because they have no occasion for them: choosing rather, no doubt, to suffer natural evils, than the inconvenience of labour. The Arabians of our days, display no monument of genius, no productions of industry, which entitle them to hold any rank in the history of the human mind.

Their ruling passion is jealousy; that torment of impetuous, weak, and indolent minds. It might naturally be asked, whether this distrust were owing to the high or contemptible opinion they entertained of themselves? It is said to be from the Arabians that several nations of Asia, Africa, and even Europe itself, have borrowed those despicable precautions this odious passion prescribes against a sex, which ought to be the guardian, not the slave of our pleasures. As soon as a daughter is born, they unite by a kind of suture those parts which nature has separated, leaving just space enough for the natural discharges. As the child grows, the parts by degrees adhere so closely, that when they become marriageable they are obliged to be separated by an incision. Sometimes it is thought sufficient to make use of a ring. The married, as well as the unmarried women, are subjected to this outrage on the virtue of the sex; with this difference only, that the ring worn by the young women cannot be taken off, whereas that of the married women has a kind of padlock, of which the husband keeps the key. This custom, which is known in all parts of Arabia, is almost universally adopted in that part which bears the name of Petræa.

(*History of the Settlements*, Book III, 'Description of Arabia')

### 'Former and Present Condition of the Women on the Banks of the Oroonoko'

Before the arrival of the Europeans, the people who border on this river, but little distant from the burning equator, knew not the use of clothes, nor the restraints of police; neither had they any form of government. Free under the yoke of poverty, they lived chiefly by hunting and fishing, and on wild fruits. But little of their time or labour could be spent on agriculture, where they had nothing but a stick to plough with, and hatchets made of stone to cut down trees; which, after being burned, or rotted, left the soil in a proper state for bearing.

The women lived in a state of oppression on the Oroonoko [Orinoco], as they do in all barbarous regions. The savage, whose wants engage his whole attention, is employed only in providing for his safety and his subsistence. He hath no other allurement to partake of the pleasures of love, than that mere natural instinct which attends to the perpetuity of the species. The intercourse between the two sexes, which is generally casual, would scarce ever be followed by any permanent consequences, if paternal and maternal tenderness did not attach the parents to their offspring. But before the first child can provide for itself, others are born which call for the same care. At length the instant arrives, when this social reason exists no more: but then, the power of long habit, the comfort of feeling ourselves surrounded by a family more or less numerous, the hopes of being assisted in our latter years by our posterity; all these circumstances expel the idea and the wish of a separation. The men are the persons who reap the greatest advantages from this cohabitation. Among people who hold nothing in estimation but strength and courage, tyranny is always exercised over weakness, in return for the protection that is afforded it. The women live in a state of disgrace. Labours, considered as the most abject, are their portion. Men, whose hands are accustomed to the handling of arms, and to the management of the oar, would think themselves degraded, if they employed them in sedentary occupations, or even in the labours of agriculture.

Among a people of shepherds, who having a more certain existence, can bestow rather more attention upon making it agreeable, the women are less wretched. In the ease and leisure which they enjoy, these people can form to themselves an idea of beauty, they can indulge their taste in the object of their affections; and, to the idea of natural pleasure, can add that of a more noble sensation.

The connections between the two sexes are still further improved, as soon as the lands begin to be cultivated. Property, which had no existence among savages, and was of little consequence among a people of shepherds, begins to acquire a degree of importance among people engaged in agriculture. The inequality which soon introduces itself among the fortunes of men, must occasion some in the consideration they hold. The ties of marriage are then no longer formed by chance; but according to conditions in life that are suitable to each other. A man, in order to be accepted, must make himself agreeable; and this necessity brings on attentions to the women, and gives them a degree of dignity.

They receive additional importance from the establishment of the arts and of commerce. Business is then increased, and connections are complicated. Men, who are often obliged, from more extensive affairs, to quit their manufactures and their home, are under the necessity of adding to their talents the vigilance of their wives. As the habit of gallantry, luxury, and dissipation, hath not yet entirely disgusted them of solitary or serious occupations, they devote themselves, without reserve, and with success, to functions with which they think themselves honoured. The retirement which this kind of life requires, renders the practice of all the domestic virtues dear and familiar to them. The influence, the respect, and the attachment of all those that are about them, are the reward of a conduct so estimable.

At length the time comes, when men grow disgusted of labour from the increase of their fortunes. Their principal care is to prevent time from hanging heavy on their hands, to multiply their amusements, and to extend their enjoyments. At this period the women are eagerly sought after; both on account of the amiable qualities they hold from nature, and of those they have received from education. Their connections become more extensive, so that they are no longer suited for a retired life, but required to shine in a more brilliant scene. When introduced upon the stage of the world, they become the soul of every pleasure, and the primum mobile of the most important affairs. Supreme happiness consists in making one's self agreeable to them, and it is the height of ambition to obtain some distinction from them. Then it is, that the freedom which exists between the two sexes in a state of nature is revived, with this remarkable difference, that in polished cities the husband is often less attached to his wife, and the wife to her husband, than in the midst of the forests; that their offspring, trusted, at the instant of their birth, to the hands of mercenaries, are no longer a tie; and that infidelity, which would be attended with no fatal consequences among most savage people, affects domestic tranquillity and happiness amongst civilized nations; where it is one of the principal symptoms of general corruption, and of the extinction of all decent affections.

The tyranny exercised against the women upon the banks of the Oroonoko, still more than in the rest of the New World, must be one of the principal causes of the depopulation of these countries that are so much favoured by nature. Mothers have contracted the custom of destroying the daughters they bring forth, by cutting the umbilical cord so close to the body, that the children die of an haemorrhage. Christianity itself hath not even been able to put a stop to this abominable practice.

(*History of the Settlements*, Book VII, 'Former and Present
Condition of the Women on the Banks of the Oroonoko')

## JAMES COOK

Born in Yorkshire, the son of a farm labourer, James Cook (1729–79) was educated at a village school before being apprenticed to a coal trader at Whitby in 1746. Having gained experience of the Baltic and coastal trades, and learned mathematics and navigation, in 1755 he joined the navy. In 1758 as master of the 'Pembroke' he charted the St Lawrence River in preparation for James Wolfe's expedition to capture Quebec from the French in the following year. A highly regarded seaman and surveyor, in 1763 he was sent to chart the coast of Newfoundland from where, in 1766, he made observations of an eclipse of the sun which were swiftly published by the Royal Society. Keen to have accurate observations from the southern hemisphere of the transit of Venus across the sun (part of an international effort to determine the earth's distance from the sun), in 1768 the Royal Society petitioned George III to send an expedition to the Pacific. A Whitby collier, the 'Endeavour', was purchased and fitted out, and Cook appointed lieutenant in command. He was charged with observing the transit of Venus, from Tahiti ('discovered' by Captain Wallis in 1767), and 'making discoveries in the South Pacific Ocean' where it was believed there would be a great southern continent and unknown lands and people, suitable for new trades and colonies. Setting sail from Plymouth in August 1768, with an astronomer and two botanists on board, Cook landed at Tahiti in April 1769; three months later he left to 'discover' the Society Islands, circumnavigate New Zealand, explore the east coast of New Holland (Australia) and, following the decimation of his crew due to malaria and dysentery, returning home in July 1771.

A year after his return, Cook began his second epic voyage, setting out from Plymouth in July 1772 with the 'Resolution' and the 'Adventurer' (captained by Tobias Furneaux). He was accompanied by the naturalist J.R. Forster and his son; William Hodges, a landscape artist appointed by the Admiralty to make drawings and paintings of the places visited; and the astronomer William Wales, who was to make scientific observations and test a replica of John Harrison's chronometer for determining longitude at sea. From the South Atlantic, Cook sailed east along the ice-edge of the Antarctic to New Zealand, from Tahiti (September 1773) and the Friendly Islands (October 1773) to the Antarctic Circle and back in a broad sweep of many Pacific islands to New Zealand. He then surveyed Tierra del Fuego and crossed the Atlantic before returning to England in July 1775 with the great majority of his men and Omai, a native from Tahiti (who would be fêted in London, and painted in Classical dress by Joshua Reynolds).

Though Cook had put an end to 'the searching after a southern continent' and made many vital discoveries, in July 1776 he set out again in the 'Resolution' with a view to finding a short route for trade with China via a 'northwest passage' from Alaska across the north of Canada. On his way to Alaska he returned Omai to Tahiti, discovered Hawaii in 1778 and, after charting the North American coast, returned to Hawaii where he was killed during a scuffle with natives in 1779.

Accounts of each of Cook's voyages, based upon his journals, were published soon after their completion, and they became best-sellers. The two extracts chosen here are from his account of the second voyage, *A Voyage towards the South Pole, and Round the World*, published in 1777. In preparing the book for the press before setting off on his third major voyage, Cook noted that the work lacked 'the elegance of a fine writer' as it was 'the production of a man, who has not had the advantage of much school education'. Nevertheless, he hoped that, being 'the work of a plain man', 'candour and fidelity will counterbalance the want of ornament'.

In the first extract, written on his return to Tahiti in September 1773, Cook reflects upon some of the customs of the people as reported in Louis Antoine de Bougainville's famous *Voyage around the World* (1771), based on a ten-day visit in 1768. Having questioned whether Captain Wallis' British or Bougainville's French sailors had brought syphilis to the island, Cook considers the Frenchman's claims about human sacrifices and the sexual mores of the inhabitants. In the second extract, Cook summarises his view of the people of the Friendly Islands (Tonga and Eua) after a five-day stay in October 1773. During this time he was shown around the island by Attago/Otago, a Tongan whom he had met on the first day.

## A Voyage towards the South Pole and Round the World (1777)

### 'September 1773'

As I had some reason to believe, that amongst their religious customs [at Tahiti], human sacrifices were sometimes considered as necessary, I went one day to a *Marai* in Matavai, in company with Captain Furneaux; having with us, as I had upon all other occasions, one of my men who spoke their language tolerably well, and several of the natives, one of whom appeared to be an intelligent, sensible man. In the *Marai* was a *Tupapow*, on which lay a corpse and some viands; so that every thing promised success to my inquiries. I began with asking questions relating to the several objects before me, if the plantains, &c. were for the *Eatua*? If they sacrificed to the *Eatua*, hogs, dogs, fowls &c. to all of which he assured in the affirmative. I then asked, if they sacrificed men to the *Eatua*? He answered, *Taata eno*; that is, bad men they did, first *Tiparrahy*, or beating them till they were dead. I then asked him, if good men were put to death in this manner? His answer was, No, only *Taata eno*. I asked him, if any *Earees* were? He said, they had hogs to give to the *Eatua*, and again repeated *Taata eno*. I next asked him, if *Towtows*, that is, servants or slaves, who had no hogs, dogs, or fowls, but yet were good men, if they were sacrificed to the *Eatua*? His answer was, No, only bad men. I asked him several more questions, and all his answers seemed to tend to this one point, that men for certain crimes were condemned to be sacrificed to the gods, provided they had not wherewithal to redeem themselves. This, I think, implies, that, on some occasions, human sacrifices are considered as necessary; particularly when they take such men as have, by the laws of the country, forfeited their lives, and have nothing to redeem them; and such will generally be found among the lower class of people.

The man of whom I made these inquiries, as well as some others, took some pains to explain the whole of this custom to us; but we were not masters enough of their language to understand them. I have since learnt from Omai, that they offer human sacri-

The Island of OTAHEITE bearing S. E. distant one League.

*Figure 11.1* W. Hodges, 'The Island of Otaheite'

*Source*: From Cook's *A Voyage towards the South Pole* (1777).

fices to the Supreme Being. According to his account, what men shall be so sacrificed, depends on the caprice of the high priest, who, when they are assembled on any solemn occasion, retires alone into the house of God, and stays there some time. When he comes out, he informs them, that he has seen and conversed with their great God (the high priest alone having that privilege), and that he has asked for a human sacrifice, and tells them that he has desired such a person, naming a man present, whom most probably the priest has an antipathy against. He is immediately killed, and so falls a victim to the priest's resentment, who, no doubt (if necessary) has address enough to persuade the people that he was a bad man. If I except their funeral ceremonies, all the knowledge that has been obtained of their religion, has been from information; and as their language is but imperfectly understood, even by those who pretend to the greatest knowledge of it, very little on this head is yet known with certainty.

The liquor which they make from the plant called *Ava ava,* is expressed from the root, and not from the leaves, as mentioned in the narrative of my former voyage. The manner of preparing this liquor is as simple as it is disgusting to a European. It is thus: several people take some of the root and chew it till it is soft and pulpy; then they spit it out into a platter or other vessel, every one into the same; when a sufficient quantity is chewed, more or less water is put to it, according as it is to be strong or weak; the juice, thus diluted, is strained through some fibrous stuff like fine shavings; after which it is fit for drinking, and this is always done immediately. It has a pepperish taste, drinks flat, and rather insipid. But though it is intoxicating, I saw only one instance where it had that effect; as they generally drink it with great moderation, and but little at a time. Sometimes they chew this root in their mouths, as Europeans do tobacco, and swallow their spittle; and sometimes I have seen them eat it wholly.

At Ulietea they cultivate great quantities of this plant. At Otaheite [Tahiti] but very little. I believe there are but few islands in this sea, that do not produce more or less of it; and the natives apply it to the same use, as appears by Le Mair's account of Horn island, wherein he speaks of the natives making a liquor from a plant in the same manner as above mentioned.

Great injustice has been done the women of Otaheite, and the Society Isles, by those who have represented them, without exception, as ready to grant the last favour to any man who will come up to their price. But this is by no means the case; the favours of married women, and also the unmarried of the better sort, are as difficult to be obtained here, as in any other country whatever. Neither can the charge be understood indiscriminately of the unmarried of the lower class, for many of these admit of no such familiarities. That there are prostitutes here, as well as in other countries, is very true, perhaps more in proportion, and such were those who came on board the ships to our people, and frequented the post we had on shore. By seeing these mix indiscriminately with those of a different turn, even of the first rank, one is, at first, inclined to think that they are all disposed the same way, and that the only difference is in the price. But the truth is, the woman who becomes a prostitute, does not seem, in their opinion, to have committed a crime of so deep a dye as to exclude her from the esteem and society of the community in general. On the whole, a stranger who visits England might, with equal justice, draw the characters of the women there, from those which he might meet with on board the ships in one of the naval ports, or in the purlieus of Covent-Garden and Drury-Lane. I must, however, allow that they are all completely versed in the art of coquetry, and that very few of them fix any bounds to their conversation. It is, therefore, no wonder that they have obtained the character of libertines.

(*A Voyage*, Book I, ch. 15, 'September 1773')


**'October 1773'**

These islands [the Friendly Isles] were first discovered by Captain Tasman in January 1642–43; and, by him, called Amsterdam and Middleburg. But the former is called by the natives Ton-ga-ta-bu, and the latter Ea-oo-wee. They are situated between the latitude of 21° 29' and 21° 3' South, and between the longitude of 174° 40' and 175° 15' West, deduced from observations made on the spot.

Middleburg, or Eaoowe, which is the southernmost, is about ten leagues in circuit, and of a height sufficient to be seen twelve leagues. The skirts of this isle are mostly taken up in the plantations; the S.W. and N.W. sides especially. The interior parts are but little cultivated, though very fit for cultivation. However, the want of it added greatly to the beauty of the isle; for here are, agreeably dispersed, groves of cocoa-nut and other trees, lawns covered with thick grass, here and there plantations, and paths leading to every part of the island in such beautiful disorder, as greatly enlivens the prospect. […]

The island of Amsterdam or Tongotabu is wholly laid out in plantations, in which are planted some of the richest productions of nature; such as bread-fruit; cocoa-nut trees, plantains, bananoes, shaddocks, yams, and some other roots, sugar-cane, and a fruit like a nectarine, called by them *Fighega*, and at Otaheite *Ahuya*. In short, here are most of the articles which the Society Islands produce, besides some which they have not. Mr. Forster tells me, that he not only found the same plants here, that are at Otaheite and the neighbouring isles, but several others which are not to be met with there. And I probably have added to their stock of vegetables, by leaving with them an assortment of garden seeds, pulse, &c. Bread-fruit here, as well as at all the other isles, was not in season; nor was this the time for roots and shaddocks. We got the latter only at Middleburg.

The produce and cultivation of this isle is the same as at Amsterdam; with this difference, that a part only of the former is cultivated, whereas the whole of the latter is. The lanes or roads necessary for travelling, are laid out in so judicious a manner as to open a free and easy communication from one part of the island to the other. Here are no towns or villages, most of the houses are built in the plantations, with no other order than what conveniency requires; they are neatly constructed, but do not exceed those in the other isles. The materials of which they are built, are the same; and some little variation in the disposition of the framing is all the difference in their construction. The floor is a little raised, and covered with thick strong mats; the same sort of matting serves to inclose them on the windward side, the other being open. They have little areas before the most of them, which are generally planted round with trees, or shrubs of ornament, whose fragrancy perfumes the very air in which they breathe. Their household furniture consists of a few wooden platters, cocoa-nut shells, and some neat wooden pillows shaped like four-footed stools or forms. Their common clothing, with the addition of a mat, serves them for bedding. We got from them two or three earthen vessels, which were all we saw among them. One was in the shape of a bomb-shell, with

*The Landing at* MIDDLEBURGH *one of the* FRIENDLY ISLES.

*Published Feb.ʸ 1.ˢᵗ 1777, by W.ᵐ Strahan, New Street, Shoe Lane, and Tho.ˢ Cadell, in the Strand, London.*

*Figure 11.2*   W. Hodges, 'The Landing at Middleburgh'

*Source: From Cook's* A Voyage towards the South Pole *(1777).*

two holes in it opposite each other; the others were like pipkins, containing about five or six pints, and had been in use on the fire. I am of the opinion they are the manufacture of some other isle; for, if they were of their own, we ought to have seen more of them. Nor am I to suppose they came from Tasman's ships; the time is too long for brittle vessels like these to be preserved.

We saw no other domestic animals amongst them but hogs and fowls. The former are of the same sort as at the other isles in this sea; but the latter are far superior, being as large as any we have in Europe, and their flesh equally good, if not better. We saw no dogs, and believe they have none, as they were exceedingly desirous of those we had on board. My friend Attago was complimented with a dog and a bitch, the one from New Zealand, the other from Ulietea. The name of a dog with them is *kooree* or *gooree*, the same as at New Zealand, which shews that they are not wholly strangers to them. We saw no rats in these isles, nor any other wild quadrupeds except small lizards. The land birds are pigeons, turtle-doves, parrots, parroquets, owls, bald couts with a blue plumage, a variety of small birds, and large bats in abundance. The produce of the sea we know but little of; it is reasonable to suppose that the same sorts of fish are found here as at the other isles. Their fishing instruments are the same; that is, hooks made of mother of pearl, gigs with two, three, or more prongs, and nets made of a very fine thread, with the meshes wrought exactly like ours. But nothing can be a more demonstrative evidence of their ingenuity than the construction and make of their canoes, which, in point of neatness and workmanship, exceed every thing of this kind we saw in this sea. [...]

Their working tools are made of stone, bone, shells, &c. as at the other islands. When we view the work which is performed with these tools, we are struck with admiration at the ingenuity and patience of the workman. Their knowledge of the utility of iron was no more than sufficient to teach them to prefer nails to beads, and such trifles; some, but very few, would exchange a pig for a large nail, or a hatchet. Old jackets, shirts, cloth, and even rags, were in more esteem than the best edge-tool we could give them; consequently they got but few axes from us but what were given as presents. But if we include the nails which were given by the officers and crews of both ships for curiosities, &c. with those given for refreshments, they cannot have got less than five hundred weight, great and small. The only piece of iron we saw among them was a small broad awl, which had been made of a nail.

Both men and women are of a common size with Europeans; and their colour is that of a lightish copper, and more uniformly so than amongst the inhabitants of Otaheite and the Society Isles. Some of our gentlemen were of opinion these were a much handsomer race; others maintained a contrary opinion, of which number I was one. Be this as it may, they have a good shape, and regular features, and are active, brisk, and lively. The women, in particular, are the merriest creatures I ever met with, and will keep chattering by one's side, without the least invitation, or considering whether they are understood, provided one does but seem pleased with them. In general they appeared to be modest; although there was no want of those of a different stamp; and as we had yet some venereal complaints on board, I took all possible care to prevent the disorder being communicated to them. Upon most occasions they shewed a strong propensity to pilfering; in which they were full as expert as the Otaheiteans.

Their hair in general is black, but more especially that of the women. Different colours were found among the men, sometimes on the same head, caused by something they put upon it, which stains it white, red, and blue. Both sexes wear it short; I saw but two exceptions to this custom, and the most of them combed it upwards. Many of the boys had it cut very close, except a single lock on the top of the head, and a small quantity on each side. The men cut or shave their beards quite close, which operation is performed with two shells. They have fine eyes, and in general good teeth, even to an advanced age. The custom of *tattowing* or puncturing the skin prevails. The men are *tattowed* from the middle of the thigh to above the hips. The women have it only on their arms and fingers; and there but very slightly.

The dress of both sexes consists of a piece of cloth, or matting, wrapped round the waist, and hanging down below the knees. From the waist, upwards, they are generally naked; and it seemed to be a custom to anoint these parts every morning. My friend Attago never failed to do it; but whether out of respect to his friend, or from custom, I will not pretend to say; though I rather think from the latter, as he was not singular in the practice.

Their ornaments are amulets, necklaces, and bracelets of bones, shells, and beads of mother of pearl, tortoise-shell, &c. which are worn by both sexes. The women also wear on their fingers neat rings made of tortoise-shell, and pieces in their ears about the size of a small quill; but ear ornaments are not commonly worn, though all have their ears pierced. They have also a curious apron made of the outside fibres of the cocoa-nut shell, and composed of a number of small pieces sewed together in such a manner as to form stars, half-moons, little squares, &c. It is studded with beads of shells, and covered with red feathers, so as to have a pleasing effect. They make the same kind of cloth, and of the same materials, as at Otaheite; though they have not such a variety, nor do they make any so fine; but, as they have a method of glazing it, it is more durable, and will resist rain for some time, which Otaheite cloth will not. Their colours are black, brown, purple, yellow, and red; all made from vegetables. They make various sorts of matting; some of a very fine texture, which is generally used for clothing; and the thick and stronger sort serves to sleep on, and to make sails for their canoes, &c. Among other useful utensils, they have various sorts of baskets; some made of the same materials as their mats; and others of the twisted fibres of cocoa-nuts. These are not only durable but beautiful; being generally composed of different colours, and studded with beads made of shells or bones. They have many little nick-nacks amongst them, which shews that they neither want taste to design, nor skill to execute, whatever they take in hand.

How these people amuse themselves in their leisure hours, I cannot say, as we are but little acquainted with their diversions. The women frequently entertained us with songs, in a manner which was agreeable enough. They accompany the music by snapping their fingers, so as to keep time to it. Not only their voices, but their music was very harmonious, and they have a considerable compass in their notes. I saw but two musical instruments amongst them. One was a large flute made of a piece of bamboo, which they fill with their noses as at Otaheite; but these have four holes or stops, whereas those of Otaheite have only two. The other was composed of ten or eleven small reeds of unequal lengths, bound together side by side, as the Doric pipe of the ancients is said to have been; and the open ends of the reeds into which they blow with their mouths, are of equal height or in a line. They have also a drum which, without any impropriety, may be compared to an hollow log of wood. The one I saw was five feet six inches long, and thirty inches in girt, and had a slit in it, from the one end to the other, about three inches wide, by means of which it had been hollowed out. They beat on the side of this log with two drum-sticks, and produce an hollow sound, not quite so musical as that of an empty cask.

The common method of saluting one another is by touching or meeting noses, as is done in New Zealand; and their sign of peace to strangers, is the displaying a white flag or flags; at least such were displayed to us, when we first drew near the shore. But the people who came first on board brought with them some of the pepper plant, and sent it before them into the ship; a stronger sign of friendship than which one could not wish for. From their unsuspicious manner of coming on board, and of receiving us at first on shore, I am of the opinion, they are seldom disturbed by either foreign or domestic troubles. They are, however, not unprovided with very formidable weapons; such as clubs and spears, made of hard wood; also bows and arrows. The clubs are from three to five feet in length, and of various shapes, as is represented in the plate. Their bows and arrows are but indifferent; the former being very slight, and the latter only made of a slender reed pointed with hard wood. Some of their spears have many barbs, and must be very dangerous weapons where they take effect. On the inside of the bow is a groove, in which is put the arrow; from which it should seem that they use but one.

They have a singular custom of putting every thing you give them to their heads, by way of thanks as we conjectured. This manner of paying a compliment, is taught them from their very infancy; for when we gave things to little children, the mother lifted up the child's hand to its head. They also used this custom in their exchanges with us; whatever we gave them for their goods, was always applied to the head, just as if it had been given them for nothing. Sometimes they would look at our goods, and, if not approved, return them back; but whenever they applied them to the head, the bargain was infallibly struck. When I had made a present to the chief of any thing curious, I frequently saw it handed from one to another, and every one, into whose hands it came, put it to the head. Very often the women would take hold of my hand, kiss it, and lift it to their heads. From all this it should seem, that this custom which they call *fagafatie*, has various significations according as it is applied; all however complimentary.

It must be observed that the sullen chief or king did not pay me any of these compliments for the present I made him.

A still more singular custom prevails in these isles. We observed that the greater part of the people, both men and women, had lost one, or both their little fingers. We endeavoured, but in vain, to find out the reason for this mutilation; for no one would take any pains to inform us. It was neither peculiar to rank, age, or sex; nor is it done at any certain age, as I saw those of all ages on whom the amputation had been just made; and, except some young children, we found few who had both hands perfect. As it was more common among the aged than the young, some of us were of opinion that it was occasioned by the death of their parents, or some other near relation. But Mr. Wales one day met with a man, whose hands were both perfect, of such an advanced age, that it was hardly possible his parents could be living. They also burn or make incisions in their cheeks, near the cheek bone. The reason of this was equally unknown to us. In some, the wounds were quite fresh; in others, they could only be known by the scars, or colour of the skin. I saw neither sick nor lame amongst them; all appeared healthy, strong and vigorous; a proof of the goodness of the climate in which they live.

I have frequently mentioned a King, which implies the government being in a single person, without knowing for certain whether it is so or not. Such an one was, however, pointed out to us; and we had no reason to doubt it. From this, and other circumstances, I am of opinion that the government is much like that of Otaheite: that is, in a king or great chief, who is here called Areeke, with other chiefs under him, who are lords of certain districts, and perhaps sole proprietors, to whom the people seem to pay great obedience. I also observed a third rank, who had not a little authority over the common people; my friend Attago was one of these. I am of opinion that all the land on *Tongatabu* is private property, and that there are here, as at Otaheite, a set of people, who are servants or slaves, and have no property in land. It is unreasonable to suppose every thing in common in a country so highly cultivated as this. Interest being the greatest spring which animates the hand of industry, few would toil in cultivating and planting the land, if they did not expect to reap the fruit of their labour: were it otherwise, the industrious man would be in a worse state than the idle sluggard. I frequently saw parties of six, eight, or ten people, bring down to the landing-place, fruit and other things to dispose of, where one person, a man or woman, superintended the sale of the whole; no exchanges were made but with his or her consent; and, whatever we gave in exchange, was always given to them, which, I think, plainly shewed them to be the owners of the goods, and the others no more than servants. Though benevolent Nature has been very bountiful to these isles, it cannot be said that the inhabitants are wholly exempt from the curse of our forefathers: part of their bread must be earned with the sweat of their brows. The high state of cultivation their lands are in, must have cost them immense labour. This is now amply rewarded by the great produce, of which every one seems to partake. No one wants the common necessaries of life; joy and contentment are painted in every face. Indeed, it can hardly be otherwise; an easy freedom prevails among all ranks of people, they feel no wants which they do not enjoy the means of gratifying; and they live in a clime where the painful extremes of heat and cold are equally unknown. If Nature has been wanting in any thing, it is in the article of fresh water, which, as it is shut up in the bowels of the earth, they are obliged to dig for. A running stream was not to be seen, and but one well, at Amsterdam. At Middleburg, we saw no water but what the natives had in vessels; but, as it was sweet and cool, I had no doubt of its being taken up upon the island; and, probably, not far from the spot where I saw it.

So little do we know of their religion, that I hardly dare mention it. The buildings called *Afiatoucas*, before mentioned, are undoubtedly set apart for this purpose. Some of our gentlemen were of opinion, that they were merely burying-places. I can only say, from my own knowledge, that they are places to which particular persons directed set speeches, which I understood to be prayers, as hath been already related. Joining my opinion with that of others, I was inclined to think that they are set apart to be both temples and burying-places, as at Otaheite, or even in Europe. But I have no idea of the images being idols; not only from what I saw myself, but from Mr. Wales's informing me that they set one of them up, for him and others to shoot at.

One circumstance showed that these *Afiatoucas* were frequently resorted to, for one purpose or other. The areas, or open places, before them, being covered with a green sod, the grass on which was very short. This did not appear to have been cut, or reduced by the hand of man, but to have been prevented in its growth, by being often trod, or sat upon.

It cannot be supposed that we could know much, either of their civil or religious policy, in so short a time as four or five days, especially as we understood but little of their language; even the two islanders we had on board could not at first understand them; and yet as we became the more acquainted with them, we found their language was nearly the same spoken at Otaheite and the Society Isles. The difference not being greater than what we find betwixt the most northern and western parts of England, as will more fully appear by the vocabulary.

(*A Voyage*, Book II, ch. 3, 'October 1773')


## DENIS DIDEROT

Like many other *philosophes*, Diderot (see p. 20) was fascinated by the idea of 'primitive' other societies, such as those 'discovered' in the Pacific by Bougainville and Cook. Early in his literary career, he had invented a despotic and sexually-exploitative foreign country to provide the setting for his erotic tale *Les Bijoux Indiscrets* (*The Indiscreet Jewels*) published anonymously in 1748. Such exotic societies (real or imagined) provided a means of rethinking human nature and its relationship to the natural world, and a yardstick for gauging the character and apparent 'progress' of European civilisation. When Bougainville's *Voyage around the World* was published in 1771, Diderot began writing a review of it which he soon developed into a substantial text inspired by Bougainville's two chapters on Tahiti. The new text was based upon a dialogue between two fictitious men (A and B) who reflect upon the *Voyage* and present additional material on Tahiti that Bougainville had allegedly suppressed.

Although the *Supplement to the Voyage of Bougainville, or a dialogue between A and B on the inappropriateness of attaching moral ideas to certain physical actions that do not accord with them* was not published until 1796, it was circulated in manuscript copies in 1772. The *Supplement* begins with A and B's discussion of Bougainville's *Voyage* (part I), which introduces an oration by one of the island's chiefs on the departure of Bougainville's crew (II). This is followed by a dialogue between the ship's chaplain and a Tahitian, Orou (III), and then by further discussions between them and by the reflections of A and B (IV and V). Two extracts are provided here from a modern translation. The first is taken from part II, 'The Old Man's Farewell'; a hearty condemnation of colonialism. The second extract is from part III, 'The Conversation between the Chaplain and Orou', in which the natural freedoms, sexuality and morals of the Tahitians are compared with the artificial, civilised and Christian mores of Europeans.

## Supplement to the Voyage of Bougainville (1796)

### 'The Old Man's Farewell'

The speaker is an old man. He was the father of a large family. When the Europeans arrived he looked upon them with scorn, showing neither astonishment, nor fear, nor curiosity. On their approach he turned his back and retired to his hut. Yet his silence and anxiety revealed his thoughts only too well; he was inwardly lamenting the eclipse of his countrymen's happiness. When Bougainville was leaving the island, as the natives swarmed on the shore, clutching his clothes, clasping his companions in their arms and weeping, the old man made his way forward and proclaimed solemnly, 'Weep, wretched natives of Tahiti, weep. But let it be for the coming and not the leaving of these ambitious, wicked men. One day you will know them better. One day they will come back, bearing in one hand the piece of wood you see in that man's belt, and, in the other, the sword hanging by the side of that one, to enslave you, slaughter you, or make you captive to their follies and vices. One day you will be subject to them, as corrupt, vile and miserable as they are. But I have this consolation. My life is drawing to its close, and I shall not see the calamity I foretell. Oh fellow Tahitians, oh my friends! There is one way to avert a dreadful fate, but I would rather die than counsel you to take it. Let them leave, and let them live.'

Then turning to Bougainville, he continued, 'And you, leader of the ruffians who obey you, pull your ship away swiftly from these shores. We are innocent, we are content, and you can only spoil that happiness. We follow the pure instincts of nature, and you have tried to erase its impression from our hearts. Here, everything belongs to everyone, and you have preached I can't tell what distinction between "yours" and "mine". Our daughters and our wives belong to us all. You shared that privilege with us, and you enflamed them with a frenzy they had never known before. They have become wild in your arms, and you have become deranged in theirs. They have begun to hate each other. You have butchered one another for them, and they have come back stained with your blood. We are free, but into our earth you have now staked your title to our future servitude. You are neither a god nor a demon. Who are you, then, to make them slaves? Orou, you who understand the language of these men, tell us all, as you have told me, what they have written on that strip of metal: *This land is ours*. So this land is yours? Why? Because you set foot on it! If a Tahitian should one day land on your shores and engrave on one of your stones or on the bark of one of your trees, *This land belongs to the people of Tahiti*, what would you think then? You are stronger than we are, and what does that mean? When one of the miserable trinkets with which your ship is filled was taken away, what an uproar you made, what revenge you exacted! At that very moment, in the depths of your heart, you were plotting the theft of an entire country! You are not a slave, you would rather die than be one, and yet you wish to make slaves of us. Do you suppose, then, that a Tahitian cannot defend his own liberty and die for it as well? This inhabitant of Tahiti, whom you wish to ensnare like an animal, is your brother. You are both children of Nature. What right do you have over him that he does not have over you? You came; did we attack you? Have we plundered your ship? Did we seize you and expose you to the arrows of our enemies? Did we harness you to work with our animals in the fields? We respected our own image in you.

(*Supplement to the Voyage*, II, 'The Old Man's Farewell')

### 'The Conversation between the Chaplain and Orou'

In the division of Bougainville's crew by the Tahitians, the chaplain was allotted to Orou. They were roughly the same age, around thirty-five or thirty-six years old. At the time Orou had only his wife and three children, who were called Asto, Palli and Thia. They undressed the chaplain, washed his face, hands and feet, and served him a wholesome and frugal meal. When he was about to go to bed, Orou, who had stepped out with his family, reappeared, presented him with his wife and three daughters, each of them naked, and said, 'You have eaten, you are young and in good health; if you go to bed alone, you will sleep badly. At night a man needs a companion beside him. Here is my wife; here are my daughters. Choose whomever you prefer; but if you wish to oblige me you will select the youngest of my daughters, who is still childless.' 'Alas', added the mother, 'I don't hold it against her, poor Thia! It's not her fault.'

The chaplain replied that his religion, his holy orders, morality and decency all prohibited him from accepting Orou's offer.

Orou answered: 'I don't know what you mean by "religion", but I can only think ill of it, since it prevents you from enjoying an innocent pleasure to which Nature, that sovereign mistress, invites every person: that is, of bringing into the world one of your own kind; rendering a service which the father, mother and children all ask of you; repaying a gracious host, and enriching a nation by adding one more subject to it. I don't know what you mean by "holy orders", but your first duty is to be a man and to show gratitude. I'm not asking you to take back the ways of Orou to your country, but Orou, your host and friend, begs that here you accept the ways of Tahiti. Whether the ways of Tahiti are better or worse than yours is an easy question to settle. Has the land of your birth more people than it can feed? In that case your ways are neither worse nor better than ours. Can it feed more than it has? In that case our ways are better than yours. As for the decency which holds you back, I quite understand. I admit I'm wrong and ask that you forgive me. I don't insist that you put your health in danger. If you are tired, you must rest; but I trust that you will not continue to disappoint us. Look at the sorrow you've brought to all these faces. They're afraid you have detected blemishes in them which have aroused your distaste. But even if that were so, wouldn't the pleasure of doing a good deed, of ensuring that one of my daughters was honoured among her companions and sisters, wouldn't that suffice for you? Be generous.'

THE CHAPLAIN  It's not that. They are all four of them equally beautiful. But my religion! My holy orders!

OROU  They are mine, and I'm offering them to you. They are their own as well and give themselves up to you freely. Whatever purity of conscience is prescribed to you by that thing you call 'religion' and that thing you call 'holy orders', you may accept them without scruple. I am in no way exceeding my authority, and you may be sure that I know and respect the rights of individuals.

At this point the truthful chaplain acknowledges that Providence had never exposed him to such strong temptation. He was young, agitated, vexed. He averted his eyes from the delightful supplicants and then gazed at them again; he raised his eyes and hands to the heavens. Thia, the youngest, threw her arms around his knees and said to him,

'Stranger, do not make my father unhappy, nor my mother, nor me. Honour me in this hut and within my family. Lift me up to the status of my sisters, who make fun of me. Asto, the eldest, already has three children; Palli, the second, has two; but Thia has none. Stranger, good stranger, do not reject me. Make me a mother. Make me bear a child whom I can one day lead by the hand, by my side, in Tahiti, who in nine months' time will be seen suckling at my breast, who will make me proud and who will be a part of my dowry, when I pass from my father's hut to another. I may be more fortunate with you than with our young Tahitians. If you grant me this favour, I shall never forget you. I shall bless you all my life; I shall write your name on my arm and on that of your son. We shall forever utter it with joy; and when you leave these shores my prayers will accompany you across the seas, until you reach your own land.'

The artless chaplain says that she clasped his hands, that she fastened her eyes on his with glances so touching and expressive that she wept, that her father, mother and sisters withdrew, that he remained alone with her, and that, still calling out 'But my religion, but my holy orders', he found himself at dawn lying beside this young girl who overwhelmed him with caresses and who invited her father, and sisters, when in the morning they came to his bed, to add their own gratitude to hers.

Asto and Palli, after withdrawing for a time, returned with native food, drinks and fruits. They embraced their sister and wished her good fortune. They breakfasted together; then Orou remained alone with the chaplain and said to him, 'I see that my daughter is pleased with you, and I thank you. But could you tell me just what is the meaning of the word "religion" which you have expressed so many times and with such sadness?'

The chaplain (after reflecting for a moment, replied) 'Who made your hut and all the things that furnish it?'

OROU  I did.

THE CHAPLAIN  Well, we think that this world and everything in it is the work of one craftsman.

OROU  Does he then have feet, hands, a head?

THE CHAPLAIN  No.

OROU  Where does he live?

THE CHAPLAIN  Everywhere.

OROU  Here, even?

THE CHAPLAIN  Here.

OROU  We have never seen him.

THE CHAPLAIN  He cannot be seen.

OROU  What a pretty poor father. He must be aged, because he must be at least as old as what he's made.

THE CHAPLAIN  He never grows old. He spoke to our ancestors; he gave them laws; he prescribed the way he wished to be honoured; he ordained that certain actions were good and forbade others as evil.

OROU  I understand. And one of those actions he forbade as evil is to lie with a woman or girl. But why then did he make two sexes?

THE CHAPLAIN   So that they may be united, but subject to certain conditions, following preliminary ceremonies, by virtue of which a man belongs to a woman and only to her; and a woman belongs to a man and only to him.

OROU   For as long as they live?

THE CHAPLAIN   For as long as they live.

OROU   So that if a woman should happen to lie with someone other than her husband, or a husband should lie with someone other than his wife ... But that doesn't happen, since he's there and whatever displeases him he knows how to stop.

THE CHAPLAIN   No, he lets them do it, and so they sin against the law of God, for that is the name we give to the great craftsman. Against the law of the country what we commit is a crime.

OROU   I should be sorry to offend you by what I say, but if you'll permit me, let me tell you what I think.

THE CHAPLAIN   Speak.

OROU   I find these strange precepts contrary to Nature, an offence against reason, certain to breed crime and bound to exasperate at every turn the old craftsman who, without a head, hand or tools has made everything; and who is everywhere but nowhere to be seen; who exists today and endures tomorrow without ever ageing a single moment; who commands and is not obeyed; who does not prevent occurrences which it is in his power to stop. Contrary to Nature, because they assume that a being which feels, thinks and is free may be the property of another being like himself. On what could such a right be based? Don't you see that in your country you have confused something which cannot feel or think or desire or will; which one takes or leaves, keeps or sells, without it suffering or complaining, with a very different thing that cannot be exchanged or acquired; which *does* have freedom, will, desire; which has the ability to give itself up or hold itself back forever; which complains and suffers; and which can never be an article of exchange unless its character is forgotten and violence is done to its nature. Such rules are contrary to the general order of things. What could seem more ridiculous than a precept which forbids any change of our affections, which commands that we show a constancy of which we're not capable, which violates the nature and liberty of male and female alike in chaining them to one another for the whole of their lives? What could be more absurd than a fidelity restricting the most capricious of our pleasures to a single individual; than a vow of immutability taken by two beings formed of flesh and blood, under a sky that doesn't remain fixed for an instant, beneath caverns poised on the edge of collapse, under a cliff crumbling into dust, at the foot of a tree shedding its bark, beneath a quivering stone? Believe you me, you have made the plight worse than that of an animal. I've no understanding of your great craftsman, but I rejoice in his never having addressed our forefathers, and I hope he will never speak to our children; for he might by chance tell them the same nonsense, and they might commit the folly of believing him.

Yesterday at supper you talked to us about magistrates and priests. I don't know what you mean by 'magistrates' and 'priests', who have the authority to regulate your conduct, but tell me, are they masters of good and evil? Can they make what is just unjust, and transform what is unjust into what's just? Can they make harmful actions good, and innocent and useful ones evil? One would hardly think so, since nothing could then be true or false, good or evil, beautiful or ugly, unless it pleased your great craftsman and his magistrates and priests to deem them so; in which case you'd be obliged, from one moment to another to change your beliefs and conduct. One day, on behalf of one of your three masters you'd be told, 'Kill', and you'd then be obliged in conscience to kill; another day, 'Steal', and you'd then have to steal; or 'Do not eat this fruit', and you wouldn't dare eat it; 'I forbid you this plant or ani-mal', and you'd refrain from touching them. There's nothing good that couldn't be forbidden, nothing evil that might not be required of you. And where would you be if your three masters, out of sorts with one another, took it upon themselves to commit you, command you, and forbid you the very same thing, as I suspect must happen often? Then, to please the priest, you'll be forced to oppose the magistrate; to satisfy the magistrate, you'll be forced to displease the great craftsman; (and to satisfy the great craftsman) you'll have to abandon Nature. And do you know what will happen then? You'll come to despise all three of them, and you'll be neither a man, nor a citizen, nor a true believer. You'll be nothing. You'll be out of favour with each form of authority, at odds with yourself, malicious, tormented by your heart, miserable and persecuted by your senseless masters, as I saw you yesterday when I offered my daughters (and wife) to you, and you cried out, 'But my religion; but my holy orders!'

Would you like to know what's good and what's bad at all times and in all places? Stick to the nature of things and of actions, to your relations with your fel-low-man, to the effect of your conduct on your own well-being and on the gener-al welfare. You're mad if you suppose there can be anything high or low in the uni-verse which can add to or take away from the laws of Nature. Her eternal will is that good should be preferred to evil and the general good to the particular. You may decree the opposite, but you will not be obeyed. You will merely breed rascals and wretches, inspired by fear, punishment and remorse, depraving their con-science, corrupting their character. People will no longer know what they should do and what they should avoid. Anxious when innocent, calm only in crime, they will have lost sight of the pole star which should have guided their way. Answer me truthfully. Despite the express commands of your three legislators, doesn't a young man in your country ever lie with a young woman without their permission?

THE CHAPLAIN  I should be lying if I assured you this never happens.

OROU  Doesn't the woman who has sworn to belong to her husband give herself to another?

THE CHAPLAIN  Nothing is more common.

OROU  Your legislators must be either severe in meting out punishment, or not severe. If severe, they're wild beasts fighting against nature. If not severe, they're imbeciles whose useless prohibitions have subjected their authority to scorn.

THE CHAPLAIN  Culprits who escape the severity of the laws are punished by public cen-sure.

OROU  This amounts to saying that justice is administered without benefit of the whole nation's common sense, and that in place of laws you adopt the folly of opinion.

THE CHAPLAIN  A girl who's lost her honour can no longer find a husband.

OROU  Lost her honour! Why?

THE CHAPLAIN  An unfaithful woman is more or less despised.

OROU  Despised! And why?

THE CHAPLAIN  The young man is called a cowardly seducer.

OROU  A coward, a seducer! And why?

THE CHAPLAIN  The father, mother and poor child are disconsolate. The unfaithful husband is a libertine. The betrayed husband shares the shame of his wife.

OROU  What a monstrous web of delirium you describe, and yet you've not told me everything. For as soon as it's permitted to settle ideas of justice and property according to one's fancy, to ascribe or strike out the traits of things as if they were arbitrary, to attribute or deny good and evil to actions on no other grounds than whim, each person blames, accuses, suspects another; everyone tramples upon each other, becomes envious, jealous, deceitful, distressed, secretive, covert, spying upon another to take him or her by surprise; everyone quarrels and lies. Daughters deceive their parents, husbands cheat their wives, wives their husbands. Daughters — yes, I'm sure of it — will suffocate their children, suspicious fathers will scorn and neglect theirs, mothers will abandon them and leave them to the mercy of fate, and the crime of debauchery will appear in every shape and form. I know all this as plainly as if I'd lived among you. It's just so because it could not be otherwise; and the society whose splendid order your leader acclaims will be nothing but a swarm of hypocrites who secretly trample on the laws, or unfortunates who are themselves the willing instruments of their own torture; or imbeciles in whom prejudice has altogether stifled the voice of Nature; or misshapen creatures in whom Nature does not lay claim to her rights.

THE CHAPLAIN  It's a fair likeness. But do you therefore never marry?

OROU  We marry.

THE CHAPLAIN  What does your marriage consist of?

OROU  A mutual consent to live in the same hut and to share the same bed, for as long as we find it good to do so.

THE CHAPLAIN  And when you come to find it bad?

OROU  We separate.

THE CHAPLAIN  What becomes of the children?

OROU  Oh stranger! That last question reveals to me your country's depths of misery. You must understand, my friend, that here the birth of a child is always a source of joy, and a child's death an occasion for sorrow and tears. A child is a precious thing because it will grow up to be an adult. We thus have an interest in caring for it altogether different from that shown in our plants and animals. The birth of a child brings domestic and public joy. It will mean an increase of wealth for the hut, and of strength for the nation. It means another pair of arms and hands in Tahiti. We see in him a future farmer, fisherman, hunter, soldier, husband, father. In returning from her husband's hut to that of her parents, a woman brings back the children she had taken with her as a dowry; those born during the companionship are shared, males and females equally, as far as possible, so that each parent has more or less the same number of boys and girls.

THE CHAPLAIN  But children are a burden for many years before they can make themselves useful.

OROU  For their maintenance and that of the aged we set aside one part in six of all our harvests. This allowance always goes with them. So you see that the larger a Tahitian's family, the richer he is.

THE CHAPLAIN  One part in six!

OROU  Yes. It encourages the growth of population and respect for the elderly and the welfare of children.

THE CHAPLAIN  Do your husbands and wives sometimes take each other back?

OROU  Very often. The shortest length of a marriage, however, is one month.

THE CHAPLAIN  Assuming, of course, that the mother's not with child; for then they must live together for at least nine months.

OROU  You're mistaken. The child's paternity, like its allowance, follows it everywhere.

THE CHAPLAIN  You speak to me of children which a wife brings to her husband as a dowry.

OROU  Exactly. Take my eldest daughter here, who has three children. They can walk, they're healthy and attractive. They promise to be strong. When she comes to fancy getting married, she'll take them with her; they're hers. Her husband will accept them with joy and could only regard his wife as more dear to him if she were pregnant with a fourth.

THE CHAPLAIN  By him?

OROU  By him or another. The more our girls have children, the more sought after they are. The more lusty and handsome our boys, the richer they are. Before they've reached the age of sexual maturity, we're careful to keep girls away from men, and boys from intercourse with women, but once they've passed puberty we exhort them to produce children. You can't imagine the importance of the service you will have rendered to my daughter Thia, if she's now with child. Her mother will no longer say to her each month, 'But Thia, what are you thinking of? You never get pregnant. You're nineteen years old; you should already have two children, and you've none. Who will look after you? If you let your youth pass in this way, what will you do in your old age? Thia, there must be something wrong with you that puts men off. Cure yourself of it, my child. At your age, I'd already been a mother three times.'

THE CHAPLAIN  What precautions do you take to safeguard your adolescent girls and boys?

OROU  That's the main object of domestic education, and the most important item of public morality. Up to the age of twenty-two, that is, two or three years past puberty, our boys wear a long tunic which covers them, their loins clasped by a little chain. Before they become nubile, our girls daren't go out without a white veil. To take off one's chain or remove one's veil is a wrong seldom committed, because we teach our children at an early age what harmful effects will follow. But as soon as the male has attained his full strength, when the symptoms of his virility appear durable, and when the frequent emission and quality of his seminal fluid confirm it; just when the young girl becomes languid, bored and sufficiently mature to feel passion, to inspire and satisfy it usefully; then the father unfastens his son's chain and cuts the nail of the middle finger of his right hand; while the mother removes her daughter's veil. The young man may henceforth seek a woman's favours and be sought out in turn himself; the woman may thereafter walk about freely, her face and breasts uncovered. She may accept or reject a man's caresses. We merely indicate in advance to the boy, which girls, and to the girl, which boys, they should prefer. The (day of) emancipation for a boy or girl is a great holiday. If it's a girl, the young men assemble round her hut the evening before, filling the air the whole night long with their singing and the sound of musical instruments. On the appointed day, she's led by her father and mother into an enclosure where there's dancing and exercises of jumping, wrestling and running. The naked man is displayed before her, from all sides and in all attitudes. If it's a boy, then the girls undertake to please and do the honours of the ceremony, presenting before his eyes the nude female body, without reserve or furtiveness. The rest of the ceremony is enacted on a bed of leaves, as you saw on your arrival here. At sunset the girl returns to her parents' hut or to the hut of the young man she's chosen, and she remains there as long as she pleases.

THE CHAPLAIN  So is this ceremony a wedding-day or not?

OROU  Just so.

(*Supplement to the Voyage*, III,
'The Conversation between the Chaplain and Orou')

# Chapter 12

# Radicalism and revolution

**A**LONGSIDE THE DEVELOPMENT OF 'Enlightened' philosophies of law, government and kingship, the eighteenth century witnessed major social changes, political unrest and conflict – most famously in North America and France, but also in England, Ireland, Switzerland, Corsica, the Austrian Netherlands and other places. There were also numerous slave rebellions in North America and the Caribbean, peasant revolts in Hungary, Russia, Bohemia and Sweden, and a very long catalogue of wars, conquests and invasions in Europe, and by European powers around the world. Shortly after the close of the century, the great revolutionary leader Simón Bolívar, well schooled in the Enlightenment, would begin the process of liberating half of South America from Spanish rule. Of course, these conflicts were not all inspired by Enlightenment texts and reasonings. However, through the North American and French revolutions – particularly the latter – new thinking emerged about the power and rights of people to transform their societies, rather than seek the restoration of a prior order, and to become the citizens of secular republics rather than the subjects of ancient monarchies. These radical ideas were rehearsed (and often rejected) in many works of the Enlightenment, but they became explosive through the experience of revolution and would give rise to new ways of thinking and writing about human society and history.

The American War of Independence arose from tensions between Britain and its American colonies. Britain had increased control over the thirteen colonies along the Atlantic coastline, when, at the end of the Seven Years War in 1763 it took over Canada from the French and Florida from the Spanish. The relationship between the British government and the 'land of opportunities' then began to deteriorate, as the desire to maintain control and to levy taxes that would require the colonists to share the costs of the Empire prompted a period of revolt. A Revenue Act in 1767 led to duties being imposed on lead, glass, paper and tea, a reorganised customs and a suspended New York Assembly. A number of protests, such as boycotts in Boston, led to the repeal of taxes on commodities, but tea tax was retained, and smuggling ensued. Following the Boston Tea Party in December 1773, when 340 chests of tea were dumped into the harbour, the port was closed and occupied by British troops. By September 1774 the first Continental Congress had been convened in Philadelphia, and the first shots in the War of Independence were fired in the Spring of 1775.

The publication of Thomas Paine's *Common Sense* (1776) lent support to the idea of independence, which was delivered on 2 July 1776. Two days later, Congress passed a 'Declaration of Independence'. In response, the British blocked the port of New York and embarked on a succession of defeats of the American army, made up of volunteers and led by George Washington. By Christmas 1776, Washington had retreated across the Delaware River, but in 1777 he defeated the British at Saratoga, and in 1781, with the help of the French, he trapped the British General, Lord Cornwallis, at Yorktown. Two years later, the Treaty of Paris (1783) sealed the achievement of independence, but it would take another seven years before all thirteen of the original rebel states had agreed to join the union. Immediately after the War of Independence, the states were weak and divided, struggling with bankruptcy and a lack of military cohesion, and without a government with the power to deal with these problems. At a Constitutional Convention held in 1787, a new system of government, based upon a written constitution, began to be devised in which the power of federal government was balanced with that of the individual states. In 1789 George Washington was elected president of the new nation.

The ideas of Locke and Rousseau were a direct influence on the 'founding fathers' of the United States of America as they formulated the claims to, and guiding principles of, their new country. The Declaration of Independence argued, in Lockean fashion, for the 'self-evident' equality of all (white) men and the inalienable rights of all men to 'life, liberty and the pursuit of happiness', as well as for the right to revolt when those natural rights were overruled. From the outset, the war was presented as a heroic process of liberation. Even so, this interpretation has been challenged, particularly in the twentieth century. In the 1930s and '40s, examination of the British imperial system which created the conditions for revolt, and studies of the private interests of the central figures of the Revolution, led to some less heroic narratives. Later, scholarly focus on the Revolution examined the level of pragmatic consensus displayed by the revolutionaries (and their commonalities with other revolutionaries), their ideological fervour, and the social and material conflicts that made up the War of Independence. More recently, the struggle for independence has been seen as America's first civil war, and of doubtful benefit either to the North American Indians or to the half a million African-American slaves who were not emancipated by it.

The relationship between the Enlightenment and the French Revolution is one that has always been debated. For conservative contemporaries such as Edmund Burke, and many nineteenth-century historians, the violence of the revolution was a direct result of the *philosophes'* undermining of the social order. While it is clear that many *philosophes* believed that improvements could be made by embracing new ideas and opportunities, and some, such as Rousseau and Voltaire, were widely cited and championed during the Revolution, the claim for a simple causal relationship between the Enlightenment and Revolution now appears largely rhetorical, in that it fails to take account of the complexity of either phenomenon. While many scholars would regard the Enlightenment as an essential precursor of the Revolution, few would probably regard it now as a wholly sufficient or even the most important cause.

The political events of the Revolution can be traced to the financial crisis of the French state at the beginning of the eighteenth century, due at least in part to the ambitions and extravagances of court life under Louis XIV and his successors. The repeated failure to resolve this crisis meant that in 1788, Louis XVI was forced to call the Estates General, a body made up of three social orders: the first estate consisting of the clergy, the second of the nobility, and the third of the commoners, represented largely by tradesmen, lawyers, artisans and bankers. The first two estates, though a minority, were exempt from taxes and held the majority of votes. In a lengthy pamphlet *Qu'est-ce que le Tiers-État?* (*What is the Third Estate?*) circulated in January 1789, the constitutional theorist Abbé Sieyès provided what for many people was a succinct summary of the problem: '(1) What is the Third Estate? – Everything. (2) What has its role been so far in the political order? – Nothing. (3) What does it demand? – To be something.' As Tom Paine tried to explain in *The Rights of Man* (1791–92), because no agreement could be reached between the groups, the third estate declared itself to be a National Assembly in 1789, the representative body which then proclaimed the Declaration of the Rights of Man and the Citizen. Until this time, the movement for reform had been quite unified and supported by popular mass protests. However, under the strains of division and (after 1792) of war, revolutionary fervours soon became inflamed, leading to many radical developments, such as the creation of a revolutionary calendar in 1792. Thus the nomenclature of the new thirty-day months related to the weather (*nivôse*, referring to the snow of winter; *thermidor*, the warmth of summer) or the cycle of growth (*floréal*, referring to flowering days of spring; *fructidor*, to the fruits of autumn). By the autumn of 1793 the Committee of Public Safety had instituted a dramatic process of dechristianisation, which, by the Spring of 1794, the revolutionary leader Robespierre had transformed into the Cult of the Supreme Being – a state-directed secular religion based, like deism, upon belief in reason.

By 1792, the Convention was ousting its moderates, the Girondins, and later the Jacobins themselves would split into factions. In this way, the Revolution's basis for consensus was diminished, and in July 1794 Robespierre himself was guillotined. Great problems were now encountered in matching abstract claims to human rights with the urgent and practical difficulties of defending the Revolution and providing stable government. Following the execution of Louis XVI in 1793, the deterioration of revolutionary ideology and the basis for consensus culminated in a general intimidation and violence that became known as the 'Great Terror' (1793–94). This extreme response to securing the legitimacy of the ideals of the Revolution, and its imposition of the 'general will', has prompted extensive controversy on the nature of the revolution, and on the possibility and meaning of revolutionary change. For Burke and many others, violence was always a feature of the revolutionary days in France, which through a turbulent decade eventually led to Napoléon Bonaparte becoming First Consul and *de facto* ruler in 1799.

Since the French Revolution became the moment from which Europeans tended to define and date the birth of modern political history, its causes and dynamics have always been fiercely contested. For some historians, the Revolution dislodged paternalism as a political model in favour of a 'collective representation of fraternity'. Others have focused on the conservatism of some aspects of the Revolution, such as its denial of voting rights to women. For many years, the Revolution was viewed as a social phenomenon: essentially a class conflict, the classic Marxist struggle of a bourgeoisie to establish itself; an historical event which ushered in modern capitalism and its attendant social practices and values. Recently, more 'political' interpretations have been advanced, focusing on political processes (mobilisation, the politicisation of everyday life) and cultural processes such as the rise of new forms of sociability through festivals and clubs. This has stimulated the study of popular culture, citizenship and 'mentalités' during the Enlightenment and the Revolution.

The first two texts selected here come from the American revolution. The first is the catalogue of grievances against Britain as espoused by the rhetoric of Thomas Jefferson's *Summary View of the Rights of British America*, written at the height of the struggle for independence in 1774. The second extract is from Jefferson's *Notes on the State of Virginia* (1787) written in the aftermath of the war when a workable balance between democracy and governance had still to be agreed. The third extract is from Thomas Paine's *The Rights of Man* (1791–92), in which he narrates the outbreak of the French Revolution up until the symbolic moment of the storming of the Bastille and the Declaration of the Rights of Man and of Citizens in 1789. The final extract is from William Godwin's *An Enquiry concerning Political Justice* (1793). Here, Godwin offers an anarchist view of power as residing in the individual, but he rejects violent political revolution as an effective means of social change. This is because he believes 'there is no effectual way of improving the institutions of any people but by enlightening their understandings'.

## THOMAS JEFFERSON

The diplomat, architect, philosopher and third president of the United States, Thomas Jefferson (1743–1826) is probably most celebrated as the man who, at the age of thirty-three, drew up the first draft of the American Declaration of Independence in 1776. Born in Albemarle County, Virginia, into a well-established family, he inherited 5,000 acres of land on which he was later to construct his mountain-top home, Monticello. He studied at the College of William and Mary, and was admitted to the bar in 1767, practising until the courts were closed by the War of Independence. He sat in the Virginia House of Burgesses (set up in 1619, the first self-governing body in America, subject to the British Crown) from 1769 to 1775, and then became a delegate of the Continental Congress from 1775–76, during which time he wrote the Declaration of Independence. He became one of the delegates of the Virginia legislature and, subsequently, governor for Virginia until 1785, penning the bill for the Virginia Statute for Religious Freedom (1786). He then succeeded Benjamin Franklin as Minister for France, staying till the brink of the French Revolution. Under George Washington the first President of the USA, he was Secretary of State, resigning in 1793 over his support for the French Revolution. His support for state rights, a centralised government and agrarian interests led him to assume the leadership of the emerging Democratic–Republican Party. Coming second to John Adams in the 1796 presidential elections, he became Vice-President to a Federalist President, as the Constitution then allowed. He also became president of the American Philosophical Society in 1797. In 1801 he became third president of the United States, greatly increasing the territory of the USA by purchasing Louisiana from the French in 1803. In his second term, he struggled with unpopular measures to keep America out of the Napoleonic wars. In 1809 he retired to Monticello, dedicating himself to the foundation of the University of Virginia and to writing, including a lengthy correspondence to his former rival, John Adams. He died on 4 July 1826.

In 1774, while a lawyer and member of the Virginia House of Burgesses, Jefferson wrote, and then sent to a Convention that he was unable to attend, a text that was soon to be published in Williamsburg and London as *A Summary View of the Rights of British America*. Suffused with the Enlightenment discourse of natural rights and universal truths, this short pamphlet was a strong rebuke of King George III's authority and British policies in America. It asserted that a 'society must at all times possess within itself the sovereign powers of legislation'. It was considered too radical for the Convention at the time, but was still published by it. In *A Summary View*, Jefferson speaks out against trade restrictions and customs duties imposed on America, and British interference in internal affairs, and he addresses the question of land ownership. Prefiguring his later comments in the Declaration of Independence (omitted from the final draft), Jefferson also condemned the practice of slavery – an issue on which, in private, he was ambivalent. Publicly, he later noted his 'suspicion' that African-Americans were 'inferior to the whites in the endowments both of body and of mind' (*Notes on Virginia*). Similarly, with regard to North American Indians, he was prepared to consider their 'extermination' if they resisted European settlers, noting 'The world will scarcely do for them and us'. Nor was he prepared to tolerate women in politics or public office, since he believed that nature had intended them for the domestic sphere: 'The tender breasts of ladies were not formed for political convulsion'. The passage from *A Summary View* reproduced here is the first third of that pamphlet.

*Notes on the State of Virginia* (1787), Jefferson's only book-length publication, began as a statistical survey for the French government and grew to become a pioneering, informed and philosophical account of various aspects of eighteenth-century American life. The book was written during his difficult governorship of invaded and wartime Virginia and after the death of his daughter. Once given to the secretary of the French legation, interest in the text encouraged Jefferson to have it printed at Paris in 1785 for private distribution. Continued interest and the threat of a 'pirate' translation prompted him to make revisions to the original text, and a new edition was published in 1787.

The care with which Jefferson explores geography, climate, the military, laws, religion, manners, history and economics may be regarded as evidence of his attempt to impose a unity and order on the world. He ranges from the empirical to the speculative, expressing his thoughts on such topics as slavery and the relationship of the Church and state, and these sections would gain him notoriety as he grew to prominence. Jefferson also refuted Raynal's and Buffon's claims that the species of 'colonies' were degenerations of European ones. *Notes on the State of Virginia* thus served as a powerful statement of American virtues and the integrity of American territory. It also quickly established Jefferson's reputation as a scholar of natural history.

The text is structured around a number of queries arising from the original questionnaire. The section on the constitution, from which the extract here is taken, gives the reader an insight into political processes in the newly independent states. Initially, the national governing body of Congress had limited powers. Local governments in the form of the states controlled taxation and trade regulations, for example. State governments (with the exception of Pennsylvania) were formed with powerful bicameral legislatures. Most states therefore found it necessary to adopt a Bill of Rights or to make additions to their constitutions in order to balance the power of the legislatures. After 1787 the need for a stronger national government paved the way for an American constitution which divided legislative power between two national bodies: a House of Representatives elected by 'the people', and a Senate elected by the state legislatures. In the extract from *Notes on the State of Virginia* selected here, Jefferson surveys the state of Virginia at a time when questions of political representation were acute, and the relationships between individuals, community and government were hotly contested. The text reveals some of the limits of the revolutionary moment: political participation remained in the hands of white male property-owners.

## A Summary View of the Rights of British America (1774)

Resolved, that it be an instruction to the said deputies, when assembled in general congress with the deputies from the other states of British America, to propose to the said congress that an humble and dutiful address be presented to his majesty, begging leave to lay before him, as chief magistrate of the British empire, the united complaints of his majesty's subjects in America; complaints which are excited by many unwarrantable encroachments and usurpations, attempted to be made by the legislature of one part of the empire, upon those rights, which God and the laws have given equally and independently to all. To represent to his majesty that these his states have often individually made humble application to his imperial throne to obtain, through its intervention, some redress of their injured rights, to none of which was ever even an answer condescended; humbly to hope that this their joint address, penned in the language of truth, and divested of those expressions of servility which would persuade his majesty that we are asking favours, and not rights, shall obtain from his majesty a more respectful acceptance. And this his majesty will think we have reason to expect when he reflects that he is no more than the chief officer of the people, appointed by the laws, and circumscribed with definite powers, to assist in working the great machine of government, erected for their use, and consequently subject to their superintendance. And in order that these our rights, as well as the invasions of them, may be laid more fully before his majesty, to take a view of them from the origin and first settlement of these countries.

To remind him that our ancestors, before their emigration to America, were the free inhabitants of the British dominions in Europe, and possessed a right which nature has given to all men, of departing from the country in which chance, not choice, has placed them, of going in quest of new habitations, and of there establishing new societies, under such laws and regulations as to them shall seem most likely to promote public happiness. That their Saxon ancestors had, under this universal law, in like manner left their native wilds and woods in the north of Europe, had possessed themselves of the island of Britain, then less charged with inhabitants, and had established there that system of laws which has so long been the glory and protection of that country. Nor was ever any claim of superiority or dependence asserted over them by that mother country from which they had migrated; and were such a claim made, it is believed that his majesty's subjects in Great Britain have too firm a feeling of the rights derived to them from their ancestors, to bow down the sovereignty to their state before such visionary pretensions. And it is thought that no circumstance has occurred to distinguish materially the British from the Saxon emigration. America was conquered, and her settlements made, and firmly established, at the expense of individuals, and not of the British public. Their own blood was spilt in acquiring lands for their settlement, their own fortunes expended in making that settlement effectual; for themselves they fought, for themselves they conquered, and for themselves alone they have right to hold. Not a shilling was ever issued from the public treasures of his majesty, or his ancestors, for their assistance, till of very late times, after the colonies had become established on a firm and permanent footing. That then, indeed, having become valuable to Great Britain for her commercial purposes, his parliament was pleased to lend them assistance against an enemy, who would fain have drawn to herself the benefits of their commerce, to the great aggrandizement of herself, and danger of Great Britain. Such assistance, and in such circumstances, they had often before given to Portugal, and other allied states, with whom they carry on a commercial intercourse; yet these states never supposed, that by calling in her aid, they thereby submitted themselves to her sovereignty. Had such terms been proposed, they would have rejected them with disdain, and trusted for better to the moderation of their enemies, or to a vigorous exertion of their own force. We do not, however, mean to under-rate those aids, which to us were doubtless valuable, on whatever principles granted; but we would show that they cannot give a title to that authority which the British parliament would arrogate over us, and that they may amply be repaid by our giving to the inhabitants of Great Britain such exclusive privileges in trade as may be advantageous to them, and at the same time not too restrictive to ourselves. That settlements having been thus effected in the wilds of America, the emigrants thought proper to adopt that system of laws under which they had hitherto lived in the mother country, and to continue their union with her by submitting themselves to the same common sovereign, who was thereby made the central link connecting the several parts of the empire thus newly multiplied.

But that not long were they permitted, however far they thought themselves removed from the hand of oppression, to hold undisturbed the rights thus acquired, at the hazard of their lives, and loss of their fortunes. A family of princes [Stuarts] was then on the British throne, whose treasonable crimes against their people brought on them afterwards the exertion of those sacred and sovereign rights of punishment reserved in the hands of the people for cases of extreme necessity, and judged by the constitution unsafe to be delegated to any other judicature. While every day brought forth some new and unjustifiable exertion of power over their subjects on that side of the water, it was not to be expected that those here, much less able at that time to oppose the designs of despotism, should be exempted from injury.

Accordingly that country, which had been acquired by the lives, the labours, and the fortunes, of individual adventurers, was by these princes, at several times, parted out and distributed among the favourites and followers of their fortunes [a footnote here describes how Maryland, Pennsylvania and Carolina were granted to British nobles], and, by an assumed right of the crown alone, were erected into distinct and independent governments; a measure which it is believed his majesty's prudence and understanding would prevent him from imitating at this day, as no exercise of such a power, of dividing and dismembering a country, has ever occurred in his majesty's realm of England, though now of very ancient standing; nor could be justified or acquiesced under there, or in any other part of his majesty's empire.

That the exercise of a free trade with all parts of the world, possessed by the American colonists, as of natural right, and which no law of their own had taken away or abridged, was next the object of unjust encroachment. Some of the colonies having thought proper to continue the administration of their government in the name and under the authority of his majesty King Charles the first, whom, notwithstanding his late deposition by the commonwealth of England, they continued in the sovereignty of their state; the parliament for the commonwealth took the same in high offence, and assumed upon themselves the power of prohibiting their trade with all other parts of the world, except the island of Great Britain. This arbitrary act, however, they soon recalled, and by solemn treaty, entered into on the 12$^{th}$ day of March, 1651, between the said commonwealth by their commissioners, and the colony of Virginia by their house of burgesses, it was expressly stipulated, by the 8$^{th}$ article of the said treaty, that they should have 'free trade as the people of England do enjoy to all places and with all nations, according to the laws of that commonwealth'. But that, upon the restoration [in 1660] of his majesty King Charles the second, their rights of free commerce fell once more a victim to arbitrary power; and by several acts of his reign, as well as of some of his successors, the trade of the colonies was laid under such restrictions, as show what hopes they might form from the justice of a British parliament, were its uncontrolled power admitted over these states. History has informed us that bodies of men, as well as individuals, are susceptible of the spirit of tyranny. A view of these acts of parliament for regulation, as it has been affectedly called, of the American trade, if all other evidence were removed out of the case, would undeniably evince the truth of this observation. Besides the duties they impose on our articles of export and import, they prohibit our going to any markets northward of Cape Finesterre, in the kingdom of Spain, for the sale of commodities which Great Britain will not take from us, and for the purchase of others, with which she cannot supply us, and that for no other than the arbitrary purposes of purchasing for themselves, by a sacrifice of our rights and interests, certain privileges in their commerce with an allied state, who in confidence that their exclusive trade with America will be continued, while the principles and power of the British parliament be the same, have indulged themselves in every exorbitance which their avarice could dictate, or our necessities extort; have raised their commodities, called for in America, to the double and treble of what they sold for before such exclusive privileges were given them, and of what better commodities of the same kind would cost us elsewhere, and at the same time give us much less for what we carry thither than might be had at more convenient ports. That these acts prohibit us from carrying in quest of other purchasers the surplus of our tobaccos remaining after the consumption of Great Britain is supplied; so that we must leave them with the British merchant for whatever he will please to allow us, to be by him reshipped to foreign markets, where he will reap the benefits of making sale of them for full value. That to heighten still the idea of parliamentary justice, and to show with what moderation they are like to exercise power, where themselves are to feel no part of its weight, we take leave to mention to his majesty certain other acts of British parliament, by which they would prohibit us from manufacturing for our own use the articles we raise on our own lands with our own labour. By an act passed in the $5^{th}$ year of the reign of his late majesty King George the second [1727–60], an American subject is forbidden to make a hat for himself of the fur which he has taken perhaps on his own soil; an instance of despotism to which no parallel can be produced in the most arbitrary ages of British history. By one other act, passed in the $23^{rd}$ year of the same reign, the iron which we make we are forbidden to manufacture, and heavy as that article is, and necessary in every branch of husbandry, besides commission and insurance, we are to pay freight for it to Great Britain, and freight for it back again, for the purpose of supporting not men, but machines, in the island of Great Britain. In the same spirit of equal and impartial legislation is to be viewed the act of parliament, passed in the $5^{th}$ year of the same reign, by which American lands are made subject to the demands of British creditors, while their own lands were still continued unanswerable for their debts; from which one of these conclusions must necessarily follow, either that justice is not the same in America as in Britain, or else that the British parliament pay less regard to it here than there. But that we do not point out to his majesty the injustice of these acts, with intent to rest on that principle the cause of their nullity; but to show that experience confirms the propriety of those political principles which exempt us from the jurisdiction of the British parliament. The true ground on which we declare these acts void is, that the British parliament has no right to exercise authority over us.

(Summary View)

## Notes on the State of Virginia (1787)

### 'Constitution'

It is unnecessary [...] to glean up the several instances of injury, as scattered through American and British history, and the more especially as, by passing on to the accession [in 1760] of the present king [George III] we shall find specimens of them all, aggravated, multiplied and crowded within a small compass of time, so as to evince a fixed design of considering our rights natural, conventional and chartered as mere nullities. The following is an epitome of the first sixteen years of his reign. The colonies were taxed internally and externally; their essential interests sacrificed to individuals in Great Britain; their legislatures suspended; charters annulled; trials by juries taken away; their persons subjected to transportation across the Atlantic, and to trial before foreign judicatories; their supplications for redress thought beneath answer; themselves published as cowards in the councils of their mother country and courts of Europe; armed troops sent among them to enforce submission to these violences; and actual hostilities commenced against them. No alternative was presented but resistance, or unconditional submission. Between these could be no hesitation. They closed in the appeal to arms. They declared themselves independent states. They confederated together into one great republic; thus securing to every state the benefit of an union of their whole force. In each state separately a new form of government was established. Of ours particularly the following are the outlines. The executive powers are lodged in the hands of a governor, chosen annually, and incapable of acting more than three years in seven. He is assisted by a council of eight members. The judiciary powers are divided among several courts, as will be hereafter explained [in Query XIV, 'Laws']. Legislation is exercised by two houses of assembly, the one called the house of Delegates, composed of two members from each county, chosen annually by the citizens, possessing an estate for life in 100 acres of uninhabited land, or 25 acres with a house on it, or in a house or lot in some town: the other called the Senate, consisting of 24 members, chosen quadrennially by the same electors, who for this purpose are distributed into 24 districts. The concurrence of both houses is necessary to the passage of a law. They have the appointment of the governor and council, the judges of the superior courts, auditors, attorney general, treasurer, register of the land office, and delegates to congress. As the dismemberment of the state had never had its confirmation, but, on the contrary, had always been the subject of protestation and complaint, that it might never be in our own power to raise scruples on that subject, or to disturb the harmony of our new confederacy, the grants to Maryland, Pennsylvania and the two Carolinas were ratified.

This constitution was formed when we were new and unexperienced in the science of government. It was the first, too, which was formed in the whole United States. No wonder then that time and trial have discovered very capital defects in it.
1. The majority of the men in the state, who pay and fight for its support, are unrepresented in the legislature, the roll of freeholders entitled to vote, not including generally the half of those on the roll of the militia, or of the tax-gatherers.

2. Among those who share the representation, the shares are very unequal. Thus the county of Warwick, with only one hundred fighting men, has an equal representation with the county of Loudon, which has 1,746. So that every man in Warwick has as much influence in the government as 17 men in Loudon. But lest it should be thought that an equal interspersion of small among large counties, through the whole state, may prevent any danger of injury to particular parts of it, we will divide it into districts, and show the proportions of land, of fighting men, and of representation in each:

An inspection of this table will supply the place of commentaries on it. It will appear at once that nineteen thousand men, living below the falls of the rivers, possess half of the senate, and want four members only of possessing a majority of the house of delegates; a want more than supplied by the vicinity of their situation to the seat of government, and of course the greater degree of convenience and punctuality with which their members may and will attend in the legislature. These nineteen thousand, therefore, living in one part of the country, give law to upwards of thirty thousand living in another, and appoint all their chief officers, executive and judiciary. From the difference of their situation and circumstances, their interests will often be very different.

3. The senate is, by its constitution, too homogeneous with the house of delegates. Being chosen by the same electors, at the same time, and out of the same subjects, the choice falls of course on men of the same description. The purpose of establishing different houses of legislation is to introduce the influence of different interests or different principles. Thus in Great Britain it is said their constitution relies on the house of commons for honesty, and the lords for wisdom; which would be a rational reliance, if honesty were to be bought with money, and if wisdom were hereditary. In some of the American states, the delegates and senators are so chosen, as that the first represent the persons, and the second the property of the state. But with us, wealth and wisdom have equal chance for admission into both houses. We do not, therefore, derive from the sep-

*Table 12.1*  Notes on the State of Virginia

|  | Square miles | Fighting men | Delegates | Senators |
|---|---|---|---|---|
| Between the sea-coast and falls of the rivers | [1]11,205 | 19,012 | 71 | 12 |
| Between the falls of the rivers and Blue Ridge of mountains | 18,759 | 18,828 | 46 | 8 |
| Between the Blue Ridge and the Alleghany | 11,911 | 7,673 | 16 | 2 |
| Between the Alleghany and Ohio | [2]79,650 | 4,458 | 16 | 2 |
| Total | 121,525 | 49,971 | 149 | 24 |

*Notes*:

[1]  Of these, 542 are on the eastern shore

[2]  Of these, 22,616 are Eastward of the meridian of the mouth of the Great Kanhaway

aration of our legislature into two houses, those benefits which a proper complication of principles is capable of producing, and those which alone can compensate the evils which may be produced by their dissensions.

4. All the powers of government, legislative, executive, and judiciary, result to the legislative body. The concentrating these in the same hands is precisely the definition of despotic government. It will be no alleviation that these powers will be exercised by a plurality of hands, and not by a single one. 173 despots would surely be as oppressive as one. Let those who doubt it turn their eyes on the republic of Venice. As little will it avail us that they are chosen by ourselves. An *elective despotism* was not the government we fought for, but one which should not only be founded on free principles, but in which the powers of government should be so divided and balanced among several bodies of magistracy, as that no one could transcend their legal limits, without being effectually checked and restrained by the others. For this reason that convention, which passed the ordinance of government, laid its foundation on this basis, that the legislative, executive and judiciary departments should be separate and distinct, so that no person should exercise the powers of more than one of them at the same time. But no barrier was provided between these several powers. The judiciary and executive members were left dependent on the legislative, for their subsistence in office, and some of them for their continuance in it. If therefore the legislature assumes executive and judiciary powers, no opposition is likely to be made; nor, if made, can it be effectual; because in that case they may put their proceedings into the form of an act of assembly, which will render them obligatory on the other branches. They have accordingly, in many instances, decided rights which should have been left to judiciary controversy: and the direction of the executive, during the whole time of their session, is becoming habitual and familiar. And this is done with no ill intention. The views of the present members are perfectly upright. When they are led out of their regular province, it is by art in others, and inadvertence in themselves. And this will probably be the case for some time to come. But it will not be a very long time. Mankind soon learn to make interested uses of every right and power which they possess, or may assume. The public money and public liberty intended to have been deposited with three branches of magistracy, but found inadvertently to be in the hands of one only, will soon be discovered to be sources of wealth and dominion to those who hold them; distinguished, too, by this tempting circumstance, that they are the instrument, as well as the object, of acquisition. With money we will get men, said Cæsar, and with men we will get money. Nor should our assembly be deluded by the integrity of their own purposes, and conclude that these unlimited powers will never be abused, because themselves are not disposed to abuse them. They should look forward to a time, and that not a distant one, when a corruption in this, as in the country from which we derive our origin, will have seized the heads of government, and be spread by them through the body of the people; when they will purchase the voices of the people, and make them pay the price. Human nature is the same on every side of the Atlantic, and will be alike influenced by the same causes. The time to guard against corruption and tyranny, is before they shall have gotten hold of us. It is better to keep the wolf out of the fold, than to trust

to drawing his teeth and talons after he shall have entered. To render these considerations the more cogent, we must observe in addition:

5. That the ordinary legislature may alter the constitution itself. On the discontinuance of assemblies, it became necessary to substitute in their place some other body, competent to the ordinary business of government, and to the calling forth the powers of the state for the maintenance of our opposition to Great Britain. Conventions were therefore introduced, consisting of two delegates from each county, meeting together and forming one house, on the plan of the former house of Burgesses [set up in 1619], to whose places they succeeded. These were at first chosen anew for every particular session. But in March 1775, they recommended to the people to choose a convention, which should continue in office a year. This was done, accordingly, in April 1775, and in the July following that convention passed an ordinance for the election of delegates in the month of April annually. It is well known, that in July 1775, a separation from Great Britain and establishment of republican government, had never yet entered into any person's mind. A convention, therefore, chosen under that ordinance, cannot be said to have been chosen for the purposes which certainly did not exist in the minds of those who passed it. Under this ordinance, at the annual election in April 1776, a convention for the year was chosen. Independence, and the establishment of a new form of government, were not even yet the objects of the people at large. One extract from the pamphlet called *Common Sense* [by Thomas Paine] had appeared in the Virginia papers in February, and copies of the pamphlet itself had got in a few hands. But the idea had not been opened to the mass of the people in April, much less can it be said that they had made up their minds in its favor. So that the electors of April 1776, no more than the legislators of July 1775, not thinking of independence and a permanent republic, could not mean to vest in these delegates powers of establishing them, or any authorities other than those of the ordinary legislature. So far as a temporary organization of government was necessary to render our opposition energetic, so far their organization was valid. But they received in their creation no powers but what were given to every legislature before and since. They could not, therefore, pass an act transcendent to the powers of other legislatures. If the present assembly pass an act, and declare it shall be irrevocable by subsequent assemblies, the declaration is merely void, and the act repealable, as other acts are. So far, and no farther authorized, they organized the government by the ordinance entituled a Constitution or Form of government. It pretends to no higher authority than the other ordinance of the same session; it does not say that it shall be perpetual; that it shall be unalterable by other legislatures; that it shall be transcendent above the powers of those who they knew would have equal power with themselves. Not only the silence of the instrument is a proof they thought it would be alterable, but their own practice also; for this very convention, meeting as a House of Delegates in General Assembly with the new Senate in the autumn of that year, passed acts of assembly in contradiction to their ordinance of government; and every assembly from that time to this has done the same. I am safe therefore in the position, that the constitution itself is alterable by the ordinary legislature.

(*Notes on the State of Virginia*, Query XIII, 'Constitution')

## THOMAS PAINE

Thomas Paine (1737–1809) was born in Norfolk, the son of a Quaker, and educated at a local grammar school. After moving to London and working as an exciseman and shopkeeper he became involved in radical circles before emigrating (to avoid imprisonment for debt) to America in 1774 with a letter of recommendation from Benjamin Franklin, the American colonists' leading representative in England. Paine became well known as the author of the radical republican pamphlet *Common Sense: addressed to the inhabitants of America* (1776) which supported American independence from Britain, and of which, in 1776, George Washington would write: 'I find that *Common Sense* is working a powerful change here in the minds of men'. In 1779 he became clerk to the Pennsylvania Assembly. He returned to Europe from 1787 to 1802, writing the hugely popular *The Rights of Man* (1791–92), which defended the French Revolution and responded to Edmund Burke's criticisms of it in *Reflections on the Revolution in France* (1790). In *The Rights of Man* Paine recounts the events of the Revolution, and this leads to an exposition and discussion of the Declaration of the Rights of Man (1789) and concluding remarks about forms of government – the passages that are selected here. Almost a year later, Paine published a second part of *The Rights of Man*, dealing more theoretically with government (which he felt to be a 'necessary evil') and society. Here, he put forward a positive view of commerce, and made detailed economic proposals. His proposals for taxation, for example, included the care of the elderly and a summary of general welfare. Indicted for treason, in 1792 Paine fled to France, where through Lafayette and Thomas Jefferson he had already met the *philosophe* Condorcet with whom he now worked and took an active part in the Revolution. He was elected to the National Convention, but, following his opposition to the execution of Louis XIV, he was imprisoned (1792–93) during the Terror. In 1794–95 he published a deist work *The Age of Reason*, which consisted of such a powerful assault on Christianity it made him generally unpopular when he returned to America in 1802. His last great work, the pamphlet *Agrarian Justice*, developing his economic thought, was published in French and English in 1797.

In the following passages from *The Rights of Man*, Part 1, Paine recounts the outbreak of the Revolution in 1789, from the meeting of the States-General (consisting of three hundred representatives for each of the Aristocracy and Clergy, and six hundred members of the 'Third Estate' or Commons) to the passing of the Declaration of the Rights of Man and of Citizens.

### *The Rights of Man* (1791–92)

Societies were formed in Paris, and committees of correspondence and communication established throughout the nation, for the purpose of enlightening the people, and explaining to them the principles of civil government; and so orderly was the election [to the States-General] conducted, that it did not give rise even to the rumour of tumult.

The States-General were to meet at Versailles, in April 1789, but did not assemble till May. They situated themselves in three separate chambers; or rather the Aristocracy and the Clergy withdrew each into a separate chamber. The majority of the Aristocracy claimed what they called the privilege of voting as a separate body, and of giving their consent or negative in that manner; and many of the Bishops, and the high-beneficed Clergy, claimed the same privilege on the part of their order.

The *Tiers État*, as they were then called, disowned any knowledge of artificial orders, and artificial privileges; and they were not only resolute on this point, but somewhat disdainful. They began to consider Aristocracy as a kind of fungus growing out of society, that could not be admitted even as a branch of it; and from the disposition the Aristocracy had shown, by upholding *lettres de cachet* [king's warrants for arrest without trial] and in sundry other instances, it was manifest that no Constitution could be formed, by admitting men in any other character than as National men.

After various altercations on this head, the *Tiers État* or Commons, as they were then called, declared themselves, on a motion made for that purpose, by the Abbé Sieyès [constitutional theorist and author of the influential pamphlet, *What is the Third Estate?* (1789)], THE REPRESENTATIVES OF THE NATION; and that the two orders could be considered but as deputies of corporations, and could only have a deliberate voice but when they assembled in a National character with the National representatives. This proceeding extinguished the style of *États-Généraux*, or States-General, and erected it into the style it now bears, that of *L'Assemblée Nationale*, or National Assembly.

This motion was not made in a precipitate manner. It was the result of cool deliberation, and concerted between the National representatives, and the patriotic members of the two chambers, who saw into the folly, mischief, and injustice of artificial privileged distinctions. It was become evident, that no Constitution, worthy of being called by that name, could be established on any thing less than a National ground. The Aristocracy had hitherto opposed the despotism of the Court, and affected the language of patriotism; but it opposed it as its rival (as the English Barons opposed King John), and it now opposed the Nation from the same motives.

On carrying this motion, the National representatives, as had been concerted, sent an invitation to the two chambers, to unite with them in a National character, and to proceed to business. A majority of the Clergy, chiefly of the parish priests, withdrew from the clerical chamber, and joined the Nation; and forty-five from the other chamber joined in like manner. [...]

The King, who, very different from the general class called by that name, is a man of a good heart, showed himself disposed to recommend an union of the three chambers on the ground the National Assembly had taken; but the malcontents exerted themselves to prevent it; and began now to have another object in view.

Their numbers consisted of a majority of the aristocratical chamber, and a minority of the clerical chamber, chiefly of bishops and high-beneficed clergy; and these men were determined to put everything to issue, as well by strength, as by stratagem. They had no objection to a constitution; but it must be such a one as themselves should dictate, and suited to their own views and peculiar situations. On the other hand, the Nation disowned knowing anything of them but as citizens; and was determined to shut out all such upstart pretensions. The more aristocracy appeared, the more it was despised; there was a visible imbecility and want of intellect in the majority — a sort of *je ne sais quoi*, that while it affected to be more than citizen, was less than man. It lost ground from contempt more than from hatred; and was rather jeered at as an ass, than dreaded as a lion. This is the general character of aristocracy, or what are called nobles, or nobility, or rather no-ability, in all countries.

The plan of the malcontents consisted now of two things; either to deliberate and vote by chambers (or orders) more especially on all questions respecting a constitution (by which the aristocratical chamber would have had a negative on any article of the constitution); or, in case they could not accomplish this object, to overthrow the National Assembly entirely.

To effect one of other of these objects, they now began to cultivate a friendship with the despotism they had hitherto attempted to rival, and the Count d'Artois [the king's brother] became their chief. The King, who has since declared himself deceived into their measures, held, according to the old form, a *Bed of Justice* [*lit de justice*], in which he accorded to the deliberation and vote *par tête* (by head) upon several subjects: but reserved the deliberation and vote upon all questions respecting a constitution, to the three chambers separately. This declaration of the King was made against the advice of M. Necker [the Swiss banker, Jacques Necker, Controller of Finance 1777–83, recalled to office in 1788], who now began to perceive that he was growing out of fashion at Court, and that another minister was in contemplation.

As the form of sitting in separate chambers was yet apparently kept up, though essentially destroyed, the National representatives, immediately after this declaration of the King, resorted to their own chambers to consult on a protest against it; and the minority of the chamber calling itself the nobles, who had joined the National cause, retired to a private house to consult in like manner.

The malcontents had by this time concerted their measures with the Court, which the Count d'Artois undertook to conduct; and as they saw from the discontent which the declaration excited, and the opposition making against it, that they could not obtain a control over the intended constitution by a separate vote, they prepared themselves for their final object — that of conspiring against the National Assembly, and overthrowing it.

The next morning, the door of the chamber of the National Assembly was shut against them, and guarded by troops, and the members were refused admittance. On this, they withdrew to a tennis-ground in the neighbourhood of Versailles, as the most convenient place they could find, and after renewing their session, they took an oath, never to separate from each other, under any circumstance whatever, death excepted, until they had established a constitution. As the experiment of shutting up the house had no other effect than that of producing a closer connection in the members, it was opened again the next day, and the public business recommenced in the usual place.

We are now to have in view the formation of the new Ministry, which was to accomplish the overthrow of the National Assembly. But as force would be necessary, orders were issued to assemble thirty thousand troops, the command of which was given to [Marshall de] Broglie, one of the new-intended Ministry, who was recalled from the country for this purpose. But as some management was also necessary, to keep this plan concealed till the moment it should be ready for execution, it is to this policy that a declaration made by the Count d'Artois must be attributed, and which it is here proper to introduce.

It could not but occur, that while the malcontents continued to resort to their chambers, separate from the National Assembly, more jealousy would be excited than if they were mixed with it; and that the plot might be suspected. But, as they had taken their ground, and now wanted a pretext for quitting it, it was necessary that one should be devised. This was accomplished in the declaration made by the Count d'Artois, 'That if they took not a part in the National Assembly, the life of the King would be endangered'; on which they quitted their chambers, and mixed with the Assembly in one body.

At the time this declaration was made, it was generally treated as a piece of absurdity in Count d'Artois; and calculated merely to relieve the outstanding members of the two chambers, from the diminutive situation they were put in; and if nothing more had followed, this conclusion would have been good. But as things best explain themselves by their events, this apparent union was only a cover to the machinations which were secretly going on; and the declaration accommodated itself to answer that purpose. In a little time the National Assembly found itself surrounded by troops, and thousands more were daily arriving. On this a very strong declaration was made by the National Assembly to the King, remonstrating on the impropriety of the measure, and demanding the reason.

The King, who was not in the secret of this business, as himself afterwards declared, gave substantially for answer, that he had no other object in view than to preserve the public tranquillity, which appeared to be very much disturbed.

But in a few days from this time, the plot unravelled itself. M. Necker, and the Ministry were displaced, and a new one formed, of the enemies of the revolution; and Broglie, with between twenty-five and thirty thousand foreign troops, was arrived to support them. The mask was now thrown off, and matters were come to a crisis. The event was, that in the space of three days, the new Ministry and their abettors found it prudent to fly the nation: the Bastille was taken, and Broglie and his foreign troops dispersed. [...]

The conspiracy being thus dispersed, one of the first works of the National Assembly, instead of vindictive proclamations as has been the case with other governments, published a Declaration of the Rights of Man, as the basis on which the new constitution was to be built, and which is here subjoined.

## 'Declaration of the Rights of Man and Citizens'

By the National Assembly of France

The representatives of the people of France, formed into a National Assembly, considering that ignorance, neglect, or contempt of human rights, are the sole causes of public misfortunes and corruptions of government, have resolved to set forth, in a solemn declaration, these natural, imprescriptible, and inalienable rights: that this declaration being constantly present to the minds of the body social, they may be ever kept attentive to their rights and their duties: that the acts of the legislative and executive powers of government, being capable of being every moment compared with the end of political institutions, may be more respected: and also, that the future claims of the citizens, being directed by simple and incontestable principles, may always tend to the maintenance of the constitution and the general happiness.

For these reasons the National Assembly doth recognize and declare, in the presence of the Supreme Being, and with a hope of his blessing and favour, the following *sacred* rights of men and of citizens:

I. Men are born and always continue free and equal in respect of their rights. Civil distinctions, therefore, can only he founded on public utility.

II. The end of all political associations is the preservation of the natural and imprescriptible rights of man; and these rights are liberty, property, security, and resistance of oppression.

III. The nation is essentially the source of all sovereignty: nor can any *individual* or *any body of men*, be entitled to any authority which is not expressly derived from it.

IV. Political liberty consists in the power of doing whatever does not injure another. The exercise of the natural rights of every man has no other limits than those which are necessary to secure to every *other* man the free exercise of the same rights; and these limits are determinable only by the law.

V. The law ought to prohibit only actions hurtful to society. What is not prohibited by the law, should not be hindered; nor should anyone be compelled to that which the law does not require.

VI. The law is an expression of the will of the community. All citizens have a right to concur, either personally, or by their representatives, in its formation. It should be the same to all, whether it protects or punishes; and all being equal in its sight, are equally eligible to all honours, places, and employments, according to their different abilities, without any other distinction than that created by their virtues and talents.

VII. No man should be accused, arrested, or held in confinement, except in cases determined by the law, and according to the forms which it has prescribed. All who promote, solicit, execute, or cause to be executed, arbitrary orders, ought to be punished; and every citizen called upon or apprehended by virtue of the law, ought immediately to obey, and not render himself culpable by resistance.

VIII. The law ought to impose no other penalties than such as are absolutely and evidently necessary: and no one ought to be punished, but in virtue of a law promulgated before the offence, and legally applied.

IX. Every man being presumed innocent till he has been convicted, whenever his detention becomes indispensable, all rigour to him, more than is necessary to secure his person, ought to be provided against by the law.

X. No man ought to be molested on account of his opinions, not even on account of his *religious* opinions, provided his avowal of them does not disturb the public order established by law.

XI. The unrestrained communication of thoughts and opinions being one of the most precious rights of man, every citizen may speak, write, and publish freely, provided he is responsible for the abuse of this liberty in cases determined by the law.

XII. A public force being necessary to give security to the rights of men and of citizens, that force is instituted for the benefit of the community, and not for the particular benefit of the persons with whom it is entrusted.

XIII. A common contribution being necessary for the support of the public force, and for defraying the other expenses of government, it ought to be divided equally among the members of the community, according to their abilities.

XIV. Every citizen has a right either by himself or his representative, to a free voice in determining the necessity of public contributions, the appropriation of them, and their amount, mode of assessment, and duration.

XV. Every community has a right to demand of all its agents, an account of their conduct.

XVI. Every community in which a separation of powers and a security of rights is not provided for, wants a constitution.

XVII. The right to property being inviolable and sacred, no one ought to be deprived of it except in cases of evident public necessity legally ascertained, and on condition of a previous just indemnity.

### Observations on the Declaration of Rights

While the Declaration of Rights was before the National Assembly, some of its members remarked that if a Declaration of Rights was published it should be accompanied by a Declaration of Duties. The observation discovered a mind that reflected, and it only erred by not reflecting far enough. A Declaration of Rights is, by reciprocity, a Declaration of Duties also. Whatever is my right as a man, is also the right of another; and it becomes my duty to guarantee, as well as to possess.

The three first articles are the basis of liberty, as well individual as national; nor can any country be called free whose government does not take its beginning from the principles they contain, and continue to preserve them pure; and the whole of the Declaration of Rights is of more value to the world, and will do more good, than all the laws and statutes that have yet been promulgated.

In the declaratory exordium which prefaces the Declaration of Rights, we see the solemn and majestic spectacle of a nation opening its commission, under the auspices of its Creator, to establish a government; a scene so new, and so transcendently unequalled by anything in the European world, that the name of a Revolution is diminutive of its character, and it rises into a Regeneration of man. What are the present governments of Europe, but a scene of iniquity and oppression? What is that of England? Do not its own inhabitants say, It is a market where every man has his price, and where corruption is common traffic, at the expense of a deluded people? No wonder, then, that the French Revolution is traduced. Had it confined itself merely to the destruction of flagrant despotism, perhaps Mr Burke and some others had been silent. Their cry now is, 'It has gone too far': that is, it has gone too far for them. It stares corruption in the face, and the venal tribe are all alarmed. Their fear discovers itself in their outrage, and they are but publishing the groans of a wounded vice. But from such opposition, the French Revolution, instead of suffering, receives an homage. The more it is struck, the more sparks it will emit; and the fear is, it will not be struck enough. It has nothing to dread from attacks: Truth has given it an establishment; and Time will record it with a name as lasting as his own.

*(Rights of Man*, Part 1)

## WILLIAM GODWIN

Born into a non-conformist family in Cambridgeshire, William Godwin (1756–1836) was educated at Hoxton Academy, and became a dissenting minister before encountering the texts of d'Holbach, Helvétius and Rousseau and turning to deism, and then perhaps to atheism. In 1782 he moved to London and launched himself into a literary career, attaining fame (and notoriety, as hostility to the French Revolution spread) with publication of *An Enquiry Concerning Political Justice and its Influence on Morals and Happiness* in 1793, and a novel, *The Adventures of Caleb Williams* in 1794. In 1796 he started a relationship with the feminist writer Mary Wollstonecraft (whom he had met five years earlier), and they were soon married. Godwin was distraught at her death following the birth of their daughter Mary Godwin in 1797, and in 1798 he wrote the *Memoirs of the Author of the Vindication of the Rights of Woman*. Despite the immediate success of *Enquiry Concerning Political Justice*, repeated attacks on and parodies of his ideas led Godwin to focus on writing novels: notably, *Mandeville* (1817), *Cloudesley* (1820), and *Deloraine* (1833). His work exercised a powerful influence over the Romantic poets, particularly Shelley (his son-in-law), Wordsworth, Southey and Coleridge.

An Enquiry Concerning Political Justice investigates political institutions and their capacity to obstruct and pervert the rise of individual good and the perfectibility of man, for Godwin held that 'individuality is of the very essence of intellectual excellence'. The book dismisses divine right, patriarchal descent and despotism, but it also attacks the idea of natural rights. Godwin followed Tom Paine's distinction in *Common Sense*, between society (which is seen as a blessing) and government (which is never more than a 'necessary evil'), but he went much further, calling not so much for the reform of government as for its abolition. He remained unconvinced about social contract theory, and his book launched a vehement assault on law and political authority, as well as on punishment, private property and marriage. He argued that the basic moral principles are justice, equality and private judgement: 'Each man should be wise enough to govern himself, without the intervention of any compulsory restraint'. In particular, he advocated that 'arbitrary distinctions' be removed and that human beings be encouraged to live rationally and morally, engaging in a constant process of self-critical dialogue and public discussion. The *Enquiry*'s rational account of anarchism meant that it became, and remains, a founding text of radical thought.

The *Enquiry*, originally published in two volumes in 1793, consists of eight main sections ('books'), each subdivided into several chapters. Following its success, in 1796 Godwin produced a revised edition with a new Preface, noting that the first edition had been 'treated by some persons as of a seditious and inflammatory nature', and adding, 'This is probably an aspersion.' He continued:

> No man can more fervently deprecate scenes of commotion and tumult than the author of this book; no man would more anxiously avoid the lending his assistance in the most distant manner to animosity and bloodshed; but he persuades himself that, whatever may be the events with which the present

crisis of human history shall be distinguished, the effect of his writings, as far as they are in any degree remembered, will be found favourable to the increase and preservation of general kindness and benevolence.

The following three extracts (based upon the 1796 edition) are taken from books 2, 3 and 4 of the *Enquiry*.

## An Enquiry Concerning Political Justice (1793)

### 'Principles of Society – Of Justice'

Society is nothing more than an aggregation of individuals. Its claims and duties must be the aggregate of their claims and duties, the one no more precarious and arbitrary than the other. What has the society a right to require from me? The question is already answered: everything that it is my duty to do. Anything more? Certainly not. Can it change eternal truth, or subvert the nature of men and their actions? Can it make my duty consist in committing intemperance, in maltreating or assassinating my neighbour? Again, what is it that the society is bound to do for its members? Everything that is requisite for their welfare. But the nature of their welfare is defined by the nature of mind. That will most contribute to it which expands the understanding, supplies incitements to virtue, fills us with a generous consciousness of our independence, and carefully removes whatever can impede our exertions.

Should it be affirmed 'that it is not in the power of political system to secure to us these advantages', the conclusion will not be less incontrovertible. It is bound to contribute everything it is able to these purposes. Suppose its influence in the utmost degree limited; there must be one method approaching nearer than any other to the desired object, and that method ought to be universally adopted. There is one thing that political institutions can assuredly do, they can avoid positively counteracting the true interests of their subjects. But all capricious rules and arbitrary distinctions do positively counteract them. There is scarcely any modification of society but has in it some degree of moral tendency. So far as it produces neither mischief nor benefit, it is good for nothing. So far as it tends to the improvement of the community, it ought to be universally adopted.

(*Enquiry*, Book II 'Principles of Society', ch. 2 'Of Justice')

### 'Principles of Government – Of Forms of Government'

There is one other topic relative to general principles of government, which it seems fitting and useful to examine in this place. 'Is there a scheme of political institution which, as coming nearest to perfection, ought to be prescribed to all nations; or, on the other hand, are different forms of government best adapted to the condition of different nations, each worthy to be commended in its peculiar place, but none proper to be transplanted to another soil?'

The latter part of this alternative is the creed which has ordinarily prevailed; but it is attended with obvious objections.

If one form of government makes one nation happy, why should it not equally contribute to the felicity of another?

The points in which human beings resemble are infinitely more considerable than those in which they differ. We have the same senses; and the impressions on those senses which afflict me may ordinarily be expected to be sources of anguish to you. It is true that men differ in their habits and tastes. But these are accidental varieties. There is but one perfection to man; one thing most honourable; one thing that, to a well organized and healthful mind, will produce the most exquisite pleasure. All else is deviation and error; a disease, to be cured, not to be encouraged. Sensual pleasure on the one hand, or intellectual on the other, is, absolutely speaking, the highest and most desirable. We are not to make too much account of the perversions of taste. Men long inured to slavery, for example, undoubtedly have a less exquisite sense of its hatefulness; perhaps instances may be found where it is borne without a murmur. But this is by no means a proof that it is the fit and genuine state of the beings who suffer it. To such men we ought to say, 'You are satisfied with an oblivion of all that is eminent in man; but we will awake you. You are contented with ignorance; but we will enlighten you. You are not brutes: you are not stones. You sleep away existence in a miserable neglect of your most valuable privileges: but you are capable of exquisite delights; you are formed to glow with benevolence, to expatiate in the fields of knowledge, to thrill with disinterested transport, to enlarge your thoughts, so as to take in the wonders of the material universe, and the principles that bound and ascertain the general happiness.'

If then it appears that the means which are beneficial to one man ought, in the most important instances, to be deemed most desirable for others, the same principle which applies to all other sources of moral influence will also apply to government. Every political system must have a certain influence upon the moral state of the nation among whom it exists. Some are more favourable, or less inimical, to the general interest than others. That form of society which is most conducive to improvement, to the exalted and permanent pleasure of man, the sound politician would wish to see universally realized.

Such is the true theory of this subject, taken in its most absolute form; but there are circumstances that qualify the universality of these principles.

The best gift that can be communicated to man is valuable only so far as it is esteemed. It is in vain that you heap upon me benefits that I neither understand nor desire. The faculty of understanding is an essential part of every human being, and cannot with impunity be overlooked, in any attempt to alter or meliorate his condition. Government, in particular, is founded in opinion; nor can any attempt to govern men otherwise than in conformity to their own conceptions be expected to prove salutary. A project therefore to introduce abruptly any species of political institution, merely from a view to its absolute excellence, and without taking into account the state of the public mind, must be absurd and injurious. The best mode of political society will, no doubt, be considered by the enlightened friend of his species, as the ultimate object of his speculations and efforts. But he will be on his guard against precipitate measures. The only mode for its secure and auspicious establishment is through the medium of a general preference in its favour. [...]

'Different forms of government are best adapted to the condition of different nations.' Yet there is one form, in itself considered, better than any other form. Every other mode of society, except that which conduces to the best and most pleasurable state of the human species, is at most only an object of toleration. It must of necessity be ill in various respects; it must entail mischiefs; it must foster unsocial and immoral prejudices. Yet upon the whole, it may be, like some excrescences and defects in the human frame, it cannot immediately be removed without introducing something worse. In the machine of human society all the wheels must move together. He that should violently attempt to raise any one part into a condition more exalted than the rest, or force it to start away from its fellows, would be the enemy, and not the benefactor, of his contemporaries.

It follows however, from the principles already detailed, that the interests of the human species require a gradual, but uninterrupted change. He who should make these principles the regulators of his conduct would not rashly insist upon the instant abolition of all existing abuses. But he would not nourish them with false praise. He would show no indulgence to their enormities. He would tell all the truth he could discover, in relation to the genuine interests of mankind. Truth, delivered in a spirit of universal kindness, with no narrow resentments or angry invective, can scarcely be dangerous, or fail, so far as relates to its own operation, to communicate a similar spirit to the hearer. Truth, however unreserved be the mode of its enunciation, will be sufficiently gradual in its progress. It will be fully comprehended only by slow degrees by its most assiduous votaries; and the degrees will be still more temperate by which it will pervade so considerable a portion of the community as to render them mature for a change of their common institutions.

Again, if conviction of the understanding be the compass which is to direct our proceedings in the general affairs, we shall have many reforms, but no revolutions. As it is only in a gradual manner that the public can be instructed, a violent explosion in the community is by no means the most likely to happen as the result of instruction. Revolutions are the produce of passion, not of sober and tranquil reason. There must be an obstinate resistance to improvement on the one side, to engender a furious determination of realizing a system at a stroke on the other. The reformers must have suffered from incessant counteraction, till, inflamed by the treachery and art of their opponents, they are wrought up to the desperate state of imagining that all must be secured in the first favourable crisis, as the only alternative for its being ever secured. It would seem therefore that the demand of the effectual ally of the public happiness, upon those who enjoy the privileges of the state, would be, 'Do not give us too soon; do not give us too much; but act under the incessant influence of a disposition to give us something.'

Government, under whatever point of view we examine this topic, is unfortunately pregnant with motives to censure and complaint. Incessant change, everlasting innovation, seem to be dictated by the true interests of mankind. But government is the perpetual enemy of change. What was admirably observed of a particular system of government (the Spartan) is in a great degree true of all: they 'lay their hand on the spring there is in society, and put a stop to its motion'. Their tendency is to perpetuate abuse. What was once thought right and useful they undertake to entail to the latest posterity. They reverse the genuine propensities of man, and, instead of suffering us to proceed, teach us to look backward for perfection. They prompt us to seek the public welfare, not in alteration and improvement, but in a timid reverence for the decisions of our ancestors, as if it were the nature of the human mind always to degenerate, and never to advance.

Man is in a state of perpetual mutation. He must grow either better or worse, either correct his habits or confirm them. The government under which we are placed must either increase our passions and prejudices by fanning the flame, or, by gradually discouraging, tend to extirpate them. In reality, it is impossible to conceive a government that shall have the latter tendency. By its very nature, positive institution has a tendency to suspend the elasticity and progress of mind. Every scheme for embodying imperfection must be injurious. That which is today a considerable melioration will at some future period, if preserved unaltered, appear a defect and disease in the body politic. It is earnestly to be desired that each man should be wise enough to govern himself, without the intervention of any compulsory restraint; and, since government, even in its best state, is an evil, the object principally to be aimed at is that we should have as little of it as the general peace of human society will permit.

(*Enquiry*, Book III 'Principles of Government',
ch. 7 'Of Forms of Government')

### 'Of the Operation of Opinion in Societies and Individuals – Of Resistance'

The strong hold of government has appeared hitherto to have consisted in seduction. However imperfect might be the political constitution under which they lived, mankind have ordinarily been persuaded to regard it with a sort of reverential and implicit respect. The privileges of Englishmen, and the liberties of Germany, the splendour of the most Christian, and the solemn gravity of the Catholic king, have each afforded a subject of exultation to the individuals who shared, or thought they shared, in the advantages these terms were conceived to describe. Each man was accustomed to deem it a mark of the peculiar kindness of providence that he was born in the country, whatever it was, to which he happened to belong. The time may come which shall subvert these prejudices. The time may come when men shall exercise the piercing search of truth upon the mysteries of government, and view without prepossession the defects and abuses of the constitution of their country. Out of this new order of things a new series of duties will arise. When a spirit of impartiality shall prevail, and loyalty shall decay, it will become us to enquire into the conduct which such a state of thinking shall make necessary. We shall then be called upon to maintain a true medium between blindness to injustice and calamity on the one hand, and an acrimonious spirit of violence and resentment on the other. It will be the duty of such as shall see these subjects in the pure light of truth to exert themselves for the effectual demolition of monopolies and usurpation; but effectual demolition is not the offspring of crude projects and precipitate measures. He who dedicates himself to these may be suspected to be under the domination of passion, rather than benevolence. The true friend of equality will do nothing unthinkingly, will cherish no wild schemes or uproar and confusion, and will endeavour to discover the mode in which his faculties may be laid out to the greatest and most permanent advantage.

(*Enquiry*, Book IV 'Of the Operation of Opinion in
Societies and Individuals', ch. 1 'Of Resistance')

# Chapter 13

# Autobiographical reflections

**T**HE EIGHTEENTH CENTURY has often been regarded as the historical moment when an ideology of human rights became politically and culturally enshrined. These rights were based upon various ideas about human nature and identity that, while often seeking comprehensive explanations for the proposed unity and diversity of humankind, nevertheless raised many questions.

Due to his influence upon other writers, John Locke's claims in the second edition (1694) of his *Essay Concerning Human Understanding* and in his *Two Treatises of Government* (1690) were especially pivotal in this new explication of what it meant to be a human. For Locke, a person could be defined as 'a thinking intelligent Being, that has reason and reflection, and can consider itself as itself, the same thinking thing in different times and places'. The self-identity of a person over time was dependent upon a unity of consciousness: 'Since consciousness always accompanies thinking, and 'tis that, that makes every one to be, what he calls "self" and thereby distinguishes himself from all other thinking things, in this alone consists personal identity' (*Essay*, Book II). In political terms, each individual was also conceived by Locke as having a God-given and distinctive mind and body (each person's inalienable property) which, through labour, could be used to establish further property rights and possessions in society. What it meant to be 'human' was therefore explained largely in terms of each individual's body, experience and consciousness, and each person's original (and divinely ordained) possession of, and right to, private property.

Of course, Locke's views of personal identity were not shared by everybody. But although Leibniz and many others objected, Locke's views made a great impression on later thinkers. David Hume reworked Locke's ideas, reaching the unsettling conclusion that personal identity consisted of 'nothing but a bundle or collection of different perceptions, which succeed each other with an inconceivable rapidity, and are in a perpetual flux and movement' (*Treatise of Human Nature*, 1739). Diderot, like

Hume, emphasised the importance of memory in creating a sense of self, and Kant stressed the importance of people thinking of themselves as moral agents in their societies. Above all, however, it was Locke's view that knowledge was based upon sensory experience – and that only experience could be trusted in the search for truth – that gave a tremendous boost to the study of 'the individual', for it seemed that sensory experience could only be located in the individual self. As Locke put it: 'the general and universal belong not to the real existence of things; but are the inventions and creatures of the understanding ... universality belongs not to things themselves, which are all of them particular in their existence' (*Essay*, Book III).

By no means confined to philosophical discussions, this growing interest in exploring the individual's experience of the world was reflected in many of the most popular novels of the century. Marivaux's *La Vie de Marianne* (1731–36), Richardson's *Pamela, or Virtue Rewarded* (1740) and *Clarissa, or the History of a Young Woman* (1747–48), Sterne's *The Life and Opinions of Tristram Shandy* (1759–67) and Goethe's *The Sorrows of Young Werther* (1774) were all either written in epistolary form or with first-person narrators, and focused upon individual protagonists. Though the novel rose from humble beginnings as a largely despised prose-form, which often seemed more concerned with the worldly lives, feelings and experiences of 'ordinary' people, rather than with important historical events or the mythological or religious themes of Classical or Christian art, novels became increasingly respectable as a literary genre. Supported by a socially diverse readership (though predominantly middle class and female), novels were also part of the growing commercialisation of art and literature, whereby artists and authors did not depend so much as before upon aristocratic patrons and subscribers in order to make a living, but could look increasingly to the tastes of the new marketplace for art. Some scholars have seen the rise of the novel as part of the general development of bourgeois identity in the period, creating a new and more private domain of culture that helped to forge a seemingly more personal sense of human identity, freed from the restrictions and status distinctions of traditional society. Novels often appeared to be about personal experiences, were read primarily for pleasure, and were often associated with women's leisure. Thus for some eighteenth-century critics and observers, they were a thoroughly idle and decadent pursuit. Furthermore, the tendency of many Enlightenment figures to tolerate and advocate a new love of personal pleasure did not help to elevate the novel as a serious art form. Indeed, the growth of intimate and erotic fiction narrated in the first person, from John Cleland's *Memoirs of a Woman of Pleasure* (popularly known as *Fanny Hill*, 1749) to the writings of the Marquis de Sade, can be seen as evidence of the rising interest in personal identity and the pursuit of worldly happiness. There were, however, many different kind of 'Enlightenment' novels, ranging from philosophical tales, such as Voltaire's *Candide* (1759) or Samuel Johnson's *The History of Rasselas* (1759), to 'realistic' novels that seemed to portray human experiences in a generally credible or probable manner, such as Henry Fielding's *The History of Tom Jones* (1749), to fantastic works, such as Horace Walpole's Gothic novel *The Castle of Otranto* (1765) and Mary Shelley's exploration of the self in *Frankenstein* (1818).

Another form of story-telling – autobiographical writing – in evidence since the Renaissance, also came to flourish in the eighteenth century, though the term 'autobiography' was not in use before Robert Southey coined the word in 1809. These autobiographies, like novels, usually focused on the creation of an individual in her or his environment, and used plot mechanisms which privileged a causal relation between character motivation and effect. Modelled on historical forms, they characteristically displayed preoccupations with facticity and a temporal model of identity. Consciousness was depicted as having an origin in the past and as a phenomenon which developed over time. Textual inscriptions of birth, geneal-ogy, tastes and memory helped to construct the new vision of the self, and it has been argued that autobiography grew from the novel, reproducing its models of describing selfhood – though notions of 'truthfulness' help readers to distinguish between the genres. The novel itself was also stimulated by the idea of autobio-graphical writing. Thus Sterne's *Tristram Shandy* plays with new notions of the self and authorial identity as the text performs a playful self-commentary on the nature of the book, with appeals to the reader, visual tricks (e.g. missing pages), and trans-gressive narrative structures (inspired by Locke's concept of the association of ideas). Autobiography may also be seen as literary evidence of the 'individual' mov-ing to centre stage in political liberalism, an effect of the increasing emphasis on the 'individual' which becomes prevalent with the long rise of Protestantism and capitalism. Eighteenth-century novels and autobiographies can thus be seen as expressions of the new challenges facing individuals, enabling readers to identify with the personal experiences and circumstances of the central figures, and to explore the changing social conditions of contemporary life. In this way, Benjamin Franklin's rags-to-riches story can be read as a heroic struggle that was both a per-sonal and a social parable.

From various socialist, feminist and postmodernist perspectives, notions of the individual at the centre of liberal political thought, of individuals largely control-ling their own destiny, and of a stable and permanent personal identity, have all been rigorously critiqued. The dependence of individuals upon other people, social traditions and relationships, has been re-emphasised. Psychoanalytic understand-ings of the 'subject' as shot through with unconscious and irrational motivations, and postmodern notions of the construction of the self in language, have also emerged. Seeing everything as originating and revolving around individuals, and being preoccupied with individuals' rights, may be as debilitating and self-deluding as it may be liberating. Moreover, for Foucauldians, the notion of 'the individual' enables modern states to lock their subjects into the bureaucratic and administra-tive systems upon which modernity depends: family, schools, prisons, medical care and provision, the police, etc. Nevertheless, the 'individual' remains the fulcrum of basic freedoms enshrined in various declarations of human rights.

Of course, autobiographical writing, reflection and introspection took many dif-ferent forms during the Enlightenment, ranging from Gibbon's famous *Memoirs* to Vico's *Autobiography*, Hogarth's *Anecdotes*, Jefferson's *Autobiography* and Princess Dashkova's *Memoirs* – as well as Rousseau's *Confessions*, Franklin's *Autobiography* and Madame de Roland's *An Appeal to Impartial Posterity*, the three texts selected here. Autobiographies were also written for many different purposes, and utilised a great variety of methods in the construction of their narrators and narratives. Mary Wollstonecraft began her literary exploration of herself in *Mary, A Fiction* (1788) by stating that 'In delineating the heroine of this fiction, the author attempts to develop a character different from those generally portrayed', as in works such as *Clarissa*. But Princess Dashkova preferred a simple opening statement – 'I was born in St Petersburg in the year 1744' – which was no less invented, as she was actually born a year before. In the following extracts from the autobiographical writings of Rousseau, Franklin and Madame de Roland, the self is constructed using a great variety of tools and methods to understand experiences as complex and diverse as childhood, fame and imprisonment. Each of these authors also examines the extent and limits of their individual agency, and their texts allow us to see how social changes were related to changes in individuals' personal lives and self-perceptions. In discussing such things as reading, writing letters and memoirs, hosting a salon, founding a public library and publishing a scientific paper, the authors show us some of the spaces of interiority and sociability during the Enlightenment. They also show us how keen they are to see themselves, and to be seen, as fundamentally good and honest people. It is not surprising, then, that each should claim to have been impressed during their childhood reading by the biographies of eminent Greeks and Romans, as narrated by Plutarch [*c*.46–120 AD] in his *Parallel Lives*. Each of their texts is deeply concerned with the idea and practice of 'virtue' as a member of society – a common and fundamental theme of eighteenth-century art and of Enlightenment reasoning and reflection.

Rousseau begins his *Confessions* (1781) with a challenging claim to the truthfulness and uniqueness of his autobiography. From his bold attempt to 'bare his soul', we can read the beginnings of Romantic and modern ideas of the journey of discovery of a problematic and passionate selfhood that seeks to express itself. The special attention that Rousseau gave to his experiences of childhood was an innovation, though it has become fundamental to modern thinking about personal identity. Franklin's memoirs begin with his tracing of his English genealogy. The extracts here from his *Autobiography* (1791) reveal his efforts to understand and explain the world in terms of his personal thoughts and experiences. We read him celebrating his achievements as a 'self-made' man who also likes to make genuine contributions to the progress of society. The use of writing to come to terms with social change may help to account for the wealth of confessional writing in post-revolutionary France. In *An Appeal to Impartial Posterity* (1795), Madame de Roland makes sense of the cataclysm of the Revolution through the act of writing during her imprisonment. She begins by reflecting on her role in the recent political events of the Revolution, and then proceeds to examine her childhood and character.

## JEAN-JACQUES ROUSSEAU

Rousseau (see p. 17) wrote his autobiography *Les Confessions* – an immense project of self-revelation, self-explanation, and self-justification – towards the end of his life. Completed in 1770 and published posthumously in 1781, the work inspired many other eighteenth-century writers, such as Madame de Roland (1754–93) and Goethe (1749–1832). Since then, confessional narratives championing self-expression and individuation have become familiar forms of writing. Earlier models were St Augustine's *Confessions* and St Teresa of Avila's *Life of Herself*, but Rousseau pioneered a self-analysis in writing that was concerned primarily with worldly feelings and experience, rather than with the demands and rewards of a Christian life. Thus he laid the foundations for modern autobiographical writing involving a retrospective analysis and narration of the development of the individual.

The *Confessions* recounts Rousseau's life up to 1765, when he was fifty-three; a life troubled by his sensuality, ill-health and hypochondria, spiritual restlessness and travels, and the extraordinary talents and convictions that inspired his writings. Above all, Rousseau wanted the *Confessions* to express his feelings about himself, about the difficulties of his personal relationships, not least with many of the *philosophes* (notably Diderot, d'Alembert, d'Holbach and Grimm) whom he imagined were in a conspiracy to ruin him. After the publication of the *Social Contract* and *Emile* in 1762, a warrant was issued in France for his arrest, and he fled with his companion, Thérèse Levasseur, first to Neuchâtel, a small principality under Frederick II's protection, and later, in January 1766 – after the publication of his *Lettres Écrites de la Montagne* (*Letters from the Mountain*, 1764) had further upset the Protestant clergy of Geneva and Neuchâtel, stones had been thrown at his house (1765) and a short stay on Bernese territory had been terminated – to England.

Rousseau had been invited to England by David Hume, who also secured a pension for him from George III, but he soon became suspicious that Hume (like Voltaire in 1764) had been secretly mocking him in a pamphlet (actually written by Horace Walpole). It was while he was living in Derbyshire, however, that Rousseau began his *Confessions*, and he completed the first six (of twelve) 'books' there, before leaving for France in May 1767. Over the next few years, living under a false name, he took refuge at the Prince de Conti's chateau at Tyre, and then at several places near Grenoble and Lyons where he completed his *Confessions*. In 1770 he was allowed to return to Paris where he lived and wrote his *Reveries of the Solitary Walker* (see p. 118) before moving to a country estate at Ermenonville two months before his death in 1778.

The passages selected here are based upon an English translation of the *Confessions* published in 1783. In the first extract, from the beginning of Book 1, Rousseau sets out the objectives of his work. In the second extract from Book 1, he recalls his first and traumatic experience of being unjustly punished. This was when he was an eight-year-old lodging at the house of his teacher, the pastor Mr Lambercier, whose sister's physical punishments (so Rousseau confesses) had previously been a source of great pleasure. The extract from Book 2 follows shortly after Rousseau's conversion to Catholicism in 1728 at Turin. He confesses the theft of a ribbon while working as a footman at the house of the Countess of Vercellis, who, due to her illness, had been governed by her avaricious servants Mr and Mrs

Lorenzini and their niece Miss Pontal. When questioned by the Countess's heir, Count de la Roque, Rousseau lies about his crime, leading to an abiding fear that he may have condemned an honest girl to disgrace and misery. In the extract from Book 3, he explains his distinctive way of thinking and writing. In the passage from Book 6, he describes his happiness in the late 1730s at Les Charmettes, an estate near Chambéry, a time when he was with 'Mamma', Louise de Warens, 'more than a sister, more than a mother, more than a friend, more even than a mistress'.

## Confessions (1781)

I am undertaking a work which has no example and whose execution will have no imitator. I mean to lay open to my fellow mortals a man just as nature wrought him, and that man is myself. I alone. I know my heart and I am acquainted with mankind. I am not made like anyone I have seen, I dare believe I am not made like anyone existing. If I am not better, at least I am quite different. Whether Nature has done well or ill in breaking the mould she cast me in can only be determined only after having read me.

Let the trumpet of the day of judgement sound when it will, I shall appear with this book in my hand before the Sovereign Judge, and cry with a loud voice: 'This is my work, these were my thoughts, and thus was I. I have freely told the good and the bad, and have hid nothing wicked, added nothing good; and if I have happened to make use of an insignificant ornament, 'twas only to fill a void occasioned by a short memory. I may have supposed true what I knew might be so, never what I knew was false. I have exposed myself as I was, contemptible and vile sometimes; at others good, generous and sublime. I have revealed my heart as Thou sawest it thyself. Eternal Being! Assemble around me the numberless throng of my fellow-mortals and let them listen to my confessions, let them lament at my unworthiness, let them blush at my misery. Let each of them, in his turn, lay open his heart with the same sincerity at the foot of Thy throne, and then say, if he dare, "I was better than that man."'

(*Confessions*, Book 1, 1712–19)

### 'Book 1, 1712–19'

I was studying [at Bossey, near Geneva] one day alone in the chamber contiguous to the kitchen; the maid had put some of Miss Lambercier's combs to dry by the fire; when she came to fetch them, she found the teeth of one broke. Who [was] suspect of this havock? None besides myself had entered the room. They question me; I deny having touched the comb. Mr and Miss Lambercier consult, exhort, press, threaten. I persist obstinately; but conviction was too strong, and carried it against all my protestations, though this was the first time they caught me in so audacious lies. The affair was thought serious; it deserved it. The wickedness, the lie, the obstinacy were thought equally worthy of punishment; but this time it was not Miss Lambercier that inflicted it. My Uncle Bernard was wrote to; he came. My poor cousin was charged with another crime not less serious. We were taken to the same execution. It was terrible. If, seeking the remedy even in the evil, they had intended for ever to allay my depraved senses, they could not have taken a shorter method; and I assure you, my desires left me a long time at peace.

They could not force from me the acknowledgement they sought: this renewed several times, and thrown into the most dreadful situation, I was immoveable. I would have suffered death, and I was resolved on it. Force itself was obliged to yield to the diabolical infatuation of a child; for no other name was given to my constancy. In time, I came out from this cruel ordeal in pieces, but triumphant.

It is now near fifty years since this adventure, and I am not afraid of being in future punished for the same act. Well I declare in the face of Heaven, I was innocent; that I neither broke, nor touched the comb, that I never came near the fire, never thought of it. Let me not be asked how it happened; I know not, nor can comprehend it; all that I know of it is that I was innocent.

(*Confessions*, Book 1, 1719–23)

### 'Book 2, 1728–31'

The dissolution of a family seldom happens without causing some confusion in the house, and many things to be missed [mislaid]. Such, however was the fidelity of the servants and the vigilance of M. and Madame Lorenzini that nothing was found short of the inventory [following the death of Madame de Vercellis]. Mademoiselle Pontal only lost a ribbon of white and rose colour, already much worn. Many better things were within my reach: this ribbon only tempted me. I stole it; as I did not much hide it, they soon found it on me. They wanted to know when I got it. I am confused, I hesitate, and I flutter. At last I said, with redness in my face, ''Twas Marion gave it me'. Marion was a young Moor, whom Madame de Vercellis had made her cook when, ceasing to give entertainments, she had discharged her own, having more occasion for good broths than fine ragouts [stews]. Marion was not only pretty, but had a freshness of colour to be found only in the mountains, and particularly an air of modesty, a mildness that one could not see without loving. Besides, [she was a] good girl, prudent and of an approved fidelity. This surprised them when I named her. They had as much confidence in me as in her, and it was judged of importance to know which of the two was a thief. She was sent for; there were many gathered, and the Count de la Roque was present. She comes, they show her the ribbon, I accused her boldly. She remains speechless and astonished, casts a look at me which would have appeased a devil, but which my barbarous heart resists. She denies in fine [in the end], with assurance, the theft, but without anger, turns towards me, begs me to consider, not disgrace an innocent girl who never wished me ill. I, with an infernal impudence, confirm my declaration, and maintain to her face that she gave me the ribbon. The poor creature began crying, and said but these words, 'Ah, Rousseau! I thought you of a good disposition; you reduce me to misery, but I would not be in your place. That's all'. She continued defending herself with as much simplicity as steadiness, but without using against me the least invective. This moderation, compared to my decisive tone, hurt her [defence]. It did not seem natural to suppose on one side an audaciousness so diabolical, and on the other a mildness so angelical. They did not seem to determine entirely, but prejudice was for me. In the bustle [in which] they were engaged, they did not give themselves time to sound the affair; and the Count de la Roque, in sending us both away, contented himself with saying, the conscience of the culpable would revenge the innocent. [...]

This cruel remembrance so much troubles me sometimes, and disorders me to such a degree, that I perceive in my endeavours to sleep, this poor girl coming to upbraid me of my crime, as if it was committed yesterday. Whilst I lived happy it tormented me less; but in the midst of a life of troubles it robs me of the sweet consolation of persecuted innocence. It makes me feel to the quick what I believe I have mentioned in some of my works, that remorse sleeps during a prosperous life, but awakens in adversity. I never could determine, however, to disburden my heart of this load in the breast of a friend. The strictest intimacy never induced me to tell it to anyone, not even to Madame de Warens. The most I could do was to own I upbraided myself of an atrocious action, but never said in what it consisted. The weight has therefore remained to this day on my conscience without alleviation; and I may say, that the desire of delivering myself from it in some degree, has greatly contributed to the resolution I have taken of writing my *Confessions*.

(*Confessions*, Book 2, 1728–31)

### 'Book 3, 1731–32'

This slowness of thought, joined to the vivacity of feeling, is not in my conversation only. I have it when alone also, and when I write. My ideas are disposed in my head with the greatest difficulty; they circulate dully; and they ferment till they move me, heat me, give me palpitations. And amidst all this emotion I see nothing clearly; I cannot write a single word; I must wait. Insensibly this vast emotion is suppressed, chaos dispersed; each thing takes its place, but slowly, and after long and confused agitation. Have you ever seen an opera in Italy? In changing the scenes there reigns a disagreeable disorder on those grand theatres, which lasts a considerable time. Decorations are all intermixed; you see in every part a pulling and hauling about which gives pain; you think the whole is turning topsy-turvy. By degrees, everything is, however, brought to its place, nothing is wanting and, you are greatly surprised to find a ravishing sight succeeds this long tumult. This piece of work nearly resembles that which operates in my brain, when I would write. Had I first known how to wait, and then render with all their beauties the scenes thus painted there, few authors would have surpassed me.

Thence comes the extreme difficulty I find in writing. My manuscripts, scratched out, blotted, mixed, not legible, attest the trouble they cost me. Not one but I was obliged to transcribe four or five times before it went to the press. I never could do anything, the pen in hand, opposite a table and paper: 'twas in my walks, amidst the rocks and woods, 'twas in the night during my slumbers; I wrote in my brain, you may judge how slowly, particularly to a man deprived of verbal memory, and who, in his life, never could retain six verses by heart. Some of my periods [sentences] I have turned and winded five or six nights in my head before they were in a state for going on paper. From thence, likewise, I succeed better in works that demand labour, than in those which must have a certain airiness; as letters, a style I could never get the tone of, and whose occupation is to me the greatest of punishments. I write no letters on the most trifling subject, which do not cost me hours of fatigue. Or, if I would write immediately what strikes me, I can neither begin nor end; my letter is a long and confused verbosity; with trouble I am understood when it is read.

I am not only troubled to render my ideas, but even in receiving them I find them equally difficult to take in. I have studied mankind, and think myself a tolerable good observatory. Nevertheless, I cannot see anything in what I perceived; I see clearly that only I recollect, and I have no knowledge but in my recollections. Of all that's said, of all that's done, of all that passes in my presence, I know nothing. I penetrate nothing. The external sign is all that strikes me. [When] the whole returns again; the time calls to mind the place, the tone, look, gesture and circumstance; nothing escapes me. Then, from what they said or did, I find out what they thought, and it is very seldom I mistake.

(*Confessions*, Book 3, 1731–32)

### 'Book 6, 1738'

Here begins the short happiness of my life; now come the peaceable rapid moments which give me a right to say I have lived. Precious and regretted moments! Ah, begin again your lovely course; glide more gently through my memory, if possible, than you really did in your fugitive succession. What shall I do to prolong to my wish this recital so; to tell over and over the same things and not tire my readers by repeating them more than I myself was tired by incessantly recommencing them? Besides, did this consist in facts, in actions, in words, I might describe and render them somehow. But how say that which was never done, nor thought, but tasted and felt without my being able to express any other object of my happiness but this feeling only? I rose with the sun, and I was happy; I walked, and I was happy; I saw Mamma, and was happy; I quitted her, and was happy; I ran over the woods, the hills, strayed through the valleys; I read, I rested, worked in the garden, gathered fruit, assisted house, and happiness followed me to every place; it was not in anything assignable within me; it could not leave me a single instant.

Not the least thing which happened to me during this lovely period, nothing I did, said, or thought, has escaped my memory. The years which precede or follow it present themselves to me at intervals; I recollect them unequally and confusedly; but I entirely remember it [as if it] still existed. My imagination, which in my youth was always beforehand and [is] now retrograde, compensates by this sweet recollection, the hope I have for ever lost. I see nothing in futurity that can tempt me; reflecting only on the past can soothe me, and thus reflection so lively and so real in the period I speak of often makes my life comfortable in spite of my misfortunes.

(*Confessions*, Book 6, 1738)

## BENJAMIN FRANKLIN

Benjamin Franklin (1706–90) was born into a large family in Boston, the son of a tallow-chandler who had emigrated from England in 1683. He would become an important American printer and publisher, as well as a very famous author, inventor, scientist, entrepreneur and diplomat. However, he is principally remembered as an exemplary 'Enlightened' man, and one of the 'founding fathers' of the United States whose signature came to be on several of the most important documents of early American history: the Declaration of Independence (1776), the Treaty of

Alliance with France (1778), the Treaty of Peace with Great Britain (1783), and the Constitution of the United States (1787). For many later commentators, Franklin's rags-to-riches story came to embody the 'American dream', and for the sociologist Max Weber, his life was the epitome of the Protestant ethic that was the basis of modern capitalism.

Franklin received no formal education after the age of ten and was apprenticed to his brother at the age of seventeen, running away to Philadelphia, finishing his training as a printer in London (1724–26) and setting up his own business back in Philadelphia in 1726. Possessing an extraordinary range of talents, and enthusiasm for hard work and thrift, he succeeded in a wide range of ventures, such as the founding of America's first public library (1731), the American Philosophical Society (1744), and the first American fire-insurance company (1752). He was also a keen scientist and inventor, creating the open stove, the lightning-rod conductor and bifocal glasses. He never patented these inventions, arguing that 'as we enjoy great advantages from the inventions of others, we should be glad of an opportunity to serve others by any invention of ours; and this we should do freely and generously'. His experiments and theories on electricity were published as *Experiments and Observations on Electricity* (1751–54). In 1756 he became a fellow of the Royal Society, and was elected to the French Academy of Sciences in 1772, where he met Voltaire at a celebrated meeting in 1778. Following his death in 1790, the French National Assembly declared that 'The name of Benjamin Franklin will be immortal in the records of freedom and philosophy'.

As a diplomat in London and in Paris, Franklin won high praise for his achievements, such as the repeal of the Stamp Act in 1766. An advocate of strong federal government, he was called upon to negotiate such events as Britain's recognition of the American colonies as a sovereign nation, to serve as a diplomat in France (1776–85) and to contribute to the drafting of the Declaration of Independence and the Constitution. Towards the end of his career, he was president of the executive council of Pennsylvania, and of the first American anti-slavery society. Aside from thousands of letters and papers, among his many published writings are *A Modest Enquiry into the Nature and Necessity of Paper Currency* (1729), *Poor Richard's Almanac* (1732–57), and *Proposal Relating to the Education of Youth in Pennsylvania* (1749). Part of his *Autobiography* was first published at Paris in 1791, a year after his death; the first English versions appearing in London in 1793.

The following passages are taken from the unfinished *Autobiography*, which Franklin began when he was sixty-five, and wrote in England, France and America between 1771 and 1789. In the first extract, written in 1771 at Twyford, the home of his friend Jonathan Shipley, Bishop of St Asaph, Franklin introduces his work by ostensibly addressing it to his forty-year-old natural son, William, whom he had raised with his wife's children. In the second extract, written near Paris in 1784, he describes the foundation of the public library at Philadelphia and (at the request of a Quaker friend) the virtues by which he had tried to live his life – though he did not hide his shortcomings. In the third and fourth extracts, written at his home in Philadelphia in 1788–89, Franklin relates his thoughts on the cleaning of London's streets and the origins and reception of his pioneering study of electricity. Like Rousseau and Madame de Roland, he had been greatly impressed by reading Plutarch's *Parallel Lives*, as well as by the works of Bunyan and Defoe. However, the 'self-made' man, evidently a public do-gooder and private moralist, that emerges from Franklin's story is very much his own construction; it is a warm and subtle narrative in which fact and fiction are united to create a celebrated literary self.

## *Autobiography* (1791)

Dear Son, I have ever had pleasure in obtaining any little anecdotes of my ancestors. You may remember the inquiries I made among the remains of my relations when you were with me in England, and the journey I undertook for that purpose. Imagining it may be equally agreeable to you to know the circumstances of my life, many of which you are yet unacquainted with, and expecting the enjoyment of a week's uninterrupted leisure in my present country retirement, I sit down to write them for you. To which I have besides some other inducements. Having emerged from the poverty and obscurity in which I was born and bred, to a state of affluence and some degree of reputation in the world, and having gone so far through life with a considerable share of felicity, the conducing means I made use of, which with the blessing of God so well succeeded, my posterity may like to know, as they may find some of them suitable to their own situations, and therefore fit to be imitated.

That felicity, when I reflected on it, has induced me sometimes to say, that were it offered to my choice, I should have no objection to a repetition of the same life from its beginning, only asking the advantages authors have in a second edition to correct some faults of the first. So I might, besides correcting the faults, change some sinister accidents and events of it for others more favourable. But though this were denied, I should still accept the offer. Since such a repetition is not to be expected, the next thing most like living one's life over again seems to be a recollection of that life, and to make that recollection as durable as possible by putting it down in writing.

Hereby, too, I shall indulge the inclination so natural in old men, to be talking of themselves and their own past actions; and I shall indulge it without being tiresome to others, who, through respect to age, might conceive themselves obliged to give me a hearing, since this may be read or not as any one pleases. And, lastly (I may as well confess it, since my denial of it will be believed by nobody), perhaps I shall a good deal gratify my own *vanity*. Indeed, I scarce ever heard or saw the introductory words, 'Without vanity I may say,' etc., but some vain thing immediately followed. Most people dislike vanity in others, whatever share they have of it themselves; but I give it fair quarter wherever I meet with it, being persuaded that it is often productive of good to the possessor, and to others that are within his sphere of action; and therefore, in many cases, it would not be altogether absurd if a man were to thank God for his vanity among the other comforts of life.

(*Autobiography*, Part One, written at Twyford, near Winchester, 1771)

Not having any copy here [in France] of what is already written [in 1771], I know not whether an account is given of the means I used to establish the Philadelphia public library, which, from a small beginning, is now become so considerable, though I remember to have come down to near the time of that transaction, 1730. I will therefore begin here with an account of it, which may be struck out if found to have been already given.

At the time I established myself in Pennsylvania, there was not a good bookseller's shop in any of the colonies to the southward of Boston. In New York and Philadelphia the printers were indeed stationers; they sold only paper, etc., almanacs, ballads, and a few common school-books. Those who loved reading were obliged to send for their books from England; the members of the Junto [club] had each a few. We had left the alehouse, where we first met, and hired a room to hold our club in. I proposed that we should all of us bring our books to that room, where they would not only be ready to consult in our conferences, but become a common benefit, each of us being at liberty to borrow such as he wished to read at home. This was accordingly done, and for some time contented us.

Finding the advantage of this little collection, I proposed to render the benefit from books more common, by commencing a public subscription library. I drew a sketch of the plan and rules that would be necessary, and got a skilful conveyancer, Mr. Charles Brockden [a scrivener], to put the whole in form of articles of agreement to be subscribed, by which each subscriber engaged to pay a certain sum down for the first purchase of books, and an annual contribution for increasing them. So few were the readers at that time in Philadelphia, and the majority of us so poor, that I was not able, with great industry, to find more than fifty persons, mostly young tradesmen, willing to pay down for this purpose forty shillings each, and ten shillings per annum. On this little fund we began. The books were imported; the library was opened one day in the week for lending to the subscribers, on their promissory notes to pay double the value if not duly returned. The institution soon manifested its utility, was imitated by other towns, and in other provinces. The libraries were augmented by donations; reading became fashionable; and our people, having no public amusements to divert their attention from study, became better acquainted with books, and in a few years were observed by strangers to be better instructed and more intelligent than people of the same rank generally are in other countries. [...]

In the various enumerations of the moral virtues I had met with in my reading, I found the catalogue more or less numerous, as different writers included more or fewer ideas under the same name. Temperance, for example, was by some confined to eating and drinking, while by others it was extended to mean the moderating every other pleasure, appetite, inclination, or passion, bodily or mental, even to our avarice and ambition. I proposed to myself, for the sake of clearness, to use rather more names, with fewer ideas annexed to each, than a few names with more ideas; and I included under thirteen names of virtues all that at that time occurred to me as necessary or desirable, and annexed to each a short precept, which fully expressed the extent I gave to its meaning.

These names of virtues, with their precepts, were:

1. Temperance
   Eat not to dullness; drink not to elevation.
2. Silence
   Speak not but what may benefit others or yourself; avoid trifling conversation.

3. Order
   Let all your things have their places; let each part of your business have its time.
4. Resolution
   Resolve to perform what you ought; perform without fail what you resolve.
5. Frugality
   Make no expense but to do good to others or yourself; *i.e.*, waste nothing.
6. Industry
   Lose no time; be always employed in something useful; cut off all unnecessary actions.
7. Sincerity
   Use no hurtful deceit; think innocently and justly, and, if you speak, speak accordingly.
8. Justice
   Wrong none by doing injuries, or omitting the benefits that are your duty.
9. Moderation
   Avoid extremes; forbear resenting injuries so much as you think they deserve.
10. Cleanliness
    Tolerate no uncleanliness in body, clothes, or habitation.
11. Tranquility
    Be not disturbed at trifles, or at accidents common or unavoidable.
12. Chastity
    Rarely use venery but for health or offspring, never to dullness, weakness or the injury of your own or another's peace or reputation.
13. Humility
    Imitate Jesus and Socrates.

My intention being to acquire the *habitude* of all these virtues, I judged it would be well not to distract my attention by attempting the whole at one, but to fix it on one of them at a time; and, when I should be master of that, then to proceed to another, and so on, till I should have gone through the thirteen; and, as the previous acquisition of some might facilitate the acquisition of certain others, I arranged them with that view, as they stand above. [...]

I made a little book [1 July 1733], in which I allotted a page for each of the virtues. I ruled each page with red ink, so as to have seven columns, one for each day of the week, marking each column with a letter for the day. I crossed these columns with thirteen red lines, marking the beginning of each line with the first letter of one of the virtues, on which line, and in its proper column, I might mark, by a little black spot, every fault I found upon examination to have been committed respecting that virtue upon that day.

I determined to give a week's strict attention to each of the virtues successively. Thus, in the first week, my great guard was to avoid every the least offence against *Temperance*, leaving the other virtues to their ordinary chance, only marking every evening the faults of the day. Thus, if in the first week I could keep my first line, marked T, clear of spots, I supposed the habit of that virtue so much strengthened, and its opposite weakened, that I might venture extending my attention to include the next, and for the following week keep both lines clear of spots. Proceeding thus to the last, I could go through a course complete in thirteen weeks, and four courses in a year.

(*Autobiography*, Part Two, written at Passy, near Paris, 1784)

I have sometimes wondered that the Londoners did not, from the effect holes in the bottom of the globe lamps used at Vauxhall have in keeping them clean, learn to have such holes in their street lamps. But, these holes being made for another purpose, viz., to communicate flame more suddenly to the wick by a little flax hanging down through them, the other use, of letting in air, seems not to have been thought of; and therefore, after the lamps have been lit a few hours, the streets of London are very poorly illuminated.

The mention of these improvements puts me in mind of one I proposed, when in London, to Dr. [John] Fothergill [1712–80], who was among the best men I have known, and a great promoter of useful projects. I had observed that the streets, when dry, were never swept, and the light dust carried away; but it was suffered to accumulate till wet weather reduced it to mud, and then, after lying some days so deep on the pavement that there was no crossing but in paths kept clean by poor people with brooms, it was with great labour raked together and thrown up into carts open above, the sides of which suffered some of the slush at every jolt on the pavement to shake out and fall, sometimes to the annoyance of foot-passengers. The reason given for not sweeping the dusty streets was, that the dust would fly into the windows of shops and houses.

An accidental occurrence had instructed me how much sweeping might be done in a little time. I found at my door in Craven Street [off the Strand], one morning, a poor woman sweeping my pavement with a birch broom; she appeared very pale and feeble, as just come out of a fit of sickness. I asked who employed her to sweep there; she said, 'Nobody; but I am very poor and in distress, and I sweeps before gentlefolkes doors, and hopes they will give me something.' I bid her sweep the whole street clean, and I would give her a shilling; this was at nine o'clock; at 12 she came for the shilling. From the slowness I saw at first in her working, I could scarce believe that the work was done so soon, and sent my servant to examine it, who reported that the whole street was swept perfectly clean, and all the dust placed in the gutter, which was in the middle; and the next rain washed it quite away, so that the pavement and even the kennel [gutter] were perfectly clean.

I then judged that, if that feeble woman could sweep such a street in three hours, a strong, active man might have done it in half the time. And here let me remark the convenience of having but one gutter in such a narrow street, running down its middle, instead of two, one on each side, near the footway; for where all the rain that falls on a street runs from the sides and meets in the middle, it forms there a current strong enough to wash away all the mud it meets with; but when divided into two channels, it is often too weak to cleanse either, and only makes the mud it finds more fluid, so that the wheels of carriages and feet of horses throw and dash it upon the foot-pavement, which is thereby rendered foul and slippery, and sometimes splash it upon those who are walking. My proposal communicated to the good doctor [Fothergill] was as follows:

For the more effectual cleaning and keeping clean the streets of London and Westminster, it is proposed that the several watchmen be contracted with to have the dust swept up in dry seasons, and the mud raked up at other times, each in the several streets and lanes of his round; that they be furnished with brooms and other proper instruments for these purposes, to be kept at their respective stands, ready to furnish the poor people they may employ in the service.

That in the dry summer months the dust be all swept up into heaps at proper distances, before the shops and windows of houses are usually opened, when the scavengers, with close-covered carts, shall also carry it all away.

That the mud, when raked up, be not left in heaps to be spread abroad again by the wheels of carriages and trampling of horses, but that the scavengers be provided with bodies of carts, not placed high upon wheels, but low upon sliders, with lattice bottoms, which, being covered with straw, will retain the mud thrown into them, and permit the water to drain from it, whereby it will become much lighter, water making the greatest part of its weight; these bodies of carts to be placed at convenient distances, and the mud brought to them in wheel-barrows; they remaining where placed till the mud is drained, and then horses brought to draw them away.

I have since had doubts of the practicability of the latter part of this proposal, on account of the narrowness of some streets, and the difficulty of placing the draining-sleds so as not to encumber too much the passage; but I am still of opinion that the former, requiring the dust to be swept up and carried away before the shops are open, is very practicable in the summer, when the days are long; for, in walking through the Strand and Fleet Street one morning at seven o'clock, I observed there was not one shop open, though it had been daylight and the sun up above three hours; the inhabitants of London choosing voluntarily to live much by candlelight, and sleep by sunshine, and yet often complain, a little absurdly, of the duty on candles, and the high price of tallow.

Some may think these trifling matters not worth minding or relating; but when they consider that though dust blown into the eyes of a single person, or into a single shop on a windy day, is but of small importance, yet the great number of the instances in a populous city, and its frequent repetitions give it weight and consequence, perhaps they will not censure very severely those who bestow some attention to affairs of this seemingly low nature. Human felicity is produced not so much by great pieces of good fortune that seldom happen, as by little advantages that occur every day. Thus, if you teach a poor young man to shave himself, and keep his razor in order, you may contribute more to the happiness of his life than in giving him a thousand guineas. The money may be soon spent, the regret only remaining of having foolishly consumed it; but in the other case, he escapes the frequent vexation of waiting for barbers, and of their sometimes dirty fingers, offensive breaths, and dull razors; he shaves when most convenient to him, and enjoys daily the pleasure of its being done with a good instrument. With these sentiments I have hazarded the few preceding pages, hoping they may afford hints which some time or other may be useful to a city I love, having lived many years in it happily, and perhaps to some of our towns in America.

(*Autobiography*, Part Three, written at Philadelphia, 1788–89)

In 1746 [1743], being at Boston, I met there with a Dr. Spence [Archibald Spencer, c. 1698–1760], who was lately arrived from Scotland, and showed me some electric experiments. They were imperfectly performed, as he was not very expert; but, being on a subject quite new to me, they equally surprised and pleased me. Soon after my return to Philadelphia, our library company received from Mr. P[eter] Collinson [1694–1763], Fellow of the Royal Society of London, a present of a glass tube, with some account of the use of it in making such experiments. I eagerly seized the opportunity of repeating what I had seen at Boston; and, by much practice, acquired great readiness in performing those, also, which we had an account of from England, adding a number of new ones. I say much practice, for my house was continually full, for some time, with people who came to see these new wonders.

To divide a little this incumbrance among my friends, I caused a number of similar tubes to be blown at our glass-house, with which they furnished themselves, so that we had at length several performers. Among these, the principal was Mr. [Ebenezer] Kinnersley [1711–78], an ingenious neighbor, who, being out of business, I encouraged to undertake showing the experiments for money, and drew up for him two lectures, in which the experiments were ranged in such order, and accompanied with such explanations in such method, as that the foregoing should assist in comprehending the following. He procured an elegant apparatus for the purpose, in which all the little machines that I had roughly made for myself were nicely formed by instrument-makers. His lectures were well attended, and gave great satisfaction; and after some time he went through the colonies, exhibiting them in every capital town, and picked up some money. In the West India islands indeed, it was with difficulty the experiments could be made, from the general moisture of the air.

Obliged as we were to Mr. Collinson for his present of the tube etc., I thought it right he should be informed of our success in using it, and wrote him several letters containing accounts of our experiments. He got them read in the Royal Society, where they were not at first thought worth so much notice as to be printed in their *Transactions*. One paper, which I wrote for Mr. Kinnersley, on the sameness of lightning with electricity, I sent to Dr. Mitchel [John Mitchell, d. 1768], an acquaintance of mine, and one of the members also of that society, who wrote me word that it had been read, but was laughed at by the connoisseurs. The papers, however, being shown to Dr. Fothergill, he thought them of too much value to be stifled, and advised the printing of them. Mr. Collinson then gave them to [Edward] Cave [1691–1754] for publication in his *Gentleman's Magazine*; but he chose to print them separately in a pamphlet [*Experiments and Observations on Electricity*, 1751], and Dr. Fothergill wrote the Preface. Cave, it seems, judged rightly for his profit, for by the additions that arrived afterward they swelled to a quarto volume, which has had five editions, and cost him nothing for copy-money.

It was, however, some time before those papers were much taken notice of in England. A copy of them happening to fall into the hands of the Count de Buffon [1707–88], a philosopher deservedly of great reputation in France, and, indeed, all over Europe, he prevailed with M. [Thomas-François] Dalibard [1703–99] to translate them into French, and they were printed at Paris. The publication offended the Abbé [Jean-Antoine] Nollet [1700–70], Preceptor in Natural Philosophy to the royal family, and an able experimenter, who had formed and published a theory of electricity, which then had the general vogue. He could not at first believe that such a work came from America, and said it must have been fabricated by his enemies at Paris, to decry his system. Afterwards, having been assured that there really existed such a person as Franklin at Philadelphia, which he had doubted, he wrote and published a volume of letters, chiefly addressed to me, defending his theory, and denying the verity of my experiments, and of the positions deduced from them.

I once purposed answering the abbé, and actually began the answer; but, on consideration that my writings contained a description of experiments which any one might repeat and verify, and if not to be verified, could not be defended; or of observations offered as conjectures, and not delivered dogmatically, therefore not laying me under any obligation to defend them; and reflecting that a dispute between two persons, writing in different languages, might be lengthened greatly by mistranslations, and thence misconceptions of one another's meaning, much of one of the abbé's letters being founded on an error in the translation, I concluded to let my papers shift for themselves, believing it was better to spend what time I could spare from public business in making new experiments, than in disputing about those already made. I therefore never answered M. Nollet, and the event gave me no cause to repent my silence; for my friend M. [Jean-Baptiste] le Roy [1720–1800], of the Royal Academy of Sciences, took up my cause and refuted him; my book was translated into the Italian, German, and Latin languages; and the doctrine it contained was by degrees universally adopted by the philosophers of Europe, in preference to that of the abbé; so that he lived to see himself the last of his sect, except M.B. [Maturin-Jacques Brisson, 1723–1806], of Paris, his *élève* and immediate disciple.

What gave my book the more sudden and general celebrity, was the success of one of its proposed experiments, made by Messrs Dalibard and De Lor at Marly, for drawing lightning from the clouds. This engaged the public attention everywhere. M. De Lor, who had an apparatus for experimental philosophy, and lectured in that branch of science, undertook to repeat what he called the Philadelphia Experiments; and, after they were performed before the king and court, all the curious of Paris flocked to see them. I will not swell this narrative with an account of that capital experiment, nor of the infinite pleasure I received in the success of a similar one I made soon after with a kite at Philadelphia, as both are to be found in the histories of electricity.

Dr. [Edward] Wright [d. 1761], an English physician, when at Paris, wrote to a friend, who was of the Royal Society, an account of the high esteem my experiments were in among the learned abroad, and of their wonder that my writings had been so little noticed in England. The society, on this, resumed the consideration of the letters that had been read to them; and the celebrated Dr. [William] Watson [1715–87] drew up a summary account of them, and of all I had afterwards sent to England on the subject, which he accompanied with some praise of the writer. This summary was then printed in their *Transactions*; and some members of the society in London, particularly the very ingenious Mr. [John] Canton [1718–72], having verified the experiment of procuring lightning from the clouds by a pointed rod, and acquainting them with the success, they soon made me more than amends for the slight with which they had before treated me. Without my having made any application for that honor, they chose me a member, and voted that I should be excused the customary payments, which would have amounted to twenty-five guineas; and ever since have given me their *Transactions* gratis.

*(Autobiography*, Part Three, written at Philadelphia, 1788–89)

## MADAME DE ROLAND

Marie-Jeanne Roland (1754–93) was born in Paris, the only surviving child of Marguerite Bimont and her husband, a master engraver Gatien Phlipon. In 1765, at the age of eleven, she was sent to a convent for a year. There, she became an avid reader and began a strong friendship and correspondence with Sophie Cannet (whom she would later ask to witness her execution). When her mother died in 1775, Marie recovered from what was a traumatic bereavement by reading Rousseau's *Julie, or the New Héloise* (1761): 'I was twenty-one, I had read widely and was familiar with many writers, historians and philosophers, but Rousseau made an impression upon me at that time that was comparable to the impression that Plutarch had made when I was eight.' The following year she met Jean-Marie Roland (1734–93), whom she admired, respected, and married in 1780, and by whom she would have a daughter. In 1792 she fell in love with the politician François Buzot, though she evidently remained faithful to her husband.

Madame de Roland became involved in politics through her husband, who had been elected to the municipal council of Lyons in 1790. This post brought the Rolands to Paris in 1791 where their home soon became a meeting place for Girondins and Jacobins. At the end of 1791 Roland became secretary of the Jacobin society, and in 1792 he served for two short spells (23 March–13 June 1792, and 10 August 1792–22 January 1793) as Minister of the Interior. Though they welcomed the Revolution, believing that it would revive French society and bring the sufferings of the poor to an end, following the execution of Louis XVI and Roland's resignation in January 1793, they soon came under attack from radicals such as Danton and Robespierre. On 1 June 1793 Madame de Roland was arrested for conspiracy, while her husband and Buzot fled. After five months in prison, on 8 November she was guillotined. On hearing of her death, Roland committed suicide, as did Buzot in the following year. In its report on her death, the *Moniteur Universel* grouped Madame de Roland with Marie-Antoinette and Olympe de Gouges as women justifiably executed for transgressing 'the virtues of their sex'.

It was during her months in prison that Madame de Roland wrote her memoirs, on hundreds of small sheets of paper smuggled out from time to time by visitors. She began by writing 'Historical Notices', protesting her innocence and describing the political developments that had led to her imprisonment. On hearing a false report that these notebooks had been burned, she began to recast them as 'Portraits and Anecdotes', and to write the 'Private Memoirs' of her life. In 1795 a friend arranged and edited these writings for publication as *Appel à l'Impartiale Postérité*. They were translated as *An Appeal to Impartial Posterity*, 'a collection of tracts written during her confinement in the prisons of the Abbey and St Pélagie in Paris, in four parts … published for the benefit of her daughter, deprived of the fortune of her parents by sequestration', and published in London in 1796.

As an author, Roland struggled to construct a self that was at once stoic and sensuous, intellectual and female. Above all, she wanted to embody what she regarded as the feminine virtues. In the passages selected here from the 1796 London edition of her *Appeal*, she explains her interest and involvement in politics and learning, and her thoughts about women's roles, politics and philosophy. She claims that political adversity released her from her own conception of 'woman' and brought her boldly to inscribe a problematic female self with the express purpose of publication. Passages relating to her love for Buzot, and her frank accounts of her sexuality were considered scandalous, however, and expurgated from early editions of her work. In the extracts here, Madame de Roland reflects upon her role in supporting her husband's political activities, and on her personal principles.

## An Appeal to Impartial Posterity (1795)

As soon as my husband was in the ministry [23 March 1792], I came to a fixed determination, neither to pay nor receive visits, nor invite any female to my table. I had not great sacrifices to make on that head: for, not residing constantly at Paris, my acquaintance was not extensive; besides, I had nowhere kept a great deal of company, because my love of study is as great as my detestation of cards, and because the society of silly people affords me no diversion. Accustomed to spend my days in domestic retirement, I shared the labours of Roland, and pursued the studies most suited to my own particular taste. The establishment of so severe a rule served then at once to keep up my accustomed style of life, and to prevent the inconveniences which an interested crowd throws in the way of people occupying important posts. Properly speaking, I never received company in my hotel [apartment]: twice a week, indeed, I gave a dinner to some of the ministers, a few members of the [Legislative] Assembly, and the persons with whom my husband had anything to talk over, or whose acquaintance he wished to preserve. Business was talked of in my presence; because I had not the rage of interfering, and was not surrounded with such company as could excite distrust. Out of all the rooms of a spacious apartment, I had chosen, for my daily habitation, the smallest parlour, which I had converted into a study, by removing into it my books and a bureau. It often happened, that Roland's friends or colleagues, when they wanted to speak to him confidentially, instead of going to his apartment, where he was surrounded by his clerks or by the public, would come to mine, and request me to send for him. By these means I found myself drawn into the vortex of public affairs, without intrigue or idle curiosity. Roland had a pleasure in afterwards conversing with me about them in private, with that confidence which we ever place in each other, and which established between us an intercommunity of knowledge and opinions. And it sometimes happened also, that friends, who had only some information to give, or a few words to say, being always sure of finding me, came and requested I would make the necessary communication to Roland as soon as an opportunity might occur.

(*An Appeal*, Part 1)

As to me [in June 1792], I felt a kind of agitation difficult to describe; delighted with the Revolution; persuaded that, with all its faults, it was necessary to enforce the constitution; and ardently desiring to see my country prosper, the lowering [threatening] aspect of public affairs gave me a moral fever, which raged without intermission. The king's delays demonstrated his duplicity; and Roland had no longer any doubt upon the subject: there remained then but one resolution for an honest minister to take, and that was to go out of office, in case Louis XVI should obstinately refuse to take the measures necessary for the salvation of the state.

That step, unattended by any other, might perhaps have satisfied the conscience of a timid man. But for a zealous citizen, it is not enough to renounce a post in which good is no longer to be done; it behoves him to say so with energy, that he may throw light upon the public calamities, and render his resignation beneficial to his country – Roland and I had long lamented the weakness of his colleagues. The tardiness of the king had suggested the idea, that it might be of great use to address a letter to him from the ministers collectively, setting forth the reasons which had already been given in the Council, but which, when expressed upon paper, and signed by them all, with the offer of their resignation in case his majesty should not think proper to listen to their representations, might either force him to compliance, or expose him to the eyes of all France. I drew up a letter [on 11 June], after having agreed upon the fundamental points with Roland, and Roland made the proposal to his [ministerial] colleagues – All approved of the idea, but most of them differed as to the execution. [Étienne] Clavière [1735–93] objected to some phrase or other; [Antoine] Duranthon [1736–93] was inclined to temporise; and [Jean de] Lacoste [1730–1820] was in no haste to subscribe his name. As such a measure should be the effect of a first glance and of a lively sense of its propriety, the failure of our attempt was a hint not to repeat it. It became then necessary to act in an insulated character, and since the Council had not spirit enough to stand forth together, it behoved the man who set the events at a defiance to take upon himself a task which the whole body should have fulfilled. The question was no longer to resign, but to deserve to be dismissed – to say, do thus or we will retire; but to assert that all was lost unless a proper line of conduct were pursued. I composed the famous letter.

Here I must digress for a moment to clear up the doubts, and to fix the opinion of a number of persons, of whom the greater part only allow me a little merit, that they may deny it to my husband, while many others suppose me to have a kind of influence in public affairs entirely discordant with my turn of mind. Studious habits and a taste for literature made me participate in his labours, as long as he remained a private individual – I wrote with him as I ate with him, because one was almost as natural to me as the other, and because my existence being devoted to his happiness, I applied myself to those things which gave him the greatest pleasure. Roland wrote treatises on the arts; I did the same, although the subject was tedious to me. He was fond of erudition; I helped him to pursue his critical researches. Did he wish, by way of recreation, to compose an essay for some academy? We sat down to write in concert, or else separately, that we might afterwards compare our productions, choose the best, or compress them into one. If he had written homilies, I should have written homilies also. When he became minister I did not interfere with his administration; but if a circular letter, a set of instructions, or an important state paper, were wanting, we talked the matter over with our usual freedom, and impressed with his ideas, and pregnant with my own, I took up the pen, which I had more leisure to conduct than he had.

Our principles and our turn of mind being the same, we came to a final agreement as to the form, and my husband ran no risk in passing it through my hands. I could advance nothing warranted by justice or reason, which he was not capable of realizing, or supporting by his energy and conduct; but my language expressed more strongly than his words, what he had done or what he promised to do. Roland *without me* would not have been a worse minister; his activity, and his knowledge, as well as his probity, were all his own. But *with me* he attracted more attention, because I infused into his writings that mixture of spirit and of softness, of authoritative reason, and of seducing sentiment, which are perhaps only to be found in a woman endowed with a clear head and a feeling heart. I composed with delight such pieces as I deemed likely to be of use, and felt greater pleasure in so doing than if I had been known as the author. I am avaricious of happiness: with me it consists in the good I do. I do not even stand in need of glory; nor can I find any part in this world that suits me, but that of Providence. I allow the malicious to look upon this confession as a piece of impertinence which it must somewhat resemble; those who know me, however, will see nothing in it but what is sincere, like myself.

(*An Appeal*, Part 2)

A gentle disposition, a strong mind, a solid understanding, an extremely affectionate heart, and an exterior which announced these qualities, rendered me dear to all those with whom I was acquainted. The situation [prison] into which I have been thrown has created me enemies; personally I have none: to those who have spoken the worst of me I am utterly unknown.

It is so true that things are seldom what they appear to be, that the periods of my life in which I have felt the most pleasure, or experienced the greatest vexation, were often the very contrary of those that others might have supposed: the solution is, that happiness depends on the affections more than on events.

It is my purpose to employ the leisure of my captivity in retracing what has happened to me from my tenderest infancy to the present moment. Thus to tread over again all the steps of our career, is to live a second time; and what, in the gloom of a prison, can we do better than to transport our existence elsewhere by pleasing fictions, or by the recollection of interesting occurrences?

If we gain less experience by acting, than by reflecting on what we see and do, mine will be greatly augmented by my present understanding. Public affairs, and my own private sentiments, afforded me ample matter for thinking, and subjects enough for my pen, during two months imprisonment [June and July 1793], without obliging me to have recourse to distant times. Accordingly, the first five weeks were devoted to my Historic Notices, which formed perhaps no uninteresting collection. They have just been destroyed; and I have felt all the bitterness of a loss, which I shall never repair. But I should despise myself, could I suffer my mind to sink in any circumstances whatever. In all the troubles I have experienced, the most lively impression of sorrow has been almost immediately accompanied by the ambition of opposing my strength to the evil, and of surmounting it, either by doing good to others, or by exerting my own fortitude to the utmost. Thus misfortune may pursue, but cannot overwhelm me; tyrants may persecute, but never, no never shall they debase me. My Historic Notices are gone: I mean to write my [Private] Memoirs; and, prudently accommodating myself to my weakness, at a moment when my feelings are acute, I shall talk of my own person, that my thoughts may be the less at home. I shall exhibit my fair and my unfavourable side with equal freedom. He who dares not speak well of himself is almost always a coward, who knows and dreads the ill that may be said of him; and he who hesitates to confess his faults, has neither spirit to vindicate, nor virtue to repair them. Thus frank with respect to myself, I shall not be scrupulous in regard to others: father, mother, friends, husband, I shall paint them all in their proper colours, or in the colours at least in which they appeared to me.

While I remained in a quiet and retired station, my natural sensibility so absorbed my other qualities, that it displayed itself alone, or governed all the rest. My first objects were to please and to do good. [...]

Since the energy of my character has been unfolded by circumstances, by political and other storms, my frankness takes place of everything, without considering too nicely the little scratches it may give in its way. Still, however, I deal not in epigrams; they indicate a mind pleased at irritating others by satirical observations; and, as to me, I never yet could find amusement in killing flies. But I love to do justice by the utterance of truths, and refrain not from the most severe, in presence of the parties concerned, without suffering myself to be alarmed, or moved, or angry, whatever may be the effects they produce.

(*An Appeal*, Part 3, section 1)

At the time of the dissension between the Court and the Parlement in 1771, my disposition and opinions attached me to the party of the latter; I procured all their remonstrances, and was most pleased with those which contained the strongest things expressed in the boldest style. The sphere of my ideas continually enlarged. My own happiness, and the duties to the performance of which it might be attached, occupied my mind at a very early period. The love of knowledge made me afterwards study history, and turn my thoughts to everything about me, the relation of our species to the divinity so variously represented, caricatured, and disfigured, attracted my attention; and at length the welfare of man in society fixed it to a determinate point.

In the midst of doubts, uncertainty, and investigation, relative to these important matters, I readily concluded, that the unity of the individual, if I may so express myself, that is to say, the most entire harmony between his opinions and actions, was necessary to his personal happiness. Accordingly, we ought to examine well what is right, and when we have found it, we should practise it rigorously. There is a kind of justice due to a man's self, even were he living in the world alone: it is incumbent on him so to regulate all his affections and habits, that he may be the slave of none. A being is *good* in itself, when all its parts concur to its preservation, its maintenance, or its perfection: this is not less true in the moral, than in the physical world. Justness of organization [constitution], and an equipoise of humours [balance of life forces], constitute health: wholesome aliments [foods], and moderate exercise, preserve it. The due proportion of our desires, and the harmony of the passions, form the moral constitution, of which wisdom alone can secure the excellence and duration. Its first principles originate in the interest of the individual; and in this respect it may be truly said, that virtue is nothing more than good sense applied to moral purposes. But virtue, properly so called, can only spring from the relations of a being with his fellow-creatures: a man is prudent as far as self is concerned, virtuous in regard to other people. In society everything is relative; there is no independent happiness. We are obliged to sacrifice a part of what we might enjoy, in order to run no risk of losing the whole, and to keep a portion out of the reach of accident. Even here the balance is in favour of reason. However laborious may be the life of the honest, that of the vicious must be still more so. That man can seldom be tranquil, who stands in opposition to the interest of the majority; it is impossible for him not to feel that he is surrounded by enemies, or by individuals about to become so; and this situation is always painful, however flattering may be its appearances. Let us add to these considerations the sublime instinct, which corruption may mislead, but which no false philosophy can ever annihilate; which impels us to admire and love wisdom and generosity of conduct, as we do grandeur and symmetry in nature and the arts – and we shall have the source of human virtue independent of every religious system, of the idle fancies of metaphysics, and of the imposture of priests.

As soon as I had combined and demonstrated these truths, my heart expanded with joy; they offered me a port in the storm, and I could now examine with less anxiety the errors of national creeds and social institutions. Can the sublime idea of a divine Creator, whose providence watches over the world, the immateriality of the soul, and its immortality, that consolatory hope of persecuted virtue, be nothing more than amiable and splendid chimeras? But in how much obscurity are these difficult problems involved? What accumulated objections arise when we wish to examine them with mathematical rigour! No; it is not given to the human mind to behold these truths in the full day of perfect evidence: but why should the man of sensibility repine at not being able to demonstrate what he feels to be true?

In the silence of the closet, and the dryness of discussion, I can agree with the atheist or the materialist, as to the insolubility of certain questions. But when in the country, and contemplating nature, my soul, full of emotion, soars aloft to the vivifying principle that animates them, to the almighty intellect that pervades them, and the goodness that makes the scene so delightful to my senses. Now, when immense walls separate me from all I love, and when all the evils of society fall upon us together, as if to punish us for having desired its greatest blessings, I see beyond the limits of life the reward of our sacrifices. How? In what manner? – I cannot say; I only feel that so it ought to be.

The atheist is not, in my eyes, an evil-minded man: I can live with him as well, nay better than with the devotee; for he reasons more. But he wants a certain sense that I possess, and my mind does not perfectly harmonize with his. He is unmoved at the most enchanting spectacle, and is seeking for a syllogism, while I am offering up my thanksgivings.

*Note*: I write this on the 4th of September [1793] at eleven at night, the apartment next to me resounding with peals of laughter. The actresses of the Théâtre Français were arrested yesterday, and conducted to St Pélagie. Today they were taken to their own apartments, to witness the ceremony of the taking off the seals, and are now returned to the prison, where the peace-officer is supping and amusing himself in their company. The repast is noisy and frolicsome; I catch the sound of coarse jests, while foreign wines sparkle in the goblet. The place, the object, the persons, and my occupation, form a contrast not a little curious.

(*An Appeal*, Part 3, section 2)

PART TWO

# Reader

# Chapter 14

# Modern critical reflections

**D** EFINING THE ENLIGHTENMENT has always been a tricky business, characterised by a diversity of views even during the historic period of the Enlightenment itself. Indeed, the most famous and influential essay on the subject, Kant's 'What is Enlightenment?' (see p. 54) began as a reply to that very question, posed by the journal *Berlinische Monatsschrift* (*Berlin Monthly*) in 1783. Since then, many new approaches to, and assessments of the Enlightenment have emerged, questioning almost everything, from its origins, unity and diversity, to its philosophy, politics and ethics, and – not least – its legacy and relationship to modernity. Nor is there general agreement about who or what should be the focus of attention. Distinctive but 'awkward' figures such as Rousseau and Vico have sometimes been brushed aside or portrayed as part of a 'counter-Enlightenment', rather than part of 'the canon of great thinkers' traditionally depicted at the core of the phenomenon. Other scholars have turned attention to professional writers, travellers and artists and to the social and commercial contexts in which ideas were shaped and shared.

Because it has predominantly been defined as an intellectual movement and has come to be seen, for good or ill, as crucial to the development of modern society and culture, investigations of the subject and the nature of its legacy have given rise to many historical, philosophical and critical debates. Yet, from the outset, most of the ideas and activities that came to be associated with the Enlightenment received a mixed response – ranging, in official circles, from the burning of books and the outlawing of their authors, to the bestowal of prizes and public offices. Less formally, there were Catholic clergy who corresponded with the *philosophes* and who took delight in reading and contributing to some of their works, and crowds whose hostility to what they had heard about the writings of men like Toland, Rousseau and Priestley sometimes led to violent confrontations. During the French Revolution, radicals such as Robespierre would champion some of the *philosophes*, a few would be hounded to their death, and critics such as Edmund Burke would denounce what they saw as the false ideals of the Enlightenment that had led to Revolution. Indeed, in many respects it was the Revolution that fashioned a new kind of reflection upon, and construction of the Enlightenment, for all subsequent understandings would be coloured by knowledge of the general importance of that event. In the nineteenth century, writers of the Romantic movement inveighed against what they saw as the excessive rationalism of Enlightened thinking, and Engels referred to the 'kingdom of reason' as 'the idealised kingdom of the bourgeoisie'. Many ideas about and attitudes towards the Enlightenment had thus been forged well before scholars in the twentieth century picked up the discussion and developed new insights and debates.

Only a small selection of seminal writings reflecting on the Enlightenment from the vantage of the twentieth century can be included here, beginning with the work of Ernst Cassirer. His influential thesis emphasised the importance and unity of a small group of French *philosophes* and the audacious, secularising nature of their work. Writing an 'intellectual history' largely divorced from social context, Cassirer reiterated what he saw as the *philosophes'* vision of reason as part of the essence of the human, and of objective science and universal morality as emancipatory. Subsequent scholarship would both widen this field of vision – not least to incorporate much more than the elite and largely male collective of *philosophes* that interested Cassirer and his followers – and work through the contradictions and limits of seeing the Enlightenment as secularisation and modernisation, or both.

After the Second World War, the experiences of totalitarianism and the holocaust undermined many scholars' confidence in progress and the whole idea of modernity. It was in this context that Theodore Adorno and Max Horkheimer explored the 'dark side' of a movement that had usually been signified in terms of metaphors of light. They found that the rational understanding and control, evidently championed by the Enlightened, led to persecution and exploitation. No less influential was the work of the German philosopher Jürgen Habermas, who is most closely associated with the contention that the problems identified by Adorno and Horkheimer had arisen because the 'enlightenment project', as he called it, was still unfinished. His work is also an example of an approach that widened the scope of Enlightenment studies and, like that of Michel Foucault and Robert Darnton, focused more attention on the social practices that were now considered a vital part of the Enlightenment, rather than concentrating largely on the great philosophical texts and major thinkers of the period.

The flourishing of modernism in the arts at the beginning of the twentieth century, challenging notions of fixity and coherence in aesthetic representation, undermined some of the apparent premises of Enlightenment thought. From the 1970s, the advent of second-wave feminism and postcolonialism created a climate in which feminists and post-colonialists developed fresh critiques of what appeared to be the gender-bias and culture-specificity of the Enlightenment. Similarly, academic interest in post-structuralism and postmodernism encouraged both the denunciation of abstract reason and the unified humanist subject, and a growing disillusionment with totalising strategies for emancipation, autonomy, justice and equality. By highlighting the exclusions and ideological conflicts under the apparent consensus of Enlightenment thought, recent scholarship has illuminated 'other' Enlightenments and the 'others' of the Enlightenment: notably by broadening the geographical range, social classes and contexts studied; exploring the influence of, and impact on, non-Europeans and Europe's colonies; examining the distinctiveness of regional and national contexts; and investigating the representation and roles of women. In the small collection of critical reflections selected here, it is not possible to gain more than a taste of some of these modern studies. However, an excellent introduction to the historiography of the subject has recently been provided by Dorinda Outram in *The Enlightenment* (1995), and to its social contexts by Thomas Munck in *The Enlightenment: A Comparative Social History, 1721–1794* (2000). Outram's approach is to present the Enlightenment as 'a *capsule* containing sets of debates, stresses and concerns, which however differently formulated or responded to, do appear to be characteristic of the way in which ideas, opinions and social and political structures interacted and changed in the eighteenth century'. In his conclusion, Munck comments: 'If the enlightenment was anything, it was about exposing all inherited beliefs to reason and open debate, and ultimately replacing passive acceptance with active participation'. Roy Porter's pamphlet *The Enlightenment* (2001) also includes some historiographical discussion and a useful annotated bibliography.

As Porter noted in his pamphlet, there is no sign of 'the scholarly attention lavished on the Enlightenment' abating. Indeed, as one of the outstanding scholars of the eighteenth century, Porter himself published a major new study *Enlightenment: Britain and the Creation of the Modern World* in 2000. Tackling the long tradition – upheld by Cassirer, Gay, Darnton and many others – of seeing the Enlightenment as a predominantly French affair, he set out to demonstrate the central and distinctive role of Britain as 'the *true* home of modernity'. His view of 'Foucauldian and postmodernist readings' of the Enlightenment is that they are 'wilfully lopsided'. As to Horkheimer and Adorno's text, a footnote reads: 'However good as polemic, it is historical baloney; after all, the Nazis loathed the *philosophes*'. For Porter, 'The Enlightenment is not a good thing or a bad thing, to be cheered or jeered … there never was a monolithic "Enlightenment project". Enlightened thinkers were broad-minded, they espoused pluralism, their register was ironic rather than dogmatic.'

Though equally enthusiastic about the virtues of the Enlightenment, in 2001 another distinguished historian Jonathan Israel set out a very different account of its intellectual and geographical origins. Reflecting on the historiography of the subject, Israel rejects a primarily 'French' perspective, due to the 'philosophical and scientific borrowing' that French thinkers were engaged in. An alternative approach – conceived by several *philosophes*, and notably advanced by the American historian Margaret Jacob – that looks to England as the source of Enlightened thinking, is regarded as flawed due to the slow and mixed reception that Locke and Newton received outside Britain. The view – expressed by some scholars, such as Henry May and John Pocock – that there was not one movement but 'a family of Enlightenments', that emerged each in different national contexts, is rejected on the grounds that such a 'national history' approach fails to address 'the common impulses and concerns' that shaped what was an international phenomenon. And the recent tendency to distinguish a main 'moderate' Enlightenment from a more radical but marginal one, is also regarded as mistaken. For Israel, the European Enlightenment was 'a single highly integrated intellectual and cultural movement' which owed its radical origins to the writings of Baruch Spinoza in seventeenth-century Holland. In the Preface to this grand thesis, *Radical Enlightenment: Philosophy and the Making of Modernity, 1650–1750*, Israel concludes:

> the Enlightenment – European and global – not only attacked and severed the roots of traditional European culture in the sacred, magic, kingship, and hierarchy, secularizing all institutions and ideas, but (intellectually and to a degree in practice) effectively demolished all legitimation of monarchy, aristocracy, woman's subordination to man, ecclesiastical authority, and slavery, replacing these with the principles of universality, equality, and democracy. This implies the Enlightenment was of a different order of importance for understanding the rise of the modern world than the Reformation and Renaissance, and that there is something disproportionate and inadequate about its coverage in the existing historiography. But to assess its assuredly overriding global significance one must first gauge the Enlightenment as a whole, which means, in my view, giving due weight to the Radical Enlightenment and, equally, emancipating ourselves from the deadly compulsion to squeeze the Enlightenment, radical and mainstream, into the constricting strait-jacket of 'national history'.

The short extracts from nine modern works presented here (with selected author notes incorporated within the text) offer brief insights into some of the many questions that the twentieth century pursued and raised about the Enlightenment. Full bibliographical details for these critical reflections are provided in the Acknowledgements at the beginning of this book.

## ERNST CASSIRER

Keen to save the Enlightenment from the adverse assessment of the Romantic movement, in the 1930s the German scholar Ernst Cassirer argued that the Enlightenment was essentially a united and self-reflexive intellectual movement concerned with understanding the very processes of thought. *The Philosophy of the Enlightenment* (1932), insisted that, despite their various philosophical positions, the 'great' Enlightenment thinkers constituted 'an essentially homogeneous formative power' that broke with the transcendental and systematic philosophy of the seventeenth century. For Cassirer, this unity of the Enlightenment was based upon a preoccupation with reason, the elaboration of historicity and teleology, descriptive natural science, empiricism, tolerance, the development of civil rights, and the beginnings of aesthetic theory. Thus, he created a unified, empirical and teleological study of Enlightenment philosophy, and focused exclusively on the writings of philosophers, scarcely referring to wider social contexts. He often refers to Enlightenment thought as having an agency of its own: 'Thought no longer wants to accept the world as empirically given'. His use of the present tense and of a rhetorical 'we' (perhaps referring to himself, the implied reader and Enlightenment philosophers) assumes a community of scholars in agreement with the evident 'truths' of Enlightenment thought. The passages chosen here are less expository, and show Cassirer's elaboration of a general theory of the Enlightenment.

## The Philosophy of the Enlightenment (1932)

The philosophy of the eighteenth century takes up this particular case, the methodological pattern of Newton's physics, though it immediately begins to generalize. It is not content to look upon analysis as the great intellectual tool of mathematico-physical knowledge; eighteenth century thought sees analysis rather as the necessary and indispensable instrument of all thinking in general. This view triumphs in the middle of the century. However much individual thinkers and schools differ in their results, they agree in this epistemological premise. Voltaire's *Treatise on Metaphysics*, d'Alembert's *Preliminary Discourse*, and Kant's *Inquiry concerning the Principles of Natural Theology and Morality* all concur on this point. All these works represent the true method of metaphysics as in fundamental agreement with the method which Newton, with such fruitful results, introduced into natural science. Voltaire says that man, if he presumes to see into the life of things and know them as they really are in themselves, immediately becomes aware of the limits of his faculties; he finds himself in the position of a blind man who must judge the nature of color. But analysis is the staff which a benevolent nature has placed in the blind man's hands. Equipped with this instrument he can feel his way forward among appearances, discovering their sequence and arrangement; and this is all he needs for his intellectual orientation to life and knowledge. 'We must never make hypotheses; we must never say: Let us begin by inventing principles according to which we attempt to explain everything. We should say rather: Let us make an exact analysis of things ... When we cannot utilize the compass of mathematics or the torch of experience and physics, it is certain that we cannot take a single step forward' (Voltaire, *Traité de Métaphysique*, chs III and V). But provided with such instruments as these, we can and should venture upon the high seas of knowledge. We must, of course, abandon all hope of ever wresting from things their ultimate mystery, of ever penetrating to the absolute being of matter or of the human soul. If, however, we refer to empirical law and order, the 'inner core of nature' proves by no means inaccessible. In this realm we can establish ourselves and proceed in every direction. The power of reason does not consist in enabling us to transcend the empirical world but rather in teaching us to feel at home in it. [...]

What reason is, and what it can do, can never be known by its results but only by its function. And its most important function consists in its power to bind and to dissolve. It dissolves everything merely factual, all simple data of experience, and everything believed on the evidence of revelation, tradition and authority; and it does not rest content until it has analyzed all these things into their simplest component parts and into their last elements of belief and opinion. Following this work of dissolution begins the work of construction. Reason cannot stop with the dispersed parts; it has to build from them a new structure, a true whole. But since reason creates this whole and fits the parts together according to its own rule, it gains complete knowledge of the structure of its product. Reason understands this structure because it can reproduce it in its totality and in the ordered sequence of its individual elements. Only in this twofold intellectual movement can the concept of reason be fully characterized, namely as a concept of agency, not of being.

This conviction gains a foothold in the most varied fields of eighteenth century culture. Lessing's famous saying that the real power of reason is to be found not in the possession but in the acquisition of truth has its parallels everywhere in the intellectual history of the eighteenth century. Montesquieu attempts to give a theoretical justification for the presence in the human soul of an innate thirst for knowledge, an insatiable intellectual curiosity, which never allows us to be satisfied with any conception we have arrived at, but drives us on from idea to idea. 'Our soul is made for thinking, that is, for perceiving,' said Montesquieu; 'but such a being must have curiosity, for just as all things form a chain in which every idea precedes one idea and follows another, so one cannot want to see the one without desiring to see the other.' The lust for knowledge, the *libido sciendi*, which theological dogmatism had outlawed and branded as intellectual pride, is now called a necessary quality of the soul as such and restored to its original rights. The defense, reinforcement, and consolidation of this way of thinking is the cardinal aim of eighteenth century culture; and in this mode of thinking, not in the mere acquisition and extension of specific information, the century sees its major task. This fundamental tendency can also be traced unambiguously in the *Encyclopedia*, which became the arsenal of all such information. Diderot himself, originator of the *Encyclopedia*, states that its purpose is not only to supply a certain body of knowledge but also to bring about a change in the mode of thinking – *pour changer la façon commune de penser*. Consciousness of this task affects all the minds of the age and gives rise to a new sense of inner tension. [...]

A fundamental feature of the philosophy of the Enlightenment appears in the fact that, despite its passionate desire for progress, despite its endeavors to break the old tables of the law and to arrive at a new outlook on life, it returns again and again to the persistent problems of philosophy. Descartes had answered the objection that he was trying to found an entirely new philosophy by declaring that his doctrine could lay claim to the prerogative of age since it was grounded in reason and constructed according to strictly rational principles. For reason possesses the true right of the first-born, and it is older than any opinion or prejudice which has obscured it in the course of the centuries. The philosophy of the Enlightenment adopts this motto. It opposes the power of convention, tradition, and authority in all the fields of knowledge. But it does not consider this opposition as merely a work of negation and destruction; it considers rather that it is removing the rubble of the ages in order to make visible the solid foundations of the structure of knowledge. These foundations are looked upon as immutable and unshakable; they are as old as mankind itself. The philosophy of the Enlightenment, accordingly, does not understand its task as an act of destruction but as an act of reconstruction. In its very boldest revolutions the Enlightenment aims only at 'restitution to the whole' (*restitutio in integrum*), by which reason and humanity are to be re-installed in their ancient rights. Historically, this twofold tendency appears in that the Enlightenment, despite its struggle with the existing order and the immediate past, constantly goes back to the trends of thought and problems of antiquity. In this respect it follows the example of the Renaissance whose intellectual possessions it inherits. But as a purely philosophical movement, the Enlightenment disposes much more freely of its heritage than Humanism within the sphere of mere scholarly research had ever done. It selects only certain basic features which suit its own way of thinking and leaves the rest alone. But in this very selection the Enlightenment often succeeds in penetrating to the real source of its problems. [...]

Diderot and the Encyclopaedists are convinced that one can entrust himself to the progress of culture because such progress, simply by virtue of its immanent tendency and law, will of itself bring about a better form of the social order. The refinement of manners and the growth and extension of knowledge will and must finally transform morality and give it a firmer foundation. This faith is so strong that for most of these thinkers the concept of the community which they are endeavoring to formulate and justify becomes synonymous not only with the concept of society but even with that of sociability. In the French expression *société* these two meanings constantly overlap. A sociable philosophy and a sociable science are here in request. Not only political, but also theoretical, ethical and aesthetic ideals are formed by and for the salons. Urbanity becomes a criterion of real insight in science. Only that which can be expressed in the language of such urbanity has stood the test of clarity and distinctness.

In his 'Preliminary Discourse' in the *Encyclopaedia* d'Alembert declares that the essential advantage of the eighteenth century over the preceding era consists in the fact that it has brought forth more geniuses, more truly creative minds. Nature always remains the same; hence every age has great geniuses. But what can they achieve if they live in isolation and are left to their own thoughts? 'The ideas which one acquires from reading and society are the germ of almost all discoveries. It is an air which one breathes without thinking about it and to which one owes his life.' The vital and intellectual atmosphere of the *Encyclopaedia* finds perhaps its most precise and pregnant expression in these words. Society is the vital air in which alone true science, true philosophy, and true art can thrive. The *Encyclopaedia* endeavors to produce and establish this union. It conceives knowledge for the first time consciously as a social function, declaring that its development is possible only on the basis of a sound social organization. All political and social enterprise must stand on the same foundation, and a renaissance of political and moral life can be expected only from the growth and spread of intellectual and social culture.

(pp. 13–14, 234–235, 268–269)

## THEODOR W. ADORNO AND MAX HORKHEIMER

In 1947, as the world emerged from war and the holocaust, a sombre new interpretation of the Enlightenment was produced by Adorno and Horkheimer of the 'Frankfurt School'. Their *Dialektik der Aufklärung* (1947, translated as *Dialectic of Enlightenment* in 1972) broke with a premise on which Cassirer's (and later, Gay's) work had been established: that Enlightenment reasoning and the pursuit of rational mastery of nature and the world is impartial, and opens out to a rational, objective and liberating truth. For Horkheimer and Adorno, Enlightenment thought created its own forms of domination, with direct and dire historical effects. The first chapter of their study, from which the following extract is taken, explores how the Enlightenment proposed to do away with mythological thinking – 'The programme of the Enlightenment was the disenchantment of the world' – but in fact produced its own brand of myth. The authors argue that the abstraction of Enlightenment thinking denies individual thought and paves the way for a deceived and 'manipulated collective'. The Enlightenment may have removed the symbols of metaphysics, but it retained from mythology a basic fear of nature. For Adorno and Horkheimer, the Enlightenment emphasis on the separation of subject and object, secured the alienation and domination both of 'man' and of nature. In subsequent chapters they explore how, even in Homer's *Odyssey*, this dialectic was inherent; how the writings of the Marquis de Sade are indicative (and predictive) of the destructive effects of 'cold reason'; and the standardisation and hollowness of mass culture (their much-cited analysis of the 'culture industry'). Far from being truly tolerant of different ways of thinking, and being liberating, the Enlightenment was profoundly totalitarian, producing a managerial rationality that would eventually lead to the creation of concentration camps. The final chapter of *Dialectic of Enlightenment* brings together these elements as being present in the expression of anti-semitism, and ends with the hope that 'Enlightenment which is in possession of itself and coming to power can break the bounds of enlightenment'.

## *The Dialectic of Enlightenment* (1947)

For enlightenment is as totalitarian as any system. Its untruth does not consist in what its romantic enemies have always reproached it for: analytical method, return to elements, dissolution through reflective thought; but instead in the fact that for enlightenment the process is always decided from the start. When in mathematical procedure the unknown becomes the unknown quantity of an equation, this marks it as the well-known even before any value is inserted. Nature, before and after the quantum theory, is that which is to be comprehended mathematically; even what cannot be made to agree, indissolubility and irrationality, is converted by means of mathematical theorems. In the anticipatory identification of the wholly conceived and mathematized world with truth, enlightenment intends to secure itself against the return of the mythic. It confounds thought and mathematics. In this way the latter is, so to speak, released and made into an absolute instance. 'An infinite world, in this case a world of idealities, is conceived as one whose objects do not accede singly, imperfectly, and as if by chance to our cognition, but are attained by a rational, systematically unified method – in a process of infinite progression – so that each object is ultimately apparent according to its full inherent being ... In the Galilean mathematization of the world, however, *this selfness* is idealized under the guidance of the new mathematics: in modern terms, it becomes itself a mathematical multiplicity' (Edmund Husserl, 'Die Krisis der Europäischen

Wissenschaften und die transzendentale Phänomenologie,' in *Philosophia*, Belgrade, 1936, p. 95ff). Thinking objectifies itself to become an automatic, self-activating process; an impersonation of the machine that it produces itself so that ultimately the machine can replace it. Enlightenment has put aside the classic requirement of thinking about thought – Fichte as its extreme manifestation – because it wants to avoid the precept of dictating practice that Fichte himself wished to obey. Mathematical procedure became, so to speak, the ritual of thinking. In spite of the axiomatic self-restriction, it establishes itself as necessary and objective: it turns thought into a thing, an instrument – which is its own term for it. [...]

According to Kant, philosophic judgment aims at the new; and yet it recognizes nothing new, since it always merely recalls what reason has always deposited in the object. But there is a reckoning for this form of thinking that considers itself secure in the various departments of science – secure from the dreams of a ghost-seer: world domination over nature turns against the thinking subject himself; nothing is left of him but that eternally same *I think* that must accompany all my ideas. Subject and object are both rendered ineffectual. The abstract self, which justifies record-making and systematization, has nothing set over against it but the abstract material which possesses no other quality than to be a substrate of such possession. The equation of spirit and world arises eventually, but only with a mutual restriction of both sides. [...]

The task of cognition does not consist in mere apprehension, classification, and calculation, but in the determinate negation of each immediacy. Mathematical formalism, however, whose medium is number, the most abstract form of the immediate, instead holds thinking firmly to mere immediacy. Factuality wins the day; cognition is restricted to its repetition; and thought becomes mere tautology. The more the machinery of thought subjects existence to itself, the more blind its resignation in reproducing existence. Hence enlightenment returns to mythology, which it never really knew how to elude. For in its figures mythology had the essence of the *status quo*: cycle, fate, and domination of the world reflected as the truth and deprived of hope. [...]

Animism spiritualized the object, whereas industrialism objectifies the spirits of men. Automatically, the economic apparatus, even before total planning, equips commodities with the values which decide human behavior. Since, with the end of free exchange, commodities lost all their economic qualities except for fetishism, the latter has extended its arthritic influence over all aspects of social life. Through the countless agencies of mass production and its culture the conventionalized modes of behaviour are impressed on the individual as the only natural, respectable, and rational ones. He defines himself only as a thing, as a static element, as success or failure. His yardstick is self-preservation, successful or unsuccessful approximation to the objectivity of his function and the models established for it. Everything else, idea and crime, suffers the force of the collective, which monitors it from the classroom to the trade union. But even the threatening collective belongs only to the deceptive surface, beneath which are concealed the powers which manipulate it as the instrument of power. Its brutality, which keeps the individual up to scratch, represents the quality of men as little as value represents the things which he consumes.

(pp. 24–28)

## JÜRGEN HABERMAS

The German philosopher, Jürgen Habermas brings to critical reflection on the Enlightenment a conception of Enlightenment culture as a process created by a number of social practices, including developments in economics, engaged in by a community of participants, not solely singular intellectuals. His most sustained analysis of the eighteenth century is his *Strukturwandel der Öffentlichkeit* (1962) translated as *The Structural Transformation of the Public Sphere: An Enquiry into a Category of Bourgeois Society* in 1989. In this text, he details the emergence in the eighteenth century of what he terms a 'public sphere'. The rise of the novel and the press, and alongside this, spaces for their reading and discussion in the family home, the salon, coffee houses and *Tischgesellschaften* (table societies) formed a private, domestic and audience-orientated subjectivity that used 'reason' in public. Habermas argues that the literary focus on personal experience became a 'training ground for critical public reflection' in the political, public sphere, and that this critical process of public communication can still be used to gauge the process of democratisation.

The family unit and autonomous personhood were based on property and participation in the market economy, thus creating an overlap between property ownership and functioning as an individuated person in the public sphere. Habermas delineates the progressive weakening of the public sphere since the eighteenth century. Twentieth-century mass culture is not a sphere of literary/political debate for Habermas. Leisure, in particular, becomes the space of an externalised private sphere – what he calls 'the pseudo-public or sham-private world of culture consumption'. Thus, while calls 'the communicative network of a public made up of rationally debating private citizens has collapsed', Habermas holds out hope for the 'critical publicity' elaborated in the eighteenth century, so that (unlike most postmodern thinkers) he champions the Enlightenment and the 'project' of modernity as a whole. Unlike Adorno and Horkheimer, he retains a belief in the rationalisation of life, while continuing the dismissive stance of the Frankfurt School towards contemporary and popular culture.

## *The Structural Transformation of the Public Sphere* (1962)

The elements of early capitalist commercial relations, that is, the traffic in commodities and news, manifested their revolutionary power only in the mercantilist phase in which, simultaneously with the modern state, the national and territorial economies assumed their shapes. [...]

The reduction in the kind of publicity involved in representation that went hand in hand with the elimination of the estate-based authorities by those of the territorial ruler created room for another sphere known as the public sphere in the modern sense of the term: the sphere of public authority. The latter assumed objective existence in a *permanent* administration and a *standing* army. Now continuous state activity corresponded to the continuity of contact among those trafficking in commodities and news (stock market, press). Public authority was consolidated into a palpable object confronting those who were merely subject to it and who at first were only negatively defined by it. For they were the private people who, because they held no office, were excluded from any share in public authority. 'Public' in this narrower sense was synonymous with 'state-related'; the attribute no longer referred to the representative 'court' of a person endowed with authority but instead to the functioning of an apparatus with regulated spheres of jurisdiction and endowed with a monopoly over the legitimate use of coercion. The manorial lord's feudal authority was transformed into the authority to 'police'; the private people under it, as the addressees of public authority, formed the public. [...]

However much the *Tischgesellschaften*, *salons*, and coffee houses may have differed in the size and composition of their publics, the style of their proceedings, the climate of their debates, and their topical orientations, they all organized discussion among private people that tended to be ongoing; hence they had a number of institutional criteria in common. First, they preserved a kind of social intercourse that, far from presupposing the equality of status, disregarded status altogether. The tendency replaced the celebration of rank with a tact befitting equals. The parity on whose basis alone the authority of the better argument could assert itself against that of social hierarchy and in the end can carry the day meant, in the thought of the day, the parity of 'common humanity' ('*bloss Menschliche*'). *Les hommes*, private gentlemen, or *die Privatleute* made up the public not just in the sense that power and prestige of public office were held in suspense; economic dependencies also in principle had no influence. Laws of the market were suspended as were laws of the state. Not that this idea of the public was actually realized in earnest in the coffee houses, the *salons*, and the societies; but as an idea it had become institutionalized and thereby stated as an objective claim. If not realized, it was at least consequential.

*Secondly*, discussion within such a public presupposed the problematization of areas that until then had not been questioned. The domain of 'common concern' which was the object of public critical attention remained a preserve in which church and state authorities had the monopoly of interpretation not just from the pulpit but in philosophy, literature, and art, even at a time when, for specific social categories, the development of capitalism already demanded a behavior whose rational orientation required ever more information. To the degree, however, to which philosophical and literary works and works of art in general were produced for the market and distributed through it, these culture products became similar to that type of information: as commodities they became in principle generally accessible. They no longer remained components of the Church's and court's publicity of representation; that is precisely what was meant by the loss of their aura of extraordinariness and by the profaning of their once sacramental character. The private people for whom the cultural product became available as a commodity profaned it inasmuch as they had to determine its meaning on their own (by way of rational communication with one another), verbalize it, and thus state explicitly what precisely in its implicitness for so long could assert its authority. As Raymond Williams demonstrates, 'art' and 'culture' owe their modern meaning of spheres separate from the reproduction of social life to the eighteenth century (Williams, *Culture and Society 1870–1950*, 1958).

*Thirdly*, the same process that converted culture into a commodity (and in this fashion constituted it as a culture that could become an object of discussion to begin with) established the public as in principle inclusive. However exclusive the public might be in any given instance, it could never close itself off entirely and become consolidated as a clique; for it always understood and found itself immersed within a more inclusive public of all private people, persons who – insofar as they were propertied and educated – as readers, listeners, and spectators could avail themselves via the market of the objects that were subject to discussion. The issues discussed became 'general' not merely in their significance, but also in their accessibility: everyone had to *be able* to participate. Wherever the public established itself institutionally as a stable group of discussants, it did not equate itself with *the* public but at most claimed to act as its mouthpiece, in its name, perhaps even as its educator – the new form of bourgeois representation. The public of the first generations, even when it constituted itself as a specific circle of persons, was conscious of being part of a larger public. Potentially it was always also a publicist body, as its discussions did not need to remain internal to it but could be directed at the outside world – for this, perhaps, the *Diskurse der Mahlern*, a moral weekly published from 1721 on by Bodmer and Breitinger in Zurich, was one among many examples.

In relation to the mass of the rural population and the common 'people' in the towns, of course, the public 'at large' that was being formed diffusely outside the early institutions of the public was still extremely small. Elementary education, where it existed, was inferior. The proportion of illiterates, at least in Great Britain, even exceeded that of the preceding Elizabethan epoch (R.D. Altick, *The English Common Reader: A Social History of the Mass Reading Public*, 1957). Here, at the start of the eighteenth century, more than half of the population lived on the margins of subsistence. The masses were not only largely illiterate but also so pauperized that they could not even pay for literature. They did not have at their disposal the buying power needed for even the most modest participation in the market of cultural goods (I. Watt, *The Rise of the Novel*, 1957). Nevertheless, with the emergence of the diffuse public formed in the course of the commercialization of cultural production, a new social category arose. [...]

A political consciousness developed in the public sphere of civil society which, in opposition to absolute sovereignty, articulated the concept of and demand for general and abstract laws and which ultimately came to assert itself (i.e. public opinion) as the only legitimate source of this law. In the course of the eighteenth century public opinion claimed the legislative competence for those norms whose polemical-rationalist conception it had provided to begin with.

The criteria of generality and abstractness characterizing legal norms had to have a peculiar obviousness for privatized individuals who, by communicating with each other in the public sphere of the world of letters, confirmed each other's subjectivity as it emerged from their spheres of intimacy. For as a public they were already under the implicit law of the parity of all cultivated persons, whose abstract universality afforded the sole guarantee that the individuals subsumed under it in an equally abstract fashion, as 'common human beings', were set free in their subjectivity precisely by this parity. The clichés of 'equality' and 'liberty,' not yet ossified into revolutionary bourgeois propaganda formulae, were still imbued with life. The bourgeois public's critical public debate took place in principle without regard to all preexisting social and political rank and in accord with universal rules. These rules, because they remained strictly external to the individuals as such, secured space for the development of these individuals' interiority by literary means. These rules, because universally valid, secured a space for the individuated person; because they were objective, they secured a space for what was most subjective; because they were abstract, for what was most concrete. At the same time, the results that under these conditions issued from the public process of critical debate lay claim to being in accord with reason; intrinsic to the idea of a public opinion born of the power of the better argument was the claim to that morally pretentious rationality that strove to discover what was at once just and right. Public opinion was supposed to do justice to the nature of the case. For this reason the 'laws', which it now also wanted to establish for the social sphere, could also lay claim to substantive rationality besides the formal criteria of generality and abstractness. In this sense, the physiocrats declared that *opinion publique* alone had insight into and made visible the *ordre naturel* so that, in the form of general norms, the enlightened monarch could then make the latter the basis of his action; in this way they hoped to bring rule into convergence with reason.

The self-interpretation of the public in the political realm, as reflected in the crucial category of the legal norm, was the accomplishment of a consciousness functionally adapted to the institutions of the public sphere in the world of letters. In general, the two forms of public sphere blended with each other in a peculiar fashion. In both, there formed a public consisting of private persons whose autonomy based on ownership of private property wanted to see itself represented as such in the sphere of the bourgeois family and actualized inside the person as love, freedom, and cultivation – in a word, as humanity.

(pp. 17–18, 36–38, 54–55)

## PETER GAY

Peter Gay's celebrated two-volume work *The Enlightenment: An Interpretation* was published in the late 1960s. Like Cassirer, Gay concentrated on elucidating a coherent philosophy from the writings of the *philosophes*, who emerge as a 'party of humanity' headed by Voltaire, opposed to religious authority and injustice, and committed to the progressive emancipation of mankind through the pursuit of knowledge. His work begins with the following statement:

> There were many philosophes in the eighteenth century, but there was only one Enlightenment. A loose, informal, wholly unorganised coalition of cultural critics, religious sceptics, and political reformers from Edinburgh to Naples, Paris to Berlin, Boston to Philadelphia, the philosophes made up a clamorous chorus, and there were some discordant voices among them, but what is striking is their general harmony, not their occasional discord. The men of the Enlightenment united on a vastly ambitious program, a program of secularism, humanity, cosmopolitanism, and freedom, above all, freedom in its many forms – freedom from arbitrary power, freedom of speech, freedom of trade, freedom to realise one's talents, freedom of aesthetic response, freedom, in a word, of moral man to make his own way in the world.

Gay's thesis in the first volume, *The Rise of Modern Paganism* (1966), is to explain the 'dialectical interplay of [the *philosophes*'] appeal to antiquity, their tension with Christianity and their pursuit of modernity'. He focuses on the inter-actions between the *philosophes*, paying attention to the letters, friendships, per-sonal crises and influences on the writers that contributed to their forging of a 'family' of 'modern pagans'. This approach permits reference to some women, such as Emilie de Châtelet or those associated with the philosophical 'salon', and to refer copiously to Diderot's letters to Sophie Volland.

In the second volume, *The Science of Freedom* (1969), Gay focuses primarily on the rise of a scientific method and its secularising effect on intellectual enquiry, and looks at economic changes, the nascent industrial society, the social backdrop of journals, taverns, coffee houses and academies, and the social position of the *philosophes*. Here, he characterises Enlightenment thought as confident and forward-looking; the *philosophes* proclaiming a 'recovery of nerve' and sensing an increased mastery of the world. He concludes that the effect of the Enlightenment, in fields as diverse as natural sciences, art criticism and sociology, also came to fruition in the American Revolution. He also pays attention to the contradictions and paradoxes of Enlightenment thought, such as the limits of the 'latent rhetori-cal humanity' of the *philosophes*' programmes for educational and political change, their choice of injustices against which to fight, and their ambivalent relation to absolutism. But, in the main, his thesis is to show the 'permanent value of the Enlightenment's humane and libertarian vision and the permanent validity of its critical method'. Thus he explores the élite nature of Enlightenment thought, and concludes that the *philosophes* were 'men of their day', pessimistic about 'the capacities of the canaille', and hoping for change through the spread of education. Similarly, in the extract selected here, he acknowledges the flaws and limitations of Enlightenment historiography, but defends its polemical nature for its usefulness to modernity.

## The Enlightenment: An Interpretation (1969)

The *philosophes*' view that history was pervaded by struggles between virtue and vice, reason and unreason, philosophy and superstition, has come to seem naïve, but it was a purely human struggle, open to scientific inquiry and criticism. The struggle the Christian saw dominating history had its origins and pursued its course in the shadow of the supernatural. Wherever history was enacted – in the minds of men or on the fields of battle – it was somehow a reenactment of the very beginning of history, which was the seduction of Eve by the serpent; it was the working out, in myriad forms, of the war of Satan against God and His children. More than merely seeing history as justifi-cation for their particular version of Christianity, Christian historians saw it as part, and proof, of the supreme truths enshrined in religion. Events were on the one hand fore-tastes or repetitions of transcendent religious moments in the life of the world – the expulsion from Paradise, the Incarnation of Christ, the Second Coming – or on the other hand demonstrations of divine power, no matter which way they went: if heretics swarmed across Europe, this was a sign of God's anger at the faithful; if they retreated, it was a sign of His good will. However gravely the *philosophes* sinned in converting the events of history into a usable past, Christian historians had anticipated and in every way outdone them in this dubious enterprise.

It is true that Christian historians were coming to visualize God as acting not directly, by intermittent personal appearances, but indirectly, through human instruments. But inevitably, in their histories, the most significant human shapers of history were mere marionettes; they fulfilled God's designs without wishing to, or knowing it. Despite his attempts to portray divine action in history as indirect, the most influential, eloquent, and, to the *philosophes*, most provocative of Christian historians – Bossuet – regarded the Bible as more authoritative than the most reliable of secular histories, Moses as the first historian, the Creation, the Deluge, or worldly events with religious implications (like the reign of Constantine) as the decisive events in the past. Bossuet was not alone, and by his time no longer wholly typical, but the most philosophical of Christian historians were, like Bossuet, compelled to give religious – which is to say, incomplete, incorrect, inadequate, and often irrelevant – answers to questions men were beginning to ask about historical causation.

The *philosophes* changed all this, and their act is a decisive moment in the history of history. Barely emerged from the chrysalis of credulity, the *philosophes* were themselves sometimes credulous enough; they would ascribe great importance to world-historical individuals and the rational plans of statesmen rather than the confluence of historical forces, and they liked to attribute large events to trivial causes. D'Alembert traced the Renaissance to the Greek scholars whom the Fall of Constantinople had driven to Italy, and Voltaire took a dramatist's delight in small incidents productive of vast consequences: the messenger who, during the disorders of 1651, reaches the Prince de Condé too late and thus plunges France into civil war is a characteristic figure in Voltaire's histories, and in other Enlightenment histories.

But the *philosophes* did not make this kind of pragmatic history into a system. They had no system. The list of causes that Gibbon offers for the decline and fall of the Roman Empire scattered through his book – and revealed in isolated pronouncements and asides – is impressively diverse: as Gibbon sees it, the long period of peace induced torpor, effeminacy, and a decline in public spirit; the vast territory of the empire and the lack of real freedom froze institutions into rigidity; economic exploitation produced a populace reluctant to defend a Rome in which it had no stake – and all these conditions, reinforcing one another, made the incursions of the German barbarians and the spread of Christianity, the two decisive causes of the fall, irresistible.

Gibbon's list of causes, like lists of causes adduced by other philosophic historians for other events, was incomplete and uncoordinated; the *philosophes* had no overriding explanation of historical change that would have permitted them to show how causes interacted or how they could be arranged in a hierarchy of importance. Their theory of society was too primitive, and their idea of history as sheer battle too deeply engrained, to permit them to discover a really convincing theory of development. Uncertainty marks much of their work. It is instructive to see Voltaire's treatment of the Glorious Revolution of 1688: as he interpreted the event, it had been largely determined by the characters of James II and William III, and he offered it as a good example to those 'who like to see the cause of events in the conduct of men.' But while this one event gave support to this particular theory of historical causation, Voltaire's language makes it plain that he cannot commit himself to it in explaining other events. In fact, elsewhere Voltaire shows himself to be a supporter of the larger view that historical changes arise from an interaction among massive impersonal forces: in his *Lettres philosophiques* he traces the splendor of England to a happy congruence of prosperity, freedom, and the dominance of commercial values; elsewhere he argues that the motive power of history must be sought in changes of religion or forms of government. Other Enlightenment historians offered similar causes; in his *De l'esprit des lois*, Montesquieu suggests that 'men are governed' by 'several things'; he lists them as 'climate, religion, the laws, the principles of government, the example of the past, manners, and fashions,' and adds that one or two of these causes will take prominence in the history of one society or another, depending on its general state of culture. The *philosophes* had a sense that history is more than a drama of towering individuals. Yet their sociology is likely to be impressionistic; they had no way of converting their intuitions into formal arguments. Face to face with great historical questions, the *philosophes* often seem to be at play; they describe an event, list some plausible causes with an air of confidence, and move on.

This cavalier evasion of analysis or, rather, this substitution of literary elegance for analysis, which is often irritating, should not obscure the magnitude of their achievement. In offering a secular alternative to the theological determinism of Christian historians (whether in its rationalist version showing God clearly at work, or its mystical version according to which God manipulates events shrouded in mystery), the *philosophes*, whatever the inadequacies of their own analyses, opened the possibility for an all-embracing causal understanding of historical events and historical change. Their character sketches, the great set pieces about Luther or Cromwell, and their extended comparisons between William III and Louis XIV, are often psychologically improbable; accounts of great moments in history – the decline of the Roman Empire, the ascendancy of Louis XIV, the Spanish conquest of the New World often suffer from a certain rationalism, and a disturbing if unconscious refusal to see the issues in all their complexity. But the expulsion of God from the historical stage remained an enormous gain for historical science. History became what Lenglet du Fresnoy called *érudition profane*, with no reserved precincts, no privileged subjects, no figures exempt from criticism. Historians could now address themselves, without reserve and without fear, to what Montesquieu called 'general causes, whether moral or physical.' God's disappearance left a vacuum that the secular intelligence was called upon to fill.

(vol. II, pp. 385–390)

## ROBERT DARNTON

Interest in the social movements, uses and contexts of the Enlightenment became much greater during the 1970s and '80s, led by the work of historians such as Robert Darnton and Roger Chartier. The American historian Darnton's *The Business of Enlightenment: A Publishing History of the 'Encyclopédie', 1775–1800* (1979) focuses on the publication history of a work which exercised a seminal influence in the Enlightenment's 'rethinking of the world'. Darnton sees the *Encyclopédie* as an economic as well as ideological phenomenon: it was a best seller in its time (he estimates 25,000 copies were in print by 1789), and thus a hugely successful commercial venture for its publishers. By paying attention to the book as a commodity and to contract disputes, pirate copies, trade wars, editorial work, wages, labour relations, the marketing of the book and the collection of sub-scriptions, Darnton examines the process of eighteenth-century bookmaking in France in general, and of the *Encyclopédie* in particular. The successive publishers' negotiations for permission to print show how, at its beginning, the *Encyclopédie* was a book that barely existed within the law – being largely printed outside France. The last edition, Panchouke's huge, largely forgotten, and thematically (not alphabetically) organised *Encyclopédie Méthodique*, however, constitutes a moment when Encyclopedism and orthodoxy meet. Its contributors tended to be high officials in Louis XVI's administration, sympathetic to the principles of ration-alism and reform. Darnton concludes that this reflects the growing professionalism of the intellectual élite and the cultural acceptance of the *Encyclopédie*'s message that the world could be 'ordered by rational principles derived from experience'.

## The Business of Enlightenment (1979)

Publishers said what they pleased in their advertising. The publicity for the *Encyclopédie*, from the first prospectus of 1751 to the last flier about the *Méthodique* around 1830, is a series of half truths, falsehoods, broken promises, and fake announcements about phony editions. The publishers lied so often and so casually that one wonders whether they ever considered honesty as a policy. It probably never occurred to them that they should feel responsible for keeping the public accurately informed. Indeed, the French state encour-aged them to use false information in their prospectuses and title pages, so that it could turn a blind eye to books that the clergy and parlements wanted it to confiscate. [...]

If read as historical documents, slanted advertisements can be more revealing than straight *avis* because they show how sellers thought their products would appeal to the public. In the propaganda for the quarto [editions, 1777–79], the publishers emphasized that their customers would get a compendium of modern knowledge and a synthesis of modern philosophy, all in one. In this respect, they carried out the strategy of Diderot and d'Alembert, who wanted to promote *philosophie* by identifying it with knowledge. To ask whether the *Encyclopédie* was a reference work or a manifesto of Enlightenment is to pose a false problem, for it was meant to combine those characteristics, and it was presented as a combination of them, by its promoters as well as its authors. Insofar as one can know anything about the response of the readers, it seems that they, too, saw the *Encyclopédie* in this fashion. They wanted *philosophie* as much as information, and they did not treat the *Encyclopédie* as modern encyclopedias are treated – that is, as a neutral compilation about everything from A to Z. The contemporary understanding of the book should be taken seriously because it shows the extent to which the *Encyclopédie* was identified with the Enlightenment in the eighteenth century. The publishers predicated their sales campaign on that identification. They expected the public to buy the book for the reasons they cited in their advertising: a quarto on the shelf would proclaim its owner's standing as a man of knowledge and a philosophe. *Philosophie* had become fashionable by 1777; the commercialization of intellectual vogues had become quite advanced; and the advance had occurred along lines laid out by Diderot and d'Alembert. In short, the Enlightenment seemed to be penetrating rather far into French society, but how far?

Book consumption can serve as only a crude indicator of tastes and values among the reading public, and it may appear impertinent to talk about 'consuming' books in the first place. But the purchase of a book is a significant act, when considered culturally as well as economically. It provides some indication of the spread of ideas beyond the intellectual milieu within which intellectual history is usually circumscribed. And as there has never been a study of the sales of any eighteenth-century book, a sales analysis of the most important work of the Enlightenment ought to be worthwhile.

The price of the *Encyclopédie* set a limit to its diffusion, for the book remained beyond the purchasing power of peasants and artisans, even though some of them might have consulted it in *cabinets littéraires*. But as the *Encyclopédie* progressed from edition to edition, its format decreased in size, it contained fewer plates, its paper declined in quality, and its price went down. And as the publishing consortia succeeded one another, they cast their nets more and more widely, reaching out with each new edition to remoter sections of the reading public. By the time they launched the quarto, they proclaimed that the *Encyclopédie* had ceased to be a luxury item and had come within the range of ordinary readers. But who were the *Encyclopédie* readers of eighteenth-century France, and what part of the kingdom and the social order did they inhabit?

To identify them, it is necessary to compile statistics from the subscription list of the quarto, which covers about three-fifths of the *Encyclopédies* that existed in France and nearly one-third of those everywhere in the world before 1789. A map of subscriptions shows that the quartos spread throughout the country, but they sold better in some places than in others — better in towns than in villages, better along commercial arteries than in the hinterlands, better in the valleys of the Rhône and the Garonne than in those of the Loire and the Meuse, and best of all in the great provincial capitals: Lyons, Montpellier, Toulouse, Bordeaux, Rennes, Caen, Nancy, Dijon and Besançon. The only areas that the quarto did not reach were Brittany beyond Rennes, the Landes below Bordeaux, and the rural region of the southwest encircled by the Loire, the Cher, and the Dordogne. It is perilous to argue from geographical to social distribution, but some of the puzzling points on the map can be clarified by the correspondence of the booksellers. After weighing both sorts of evidence, it seems clear that the demand for the *Encyclopédie* came primarily from ancient cities that had acquired rich endowments of ecclesiastical and educational institutions during the late Middle Ages or that rose with the Bourbon monarchy to become administrative and cultural centers — seats of parlements, academies, and intendancies. The quarto did not sell well in the cities of the future, where the stirrings of industrialization could already be felt.

The two extremes in the market for the *Encyclopédie* are represented by Besançon, an old-fashioned provincial capital of about 28,000 inhabitants, which absorbed 338 quartos, and Lille, a burgeoning industrial center of 61,000, which absorbed only 28. If the

STN's [Société Typographique Nationale] correspondents are to be believed, the explanation for this disparity is simple: manufacturers and merchants had no interest in literature. Actually the subscribers of the quarto did include a few merchants, certainly in Marseilles and probably in Lyons and Bordeaux, although their poor showing in the north and the northeast suggests that they may have belonged to the commercial oligarchies of the older trading cities rather than to any emerging industrial society. In the case of the Franche-Comté, 253 subscribers or 65 percent of the total can be identified. Only 15 of them were merchants. The vast majority came from the traditional elite: men of the robe, led by the councillors of the parlement, and men of the sword, led by the officers in the garrison of Besançon. Royal officials subscribed so heavily that the book seems to have penetrated the entire administration of the province. In the small towns, it appealed to an intelligentsia of lawyers, administrators, and even curés. In Besançon, it went into the libraries of *parlementaires*, civil and military officers, lawyers, doctors, and priests. Half the Bisontin subscribers came from the first two estates, although the eventual readership of the book probably extended down to the lower middle classes, thanks to borrowing and Lépagnez's *cabinet littéraire*. In general, however, the *Encyclopédie* did not seep into the base of society: it circulated through the middle sectors and saturated those at the top.

This view of a top-heavy diffusion process corresponds to the strategy of Enlightenment formulated by Voltaire and d'Alembert — an Enlightenment from above, which would filter down through the superstructure from the salons and academies into the world of small-town notables and country gentlemen — but not farther. Thus the *Encyclopédie* began as a luxury limited primarily to the élite of the court and capital. But after it assumed a more modest form and acquired a price that suited middle-class budgets, it spread through the *bourgeoisie d'Ancien Régime*, a bourgeoisie that lived off *rentes*, offices, and services rather than industry and commerce. The modern capitalist bourgeoisie also could have afforded the later *Encyclopédie*, and a few enlightened merchants did buy it — but so few that they seem trivial in comparison with the *privilégiés* and professional men, who bought most of the copies. Voltaire's prescription for the Enlightenment therefore appears to be rather close to what actually happened — closer than the interpretation of some of the most eminent historians in France today, who usually rivet the Enlightenment to the industrializing bourgeoisie and treat the *Encyclopédie* as the expression of class consciousness. Nothing could have been more cutthroat and capitalistic than the *Encyclopédie* as an enterprise, but the audience of the *Encyclopédie* did not consist of capitalists. The readers of the book came from the sectors of society that were to crumble quickest in 1789, from the world of parlements and bailliages, from the Bourbon bureaucracy and the army and the church. It may seem paradoxical that a progressive ideology should have infiltrated the most archaic and eroded segments of the social structure, but the Revolution began with a paradox — with collapse at the top before upheaval from below. And although some of the *Encyclopédie* subscribers may have been devastated by the Revolution, most of them probably gained by it, at least in the long run, for it ultimately came under the control of lawyers and notables who directed it in their own interests and who continued to dominate France for the next hundred years, if not longer.

(pp. 522–527)

# JEAN-FRANÇOIS LYOTARD

Jean-François Lyotard's *La Condition Postmoderne: rapport sur le savoir* (1979), translated as *The Postmodern Condition: A Report on Knowledge* in 1984, became central to the philosophical and theoretical debate about postmodernism. Lyotard argues that a fragmented 'contemporary knowledge' constitutes a questioning of, and a break from, Enlightenment thought. The Enlightenment is defined as a project based on a notion of a stable subject and the narrative of history. It led to myths about the progressive liberation of humankind and the growth and unity of knowledge. In the passages selected here, Lyotard contrasts the narrative of the Enlightenment, which functions to legitimate science, and its 'hero' of knowledge – the rational individual – with the heterogeneous, fragmented language games of the postmodern condition, famously defined as 'incredulity towards metanarratives'.

## *The Postmodern Condition* (1979)

The object of this study is the condition of knowledge in the most highly developed societies. I have decided to use the word *postmodern* to describe that condition. The word is in current use on the American continent among sociologists and critics; it designates the state of our culture following the transformations which, since the end of the nineteenth century, have altered the game rules for science, literature, and the arts. The present study will place these transformations in the context of the crisis of narratives.

Science has always been in conflict with narratives. Judged by the yardstick of science, the majority of them prove to be fables. But to the extent that science does not restrict itself to stating useful irregularities and seeks the truth, it is obliged to legitimate the rules of its own game. It then produces a discourse of legitimation with respect to its own status, a discourse called philosophy. I will use the term *modern* to designate any science that legitimates itself with reference to a metadiscourse of this kind making an explicit appeal to some grand narrative, such as the dialectics of the Spirit, the hermeneutics of meaning, the emancipation of the rational or working subject, or the creation of wealth. For example, the rule of consensus between the sender and addressee of a statement with truth-value is deemed acceptable if it is cast in terms of a possible unanimity between rational minds: this is the Enlightenment narrative in which the hero of knowledge works towards a good ethico-political end – universal peace. As can be seen from this example, if a metanarrative implying a philosophy of history is used to legitimate knowledge, questions are raised concerning the validity of the institutions governing the social bond: these must be legitimated as well. Thus justice is consigned to the grand narrative in the same way as truth. [...]

With modern science, two new features appear in the problematic of legitimation. To begin with, it leaves behind the metaphysical search for a first proof of transcendental authority as a response to the question: 'How do you prove the proof?' or, more generally, 'Who decides the conditions of truth?' It is recognized that the conditions of truth, in other words, the rules of the game of science, are immanent in that game, that they can only be established within the bonds of a debate that is already scientific in nature, and that there is no other proof that the rules are good than the consensus extended to them by the experts.

Accompanying the modern proclivity to define the conditions of a discourse in a discourse on those conditions is a renewed dignity for narrative (popular) cultures, already noticeable in Renaissance Humanism and variously present in the Enlightenment, the *Sturm und Drang*, German idealist philosophy, and the historical school in France. Narration is no longer an involuntary lapse in the legitimation process. The explicit appeal to narrative in the problematic of knowledge is concomitant with the liberation of the bourgeois classes from the traditional authorities. Narrative knowledge makes a resurgence in the West as a way of solving the problem of legitimating the new authorities. It is natural in a narrative problematic for such a question to solicit the name of a hero as its response: *Who* has the right to decide for society? Who is the subject whose prescriptions are norms for those they obligate?

This way of inquiring into sociopolitical legitimacy combines with the new scientific attitude: the name of the hero is the people, the sign of legitimacy is the people's consensus, and their mode of creating norms is deliberation. The notion of progress is a necessary outgrowth of this. It represents nothing other than the movement by which knowledge is presumed to accumulate — but this movement is extended to the new sociopolitical subject. The people debate among themselves about what is just or unjust in the same way that the scientific community debates about what is true or false; they accumulate civil laws just as scientists accumulate scientific laws; they perfect their rules of consensus just as the scientists produce new 'paradigms' to revise their rules in light of what they have learned.

It is clear that what is meant here by 'the people' is entirely different from what is implied by traditional narrative knowledge, which ... requires no instituting deliberation, no cumulative progression, no pretension to universality; these are the operators of scientific knowledge. It is therefore not at all surprising that the representatives of the new process of legitimation by 'the people' should be at the same time actively involved in destroying the traditional knowledge of peoples, perceived from that point forward as minorities or potential separatist movements destined only to spread obscurantism.

We can see too that the real existence of this necessarily abstract subject (it is abstract because it is uniquely modelled on the paradigm of the subject of knowledge — that is, one who sends–receives denotative statements with truth-value to the exclusion of other language games) depends on the institutions within which that subject is supposed to deliberate and decide, and which comprise all or part of the State. The question of the State becomes intimately entwined with that of scientific knowledge.

But it is also clear that this interlocking is many sided. The 'people' (the nation, or even humanity), and especially their political institutions, are not content to know — they legislate. That is, they formulate prescriptions that have the status of norms. They therefore exercise their competence not only with respect to denotative utterances concerning what is true, but also prescriptive utterances with pretensions to justice. As already said, what characterizes narrative knowledge, what forms the basis of our conception of it, [is] precisely that it combines both of these kinds of competence, not to mention all the others.

The mode of legitimation we are discussing, which reintroduces narrative as the validity of knowledge, can thus take two routes, depending on whether it represents the subject of the narrative as cognitive or practical, as a hero of knowledge or a hero of liberty. Because of this alternative, not only does the meaning of legitimation vary, but it is already apparent that narrative itself is incapable of describing that meaning adequately.

(pp. xxiii–xxiv, 29–31)

# MICHEL FOUCAULT

The French philosopher Michel Foucault characterised himself as a historian of 'systems of thought' and has produced influential critiques of modern Western conceptions of normality and abnormality in sexuality, criminality, and mental illness. In *Madness and Civilization* (1965) he claimed that Enlightenment 'reason' was (far from promoting liberation) an instrument of control – silencing 'unreason'. In *Discipline and Punish* (1977) he examined Enlightenment views of punishment and how individuals are 'disciplined' by social institutions. His assertion in the conclusion of *The Order of Things* (1966) that the centrality of the concept of 'man' was an eighteenth-century invention that was historically on the wane is particularly relevant to a consideration of the Enlightenment. Partly reflecting upon his earlier work, his essay 'What is Enlightenment?', first published in 1984, is both an attempt to define an attitude of modernity and to produce a programme for a historico-critical method that can reflect on various material practices. His attempt to be neither 'for' nor 'against' the Enlightenment, but to consider it as part of a shift crucial to the development of an 'attitude of modernity' adds another perspective to Enlightenment debates.

## 'What is Enlightenment?' (1984)

I do not pretend to be summarizing in these few lines either the complex historical event that was the Enlightenment, at the end of the eighteenth century, or the attitude of modernity in the various guises it may have taken on during the last two centuries.

I have been seeking, on the one hand, to emphasize the extent to which a type of philosophical interrogation – one that simultaneously problematizes man's relation to the present, man's historical mode of being, and the constitution of the self as an autonomous subject – is rooted in the Enlightenment. On the other hand, I have been seeking to stress that the thread that may connect us with the Enlightenment is not faithfulness to doctrinal elements, but rather the permanent reactivation of an attitude – that is, of a philosophical ethos that could be described as a permanent critique of our historical era. I should like to characterize this ethos very briefly.

A. *Negatively*

1.   This ethos implies, first, the refusal of what I like to call the 'blackmail' of the Enlightenment. I think that the Enlightenment, as a set of political, economic, social,

institutional, and cultural events on which we still depend in large part, constitutes a privileged domain for analysis. I also think that, as an enterprise for linking the progress of truth and the history of liberty in a bond of direct relation, it formulated a philosophical question that remains for us to consider. I think, finally, as I have tried to show with reference to Kant's text [*What is Enlightenment?*], that it defined a certain manner of philosophizing.

But that does not mean that one has to be 'for' or 'against' the Enlightenment. It even means precisely that one has to refuse everything that might present itself in the form of a simplistic and authoritarian alternative: you either accept the Enlightenment and remain within the tradition of its rationalism (this is considered a positive term by some and used by others, on the contrary, as a reproach); or else you criticize the Enlightenment and then try to escape from its principle of rationality (which may be seen once again as good or bad). And we do not break free of this blackmail by introducing 'dialectical' nuances while seeking to determine what good and bad elements there may have been in the Enlightenment.

We must try to proceed with the analysis of ourselves as beings who are historically determined, to a certain extent, by the Enlightenment. Such an analysis implies a series of historical inquiries that are as precise as possible; and these inquiries will not be oriented retrospectively toward the 'essential kernel of rationality' that can be found in the Enlightenment, and that would have to be preserved in any event; they will be oriented toward 'the contemporary limits of the necessary,' that is, toward what is not or is no longer indispensable for the constitution of ourselves as autonomous subjects.

2.   This permanent critique of ourselves has to avoid the always too facile confusions between humanism and Enlightenment.

We must never forget that the Enlightenment is an event, or a set of events and complex historical processes, that is located at a certain point in the development of European societies. As such, it includes elements of social transformation, types of political institution, forms of knowledge, projects of rationalization of knowledge and practices, technological mutations that are very difficult to sum up in a word, even if many of these phenomena remain important today. The one I have pointed out, which seems to me to have been at the basis of an entire form of philosophical reflection, concerns only the mode of reflective relation to the present.

Humanism is something entirely different. It is a theme or, rather, a set of themes that have reappeared on several occasions, over time, in European societies; these themes, always tied to value judgments, have obviously varied greatly in their content, as well as in the values they have preserved. Furthermore, they have served as a critical principle of differentiation. In the seventeenth century, there was a humanism that presented itself as a critique of Christianity or of religion in general; there was a Christian humanism opposed to an ascetic and much more theocentric humanism. In the nineteenth century, there was a suspicious humanism, hostile and critical toward science, and another that, to the contrary, placed its hope in that same science. Marxism has been a humanism; so have existentialism and personalism; there was a time when people supported the humanistic values represented by National Socialism, and when the Stalinists themselves said they were humanists.

From this, we must not conclude that everything that has ever been linked with humanism is to be rejected, but that the humanistic thematic is in itself too supple, too diverse, too inconsistent to serve as an axis for reflection. And it is a fact that, at least since the seventeenth century, what is called humanism has always been obliged to lean on certain conceptions of man borrowed from religion, science, or politics. Humanism serves to color and to justify the conceptions of man to which it is, after all, obliged to take recourse.

Now, in this connection, I believe that this thematic, which so often recurs, and which always depends on humanism, can be opposed by the principle of a critique and a permanent creation of ourselves in our autonomy: that is, a principle at the heart of the historical consciousness that the Enlightenment has of itself. From this standpoint, I am inclined to see Enlightenment and humanism in a state of tension rather than identity.

In any case, it seems to me dangerous to confuse them; and further, it seems historically inaccurate. If the question of man, of the human species, of the humanist, was important throughout the eighteenth century, this is very rarely, I believe, because the Enlightenment considered itself a humanism. It is worthwhile, too, to note that throughout the nineteenth century, the historiography of sixteenth-century humanism, which was so important for people like Saint-Beuve or Burckhardt, was always distinct from and sometimes explicitly opposed to the Enlightenment and the eighteenth century. The nineteenth century had a tendency to oppose the two, at least as much as to confuse them.

In any case, I think that, just as we must free ourselves from the intellectual blackmail of 'being for or against the Enlightenment', we must escape from the historical and moral confusionism that mixes the theme of humanism with the question of the Enlightenment. An analysis of their complex relations in the course of the last two centuries would be a worthwhile project, an important one if we are to bring some measure of clarity to the consciousness that we have of ourselves and of our past.

(pp. 42–45)


## SYLVANA TOMASELLI

In 1982, *History Workshop* changed its subtitle from 'a journal of socialist historians' to 'a journal of socialist and feminist historians', to encourage and widen debate on the history of women. In 1985, Sylvana Tomaselli made an incisive contribution to this discussion through her essay 'The Enlightenment Debate on Women', which sought 'to put women back in their place in history by examining a forgotten tradition which linked women, not, as is all too swiftly done, to nature, but to culture and the process of historical development'. Having reviewed several recent books which had continued a tradition of linking women primarily with nature, Tomaselli states:

> In fact, the view that woman civilises, that she cultivates, refines, perhaps even adulterates and corrupts is as recurrent as the view that she is nature's most dutiful and untouched daughter, or to put it less palatably, a being closer to animals, one link, at least, lower than man in the Great Chain of Beings. Were the connection between woman and nature as unproblematic as some writers

seem to think it is within our culture, there simply would be no language in which to articulate the questions which make up feminist discourse.

## 'The Enlightenment Debate on Women' (1985)

Few periods gave as much consideration to the issue of the merit and demerit of the growth of society, of culture and civilisation as the eighteenth century. The categories of nature and culture were absolutely pivotal to nearly every aspect of the Enlightenment. It produced perhaps the greatest reassessment of the value of society by contrasting it with a hypothetical state of nature out of which social life emerged in distinctive and progressive stages. It is often assumed that when writing the history of Man and society, eighteenth century thinkers were subsuming woman within the notion of man – yet one more example of the sexist categories of male political thought. But this was by no means always the case. We need not be shy. We can actually ask whether the history of society told the same tale for man as for woman, because that is a question which the eighteenth century itself asked.

For those who gave the matter any thought, the history of civilisation, when written with women in mind, could only be viewed positively. Whatever the advantages or disadvantages of the progress of the arts and sciences, of the coming of commercial society and of the growth of manners and politeness, all were agreed that there was nothing in the infancy of mankind about which women need feel nostalgic. Woman's life in the state of nature or in primitive societies was not only confined to securing the means of subsistence, but it was marked in addition by their subjugation to the unremitting and universal tyranny of men. As long as commentators focused on women, the history of the species was unquestionably one of progress towards liberty. The issue of the condition of women present or past could be passed over in silence of course, but once raised, the question of the comparative freedom, and indeed happiness, of the savage and civilised woman seems to have afforded only one answer.

This was true of such critics of the relation between the sexes and the condition of women in the eighteenth century as Catherine Macaulay (1731–91), as it was of critics of civilisation like Denis Diderot (1713–84). Thus, Macaulay contends in her *Letters on Education*:

> But whatever might be the wise purpose intended by Providence in such a disposition of things, certain it is, that some degree of inferiority, in point of corporal strength, seems always to have existed between the two sexes; and this advantage in the barbarous ages of mankind, was abused to such a degree, as to destroy all the natural rights of the female species, and reduce them to a state of abject slavery.
> (*Letters on Education*, Letter XXII, 'No Characteristic Difference in Sex',
> London, 1790, p. 206)

Unlike the writers with whom we shall be principally concerned, Macaulay wasn't interested in tracing the history of the surpassing of these uncultivated ages. 'What accidents', she writes,

have contributed in Europe to better their condition, would not be to my purpose
to relate; for I do not intend to give you a history of women; I mean only to trace
the sources of their peculiar foibles and vices; and these I firmly believe to originate in situation and education only: for so little did a wise and just Providence
intend to make the condition of slavery an unalterable law of female nature, that in
the same proportion as the male sex have consulted the interest of their own happiness, they have relaxed in their tyranny over women.

(Macaulay, Letters on Education, pp. 206–207)

Had this historian of politics been a little more inclined to write the history of women,
she might have been led to think of them as the agents, and not just the objects, of the
process by which their condition was improved. Writers like Diderot, however, did not
fail to take up the opportunity, when it presented itself, of thinking through the stages
of the history of woman.

Reviewing Antoine-Léonard Thomas's (1732–85) *Essai sur le Caractère, les Moeurs et
l'Esprit des Femmes dans les différents Siècles* (Essay on the Character, Manners and Spirit of
Women throughout the Ages), Diderot did have a lot of abuse to vent. Thomas, or so
the review seems to indicate, had essentially wasted a brilliant chance to treat a subject
of great interest and importance. On a topic such as this, Diderot thought, there was no
excuse for being as excruciatingly dull as Thomas. But however boring Thomas might
have been, Diderot did not dispute his thesis. In fact, he accepted the claim that:

> In nearly every land the cruelty of positive laws has united with the cruelty of
> nature against women. They have been treated as imbecile children. There is no
> manner of vexation which man cannot with impunity exercise against woman
> amongst civilised people; the only retribution which she can exert leads to domes-
> tic trouble and contempt the extent of which varies with the level of civility the
> nation has reached. There is no manner of vexation which the savage doesn't exert
> against his woman; the unhappy woman in the cities is far unhappier still in the
> midst of the forests. Listen to the speech of an Indian woman from the banks of the
> Orenoco, and listen to it, if you can, without being moved by it.

(Denis Diderot, 'Sur les Femmes', review of Essai sur le Caractère … par Thomas,<br>
written for the Correspondance Littéraire, 1 April 1771, Oeuvres Complètes, ed.<br>
Roger Lewinter, Paris, 1971, vol. 10, pp. 28–53)

There followed the often cited account of North-American Indian mothers strangling
their baby daughters to spare them the ignominy and suffering of a life of enslavement
to men. It was indeed a very moving speech.

The point behind such travellers' tales always remained the same. It was not that
Diderot, or Thomas or the many other writers who dealt with the issue felt that modernity could be self-congratulatory with respect to the status of women. There was scarcely any discussion of women in the eighteenth century which did not find much to
criticise and in the age of Enlightenment, education was the most frequent target of
such criticisms. Even if the ideal curriculum for women was a subject on which there
was considerable disagreement, no one in the period seems to have been pleased with

what education they did receive. Catherine Macaulay and Mary Wollstonecraft are but two representatives of this critique. [...]

Women are less unhappy amongst pastoral peoples, in Diderot's view, for the greater ease such peoples have in securing the means of subsistence entails that they also have greater leisure and this, in turn, makes for the conditions in which beauty arises. In such societies women and men can, in Diderot's words 'make some choice as to the object of their desire and add the idea of a nobler sentiment to that of physical pleasure'.

Nor did the logic of the argument cease here. It was extended to welcome the beginnings of agriculture. Thus Diderot argued that the relations between the sexes were further improved as soon as land began to be cultivated. While [William] Alexander [1726–83] noted that

> though pasturages, agriculture and every thing that brings mankind into society, is generally in favour of women; yet the first efforts of a people in agriculture, commonly lay an additional load of labour on the shoulders of that sex; so that they lose, in the beginning, by an institution, which afterwards turns greatly to their advantage.
>
> (*The History of Women from the Earliest Antiquity, to the Present Time*, 1782 edn, vol. I, p. 283)

Nor did women benefit any the less from the growth of commercial society. Turning to Diderot again we find him arguing that women acquire a new importance with the advent of the arts and of commerce as men grow increasingly dependent on women in the daily running of their business – an activity at which women excel. Not even luxury, in Diderot's view, puts an end to the progress of women, for when labour is scorned and wealth increases, mankind has only one obsessive concern: 'In such times, women are eagerly sought after, both on account of the attributes which they owe to nature and of those they acquire by education'.

Each step towards the full development of commercial society could thus be happily undertaken by women. Now, this is by no means as obvious as it might first appear. In order to come to appreciate that this argument about the absolute gain which women made out of the growth of civilisation isn't simply a special case within a wider brief for the rise of commercial society, we must first turn back to the descriptions given within this discourse of the beginnings of society. We must in particular note the extent to which something like a master-slave dialectic is pervasive in such accounts of the early stages of the natural history. Here Thomas's *Essai* offers us what is possibly the best point of departure:

> If one surveys the course of nations through the ages, one will see almost everywhere women both adored and oppressed. Man, who has never missed an opportunity to abuse his power in rendering homage to beauty, has everywhere taken advantage of their weakness. He has been their tyrant and their slave.
>
> (*Essai*, p. 1)

This conceptualisation of the condition of women as one of slavery is so frequent as to be almost a common-place in the Enlightenment. Condorcet's (1743–94) *Esquisse d'un Tableau Historique des Progrès de l'Esprit Humain* (Sketch of a Historical Table of the Progress of the Human Mind) told of the slow development from a state in which 'women were condemned to a kind of slavery'. Much earlier in the century, even Rousseau (1712–78), in his collaboration with Mme Dupin (as their secretary, Rousseau collaborated with both Mme and M. Dupin, during the period from 1745–49), on her projected history of women, urged us to conceive of the matter in these very terms. Men had first deprived women of their liberty, according to him. Masters of all things they had grounded their tyranny in a theory of natural right which had no foundation other than their superior might. Had it not been for this original enslavement, women would have surpassed men in every act of virtue and courage. In fact, they often had. But men were careful to suppress any mention of it. And as they most often wrote the histories of the race, this censorship was almost entirely successful in its aim (Rousseau, 'Sur les Femmes', *Oeuvres Complètes*, II, Pléiade edition, Paris, 1961, pp. 1254–1255).

These are startling terms indeed for someone so often thought of as the arch-misogynist and arch-sexist of the Enlightenment period. But what has been said above, is not intended to absolve him of any such charges. We will have further occasion to discuss Rousseau's views of the relationship between women and men taken in their historical context. For the moment, it suffices to note that *even* Rousseau was no exception to this discourse of the history of the power relations between woman and men.

Eighteenth century histories of women thus began with their loss of liberty. They continued with an account of how and to what extent the master-slave or tyrant-slave relation was redressed, if not reversed. Power and freedom were the central categories through which the relation between the sexes were analysed. The history of women therefore was the history of their conflict with men, of the conflict between the sexes, to borrow a phrase.

Montesquieu's (1689–1755) *L'Esprit des Lois* (The Spirit of the Laws) (1748) provides the classical statement of this vision of the relation between men and women. The concept of liberty and its appendant register of captivity, servitude and enslavement lie at the heart of his treatment of what he calls 'le gouvernement domestique' (domestic rule), no less than they do that of his analysis of any other form of government. In his view, in fact, the two, political and domestic, were indissolubly intertwined:

> Everything is closely related: the despotism of the prince is naturally conjoined to the servitude of women; just as the liberty of women is tied to the spirit of the monarch.

> (Montesquieu, *Oeuvres Complètes*, ed. Daniel Oster, Paris, 1964, book XIX, ch. 15, p. 644)

The language of liberty and servitude, the interconnection between the status of women and the spirit prevailing in a nation was not restricted to these two forms of government, despotism and monarchy. Montesquieu's description of republics exhibited no less of an awareness of the consequences which the near equality of citizens had on the condition of women – it provided a check to the tyranny of men. Free under the law, women in republics were restrained by its mores: as luxury was banned, corruption could not find its nest. The conflict between men and women was therefore neutralised. The laws protected women against the tyranny of men, while men were themselves assured that they would not fall prey to the ensnarement of women through what we might call commodity fetishism. The condition then of all citizens was therefore genuinely equal and free, though men and women retained their gender differences, a fact reflected in the very nature of the laws which governed them.

But Montesquieu did not stop there in his use of the tyrant-slave dialectic. He applied his description of the nature of the slavery of women, domestic slavery, to help conceptualise what he called 'real slavery' – productive labour. True degradation resided in the addition of domestic slavery to the burden of real slavery – such had been the condition of the Helots in Spartan society. The status of women therefore informed Montesquieu's theory at all levels. It was part and parcel of his conceptual framework. Reading him, there is no doubt as to how to think of the position of women. His use of the extent of their slavery or enfranchisement as the measure of the liberty prevalent in any one form of government can be found in the writings of a very wide range of eighteenth century thinkers, amongst whom [John] Millar is perhaps the most well-known example. Alexander, however, gives the thesis its most succinct form:

> we shall almost constantly find women among savages condemned to every species of servile, or rather of slavish drudgery; and shall as constantly find them emerging from this state, in the same proportion as we find the men emerging from ignorance and brutality; the rank, therefore, and condition, in which we find women in any country, mark out to us with the greatest precision, the exact point in the scale of civil society, to which the people of such country have arrived; and were their history entirely silent on every other subject, and only mentioned the manner in which they treated their women, we would, from thence, be enabled to form a tolerable judgement of the barbarity, or culture of their manners.
>
> (*History*, vol. I, p. 151)

Alexander's confidence would have been shared by Diderot, Thomas, Millar and the like, for the idea that women were the barometers on which every aspect of society, its morals, its laws, its customs, its government, was registered had gained much ground since the publication of Montesquieu's *De L'Esprit des Lois* in the middle of the century. The nature and extent of their subjection or liberty said everything.

(pp. 106–109, 111–114)

# JOAN WALLACH SCOTT

New approaches to the Enlightenment did not always question the canon of authors studied. Feminist inquiry has both rediscovered and examined the role of women in the Enlightenment and explored the practices through which social suppression and understandings of femininity and masculinity were formulated.

In this extract from Joan Wallach Scott's essay 'French Feminists and the Rights of "Man": Olympe de Gouges' Declaration' (1989) the author questions the universalism of the Enlightenment subject, focusing particularly on sexual difference. She explores the problems and paradoxes of a feminism caught up in a language of rights that excludes women's embodiment.

## 'French Feminists and the Rights of "Man" ' (1989)

For women, the legacy of the French Revolution was contradictory: a universal, abstract, rights-bearing individual as the unit of national sovereignty, embodied, however, as a man. The abstraction of a genderless political subject made it possible for women to claim the political rights of active citizens and, when denied them in practice, to protest against exclusion as unjust, a violation of the founding principles of the republic. The equally abstract gesture of embodiment – the attribution of citizenship to (white) male subjects – complicated enormously the project of claiming equal rights, for it suggested either that rights themselves, or at least how and where they were exercised, depended on the physical characteristics of human bodies. [...]

There were many different contests about bodies and rights in the course of the Revolution and few were definitively resolved. Under the first constitution, passive citizens were distinguished from active according to levels of property ownership and wealth; the distinction disappeared with the monarchy and reappeared in different language under the Directory. 'Men of colour' were initially excluded from and then included in the category of citizen. Slaves were denied and then granted the rights of free men, only to lose them again under Napoleon. Women were systematically barred from formal political rights; but were granted rights to divorce and some control of marital property in 1792, only to have them restricted under the Code Napoleon and revoked by the Restoration. Each of these instances was characterized by different kinds of arguments; each has a complicated, contextual explanation – the abolition of slavery, for example, took place as the French sought to repel a British conquest of Santo Domingo by enlisting all male inhabitants of the island in the army. What they have in common, however, is the persistent question of the relationship of specific, marked groups to the embodied universal: how could the rights of the poor, of mulattos, blacks, or women be figured as the rights of Man?

The general answer is: with difficulty. There was no simple way either to expand the category of Man to take in all his Others or to disembody the abstract individual so that literally anyone could represent him. Specific contests about the rights of excluded groups did not resolve this paradox, but exposed it; the terms of debate and the strategies of the contenders show equality to be a more elusive ideal in both its formulation and achievement than was ever acknowledged by the Revolution's most visionary architects or, for that matter, by many of its historians. Women are a case in point. From the outset of the Revolution, there were scattered demands for women's rights. These were most often passed over in revolutionary legislation until 1793 (several days after the execution of Marie-Antoinette), when the question of women's political role was directly addressed. Using the occasion of a street disturbance between market women and members of the Society of Revolutionary Republican women, the National Convention outlawed all women's clubs and popular societies, invoking Rousseauist

themes to deny women the exercise of political rights and to end, some hoped definitively, persistent feminist agitation. 'Should women exercise political rights and meddle
in the affairs of government?' asked André Amar, the representative of the Committee
of General Security. 'In general, we can answer, no.' He went on to consider whether
women could meet in political associations and again answered negatively: 'because they
would be obliged to sacrifice the more important cares to which nature calls them. The
private functions for which women are destined by their very nature are related to the
general order of society; this social order results from the differences between man and
woman. Each sex is called to the kind of occupation which is fitting for it; its action is
circumscribed within this circle which it cannot break through, because, nature, which
has imposed these limits on man, commands imperiously and receives no law' (see
*Women in Revolutionary Paris, 1789–1795*, 1979, ed. D.G. Levy, H.B. Applewhite and
M.D. Johnson, p. 215). [...]

   In the intersecting discourses of biology and politics, theories of complementarity
resolved the potentially disruptive effects of sexual difference. Species reproduction and
social order were said to depend on the union of the opposite elements, male and
female, on a functional division of labour that granted nature her due. Although it was
logically possible to present complementarity as an egalitarian doctrine, in fact it served
in the predominant political rhetoric of this period to justify an asymmetrical relationship between men and women. The goals of the revolution, after all, were liberty, sovereignty, moral choice informed by reason, and active involvement in the formation of
just laws. All of these were firmly designated male prerogatives, defined in contrast to
the female. The contrasting elements were:

| | |
|---|---|
| active | passive |
| liberty | duty |
| individual sovereignty | dependency |
| public | private |
| political | domestic |
| reason | modesty |
| speech | silence |
| education | maternal nurture |
| universal | particular |
| male | female |

The second column served not only to define the first, but provided the possibility for
its existence. 'Natural' sexual differences permitted a resolution of some of the knotty
and persistent problems of inequalities of power in political theory by locating individual freedom in male subjects and associating social cohesion with females. Maternal nur-
ture awakened or instilled human empathy (pity) and love of virtue, the qualities that
tempered selfish individualism; modesty at once equipped women to perform their roles
and served as a corrective to their inability otherwise to restrain (sexual) desire.
Women's modesty was, furthermore, a precondition for the successful exercise of male
reason in restraint of desire. The dependency of the domestic sphere elicited from men
the fulfilment of their social duty; indeed duty denoted here not women's obligations but

their position as the objects of male obligation. The active/passive distinction, in fact, resting as it did on contrasting theories of natural rights, summed up the differences: those who enjoyed active rights were individual agents, making moral choices, exercising liberty, acting (speaking) on their own behalf. They were, by definition, political subjects. Those who enjoyed passive rights had the 'right to be given or allowed something by someone else' (R. Tuck, *Natural Rights Theories: Their Origin and Development*, 1979, pp. 5–6). Their status as political subjects was ambiguous, if not wholly in doubt.

Historians of natural rights theories rightly describe active and passive rights as antithetical paradigms; but they often also imply that these logically conflicting notions could not prevail simultaneously. Political regimes, they suggest, have been premised historically on one or another of these theories; from this perspective, the age of democratic revolutions was quintessentially the age of liberty and active rights. These characterizations reckon, however, neither with the ingenuity of the French revolutionaries who, in their first effort at constitution-making in 1791, reconciled their fear of democracy and their commitment to liberty by establishing two categories of citizen – the active and the passive – nor with the operations of gender within the universal languages of political theory.

In the constitution of 1791, active citizens were men over 25 who were independent (they could not be domestic servants) and who possessed measurable wealth (they had to pay a direct tax equivalent to three days of labour). The prerequisite was property – in land or money and the self. After the fall of the monarch in 1792, citizenship was granted to all men who were over 21 and self-supporting. The means test was dropped, leaving as the operative concept property in the self. But, I would argue, the active/passive distinction did not disappear, even if it was no longer explicitly articulated in official political documents. Instead, it was employed to differentiate between the rights of those with and without autonomy or agency, and these were largely, though not exclusively, men and women.

Unlike distinctions of wealth, those of sex were considered natural; they were therefore taken for granted, treated as axiomatic, assumed to be unalterable rules of 'imperious' nature, hence left outside the legislative arena. Constitutions and legal decrees dealt, for the most part, with the rules of (active) political participation and so dropped reference to those whose rights were taken care of for them by others. Invisibility, however, did not mean absence. The terms *citoyen* and *citoyenne* often carried the active/passive contrast, and from time to time it was clearly invoked – by the exasperated Chaumette, for example, in October 1793: 'Impudent women who want to become men,' (I imagine) he shouted, 'aren't you well enough provided for? What else do you need?' (*Women in Revolutionary Paris*, ed. Levy, Applewhite and Johnson, p. 220).

This rather crude form of political theorizing sums up the outlook I have been describing. For from the outset, there were feminist critics of these theories, women and men who argued for genuine equality of political rights. There were also, of course, women who paid no heed to the arguments and whose participation in the events of the Revolution has offered social historians ample evidence both for insisting that women were active historical subjects and for rejecting the importance of political theory in the practice of 'real' politics. The presence of women in crowds, their centrality in the march to Versailles, their membership in clubs (and the prominence of figures like

Pauline Léon and Claire Lacombe among the Jacobins), their proposals to the various legislatures, their actions on behalf of and in opposition to the Revolution, all support the claim made by Camille Desmoulins in 1791 that action established agency: 'The active citizens,' he reminded his colleagues, 'are those who took the Bastille' (M.J. Sydenham, *The French Revolution*, 1966, p. 67).

Yet action by women was insufficient, either during the Revolution or long after it, to secure formal recognition of this point. Some of the explanation for the legal disempowerment of women and their invisibility in the historical record must come from analyses of the discourse that established and justified exclusion. Sometimes feminists provided those analyses; more often their formulations furnish material from which such analyses can be fashioned. In their search for ways out of the paradox of an embodied equality, feminists show us the dead-ends, the limits of certain paths, and the complexity of others – all effects of the paradox itself.

(pp. 1–6)

# PART THREE

# Chronology and further reading

# Chronology

*Selected works are in bold*

| | |
|---|---|
| 1682 | Founding of Philadelphia by William Penn |
| 1684 | Thomas Burnet, *Sacred Theory of the Earth* |
| 1685 | Edict of Nantes revoked by Louis XIV |
| 1687 | **Newton, *Mathematical Principles of Natural Philosophy*** |
| 1689 | 'Glorious Revolution' in Britain leads to reign of William III and Mary |
| | John Locke, *Letter Concerning Toleration* |
| 1690 | **Locke, *Two Treatises of Government* and *Essay Concerning Human Understanding*** |
| | Battle of the Boyne |
| 1693 | John Locke, *Some Thoughts Concerning Education* |
| 1694 | **Astell, *Serious Proposal to the Ladies*** |
| 1695 | Lapsing of pre-publication censorship in Britain |
| 1696 | **Toland, *Christianity not Mysterious*** |
| 1697 | Pierre Bayle, *Historical and Critical Dictionary* |
| 1701 | War of the Spanish Succession (1701–13) |
| | Foundation of Yale College, New Haven |
| 1702 | Anne becomes Queen of England, Scotland and Ireland |
| 1703 | Founding of St Petersburg by Peter the Great |
| 1704 | Isaac Newton, *Optics* |
| 1707 | Act of Union (England and Scotland) |
| | Abraham Darby introduces coke-fired iron smelting |
| 1708 | Hermann Boerhaave, *Institutiones Medicae* |
| 1709 | **Steele, *Tatler* (1709–11)** |
| | Major famine in France |

| | |
|---|---|
| 1710 | **Leibniz, *Essays on Theodicy*** |
| | George Berkeley, *Principles of Human Knowledge* |
| 1711 | **Steele, *Spectator* (1711–12)** |
| | Thomas Newcomen produces pumping steam-engine |
| 1712 | **Steele, *Englishman* (1713–14)** |
| | Papal Bull *Unigenitus* condemns Jansenism |
| 1714 | George I becomes King of Great Britain (1714–27) |
| 1715 | Jacobite Rebellion begins in Britain (1715–16) |
| | Death of Louis XIV of France (ruled 1643–1715) |
| | Accession of Louis XV of France (1715–74), under Regency of Duke of Orléans (1715–23) |
| 1717 | First Freemasons' lodge established in London |
| 1719 | Daniel Defoe, *Robinson Crusoe* |
| 1720 | Major plague at Marseilles |
| 1721 | Baron de Montesquieu, *Persian Letters* |
| | Robert Walpole becomes Prime Minster (1721–42) |
| 1722 | Daniel Defoe, *Moll Flanders* |
| 1725 | **Vico, *New Science* (1st edn)** |
| 1726 | Jonathan Swift, *Gulliver's Travels* |
| | Famine in Ireland (1726–29) |
| 1727 | **Hales, *Vegetable Statics*** |
| | George II becomes King of Great Britain (1727–60) |
| 1728 | **Chardin, *The Rayfish* exhibited at the Louvre** |
| | John Gay, *The Beggar's Opera* |
| 1729 | John Wesley founds the Methodist Society |
| | First performance of J. S. Bach's *St Matthew Passion* |
| 1730 | James Thomson, *The Seasons* |
| 1733 | **Pope, *Essay on Man*** |
| | **Voltaire, *Letters Concerning the English Nation*** |
| | War of the Polish Succession begins (1733–35) |
| 1735 | **Linnaeus, *System of Nature*** |
| 1736 | Porteous Riots in Edinburgh |
| | Excavation begins of the ruins of Herculaneum (1736–66) |
| 1738 | John Kay patents 'flying shuttle' for cloth-weaving industry |
| 1739 | **Hume, *Treatise of Human Nature*** |
| | Anglo-Spanish War of Jenkins' Ear (1739–48) |
| 1740 | **Chardin, *Saying Grace* exhibited at the Louvre** |
| | Gabrielle Émilie, Marquise du Châtelet, *Institutions of Physics* |
| | Frederick II becomes King of Prussia (1740–86) and invades Silesia, leading to War of the Austrian Succession (1740–48) |
| | Samuel Richardson, *Pamela, or Virtue Rewarded* |
| 1742 | First performance, in Dublin, of George Frederic Handel's *Messiah* |
| 1743 | Jean d'Alembert, *Treatise on Dynamics* |
| 1745 | William Hogarth, *Marriage à la Mode* series |
| | Jacobite Rebellion begins in Britain (1745–46) |

| | |
|---|---|
| 1746 | Pierre Louis Moreau de Maupertius appointed President of the Berlin Academy of Sciences |
| 1747 | **La Mettrie, *Man a Machine*** |
| | Jean-Jacques Burlamaqui, *Principles of Natural Right* |
| | Frederick II completes his palace of Sans-Souci, Potsdam |
| 1748 | **Hume, *Enquiry Concerning Human Understanding*** |
| | **Montesquieu, *Spirit of the Laws*** |
| | **Gainsborough, *Mr and Mrs Robert Andrews*** |
| | Discovery of the ruins of Pompeii |
| 1749 | **Buffon, *Natural History* (1749–1804)** |
| | Henry Fielding, *Tom Jones* |
| 1750 | **Rousseau, *Discourse on the Arts and the Sciences*** |
| 1751 | **D'Alembert, '*Preliminary Discourse*' from the *Encyclopédie* (28 vols, 1751–72)** |
| | **Jaucourt, 'Invention' from the *Encyclopédie*** |
| | **Hogarth, *Beer Street* and *Gin Lane*** |
| | Benjamin Franklin, *Experiments and Observations on Electricity* (1751–54) |
| | Giovanni Battista Piranesi's engravings, *Prisons*, are published |
| 1753 | **Buffon, *History of Man and the Quadrupeds*** |
| | **Diderot, *Thoughts on the Interpretation of Nature*** |
| | **Laugier, *Essay on Architecture*** |
| | Hogarth, *Analysis of Beauty* |
| 1754 | Étienne Bonnot de Condillac, *Treatise on Sensations* |
| 1755 | **Rousseau, *Discourse on Inequality*** |
| | Lisbon Earthquake |
| | Samuel Johnson, *Dictionary of the English Language* |
| | Building begins on Jacques Soufflot's church of St Geneviève (later the Panthéon), Paris |
| | Johann Joachim Winckelmann, *On the Imitation of Greek Art* |
| 1756 | **Voltaire, *On the Lisbon Disaster*** |
| | The Seven Years War begins (1756–63) |
| 1757 | **Hume, *Enquiry Concerning the Principles of Morals*** |
| | Edmund Burke, *Enquiry on the Sublime and Beautiful* |
| | Albrecht von Haller, *Elements of Physiology* (1757–66) |
| 1758 | François Quesnay, *Economic Tableau* |
| | Claude-Adrien Helvétius, *On the Mind* |
| 1759 | **Chambers, *Treatise on Civil Architecture*** |
| | **Diderot, *Salons* (1759–81)** |
| | **Reynolds, 'The Grand Style of Painting' from Johnson's *Idler, no. 79*** |
| | Adam Smith, *Theory of Moral Sentiments* |
| | Voltaire, *Candide, or Optimism* |
| | Laurence Sterne, *Tristram Shandy* (1759–67) |

Clement XIII puts the *Encyclopédie* and Helvétius's *Essay on the Mind* on the Index of forbidden books

British capture of Quebec

Opening of the British Museum, London

1760 George III becomes King of Great Britain (1760–1820)

1762 **Rousseau, *Emile*** and *The Social Contract*

**Walpole, *Anecdotes of Painting* (1762–71)**

Catherine II becomes Empress of Russia (1762–96)

Jean Calas, a Huguenot, is tortured and executed at Toulouse

1763 **Wortley Montagu, *Embassy Letters***

Britain acquires Canada and Florida, by the Treaty of Paris

1764 **Beccaria, *On Crimes and Punishments***

**Voltaire, *Philosophical Dictionary***

Walpole, *The Castle of Otranto*

Foundation of the Hermitage Museum, St Petersburg

James Hargreaves invents the Spinning Jenny

1765 Joseph II becomes Holy Roman Emperor (1765–90) and joint ruler of the Austrian empire with his mother Maria Theresa

James Watt invents the steam engine

1766 Henry Cavendish discovers hydrogen

1767 **Catherine the Great, *Instruction***

**Ferguson, *Essay on the History of Civil Society***

Samuel Wallis 'discovers' Tahiti

Joseph Priestley, *History and Present State of Electricity*

Johann Gottfried von Herder, *Fragments on a New German Literature*

1768 Royal Academy of Arts is founded in London

**Wright, *Experiment on a Bird in an Air Pump* exhibited in London**

James Cook sets sail on the first of his three great voyages (1768–71, 1772–75, 1776–79)

Thomas Jefferson begins the building of Monticello, Virginia

1769 Richard Arkwright invents a water-powered spinning-frame

1771 First edition of *Encyclopedia Britannica*

Gustav III becomes King of Sweden (1771–92)

1772 **D'Holbach, *Common Sense***

**Raynal, *Philosophical and Political History of the Settlements***

First partition of Poland

Daniel Rutherford isolates nitrogen

1773 The Boston 'Tea Party'

1774 **Jefferson, *Summary View of the Rights of British America***

Accession of Louis XVI of France (1774–92)

Joseph Priestley isolates oxygen

Johann Wolfgang von Goethe, *Sorrows of Young Werther*

1775 American War of Independence begins (1775–83)

1776 **Gibbon, *Decline and Fall of the Roman Empire* (1776–88)**

**Smith,** *Wealth of Nations*

Johann Friedrich Blumenbach, *On the Natural Varieties of Mankind*

Thomas Paine, *Common Sense*

American Declaration of Independence, drafted by Thomas Jefferson

1777   **Cook,** *Voyage Towards the South Pole and Around the World*

**Frederick II,** *Essay on the Forms of Government*

William Robertson, *History of America*

1778   Fanny Burney, *Evelina*

1779   Gotthold Ephraim Lessing, *Nathan the Wise*

1780   Gordon Riots in London

1781   **Rousseau,** *Confessions*

Immanuel Kant, *Critique of Pure Reason*

William Herschel discovers Uranus

1782   **Rousseau,** *Reveries of a Solitary Walker*

**Gainsborough,** *Girl with Pigs*

Pierre Choderlos de Laclos, *Dangerous Acquaintances*

1783   Moses Mendelssohn, *Jerusalem: Or Religious Power and Judaism*

1784   **Kant,** *What is Enlightenment?*

Pierre-Augustin Caron de Beaumarchais, *Marriage of Figaro*

Jacques-Louis David, *Oath of the Horatii* (painting, 1784–85)

Johann Gottfried Herder, *Ideas for a Philosophy of the History of Mankind* (1784–91)

1785   **Kant,** *Fundamental Principles of the Metaphysics of Morals*

1786   First performance, in Vienna, of Mozart's *Marriage of Figaro*

1787   **Jefferson,** *Notes on the State of Virginia*

First meeting of the Assembly of Notables in France

Establishment of the Association for Abolition of Slavery, in Britain

1788   Immanuel Kant, *Critique of Practical Reason*

A penal colony is founded at Botany Bay (Australia)

1789   **Bentham,** *Introduction to the Principles of Morals and Legislation*

**Reynolds, 'Gainsborough', from** *Discourses on Art* **(1778, 1797)**

Start of the French Revolution: meeting of the Estates General (later National Assembly); Fall of the Bastille; Declaration of the Rights of Man and the Citizen

George Washington becomes first President of the United States (1789–97)

Antoine Laurent Lavoisier, *Elements of Chemistry*

Olaudah Equiano, *Interesting Narrative of the Life of Olaudah Equiano*

William Blake, *Songs of Innocence*

1790   **Macaulay,** *Letters on Education*

Edmund Burke, *Reflections on the French Revolution*

1791   **De Gouges,** *The Rights of Woman*

**Franklin,** *Autobiography*
**Paine,** *The Rights of Man* **(1791–92)**
James Boswell, *Life of Johnson*

1792      **Wollstonecraft,** *Vindication of the Rights of Woman*
Building of the Capitol, Washington, begins

1793      **Godwin,** *Enquiry Concerning Political Justice*
Execution of Louis XVI; 'Reign of Terror' begins in France
Second Partition of Poland

1794      **Darwin,** *Zoonomia* **(1794–96)**

1795      **De Roland,** *Appeal to Impartial Posterity*
**Condorcet,** *Sketch of a Historical Picture of the Human Mind*
**De Sade,** *Philosophy in the Boudoir*
Mungo Park begins expedition of the Niger

1796      **Diderot,** *Supplement to the Voyage of Bougainville*
Edward Jenner produces smallpox vaccination

1798      Rebellion in Ireland
Napoléon Bonaparte conquers Egypt
Samuel Taylor Coleridge and William Wordsworth, *Lyrical Ballads*

1799      First performance of Franz Joseph Haydn's *The Creation*
Francisco Goya, *Caprices*
Napoléon Bonaparte becomes First Consul and *de facto* ruler of
France (1799–1804), and emperor (1804–1814, 1815)

1801      Thomas Jefferson becomes third President of the United States
(1801–9)
Act of Union (Ireland with England and Scotland)

1803      The Louisiana purchase by USA

# Further reading

Scholarship on and relating to the Enlightenment is massive – a tribute both to the importance of the subject and its continuing fascination to writers and researchers from a wide range of disciplines. The following list of texts in English (wherever possible) is divided into four main sections: I, General Works – reference, primary, and secondary materials; II, National Contexts; III, Works and Studies of Selected Figures (e.g. 'Rousseau'); IV, Chapter Topics (e.g. 'Human Nature'). Articles in scholarly journals have not been included. Among the leading journals devoted to this period are *Eighteenth-Century Studies*, *Studies in Eighteenth-Century Culture*, *The British Journal for Eighteenth-Century Studies*, and *Studies on Voltaire and the Eighteenth Century*. There are also several periodicals that focus on individuals, such as *Diderot Studies* and *Locke Studies*.

## I  GENERAL WORKS

### Reference material

Black, J. and Porter, R. (eds), *A Dictionary of Eighteenth-Century World History* (Oxford: Blackwell, 1994).

Kors, A.C. (ed.), *Encyclopedia of the Enlightenment,* 4 vols (Oxford: Oxford University Press, 2002).

Yolton, J.W. (ed.), *The Blackwell Companion to the Enlightenment* (Oxford: Blackwell, 1991).

Yolton, J.W., Price, J. V. and Stephens, J. (eds), *The Dictionary of Eighteenth-century Philosophers*, 2 vols (Bristol: Thoemmes Press, 1999).

### Primary material

Berlin, I. (ed.), *The Age of Enlightenment* (New York: Mentor, 1956).

Brinton, C. (ed.), *The Portable Age of Reason Reader* (New York: Viking, 1956).

Cowie, L.W. (ed.), *Eighteenth-Century Europe* (London: Macmillan, 1989).

Croker, L.G. (ed.), *The Age of Enlightenment* (London: Macmillan, 1969).

Eliot, S. and Stern, B. (eds), *The Age of Enlightenment*, 2 vols (Milton Keynes: Open University Press, 1979).

Gay, P. (ed.), *The Enlightenment* (New York: Simon and Schuster, 1973).

Jacob, M.C. (ed.), *The Enlightenment: A Brief History with Documents* (Boston: Bedford/St Martin's, 2001).

Kramnick, I. (ed.), *The Portable Enlightenment Reader* (New York: Penguin, 1995).

Lively, J.F. (ed.), *The Enlightenment* (London: Longman, 1966).

Marsak, L. (ed.), *The Enlightenment* (New York: Wiley, 1972).

Williams, D. (ed.), *The Enlightenment* (Cambridge: Cambridge University Press, 1999).

## Secondary material

Adorno, T.W. and Horkheimer, M., *Dialectic of Enlightenment*, trans. J. Cumming ([1947]; New York: Continuum, 1995).

Anchor, R., *The Enlightenment Tradition* (New York: Harper and Row, 1967).

Barber, G., *Studies in the Booktrade of the European Enlightenment* (London: Pindar, 1994).

Baker, K.M. and Reill, P.H. (eds), *What's Left of Enlightenment? A Postmodern Question* (Stanford: Stanford University Press, 2001).

Baxandall, M., *Shadows and Enlightenment* (New Haven: Yale University Press, 1995).

Blanning, T.C.W., *The Culture of Power and the Power of Culture: Old Regime Europe, 1660–1789* (Oxford: Oxford University Press, 2001).

Brown, S. (ed.), *Routledge History of Philosophy*, vol. V, *British Empiricism and the Enlightenment* (London: Routledge, 1995).

Brown, S.C. (ed.), *Philosophers of the Enlightenment* (Brighton: Harvester Press, 1979).

Cassirer, E., *The Philosophy of the Enlightenment*, trans. F.C.A. Koelln and J.P. Pettegrove ([1932]; Princeton: Princeton University Press, 1951).

Chartier, R., *Cultural History: Between Practices and Representations* (Ithaca: Cornell University Press, 1988).

Cobban, A., *In Search of Humanity: The Role of the Enlightenment in Modern History* (London: Cape, 1960).

Dunthorne, H., *The Enlightenment* (London: Historical Association, 1991).

Foucault, M., *The Order of Things: An Archaeology of the Human Sciences* ([1970]; London: Routledge, 1989).

—— *Madness and Civilization: A History of Insanity in the Age of Reason* (London: Routledge, 2001).

Fox, C., Porter. R. and Wokler, R. (eds), *Inventing Human Science: Eighteenth-century Domains* (Berkeley: University of California Press, 1995).

Gay, P., *The Enlightenment: An Interpretation*, vol. I, *The Rise of Modern Paganism* (London: Weidenfeld and Nicolson, 1967); vol. II, *The Science of Freedom* (London: Weidenfeld and Nicolson, 1969).

Goldgar, A., *Impolite Learning. Conduct and Community in the Republic of Letters 1680–1750* (New Haven: Yale University Press, 1995).

Goldmann, L., *The Philosophy of the Enlightenment: The Christian Burgess and the Enlightenment* (Cambridge, Mass.: Harvard University Press, 1973).

Gordon, L. (ed.), *Postmodernism and the Enlightenment: New Perspectives in Eighteenth-century French Intellectual History* (London: Routledge, 2001).

Gray, J. *Enlightenment's Wake: Politics and Culture at the Close of the Modern Age* (London: Routledge, 1995).

Habermas, J., *The Structural Transformation of the Public Sphere: An Inquiry into a Category of Bourgeois Society*, trans. T. Burger ([1962]; Cambridge: Polity. Press, 1989).

Hampson, N., *The Enlightenment* (Harmondsworth: Penguin, 1968).

Hayes, J.C., *Reading the Enlightenment: System and Subversion* (Cambridge: Cambridge University Press, 1999).

Hazard, P., *The European Mind, 1680–1715*, trans. J.L. May ([1935]; Harmondsworth: Penguin, 1964).

——— *European Thought in the Eighteenth Century*, trans. J.L. May ([1946]; Harmondsworth: Penguin, 1965).

Hulme, P. and Jordanova, L. (eds), *The Enlightenment and Its Shadows* (London: Routledge, 1990).

Im Hof, U., *The Enlightenment*, trans. W.E. Yuill (Oxford: Blackwell, 1994).

Israel, J.I., *Radical Enlightenment: Philosophy and the Making of Modernity 1650–1750* (Oxford: Oxford University Press, 2001).

Koselleck, R., *Critique and Crisis: Enlightenment and the Pathogenesis of Modern Society* ([1959], Oxford: Berg, 1988).

Livingstone, D.N. and Withers, C.W.J. (eds), *Geography and Enlightenment* (Chicago: Chicago University Press, 2000).

Micale, M.S. and Dietle, R.L. (eds), *Enlightenment, Passion, Modernity: Historical Essays in European Thought and Culture* (Stanford: Stanford University Press, 2000).

Munck, T., *The Enlightenment: A Comparative Social History, 1721–1794* (London: Arnold, 2000).

Outram, D., *The Enlightenment* (Cambridge: Cambridge University Press, 1995).

Porter, R., *The Enlightenment* (London: Macmillan, 1990).

Racevskis, K., *Postmodernism and the Search for Enlightenment* (Charlottesville: University Press of Virginia, 1993).

Venturi, F., *Utopia and Reform in the Enlightenment* (Cambridge: Cambridge University Press, 1971).

Vereker, C.H., *Eighteenth-Century Optimism: A Study of the Interrelations of Moral and Social Theory in English and French Thought between 1689 and 1789* (Liverpool: Liverpool University Press, 1967).

Wuthnow, R., *Communities of Discourse: Ideology and Social Structure in the Reformation, the Enlightenment, and European Socialism* (Cambridge, Mass.: Harvard University Press, 1989).

Yolton, J.W. (ed.), *Philosophy, Religion and Science in the Seventeenth and Eighteenth Centuries* (Rochester, N.Y.: University of Rochester Press, 1990).

## II NATIONAL CONTEXTS

Aldridge, A.O. (ed.), *The Ibero-American Enlightenment* (Urbana: University of Illinois Press, 1971).

Barton, H.A., *Scandinavia in the Revolutionary Era, 1760–1815* (Minneapolis: University of Minnesota Press, 1986).

Behrens, C.B.A. (ed.), *Society, Government and the Enlightenment: The Experiences of Eighteenth-Century France and Prussia* (New York: Harper and Row, 1985).

Black, J., *Eighteenth Century Europe, 1700–1789* (London: Macmillan, 1990).

——— *The British Abroad: The Grand Tour in the Eighteenth Century* (London: Alan Sutton, 1992).

Brewer, J., *The Pleasures of Imagination: English Culture in the Eighteenth Century* (London: HarperCollins, 1997).

Broadie, A. (ed.), *The Scottish Enlightenment: An Anthology* (Edinburgh: Canongate, 1997).

Bruford, W.H., *Germany in the Eighteenth Century: The Social Background of the Liberal Revival* (Cambridge: Cambridge University Press, 1952).

Brunschwig, H., *Enlightenment and Romanticism in Eighteenth-Century Prussia* (Chicago: Chicago University Press, 1974).

Campbell, R.H. and Skinner, A.S. (eds), *The Origins and Nature of the Scottish Enlightenment* (Edinburgh: Edinburgh University Press, 1982).

Carpanetto, D. and Ricuperati, G., *Italy in the Age of Reason, 1685–1789* (London: Longman, 1972).

Cassara, E., *The Enlightenment in America* (Lanham: University Press of America, 1988).

Censer, J.R., *The French Press in the Age of Enlightenment* (London: Routledge, 1994).

Chitnis, A.C., *The Scottish Enlightenment: A Social History* (London: Croom Helm, 1976).

Clark, J.C.D., *English Society, 1688–1832: Ideology, Social Structure and Political Practice during the Ancien Régime* (Cambridge: Cambridge University Press, 1985).

Cobban, A. (ed.), *The Eighteenth Century: Europe in the Age of Enlightenment* (London: Thames and Hudson, 1969).

Colley, L., *Britons: Forging the Nation 1707–1837* (New Haven: Yale University Press, 1992).

Commager, H.S., *The Empire of Reason: How Europe Imagined and America Realized the Enlightenment* (London: Weidenfeld and Nicolson, 1978).

Cottom, D., *Cannibals and Philosophers: Bodies of Enlightenment* (Baltimore: Johns Hopkins University Press, 2001).

Daiches, D., Jones, P., and Jones, J. (eds), *A Hotbed of Genius: The Scottish Enlightenment 1730–1790* (Edinburgh: Edinburgh University Press, 1986).

Darnton, R., *The Literary Underground of the Old Regime* (Cambridge, Mass.: Harvard University Press, 1982).

—— *The Great Cat Massacre and Other Episodes in French Cultural History* (Harmondsworth: Penguin, 1985).

Dickinson, H.T., *Liberty and Property: Political Ideology in Eighteenth-Century Britain* (London: Methuen, 1979).

Dixon, S., *The Modernization of Russia, 1676–1825* (Cambridge: Cambridge University Press, 1999).

Donnert, E., *Russia in the Age of Enlightenment* (Leipzig: Edition Leipzig, 1986).

Doyle, W., *The Ancien Régime* (London: Macmillan, 1986).

Dukes, P., *The Making of Russian Absolutism, 1613–1801* (London: Longman, 1982).

Dülmen, R. van, *The Society of the Enlightenment: The Rise of the Middle Class and Enlightenment Culture in Germany*, trans. A. Williams (Cambridge: Polity Press, 1992).

Ferguson, R.A., *The American Enlightenment 1750–1820* (Cambridge, Mass.: Harvard University Press, 1997).

Ferrone, V., *The Intellectual Roots of the Italian Enlightenment: Newtonian Science, Religion, and Politics in the Early Eighteenth Century*, trans. S. Brotherton (Atlantic Highlands, N.J.: Humanities Press, 1995).

Frankel, C., *The Faith of Reason: the Idea of Progress in the French Enlightenment* (New York: Octagon Books, 1969).

Gagliardo, J., *Germany under the Old Regime, 1600–1790* (London: Longman, 1991).

Gargett, G. and Sheridan, G. (eds), *Ireland and the French Enlightenment, 1700–1800* (Basingstoke: Macmillan, 1999).

Gearhart, S., *The Open Boundary of History and Fiction: A Critical Approach to the French Enlightenment* (Princeton, Princeton University Press, 1984).

Golinski, J., *The Republic of Letters: A Cultural History of the French Enlightenment* (Ithaca, N.Y.: Cornell University Press, 1994).

Goodman, D., *The Republic of Letters: A Cultural History of the French Enlightenment* (Ithaca, N.Y.: Cornell University Press, 1994).

Grave, S.A., *The Scottish Philosophy of Common Sense* (Oxford: Clarendon Press, 1960).

Herman, A., *The Scottish Enlightenment: the Scots' Invention of the Modern World* (London: Fourth Estate, 2002).

Herr, R., *The Eighteenth Century Revolution in Spain* (Princeton: Princeton University Press, 1958).

Hont, I. and Ignatieff, M. (eds), *Wealth and Virtue: The Shaping of Political Economy in the Scottish Enlightenment* (Cambridge: Cambridge University Press, 1983).

Hunter, I., *Rival Enlightenments: Civil and Metaphysical Philosophy in Early Modern Germany* (Cambridge: Cambridge University Press, 2001).

Jacob, M.C. and Mijnhardt, W.W. (eds), *The Dutch Republic in the Eighteenth Century: Decline, Enlightenment and Revolution* (Ithaca: Cornell University Press, 1992).

Langford, P., *A Polite and Commercial People: England 1727–1783* (Oxford: Oxford University Press, 1989).

Kors, A.C. and Korshin, P.J. (eds), *Anticipations of the Enlightenment in England, France, and Germany* (Philadelphia: University of Pennsylvania Press, 1987).

Mason, H.T. (ed.), *The Darnton Debate: Books and Revolution in the Eighteenth Century* (Oxford: Voltaire Foundation, 1998).

May, H.F., *The Enlightenment in America* (New York: Oxford University Press, 1976).

McKay, D. and Scott, H.M., *The Rise of the European Powers 1679–1793* (London: Arnold, 1990).

McKendrick, N., Brewer, J. and Plumb, J.H., *The Birth of a Consumer Society: The Commercialisation of Eighteenth-Century England* (London: Europa, 1982).

Porter, R., *Enlightenment: Britain and the Creation of the Modern World* (Harmondsworth: Penguin, 2000).

Porter, R. and Teich, M. (eds), *The Enlightenment in National Context* (Cambridge: Cambridge University Press, 1981).

Raeff, M., *The Well-Ordered Police State: Social and Institutional Change through Law in the Germanies and Russia, 1600–1800* (New Haven: Yale University Press, 1984).

Redwood, J., *Reason, Ridicule and Religion: The Age of Enlightenment in England, 1660–1750* (London: Thames and Hudson, 1976).

Rendall, J. (ed.), *The Origins of the Scottish Enlightenment 1707–76* (London: Macmillan, 1978).

Robertson, R. and Timms, E., *The Austrian Enlightenment and its Aftermath* (Edinburgh: Edinburgh University Press, 1991).

Roche, D., *France in the Age of Enlightenment* (Cambridge, Mass.: Harvard University Press, 1998).

Rothcrug, H., *The Opposition to Louis XIV; the Political and Social Origins of the French Enlightenment* (Princeton: Princeton University Press, 1966).

Schama, S., *The Embarrassment of Riches: An Interpretation of Dutch Culture in the Golden Age* (London: Fontana, 1988).

Schmidt, L., *Hearing Things: Religion, Illusion and the American Enlightenment* (Cambridge, Mass.: Harvard University Press, 2000).

Sher, R. and Smitten, J., *Scotland and America in the Age of the Enlightenment* (Edinburgh: Edinburgh University Press, 1990).

Spadafora, D., *The Idea of Progress in Eighteenth-century Britain* (New Haven: Yale University Press, 1990).

Stephen, L., *History of English Thought in the Eighteenth Century*, 2 vols ([1876]; London: Harbinger, 1962).

Teich, P. and Teich, M. (eds), *Romanticism in National Context* (Cambridge: Cambridge University Press, 1988).

Venturi, F., *Italy and the Enlightenment: Studies in a Cosmopolitan Century*, ed. S. Woolf (London: Longman, 1972).

Wade, I.O., *The Intellectual Origins of the French Enlightenment* (Princeton: Princeton University Press, 1971).

Wangermann, E., *The Austrian Achievement, 1700–1800* (New York: Harcourt, Brace, Jovanovich, 1973).

Wilson, K., *The Sense of the People: Politics, Culture and Imperialism in England, 1715–1785* (Cambridge: Cambridge University Press, 1995).

Wolff, L., *Inventing Eastern Europe: The Map of Civilization on the Mind of the Enlightenment* (Stanford: Stanford University Press, 1994).

## III Works and Studies of Selected Figures

### D'Alembert (Jean le Rond)

—— *Preliminary Discourse to the Encyclopedia of Diderot*, trans. R.N. Schwab (Chicago: Chicago University Press, 1995).

Grimsley, R., *Jean D'Alembert: 1717–83* (Oxford: Clarendon Press, 1963).

Hankins, T.L., *Jean D'Alembert: Science and the Enlightenment* (Oxford: Clarendon Press, 1970).

Pappas, J.N., *Voltaire and D'Alembert* (Bloomington: Indiana University Press, 1962).

### Astell (Mary)

—— *Political Writings*, ed. P. Springborg (Cambridge: Cambridge University Press, 1996).

Hill, B. (ed.), *The First English Feminist: 'Reflections upon Marriage' and Other Writings by Mary Astell* (Aldershot: Gower, 1986).

Perry, R., *The Celebrated Mary Astell: An Early English Feminist* (Chicago: University of Chicago Press, 1986).

### Beccaria (Cesare)

—— *'On Crimes and Punishments' and Other Writings*, ed. R. Bellamy (Cambridge: Cambridge University Press, 1995).

Hart, H.L.A., *Beccaria and Bentham* (Torino: Academy of Science, 1966).

Maestro, M., *Cesare Beccaria and the Origins of Penal Reform* (Philadelphia: Temple University Press, 1973).

### Bentham (Jeremy)

—— *An Introduction to the Principles of Morals and Legislation*, ed. J.H. Burns and H.L.A. Hart (Oxford: Clarendon Press, 1996).

—— *Correspondence*, 11 vols, ed. J.R. Dinwiddy *et al.* (Oxford: Clarendon Press, 1984–2000).

—— *Deontology, Together with a Table of the Springs of Action and The Article on Utilitarianism*, ed. A. Goldworth (Oxford: Clarendon Press, 1983).

—— *Legislator of the World: Writings on Codification, Law and Education*, ed. P. Schofield and J. Harris (Oxford: Clarendon Press, 1998).

Baumgardt, D., *Bentham and the Ethics of Today* (Princeton: Princeton University Press, 1952).

Crimmins, J.E., *Secular Utilitarianism: Social Science and the Critique of Religion in the Thought of Jeremy Bentham* (Oxford: Clarendon Press, 1990).

Dinwiddy, J., *Bentham* (Oxford: Oxford University Press, 1989).

Harrison, R., *Bentham* (London: Routledge and Kegan Paul, 1983).

Lyons, D., *In the Interest of the Governed: A Study in Bentham's Philosophy of Utility and Law* (Oxford: Oxford University Press, 1991).

Mack, M.P., *Jeremy Bentham*, 2 vols (London: Heinemann, 1962).

Manning, D.J., *The Mind of Jeremy Bentham* (London: Longman, 1968).

Semple, J., *Bentham's Prison: A Study of the Panopticon Penitentiary* (Oxford: Clarendon Press, 1993).

## Buffon (Comte de)

—— *From Natural History to the History of Nature; Readings from Buffon and his Critics*, trans. and ed. J. Lyon and P.R. Sloan (Notre Dame, Ind.: Notre Dame University Press, 1981).

Fellows, O. and Milliken, S., *Buffon* (New York: Twayne, 1972).

Loveland, J., *Rhetoric and Natural History – Buffon in Polemical and Literary Context* (Oxford: Voltaire Foundation, 2001).

Roger, J., *Buffon: A Life in Natural History*, ed. L.P. Williams, trans. S.L. Bonnefoi (Ithaca: Cornell University Press, 1997).

## Catherine II

—— *Catherine the Great's Instruction (Nakaz) to the Legislative Commission, 1767*, ed. P. Dukes (Newtonville, Mass.: Oriental Research Partners, 1977).

—— *Documents of Catherine the Great*, ed. W.F. Reddaway (Cambridge: Cambridge University Press, 1971).

—— *The Memoirs of Catherine the Great*, ed. D. Maroger (London: Hamish Hamilton, 1961).

Alexander, J.T., *Catherine the Great: life and legend* (Oxford: Oxford University Press, 1989).

Dixon, S., *Catherine the Great* (Harlow: Longman, 1997).

Dukes, P. (ed.), *Russia under Catherine the Great. Vol. I, Selected Documents on Government and Society* (Newtonville, Mass.: Oriental Research Partners, 1978).

Oliva, L.J. (ed.), *Catherine the Great* (Englewood Cliffs, N.J.: Prentice-Hall, 1971).

Madariaga, I. de, *Russia in the Age of Catherine the Great* (London: Weidenfeld and Nicolson, 1981).

—— *Catherine the Great* (New Haven: Yale University Press, 1990).

Raeff, M. (ed.), *Catherine the Great: a profile* (London: Macmillan, 1972).

## Chambers (William)

—— *A Treatise on the Decorative Part of Civil Architecture* (Farnborough: Gregg Press, 1969).

—— *A Dissertation on Oriental Gardening* (Farnborough: Gregg Press, 1972).

Harris, J., *Sir William Chambers: Knight of the Polar Star* (London: Zwemmer, 1970).

—— and Snodin, M. (eds), *Sir William Chambers: architect to George III* (New Haven: Yale University Press, 1996).

## Chardin (Jean Siméon)

—— *Chardin: catalogue raisonné*, ed. D. Wildenstein, trans. S. Gilbert (Oxford: Cassirer, 1969).

Naughton, G., *Chardin* (London: Phaidon, 1996).

Prigent, H. and Rosenberg, P., *Chardin: An Intimate Art*, trans. J. Brenton (London: Thames and Hudson, 2000).

Royal Academy of Arts, *Chardin* (London: Royal Academy of Arts, 2000).

## Condorcet (Marquis de)

—— *Foundations of Social Choice and Political Theory*, ed. and trans. I. McLean and F. Hewitt (Aldershot: Elgar, 1994).
—— *Sketch for a Historical Picture of the Progress of the Human Mind*, trans. J. Barraclough (London: Weidenfeld and Nicolson, 1955).
—— *Condorcet: Selected Writings*, ed. K.M. Baker (Indianapolis: Bobbs-Merrill, 1976).
Avery, J., *Progress, Poverty and Population: Re-reading Condorcet, Godwin and Malthus* (London: Frank Cass, 1997).
Baker, K.M., *Condorcet: From Natural Philosophy to Social Mathematics* (Chicago: University of Chicago Press, 1975).
Goodell, E., *The Noble Philosopher: Condorcet and the Enlightenment* (Buffalo, N.Y.: Prometheus Books, 1994).
Lukes, S., *The Curious Enlightenment of Professor Caritat. A Novel* (London: Verso, 1995).
Schapiro, J.S., *Condorcet and the Rise of Liberalism* (New York: Octagon, 1978).

## Cook (James)

—— *The Journals of Captain James Cook on his Voyages of Discovery*, 4 vols, ed. J.C. Beaglehole (Cambridge: Cambridge University Press, 1955–74).
—— *The Journals of Captain Cook*, ed. P. Edwards (Harmondsworth: Penguin, 1999).
Beaglehole, J.C. (ed.), *The Life of Captain James Cook* (Stanford: Stanford University Press, 1974).
David, A., *The Charts and Coastal Views of Captain Cook's Voyages*, 3 vols (Aldershot: Ashgate, 1988–97).
Hough, R., *Captain James Cook: A Biography* (London: Hodder and Stoughton, 1994).
Joppien, R. and Smith, B., *The Art of Captain Cook's Voyages*, 3 vols (New Haven: Yale University Press, 1985–88).
Obeyesekere, G., *The Apotheosis of Captain Cook: European Mythmaking in the Pacific* (Princeton: Princeton University Press, 1992).
Smith, B., *Imagining the Pacific: In the Wake of the Cook Voyages* (New Haven: Yale University Press, 1992).
Withey, L., *Voyages of Discovery: Captain Cook and the Exploration of the Pacific* (Berkeley: University of California Press, 1988).

## Darwin (Erasmus)

—— *The Essential Writings of Erasmus Darwin*, ed. D. King-Hele (London: McGibbon and Kee, 1968).
—— *The Letters of Erasmus Darwin*, ed. D. King-Hele (Cambridge: Cambridge University Press, 1981).
Darwin, C., *Life of Erasmus Darwin* (London: John Murray, 1887).
King-Hele, D., *Doctor of Revolution: The Life and Genius of Erasmus Darwin* (London: Faber and Faber, 1977).
—— *Erasmus Darwin: A Life of Unequalled Achievement* (London: DLM, 1999).
McNeil, M., *Under the Banner of Science: Erasmus Darwin and His Age* (Manchester: Manchester University Press, 1987).

## Diderot (Denis)

—— *Salons*, ed. J. Seznec and J. Adhémar, 4 vols (Oxford: Clarendon Press, 1957–67).

—— *Diderot on Art*, ed. and trans. J. Goodman, 2 vols (New Haven: Yale University Press, 1995).

—— *Diderot's Letters to Sophie Volland: a selection*, trans. P. France (Oxford: Oxford University Press, 1972).

—— *Encyclopedia: Selections*, ed. N.S. Hoyt and T. Cassirer (Indianapolis: Bobbs-Merrill, 1965).

—— *Encyclopédie* http://tuna.uchicago.edu/homes/mark/ENC_DEMO/.

—— *Pictorial Encyclopedia of Trades and Industry*, ed. C.C. Gillespie, 2 vols (New York: Dover, 1993).

—— *Political Writings*, ed. J. Mason and R. Wokler (Cambridge: Cambridge University Press, 1992).

—— *'Rameau's Nephew' and 'D'Alembert's Dream'*, trans. L. Tancock (Harmondsworth: Penguin, 1976).

—— *Thoughts on the Interpretation of Nature; and other philosophical works*, introduced and annotated by D. Adams (Manchester: Clinamen, 1999).

—— *Diderot: Interpreter of Nature. Selected Writings*, ed. J. Kemp (London: Lawrence and Wishart, 1937).

Barker, J.E., *Diderot's Treatment of the Christian Religion in the Encyclopédie* (New York: King's Crown Press, 1941).

Bremner, G., *Order and Change: the Pattern of Diderot's Thought* (Cambridge: Cambridge University Press, 1983).

Brewer, D., *The Discourse of Enlightenment in Eighteenth Century France: Diderot and the Art of Philosophizing* (Cambridge: Cambridge University Press, 1993).

Curran, A., *Sublime Disorder: Physical Monstrosity in Diderot's Universe* (Oxford: Voltaire Foundation, 2001).

Darnton, R., *The Business of the Enlightenment: A Publishing History of the Encyclopédie, 1755–1800* (Cambridge, Mass.: Harvard University Press, 1979).

France, P., *Diderot* (Oxford: Oxford University Press, 1983).

Furbank, P.N., *Diderot: A Critical Biography* (London: Secker and Warburg, 1992).

Kafker, F., *The Encyclopedists as a Group: A Collective Biography of the Authors of the Encyclopédie* (Oxford: Voltaire Foundation, 1996).

Lough, J., *Essays on the Encyclopédie of Diderot and D'Alembert* (London: Oxford University Press, 1968).

Mason, J.H. (ed.), *The Irresistible Diderot* (London: Quartet Books, 1982).

Vartanian, A., *Diderot and Descartes. A Study of Scientific Naturalism in the Enlightenment* (Princeton: Princeton University Press, 1953).

Wilson, A.M., *Diderot* (Oxford: Oxford University Press, 1972).

## Ferguson (Adam)

—— *An Essay on the History of Civil Society*, ed. F. Ox-Salzberger (Cambridge: Cambridge University Press, 1995).

—— *The Correspondence of Adam Ferguson*, 2 vols, ed. V. Merolle (London: William Pickering, 1995).

Kettler, D., *The Social and Political Thought of Adam Ferguson* (Columbus: Ohio State University Press, 1965).

Lehmann, W.C., *Adam Ferguson and the Beginning of Modern Sociology* (New York: Columbia University Press, 1930).

## Franklin (Benjamin)

—— *Autobiography and Other Writings*, ed. K. Silverman (Harmondsworth: Penguin, 1986).

—— *The Autobiography of Benjamin Franklin*, ed. L.W. Labaree *et al.* (New Haven: Yale University Press, 1964).

—— *Benjamin Franklin: His Life As He Wrote It*, ed. E. Wright (Cambridge, Mass.: Harvard University Press, 1990).

—— *Selected Writings of Benjamin Franklin*, 3 vols (London: Pickering, 1996).

—— *The Ingenious Dr. Franklin: Selected Scientific Letters of Benjamin Franklin*, ed. N.G. Goodman (Philadelphia: University of Pennsylvania Press, 2000).

—— *The Papers of Benjamin Franklin*, 36 vols (New Haven: Yale University Press, 1990–).

Anderson, D., *The Radical Enlightenments of Benjamin Franklin* (Baltimore: Johns Hopkins University Press, 1997).

Clark, R.W., *Benjamin Franklin: A Biography* (New York: Random House, 1983).

Cohen, I.B., *Franklin and Newton* (Cambridge, Mass.: Harvard University Press, 1966).

Durham, J.L., *Benjamin Franklin: A Biographical Companion* (Santa Barbara, Calif.: ABC-Clio, 1997).

Jacobs, W.R. (ed.), *Benjamin Franklin: Statesman-Philosopher or Materialist?* (New York: Holt, Rinehart and Winston, 1972).

Jennings, F., *Benjamin Franklin, Politician* (New York: W.W. Norton, 1996).

Middlekauff, R., *Benjamin Franklin and His Enemies* (Berkeley: University of California Press, 1996).

Walters, K.S., *Benjamin Franklin and His Gods* (Urbana: University of Illinois Press, 1999).

Wright, E., *Franklin of Philadelphia* (Cambridge, Mass.: Belknap, 1986).

## Frederick II

—— *Frederick the Great: Letters and Documents*, ed. A. Lentin (Milton Keynes: Open University Press, 1979).

—— *Frederick the Great on the Art of War*, ed. and trans. J. Luvaas (New York: De Capo Press, 1999).

Duffy, C., *Frederick the Great: A Military Life* (London: Routledge and Kegan Paul, 1985).

Fraser, D., *Frederick the Great: King of Prussia* (Harmondsworth: Penguin, 2000).

MacDonogh, G., *Frederick the Great: A Life in Deed and Letters* (London: Weidenfeld and Nicolson, 1999).

Ritter, G., *Frederick the Great: A Historical Profile*, trans. P. Paret (Berkeley: University of California Press, 1970).

Schieder, T., *Frederick the Great*, trans. S. Berkeley and H.M. Scott (London: Longman, 2000).

## Gainsborough (Thomas)

—— *The Letters of Thomas Gainsborough*, ed. J. Hayes (New Haven; London: Yale University Press, 2001).

Hayes, J., *Gainsborough* (London: Tate Gallery, 1981)

—— *The Landscape Paintings of Thomas Gainsborough*, 2 vols (London: Sotheby, 1982).

Rosenthal, M., *The Art of Thomas Gainsborough* (New Haven: Yale University Press, 1999).

Sloman, S., *Gainsborough in Bath* (New Haven: Yale University Press, 2002).

## Gibbon (Edward)

—— *The History of the Decline and Fall of the Roman Empire*, ed. D. Womersley, 3 vols (London: Allen Lane, 1994).

—— *Autobiography* (London: Routledge, 1971).
Burrow, J.W., *Gibbon* (Oxford: Oxford University Press, 1985).
Carnochan, W.B., *Gibbon's Solitude: The Inward World of the Historian* (Stanford: Stanford University Press, 1987).
Craddock, P.B., *Edward Gibbon: Luminous Historian, 1772–94* (Baltimore: Johns Hopkins University Press, 1989).
Gossman, L., *The Empire Unpossess'd. An Essay on Gibbon's Decline and Fall* (Cambridge: Cambridge University Press, 1981).
Porter, R., *Edward Gibbon: Making History* (London: Weidenfeld and Nicolson, 1988).
McKitterick, R. (ed.), *Edward Gibbon and Empire* (Cambridge: Cambridge University Press, 1997).
Womersley, D. (ed.), *Edward Gibbon. Bicentenary Essays* (Oxford: Voltaire Foundation, 1997).
—— *Gibbon and the 'Watchmen of the Holy city': the Historian and his Reputation, 1776–1815* (Oxford: Oxford University Press, 2002).
—— *The Transformation of the Decline and Fall of the Roman Empire* (Cambridge: Cambridge University Press, 1988).

## Godwin (William)

—— *An Enquiry Concerning Political Justice and Its Influence on Modern Morals and Happiness*, ed. I. Kramnick (Harmondsworth: Penguin, 1985).
—— *Political and Philosophical Writings*, 7 vols, ed. M. Philp (London: Pickering, 1993).
—— *The Enquirer. Reflections on Education, Manners and Literature* (New York: Augustus M. Kelley, 1965).
Clark, J.P., *The Philosophical Anarchism of William Godwin* (Princeton: Princeton University Press, 1977).
Graham, K.W., *William Godwin Reviewed: A Reception History, 1783–1834* (New York: AMS Press, 1999).
Locke, D., *A Fantasy of Reason: The Life and Thought of William Godwin* (London: Routledge and Kegan Paul, 1980).
Marshall, P.H., *William Godwin* (New Haven: Yale University Press, 1984).
Monro, D.H., *Godwin's Moral Philosophy* (Oxford: Oxford University Press, 1953).
Philp, M., *Godwin's Political Justice* (London: Duckworth, 1986).

## Gouges (Olympe de)

—— *The Rights of Woman*, trans. V. Stevenson (London: Pythia Press, 1989).
Kadish, D.Y. and Massardier-Kenney, F. (eds), *Translating Slavery Gender and Race in French Women's Writing, 1783–1823* (Kent, Ohio: Kent State University Press, 1994).

## Hales (Stephen)

—— *Vegetable Staticks*, ed. M.A. Hoskin (London: Scientific Book Guild, 1961).
Allen, D.E.G. and Schofield, R.E., *Stephen Hales: Scientist and Philanthropist* (London: Scolar, 1980).
Clark-Kennedy, A.E., *Stephen Hales: an Eighteenth-Century Biography* (Ridgewood, N.J.: Gregg, 1965).

## Hobbes (Thomas)

—— *Elements of Law, Natural and Politic*, ed. J.C.A. Gaskin (Oxford: Oxford University Press, 1994).

—— *Leviathan*, ed. J.C.A. Gaskin (Oxford: Oxford University Press, 1998).

—— *Leviathan*, ed. C.B. Macpherson (Harmondsworth: Penguin, 1968).

—— *The Collected English Works of Thomas Hobbes*, ed. W. Molesworth (London: Routledge, 1997).

King, P. (ed.), *Thomas Hobbes: critical assessments*, 4 vols (London: Routledge, 1993).

Kramer, M.H., *Hobbes and the Paradoxes of Political Origins* (Basingstoke: Macmillan, 1997).

Kraynak, R.P., *History and Modernity in the Thought of Thomas Hobbes* (Ithaca: Cornell University Press, 1990).

Martinich, A.P., *A Hobbes Dictionary* (Oxford: Blackwell, 1995).

—— *Thomas Hobbes* (London: Macmillan, 1997).

Rogers, G.A.J. (ed.), *Hobbes and History* (London: Routledge, 2000).

Skinner, Q., *Reason and Rhetoric in the Philosophy of Hobbes* (Cambridge: Cambridge University Press, 1996).

Slomp, G., *Thomas Hobbes and the Political Philosophy of Glory* (Basingstoke: Macmillan, 2000).

Sorell, T. (ed.), *The Cambridge Companion to Hobbes* (Cambridge: Cambridge University Press, 1996).

Warrender, H., *The Political Philosophy of Hobbes: his theory of obligation* (Oxford: Oxford University Press, 2000).

## Hogarth (William)

—— *Hogarth's Graphic Works: The Complete Engravings*, ed. R. Paulson, 2 vols (London: Print Room, 3rd rev. edn 1989).

—— *The Analysis of Beauty*, ed. R. Paulson (New Haven: Yale University Press, 1997).

Antal, F., *Hogarth and his Place in European Art* (London: Routledge and Kegan Paul, 1962).

Craske, M., *William Hogarth* (Princeton: Princeton University Press, 2000).

Dabydeen, D., *Hogarth's Blacks: Images of Blacks in Eighteenth-century English Art* (Kingston, Surrey: Dangeroo Press, 1985).

Fort, B. and Rosenthal, A. (eds), *The Other Hogarth: Aesthetics of Difference* (Princeton: Princeton University Press, 2001).

Hallett, M., *The Spectacle of Difference: Graphic Satire in the Age of Hogarth* (New Haven: Yale University Press, 1999).

Jarrett, D., *The Ingenious Mr Hogarth* (London: Joseph, 1976).

Paulson, R., *Hogarth: His Life, Art and Times*, 3 vols (New Brunswick: Rutgers University Press, 1991–93).

—— *The Art of Hogarth* (London: Phaidon Press, 1975).

Uglow, J., *Hogarth: A Life and a World* (London: Faber and Faber, 1997).

## Holbach (Baron d')

—— *Superstition in all Ages; Common Sense* by Jean Meslier (New York: Truthseeker, 1950).

—— *The System of Nature,* intro. M. Bush (Manchester: Clinamen, 1999).

Kors, A.C., *D'Holbach's Coterie: An Enlightenment in Paris* (Princeton: Princeton University Press, 1976).

Topazio, V., *D'Holbach's Moral Philosophy: Its Background and Development* (Geneva: Institut et Musée Voltaire, 1956).

Wickwar, W.H., *Baron d'Holbach: A Prelude to the French Revolution* (New York: A.M. Kelley, 1968).

## Hume (David)

—— *An Enquiry Concerning Human Understanding*, ed. and intro. T.L. Beauchamp (Oxford: Oxford University Press, 1999).
—— *An Enquiry Concerning the Principles of Morals*, ed. and intro. T.L. Beauchamp (Oxford: Oxford University Press, 1998).
—— *A Treatise of Human Nature*, ed. L.A. Selby-Bigge (Oxford: Clarendon Press, 1978).
—— *Political Essays*, ed. K. Haakonssen (Cambridge: Cambridge University Press, 1994).
—— *Principal Writings on Religion, including Dialogues concerning Natural Religion and The Natural History of Religion*, ed. J.C.A. Gaskin (Oxford: Oxford University Press, 1993).
—— *David Hume's Dialogues Concerning Natural Religion in Focus*, ed. S. Tweyman (London: Routledge, 1990).
Ayer, A.J., *Hume* (Oxford: Oxford University Press, 1980).
Baier, A., *A Progress of Sentiments: Reflections on Hume's Treatise* (Cambridge, Mass.: Harvard University Press, 1991).
Baillie, J., *Hume on Morality* (London: Routledge, 2000).
Capaldi, N., *Hume's Place in Moral Philosophy* (New York: Peter Lang, 1989).
Christensen, J., *Practising Enlightenment: Hume and the Formation of a Literary Career* (Madison: University of Wisconsin Press, 1987).
Fogelin, R., *Hume's Skepticism in the Treatise of Human Nature* (London: Routledge and Kegan Paul, 1985).
Gaskin, J.C.A., *Hume's Philosophy of Religion* (Basingstoke: Macmillan, 1988).
Mackie, J.L., *Hume's Moral Theory* (London: Routledge, 1980).
Mossner, E.C., *The Life of David Hume* (Oxford: Clarendon Press, 1980).
Norton, D.F., *David Hume: Common-sense Moralist, Sceptical Metaphysician* (Princeton: Princeton University Press, 1982).
—— (ed.), *The Cambridge Companion to Hume* (Cambridge: Cambridge University Press, 1993).
O'Connor, D., *Hume on Religion* (London: Routledge, 2001).
Phillipson, N., *Hume* (London: Weidenfeld and Nicolson, 1989).
Price, H.H., *Hume's Theory of the External World* (Oxford: Oxford University Press, 1940).
Stroud, B., *Hume* (London: Routledge, 1988).

## Jaucourt (Louis)

Haechler, J., *L'Encyclopédie de Diderot et de ... Jaucourt: Essai bibliographique sur le chevalier Louis de Jaucourt* (Paris: Champion, 1995).
Lough, J., *The Encyclopédie in Eighteenth Century England and Other Studies* (Newcastle: Oriel Press, 1970).

## Jefferson (Thomas)

—— *Notes on the State of Virginia*, ed. F. Shuffleton (New York: Penguin, 1999).
—— *Political Writings*, ed. J. Appleby and T. Ball (Cambridge: Cambridge University Press, 1999).
—— *The Papers of Thomas Jefferson*, 28 vols, ed. J.P. Boyd (Princeton: Princeton University Press, 1950).
—— *The Portable Thomas Jefferson*, ed. M.D. Peterson (Harmondsworth: Penguin, 1977).

—— Thomas Jefferson Papers at the Library of Congress: http://memory.loc.gov/ammem/mtjhtml/mtjhome.html.

Adams, W.H. (ed.), *The Eye of Thomas Jefferson* (Washington D.C.: National Gallery of Art, 1976).

Bedini, S.A., *Thomas Jefferson: Statesman of Science* (New York: Macmillan, 1990).

Berman, E.D., *Thomas Jefferson Among the Arts* (New York: Philosophical Library, 1947).

Boorstin, D.J., *The Lost World of Thomas Jefferson* (Chicago: University of Chicago Press, 1993).

Bottorff, W.K., *Thomas Jefferson* (Boston: Twayne Publishers, 1979).

Brodie, F.M., *Thomas Jefferson: An Intimate History* (New York: W.W. Norton, 1998).

Cunningham, N., *In Pursuit of Reason: The Life of Thomas Jefferson*, 3 vols (Baton Rouge: Louisiana State University Press, 1987).

Engeman, T.S., *Thomas Jefferson and the Politics of Nature* (Notre Dame, Ind.: University of Notre Dame Press, 2000).

Fliegelman, J., *Declaring Independence: Jefferson, Natural Language, and the Culture of Performance* (Stanford: Stanford University Press, 1993).

Lerner, M., *Thomas Jefferson: America's Philosopher-King* (New Brunswick, N.J.: Transaction Publishers, 1996).

Malone, D., *Jefferson in his Time*, 6 vols (Boston: Little, Brown, 1948–81).

Miller, C.A., *Jefferson and Nature: An Interpretation* (Baltimore: Johns Hopkins University Press, 1988).

Peterson, M.D., *Thomas Jefferson and the New Nation* (New York: Oxford University Press, 1970).

Shackelford, G.G., *Thomas Jefferson's Travels in Europe 1784–1789* (Baltimore: Johns Hopkins University Press, 1995).

Sheldon, G.W., *The Political Philosophy of Thomas Jefferson* (Baltimore: Johns Hopkins University Press, 1991).

Smith, J.M. (ed.), *The Republic of Letters: The Correspondence between Thomas Jefferson and James Madison, 1776–1826*, 3 vols (New York: Norton, 1995).

Risjord, N.K., *Jefferson's America, 1760–1815* (Madison: Madison House, 1991).

Willis, G., *Inventing America: Jefferson's Declaration of Independence* (New York: Doubleday, 1978).

## Kant (Immanuel)

—— *The Works of Immanuel Kant*, 3 vols, ed. P. Heath and J.B. Schneewind (Cambridge: Cambridge University Press, 1997).

—— *Political Writings*, ed. H. Reiss (Cambridge: Cambridge University Press, 1990).

—— *The Metaphysics of Ethics*, trans. J.W. Semple (Edinburgh: T. and T. Clark, 1979).

Cassirer, E., *Kant: His Life and Thought* (New Haven: Yale University Press, 1981).

Covell, C., *Kant and the Law of Peace* (New York: St Martin's Press, 1997).

Guyer, P., *Kant and the Claims of Knowledge* (Cambridge: Cambridge University Press, 1987).

Körner, S., *Kant* (London: Penguin, 1955).

Kuehn, M., *Kant: A Biography* (Cambridge: Cambridge University Press, 2001).

Louden, R.B., *Kant's Impure Ethics: from Rational Beings to Human Beings* (Oxford: Oxford University Press, 2000).

Paton, H.J., *The Categorical Imperative: A Study of Kant's Moral Philosophy* (London: Hutchinson's University Library, 1947).

Ross, W.D., *Kant's Ethical Theory* (Oxford: Clarendon Press, 1965).

Scruton, R., *Kant* (Oxford: Oxford University Press, 1982).

Shell, S.M., *The Embodiment of Reason: Kant on Spirit, Generation, and Community* (Chicago: University of Chicago Press, 1996).

Sullivan, R.J., *An Introduction to Kant's Ethics* (Cambridge: Cambridge University Press, 1994).
Wood, A.W., *Kant's Ethical Thought* (Cambridge: Cambridge University Press, 1999).
Williams, H., *Kant's Political Philosophy* (Oxford: Blackwell, 1983).
Zammito, J.H., *The Genesis of Kant's Critique of Judgement* (Chicago: Chicago University Press, 1992).

## La Mettrie (Julien Offray de)

—— *Machine Man and Other Writings*, ed. and trans. A. Thomson (Cambridge: Cambridge University Press, 1996).
Vartanian, A., *La Mettrie's 'L'Homme Machine': A Study in the Origins of an Idea* (Princeton: Princeton University Press, 1960).
Wellman, K., *La Mettrie: Medicine, Philosophy and the Enlightenment* (Durham: Duke University Press, 1992).

## Laugier (Marc-Antoine)

—— *An Essay on Architecture*, trans. W. and A. Herrmann (Los Angeles: Hennessey and Ingalls, 1977).
Hermann, W., *Laugier and Eighteenth-Century French Theory* (London: A. Zwemmer, 1962).

## Leibniz (Gottfried Wilhelm)

—— *Philosophical Texts*, trans. and intro. R.S. Woolhouse and R. Francks (Oxford: Oxford University Press, 1998).
—— *Theodicy: Essays on the Goodness of God, the Freedom of Man, and the Origin of Evil*, ed. A. Farrer, trans. E.M. Huggard (La Salle: Open Court, 1985).
—— *Leibniz: Political Writings*, ed. and trans. P. Riley (Cambridge: Cambridge University Press, 1988).
—— *The Leibniz–Clarke Correspondence*, ed. H.G. Alexander (Manchester: Manchester University Press, 1976).
—— *Philosophical Papers: A Selection*, ed. G. Parkinson (Oxford: Clarendon Press, 1969).
Adams, R.M., *Leibniz: determinist, theist, idealist* (Oxford: Oxford University Press, 1998).
Barber, W.H., *Leibniz in France: from Arnauld to Voltaire* (London: Garland, 1985).
Brown, S., *Leibniz* (Minneapolis: University of Minneapolis Press, 1984).
Hooker, M. (ed.), *Leibniz: Critical and Interpretive Essays* (Minneapolis: University of Minnesota Press, 1982).
Hostler, J., *Leibniz's Moral Philosophy* (London: Duckworth, 1975).
Jolley, N., *Leibniz and Locke: A Study of the 'New Essays on Human Understanding'* (Oxford: Oxford University Press, 1984).
Jolley, N., *The Cambridge Companion to Leibniz* (Cambridge: Cambridge University Press, 1994).
Mates, B., *The Philosophy of Leibniz* (Oxford: Oxford University Press, 1986).
Rutherford, D., *Leibniz and the Rational Order of Nature* (Cambridge: Cambridge University Press, 1995).
Savile, A., *Leibniz and the Monadology* (London: Routledge, 2000).
Wilson, C., *Leibniz's Metaphysics* (Manchester: Manchester University Press, 1989).
Woolhouse, R.S., *Gottfried Wilhelm Leibniz: critical assessments* (London: Routledge, 1994).

## Linnaeus (Carolus)

—— *Species Plantarum*, 2 vols (London: Ray Society, 1959).
—— *Systema Naturae* (Weinheim: Cramer, 1964).
—— *The Lapland Journey*, ed. and trans. P. Graves (Edinburgh: Lockharton Press, 1995).
Blunt, W., *The Compleat Naturalist: A Life of Linnaeus* (London: Collins, 1971).
Frängsmyr, T. (ed.), *Linnaeus, the Man and his Work* (Berkeley: University of California Press, 1983).
Koerner, L., *Linneaus: Nature and Nation* (Cambridge, Mass.: Harvard University Press, 1999).
Larson, J.L., *Reason and Experience: The Representation of Natural Order in the Work of Carl von Linné* (Berkeley: University of California Press, 1971).
Stafleu, F., *Linnaeus and the Linnaeans* (Utrecht: A. Oosthoek, 1971).
Weinstock, J. (ed.), *Contemporary Perspectives on Linnaeus* (London: University Press of America, 1985).

## Locke (John)

—— *Political Essays*, ed. M. Goldie (Cambridge: Cambridge University Press, 1997).
—— *An Essay Concerning Human Understanding*, ed. P.H. Nidditch (Oxford: Clarendon Press, 1975).
—— *An Essay Concerning Human Understanding*, ed. R.S. Woolhouse (Harmondsworth: Penguin, 1997).
—— *Political Writings*, ed. D. Wootton (Harmondsworth: Penguin, 1993).
—— *Some Thoughts Concerning Education*, ed. J.W. and J.S. Yolton (Oxford: Oxford University Press, 1989).
—— *The Correspondence of John Locke*, ed. E.S. de Beer, 9 vols (Oxford: Clarendon Press, 1976–89).
—— *The Educational Writings of John Locke: A Critical Edition with Introduction and Notes*, ed. J.L. Axtell (Cambridge: Cambridge University Press, 1968).
—— *Two Treatises of Government*, ed. P. Laslett (Cambridge: Cambridge University Press, 1988).
Ashcraft, R., *Revolutionary Politics and Locke's 'Two Treatises of Government'* (Princeton: Princeton University Press, 1986).
—— (ed.), *John Locke: Critical Assessments*, 4 vols (London: Routledge, 1991).
Brown, G., *The Consent of the Governed: The Lockean Legacy in Early American Culture* (Cambridge, Mass.: Harvard University Press, 2001).
Chapell, V. (ed.), *The Cambridge Companion to Locke* (Cambridge: Cambridge University Press, 1994).
—— (ed.), *Locke* (Oxford: Oxford University Press, 1998).
Colman, J., *John Locke's Moral Philosophy* (Edinburgh: Edinburgh University Press, 1983).
Dunn, J., *Locke* (Oxford: Oxford University Press, 1984).
—— *The Political Thought of John Locke* (Cambridge: Cambridge University Press, 1969).
Franklin, J.H., *John Locke and the Theory of Sovereignty* (Cambridge: Cambridge University Press, 1978).
Goldie, M. (ed.), *The Reception of Locke's Politics: From the 1690s to the 1830s*, 6 vols (London: Pickering and Chatto, 1999).
Grant, R.W., *John Locke's Liberalism* (Chicago: University of Chicago Press, 1987).
Harris, I., *The Mind of John Locke: A Study of Political Theory in its Intellectual Setting* (Cambridge: Cambridge University Press, 1998).

Huyler, J., *Locke in America: The Moral Philosophy of the Founding Era* (Lawrence: University Press of Kansas, 1995).

Jolley, N., *Locke: His Philosophical Thought* (Oxford: Oxford University Press. 1999).

Lowe, E.J., *Locke on 'Human Understanding'* (London: Routledge, 1995).

Marshall, J., *John Locke: Resistance, Religion and Responsibility* (Cambridge: Cambridge University Press, 1994).

Schouls, P.A., *Reasoned Freedom: John Locke and the Enlightenment* (Ithaca, N.Y.: Cornell University Press, 1992).

Simmons, A.J., *The Lockean Theory of Rights* (Princeton: Princeton University Press, 1992).

Spellman, W.M., *John Locke* (New York: St Martin's Press, 1997).

Tully, J., *A Discourse on Property: John Locke and his Adversaries* (Cambridge: Cambridge University Press, 1980).

Wood, N., *The Politics of Locke's Philosophy* (Berkeley: University of California Press, 1983).

Yolton, J., *Locke: an Introduction* (Oxford: Blackwell, 1985).

—— *A Locke Dictionary* (Oxford: Blackwell, 1993).

—— *John Locke and the Way of Ideas* (Oxford: Oxford University Press, 1956).

—— (ed.), *John Locke: Problems and Perspectives* (Cambridge: Cambridge University Press, 1969).

—— *Locke and French Materialism* (Oxford: Clarendon Press, 1991).

## Macaulay (Catharine)

—— *Letters on Education* (London: Pickering and Chatto, 1996).

—— *On Burke's Reflections on the French Revolution* (Poole, Dorset: Woodstock Books, 1997).

Hill, B., *The Republican Virago: The Life and Times of Catharine Macaulay* (Oxford: Clarendon Press, 1992).

## Montagu (Mary Wortley, Lady)

—— *The Complete Letters of Lady Mary Wortley Montagu*, ed. R. Halsband, 3 vols (Oxford: Clarendon Press, 1965–67).

—— *Selected Letters*, ed. I. Grundy (Harmondsworth: Penguin, 1997).

Grundy, I., *Lady Mary Wortley Montagu: Comet of the Enlightenment* (Oxford: Oxford University Press, 1999).

Lowenthal, C., *Lady Mary Wortley Montagu and the Eighteenth Century Familiar Letter* (Athens: University of Georgia Press, 1994).

## Montesquieu (Charles de Secondat, Baron de)

—— *The Spirit of the Laws*, ed. A.M. Cohler, B.C. Miller and H.S. Stone (Cambridge: Cambridge University Press, 1989).

—— *The Persian Letters*, trans. and intro. by C.J. Betts (Harmondsworth: Penguin, 1993).

Carrithers, D.W., Mosher, M.A. and Rahe, P.A., *Montesquieu's Science of Politics: Essays on The Spirit of the Laws* (Oxford: Rowman and Littlefield, 2001).

Durkheim, E., *Montesquieu and Rousseau: Forerunners of Sociology* (Michigan: Michigan University Press, 1965).

Hulliung, M., *Montesquieu and the Old Regime* (Berkeley: University of California Press, 1976).

Shackleton, R., *Essays on Montesquieu and on the Enlightenment* (Oxford: Voltaire Foundation, 1988).

—— *Montesquieu: A Critical Biography* (Oxford: Oxford University Press, 1961).

Shklar, J.N., *Montesquieu* (Oxford: Oxford University Press, 1987).


## Newton (Isaac)

—— *The Principia: Mathematical Principles of Natural Philosophy*, trans. I.B. Cohen and A. Whitman (Berkeley: University of California Press, 1999).

—— *The Correspondence of Isaac Newton*, 7 vols, ed. H.W. Turnbull, J.F. Scott, A.R. Hall and L. Tilling (Cambridge: Cambridge University Press, 1959–77).

Butts, R.E. and Davis, J.W. (eds), *The Methodological Heritage of Newton* (Oxford: Blackwell, 1970).

Cohen, I.B., *The Newtonian Revolution* (Cambridge: Cambridge University Press, 1980).

Cohen, I.B. and Westfall, R.S. (eds), *Newton: Texts, Backgrounds, Commentaries* (New York: Norton, 1995).

Dobbs, B.J.T. and Jacob, M.C., *Newton and the Culture of Newtonianism* (Amherst, N.Y.: Prometheus Books, 2000).

Guerlac, H., *Newton on the Continent* (New York: Cornell University Press, 1981).

Hall, A.R., *All Was Light: An Introduction to Newton's Opticks* (Oxford: Clarendon Press, 1993).

—— *Isaac Newton: Eighteenth Century Perspectives* (Oxford: Oxford University Press, 1998).

—— *Isaac Newton: Adventurer in Thought* (Oxford: Blackwell, 1992).

Jacob, M.C., *The Newtonians and the English Revolution, 1689–1720* (Brighton: Harvester Press, 1976).

Manuel, F.E., *A Portrait of Isaac Newton* (Cambridge: Mass.: Harvard University Press, 1968).

Teeter Dobbs, B-J. and Jacob, M.C., *Newton and the Culture of Newtonianism* (Atlantic Highlands, N.J.: Humanities Press, 1995).

Westfall, R., *Never at Rest: A Biography of Isaac Newton* (Cambridge: Cambridge University Press, 1980).


## Paine (Thomas)

—— *Political Writings*, ed. B. Kuklick (Cambridge: Cambridge University Press, 1989).

—— *The Rights of Man, Common Sense, and other Political Writings*, ed. M. Philp (Oxford: Oxford University Press, 1998).

—— *The Rights of Man*, ed. H. Collins (Harmondsworth: Penguin, 1969).

Aldridge, A., *Thomas Paine's American Ideology* (Delaware: Dover, 1984).

Ayer, A., *Thomas Paine* (London: Secker and Warburg, 1988).

Claeys, G., *Thomas Paine. Social and Political Thought* (Winchester, Mass.: Unwin Hyman, 1989).

Hawke, D.F., *Paine* (New York: Norton, 1992).

Keane, J., *Tom Paine: A Political Life* (London: Bloomsbury, 1995).

Philp, M., *Paine* (Oxford: Oxford University Press, 1989).


## Pope (Alexander)

—— *The Poems of Alexander Pope*, ed. J. Butt (London: Methuen, 1963).

—— *Selected Poetry: Alexander Pope*, ed. P. Rogers (Oxford: Oxford University Press, 1994).

—— *The Correspondence of Alexander Pope*, ed. G. Sherburn, 5 vols (Oxford: Clarendon Press, 1956).

Baines, P., *The Complete Critical Guide to Alexander Pope* (London: Routledge, 2000).

Barnard, J. (ed.), *Alexander Pope: the Critical Heritage* (London: Routledge, 1995).

Fairer, D., *The Poetry of Alexander Pope* (Harmondsworth: Penguin, 1989).

Hammond, B.S., *Pope* (Brighton: Harvester Press, 1986).

Mack, M., *Alexander Pope: A Life* (New Haven: Yale University Press, 1985).

Rogers, P., *An Introduction to Pope* (London: Methuen, 1975).

Tillotson, G., *Pope and Human Nature* (Oxford: Clarendon Press, 1958).

## Raynal (Abbé)

—— *A Philosophical and Political History of the Settlements and Trade of the Europeans in the East and West Indies* (London: Longman, Hurst, Rees, Orme and R. Brown, 1812).

—— *Histoire des Deux Indes*, ed. Y. Benot (Paris: Maspero, 1981).

## Reynolds (Joshua)

—— *Discourses on Art*, ed. R. Wark (New Haven: Yale University Press, 1997).

—— *Discourses*, ed. P. Rogers (Harmondsworth: Penguin, 1992).

—— *The Letters of Joshua Reynolds*, ed. J. Ingamells and J. Edgcumbe (New Haven: Yale University Press, 2001).

—— *The Works*, ed. E. Malone, 2 vols (Hildesheim: Georg Olms Verlag, 1971).

Mannings, D., *Sir Joshua Reynolds: A Complete Catalogue of his Paintings*, 2 vols (New Haven: Yale University Press, 2000).

Penny, N. (ed.), *Reynolds* (London: Tate Gallery, 1986).

Postle, M.J., *Sir Joshua Reynolds: The Subject Pictures* (Cambridge: Cambridge University Press, 1995).

Wendorf, R., *Sir Joshua Reynolds: the Painter in Society* (London: National Portrait Gallery, 1996).

## Roland (Madame de)

—— *The Memoirs of Madame Roland: A Heroine of the French Revolution*, ed. and trans. E. Shuckburgh (New York: Moyer Bell, 1990).

May, G., *Madame Roland and the Age of Revolution* (New York: Columbia University Press, 1971).

## Rousseau (Jean-Jacques)

—— *The Confessions of Jean-Jacques Rousseau*, trans. J.M. Cohen (Harmondsworth: Penguin, 1971).

—— *Discourse on the Origin of Inequality*, ed. P. Coleman, trans. F. Philip (Oxford: Oxford University Press, 1999).

—— *Emile*, trans. B. Foxley (London: Everyman, 1993).

—— *The Reveries of the Solitary Walker*, trans. by C.E. Butterworth (New York: New York University Press, 1979).

—— 'The Discourses' and Other Early Political Writings, ed. V. Gourevitch (Cambridge: Cambridge University Press, 1997).

—— *The Essential Rousseau*, trans. L. Blair (New York: New American Library, 1974).

—— *'The Social Contract' and Other Later Political Writings*, ed. V. Gourevitch (Cambridge: Cambridge University Press, 1997).

Blum, C., *Rousseau and the Republic of Virtue: The Language of Politics in the French Revolution* (Ithaca: Cornell University Press, 1986).

Cassirer, E., *The Question of Jean-Jacques Rousseau*, ed. and trans. P. Gay (New Haven: Yale University Press, 1989).

Cranston, M., *Jean-Jacques: The Early Life and Work of J.-J. Rousseau 1712–1754* (London: Allen Lane, 1983).

—— *The Noble Savage: Jean-Jacques Rousseau 1754–1762* (London: Allen Lane, 1991).

—— *The Solitary Self: Jean-Jacques Rousseau in Exile and Adversity* (London: Allen Lane, 1987).

Dent, N.J.H., *A Rousseau Dictionary* (Oxford: Blackwell Reference, 1992).

—— *Rousseau: An Introduction to his Psychological, Social and Political Theory* (Oxford: Blackwell, 1988).

Duffy, E., *Rousseau in England: The Context for Shelley's Critique of the Enlightenment* (Berkeley: University of California Press, 1979).

Fralin, R., *Rousseau and Representation: A Study of the Development of his Concept of Political Institutions* (New York: Columbia University Press, 1978).

Gildin, H., *Rousseau's Social Contract: The Design of the Argument* (Chicago: Chicago University Press, 1983).

Grimsley, R., *The Philosophy of Rousseau* (Oxford: Oxford University Press, 1973).

Hendel, C.W., *Jean-Jacques Rousseau: Moralist* (Indianapolis: Bobbs-Merrill, 1962).

Hulliung, M., *The Autocritique of Enlightenment: Rousseau and the Philosophes* (Cambridge, Mass.: Harvard University Press, 1994).

Kelly, C., *Rousseau's Exemplary Life: The 'Confessions' as Political Philosophy* (Ithaca, NY: Cornell University Press, 1987).

Miller, J., *Rousseau: Dreamer of Democracy* (New Haven: Yale University Press, 1984).

Mason, J.H., *The Indispensable Rousseau* (London: Quartet Books, 1979).

Masters, R.D., *The Political Philosophy of Rousseau* (Princeton: Princeton University Press, 1968).

O'Hagan, T., *Rousseau* (London: Routledge, 1999).

Riley, P. (ed.), *The Cambridge Companion to Rousseau* (Cambridge: Cambridge University Press, 2001).

Rosenblatt, H., *Rousseau and Geneva: From the 'First Discourse' to the 'Social Contract', 1749–1762* (Cambridge: Cambridge University Press, 1997).

Shklar, J., *Men and Citizens: A Study of Rousseau's Social Theory* (Cambridge: Cambridge University Press, 1969).

Starobinski, J., *Jean-Jacques Rousseau: Transparency and Obstruction*, trans. A. Goldhammer (Chicago: University of Chicago Press, 1988).

Still, J., *Justice and Difference in the Works of Rousseau* (Cambridge: Cambridge University Press, 1993).

Strong, T., *Jean-Jacques Rousseau: The Politics of the Ordinary* (London: Sage, 1994).

Trachtenberg, Z.M., *Making Citizens: Rousseau's Political Theory of Culture* (New York: Routledge, 1993).

Wingrove, E.R., *Rousseau's Republican Romance* (Princeton: Princeton University Press, 2000).

Wokler, R., *Rousseau* (Oxford: Oxford University Press, 1995)

—— *Rousseau on Society, Politics, Music and Language: An Historical Interpretation of his Early Writings* (New York: Garland, 1987).

## Sade (Marquis de)

—— *Letters from Prison*, trans. R. Seaver (London: Harvill Press, 1999).

—— *The Complete Justine, Philosophy in the Bedroom and other Writings*, trans. R. Seaver and A. Wainhouse (New York: Grove Press, 1966).

—— *The Misfortunes of Virtue, and other early tales*, trans. and ed. D. Coward (Oxford: Oxford University Press, 1992).

—— *The Passionate Philosopher: A Marquis de Sade Reader*, trans. M. Crossland (London: Minerva, 1993).

Airaksinen, T., *The Philosophy of the Marquis de Sade* (London: Routledge, 1995).

Donald, T., *The Marquis de Sade* (London: Allison and Busby, 1992).

Hénaff, M., *Sade, the Invention of the Libertine Body* (Minneapolis: University of Minnesota Press, 1999).

Lever, M., *Marquis de Sade: A Biography*, trans. A. Goldhammer (London: Harper Collins, 1993).

Phillips, J., *Sade: The Libertine Novels* (London: Pluto, 2001).

Plessix Gray, F. du, *At Home with the Marquis de Sade* (London: Pimlico, 2000).

Schaeffer, N., *The Marquis de Sade: A Life* (London: Hamish Hamilton, 1999).

Warman, C., *Sade: From Materialism to Pornography* (Oxford: Voltaire Foundation, 2002).

## Smith (Adam)

—— *An Inquiry into the Nature and Causes of the Wealth of Nations*, ed. R.H. Campbell, A.S. Skinner and W.B. Todds, 2 vols (Oxford: Clarendon Press, 1976).

—— *Lectures on Jurisprudence*, ed. R. Meek, D. Raphael and P. Stein (Oxford: Clarendon Press, 1982).

—— *The Theory of Moral Sentiments,* ed. D.D. Raphael and A.L. Macfie (Oxford: Clarendon Press, 1976).

—— *The Wealth of Nations* (Harmondsworth: Penguin, 1982).

—— *The Essential Adam Smith*, ed. R.L. Heilbroner (Oxford: Oxford University Press, 1986).

Campbell, R.H. and Skinner, A.S., *Adam Smith* (London: Croom Helm, 1982).

Griswold, C.L., *Adam Smith and the Virtues of Enlightenment* (Cambridge: Cambridge University Press, 1999).

Lindgren, R., *The Social Philosophy of Adam Smith* (The Hague: Martinus Nijhoff, 1973).

Raphael, D.D., *Adam Smith* (Oxford: Oxford University Press, 1985).

Ross, I.S., *The Life of Adam Smith* (Oxford: Clarendon Press, 1995).

—— (ed.), *On the Wealth of Nations: Contemporary Responses to Adam Smith* (Bristol: Thoemmes Press, 1998).

Rothschild, E., *Economic Sentiments: Adam Smith, Condorcet and the Enlightenment* (Cambridge, Mass.: Harvard University Press, 2001).

## Steele (Richard)

—— *The Englishman*, ed. R. Blanchard (Oxford: Clarendon Press, 1955).

—— *The Guardian*, ed. J.C. Stephens, (Lexington, Ky.: University Press of Kentucky, 1982).

—— *The Spectator*, ed. D.F. Bond, 5 vols (Oxford: Clarendon Press, 1965).

—— *Selections from 'The Tatler' and 'The Spectator' of Steele and Addison*, ed. A. Ross (Harmondsworth: Penguin, 1982).

—— *Spectator* http://harvest.rutgers.edu/projects/spectator/search.html.

Bond, R.P., *The Tatler: The Making of a Literary Journal* (Cambridge, Mass.: Harvard University Press, 1971).

Winton, C., *Captain Steele: The Early Career of Richard Steele* (Baltimore: Johns Hopkins University Press, 1964).

—— *Sir Richard Steele, M.P.: The Later Career* (Baltimore: Johns Hopkins University Press, 1970).

## Toland (John)

—— *John Toland's 'Christianity not Mysterious'. Texts, Associated Works and Critical Essays*, ed. P. McGuinness, A. Harrison and R. Kearney (Dublin: Lilliput Press, 1997).
—— *Christianity not Mysterious*, ed. G. Gawlick (Stuttgart–Bad Cannstatt: F. Frommann Verlag, 1964).
Daniel, S.H., *John Toland: His Methods, Manners and Mind* (Kingston and Montreal: McGill–Queen's University Press, 1984).
Evans, R.R., *Pantheisticon: The Career of John Toland* (New York: Peter Lang, 1991).
Sullivan, R., *John Toland and the Deist Controversy: A Study in Adaptations* (Cambridge, Mass.: Harvard University Press, 1982).

## Vico (Giambattista)

—— *New Science*, trans. D. Marsh, intro. A. Grafton (Harmondsworth: Penguin, 1999).
—— *The Autobiography*, trans. T.G. Bergin and M.H. Fisch (Ithaca: Cornell University Press, 1975).
—— *Vico: Selected Writings*, ed. and trans. L. Pompa (Cambridge: Cambridge University Press, 1982).
Berlin, I., *Three Critics of the Enlightenment: Vico, Hamann, Herder*, ed. H. Hardy (London: Pimlico, 2000).
Burke, P., *Vico* (Oxford: Oxford University Press, 1985).
Croce, B., *The Philosophy of Giambattista Vico*, trans. R.G. Collingwood (New York: Russell and Russell, 1964).
Goetsch, J.R., *Vico's Axioms: The Geometry of the Human World* (New Haven: Yale University Press, 1995).
Lilla, M., *G.B. Vico: The Making of an Anti-Modern* (Cambridge, Mass.: Harvard University Press, 1993).
Mali, J., *The Rehabilitation of Myth. Vico's New Science* (Cambridge: Cambridge University Press, 1992).
Mazzotta, G., *The New Map of the World: The Poetic Philosophy of Giambattista Vico* (Princeton: Princeton University Press, 1998).
Pompa, L., *Vico: A Study of the 'New Science'* (Cambridge: Cambridge University Press, 1975).
Stone, H., *Vico's Cultural History: The Production and Transmission of Ideas in Naples, 1685–1750* (New York: E.J. Brill, 1997).
Tagliacozzo, G. (ed.), *Vico: Past and Present* (Atlantic Highlands, N.J.: Humanities Press, 1981).
Verene, D.P., *The New Art of Autobiography: An Essay on the Life of Giambattista Vico, Written by Himself* (Oxford: Clarendon, 1991).

## Voltaire

—— *Candide*, trans. and ed. D. Gordon (Boston, Mass.: Bedford/St Martin's Press, 1999).
—— *Candide; and Other Stories*, trans. R. Pearson (Oxford: Oxford University Press, 1998).
—— *The Selected Letters of Voltaire*, ed. and trans. R.A. Brooks (New York: New York University Press, 1973).

—— *Letters concerning the English Nation*, ed. N. Cronk (Oxford: Oxford University Press, 1994).

—— *Philosophical Dictionary*, trans. T. Besterman (Harmondsworth: Penguin, 1979).

—— *Philosophical Letters*, trans. E. Dilworth (Indianapolis: Bobbs-Merrill, 1961).

—— *Political Writings*, ed. D. Williams (Cambridge: Cambridge University Press, 1994).

—— *Voltaire: Selections*, ed. P. Edwards (London: Collier Macmillan, 1989).

Bestermann, T., *Voltaire* (Oxford: Blackwell, 1976).

Brailsford, H.N., *Voltaire* (Oxford: Oxford University Press, 1968).

Brumfitt, J.H., *Voltaire, Historian* (Oxford: Oxford University Press, 1970).

Gay, P., *Voltaire's Politics: The Poet as Realist* (Princeton: Princeton University Press, 1959).

Howells, R.J. and Mason, A. (eds), *Voltaire and His World* (Oxford: Voltaire Foundation, 1985).

Knapp, B.L., *Voltaire Revisited* (New York: Twayne, 2000)

Lanson, G., *Voltaire* (London: Wiley, 1966).

Lentin, A. (ed.), *Voltaire and Catherine the Great: Selected Correspondence* (Cambridge: Oriental Research Partners, 1974).

Mason, H.T., *Voltaire: a Biography* (Baltimore: Johns Hopkins University Press, 1981).

Torrey, N.L., *Voltaire and the English Deists* (Oxford: Marston Press, 1963).

Wade, I.O., *Voltaire and Madame du Châtelet* (New York: Octagon Books, 1967).

—— *The Intellectual Development of Voltaire* (Princeton: Princeton University Press, 1969).

## Walpole (Horace)

—— *Anecdotes of Painting in England* (New Haven: Yale University Press, 1937).

—— *The Yale Edition of Horace Walpole's Correspondence*, ed. W.S. Lewis, 48 vols (New Haven: Yale University Press, 1937–83).

Brownell, M.R., *The Prime Minister of Taste: a portrait of Horace Walpole* (New Haven: Yale University Press, 2001).

Fothergill, B., *The Strawberry Hill Set: Horace Walpole and his Circle* (London: Faber and Faber, 1983).

Kallich, M., *Horace Walpole* (New York: Twayne, 1971).

Mowl, T., *Horace Walpole: The Great Outsider* (London: John Murray, 1996).

Sabor, P., *Horace Walpole: A Reference Guide* (Boston: G.K. Hall, 1984).

—— (ed.), *Horace Walpole: The Critical Heritage* (London: Routledge and Kegan Paul, 1987).

## Wollstonecraft (Mary)

—— *The Works of Mary Wollstonecraft*, ed. J. Todd and M. Butler, 7 vols (London: William Pickering, 1989).

—— *A Vindication of the Rights of Men and A Vindication of the Rights of Woman and Hints*, ed. S. Tomaselli (Cambridge: Cambridge University Press, 1995).

—— *Thoughts on the Education of Daughters*, ed. J. Todd (Bristol: Thoemmes, 1995).

Conger, S. M., *Mary Wollstonecraft and the Language of Sensibility* (London and Toronto: Associated University Press, 1994).

Jacobs, D., *Her Own Woman: The Life of Mary Wollstonecraft* (New York: Simon and Schuster, 2001).

Johnson, C.L. (ed.), *The Cambridge Companion to Mary Wollstonecraft* (Cambridge: Cambridge University Press, 2002).

Kelly, G., *Revolutionary Feminism: The Mind and Career of Mary Wollstonecraft* (New York: St Martin's Press, 1992).

Sapiro, V., *Vindication of Political Virtue: The Political Theory of Mary Wollstonecraft* (Chicago: Chicago University Press, 1992).

Tauchert, A., *Mary Wollstonecraft and the Accent of the Feminine* (Basingstoke: Palgrave, 2002).

Todd, J., *Mary Wollstonecraft: A Revolutionary Life* (London: Weidenfeld and Nicolson, 2000).

Tomalin, C., *The Life and Death of Mary Wollstonecraft* (London: Weidenfeld and Nicolson, 1974).

Yeo, E. (ed.), *Mary Wollstonecraft and 200 Years of Feminism* (London: Rivers Oram Press, 1997).

## Wright (Joseph)

Egerton, J., *Wright of Derby*, exhibition catalogue (London: Tate Gallery, 1990).

Fraser, D., *Joseph Wright of Derby* (Derby: Derby Museum and Art Gallery, 1979).

Nicolson, B., *Joseph Wright of Derby: Painter of Light*, 2 vols (London: Routledge and Kegan Paul, 1968).

# IV  CHAPTER TOPICS

## 1  Human nature

Allen, R.C., *David Hartley on Human Nature* (New York: State University of New York Press, 1999).

Carretta, V. (ed.), *Unchained Voices: An Anthology of Black Authors in the English-speaking World of the Eighteenth Century* (Lexington: University Press of Kentucky, 1996).

Equiano, O., *Equiano's Travels*, ed. P. Edwards ([1789]; Oxford: Heinemann, 1967).

Eze, E.C. (ed.), *Race and the Enlightenment* (Oxford: Blackwell, 1997).

Faull, K.M. (ed.), *Anthropology and the German Enlightenment* (Lewisburg: Bucknell and Associated University Presses, 1994).

Fogel, R.W., *Without Consent or Contract: The Rise and Fall of American Slavery* (New York: Norton, 1989).

Hastings, H., *Man and Beast in French Thought of the Eighteenth Century* (Baltimore: Johns Hopkins Press, 1936).

Jordan, W., *White over Black: American Attitudes towards the Negro 1550–1812* (Chapel Hill: University of North Carolina Press, 1968).

Kidd, C., *British Identities before Nationalism: Ethnicity and Nationhood in the Atlantic World, 1600–1800* (Cambridge: Cambridge University Press, 1999).

Mell, D.C. Jr., Braun, T.E.D. and Palmer, L.M. (eds), *Man, God, and Nature in the Enlightenment* (Michigan: Colleagues Press, 1988).

Manuel, F.E., *The Prophets of Paris* (Cambridge, Mass.: Harvard University Press, 1962).

Passmore, J.A., *The Perfectibility of Man* (London: Duckworth, 1970).

Peabody, S., *There are No Slaves in France: The Political Culture of Race and Slavery in the Ancien Régime* (New York: Oxford University Press, 1996).

Smith, D.W., *Helvétius: A Study in Persecution* (Oxford: Clarendon Press, 1965).

Trigg, R., *Ideas of Human Nature* (Oxford: Blackwell, 1999).

Turley, D., *The Culture of English Anti-Slavery, 1780–1860* (London: Routledge, 1991).

## 2 The search for knowledge

Bayle, P., *Bayle's Dictionary: Historical and Critical*, 5 vols, intro. R. Popkin ([1697]; London: Routledge, 1997).

Buchdahl, G., *The Image of Newton and Locke in the Age of Reason* (London: Sheed and Ward, 1961).

Hall, M.B., *Promoting Experimental Learning: Experiment and the Royal Society 1660–1727* (Cambridge: Cambridge University Press, 1991).

Koestler, A., *The Sleepwalkers: A History of Man's Changing Vision of the Universe* (London: Hutchinson, 1959).

Lange, F.A., *The History of Materialism*, trans. E.C. Thomas (New York: Arno Press, 1974).

Schaffer, S. and Shapin, S., *Leviathan and the Air Pump: Hobbes, Boyle and the Experimental Life* (Princeton: Princeton University Press, 1985).

Schouls, P., *Descartes and the Enlightenment* (Kingston: McGill-Queen's University Press, 1989).

Schofield, R.E., *Mechanism and Materialism: British Natural Philosophy in an Age of Reason* (Princeton: Princeton University Press, 1970).

Stewart, L., *The Rise of Public Science: Rhetoric, Technology, and Natural Philosophy in Newtonian Britain, 1660–1750* (Cambridge: Cambridge University Press, 1992).

Taylor, R. (ed.), *The Empiricists* (London: Anchor Press/Doubleday, 1974).

Yolton, J.W., *Thinking Matter: Materialism in Eighteenth-Century Britain* (Minneapolis: University of Minnesota Press, 1983).

## 3 Religion and belief

Almond, P.C., *Heaven and Hell in Enlightenment England* (Cambridge: Cambridge University Press, 1994).

Barnett, S.J., *Idol Temples and Crafty Priests: The Origins of Enlightenment Anticlericalism* (New York: St Martin's Press, 1999).

Becker, C., *The Heavenly City of the Eighteenth Century Philosophers* (New Haven: Yale University Press, 1932).

Berman, D., *A History of Atheism in Britain from Hobbes to Russell* (London: Croom Helm, 1988).

Bien, D.D., *The Calas Affair: Persecution, Toleration, and Heresy in Eighteenth-Century Toulouse* (Princeton: Princeton University Press, 1960).

Byrne, J., *Glory, Jest and Riddle: Religious Thought in the Enlightenment* (London: SCM Press, 1996).

Callaghan, W.J. and Higgs, D. (eds), *Church and Society in Catholic Europe of the Eighteenth Century* (Cambridge: Cambridge University Press, 1979).

Clark, S.R.L., *God's World and the Great Awakening* (Oxford: Clarendon Press, 1991).

Champion, J.A.I., *The Pillars of Priestcraft Shaken: The Church of England and its Enemies, 1660–1730* (Cambridge: Cambridge University Press, 1992).

Cragg, G.R., *Reason and Authority in the Eighteenth Century* (Cambridge: Cambridge University Press, 1964).

Downey, J., *The Eighteenth Century Pulpit* (Oxford: Clarendon Press 1969).

Frei, H., *The Eclipse of Biblical Narrative* (New Haven: Yale University Press, 1974).

Gay, P., *Deism: An Anthology* (Princeton: Van Nostrand, 1968).

Grell, O.P. and Porter, R. (eds), *Toleration in Enlightenment Europe* (Cambridge: Cambridge University Press, 2000).

Haakonssen, K. (ed.), *Enlightenment and Religion: Rational Dissent in Eighteenth-century Britain* (Cambridge: Cambridge University Press, 1997).

Harrison, P., 'Religion' and the Religions in the English Enlightenment (Cambridge: Cambridge University Press, 1990).

Hunter, M. and Wootton, D. (eds), Atheism from the Reformation to the Enlightenment (Oxford: Oxford University Press, 1992).

Manuel, F.E., The Eighteenth Century Confronts the Gods (New York: Harvard University Press, 1967).

McManners, J., Church and Society in Eighteenth-Century France, 2 vols (Oxford: Oxford University Press, 1998).

—— Death and the Enlightenment: Changing Attitudes to Death among Christians and Unbelievers in Eighteenth-Century France (Oxford: Clarendon Press, 1981).

Mendelssohn, M., Jerusalem: Or on Religious Power and Judaism, ed. A. Arkush ([1783]; Hanover: University Press of New England, 1983).

Palmer, R.R., Catholics and Unbelievers in Eighteenth Century France (Princeton: Princeton University Press, 1961).

Rupp, G., Religion in England 1688–1791 (Oxford: Clarendon Press, 1986).

Sorkin, D., Moses Mendelssohn and the Religious Enlightenment (Berkeley: University of California Press, 1996).

Walters, K.S. (ed.), The American Deists: Voices of Reason and Dissent in the Early Republic (Lawrence: University Press of Kansas, 1992).

Young, B.W., Religion and Enlightenment in Eighteenth-century England: Theological Debate from Locke to Burke (Oxford: Clarendon Press, 1998).

## 4   The natural world

Bewell, A., Wordsworth and the Enlightenment: Nature, Man, and Society in the Experimental Poetry (New Haven: Yale University Press, 1989).

Charlton, D.G., New Images of the Natural in France: A Study in European Cultural History, 1750–1800 (Cambridge: Cambridge University Press, 1984).

Croker, L.G., An Age of Crisis: Man and World in Eighteenth-Century French Thought (Baltimore: Johns Hopkins University Press, 1959).

Harris, R.W., Reason and Nature in the Eighteenth Century, 1714–1780 (London: Blandford Press, 1968).

Lovejoy, A.O., The Great Chain of Being: A Study of the History of an Idea (Cambridge, Mass.: Harvard University Press, 1970).

Thomas, K., Man and the Natural World: Changing Attitudes in England, 1500–1800 (Harmondsworth: Penguin, 1983).

Willey, B., The Eighteenth Century Background: Studies on the Idea of Nature in the Thought of the Period (Harmondsworth: Penguin, 1962).

## 5   Science and invention

Adas, M., Machines as the Measure of Men: Science, Technology, and Ideologies of Western Dominance (New York: Cornell University Press, 1989).

Anderson, R.G.W. and Lawrence, C., Science, Medicine and Dissent: Joseph Priestley, 1733–1804 (London: Wellcome Trust/Science Museum, 1987).

Berg, M., The Age of Manufactures, 1700–1820: Industry, Innovation and Work in Britain (London: Routledge, 1994).

Butterfield, H., The Origins of Modern Science, 1300–1800 (London: Bell and Hyman, 1957).

Clark, W., Golinski, J. and Schaffer, S. (eds), The Sciences in Enlightened Europe (Chicago: University of Chicago Press, 1999).

Cohen, I.B., Revolution in Science (Cambridge, Mass.: Belknap Press, 1985).

Dean, D.R., *James Hutton and the History of Geology* (Ithaca, New York: Cornell University Press, 1992).

Dear, P., *Revolutionising the Sciences: European Knowledge and its Ambitions 1500–1700* (Basingstoke: Palgrave, 2001).

Donovan, A.L., *Philosophical Chemistry in the Scottish Enlightenment: the Doctrines and Discoveries of William Cullen and Joseph Black* (Edinburgh: Edinburgh University Press, 1975).

Frängsmyr, T., Heilbron, J.L., and Rider, R.E. (eds)., *The Quantifying Spirit in the Eighteenth Century* (Berkeley: University of California Press, 1990).

Golinski, J., *Science as a Public Culture: Chemistry and Enlightenment in Britain, 1760–1820* (Cambridge: Cambridge University Press, 1992).

Hahn, R., *The Anatomy of a Scientific Institution; the Paris Academy of Sciences 1666–1803* (Berkeley: University of California Press, 1971).

Hall, A.R., *Scientific Revolution 1500–1800* (London: Longman, 1954).

Hankins, T.L., *Science and the Enlightenment* (Cambridge: Cambridge University Press, 1985).

Heilbron, J.L., *Electricity in the Seventeenth and Eighteenth Centuries: A Study of Early Modern Physics* (Berkeley: University of California Press, 1979).

Henry, J., *The Scientific Revolution and the Origins of Modern Science* (London: Macmillan, 1997).

Holmes, F.L., *Eighteenth Century Chemistry as an Investigative Enterprise* (Berkeley: University of California Press, 1989).

Jacob, M.C., *Scientific Culture and the Making of the Industrial West* (Oxford: Oxford University Press, 1997).

Jones, P. (ed.), *Philosophy and Science in the Scottish Enlightenment* (Edinburgh: J. Donald, 1988).

Kiernan, C., *Enlightenment and Science in Eighteenth Century France* (Banbury: Voltaire Foundation, 1973).

Magner, L.N., *History of the Life Sciences* (New York: M. Dekker, 1979).

Porter, R. (ed.), *The Cambridge History of Science*, Vol. 4, *The Eighteenth Century* (Cambridge: Cambridge University Press, 2000).

—— *Medicine and the Enlightenment* (Amsterdam: Rodopi, 1994).

—— *The Making of the Science of Geology* (Cambridge: Cambridge University Press, 1977).

—— and Teich, M. (eds), *The Scientific Revolution in National Context* (Cambridge: Cambridge University Press, 1992).

Rousseau, G.S. and Porter, R. (eds), *The Ferment of Knowledge: Studies in the Historiography of Eighteenth-century Science* (Cambridge: Cambridge University Press, 1980).

Schofield, R.E., *The Enlightenment of Joseph Priestley: A Study of His Life and Work from 1733 to 1773* (Philadelphia: Pennsylvania State University Press, 1997).

—— *The Lunar Society of Birmingham: A Social History of Provincial Science and Industry in Eighteenth-century England* (Oxford: Clarendon Press, 1963).

Stansfield, D.A., *Thomas Beddoes MD 1760–1808, Chemist, Physician, Democrat* (Dordrecht: Reidel, 1984).

Thackray, A.W., *Atoms and Powers: An Essay on Newtonian Matter — Theory and the Development of Chemistry* (Cambridge, Mass.: Harvard University Press, 1970).

Uglow, J., *The Lunar Men: The Friends who made the Future* (London: Faber and Faber, 2002).

Vartanian, A., *Science and Humanism in the French Enlightenment* (Charlottesville: Rookwood Press, 1999).

Wolf, A., *A History of Science, Technology and Philosophy in the Eighteenth Century*, 2 vols ([1939]; London: George Allen and Unwin, 1962).

## 6  Political rights and responsibilities

Andrews, S. (ed.), *Enlightened Absolutism* (London: Longman, 1967).

Beales, D., *Joseph II* (Cambridge: Cambridge University Press, 1987).

Blanning, T.C.W., *Joseph II and Enlightened Despotism* (London: Longman, 1970).

Cranston, M., *Philosophers and Pamphleteers, Political Theorists of the Enlightenment* (Oxford: Oxford University Press, 1986).

Hochstrasser, T.J., *Natural Law Theorists in the Early Enlightenment* (Cambridge: Cambridge University Press, 2000).

Jacob, M.C., *Living the Enlightenment: Freemasonry and Politics in Eighteenth-Century Europe* (New York: Oxford University Press, 1991).

Kreiger, L., *Kings and Philosophers, 1689–1789* (New York: Norton, 1970).

Lentin, A. (ed.), *Enlightened Absolutism (1760–1790): A Documentary Sourcebook* (Newcastle-upon-Tyne: Avero Publications, 1985).

Macpherson, C.B., *The Political Theory of Possessive Individualism: Hobbes to Locke* (Oxford: Oxford University Press, 1962).

Pagden, A. (ed.), *The Languages of Political Theory in Early-Modern Europe* (Cambridge: Cambridge University Press, 1987).

Riley, P., *Will and Political Legitimacy: A Critical Exposition of Social Contract Theory in Hobbes, Locke, Rousseau, Kant and Hegel* (Cambridge, Mass.: Harvard University Press, 1982).

Scott, H.M. (ed.), *Enlightened Absolutism: Reform and Reformers in Late Eighteenth-century Europe* (London: Macmillan, 1990).

Talmon, J.L., *The Rise of Totalitarian Democracy* (London: Secker and Warburg, 1952).

Tuck, R., *Natural Rights Theories: Their Origin and Development* (Cambridge: Cambridge University Press, 1979).

Venturi, F., *The End of the Old Regime in Europe 1776–1789*, 2 vols (Princeton: Princeton University Press, 1991).

## 7  The development of civil society

Ayres, P., *Classical Culture and the Idea of Rome in Eighteenth-century England* (Cambridge: Cambridge University Press, 1997).

Barnard, F. (ed.), *Herder on Social and Political Culture* (Cambridge: Cambridge University Press, 1969).

Becker, M.B., *The Emergence of Civil Society in the Eighteenth Century* (Indiana: Indiana University Press, 1994).

Berg, M., and Clifford, H. (eds), *Consumers and Luxury: Consumer Culture in Europe 1650–1850* (Manchester: Manchester University Press, 1999).

Caton, H., *The Politics of Progress: The Origins and Development of the Commercial Republic, 1600–1835* (Gainesville: University of Florida Press, 1988).

Fox, C., Porter, R.S., and Wokler, R. (eds), *Inventing Human Science: the Eighteenth-Century Domains* (Berkeley: University of California Press, 1995).

Hont, I. and Ignatieff, M. (eds), *Wealth and Virtue: the Shaping of Political Economy in the Scottish Enlightenment* (Cambridge: Cambridge University Press, 1983).

Hundert, E.G. *The Enlightenment's Fable: Bernard Mandeville and the Discovery of Society* (Cambridge: Cambridge University Press, 1994).

Meek, R.L., *Social Science and the Ignoble Savage* (Cambridge: Cambridge University Press, 1976).

O'Brien, K., *Narratives of Enlightenment: Cosmopolitan History from Voltaire to Gibbon* (Cambridge: Cambridge University Press, 1997).

Olson, R., *The Emergence of the Social Sciences, 1642–1792* (New York: Twayne, 1993).

Payne, H.C., *The Philosophes and the People* (New Haven: Yale University Press, 1976).

Pocock, J.G.A., *Barbarism and Religion*, 2 vols: Vol. i: *The Enlightenments of Edward Gibbon, 1737–1764*; Vol. ii: *Narratives of Civil Government* (Cambridge: Cambridge University Press, 1999).

Rossi, P., *The Dark Abyss of Time: The History of the Earth and the History of Nations from Hooke to Vico* (Chicago: University of Chicago Press, 1984).

Schlereth, T., *The Cosmopolitan Ideal in Enlightenment Thought: Its Form and Function in the Ideas of Franklin, Hume and Voltaire* (Notre Dame: University of Notre Dame Press, 1977).

## 8  Moral principles and punishments

Crocker, L.G., *Nature and Culture: Ethical Thought in the French Enlightenment* (Baltimore: Johns Hopkins University Press, 1963).

Foucault, M., *Discipline and Punish: The Birth of the Prison*, trans. A. Sheridan (Harmondsworth: Penguin, 1991).

Fussell, P., *The Rhetorical World of Augustan Humanism. Ethics and Imagery from Swift to Burke* (Oxford: Clarendon Press, 1965).

Gatrell, V.A.C., *The Hanging Tree: Execution and the English People, 1700–1868* (Oxford: Oxford University Press, 1994).

Haakonssen, K., *Natural Law and Moral Philosophy* (Cambridge: Cambridge University Press, 1996).

Hay, D. (ed.), *Albion's Fatal Tree* (London: Allen Lane, 1975).

Heath, J., *Eighteenth-Century Penal Theory* (Oxford: Oxford University Press, 1963).

Hope, V., *Virtue by Consensus: The Moral Philosophy of Hutcheson, Hume, and Adam Smith* (Oxford: Clarendon Press, 1989).

Maestro, M., *Voltaire and Beccaria as Reformers of Criminal Law* (New York: Columbia University Press, 1942).

Plamenatz, J., *The English Utilitarians* (Oxford: Blackwell, 1958).

MacIntyre, A., *A Short History of Ethics* (London: Routledge, 1993).

Norman, R., *The Moral Philosophers* (Oxford: Oxford University Press, 1998).

## 9  Gender and society

Amussen, S.D., *An Ordered Society: Gender and Class in Early Modern England* (Oxford: Basil Blackwell, 1988).

Assiter, A., *Enlightened Women: Modernist Feminism in a Postmodern Age* (London: Routledge, 1996).

Barker, H. and Chalus, E. (eds), *Gender in Eighteenth-Century England: Roles, Representations and Responsibilities* (New York: Addison Wesley Longman, 1997).

Barker-Benfield, G.J., *The Culture of Sensibility: Sex and Society in Eighteenth-Century Britain* (Chicago: University of Chicago Press, 1992).

Boucé, P-G. (ed.), *Sexuality in Eighteenth-century Britain* (Manchester: Manchester University Press, 1982).

Browne, A., *The Eighteenth-century Feminist Mind* (Brighton: Harvester Press, 1987).

Davis, N.Z. and Farge, A. (eds), *A History of Women in the West*, Vol. iii: *Renaissance and Enlightenment Paradoxes* (Cambridge, Mass.: Harvard University Press, 1993).

Ehrman, E., *Mme du Châtelet* (Leamington Spa: Berg, 1986).

Eger, G., Grant, C., O'Gallchoir, C. and Warburton, P. (eds), *Women, Writing and the Public Sphere, 1700–1830* (Cambridge: Cambridge University Press, 2001).

Harvey, A.D., *Sex in Georgian England. Attitudes and Prejudices from the 1720s to the 1820s* (London: Duckworth, 1994).

Hill, B., *Eighteenth-century Women: An Anthology* (London: Routledge, 1993).

—— *Women, Work and Sexual Politics in Eighteenth-century England* (London: UCL Press, 1994).

Hitchcock, T., *English Sexualities, 1700–1800* (Basingstoke: Macmillan, 1997).

Hitchcock, T. and Cohen, M. (eds), *English Masculinities, 1660–1800* (London: Longman, 1999).

Hunt, M., *The Middling Sort: Commerce, Gender and the Family in England, 1680–1780* (Berkeley: University of California Press, 1996).

Hunt, M., Jacob, M., Mack, P. and Perry, R., *Women and the Enlightenment* (New York: Institute for Research in History, 1984).

Jones, V. (ed.), *Women in the Eighteenth Century: Constructions of Femininity* (London: Routledge, 1990).

Levy, D.G., Applewhite, H.B. and Johnson, M.D. (eds), *Women in Revolutionary Paris 1789–1795, selected documents* (Urbana: University of Illinois Press, 1980).

Maccubbin, R.P. (ed.), *'Tis Nature's Fault: Unauthorized Sexuality during the Enlightenment* (Cambridge: Cambridge University Press, 1987).

Mendelson, S. and Crawford, P., *Women in Early Modern England* (Oxford: Clarendon Press, 1998).

Myers, S.H., *The Bluestocking Circle: Women, Friendship, and the Life of the Mind in Eighteenth-century England* (Oxford: Clarendon Press, 1990).

Pekaz, J.T., *Conservative Tradition in Pre-Revolutionary France: Parisian Salon Women* (New York: Peter Lang, 1999).

Rogers, K.M., *Feminism in Eighteenth-century England* (Brighton: Harvester Press, 1982).

Rousseau, G. and Porter, R. (eds), *Sexual Underworlds of the Enlightenment* (Manchester: Manchester University Press, 1987).

Schiebinger, L., *The Mind Has No Sex: Women in the Origins of Modern Science* (Cambridge, Mass.: Harvard University Press, 1989).

Scott, J., *Only Paradoxes to Offer: French Feminists and the Rights of Man* (Cambridge, Mass.: Harvard University Press, 1996).

Shoemaker, R., *Gender in English Society, 1650–1850* (London: Longman, 1998).

Steinbrügge, L., *The Moral Sex: Women's Nature in the French Enlightenment*, trans. P. Selwyn (Oxford: Oxford University Press, 1995).

Trouille, M., *Sexual Politics and the Enlightenment: Women Writers Read Rousseau* (Albany: SUNY Press, 1997).

Uphaus, R.W. and Foster, G.M. (eds), *The 'Other' Eighteenth Century: English Women of Letters 1660–1800* (East Lansing: Colleagues Press, 1991).

Wagner, P., *Eros Revived: Erotica in the Age of Enlightenment* (London: Secker and Warburg, 1986).

Winn, C.H. and Kuizenga, D. (eds), *Women Writers in Pre-Revolutionary France: Strategies of Emancipation* (New York: Garland, 1997).

## 10 Art, architecture and nature

Ashfield, A. and Bolla, P. de (eds), *The Sublime: A Reader in British Eighteenth-century Aesthetic Theory* (Cambridge: Cambridge University Press, 1996).

Braham, A., *The Architecture of the French Enlightenment* (London: Thames and Hudson, 1980).

Burke, E., *A Philosophical Inquiry into the Origin of our Ideas of the Sublime and the Beautiful*, ed. A. Phillips ([1757] (Oxford: Oxford University Press, 1998).

Christie, C., *The British Country House in the Eighteenth Century* (Manchester: Manchester University Press, 2000).

Conisbee, P., *Painting in Eighteenth-Century France* (Oxford: Phaidon, 1981).

Craske, M., *Art in Europe 1700–1830* (New York: Oxford University Press, 1997).

Crow, T., *Painters and Public Life in Eighteenth-Century Paris* (New Haven: Yale University Press, 1985).

Denvir, B. (ed.), *A Documentary History of Taste in Britain. The Eighteenth Century: Art, Design and Society, 1689–1789* (London: Longman, 1983).

Ford, B. (ed.), *The Cambridge Cultural History: Vol. 5, Eighteenth Century Britain* (Cambridge: Cambridge University Press, 1991).

Foss, M., *The Age of Patronage: The Arts in England 1660–1750* (London: Hamish Hamilton, 1971).

Fried, M., *Absorption and Theatricality: Painting and Beholder in the Age of Diderot* (Berkeley: University of California Press, 1980).

Gilmore, T.B. (ed.), *Early Eighteenth-Century Essays on Taste* (New York: Scholars, 1972).

Goethe, J.W., *Essays on Art and Literature*, ed. J. Gearey, trans. E. and E. von Nardroff (Princeton: Princeton University Press, 1994).

Harris, J., *The Palladian Revival: Lord Burlington, His Villa and Garden at Chiswick* (London: Royal Academy of Arts, 1995).

Harrison, C., Wood, P. and Gaiger, J. (eds), *Art in Theory 1648–1815: An Anthology of Changing Ideas* (Oxford: Blackwell, 2000).

Hunt, J.D. and Willis, P. (eds), *The Genius of the Place: The English Landscape Garden 1660–1820* (London: Elek, 1975).

Keener, F.M. and Lorsch, S.E. (eds), *Eighteenth-Century Women and the Arts* (New York: Greenwood, 1988).

Levey, M. and Kalnein, W. von, *Art and Architecture in France in the Eighteenth Century* (Harmondsworth: Penguin, 1972).

Parissien, S., *Palladian Style* (London: Phaidon, 1994).

Paulson, R., *Emblem and Expression: Meaning in English Art of the Eighteenth Century* (Cambridge, Mass.: Harvard University Press, 1975).

Pears, I., *The Discovery of Painting: The Growth of Interest in the Arts in England 1680–1768* (New Haven: Yale University Press, 1988).

Perry, G., *Femininity and Masculinity in Eighteenth Century Art and Culture* (Manchester: Manchester University Press, 1994).

Ribeiro, A., *The Art of Dress: Fashion in England and France 1750–1820* (New Haven: Yale University Press, 1995).

Russell, T.M., *The Encyclopaedic Dictionary in the Eighteenth Century: Architecture, Arts and Crafts*, 5 vols (Aldershot: Ashgate, 1997).

Russell, T.M. and Thornton, A-M., *Gardens and Landscapes in the 'Encyclopédie' of Diderot and D'Alembert* (Aldershot: Ashgate, 1999).

Sambrook, J., *The Eighteenth Century: The Intellectual and Cultural Context of English Literature 1700–1789* (London: Longman, 1993).

Solkin, D.H., *Painting for Money: The Visual Arts and the Public Sphere in Eighteenth-Century England* (New Haven: Yale University Press, 1992).

Sweetman, J., *The Enlightenment and the Age of Revolution 1700–1850* (London: Longman, 1998).

Williamson, T., *Polite Landscapes: Gardens and Society in Eighteenth-Century England* (Stroud: Alan Sutton, 1995).

Winckelmann, J.J., *Writings on Art*, ed. D. Irwin (London: Phaidon, 1972).

## 11 Europeans and the wider world

Alexander, M., *Omai: Noble Savage* (London: Collins and Harvill, 1977).

Bayly, C.A., *Imperial Meridian: The British Empire and the World, 1780–1830* (London: Longman, 1989).

Beaglehole, J.C., *The Exploration of the Pacific* (London: A. and C. Black, 1966).

Bitterli, U., *Cultures in Conflict: Encounters between European and Non-European Cultures, 1492–1800*, trans. R. Robertson ([1986]; Cambridge: Polity Press, 1993).

Calder, A., *Revolutionary Empire: The Rise of the English-speaking Empires from the Fifteenth Century to the 1780s* (London: Jonathan Cape, 1981).

Clarke, J.J., *Oriental Enlightenment: The Encounter between Asian and Western Thought* (London: Routledge, 1997).

Damiani, A., *Enlightened Observers: British travellers to the Near East, 1715–1850* (Beirut: American University of Beirut, 1979).

Dolan, B., *Exploring European Frontiers: British Travellers in the Age of Enlightenment* (Basingstoke: Macmillan, 1999).

Grove, R., *Green Imperialism. Colonial Expansion, Tropical Island Edens and the Origins of Environmentalism 1600–1800* (Cambridge: Cambridge University Press, 1995).

Howse, D. (ed.), *Background to Discovery: Pacific Exploration from Dampier to Cook* (Berkeley: University of California Press, 1990).

Marshall, P.J., *Bengal. The British Bridgehead: Eastern India 1740–1828* (Cambridge: Cambridge University Press, 1988).

—— and Williams, G., *The Great Map of Mankind: British Perceptions of the World in the Age of Enlightenment* (London: Dent, 1982).

Pagden, A., *Lords of all the Worlds: Ideologies of Empire in Spain, Britain and France c.1500–c.1800* (New Haven: Yale University Press, 1995).

—— *The Fall of Natural Man: the American Indian and the Origins of Comparative Ethnology* (Cambridge: Cambridge University Press, 1988).

Parry, J.H., *Trade and Dominion: The European Overseas Empires in the Eighteenth Century* (London: Weidenfeld and Nicolson, 1971).

Rennie, N., *Far-fetched Facts: The Literature of Travel and the Idea of the South Seas* (Oxford: Clarendon Press, 1995).

Rousseau, G.S. and Porter, R. (eds), *Exoticism in the Enlightenment* (Manchester: Manchester University Press, 1989).

Russell-Wood, A.J.R. (ed.), *An Expanding World. The European Impact on World History, 1450–1800*, 31 volumes (Aldershot: Ashgate, 1995–2000).

Said, E., *Orientalism* (Harmondsworth: Penguin, 1978).

Smith, B., *European Vision and the South Pacific, 1768–1850* (Oxford: Clarendon, 1960).

Spate, O.H.K., *Paradise Lost and Found* (Minneapolis: University of Minnesota Press, 1988).

## 12  Radicalism and revolution

Appleby, J., *Capitalism and a New Social Order: The Republican Vision of the 1790s* (New York: New York University Press, 1984).

Applewhite, H.B. and Levy, D.G. (eds), *Women and Politics in the Age of Democratic Revolution* (Ann Arbor: University of Michigan Press, 1993).

Baker, K.M., *Inventing the French Revolution: Essays on French Political Culture in the Eighteenth Century* (Cambridge: Cambridge University Press, 1990).

Blanning, T.C.W., *Reform and Revolution in Mainz, 1743–1803* (Cambridge: Cambridge University Press, 1974).

—— *The French Revolution: Aristocrats versus Bourgeois?* (London: Macmillan, 1987).

Bonwick, C., *The American Revolution* (Basingstoke: Macmillan, 1991).

Butler, M. (ed.), *Burke, Paine, Godwin, and the Revolution Controversy* (Cambridge: Cambridge University Press, 1984).

Chartier, D.G., *The Cultural Origins of the French Revolution*, trans. L.G. Cochrane (Durham, NC: Duke University Press, 1991).

Comninel, G.C., *Rethinking the French Revolution. Marxism and the Revisionist Challenge* (London: Verso, 1987).

Doyle, W., *Origins of the French Revolution* (Oxford: Oxford University Press, 1980).

Dworetz, S., *The Unvarnished Doctrine: Locke, Liberalism and the American Revolution* (Durham, NC: Duke University Press, 1994).

Elliott, M., *Partners in Revolution: the United Irishmen and France* (New Haven: Yale University Press, 1982).

Goodwin, A., *The Friends of Liberty* (London: Hutchinson, 1979).

Gordon, D., *Citizens without Sovereignty: Equality and Sociability in French Thought, 1670–1789* (Princeton: Princeton University Press, 1994).

Gross, R.A., *The Minutemen and Their World* (New York: Hill and Wang, 2001).

Higonnet, P., *Sister Republics: The Origins of French and American Republicanism* (Cambridge, Mass.: Harvard University Press, 1988).

Holton, W., *Forced Founders: Indians, Debtors, Slaves, and the Making of the American Revolution in Virginia* (Chapel Hill: University of North Carolina Press, 1999).

Hunt, L., *Politics, Culture and Class in the French Revolution* (London: Methuen, 1986).

—— (ed.), *The French Revolution and Human Rights: A Brief Documentary History* (Boston: Bedford Books of St Martin's, 1996).

Jacob, M.C., *The Radical Enlightenment: Pantheists, Freemasons and Republicans* (London: Allen and Unwin, 1981).

—— *Living the Enlightenment: Freemasonry and Politics in Eighteenth Century Europe* (Oxford: Oxford University Press, 1992).

Kley, D. van (ed.), *The French Idea of Freedom: The Old Regime and the Declaration of Rights of 1789* (Stanford: Stanford University Press, 1994).

Kramnick, I., *Republicanism and Bourgeois Radicalism: Political Ideology in Late Eighteenth-century England and America* (Ithaca: Cornell University Press, 1990).

Landes, J., *Women and the Public Sphere in the Age of the French Revolution* (Ithaca: Cornell University Press, 1988).

Lough, J., *The Philosophes and Post-Revolutionary France* (Oxford: Clarendon Press, 1982).

Lutz, D.S., *The Origins of American Constitutionalism* (Baton Rouge: Louisiana State University Press, 1988).

Maier, P., *American Scripture: Making the Declaration of Independence* (New York: Knopf, 1997).

Mason, H.T. (ed.), *The Darnton Debate: Books and Revolution in the Eighteenth Century* (Oxford: Voltaire Foundation, 1998).

Mee, J., *Dangerous Enthusiasm: William Blake and the Culture of Radicalism in the 1790s* (Oxford: Clarendon Press, 1992).

Melzer, S.E. and Rabine, L.W. (eds), *Rebel Daughters: Women and the French Revolution* (New York: Oxford University Press, 1992).

Miller, P.N. (ed.), *Joseph Priestley: Political Writings* (Cambridge: Cambridge University Press, 1993).

Morgan, E.S., *Inventing the People: The Rise of Popular Sovereignty in England and America* (New York: Norton, 1988).

Outram, D., *The Body and the French Revolution: Sex, Class and Political Culture* (New Haven: Yale University Press, 1989).

Pangle, T., *The Spirit of Modern Republicanism: The Moral Vision of the American Founders and the Philosophy of Locke* (Chicago: Chicago University Press, 1988).

Palmer, R.R., *Age of the Democratic Revolution: A Political History of Europe and America 1760–1800*, 2 vols (Princeton: Princeton University Press, 1959–64).

Prickett, S., *England and the French Revolution* (London: Macmillan, 1989).

Raphael, R., *The American Revolution: A People's History* (London: Profile Books, 2001).

Robbins, C., *The Eighteenth-century Commonwealthman* (Cambridge, Mass.: Harvard University Press, 1961).

Schama, S., *Citizens: A Chronicle of the French Revolution* (London: Viking, 1989).

—— *Patriots and Liberators: Revolution in the Netherlands, 1780–1813* (London: Collins, 1977).

Schechter, R. (ed.), *The French Revolution: The Essential Readings* (Oxford: Blackwell, 2001).

Sewell, W.H., *A Rhetoric of Bourgeois Revolution: The Abbé Siéyès and What is the Third Estate?* (Durham: Duke University Press, 1994).

Wood, G., *The Radicalism of the American Revolution* (New York: Vintage Books, 1993).

## 13 Autobiographical reflections

Benstock, S. (ed.), *The Private Self: Theory and Practice of Women's Autobiographical Writings* (Chapel Hill: University of North Carolina Press, 1988).

Coleman, P., Lewis, J. and Kowalik, J. (eds), *Representations of the Self from the Renaissance to Romanticism* (Cambridge: Cambridge University Press, 2000).

Cox, S.D., *'The Stranger within Thee': The Concept of the Self in Late Eighteenth-Century Literature* (Pittsburgh: Pittsburgh University Press, 1980).

Imbarrato, S.C., *Declarations of Independency in Eighteenth-Century American Autobiography* (Knoxville: University of Tennessee Press, 1998).

Lyons, J.O., *The Invention of Self* (Carbondale: Southern Illinois University Press, 1978).

Mascuch, M., *Origins of the Individualist Self: Autobiography and Self-identity in England 1591–1791* (Stanford: Stanford University Press, 1996).

Martin, R. and Barresi, J., *Naturalisation of the Soul: Self and Personal Identity in the Eighteenth Century* (London: Routledge, 2000).

Nussbaum, F.A., *The Autobiographical Subject: Gender and Ideology in Eighteenth-century England* (Baltimore: Johns Hopkins University Press, 1989).

Porter, R. (ed.), *Rewriting the Self: Histories from the Renaissance to the Present* (London: Routledge, 1997).

Roulston, C., *Virtue, Gender, and the Authentic Self in Eighteenth-Century Fiction: Richardson, Rousseau and Laclos* (Gainesville: University of Florida Press, 1998).

Rousseau, G.S. (ed.), *The Languages of Psyche: Mind and Body in Enlightenment Thought* (Berkeley: University of California Press, 1991).

Spacks, P.M., *Imagining a Self: Autobiography and Novel in Eighteenth-Century England* (Cambridge, Mass.: Harvard University Press, 1976).

Stelzig, E.L., *The Romantic Subject in Autobiography: Rousseau and Goethe* (Charlottesville: University Press of Virginia, 2000).

Taylor, C., *Sources of the Self: The Making of the Modern Identity* (Cambridge: Cambridge University Press, 1989).

Todd, D., *Imagining Monsters: Miscreation of the Self in Eighteenth-century England* (Chicago: University of Chicago Press, 1995).

# Index